Dedicated to
Students of Plant Pathology

CROP DISEASES AND THEIR MANAGEMENT

H.S. Chaube

Professor
Department of Plant Pathology, College of Agriculture
G.B. Pant University of Agriculture and Technology
Pantnagar

V.S. Pundhir

Associate Professor
Department of Plant Pathology, College of Agriculture
G.B. Pant University of Agriculture and Technology
Pantnagar

Prentice-Hall of India Private Limited
New Delhi-110001
2005

Rs. 395.00

CROP DISEASES AND THEIR MANAGEMENT
H.S. Chaube and V.S. Pundhir

ISBN-81-203-2674-1

The export rights of this book are vested solely with the publisher.

Published by Asoke K. Ghosh, Prentice-Hall of India Private Limited, M-97, Connaught Circus, New Delhi-110001 and Printed by Jay Print Pack Private Limited, New Delhi-110015.

Contents

16. INTEGRATED PLANT DISEASE MANAGEMENT

17. KINGDOM: FUNGI

Preface

This would be a very long preface if we were to set down in detail the reasons why we attempted to write this book in present form. Suffice it to say that the text is based on courses which we have been teaching to undergraduate and postgraduate students. The purpose is to provide the basic and emerging facts whereby the students may be introduced to the scientific foundations of this noble subject called Plant Pathology. The subject of Plant Pathology has expanded tremendously. Pathogenesis and ways by which plants defend themselves are now relatively better understood. Advances in molecular Plant Pathology are providing appropriate diagnostic tools/techniques for identification of causal agents and diseases. Our knowledge of understanding the genetics of host parasite interactions have helped in evolving effective tactics of strengthening resistance of host plants. New tools and techniques of molecular biology are being appropriately used. Appropriate genes could be successfully introduced in plants and microorganism.

Keeping in view, the developments in this discipline, we undertook the task of writing an updated textbook. The text of the present book comprises three parts covering Principles of Plant Pathology, Principles of Plant Disease Management and comprehensive treatments of better known representative plant disease. We, as regular teachers of core and elective UG and PG courses, have experienced that students do not take books. They rely solely on class-notes. One of the reasons being non-availability of textbooks covering entire course contents, the way they are delivered in class. In the present book, we have tried to arrange the topics and the contents in such a manner that readers get an easy reading with due continuity. We do not claim originality in the preparation of this book and have taken help from a large number of books, journals, periodicals, bulletins, etc. We gratefully thank authors, editors, and publishers of the books, journals, etc. We express our gratitude to Dr. Jameel Akhtar and Mr. Tushar Srivastava for providing adequate help in computerization of the manuscript.

Besides our best efforts some mistakes, factual or printing, might have inadvertently crept on for which we beg sorry in anticipation and if pointed to us, shall surely correct them in subsequent print/edition. We shall also welcome suggestions and healthy criticism for the improvement of this publication.

H.S. Chaube
V.S. Pundhir

1

Plant Diseases

1.1 INTRODUCTION

There is enough evidence to believe that microorganisms were the first of biological forms to appear on this planet. The other biological forms, including plants and men, are believed to have appeared on earth several million years later. By the time men learnt to cultivate plants, microorganisms had multiplied and established universally on this planet. Their continued association with other biological systems resulted in adaptations and special features among the interacting populations. These features caused evolutionary changes to result in different biological forms and types of organisms. The association between plants and microbes is therefore, as old as the plants themselves. The inter-relationships between plants and microbes have become increasingly complex. In the process of evolution, organisms, which were not able to compete, disappeared, while more virulent and more 'fit' were selected by nature.

Man is one of the two million biological species on earth. He domesticated plants and animals to ensure his regular food supply. When he started agriculture, microorganisms were already established with plants. These relationships at different stages of evolution have created some basic associations among the interacting populations. These are given in Table 1.1.

Table 1.1 Interspecies Interactions

Interaction	Species		Nature of Interaction	Remarks
	A	B		
Positive Interactions				
Neutralism	0	0	No effect on either population	Probably uncommon
Commonsalism	+	0	One benefits while other is unaffected	Growth factor (vitamin producing organism neither suffers nor benefits)
Protocooperation	+	+	Interaction favourable to both but **not obligatory**	Free living N_2 fixing bacteria and non-fixers
Mutualism	+	+	Interaction favourable to both but **obligatory**	Various grades of mycorhizal associations
Negative Interactions				
Competition				
Direct interference	–	–	Direct inhibition	

(*Contd.*)

Table 1.1 Interspecies Interactions (*Contd.*)

Interaction	Species A	Species B	Nature of Interaction	Remarks
Resource use	–	–	Indirect when resource is limited	Most microbes specially competitive saprophytic colonizers
Amensalism	–	0	One inhibits the other but does not benefit itself	Antibiosis(*Penicillium* spp.)
Parasitism	–	+	One population benefits at the cost of other	Pathogenic fungi, bacteria, bioagents and mycoparasites
Predation	–	+	-do- but applies to feeders	Predatory nematodes and nematophagus fungi

(0 = Neither positive (+) nor negative (–) influence)

1.2 THE SCIENCE OF PLANT PATHOLOGY

Plant pathology or Phytopathology (*Phyton*-Plant; *Pathos*-ailments/suffering; *logos*-knowledge/science) is a branch of science (agricultural, botanical or biological) that deals with disease(s) in plants. The objectives of plant pathology is to establish cause(s) of disease, to elucidate mechanism of disease development, to identify factors influencing disease development, and develop technology for effective and economic management of plant diseases. Plant pathology involves the study of interacting populations (host, pathogen and vectors, if involved) under agro-ecosystem.

The science of plant pathology, 150 years old has amassed a wealth of information from which valuable knowledge has been distilled in the form of **principles of plant pathology** and **principles of plant disease management.** These principles or fundamentals guide us in developing our understanding about the phenomena of plant disease development on individual plant or in plant population and in devising suitable technology for their management. The ultimate aim is to manage the agro-ecosystem so as to minimize the crop damage (yield loss) and stabilize the production.

1.2.1 Origin of Plant Pathology

Plant pathology, a science of diseases in plants, originated as an offshoot of botany and developed to a status of recognized subject due to economic and social importance of plant diseases and the scientific achievements during last 150 years. Plant diseases and their impact were topics of interest to economic botanists in British era. The mycology (fungal pathogens), bacteriology (pathogenic bacteria), virology (virus and mollecutes) and some times nematology (parasitic nematodes) were important components of curriculum in botany at undergraduate and postgraduate levels. Thus, plant pathogens and their economic impact (plant diseases) became integral part of study in botany. One of the fallout of this origin was seen in the initial interest in basic studies on plant pathogens (taxonomy, morphology and physiology, etc.) and the focus became the diseased plant rather than plant populations. **Had the plant pathology emerged out of ecology?**, the focus would have been on population interactions and epidemiology would have been in the forefront since the beginning. But it was not to be and it took about 100 years to re-orient the pathologists attentions towards the diseased populations. A paradigm shift towards practical solutions for prevention and management of plant diseases at population level was seen. Present day epidemiology is providing logical guiding principles for strategic plant disease management.

1.2.2 Relation with Other Sciences

Knowledge of basic biological and physical sciences, as well as comprehension of agricultural, environmental and social sciences, are the foundation stones upon which the science of plant pathology rests. For instance, to understand and manage disease, plant pathologists must understand the biology, physiology, ecology, reproduction, dispersal and survival of the pathogen. They must also understand the concepts of stress and yield losses in plants when the limits of tolerance are exceeded. The interrelations of different sciences with plant pathology are illustrated in Figure 1.1.

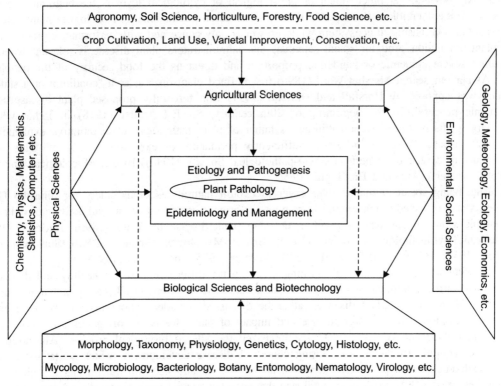

Figure 1.1 The relation of plant pathology to other sciences.

1.3 PLANT DISEASE: A CONCEPT

It is of first importance to understand that disease is a condition of abnormal physiology and that the boundary lines between the health and ill health are vague and difficult to define.

—H. Marshal Ward

Our understanding about plant disease and its description is one of the gray areas of plant pathology, by now a well-developed science in its own. Marshal Ward in 19th century said that the boundary line between health and ill health are vague and difficult to define and Agrios while entering the 21st century observed "It is difficult to pin point exactly when a plant is diseased." This tells all about our thinking on plant disease.

Lack of proper communication is the main reason for our poor understanding about 'disease' whether it is of our pet or plant. When we notice visual changes (symptoms); that is too late. A plant is diseased, by common perception, when it is not performing (growth and productivity) up to its genetic potential. Horsfall and Dimond (1959) were very judicious in their approach: "to know what is diseased … .... we should know what is normal." We feel, the possible reason for bewilderness in thinking about plant disease is due to different angles (biological and economic) applied to view the same process/phenomena: Plant disease. For a biologist plant disease is a biological process where any deviation at biochemical or physiological or cytological level is the beginning of the process. The epidemiologist's attention is only on diseased populations. For ecologists plant disease is a natural relationship in ecosystem while grower is only concerned with performance/productivity of plant population. And for social scientists and administrators plant disease is relevant when it assumes severe epidemic or pandemic proportion and threatens the food security of the people.

As per our search Marshal Ward (1896) first defined plant disease as a "condition or a state", which was opposed by Horsfall and Dimond (1959) who forcefully proposed plant disease as a 'dynamic process'. In the beginning of 20th century, Sir E.J. Butler (1918) in India, while discharging his bestowed responsibilities as father of plant pathology put quantitative explanation to plant disease "Variation which is sufficiently permanent or extensive ...." This was subsequently agreed by American Phyto-pathological Society (1940), British Mycological Society (1950), Walker (1957) and DasGupta (1977).

Man being social animal is ever eager to exploit natural resources solely for himself. This tendency was reflected in our emphasis on poor performance or cessation of vital activity or reduced economic value or survival of plant in defining plant disease by Ward (1896), Butler (1918), American Phytopathological Society (1940), British Mycological Society (1950), Stalkman and Harrar (1957), Horsfall and Dimond (1959), Wheeler (1975) and Agrios (1997).

Looking into the problems of defining precisely the difference between healthy and diseased plants and further complications brought in due to inherent variations in all plant populations Lucas (1998), did not define plant disease, rather he discussed the ideas about disease by describing damage, symptoms, causes, significance and impact of plant disease to bring home the points.

Kent (1973) and Bateman (1978) emphasized the altered biological process "Alteration of energy utilization process———" during course of disease development, which starts just at the initial outcome of host pathogen interaction at micro level and keep on magnifying in volume as disease progresses. Infact this is the vital step that can alter various plant functions and may manifest as physiological, morphological, performance and/or economic parameters used as criteria to describe disease.

The authors during classroom interactions with undergraduate and postgraduate students circulated a set of definitions by various workers. The students were asked to synthesize 'their own' definitions of plant disease. This was followed by class group discussions to reach 'consensuses'. Based on what emerged out, we do not wish to add one more definition to already existing long list. We wish to propose a precise concept about plant disease for understanding of our readers. The students of plant pathology should try to understand the facts about the phenomena: plant disease rather than choosing suitable words to frame a definition.

Plant disease is a dynamic process induced by an incitant (pathogen/abiotic factors) that disturbs the energy utilizing system in plants. This may be manifested at micro (biochemical/physiological/cytological) and/or at macro level (symptom). The diseased plant's performance to produce or survive is compromised.

1.4 CLASSIFICATION OF PLANT DISEASES

Various schemes of classifying plant diseases have been proposed from time to time. Classification of infectious plant diseases have been based on (1) **crops affected** (wheat diseases, rice diseases or cereal diseases or pulse crop diseases), (2) **organs attacked** (fruit, root, leaf or seedling diseases), (3) **symptoms** (rusts, smuts, wilts, mildews), (4) **source of inoculum** (seed-borne, soil-borne, air-borne), (5) **group of causal agent** (Fungal, bacterial, viral diseases), (6) taxonomy of the pathogen, etc. McNew (1950, 1960) proposed a system based upon seven physiological processes. Based on occurrence and consequent effects, a disease may be **endemic** (constantly present in moderate to severe form in a locality), **epidemic** (occurs widely, in severe and virulent form), **sporadic** (occurs at very irregular intervals and location), or **pandemic** (occur all over the world and cause mass mortality). Diseases have been classified according to the nature of major causal agents as **non-infectious** or **non-parasitic** or **physiological** (caused by abiotic factors) or **infectious diseases** (incited by biotic and/or mesobiotic agents).

Based on production and spread of the inoculum a disease may be a **single cycle disease** (simple interest disease) or **multiple cycle disease** (compound interest disease). In single cycle disease, the increase of disease is mathematically analogous to simple interest of money. There is only one generation of disease in the crop season. In multiple cycle diseases, the increase in disease is mathematically analogous to compound interest of money. There are several generations of the pathogen within a life cycle of a crop Figure 1.2.

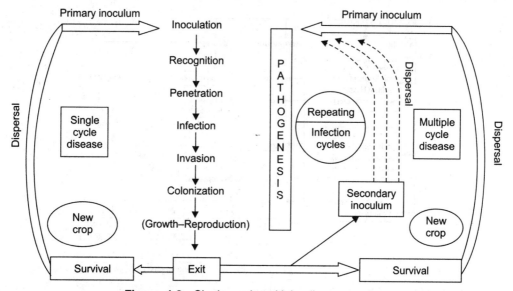

Figure 1.2 Single and multiple disease cycles.

Kommedahl and Windels (1979), based on host-pathogen dominance system, have divided diseases as 'Pathogen Dominant Diseases' (PDD) or 'Host Dominant Diseases' (HDD). In PDD, the pathogen is dominant over the host, but the relationship is transitory because host resistance is less initially than it becomes eventually. Such pathogens are tissue non-specific and attack young, immature root tissues or senescent tissues of a mature plant roots. The pathogenesis is due to the primary virulence of the pathogen. Physiological specialization is relatively uncommon. Important pathogens are *Macrophomina, Phytophthora, Pythium, Rhizoctonia, Sclerotium,* etc. In HDD, the host is dominant and the pathogen is successful only when factors favour the pathogen over the host. The resistance of the host is strong enough to keep the pathogen from advancing too rapidly against the host defenses during the vegetative growth phase and the host thereby prolongs the relationship. Damage is most severe in plants in the reproductive and senescent phases. In this group some pathogens are tissue non-specific, but most are tissue specific. Important pathogens are the species of *Armillaria, Polyporus, Poria, Helminthosporium, Fusarium,* etc.

1.5 PLANT PATHOGENS: CONCEPT AND CLASSIFICATION

Organisms suffer from diseases or disorders due to some abnormality in the functioning of their system. These abnormalities may be due to factors that have no biological activity of their own (abiotic factors) or those entities that show some biological activity (mesobiotic agents) and those that are established as cellular organisms. A pathogen can be broadly defined as any *agent or factor that induces pathos/suffering or disease in an organism,* but the term is generally used to denote biotic and mesobiotic causes. Which factor, entity or agent should be called abiotic and which one biotic or living? By intuition and experience, we have known that a thing that does not grow, reproduce, move, or show response to external stimuli is non-living and those that show these properties are living. However, when viruses appear in the picture, the whole concept of living vs. non-living becomes somewhat confused. The groups of the pathogens or causes of plant diseases are given in the following chart:

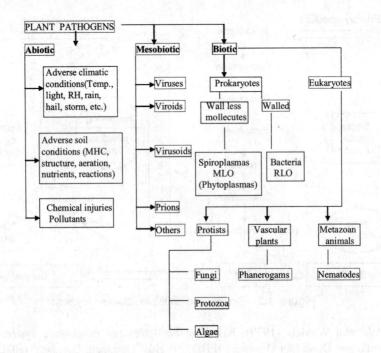

We commonly use several terms like pathogenicity, avirulence, virulence, and aggressiveness to describe attributes of the pathogens. In science the "terms" are coined or borrowed for communicating certain ideas or interpreting the facts to others. With development in our understanding about the phenomenon or the process the changes in expressions are inevitable.

Following terms should be conceived by the students of plant pathology:

Pathogenicity. Capability to cause disease; lack of pathogenicity means non-pathogenic rather than avirulence.

Virulence. Genetic ability of a pathogenic race to overcome host resistance, imparted by R genes, which may be effective against other races of the pathogen. Genetic ability of a pathogenic race to multiply on host cultivar.

Avirulence. Antonym of virulence; inability of pathogenic race to establish compatible interaction in host cv. (with R genes) in which other races may establish compatibility.

Aggressiveness. Descriptive rate at which an amount of disease is reached. Reproductive fitness of pathogen while growing in host.

Fitness. Ability of pathogen to persist in nature. It includes virulence, aggressiveness, survivability and effective dispersal.

Attributes of a successful pathogen are:

- Reproductive fitness while living in host
- Considerable amount of damage to host
- Host range of pathogen
- Survivability, in absence of host

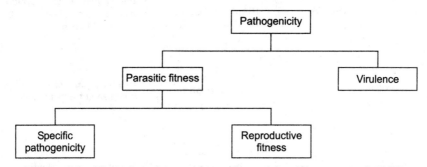

Figure 1.3 Hierarchy of terms for pathogenicity, (Shaner, et al.,1992).

1.6 EVOLUTION OF PARASITISM

Our understanding of the place and functions of the components of ecosystems has developed considerably through the application of **Trophic level concept**. The concept explains that each population in a community plays a role in the flow of energy and materials through the systems. Different kinds of organisms can be grouped into trophic levels depending on the source of energy materials they use. The basic group consists of the **producers, i.e. green plants**. Heterotrophic organisms depend on this continual input. The heterotrophs are **consumers**. They are divided into different levels. **Primary consumers** (heterotrophs and herbivores) obtain food directly from green plants; among them are cattle, insects and pathogenic fungi. **Secondary consumers** (carnivores, hyperparasites and predators) obtain their nutrients from primary consumers. In the hierarchy of parasitism, the **saprophytes** (colonize only dead organic matter) are the bottom line members. Immense competition among the saprophytes for the source of organic matter, forced some of them to develop **parasitic abilities**. The mode of parasitism had further undergone changes. They are **obligate** and **facultative** parasites. While obligate parasites infect living host organs and remain active till host cells remain active. There is more involvement of phyto-hormones and lesser dependence on toxins and enzymes, increased dependence on living host with decreased deleterious effects, narrow host range are other features of obligate parasites. Further developments probably led to the evolution of symbionts such as lichens and mycorrhizae where both host and parasite start deriving benefits from each other. The facultative parasites depend on enzymes and toxins to greater extent, as they do more damage to host tissue. The hypothetical hierarchical positioning of different plant pathogens based on their parasitic advancement is shown in Figure 1.4.

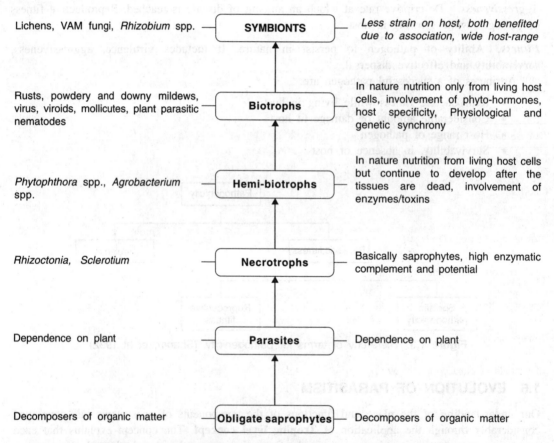

Lichens, VAM fungi, *Rhizobium* spp.	**SYMBIONTS**	Less strain on host, both benefited due to association, wide host-range
Rusts, powdery and downy mildews, virus, viroids, mollicutes, plant parasitic nematodes	**Biotrophs**	In nature nutrition only from living host cells, involvement of phyto-hormones, host specificity, Physiological and genetic synchrony
Phytophthora spp., *Agrobacterium* spp.	**Hemi-biotrophs**	In nature nutrition from living host cells but continue to develop after the tissues are dead, involvement of enzymes/toxins
Rhizoctonia, Sclerotium	**Necrotrophs**	Basically saprophytes, high enzymatic complement and potential
Dependence on plant	**Parasites**	Dependence on plant
Decomposers of organic matter	**Obligate saprophytes**	Decomposers of organic matter

Figure 1.4 Hypothetical hierarchical positioning of plant pathogens.

1.7 IMPORTANCE OF PLANT DISEASES

The increased food production to meet the requirements of the rising global human population, especially in the developing countries, is the need of the hour. Plant diseases can make a difference between a happy life and a life haunted by starvation, hunger or even death. The death from starvation of a quarter million Irish people in 1845 and the Bengal famine (1943) are examples of consequences of plant disease epidemics. Plant diseases may cause **annihilation** (chestnut blight, coffee rust), **devastation** (late blight of potato, Dutch elm disease, citrus canker), **disfiguring** (cankers, scabs) and **limiting** (root rots and wilts). Plant diseases may limit the kind of plants/crops, and the type of industry in an area. They may reduce the nutritive values of the produce or may make the plant products poisonous.

1.7.1 Impact on Human Affairs

In the history of mankind, plant diseases have been connected with a number of events. For example, wheat rust has appeared in epidemic form from time to time in many countries. This disease forced the farmers in many parts of the world to change their cropping pattern. While in Northern and Southern Europe wheat bread is more common, in Central Europe people eat rye bread. In southern part of USA, people eat corn bread, while in the northern part wheat bread is more common. The reason for these food habits is that in these parts wheat does not grow well due to rust and the farmers grow maize or rye. Several other example of diseases of historical significance and some emerging plant diseases and their geographical distribution are given in Tables 1.2 and 1.3, respectively.

Table 1.2 Some Important Examples of the Impact of Plant Diseases

Disease and the agent	*Locations and the impact*
Ergot of rye, wheat, pearl millet(*Claviceps* spp.)	857 AD Rhine Valley, Germany1089 AD France 11th, 12th and 13th century (France and Germany)
Late blight of potato (*Phytophthora infestans*)	Worldwide (cool humid climates) **Irish Famine (1845–46)**, British defeated the Germans in World War I (1916)
Brown spot of rice (*Drechslera oryzae*)	South-East Asia, Epidemics, **The great Bengal (India) rice famine** (1943–45)
Southern corn leaf blight (*Bipolaris maydis*)	USA, Epidemic (1970), crop worth $1 billion destroyed
Powdery mildew of Grapes (*Uncinula necator*)	Worldwide, European epidemics (1840–50), great financial loss.
Downy mildew of grapes (*Plasmopara viticola*)	USA, Europe, European epidemics (1870–80), threatened wine industry in France
Blue mould of Tobacco (*Peronospora tabacina*)	Europe and USA, European epidemic (1950–60), epidemic in USA (1979), substantial economic loss
Chestnut blight (*Cryphonectria parasitica*)	USA, **annihilated** American chest nut trees between 1904–1940
Dutch elm disease (*Ophiostoma novo-ulmi*)	USA, Europe, destroying elm trees since 1930, adverse ecological impact
Coffee rust (*Hemiliea vastatrix*)	South-East Asia (Sri Lanka), **annihilated** coffee bushes between 1870–80, changed human culture, spreading to Brazil and Colombia since 1970

(Contd.)

Table 1.2   Some Important Examples of the Impact of Plant Diseases (*Contd.*)

Disease and the agent	Locations and the impact
Panama disease of banana (*F. oxysporum* f. sp. *cubense*)	Central America (1930–55), destroyed plantation and caused financial losses
Jarrah die-back (*Phytophthora cinnamomi*)	Western Australia (1920), disruption of ecology and ecosystem, by 1982 forest area escalated to 14%
Apple scab (*Venturia inaequalis*)	Worldwide, epidemic in Kashmir (India) 1973, crop worth $40,000 lost
Citrus canker (*Xanthomonas axonopodis*)	Worldwide, millions of trees destroyed in Florida (USA) in 1910 and again in 1980s
Cassava bacterial blight (*X. campestris* pv. *manihotis*)	Zaire (1970–75) caused famine
Fire blight of apple and pear (*Erwinia amylovora*)	Southern Joaquin valley, between 1901–1904, 95% pear trees destroyed
Bacterial canker of stone fruits (*P. syringae* pv. *syringae*)	South Africa, annual damage exceeds $10 million
Citrus Quick decline (Tristeza virus)	Africa, America, million of trees destroyed
Cocoa swollen shoot (CSS virus)	Ghana/Nigeria, great economic loss
Peach yellows (Phytoplasma)	Eastern US, Russia, 10 million trees destroyed
Pear decline (Phytoplasma)	Pacific Coast States and Canada—million of trees destroyed
Cadang cadang of coconut palm (Viroid)	Phillipines—million of trees destroyed, huge financial losses

Table 1.3   Some Emerging Plant Diseases

Disease	Hosts	Geographic distribution
Fungal		
Late blight	Potato, tomato	Spreading worldwide
Downy mildew	Corn, sorghum	Spreading out of South-East Asia
Rust	Soyabean	Spreading from South-East Asia and Russia
Karnal bunt	Wheat	Pakistan, India, Nepal, Mexico, the USA
Monilia pod rot	Cocoa	South America
Rust	Sugarcane	The Americas
Blast	Rice	Asia
Viral		
African mosaic	Cassava	Africa
Streak disease	Maize, wheat, sugarcane	Africa
Hoja blanca (White tip)	Rice	The Americas
Bunchy top	Bananas	Asia, Australia, Egypt, Pacific Islands
Tungro	Rice	South-East Asia
Golden mosaic	Bean	Caribbean Basin, Florida, Central America
Plum pox virus	Stone fruits(Peaches, etc.)	Europe, India, Syria, Egypt, Chile
High plains virus	Cereals	Great Plains, USA
Bacterial		
Leaf blight	Rice	Japan, India
Wilt	Banana	The Americas

(Moffat, 2001, Science: 292)

1.7.2 Crop Losses by Injurious Agents

Crop destruction is the change in structure, organic existence, or condition of the crops to an extent that restoration of yield and/or quality is irreversible. In agro-ecosystem, disease is one of the factors influencing productivity, production and quality of crop produce. The producers are invariably interested only in those practices in crop production, which influence cash return per unit area. On the farms the priorities that negate the concepts of avoidance, exclusion or eradication, prevail. For example choice of crops or varieties is usually based on anticipated profitability, rather than resistance to pest/pathogens. Direct and indirect losses caused by injurious agencies are shown in the following flowchart:

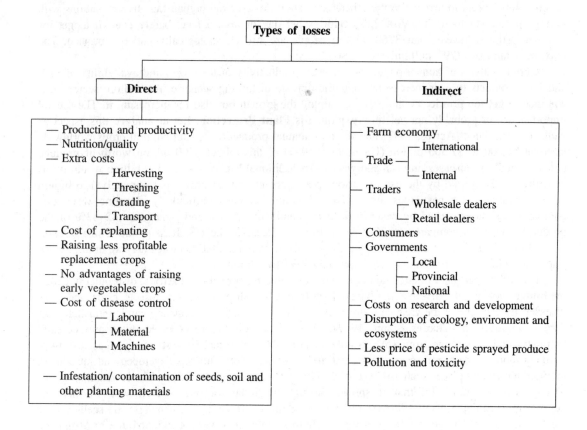

1.7.3 Crop Production: World Population and Plant Diseases

Major world crops are functioning at only 15–20% of their potential. Therefore, we must judge world agriculture sick. Its sickness is not caused by lack of genetic yield potential but by biotic and abiotic sources of stress that limit the crop production.

— Browning, J.A., 1998

The world population in the year 2000 was about 6.2 billion, and, at the current rate of 1.7% annual growth, it is expected to be 7.1 billion by 2010, and 8.5 billion by the year 2025 (Agrios, 1997).

The impact of additional mouths will be compounded by affluence. The surge in demand will occur even as evidences suggest that the **green revolution** is petering out. In the recent years, grain yields have stopped rising as fast, and plant scientists agree that they are facing physical limits as they try to coax plants to produce even more of their weight in grain. Supplies of fresh water are growing scarce. Soil quality is deteriorating. There is little unplanted arable land left to exploit. The incidence and severity of pests have increased. Thus, **we are running out of gas at the time we most need it** (Charles Mann, Science, 1997). Since the harvest of 1989–90, world grain yields have risen by just 0.5%. As a result, cereal stockpiles plunged from 383 million tons in 1992 to an estimated 281 million tons in 1997 and will be low further, the minimum necessary to safegunard world food security (FAO, Food Outlook Report, 1997). Cereal stocks held by developing countries have declined for 3 years in a row. On the other hand, about 56% of the human race live in nations with average per capita food supply of 2200 calories per day or less, a level barely enough to get by. A rough estimate reveals that 8260 million people are still chronologically under nourished. The maximum numbers (792 million) are in South Asia.

A brief analysis of human population growth, productivity of the crops, and availability of food and food products to ever increasing population create disturbing scenario. Agriculture sector must continue to get top priority for not only sustaining the growth but also for increasing it. The second important sector probably not yet fully exploited is **Plant Protection**. Let us analyze this aspect as well. It is estimated (Agrios, 1997) that the total annual production for agricultural crops worldwide is about $1,200 to $1,300 billion (US dollars, 1995) of this; about $500 billion worth of produce is lost annually to diseases, insects, and weeds. An additional loss of about $330 billion would occur annually, but is averted by the use of various plant protection measures. Approximately $26 billion is spent annually for pesticides alone. This situation becomes particularly alarming when one compares the losses caused by pests in different continents. Africa and Asia loose 42–43% of the produce to pests as compared to 25–30% in Europe, Oceania, the US, Russia, and China (Oerke, et al., 1994). In India, the annual loss is estimated to be over Rs. 20,000 crores (Jayraj, et al., 1994). Therefore, our concern should be to grow only **healthy plants**.

It would be pertinent to cite another burning example from regions of Africa, disreputably called the **hungry continent**. African agriculture suffers from a host of problems e.g. insects, birds, and plant diseases. Indeed, one of the greatest sources of crop losses in Africa is a phanerogamic parasitic plant *Striga hermonthica* (Charles Mann, 1997). *Striga* feeds on the roots of legumes and cereals. Estimates of losses range from 15% to 40% of Africa's total cereal harvest; many areas lose two-thirds or more of their crops every year. First *Striga* resistant sorghum was developed and introduced in 1995 in different places such as Chad, Mali, Niger, Rwanda, and the Sudan. The resistant sorghum variety was so successful that it spread throughout Sudan despite a civil war. Farmers in neighbouring Ethiopia wanted *Striga*—resistant sorghum badly enough to smuggle the seeds across the hostile border. The people are growing sorghum in areas that were abandoned due to *Striga* for years. The change brought about is enormous. This example signifies the importance of a parasitic entity and importance of suitable protection technology.

1.7.4 Modern Agriculture and Plant Diseases

*The **green revolution** which mainly involved raising of crops to boost crop production and productivity by introducing high-yielding varieties have resulted, in many instances, susceptibility of these varieties to new diseases.*

— Govindu, 1982

High-yielding dwarf and semi-dwarf wheat varieties developed and distributed by CIMMYT, Mexico increased wheat production (6.5 times that in 1945) in Mexico alone in the mid 1960s, thus changing Mexico from a wheat-importing to a wheat-exporting country. They also behaved very similarly and were just as productive in Africa and Asia too. To produce high yields with these varieties, many agronomic practices have to be altered drastically. Monoculture of this wheat in India, Pakistan, Afghanistan, and Turkey increased from about 23,000 acres in 1966 to 30 million acres in 1971, replacing hundreds of local varieties (Agrios, 1997). Taking the example of Indian agriculture alone, the impact of these varieties can be judged by the fact that from the total production of 11 to 12 million tons of wheat in India in 1965, it has exceeded 35 million tons, with this intensive and extensive cultivation of new varieties, the disease position has also changed from time to time. A semi-dwarf wheat variety "Kalyansona" released in 1967, was resistant to most of the then prevailing races of the black stem rust, completely resistant to yellow rust, loose smut, hill bunt and tolerant to foliar blights. It was however, susceptible to some races of brown rust (Joshi, et al., 1973). But in 1971–72 and then in 1972–73, its resistance 'broke down' to yellow rust because of appearance of new strains namely, 14-A, 20-A, and 38-A (Joshi, et al, 1980). At the same time, it also became much more susceptible to brown rust in the field. Cultivation of the same genotype possibly gave a chance to new virulence to develop at a much faster rate (Nagrajan and Joshi, 1980). Another example, showing direct influence of changing the varietal position on disease situation is provided by the fluctuations in frequency of occurrence of loose smut of wheat with the increase in area of Kalyansona between 1968 and 1975, the disease gradually dwindled down and its frequency was less than 0.5% (Joshi, et al., 1977). With its replacement by Sonalika in 1974, however, the disease once again reappeared in severe form in 1976. In the crop season of 1980–1981, the disease intensity in northern India was more than 4% (Joshi, et al., 1981). Another disease "Karnal bunt of wheat" needs special mention. In the last two decades, there has been a progressive increase in its incidence. This is due to intensive cultivation of some varieties, changes in crop management, and also frequent exchange of seed material (Govindu, 1982).

A similar *green revolution* with respect of improvement of rice varieties has been carried out by IRRI, Phillipines. Non-lodging dwarf rice varieties that respond favourably to high nitrogen fertilization and produce high yields were developed and distributed widely. Soon, however, many of these varieties became susceptible to diseases such as bacterial blight, bacterial leaf streak, sheath blight, false smut, etc. that were either unknown or unimportant when local old varieties were planted, but which now, due to high nitrogen fertilization and double cropping of large expanses of genetically homogenous varieties, reached catastrophic proportions (Govindu, 1982).

Expansion of irrigation in Venezuela made it possible to produce two rice crops in a year where only one was grown before. This resulted in serious outbreak of the virus disease "Hoja blanca" because new conditions favoured the multiplication and spread of the insect vector of the virus from one crop to another. Increased use of nitrogenous fertilizers has invariably been found to increase severity of diseases particularly those caused by biotrophs. Besides amounts, the form of nitrogen used also affects disease severity. Pesticides (insecticides, fungicides, weedicides, nematicides, etc.), alter the microbial equilibrium in the ecosystem. Use of specific pesticide often leads to increased inoculum potential of other pathogens not affected by the specific chemical. This may occur even with broad-spectrum fungicide like benomyl. Where this fungicide is used regularly and widely, it controls most but not all the pathogens like *Pythium*.

The application of pesticides to combat the pests affecting the crop, has been increasing steadily at an annual rate of 14% since the mid 1950's (Agrios, 1997). Since the year 2000 more than 3 billion kg of pesticides have been used annually worldwide. According to Agrios (1997) by 1990, nearly $25 billion was spent annually for pesticides worldwide. The use of pesticides has helped to increase production and productivity of the crops. This cannot be disputed but basically the use of pesticides is another form of loss caused by diseases and other pests. In addition to this, these pesticides have caused recurrence, resurgence and resistance in the pests besides, causing extreme pollution of agro-ecosystem and the environment.

REFERENCES

Agrios, G.N., 1997, *Plant Pathology*, 4th ed., Academic Press, New York.

American Phytopathological Society, 1940, Report of the committee on technical words, *Phytopathology*, 30:361.

British Mycological Society, 1950, Definition of some terms used in plant pathology, *Trans. Br. Mycol. Soc.*, 33:154.

DasGupta, M.K., 1977, Concept of disease in plant pathology and its application elsewhere, *Phytopathol. Z.*, 88:136.

Govindu, H.C., 1982, Green revolution—its impact on plant diseases with special reference to cereals and millets, *Indian Phytopathology*, 35:363.

Horsfall, J.G. and Dimond, E.A., 1959, Epilogue: The diseased plant, in *Plant Pathology—An advanced Treatise*, Vol. I., Horsfall, J.G., and Dimond, E.A., (Eds.), Academic Press, New York.

Joshi, L.M., Gera, S.D. and Saari, E.F., 1973, Extensive cultivation of Kalyan Sona and disease development, *Indian Phytopathology*, 26:370.

Joshi, L.M., Nagrajan, S. and Srivastava, K.D., 1977, Epidemiology of brown and yellow rusts of wheat in North India, I. Place and time of appearance and spread, *Phytopathol. Z.*, 90:116.

Kommedahl, T. and Windels, C.F., 1979, Fungi, pathogen, or host dominance in diseases, in *Ecology of Root Pathogens*, Krupa, S.V., and Dommergues, Y.R., (Eds.), Elsevier, Amsterdam, 291.

Lucas, J.A., 1998, *Plant Pathology and Plant Pathogens*, 3rd ed., Blackwell Science.

Mann, G., 1997, Reseeding the green revolution, *Science*, 277:443.

McNew, G.L., 1950, Outline of a new approach in teaching plant pathology, *Plant Dis. Reptr.* 34: 106.

Nagrajan, S. and Joshi, L.M., 1980, Further investigations on predicting wheat rust appearance in central and Peninsular India, *Phytopathol, Z.*, 98:84.

Oerke, E.C. et al., 1994, *Crop Protection and Crop Production*, Elsevier, Amsterdam.

Schumann, G.L., 1991, *Plant Disease: Their Biology and Social Impact*, APS Press, ST Paul, Minn.

Shaner, G. et al., 1992, Nomenclature and concepts of pathogenicity and virulence, *Annu. Rev. Phytopathol*, 30:47.

Stalkman, E.C. and Harrar, J.C., 1957, *Principles of Plant Pathology*, Ronald Press, New York, 581.

Walker, J.C., 1957, *Plant Pathology*, 2nd ed., McGraw-Hill, New York, 693.

Wheeler, H., 1975, *Plant Pathogenesis*, Springer-Verlag, Berlin, 104.

2 Landmarks in Development of Plant Pathology

Phytopathology like all natural sciences had its beginnings in the dawn of man's civilization.

— Whetzel, 1918

2.1 INTRODUCTION

It is reasonable, not to trace the origin of science. Plant pathology might have come into practice when man started caring about domesticated plants. His experience with crop husbandry might have refined the skills with time. But it was only in late nineteenth century that parasitic nature of plant diseases started gathering some support among the intellectuals of West. During last hundred years a lot have been achieved, several landmarks have been established during development of plant pathology into a science, and now it can be proudly stated that plant pathology has history of its own.

History records chronological account of important events, contributions of persons who significantly influenced the thinking of their era (Figure 2.1) and the interpretations of the observed facts or phenomenon over a period of time. Historical writings help us to understand systematic developments (the concepts), in any branch of science, and the problems faced by 'certain outstanding workers/thinkers' whose claims or viewpoints were unacceptable to majority of opinion makers, simply because it was 'new' and against the established 'norms' of the day. History of plant pathology is no exception, and, it is a must-read for the students of this discipline. The historical accounts will unfold the stories that may motivate the new generation to think and interpret the findings in their own way, without fear of established theories and 'dogmas' carried from the past.

There are references in the Vedas (1500 BC) to plant diseases and the methods of control. Surapal, an ancient Indian scholar wrote *Vraksha Ayurveda*, the first book in which plant diseases were discussed. People at that time knew that plant diseases were caused by 'internal and external factors'. Without experiments they practised measures like "amendments and hygiene" to control diseases. They practised tree-dressing, plant fumigation and seed treatment with some materials. There are references also in the old testament of blasting, mildews and insect pests. Kalidas, in *Raghuwansh*, and Jain authors of the *Jatakas* recorded about plant diseases. The Asian Agri–History Foundation Society (Hyderabad, India) is doing commendable work by digging out the information in old scriptures to present genuine pictures of agriculture and plant diseases of that period.

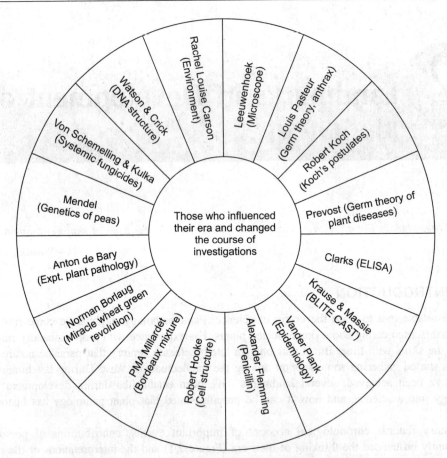

Figure 2.1 Important inventors and their contributions.

The Romans used to celebrate a festival, **Robigalia**, to ward-off rust, probably about 700 BC, and the same continued with modifications in the Christian era. Theophrastus (370–286 BC) was first to mention about diseases of trees, cereals and legumes, although his approach was **observational and speculative rather than experimental**. He was not aware that microorganisms caused diseases, and it was generally accepted that various organisms, observed to be associated with diseased or decaying plants, were the result rather than cause of the disease.

Comparatively, little was added to the knowledge of botany or plant pathology for nearly two thousand years. Anton van Leeuwenhoek (1675), invented the compound microscope and Robert Hooke, English scientist, observed the cell for the first time under microscope. These two events revolutionized the pace of scientific growth. During the 17th and 18th centuries the revival of interest in botany is reflected in the following classics produced during this period.

Gaspard Bauhin (1623) *Pinax Theatri Botanici*
P.A. Micheli (1729) *Nova Plantarum Genera*
C. Linnaeus (1707–1778) *Species Plantarum*

C.H. Persoon, who devoted most of his time in the study of fungi, produced *Synopsis Methodica Fungorum* (1793) that can be considered the major starting point for nomenclature of rusts, smuts and Gasteromycetes. E.M. Fries (1794–1878), wrote *Systema Mycologicum* (1821–1832) but regarded the rust and smut fungi as the products of diseased plants. M. Tillet (1714–1791), can be considered as first experimenter, as he demonstrated in 1755 that dusting of black smut powder on wheat seeds resulted in smutted heads. He concluded that the bunt spores contained a poisonous entity. He also demonstrated the control of disease by treating seeds with salt and lime. Tillet was an experimenter who lived ahead of his times.

Benedict Prevost, a Swiss professor of philosophy in France, studied the wheat-bunt disease for about a decade. In 1807, he published the results of his studies as *Memoir on the immediate cause of bunt or smut of wheat, and of several other diseases of plants, and on preventives of bunt.* He confirmed the findings of Tillet. He also studied and described the germination of spores, the growth of fungus within the growing wheat and the life cycle of the fungus. He showed that copper sulfate solution prevented spore germination. He distinguished between fungicidal and fungistatic effects. Prevost's results and interpretations were not accepted due to hold of the theory of spontaneous generation at that time. It has to wait some 40 years, only after the adoption of *germ theory*, that Prevost's work was recognized.

2.2 THE MODERN ERA

During mid nineteenth century, the infamous epidemic of late blight/mildew of potato devastated potato crop in Europe. The attention of scientific community as well as society was focused on plant diseases, and hence to plant pathology. Potato established as staple food and the failure of crop resulted in famine and starvation in Ireland. The **autogenetic theory** of disease was dominant at that time. John Lindley, professor of botany and editor of the *Gardener's chronicle* was the leader of autogenetists. M.J. Berkeley (1803–1889), prominent British Mycologist, after his early reservations started supporting the parasitic theory of plant diseases. Louis Pasteur (1860) furnished irrefutable evidence that **microorganisms arise from pre-existing living entities.** His discovery of the bacterial origin of anthrax buried the theory of spontaneous generation forever.

Tulasne brothers, Louis Rene and Charls (1817–1884), studied morphology of several fungi. Their illustrated accounts of rusts, smuts and ascomycetes are classics in mycology. Julius G. Kuhn (1825–1910), published his famous book for farmers in 1858 entitled, *The disease of cultivated crops: their causes and their control.* Morreu in Belgium and Montagne in France, in 1845, regarded the fungus as the major cause of the disease and described the late blight fungus as *Botrytis infestans.* Speer Schneider in 1857 and De bary in 1861 experimentally proved that the **fungus was the real cause of disease and not the result.** Anton De bary (1831–1888) was an outstanding worker in botany. Some of his notable contributions can be listed as follows:

1. Established that *P. infestans* is the cause of potato late blight
2. Discovered heteroecism in the rust fungi
3. The development and sex in a number of fungi
4. The nature of obligate and facultative parasitism
5. Role of enzymes in plant diseases
6. Detailed study on Sclerotonia diseases of vegetables
7. Research on diseases caused by Peronosporaceae fungi

Anton De bary, **the founder of modern plant pathology**, wrote his famous text *"Morphologie und Physologie der Pilze, Flechten, Und Myxomyceten"* in 1866. Most important contribution of De bary was the training he imparted to students from many parts of the world. Famous among them were M.S. Woronin of Russia, O. Brefeld of Germany, P.A. Millardet of France, H.M. Ward of England, Farlow of the USA and A. Fischer of Switzerland. These students went back and initiated phytopathological work in their countries.

Brefeld, a student of De bary, developed methods of artificial culture of microorganisms between 1875 and 1912. Tanaka (1933) established role of toxins in black spot disease of pear caused by *Alternaria*. Subsequently, the role of toxins in vascular wilt disease syndrome was established.

Robert Koch (1843–1910), a trained German physician and co-worker of Pasteur established the **germ theory** in relation to diseases of man and animals in 1876. Robert Koch in Germany published the final proof of the causal relation of the Anthrax disease in 1876. He enunciated certain rules or criteria that should be satisfied before the identity of the disease-producing organism in a particular disease can be established. These rules are known as *Koch's postulates.*

2.3 DEVELOPMENT OF PHYTOBACTERIOLOGY

The history of phytobacteriology can be traced to late 19th century. T.J. Burrill (1880) proved by an inoculation test that fire blight of pear was caused by a bacterium, which he named *Micrococcus amylovorus* in 1882. In 1883, J.H. Wakkar reported a yellowing disease in *Hyacinthi* by *Bacterium hyacinthi*. Erawin F. Smith (1894–1901) recorded several other bacterial diseases. However, German Botanist Alfred Fischer rejected Smith's observations pertaining to bacterial diseases. Nevertheless, Smith is considered **founder of phytobacteriology** for his discoveries and methodology he introduced for the study of bacterial plant diseases. Smith was also first to show in the early 1890's that crown gall disease of plants was caused by bacterium and he considered it similar to cancerous tumors in animals. Table 2.1 lists some of the noticeable milestones in phytobacteriology.

Table 2.1 Historical Events in Bacterial Plant Pathology

Name	Year	Event
T.J. Burill	1882	Publication of fire blight pathogen *Micrococcus amylovorus*
J. Omori	1896	Soft rot pathogen of wasabi *Bacillus* spp.
E.F. Smith	1901	Validation of bacteria as plant pathogens
C.O. Jensen	1910	Demonstration of evidence between crown gall of plants and cancer of animals
S. Hori	1912	Publication on soft rot pathogen
G.H. Koons and J.E. Kotila	1925	Isolation of bacteriophages of *B. carotovorus*
R.M. Klein	1954	Basic process of transformation in crown gall
A.C. Braun	1955	Wild fire toxin and its action
Y. Doi, et al.	1967	Discovery of MLOs (Phytoplasmas)
A.K. Chatterjee and M.P. Starr	1972	Conjugative gene transfer in bacteria
P.B. New and A. Kerr	1972	Biocontrol of crown gall (*A. radiobacter* Strain 84)
I. Zaenen, et al.	1974	Demonstration of Ti plasmids in *A. tumifaciens*
D.W. Dye, et al.	1980	Introduced pathovar system in taxonomy

2.4 DEVELOPMENT OF PHYTONEMATOLOGY

Existence of nematodes in nature has been traced to million of years. A plant disease with which association of a nematode could be traced, was first reported by Needham in UK in 1743 AD. He described the wheat gall nematode now known as *Anguina tritici*. However, for about a century after Needham no attention was given to the role of nematodes in plant diseases. In 1857, the life-cycle of *Anguina tritici* was studied by C. Devaine.

Root knot nematode was the second phytonematode to be discovered and reported. M.J. Berkeley in 1855 noticed galls/knots on roots of cucumber. He observed white larvae and eggs of the nematode and called them *Vibrio*. However, the first specific mention of root knot nematode was that of Cornu in 1875. He described them under the name of *Anguillula marioni*. In 1887, E.A. Goeldi published a description of *Meloidogyne exigua* (coffee root knot) and in 1889, Atkinson published a preliminary report on the life cycle of these nematodes under the name *Heterodera radicicola*. This name persisted for decades until the name *Meloidogyne*, earlier proposed by Goeldi, was accepted.

The stem nematode (*Ditylenchus dipsaci*) was reported by Kuhn in 1857. The cyst nematode of beet (*Heterodera schachtii*) was first noticed in Germany by H. Schacht in 1859. The name was given in 1871 by Schmidt. N. A. Cobb (1931) studied the structure of many nematodes and classified them. He coined the word **nematology** and developed many techniques for the study of nematodes. The association of nematodes with diseases caused by other agents had been observed as early as 1892 when Atkinson reported that Fusarial wilt of cotton was more severe in the presence of root knot nematode. In 1901, Hunger showed that Bacterial wilt of tomato was facilitated by root knot nematodes. Hewitt and associates in 1958 discovered that the grapevine fan leaf virus was transmitted by a nematode. Today, at least 18 plant viruses are known to be transmitted by species in four genera of nematodes. Developments in phytonematology have been more rapid and now the science occupies an independent position in many research centres.

2.5 MOLLICUTES AND OTHER PLANT PATHOGENS

In 1967, Doi and co-workers in Japan observed that mycoplasma-like bodies were constantly present in the phloem of plants suffering from leaf hopper transmitted yellow disease till then considered as virus disease. The same year Ishiie and colleagues reported that the mycoplasma-like bodies temporarily disappeared when the plants were treated with tetracycline antibiotics. Since then a large number of plant diseases were conclusively proved to be caused by such agents. However, they could not be characterized and Koch's postulates could not be proved in most of these diseases. Since, the MLO's associated with plants could not be grown in cell-free media, therefore, they were called **mycoplasma-like organisms (MLOs)** or more recently **phytoplasma**. In 1972, Davis and his colleagues observed a motile, helical, wall-less agent associated with corn stunt disease. They called it **spiroplasma** and this agent could be cultured and characterized.

Phytoplasma and spiroplasma are phloem inhabiting. During close examination of phloem, another group of **fastidious prokaryotes** was discovered in 1973 in citrus plant affected by greening disease. The organism had definite cell wall and was susceptible to both penicillin and tetracycline antibiotics. This suggested that the organism is true bacterium, and not MLO. *Gram (–)ve* character of the organism was confirmed in 1974. Subsequently, the organism was named as *Liberobacter asiaticum* from *Asian citrus Greening* and *Liberobacter africanum* from *African citrus greening*. Similar search for such agents in *Xylem* led to recovery of another *Gram (–)ve* bacterium in Pierce's disease of grapevine. In 1987, it was named as *Xylella fastidiosa*. Another *Gram (+)ve* xylem inhibiting bacterium was investigated from Ratoon stunting disease of sugarcane. It was named as *Clavibacter xyli*. These fastidious bacteria are often referred to as Rickettsia-like bacteria (RLB) only because of superficial resemblance to Rickettsia, but they are not Rickettsia.

2.6 DEVELOPMENT OF PHYTOVIROLOGY

The first reference to a symptom in plants, now known to be caused by a virus, is traced in a poem composed by the Empress Koken in the year 752. In this anthology the symptoms of the yellow leaf disease of *Eupatorium* were described. Later, during the 17th century in Holland, colour variegation or striping of tulip petals in plants infected with tulip mosaic virus, was much prized by Dutch tulip growers. Although the cause of tulip petal symptoms was unknown at that time, some growers knew that the condition could be grafted to a normal flower bulb. It was not until 1926 that the tulip "breaking" was found to be associated with a virus transmitted by infected sap or aphids.

The year 1882 may be considered as the beginning of the era of phytovirology when scientific studies were initiated by Adolf Eduard Mayer, a German scientist working in the Netherlands. Between 1882 and 1886 he reported that tobacco mosaic disease was neither due to microorganism nor due to nutritional imbalance. He demonstrated the contagious nature of the causal agent by artificial inoculation and also showed that boiling of the sap of infected leaves destroyed infectivity of the causal agent. In 1892 Dimitri Ivanowski, a Russian botanist working in Crimea, confirmed Mayer's findings and, in addition, had found that the causal agent could pass through filters with pores small enough to retain bacteria. The filtered sap remained infective for months. Martinus Wilhelm Beijerinck, a Dutch scientist, further confirmed the findings of Mayer and Ivanowski in 1898 and concluded that the causal agent of tobacco mosaic was something other than a microbe. The agent could pass through porcelain filters and could diffuse through agar gel. He was convinced that the agent was not a bacterium but a ***contagium vivum fluidum***, a contagious living fluid. The idea that the tobacco mosaic agent was fluid but at the same time was living, capable of reproduction and causing infection to plants, seemed extraordinary. Beijerinck is considered founder of virology, for it was he who firmly established the novel characteristics of tobacco mosaic agent, distinct from known agents of infectious diseases.

The true nature, size and shape of the virus, however, remained unknown for several decades. In 1935, W.M. Stanley added ammonium sulfate to tobacco juice extracted from infected tobacco leaves and obtained a crystalline protein which, when rubbed on tobacco, caused the tobacco mosaic disease. This led him to conclude that the virus was an autocatalytic protein that could multiply within living cells. Although his findings were later proved incorrect, Stanley received for his discovery the Nobel Prize in chemistry in 1946. In 1936, F.C. Bawden and his colleagues demonstrated that the crystalline preparations of the virus actually consisted of not only protein but also a small amount of ribonucleic acid (RNA). Kausche and colleagues saw first virus particles (tobacco mosaic virus) with electron microscope in 1939. In 1956, Gierrer and Schramm showed that the protein could be removed from the virus and that the ribonucleic acid carried all genetic information that enabled it to cause infection and to reproduce the complete virus.

Widespread use of ultra centrifuge, the electron microscope, electrophoresis, and serological techniques during 1940–1950 further helped in the understanding of plant virus structure, chemistry, replication and genetics. Quick and accurate detection and identification of virus became easier with the development of agar double diffusion serological tests in 1962 and **ELISA in 1977,** as well as production of monoclonal antibodies in 1975. Prior to 1960, the study of the viruses showed that they consisted of single stranded RNA. Later, some were found to have double stranded RNA (1963), some single stranded DNA (1977). The cauliflower mosaic virus (ds DNA) was the first virus for which the exact sequence of all its 8000 base pairs was determined in 1980. In 1982, the complete sequence (ssRNA) and some viroids were also determined.

The discovery of viroids and virusoids were additions to virology after 1970. In 1971, T.O. Diener reported that potato spinde tuber disease was caused by a small, naked, single stranded circular molecule of infectious RNA which he called **viroid**. In 1982, a circular, single stranded viroid like RNA was found encapsulated together with a single stranded linear RNA causing velvet tobacco mottle disease. The RNA molecule was called **virusoid**, which seems to form an obligatory association with the viral RNA in many plant viruses. Viroids are the smallest nucleic acid molecules to infect plants. So far they have not been found in animals although similar proteinacious infectious particles known as **prions** were reported in 1982 in scrapie disease of sheep and goats. The prions were later mentioned in connection with the "mad cow disease" in UK.

2.7 PLANT PATHOLOGY IN 20TH CENTURY

The major trends initiated in the latter half of the 19th century progressed in several directions. The rediscovery of Mendel's law in the beginning of the century had its impact and the genetics of the host as well as the pathogen received the attention of plant pathologists. Some of the major trends were in areas such as myco-physiology, fungicides, host resistance, biochemical plant pathology, ecology, biotechnology, mollecutes, bacterial pathology and epidemiology, etc.

2.7.1 Genetics of Host-Pathogen Interaction

Although Mendel had published his work on genetics of peas in 1866 and by 1898 it was known that resistance to rust in wheat was inherited, the names of Orton (1900–1909) and Biffen (1905–1912) are mentioned as pioneers in the field of resistance breeding. In 1905, Biffen described inheritance of resistance to yellow rust in two varieties of wheat and their progenies on the basis of Mendelian laws of inheritance. In 1909 Orton, working with wilt diseases of cotton, watermelon and cowpea, developed varieties that were resistant to the diseases. He also distinguished disease resistance from disease escape and disease endurance. Since then, efforts to develop resistant varieties in most crops have been continuing but there are only few crops that have varieties possessing permanent or durable resistance to a disease. One of the causes for this short-lived nature of resistance is the variability among the pathogens. Stakman called the pathogens as **shifty enemies**.

The Swedish scientist, Erickson first discovered the phenomenon of variability among fungi in 1894 when he reported the existence of physiologic races in the rust fungi. Almost at the same time Ward (1903) and Salmon (1903–1904) discovered physiologic specialization in fungi causing rust and powdery mildew of cereals. E.C. Stakman (1914) of the university of Minnesota, USA took up this aspect for further investigation. After prolonged studies he concluded that due to continuous evolution of races and biotypes in botanical species of the rust fungi, their pathogenic capabilities go on changing in their favour, as a result of which the host plant resistance also undergo changes.

In the field of host-pathogen interaction and resistance, a major development took place in 1946 when Flor, working with flax rust system, advanced the ***Gene for Gene*** hypothesis. *For every gene* *controlling resistance or susceptibility in the host, there must be matching genes for avirulence or virulence in the pathogen*. This gene for gene relationship is now demonstrated in a large number of host-parasite systems. In 1963, Vanderplank suggested that there are two kinds of resistance: one, controlled by few "major" genes, is strong but race specific (*vertical resistance*) and the other determined by many "minor" genes is partial but effective against all races of a pathogen species (*horizontal resistance*).

In 1902, Ward observed that colonization of resistant *Bromus* sp by *Puccinia dispersa* was accompanied by necrosis of the host cells adjacent to the colonizing fungus. In 1915, Stakman working on wheat-*Puccinia graminis* system, also observed rapid cell death around the sites of penetration in resistant host plants and used the term **hypersensitive** to describe the response. Gaumann later elaborated the phenomenon of resistance through hypersensitivity in 1946. Gilchirist, 1998 reported possible connection between plant disease and **programmed cell death**, cell suicide or apoptosis associated with hypersensitive reaction. In 1940, Muller and Borger, working on potato *P. infestans* system, first defined **phytoalexins** as the anti-microbial compounds synthesized and accumulating at sites of infection or stress in plants. Cruickshank (1963) confirmed accumulation of anti-microbial metabolites during pathological processes and their role in resistance.

To overcome the shortcomings of resistance breeding by conventional methods, scientists have been trying to utilize the techniques of tissue culture and genetic engineering. In 1970s, it was demonstrated that plant cells and protoplasts could be screened in culture for resistance to a pathogen toxin, and that, plants with an altered response to infection by pathogen could be regenerated from these cultured cells. Since then the techniques have improved much and a few varieties have been developed from cell culture. Of particular interest in these techniques are protoplast fusion methods, ovule and embryo culture techniques, *in-vitro* fertilization and up-take of organelles, chromosomes and DNA by protoplasts. Techniques of meristem culture have been used to obtain virus free material in sugarcane and potato.

2.7.2 Chemical Control of Plant Diseases

Greeks, Romans and Indus people used *Fungicidal materials* during 3000–2000 B.C. (Nene and Thapliyal, 1993). Although Homer (1000 B.C.) mentioned about use of sulfur as a pest averting material. Robertson recommended its use as fungicide for control of powdery mildew of peach in 1821 and Kenrich in 1833 and Grisson in 1851 recommended boiled lime sulfur. In 1902, Lowe and Parrott noticed that apple scab was controlled by lime sulfur. By 1906 it was recommended as a general fungicide. Commercial formulations of lime sulfur continue to be common protectant fungicide even today.

Homberg (1705) recommended mercuric chloride as wood preservative. Prevost recommended copper sulfate for wheat seed treatment against bunt in 1807. He for the first time demonstrated the fungitoxic value of copper compound. Copper sulfate was suggested as a possible control of late blight of potato during the 1844–45 epidemic and was recommended for roses in 1862. The use of copper sulfate admixed with lime was introduced by Dreisch in 1873 as seed treatment to control wheat bunt. The modern era of chemical control of plant diseases started with the discovery of Bordeaux mixture during the downy mildew epidemic struck grapes in France. The discovery of this fungicide has an interesting story. P.M.A. Millardet (1879–1882), a professor of botany at the university of Bordeaux, France was a man of broad interests and his contributions fell in three categories:

1. Studies on morphology, physiology, and systematic of plants
2. Investigations on the root aphid *Phylloxera* of the grapevines and hybridization experiments to develop resistant plants
3. Research on downy mildew of grapes and its control

Downy mildew of grapes was first reported in Europe in 1878 and it was discovered at about the same time in France, where it had evidently been introduced from USA during the importation of resistant rootstocks of grapevines for root aphid *Phylloxera*. The disease spread rapidly and threatened the vineyards and wine industry. Millardet started a thorough study of the disease including the methods of control. In 1882, he observed that the vines that had been sprinkled with a mixture of copper sulfate and slaked lime, to prevent the grapes from being stolen, retained their leaves whereas the untreated ones were defoliated. These observations suggested Millardet a means of controlling the disease. Subsequently, he performed extensive spraying trials with many preparations of copper, calcium and iron salts. In May 1885, Millardet published his work and gave details of spraying with a mixture of copper sulfate and slaked lime, which was later known as **Bordeaux Mixture**. Mason of France (1887) introduced Burgundy mixture using sodium carbonate in place of lime. Later, soluble copper fungicides (copper oxychloride) were discovered to overcome toxicity of Cu^{++} and gradually replaced Bordeaux mixture.

Tisdale and Williams (1934) reported fungitoxicity of dithiocarbamates. In late 1940s and during 1950s, large number of synthetic compounds were introduced in the market as fungicides. These included chlorinated hydrocarbons, organophosphates, carbamates, thiophanates, triazoles and acylanines. By 1990s, there were 113 active ingredients registered as fungicides worldwide (Knight, et al., 1997). However, all are not equally effective and safe. Salts of toxic metals and organic acids, organic compounds of mercury and sulfur, quinines and heterocyclic nitrogenous compounds have been major protectant fungicides in the latter half of the 20th century.

The introduction of systemic fungicides in 1966 was a major landmark in the history of fungicidal management of plant diseases. It started with the discovery of oxathiins in 1966 by Von Schmeling and Marshal Kulka. It was soon followed by confirmation of systemic activity of pyrimidines (1968) and benzimidazoles (1968–69). In the following year, 1969, Schroeder Provividenti reported resistance against benomyl. Metalaxyl, effective against oomycetes was developed by Ciba-Geigy in 1973 and came in use as a fungicide in 1977. During the same period, an organic phosphate fungicides, fosetyl-AL, was also developed and used against oomycetous fungi.

2.8 PLANT PATHOLOGY IN INDIA

The ancient Indians of the *Vedic* period had made observations on crop diseases and suggested several methods to control them. But they were not in a form, acceptable by western thought as scientific. Nonetheless, attempts have been made by the Asian Agri History Foundation promoted by Prof. Y.L. Nene to provide documentary explanations for the ancient observations and records.

Plant pathology developed as a science in India about hundred years ago and prior to that British officers having botany as hobby made valuable observations and noting. Major Sleeman in 1828 got the stem rust of wheat sample from Jabalpore identified from the Economic Botanist stationed in Ceylon (Sri Lanka) as *Puccinia*. This is the starting point of plant pathology in India. The coffee rust epidemic of Ceylon (Sri Lanka) and South India created economic distress for the East India Company. Coffee estates were converted into tea plantation and the British officers started recording of various diseases as free-lancers and reported them in the publications of the by-gone years. Observations of David Cunningham, on the aerobiology of Calcutta, Barclay's noting from Shimla hills. Lt. Col. K.R. Kirthikar's report on the Agaricales and Gasteromycetes fungi stimulated the growth of mycology and plant pathology in India.

Sir E.J. Butler in 1905 established the herbarium cryptogamiae at the IARI, Pusa Bihar, which later shifted to IARI, New Delhi. Butler and Bibsy in 1931 published the first edition of the Fungi of India and this has been frequently updated. The mycological support extended by J.F. Dastur, B.B. Mundhkur, C.V. Subramaniam, M.J. Thrimulachar, P.G. Patwardhan, M.S. Pavgi and K.S. Thind deserved special mention. A number of new genera of fungi have been identified from India. The type culture collection was initiated in 1963 in the Division of Mycology and Plant Pathology, IARI, New Delhi.

Sir E.J. Butler, a medical doctor, who joined IARI as the Imperial Mycologist, in 1905, served in that capacity for about 20 years and is rightly referred to as the **Father of Indian Plant Pathology.** During his tenure in India, he widely travelled and identified a number of plant diseases. He trained people and wrote a book *Fungi and Plant Diseases.* Butler is also credited for identifying and reporting the bacterial plant pathogens from India. B.B. Mundhkur is known for his contributions on the Ustilaginales, the diseases caused by Pucciniaceae, the Fusarial wilt of cotton. The most significant contribution of Mundhkur to Indian Plant Pathology will be remembered through the *Indian Phytopathological Society* which he started almost single handed in 1948 with its journal *Indian Phytopathology.* He also authored a textbook *Fungi and Plant Diseases.*

Physiology of diseased plants, effect of toxins, and role of micronutrients in the predisposition to diseases drew the attention of Prof. T.S. Sadasivan, R.N. Tandon, S.N. DasGupta and other plant pathologists during 1950's. J.C. Luthra developed solar energy based heat treatment procedure for the control of loose smut of wheat. The work on cereal rusts was initiated by K.C. Mehta of Agra College, Agra. Two monographs that he prepared laid strong foundation on the epidemiology of the *Puccinia* species infecting wheat. L.M Joshi developed new information on the spread of black, brown and yellow rusts in India through field surveys. The epidemiological investigations made by S. Nagrajan using climatic and weather based informations identified the *Puccinia* path in India.

Teaching of plant pathology as a major subject in Indian Universities started rather late. Perhaps, the University of Madras was the first to take-up plant pathology as a university science. Organized teaching in mycology and plant pathology was conducted by IARI. Agriculture College, Kanpur started postgraduate programme. First Agricultural University on land grant pattern was established in 1960 at Pantnagar (G.B. Pant University of Agriculture and Technology). Teaching in plant pathology with its supporting courses in mycology, bacteriology, virology, nematology, epidemiology, ecology, molecular plant pathology, etc. became integral part of undergraduate and postgraduate programme in agriculture.

With the onset of green revolution in early 1960, plant pathologists in India started extensive research and extension on control of plant diseases. The fungicides came in the market as an important input for disease management under intensive cultivation. Nene through his book *Fungicides in Plant Disease Control* introduced the subject to Indian readers. He also investigated the cause and control of "Khaira Disease of Paddy". R.S. Singh, a versatile writer and teacher worked on biological control and ecology of soil-borne pathogens. His book *Plant Diseases* is rightly referred as the "Bible" of plant pathology and is being read for the last forty years in India. R.K. Tripathi during his short tenure at Pantnagar developed a strong school of mycophysiology and biochemistry of plant infection.

S.Y. Padmanabhan, Anjeneyulu and A.P.K. Reddy did impressive and detailed work on rice diseases. M.M. Payak contributed significantly to maize pathology and multiple disease resistance.

C.D. Mayee contributed to the understanding of the groundnut rust, sunflower downy mildew. The research efforts in breeding and plant pathology were responsible for increased potato production in the country. The team efforts of Ramanujam led to the development of **seed plot technique** for virus free seed potato production in Indo-Gangetic plains. B.B. Nagaich made notable contributions in management of viral diseases of potato.

Systematic studies on the plant bacterial diseases started with M.K. Patel at Pune in 1948 as he identified and classified a number of plant pathogenic bacteria. The bacterial leaf blight of rice was first reported from India by Srinivasan in 1959. Variability in the different phytopathogenic bacteria has been the area of research for several scientists handling different crops such as cotton, J.P. Verma; Potato, G.S. Shekhawat; Cowpea/legume, P.N. Patel and others.

Nematology is a late starter in India, despite the fact that ufra diseases of rice and ear cockle/ tundu of wheat have attracted research efforts. Nematology started as a distinct discipline with lenience to zoology and plant pathology due to the efforts of A.R. Seshadri from Coimbatore, and Abrar M. Khan of Aligarh.

Interest in plant viruses started during 1950s and many plant pathologists initiated research programmes on plant viral diseases. R.S. Vasudera, S.N. DasGupta, T.K. Nariani, S. Mukhopadhyay, Y.L. Nene and several others contributed to the rapid growth of phytovirology in India.

Molecular plant pathology is the latest attraction and realizing the importance of it, B.M. Singh of Palampur, Anupam Verma of IARI, R. Sridhar of CRRI, A. Mahadevan of Madras and several others established schools to create competent manpower.

The pesticides and disease resistant varieties played a significant role in the success of green revolution. Pesticides soon attracted the attention of the scientific community and environmentalists due to development of pest resistance and disruption of ecology. In India, development of resistance to fungicide was noticed against dodine and ridomil (K.M. Safiulla). Biological control through introduction of antagonists like *Trichoderma harzianum* gained momentum. Production of biocontrol agents for large-scale field demonstration was standardized by Biocontrol groups at Pantnagar, Coimbatore and IARI, New Delhi. Currently there is a renewed interest in this area because of its ecofriendly nature, which is relevant to the tropical crop production systems.

REFERENCES

Agrios, G.N., 1997, *Plant Pathology,* 4th ed., Academic Press, New York.

Ainsoworth, G.C., 1981, *Introduction to the History of Plant Pathology*, Cambridge Univ. Press, Cambridge, p. 315.

Bruehl, G.W., 1991, Plant pathology, a changing profession in a changing world, *Annu. Rev. Phytopathol*, 29:1.

DasGupta, S.N., 1958, History of plant pathology and mycology in India, Burma and Ceylon Pub., *Indian Bot. Soc.*, p. 118.

Goto, M., 1992, *Fundamentals of Bacterial Plant Pathology*, Academic Press, San Diego.

Grover, R.K., 1975, Plant pathology researches in India, an introspection and prospects, *Pesticides Annual.*

Indian Council of Agric Res. 1964, *Agriculture in Ancient India*, ICAR, New Delhi, 176.

Matthews, R.E.F., 1991, *Plant Virology*, 3rd ed., Academic Press, San Diego.

Mehta, P.R., 1963, Plant pathology in India past, present and prospects, *Indian Phytopath.,* 16:1.

Orlob, G.B., 1971, History of plant pathology in the middle ages, *Annu. Rev. Phytopathol,* 9:7.

Raychaudhuri, S.P., 1967, Development of mycological and plant pathological researches education, and extension work in India, *Rev. Appl. Mycol.,* 46:577.

Raychaudhuri, S.P., 1972, History of Plant Pathology in India, *Annu. Rev. Phytopathol.,* 10:21.

Singh, R.S., 1981, Training and research in plant pathology, *Indian Phytopathol.,* 34:1

Singh, R.S., 2002, *Introduction to Principles of Plant Pathology,* 4th ed., Oxford and IBH Publishing Co. Pvt. Ltd., New Delhi.

Walker, J.C., 1957, *Plant Pathology,* 3rd ed., Tata McGraw-Hill Pub. Co. Ltd., Mumbai, p. 819.

3
Diagnosis of Plant Disease

3.1 DIAGNOSIS: THE CONCEPT

The word **diagnosis** is derived from Greek word *diagignoskein* which means to distinguish (from *dia* through, and *gignoskein*, to know). It is argued, whether diagnosis is an art or science or both. McIntyre and Sands (1977), considered diagnosis as an art. They have very rightly argued that diagnosis is done by percept and experience. The visual observations based on **experience, percept, and intuitive judgment** is still the most widely used method for identification of diseases.

3.2 THE PURPOSE OF DISEASE DIAGNOSIS

Disease diagnosis and pathogen detection may be required for the following purposes:

(a) Determine the presence and quantity of the pathogen(s).
(b) Assess the effectiveness of protection technologies.
(c) Certify planting materials for plant quarantine and certification.
(d) Determine the extent of disease incidence and consequent yield loss.
(e) Assess pathogen infection in plant materials in breeding programs.
(f) Detect and identify new pathogens rapidly to prevent further spread.
(g) Study taxonomic and evolutionary relationships of plant pathogens.
(h) Resolve the complex diseases incited by two or more pathogens.
(i) Study pathogenesis and gene functions.

3.3 METHODS OF DIAGNOSIS

In the field of human medicine, the doctors invariably use the **diagnostic tools** (physical, chemical or serological) to be sure of the ailment before starting a line of treatment. The symptoms provide the clues for possibilities, but confirmation comes only after performing diagnostic tests. In plant diseases, visual observations of the infected plant/plant parts continue to be the dominant method. Several sophisticated techniques are being used for observation, which include microscopy, isolation and identification of biotic agents associated, besides serology, immunological, biochemical and physiological analyses and genome analysis.

3.3.1 Visual Observation (Symptoms)

Symptoms are the visible expression of host-pathogen interaction. The deviation from 'normal morphology' coupled with presence of pathogen structures form the characteristic symptoms or signs, the basis for **preliminary diagnosis**.

27

Symptoms induced by parasitic fungi. Diseases caused by biotic and mesobiotic agents are identified primarily by symptoms and signs produced on host. The morphological features such as spores, fructifications, or sporophores, which differ from one fungus species to another, form important part of diagnostic programme. If desired structures of the fungus are not readily visible on the infected host surface, the parasite may be induced to sporulate by proper incubation of the infected tissue (Tuite, 1969). Major symptoms of plant diseases caused by fungal pathogen are summarized in Table 3.1, Plates 3.1–3.3.

Table 3.1 Symptoms of Diseases Caused by Fungal Parasites

Symptom	Fungus	Disease
Pathogen seen as white, gray, brownish, or purple growth on host surface; the superficial growth tangled cotton or downy growth	Downy mildew fungi; (Members of family-Peronosporaceae).	Downy mildews
Enormous numbers of spores formed on superficial growth giving host surface a dusty or powdery appearance; black fruiting bodies (cleistothecia) may also develop	Powdery mildew fungi; (members of order-Erysiphales)	Powdery mildews
Pustules of spores, usually breaking through host epidermis, dusty or compact, red brown, yellow, or black in colour	Rust fungi (order-Uredinales)	Rust diseases
Black or purplish black dusty mass formed on floral organ particularly the ovulary	Smut fungi (order-Ustilaginales)	Smut diseases
White blister-like pustules breaking open the epidermis and expose powdery mass of spores	*Albugo*	White blister or rust
Excessive growth of host tissues; abnormal increase in size due to abnormally increased cell size (hypertrophy) or increased cell divisions (hyperplasia)	*Albugo*, downy mildew fungi, root knot nematodes, MLO (Phytoplasma)	Galls, curl, pocket bladder, hairy root, knots, witche's, broom, clubbed roots, tumefaction, wart.
Reduced growth of host tissues, abnormally reduced size (atrophy)	Several fungi	Stunting, dwarfing, curling, puckering
Localized lesions on host leaves consisting of dead and collapsed cells	Several fungi	Leaf spots
Uniform, general and very rapid browning and death of foliage (leaves, branches, twigs, floral organs)	Several fungi	Blights
Necrosis and sunken ulcer like lesions on stem, leaf, flower, or fruits	*Colletotrichum* spp. *Glomerella* spp.	Anthracnose diseases
Necrosis, localized, usually surrounded by callus	Several fungi	Cankers
Disintegration or decay of part or all the root system	Many fungi	Root rots
Loss of turgidity, flaccid, dropping of leaves, or shoot due to disturbance in the vascular system of root or the stem	*Fusarium oxysporum* group, *Verticillium* spp.	Wilts
	Pythium, Rhizoctonia	Damping off of seedlings

Plate 3.1 Symptoms—diseases caused by fungi—white rust (A), leaf blight (B, C) and leaf spots (D, E, F).

Plate 3.2 Symptoms—fungal diseases [Ergot (A), mango malformation (B), bunch-rot (C), hypertrophy (D) and grain smuts (E, F)].

Plate 3.3 Symptoms caused by fungi—Powdery mildews (A, B), Downy mildews (C, D), Rusts (E), Anthracnose (F) and Fruit rot (G).

Symptoms induced by bacterial pathogens. Plant pathogenic bacteria induce water-soaked lesions in the infected tissues at the initial stages, and these lesions turn necrotic late. Formation of encrustations or bacterial ooze from infected tissues is another distinguishing feature associated with bacterial diseases. As infection progresses, leaf spots, blights, scabs, cankers, tumours, wilts, soft rots, etc. may be the prominent symptoms (Plate 3.4). Features such as cell shape, flagellation, and gram-reaction, are essentially employed for diagnosis of bacterial diseases. The characteristics of bacterial genera that are used invariably for diagnosis are summarized (Table 3.2). Detailed information regarding the cultural characteristics and different tests to be done is provided by Schaad (1988).

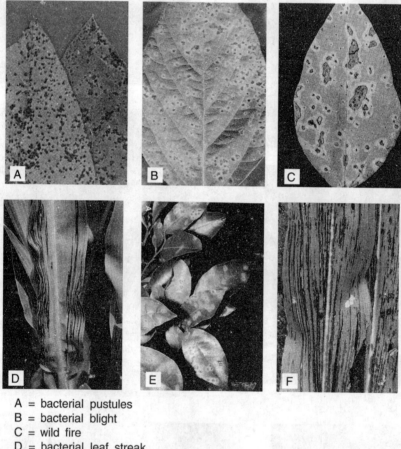

A = bacterial pustules
B = bacterial blight
C = wild fire
D = bacterial leaf streak
E = bacterial canker
F = bacterial leaf stripe

Plate 3.4 Symptoms—plant pathogenic bacteria

Symptoms induced by nematodes. Nematodes infect both root and above ground portion of plants. Root symptoms *(Plate 3.5)* may appear as root knots, root galls, root lesions, excessive root branching, injured root tips, and root rots when nematode infections are accompanied by parasitic or saprophytic fungi and bacteria. These root symptoms are usually accompanied by non-characteristic symptoms in the above ground parts of plants appearing primarily as reduced growth,

Table 3.2 Salient Features of Plant Pathogenic Genera of Bacteria

Genus or Trivial name	Gram stain	Flagellation	Morphology and size	Colony and pigmentation	G-C Mol%	Habitat and disease symptom	Reduction
Agrobacterium	Gram-negative	Peritrichous	Rods, 0.8 × 1.5-3 µm	Smooth, non-pigmented	60-63	Rhizosphere and soil-inhabitants, causes hypertrophy (Crown gall)	When growing on carbohydrate media abundant polysaccharide slime produced
Clavibacter (Coryenebacterium)	Gram-positive	None or Polar	Straight or slightly curved rods, pleomorphic, V-form 0.5-0.9 × 1.5-4.0 µm	Irregularly stained pigments or granules and club-shaped swellings	53-55	Soil-borne, produce canker, wilt, rots, and fasciation	
Erwinia	Gram-negative	Peritrichous	Straight rods, 0.5-1.0 × 1.0-3.0 µm	None or yellow ,blue or pink pigmentation	50-57	Facultative anaerobes, Necrosis, wilt diseases and soft rots	The amylovora group do not produce pectic enzymes while carotovora group has strong pectolytic activity
Pseudomonas	Gram-negative	One or many polar flagella	Straight to curved rods, 0.5-1.0 × 1.5-4.9 µm	None or green or blue	57.7-67	Inhabitants of soil, fresh water and marine environment, cause leaf spots, galls, wilt, blight canker etc.	Soluble pigments produced, no acid from lactose, some (e.g. *P. syringae*) produce yellow green diffusible fluorescent pigments on a low iron medium.
Streptomyces	Gram-positive	None	Slender-branched hyphae, 0.5-1.0 µm in diameter, spores formed	On nutrient media colonies are small (1-10 mm in diameter) smooth surface, with a weft of aerial mycelium that may appear granular, powdery or velvety, wide variety of pigments formed	69-73	Soil inhabitants, cause scab diseases	Produce one or more antibiotics active against bacteria, fungi, etc.
Xanthomonas	Gram-negative	Polar	Straight rods, 0.4-1.0 × 1.2-3.0 µ	Growth on agar media usually yellow	63-69	All species are plant pathogenic and found only in association with plants or plant materials, cause leaf spots, blight, canker, etc.	Produce acid from lactose
Xylella	Gram-negative	Non-motile, aflagellate	Straight rods, 0.3 × 1-4.0 µm	Colonies small, with smooth or finely undulated margins, non-pigmented	—	Strictly aerobic, nutritionally fastidious, habitat is xylem of plant tissue	—

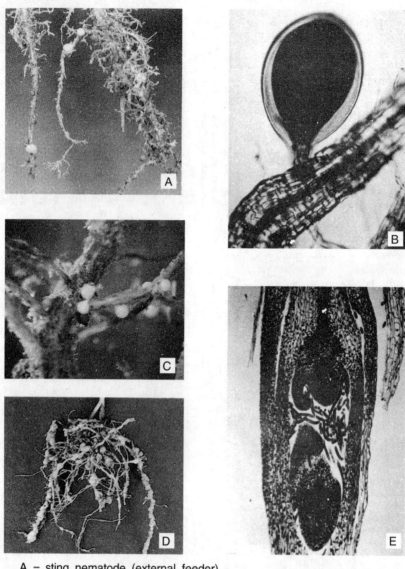

A = sting nematode (external feeder)
B = cysts of *Heterodera* attached to roots
C = lance nematode (feeds on root surface and within the roots
D = root-knot (*Meloidogyne* sp.)
E = nematode larvae within the seed

Plate 3.5 Symptoms—diseases caused by phytonematodes.

symptoms of nutrient deficiency, such as yellowing of foliage, excessive wilting in hot or dry weather, reduced yield and poor quality of products. Certain species of nematodes infect the above-ground portions of plants. They cause galls, necrotic lesions and rots, twisting and distortion of stem and leaves, and abnormal development of floral parts. Certain nematodes attack grains of grasses forming galls full of nematodes in place of seed. Diagnosis of diseases induced by sedentary nematodes is generally easier than that for migratory nematodes. Sedentary nematodes usually induce galls or enlarge sufficiently to be macroscopically visible on roots. For instance, *Meloidogyne* spp. induces variously shaped galls (Plate 3.5) and females of *Heterodera* or *Globodera* spp. (cyst nematodes) become so large that they are easily visible (Plate 3.5) on roots. One can view vermiform sedentary nematodes by microscopic examination of roots or in the rhizosphere. Nematodes extracted from plant tissues or soil can be identified using various illustrations, descriptions and keys as aids (Mai and Lyou, 1975).

Symptoms induced by viruses and viroids. Methods for identification of viral diseases have been described and reviewed (Bos, 1970; Ball, 1974; Matthews, 1991) extensively. These methods include symptomatology, mode of transmission, host-range, particle morphology, antigenicity and electrophoretic mobility in gels. Because some of these techniques require special methodology and equipment for confirmation, the symptoms and distribution patterns frequently suffice for preliminary diagnosis. Characteristics of viruses and description of symptomatology are available in several sources (CMI, 1970, Smith, 1972). Plant viruses cause a variety of symptoms, depending on the host plant species (Plate 3.6) and different unrelated viruses may induce similar symptoms in the same host plant species. The viruses induce primary symptoms on inoculated leaves, which exhibit chlorotic or necrotic local lesion or vein clearing. Later when the virus becomes systemic, secondary symptoms developed as colour changes, **teratological symptoms**, death or necrosis and abnormal growth form. Colour changes may vary from mosaic on leaves to colour breaking in flowers. Various kinds of changes in size and shape of plant part may be seen as leaf roll, leaf curl, enation, leaf crinkle, galls and tumours.

The virus infection may result in conspicuous changes in the general growth and appearance of infected plants. General stunting of branches or entire plant, rosette nature of leaves, and bunching or crowding of leaves at the apex leading to bunchy top are some of the symptoms associated with viruses, for more details Bos (1970) and Narayanasamy and Doraiswamy (1996) may be consulted. CMV, WMV-1, WMV-2, and SMV are distinguished from each other on the basis of the reaction of five indicator plants to each of them (Nelson and Tuite, 1969). For identification, host-ranges of unknowns are compared with those described for known viruses in literature (CMI, 1970; Smith, 1972; 1977) and other publications.

Symptoms induced by phytoplasmas (MLO). The MLOs cause general stunting or dwarfing of affected plant parts or whole plants. Chlorosis and reduced leaves are also frequently observed. Antholysis of floral parts is another characteristic feature; it results from virescence, phyllody, and proliferation of floral tissues. Floral parts are transformed into green leaf-like structures. Partial or total sterility of infected plants may be commonly noted. These symptoms are observed in plants infected by diseases such as aster yellows, little leaf of brinjal, sesame phyllody, and witche's broom disease of potato, peanut and grain legumes. Proliferation of auxiliary buds and formation of a large number of thin shoots are observed prominently in little of brinjal, rice yellow dwarf and sugarcane grassy shoot diseases. Reduction in leaf size and inter nodal length and tendency for the leaves to stand out stiffly, giving a spike like appearance to the infected branches are the distinguishing symptoms of sandal spike disease. Tomato big bud disease is characterized by hypertrophy of floral parts, leading to upright disposition of flower buds, which remain swollen and unopened.

Plate 3.6 Symptoms—viral diseases: (A) maize dwarf mosaic, (B) yellow mosaic, (C) yellow vein mosaic, (D) bud blight, (E) soyabean mosaic, and (F) rice tungro.

3.3.2 Chemo-diagnostic Methods

Chemo-diagnostic tests depend on the reaction between reagents and certain chemical compound(s) present in the infected plants, resulting in the development of a visible colour reaction. Detection of viruses, MLOs, fungi, and bacteria by using such tests involving the use of dyes, chemicals, selective media, and fluorescent markers have been reported.

Fungal pathogens. Plant diseases are first subjected to visual observations. The symptoms/signs are observed very closely. However, there could be instances where visual observations do not lead to conclusive identification of the disease and its cause. In such situations, techniques pertaining to isolation, pure culture and chemo-diagnostic methods are employed. The presence and viability of fungal spores can be determined by fluorescein diacetate assay (FDA). For example, lipase activity is detected consistently in the extracts of viable teliospores of *Tilletia controversa*, but not in the extracts of autoclaved spores (Chastain and King, 1990). Loose smut of wheat can be detected if seed embryos are stained with trypan blue to reveal the presence of fungal mycelia (Figure 3.1).

The usefulness of isozyme electrophoresis for detection of fungal pathogens such as *Peronospora, Phytophthora, and Fusarium* has been assessed. Cell wall analysis (glycoproteins), too, has been used for detection of fungi. Takenaka and Kawasaki (1974) used the technique to differentiate six species of *Pythium* causing snow rot of winter cereals. The electrophoretic patterns of glycoproteins, detected with coomassie brilliant blue, lectin, and antibody, exhibited sufficient interspecific polymorphism and intraspecific stability to allow identification of six species.

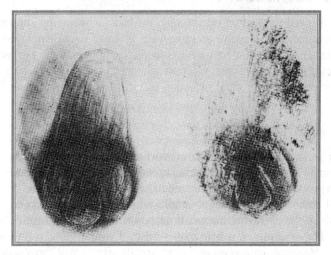

Figure 3.1   An uninfected wheat embryo (left) and mycelium of *Ustilago segetum* var. *tritici* in an excised seed embryo (right).

Bacterial pathogens. In chemo-diagnostic methods, for detection of bacterial pathogens besides use of selective media, several biochemical tests such as reduction of nitrates, hydrogen sulfide production, production of indole acetic acid, utilization of carbon and nitrogen compounds, starch hydrolysis, lipolytic activity, action on litmus milk, gelatin liquefaction, ammonia production, Kovocs's oxidase test, thornley's-arginine dehydrolase activity, tyrosinase activity, etc. are employed. Properties of bacterial cells using direct colony thin layer chromatography, polyacrylamide gel electrophoresis, and bacteriophase are also studied. Fluorescent marker substances have been used for indexing plant materials for the presence of citrus greening and exocortis. Hooker, et al. (1993) evaluated the reliability of this procedure as a method of diagnosing greening disease.

Detection of plant viruses, phytoplasmas, and viroids. Different kinds of chemicals have been used to distinguish plant infected by viruses and phytoplasmas. Linder (1961) has reviewed various chemical tests that have been used for the diagnosis of virus infection in plants. These tests depend on the reaction between the chemical used and the compounds present in infected plants, which results in the development of a recognizable colour either in the extracts or in tissues. These tests can be grouped according to the nature of compounds involved.

Various tests employed include protein test, carbohydrate test, enzyme test, polyphenol test, nucleic acid test, and fluorescent test, etc. Several histo-chemical methods have been used for the detection of infection of MLOs. Dienes's stain has been used to know the presence of MLO in rice yellow dwarf, little leaf of brinjal, sandal spike and coconut root wilt. Dark blue colour is retained in the phloem cells of MLO-infected plants, indicating the positive reaction (Narayanasamy, 1997). Floroglucinol test and poly acrylamide gel electrophoresis techniques have been used for detection of viroids.

3.4 ELECTRON MICROSCOPY

The basic principle involved in electron microscopy, methods of preparing support film, calibration of the electron microscope, and negative staining and different stains employed are described by Narayanasamy (1997). The standard electron microscopic techniques, such as metal shadowing, dip method, leaf dip serology, immuno-sorbent electron microscopy, decoration, and gold label antibody decoration, have been employed for rapid detection of viruses and phytoplasmas infected materials.

3.5 SERODIAGNOSTIC METHODS

The development of techniques based on the production of antibodies specific to individual now allow rapid and accurate identification of causal agents, and with many diseases it eliminates the problem of diagnosis based on symptoms. Immunodiagnostic procedures were first used in the crops for detection of viral pathogens, and are now employed widely for this purpose. Immunodiagnostic techniques are based on the ability of mammals to produce antibodies specific to foreign antigen entering their blood. For examples, if a mammal is injected with a virus, it will produce antibodies unique to that virus. Also, the antibodies will bind specifically to that virus alone. The antibodies can be extracted from the blood of the animal and used to detect the virus in sap from infected plants. Furthermore, antibody-producing cells can be extracted from the immunized animals and fused with perpetually dividing myeloma cells to form hybridoma cells. Hybridomas can be maintained as cell cultures and can be grown indefinitely to provide a constant supply of monoclonal antibodies specific to a particular pathogen.

The majority of immunodiagnostic tests and test kits for detection and identification of plant pathogens are based on the use of antibodies in the **enzyme-linked immuno-sorbent assay (ELISA).** Tests are usually carried out in multiwell plastic plates (Figure 3.2).

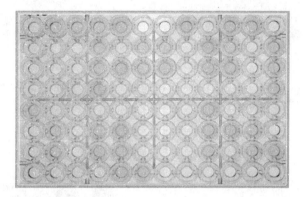

Figure 3.2 Multiwell plates used in ELISA, the dark wells show a positive response and thus presence of the pathogen.

Immunoassays can be characterized as quantitative analytical methods applied for measuring biologically important compounds/organisms using antibodies as specific analytical reagents. They are based on the unique recognition reaction between antibodies and antigens. Different types of enzyme immunoassays used in the field of diagnostics fell in two major groups: (a) **homogeneous** assays which are restricted to micromolecules of low molecular weight such as drugs, hormones and toxins, and (b) **heterogeneous** assays which are suitable for detecting macromolecules and plant or animal pathogens (Clark, 1992).

ELISA, one of the serological methods, developed in 1977 (Clark, 1977) has been used widely by pathologists and has increased tremendously their ability to study and detect plant viruses as well as other pathogens and the diseases they cause. The basic principle of ELISA is the detection of solid phase bound antigen and antibody complex by a colour reaction using specific enzyme and substrate. Based on the enzyme-labelled antibody employed, the ELISA procedure can be termed as direct or indirect. The ELISA procedure has been standardized for the detection of many plant viruses, fungi, bacteria and mycoplasma-like organisms. Also the application of ELISA in epidemiology is now increasing as it is being used more and more for studying vector relationships, investigating alternate hosts of the pathogen and studying the occurrence or distribution of various strains/races/biotypes of a pathogen. ELISA has become a preferred method for pathogen detection because of its sensitivity, economic use of antiserum, availability of quantifiable data and capacity for handling large number of samples rapidly. In spite of having a few limitations ELISA with all its versatility would remain a technique of choice for routine certification purposes.

A diagrammatic representation of the ELISA technique as it proceeds in an individual well is shown in Figure 3.3. Firstly, antibodies specific to a virus are fixed to the base of the wells. Then the sap, extracted from plant tissue, is placed in the wells. If the sap contains virus particles matching the antibodies, the virus will bind to these antibodies. Further antibodies bound to enzyme such as alkaline phosphatase, are added to the wells and these antibodies will also bind to the virus. A suitable substrate of the enzyme is added in the well. The antibody bound enzyme will react with its substrate and gives the indicator colour. A positive reaction indicates the presence of the pathogen and the extent of reaction (which is related to the intensity of colour) may give an indication of the amount of virus present in the sap.

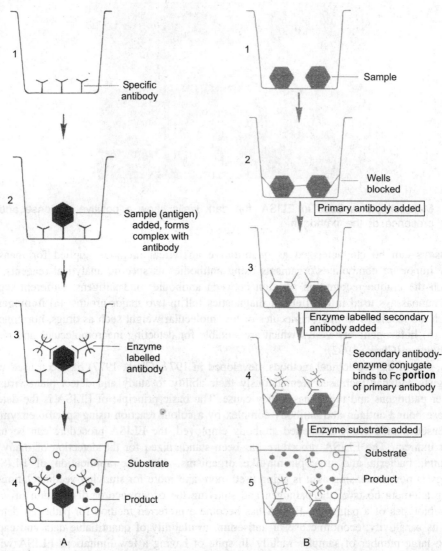

1
— Specific antibody

2
— Sample (antigen) added, forms complex with antibody

3
— Enzyme labelled antibody

4
○ — Substrate
● — Product

A

1
— Sample

2
— Wells blocked

Primary antibody added

3
— Enzyme labelled secondary antibody added

4
Secondary antibody-enzyme conjugate binds to Fc **portion** of primary antibody

Enzyme substrate added

5
— Substrate
— Product

B

Figure 3.3 (A) Direct antybody sandwich (DAS) ELISA (B) Indirect ELISA using coated wells.

Immunodiagnostic kits are now available for several important crop diseases. Early diagnosis of disease is one of the major advantages of immuno-diagnostic techniques and has led to the development of immunoassays for plant pathogenic fungi. Kits have been developed for diseases such as *Septoria* spp. On cereals, where the pathogen has a long latent period, prior to symptom expression or where symptoms may be due to attack by one of several organisms. Many kits are based on the multiwell plate procedure but some intended for field use, involve depicts or filter pad tests. With all kits, the first step is to extract sap from the diseased material. Some of the filter pad kits developed for damping-off diseases can give results in as little as 10 minutes. Readers can refer to Narayanasamy (1997) for details of the methods for all groups of plant pathogens.

3.6 NUCLEIC ACID BASED METHOD

The exploitation of nucleic acids in methods for the detection and/or identification of plant pathogens is so far limited. However, the potential advantages are so overwhelming that their wide spread, adoption seems inevitable. All that is required is the development of suitable assay systems. A variety of detection methods based on nucleic acid include: **direct visualization** of entire genomes (gel electrophoresis, Agarose gel electrophoresis), **restriction digestion** and **electrophoresis** of DNA (restriction endonuclease-cleave DNA at a particular point), hybridization of DNA and RNA and the polymerase chain reaction (PCR). The characteristics of plant pathogens and indeed all organisms are determined by the structure of their genetic material in the form of DNA (Figure 3.4) with fungi and bacteria and RNA in the case of most plant viruses. Theoretically, DNA or RNA could be extracted from a pathogen; the nucleotide sequence is determined and compared to sequences known for particular pathogens. This is, however, a long, laborious and costly process. A more realistic approach involves cutting the long nucleic acid strands into smaller pieces using endonuclease enzymes. The fragments of DNA or RNA, thus formed, may be separated by electrophoresis, the bands formed often being characteristic of a particular species.

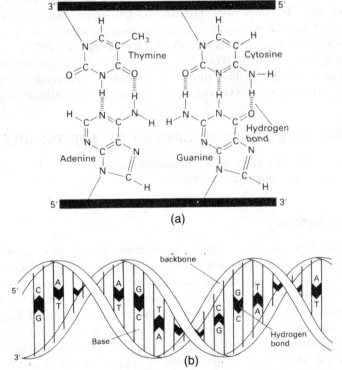

Figure 3.4 Structure of DNA, Base pairs (a) and the double helix (b).

A more sophisticated approach involves the use of nucleic acid probes. These have been employed for the rapid identification of plant viruses and offer the possibility of rapid detection of races of plant pathogenic fungi. These radioactive strands may then be used to probe nucleic acids extracted from any organism. If the radiolabelled probe recognizes the nucleic acid base sequence, to which it is complementary, it will bind to this sequence. Binding of the radiolabelled probe can be deflected with X-ray film and identification confirmed of the organism from which the nucleic acid was extracted. The development of polymerase chain reaction (PCR) may solve most of difficulties. Indeed, diagnosis by PCR may become as important as or even more important, than ELISA for detection of plant diseases. PCR involves the rapid multiplication (amplification) of DNA sequences unique to a particular organism.

3.7 THE USE OF MODERN TELECOMMUNICATIONS IN PLANT DISEASE DIAGNOSIS

Since the advent of photography in the mid 1800s, photographic images have become important and extensively used to enhance the descriptions of plant diseases and are invaluable in research, teaching, extension and diagnostics. Today photographs can be scanned, digitalized and sent around the world within seconds (Holmen, et al., 2000).

Modern telecommunication system was first used in agricultural sciences in early 1990s as Digitally Assisted Diagnosis (DAD). The equipments used are computer, digital camera, dissecting and compound microscopes with digital camera attachments, flatbed scanner and a colour inkjet printer (Briere and France, 1998, Holmen, et al., 2000). The digital images can be posted to a website or as e-mail attachment. Scientists from different countries have made computer-based diagnostic systems for different crops and diseases to ease the diagnosis and to overcome the arising risks. Some of these are PRO-PLANT for a cereal disease, VEGES for vegetables, TFRUIT. Xpert and CIT. Xpert for fruits and citrus, respectively, COTON Doc for cotton crop. Danger lies in over-reliance and unrealistic expectations. DAD is nothing more than a means of improving communication. Perhaps no other tool has had more rapid and widespread impact on plant disease diagnostics.

3.8 DIAGNOSIS OF DISORDERS CAUSED BY ABIOTIC AGENTS

Disorders induced by abiotic causes are so frequently encountered in the field that a practitioner must be knowledgeable and cognizant of them.

3.8.1 Physical Agents

Temperature. Both low and high temperature extremes impair plant growth; sometimes the symptoms and knowledge of previous year's weather enable us to diagnose the disorder easily and readily. A low temperature injures plants primarily by inducing ice formation. Affected plant organs become soft; winter injury provides avenues for wound pathogens to initiate infection. Temperatures below freezing cause a variety of injuries to plants. Such injuries include killing of buds, flowers, young fruits, and succulent twigs. Frost bands consisting of discoloured; corky tissues in a band or large area of fruit surface are often produced on apples, pears, etc., following late frost. Low temperatures may kill young roots of trees such as apples and may cause bark splitting, other symptoms include tip necrosis, leaf margin necrosis, etc. (citrus and litchi). Injuries due to high temperature are frequently accompanied by moisture stress. Sunscald of plant occurs on many plants exposed to intense solar radiation at high temperatures (citrus, litchi).

Moisture. Soil saturated with water for considerable period becomes anaerobic and affects plant growth and development in several ways. Roots can die of anoxia. They become more sensitive to soil toxicants such as nitrites which accumulate due to anaerobic microbial activity. Activities of several biotic pathogens such as *Phytophthora* and *Pythium* are enhanced in wet soils because of oxygen depletion. Diseases due to insufficient water are common, where water is chronically insufficient, plants grow poorly, and leaves may be small, abnormally pigmented, and marginally necrotic. Water deficiency retards net photosynthesis.

Light. Variation in the amount or duration of electromagnetic radiation can affect normal host physiology (Fry, 1987). Lack of sufficient light retards chlorophyll formation and promotes slender growth with long internodes, thus leading to pale green leaves, spindly growth, and premature drop of leaves and flowers. This condition is called **etiolation**.

3.8.2 Chemical Agents

Nutrient deficiency in plants. Plants require several elements for growth. When they are present in the soil in amounts smaller than the minimum levels, the plants exhibit various external and internal disorders. The kinds of symptoms produced by deficiency of a particular nutrient depend mainly on the functions of that element in plants. Major disorders/symptoms due to deficiency of elements and which could be a valid source for diagnosis are given in Table 3.3.

Table 3.3 Nutrient Deficiencies in Plants

Nutrients	Symptoms
Boron	The bases of young leaves of terminal buds become light green and finally break down. Stems and leaves become distorted. Plants are stunted. Fruits, fleshy roots, or stems may crack on the surface and/or rot in the centre, e.g. heart rot of sugar beets.
Calcium	Young leaves become distorted, with their tips hooked back and the margins curled, leaves may be irregular in shape and ragged with brown scorching or spotting, terminal buds may die and plants have poor root system, e.g. blossom end distorted. Citrus, pome, and stone fruits show dieback of twigs in summer, burning of leaf margins, chlorosis, rosetting, etc.
Iron	Young leaves become severely chlorotic, but main veins remain green, sometimes brown spots develop, part or entire leaf may dry, and leaves may be shed.
Magnesium	First the older, then the younger leaves become mottled or chlorotic, then reddish, sometimes necrotic spots appear. The tips and margins of leaves may turn upwards and the leaves appear cupped, and leaves may drop off.
Manganese	Leaves become chlorotic but their smallest veins remain green and produce a checked effect, necrotic spots may appear scattered on the leaf, and severely affected leaves turn brown and wither.
Nitrogen	Plants grow poorly and are light green in colour. The lower leaves turn yellow or light brown and the stems are short and slender.
Phosphorus	Plants grow poorly and the leaves are bluish-green with purple tints. Lower leaves sometimes turn light bronze with purple or brown spots; shoots are short, thin, upright and spindly.
Potassium	Plants have thin shoots, which in severe cases show dieback, older leaves show chlorosis with browning of tips, scorching of the margins, and many brown spots usually appear near the margins, fleshy tissues show end necrosis.
Sulfur	Young leaves are pale green or light yellow without any spots. The symptoms resemble those of nitrogen deficiency.
Zinc	Leaves show interveinal chlorosis. Later they become necrotic and show purple or reddish pigmentation. Leaves are few and small, internodes are short and shoots form rosettes, and fruit production is low. Leaves are shed progressively from base to tip.

Toxicity of Minerals. Soils often contain excessive amounts of elements, which at higher concentration may be injurious to plants, either directly (injury) or indirectly (interference with absorption or function of other elements) or both. For instance, excessive nitrogen induces deficiency of calcium in the plant, while the toxicity of Cu, Mn, or Zn is both, direct on the plant and by inducing a deficiency of iron in the plant. Excessive amount of sodium salts, especially sodium chloride, sodium sulfate and sodium carbonate, increase soil pH and affect plant growth directly or indirectly. The injuries vary in different plants and may range from chlorosis to stunting, leaf burning, wilting to death of seedlings and young plants. Some plants (wheat and apples) are very sensitive to alkali injury while sugarbeet, alfalfa, and several grasses are quite tolerant. On the other hand, when soil is too acidic, the growth of some kinds of plants is impaired and various symptoms may appear.

Herbicide injury. Pesticides, especially herbicides cause injury to plants, if used incorrectly, i.e. on the sensitive plants, at wrong time, under improper environmental condition, or at wrong dosage. Pesticide injury is often associated with cultural practices as spraying, planting, or cultivation. However, some pesticides may be transported by air or water. For example, 2, 4–D (2, 4-dichlorophenoxy acetic acid), a common broad leaf herbicide, is volatile and may drift to some distance. Among the common symptoms (Figure 3.5) observed are smaller leaves, narrowed interveinal areas, rolled leaves, distorted petioles, yellowing of veins, leaf distortions, hypertrophied inflorescence, etc. Some symptoms of herbicide injuries on various plants have been described by Streets (1972) and Lockerman, et al. (1975) and should be referred and consulted if herbicide injury is expected to be involved.

Figure 3.5 Herbicide injury.

Air pollutants. Air pollution damage can be ascertained by symptoms (Agrios, 1997; Brandt, 1965) and by proximity of diseased plants to an air pollutant. Pollutants, their source, susceptible plants and symptoms are summarized in Plate 3.7 and Table 3.4.

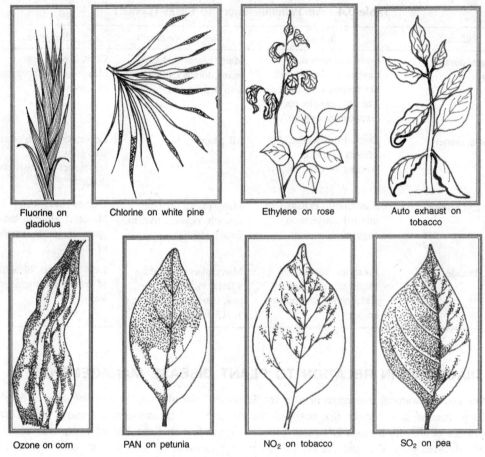

Fluorine on gladiolus

Chlorine on white pine

Ethylene on rose

Auto exhaust on tobacco

Ozone on corn

PAN on petunia

NO_2 on tobacco

SO_2 on pea

Plate 3.7 Air pollution injury to plants.

Table 3.4 Air Pollution Injury to Plants

Pollutant	Source	Susceptible plants	Symptoms
Chlorine and hydrogen chloride	Refineries, glass factories, incineration of plastic	Many plants, usually near the source of pollutant; toxic at 0.1 ppm	Leaves bleached, show interveinal necrosis, scorched, dropping prematurely
Ethylene	Automobile exhausts, burning of gas, fuel oil and coal	Many plants, toxic at 0.05 ppm	Stunted plants, abnormal leaves, premature senescence and reduced blossoms and fruits
Hydrogen fluoride	Factories processing ore or oil	Many plants including corn, peach, tulip, toxic at 0.1 to 0.2 ppm	Leaf margins (dicot) and leaf tips (monocot) turn tan to dark, die, and fall.

(Contd.)

Table 3.4 Air Pollution Injury to Plants (*Contd.*)

Pollutant	Source	Susceptible plants	Symptoms
Hydrogen dioxide (H_2O_2)	From nitrogen and oxygen in the air by hot combustion sources like furnaces, internal combustion engines	Many plants including beans, tomatoes; toxic at 2 to 3 ppm	Growth reduction, bleaching and bronzing of leaves
Particulate matter	Dusts from roads, cement factories, burning of coal, etc.	All plants	Leaves crusty, chlorotic and grow poorly, sometimes necrosis and death
Peroxyacyl nitrates (PAN)	Automobile exhausts or internal combustion engines	Many plants including spinach, petunia, tomato, lettuce, dahlia	Causes silver leaf, bleached white to bronze spots on lower surface of leaves
Sulfur dioxide	Factories, automobile exhausts, coal burning and internal combustion engines	Many plants including alfalfa, violet, conifers, pea, cotton, bean, toxic at 0.3 to 0.5 ppm	Leaf chlorosis, bleaching of interveinal tissues of leaf

3.9 DIAGNOSIS IN RELATION TO PLANT DISEASE MANAGEMENT

Effective and economical management of plant diseases is the ultimate goal of the science of plant pathology. Precise and correct diagnosis of the disease and its cause(s) are must for effective management of the diseases. It is simply because of the fact that the line of treatments could be precisely decided only after the correct diagnosis. For example, if smuts, bunts and rusts are the diseases, the user can and should opt directly for Oxathiin compounds. If the cause were other than the diseases listed earlier, application of such compounds would be shear waste of time/money. Similarly, if downy mildew is damaging the crop, Metalaxyl can be recommended directly. Many a times pollutants and phytotoxicity of pesticides create symptoms that resemble to diseases caused by phytopathogenic bacteria. Similarly, there are situations that are complex diseases having association of more than one causal agent. What is needed today for effective, sustainable and ecofriendly management of diseases is the valid and correct diagnosis of the disease(s).

3.9.1 Establishment of Pathogenicity

Diagnosis of plant diseases or identification of causal agent is a routine work for plant pathologists. Most of samples are identified based on experience or reported symptoms in literature. However, under field conditions there may be involvement/association of more than one microbes in disease samples. There may be primary as well as secondary colonizes of plant tissue. Besides, there may be a case, which is not yet reported in literature. Thus, the pathogenicity of microbe has to be established. First step in establishing pathogenicity is the isolation of microbe/pathogen in pure culture. Pathogens may be isolated into artificial culture. Seeds, for example, can be surface sterilized and placed on to suitable agar media to allow the pathogen to grow out. This method is used to detect hemibiotrophs and necrotrophs.

Robert Koch in 1880s established four principles, widely known as **Koch's postulates** for anthrax. These were adopted by plant pathologists for establishing pathogenicity in plant diseases also. The microorganism may be considered as the causal agent of disease if it fulfills the following conditions:

(a) The microorganism must be found associated with diseased tissue.

(b) The microorganism must be isolated and grown in culture, and characteristics recorded.

(c) The microorganism must reproduce the disease when inoculated in/on the host plant from which it was isolated.

(d) The microorganism, when reisolated from the artificially inoculated plants, must correspond in all its characteristics to the original isolate.

These rules have proved very useful to identify most of the diseases caused by biotic agents. However, for pathogens that do not reproduce out of the living cells certain modifications of rules have been made. The Koch's postulates for viruses are:

(a) The virus must be concomitant with the disease.

(b) It must be isolated from the diseased plant (multiplied in a propagated host, purified physico-chemically and identified for its properties).

(c) When inoculated in a healthy host plant, it must reproduce the symptoms (disease).

(d) The same virus must be demonstrated to occur in and it must be isolated from the experimental host.

Besides routine culture media, several selective and semi-selective culture media/techniques have been developed, which should be employed for identification of the pathogens. During the last four decades the development and use of selective media for isolation and enumeration of fungal and bacterial pathogens have been rising at a fast pace. Selective media have been developed for *Pythium, Phytophthora, Fusarium* (Tsao, 1970; Papavizas, 1967), *Phoma betae* (Bugbeen 1974), (*M. phaseolina* (Papavizas and Klag, 1975), *R. solani* (Ko and Horra, 1971), *S. rolfsii* (Backman and Rodriguez-Kabana, 1976), etc. have been described.

3.10 FUTURE TRENDS IN PLANT DISEASE DIAGNOSIS

In the absence of exclusive or reliable simple method of identifying pathogen or the diseases caused by them, it is likely that most diagnostic methods will continue to be used or co-exist in some form in the future. While traditional ones are sure to be used in the future, it is obvious that we are already entering a period of great change. The range of choice is relatively cheap, easy to use diagnostic kits now being developed should allow us to monitor even low level of disease on the spot under field conditions (Klausner, 1987; Miller, et al., 1988, 1990, 1992). Both immunological and nucleic acid hybridization techniques are increasingly becoming popular for the rapid detection of many of those pathogens which cannot be easily identified by other routine ways. In addition, nucleic acid hybridization technique can detect uncultivable pathogens, detect pathogens in soil or seed, and also predict virulence alleles and fungicide resistance in a pathogen population.

REFERENCES

Ball, E.M., 1974, *Serological Tests for Identification of Plant Viruses*, Am. Phytopathological Soc. ST. Paul, Minnesota, 31.

Bos, L., 1970, *Symptoms of Virus Diseases in Plants.*, Oxford & IBH, Publishing Co., New Delhi.

Briere, S.C. and France, G.D., 1998, Use of digital images to aid in disease diagnosis at the university of Wyoming, extension plant pathology lab. *Phytopathology*, 88:11.

Chastain, T.G. and King, B., 1990, A biochemical method for estimating viability of teliospore of *Tilletia Controversa*, *Phytopathology*, 80:474.

Clark, M.F. and Adams A.N., (1977), Characteristics of the microplate method of enzyme-linked immunosorbant assay for detection of plant viruses, *Jr. of Gen. Virology*, 34, 475–483.

Clark, M.F., 1992, Immunodiagnostic techniques for plant mycoplasma-like organisms. In: *Techniques for the Rapid Detection of Plant Pathogens*, Deenean, J.M. and Torance, L. (Eds.) Brit. Soc. For Plant Pathology, Blackwell Scientific, Oxford, U.K.

Commonwealth Mycological Institute, 1970, *Description of Plant Viruses*, CMT, Kew, Surrey, England.

Fry, W.E., 1987, *Principles of Plant Disease Management*, Academic Press, New York, 378.

Holmen, G.J., et al., 2000, What's a picture worth? The use of modern telecommunication in diagnosis of plant diseases, *Plant Diseases*, 84:1256.

Hooker, M.E., et al., 1993, Reliability of gentisic, a fluorescent marker for diagnosis of citrus greening, *Plant Disease*, 77:174.

Klausner, A., 1987, Immunoassays flourish in new markets, *Biotechnology* 5:551.

Linder, R.C., 1961, Chemical tests in the diagnosis of plant virus diseases, *Botanical Review*, 27:501.

Mai, W.F. and Lyou, H.H., 1975, *Pictorial Key to Genera of Plant Parasitic Nematodes*, 4th ed., Cornell Univ. Press, Ithaca, New York.

Matthews, R.E.F., 1991, *Plant Virology*, 3rd ed., Academic Press, San Diego, California.

McIntyre, J.L. and Sands, D.C., 1977, How disease is diagnosed. In Horsfall, J.G. and Cowling, E.B. (Eds.). *Plant Diseases: An Advanced Treatise*, Vol I, Academic Press, New York, 35.

Miller, S.A., et. al., 1990, Development of modern diagnostic tests and benefits to farmers. In: Shots, A. (Ed.) *Monoclonal Antibodies in Agriculture*, Pudoc. Wagenigen, Netherlands, 15.

Miller, S.A. et al., 1992, From the research bench to the market place, development of commercial diagnostic kits. In: Deencan, J.M., and Torrance, L. (Eds.), *Techniques for the Rapid Diagnosis of Plant Pathogens*, Blackwell Oxford.

Miller, S.A. and Martin, R.R., 1988, Molecular diagnosis of Plant disease, *Annu. Rev. Phytopathol.*, 26:409.

Narayanasamy, P., 1997, *Plant Pathogen Detection and Disease Diagnosis*, Marcel Dekker, Inc. New York, Basel, Hong Kong, 331.

Narayanasamy, P. and Doraiswamy, S., 1996, *Plant Viruses and Viral Diseases,* New Century Book House Pvt. Ltd., Madras, India.

Nelson, M.R. and Tuite, D.M., 1969, Epidemiology of cucumber mosaic and watermelon mosaic of cantelopes in an arid climate, *Phytopathology,* 59:849.

Schaad, N.W., 1988, *Laboratory Guide for Identification of Plant Pathogenic Bacteria,* Am. Phytopathological Society, St. Paul, Minnesota.

Smith, K.M., 1972, *A Textbook of Plant Virus Diseases,* 3rd ed., Longmans, New York, 652.

Smith, K.M., 1977, *Plant Viruses,* 6th ed., Chapman and Hall, London, 309.

Takenaka, S. and Kawasaki, S., 1974, Characterization of alanine-rich hydroxy proline containing cell wall proteins and their application for identifying *Pythium* species. *Physiological and Molecular Plant Pathology,* 45:249.

Tsao, P.H., 1970, Selective media for isolation of pathogenic fungi, *Annu. Rev. Phytopathol.* 8:157.

Tuite, J.F., 1969, *Plant Pathological Methods Fungi and Bacteria*, Minneapolis, Minnesota, 128.

4 Disease Development

4.1 INTRODUCTION

Plant disease is the outcome of interaction of the host plant with pathogen, which attacks the host basically to derive its nutrition as a parasite. This interaction is markedly influenced by the environmental factors. The role of environment in pathogenesis is important as it affects host plant, the pathogen (microbes) as well as **host-pathogen complex** (a third entity, **aegricorpus** sensu Loegering, 1966). This interaction or aegricorpus develops for certain period of time, which is decided by end of crop season or the death of the host plant. Since man for desired plant products has created agro-ecosystem, the human interference has paramount effect on occurrence and severity of plant diseases. The interactions in development of disease and the influence of various factors are represented in Figure 4.1.

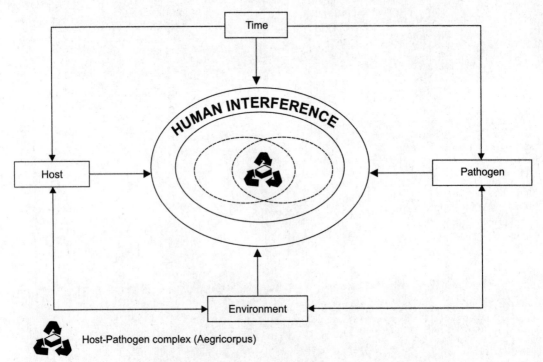

Host-Pathogen complex (Aegricorpus)

Figure 4.1 Interaction of factors responsible for disease development.

4.2 THE PATHOGENESIS

Disease development is a **dynamic process**. It is not a single step act or a condition (Horsfall and Dimond, 1959). A chain of events, in proper sequence, lead to disease development. The action(s) of pathogen and whole array of host reactions occurring in host are collectively called **pathogenesis**. The pathogenesis or the infection chain may be **continuous** or **intermittent.** The events in pathogenesis have been depicted in Figure 4.2.

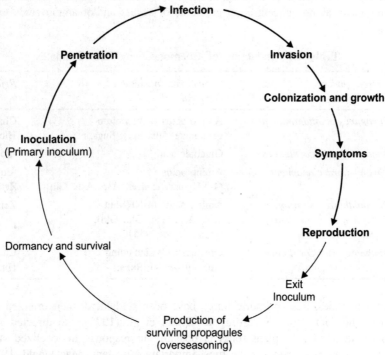

Figure 4.2 Stages in **Pathogenesis** (———►) and disease cycle.

4.2.1 Inoculum and Inoculation

The infective propagules of pathogen, capable of causing infection/disease, are known as **inoculum** and the process, which brings host and pathogen in contact, is called **inoculation**. In parasitic fungi the inoculum may be hyphal fragments, asexually and or sexually produced spores, specialized vegetative organs, etc. in bacteria, phytoplasma, RLOs, viruses, viroids and virusoids inoculum is always the whole individual. In case of nematodes, inoculum may be adults, larvae or eggs, while in phanerogams it may be plant parts or seeds. More information on inoculum production has been presented in chapter on epidemiology.

The means of survival (overwintering/oversummering) are the major link in continuation of disease cycle. The surviving structures on activation or germination produce the primary inoculum that initiates the infection chain. The initial infection that occurs from these propagules is called **primary infection**. At the end of each infection cycle, the pathogen produces new generation of propagules, as a result of growth or reproduction/multiplication. These propagules, secondary inoculum, cause secondary infection. Thus, a new infection cycle is initiated. In case of multiple cycle diseases many such infection cycles are completed in the crop season. This results in further buildup of disease in time and space.

Infection court is the site of intimate host–pathogen (inoculum) contact. Pathogen adopts several ways and means to establish contact with suitable host (infection courts). The process of pathogenesis, initiated by primary inoculum begins as soon as the inoculum comes into contact with the plant surface. Some pathogens like zoosporic fungi (*Pythium* and *Phytophthora*) possess sophisticated adaptations for locating the host, usually by responding to a particular signal. These stimuli may trigger germination of dormant propagules or attract hyphae or motile cells towards the host. Zoospores swim along concentration gradients of sugars and/or amino acids exuded by plant roots (Table 4.1).

Table 4.1 Induction of Chemotaxis by Root Exudates

Plant	Microorganisms	Chemotaxis inducing chemicals	Reference
Pea	*Phythium aphanidermatum*	Amino acids (Ammonium gentamate, Gln, Ser); Sugars	Chang-Ho and Hickman, 1970.
	Aphanomycetes cochlioides	Gluconic acid	-do-
	Phytophthora cinnamomi	Amino acids (4-NH$_2$-butyric acid, Asp, Asn, Glu)	-do- Zentmyer, 1970.
	Phytophthora cactorum, P. capsici, P. citrophthora, P. palmivora	Amino acids (4-NH$_2$-butyric acid, Asp, Asn, Glu, Gln); Sugars, Citric acid	Zentmyer, 1970.
Beet	*Aphanomycetes cochlioides*	Organic acids (including gluconic acids); Sugars	Chang-Ho and Hickman, 1970.

Plant parasitic nematodes, like zoosporic fungi, have been studied for their oriented movement and accumulation at the root zone. According to Klink, et al. (1970), the directed movement and accumulation of nematodes to plant roots is possibly in response to localized stimuli. Carbon dioxide produced by growing roots is the most important attractant (MacDonald, 1979). A number of plant parasitic nematodes such as *Meloidogyne* spp., *Aphelenchoides fragariae*, *Ditylenchus dipsaci* and *Pratylenchus penetrans* are reported to react positively in a carbon dioxide gradient and move to the source (Klinger, 1965; Edmunds and Mai, 1967). Other gradients that are produced by growing roots include water, oxygen, pH, root exudates such as aminoacids, organic acids and electricals (refer Figure 4.3).

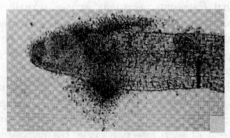

Figure 4.3 Attraction of zoospores of *Phytophthora cinnamomi* to roots. (Milholland, R.D., Phytopathology, 65:789, 1975, with permission).

4.2.2 The Recognition

Host-pathogen interaction is highly specific phenomena. Disease develops only in compatible combinations. The specificity and compatibility are components of 'recognition' an initial but significant event in host-pathogen interaction. This event of recognition differentiates between 'self' (compatibility) or 'non-self' (incompatibility).

4.2.3 Penetration Related Activities

Most of microbes are **endoparasites**; they grow and reproduce inside host tissues. Thus, they need some mechanism to penetrate the host tissue. Even powdery mildew or ecto-mycorrhizal fungi, which basically grow and reproduce on the host surface (**ectoparasite**), also require limited penetration in search of food. The plant body presents several layers of structural barriers, like medieval fort, to avoid, prevent or restrict the entry of pathogen into deeper tissues. The penetration by pathogens generally takes place at two stages:

Prepenetration phase.   The plant pathogenic propagules may be involved in some activities before they penetrate the host. Following are some of the examples:

(a) In fungi belonging to Phylum Ascomycota, the spores multiply by budding on the host surface. This is an adaptation to augment the inoculum density, thereby enhancing the inoculum potential.

(b) The sclerotia of fungus *Sclerotium rolfsii* germinate and produce mycelium on the host surface, augmentation of biomass before penetrating the host surface.

(c) The bacterial cells multiply in wound sites before making inroads into host tissues for exploitation of resources.

(d) Termination of dormancy, exogenous or endogenous, is one of the chief activities during prepenetration phase.

(e) Stimulators or inhibitors of spore germination are strategically used by several fungi as per need.

The site of initial host-pathogen interaction on host surface is called **infection court.** The pathogenic propagules of fungi, bacteria and phanerogames are intimately attached in infection court. The propagules may produce mucilaginous substance, mixture of polysaccharides, glycoproteins and fibrillar material, which becomes sticky when moistened and helps the pathogen to adhere to plant surface. Hyphae of *Rhizoctonia solani* form infection cushions to ensure firm contact with the host surface.

Penetration phase.   The pathogen may adopt any of the three modes for penetrating into the host plants. These may be **direct entry**, through pre-existing **natural openings** and through **wounds**.

Direct penetration.   Direct penetration (Plate 4.1) of herbaceous tissues requires entry through layers of wax, cutin, pectin and a network of cellulose fibrils impregnated with other wall polymers before the pathogen makes contact with host protoplasm. Biotrophic fungi (rusts, downy mildews and powdery mildews) often gain access by growing into the epidermis. Necrotrophs like *Botrytis*, under suitable conditions, enter host directly through cuticle. Direct penetration by fungi is invariably associated with the development of hyphal modifications. They are collectively known as infection structures —adhesorium, appresorium, haustorium, infection thread, etc. The formation of specialized accessory structures to facilitate passage through the cell wall has been observed in *Pythium*—type of penetration. Kraft, et al. (1967) who studied the penetration of bent grass by *P. aphanidermatum* (Plate 4.2) observed that (a) cyst germinates to produce a germ tube, and (b) the germ tube differentiates into an appresorium to achieve penetration. The simplest mechanism has been described for conidia of *Cladosporium* that involves growth of germ tube directly through the cuticle and into the middle lamella. Penetration by rust urediniospores requires two distinct stages. The first stage involves penetration by a primary penetrating hypha from an appresorium through stomata and into sub-stomatal cavity. The primary hypha develops into a sub-stomatal vesicle from which secondary hyphae arise and grow in contact with neighbouring host cells.

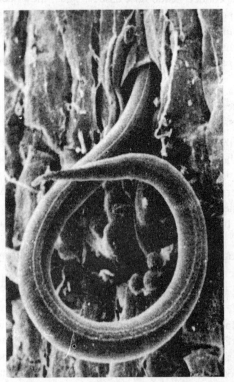 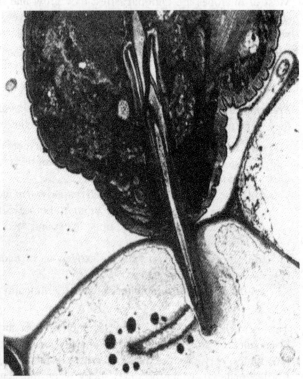

Plate 4.1 Penetration of host plant and cell by plant parasitic nematodes. (From Dropkin, V.H., *Introduction to Plant Nematology*, John Wiley and Sons, New York, 1980.)

Mechanisms of penetration. In fungal pathogens, mechanical or enzymatic actions or both achieve direct penetration through cutinized epidermal wall. In some fungi, germ tube tip swells to form **appresoria** (Plate 4.3) while in many others, hyphae as such penetrate the host surface. Appresoria formed in different species vary morphologically. They may be swollen hyphal tips to well defined, melanized, thick walled structure as found in *Magnaporthe grisea* and *Colletotrichum* spp.

The enzymes may have an equally important role in weakening the cuticle and in digesting pectin and cellulose. Enzymatic penetration of host surface has now been conclusively demonstrated at least in certain host parasite systems like papaya fruit—*Colletotrichum gloesporioides*, pea

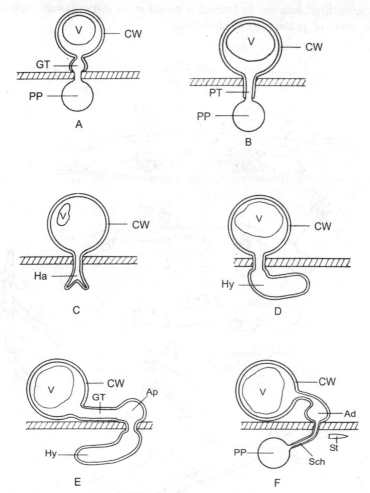

Plate 4.2 A diagrammatic comparison of penetration types exhibited by zoospores (A) *Rozella allomycis,* (B) *Olpidium brassicae,* (C) *Chytridium sp.,* (D) *Phytophthora parasitica,* (E) *Pythium aphanidermatum,* (F) Plasmodiophorales, (Ad–adhesorium, Ap–appresorium, CW–cyst wall, GT–germ tube, Ha–haustorium, Hy–hypha, PP–parasite protoplast, PT–penetration tube, Sch–schlauch, St–stachel, V–vacuole (Aist, J.R. in Physiological Plant Pathology, Heitefuss, R. and WIlliam, P.H. Eds. Springer-Verlag, Berlin, 1976, with permission).

epicotyl—*Fusarium solani,* etc. In these systems cutinases are found to be essential for penetration of intact host surface and subsequently to cause infection (Chaube and Singh, 1990). Cutinase inhibitors like anticutinase antibodies, diisopropyl fluorophosphate, organophosphorus insecticides, carbendazim, etc., provide protection against infection. Mutants incapable of producing cutinase are non-pathogenic. Moreover, they become pathogenic with exogenous application of cutinase.

Electron microscopic evidences suggest that in general cuticular penetration involves both mechanical as well as enzymatic activity. Cuticular membranes usually appear depressed inward during penetration suggesting involvement of mechanical force. On the other hand, clear holes produced without any sign of torn edges suggest that softening or erosion of the rather brittle cuticle probably occurred prior to penetration. However, at least in those cases where direct penetration occurs and no specialized structure is formed, it would seem that enzymatic action must be almost exclusively the mode of penetration (Sisler, 1986)

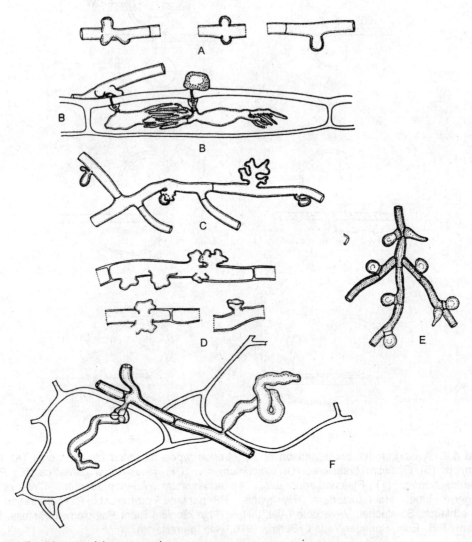

A = *Erysiphe graminis*, appresoria;
B = *Erysiphe graminis*, appresoria, penetration pegs surrounded by callose sheath, and large digitate haustoria;
C = *Microsphaera alphitoides*, appresoria and small globose to elliptical haustoria
D = *Microsphaera polonica*, appresoria
E = *Meliola s.*, hyphopodia
F = *Uromycladium tepperianum*, intercellular hypha and haustoria

(Adopted from P.B. Talbot, 1971)

Plate 4.3 Appresoria, Haustoria and Hyphopodia.

Penetration through natural openings. Many fungi and bacteria enter plants through **pre-existing natural openings,** e.g. stomata, lenticels, hydathodes and nectaries (Plate 4.4). The **stomata** are the natural openings for gaseous exchange in plant tissues. They are present in large numbers on the lower surface of the leaves. They measure about $10\text{-}20 \times 5\text{-}8$ µm and are open in the daytime but more or less closed at night. Several zoosporic fungi, e.g. *Pseudoperonospora* on hops, *Plasmopara* on vines, and *Phytophthora* on potato, produce zoospores, which are attracted to stomata where they encyst in a suitable position for their germ tubes to grow immediately between the guard cells. *Pseudoperonospora* zoospores are attracted to the open stomata but not to the closed ones. This attraction is based on recognition and partly on chemical stimulus (Lucas, 1998). The phenomenon of *Thigmotropism* (contact response to the surface topography of cells) play important role in stomatal penetration. When a rust spore germinates on a cereal leaf, the germ tube grows at right angles to the long axis of the leaf, due to thigmotropism. The germ tube will sooner or later encounter a stoma. Once stoma is contacted, the germ tube differentiates into an appresorium and an infection hypha enters the sub-stomatal cavity (Read, et al., 1992). In case of rust fungi, the signal for appresorium formation appears to be the shape of the stomatal guard cells and in particular the stomatal lip. *Uromyces appendiculatus* (bean rust), produces appresoria in response to small ridges about 0.5 µm in height, which corresponds closely to the dimensions of the stomatal lip of host plant, *Phaseolus* (Lucas, 1998). Bacterial pathogens frequently enter through stomata. Being unicellular and, if motile, they require the presence of water film, for entry.

Bacteria and fungi frequently infect their hosts through **lenticels** also. In case of bacteria and most fungi, the lenticels can act as a channel of entry only when a closing layer of suberized cells does not seal it. Fungal pathogens reported to enter through lenticels include *Spongospora subterranea* (powdery scab of potato) as zoospores, and *Armillaria mellea* as rhizomorphs on the roots of a variety of plants. *Penicillium expansum* (brown rot) attacks apple through lenticels on the fruit and *Nectria galligena* (apple canker) through stem lenticels.

Hydathodes and **nectaries** are also used by pathogens to enter the host cells. Bacterial lesions on leaves often develop at the margins, at sites where water secretes through hydathodes. The bacteria causing black rot of crucifers usually enter via hydathodes. In fact, bacteria, which accumulate in the water secreted by hydathodes, are sucked back into the plants when the water contracts as the plant dries. *Erwinia amylovora* (fire blight of apple and pears) enters through nectaries present at the base of flowers.

Penetration through wounds. Bacteria and viruses, which are incapable of entering plant, directly use wounds as most frequent or the only avenue of entry. Wounds are caused by natural agencies (wind, rain, insects and animals) as well as human activities. Fungi such as *Penicillium expansum, P. digitatum, P. italicum* cause post harvest rots of fruits. They enter fruits through mechanical wounds caused during harvesting, packing or transport. Several other examples include *Heterobasidion annosum, Nectria galligena, Phytophthora* spp., *Agrobacterium, Botrytis cinerea,* etc. Many insects/pests are important vectors of plant pathogens. Their feeding habits/activities cause wounds which serve as an entry route. *Ophiostoma novo-ulmi* (Dutch elm disease) is introduced directly into sapwood by its vector: the bark beetle. Aphids, white flies and leafhoppers are the vectors of many viruses. The aphid stylet injects the virus into the sieve cells of the host with clinical efficiency and subsequently the virus can spread freely via phloem. Soil borne viruses, bacteria or fungal pathogens enter host cells through wounds caused by nematodes or fungal pathogens.

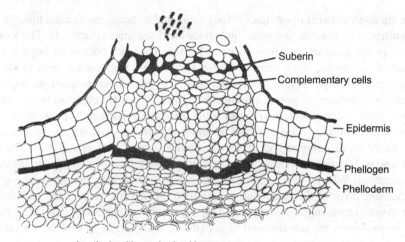

Lenticels with a suberized layer

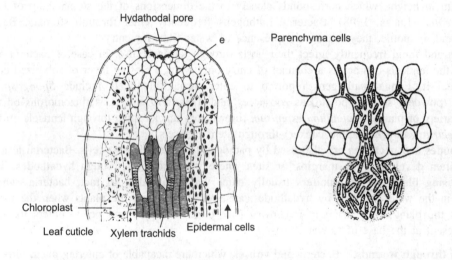

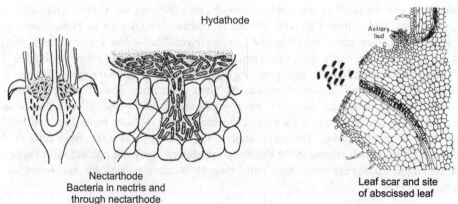

Plate 4.4 Natural openings for entry of plant pathogens.

Host-pathogen interface. The sites of intimate contact between host and pathogen are called **the interface**. The formation of haustoria presents the first interface between host and fungal pathogen. In fact, fungal pathogen makes direct contact with plasma membrane of living host cells through haustoria only as haustoria also lack the cell wall. Interface is the site at which the molecular communications between two partners take place. It is likely that recognition event determining active resistance or susceptibility to infection are initiated at the interface. The parasite starts drawing nutrients, thus a biological relationship or infection is established. Lucas (1998) described **transfer intercept infection** as the behaviour of biotrophic pathogen that invade the host tissue adjacent to vascular elements (rust fungi) or *Claviceps purpurea* colonizes developing embryo, where transfer of nutrients from the source cells is much easier.

Structure and function of haustoria. The haustoria are the specialized structures produced by fungal pathogens (rusts, powdery and downy mildews, *Phytophthora infestans* and several other facultative saprophytes) to perform vital function of absorption of nutrients from host cells. Invariably, haustoria are produced in paranchymatous host cells. However, the haustoria produced by powdery mildew fungi are confined to epidermal cells only.

The haustorium formation initiates as small protuberance from the haustorial mother cell. It grows and comes in contact with host cell wall and penetrates through it. The penetration of cell wall seems to be a chemical process (chemicals/enzymes produced by haustorial mother cell) as lack of cell wall on haustorial apparatus rules out the involvement of any mechanical force. Once the penetration is achieved, cell wall is formed around 'neck' of haustorium and the apex grows into various shapes and sizes, characteristic of the pathogen. They may be small, club shaped, lobed or branched (finger like) structures. Typically, where the haustorial neck branches the host cell, callose like material (electron high density) is deposited. In an incompatible host-pathogen combination this may extend to form a sheath completely encasing haustorium (Lucas, 1998). The discrete, electron dense ring is not observed in haustoria formed by Oomycete pathogen (downy mildew fungi and *Albugo*). The mature haustorium contains nuclei, mitochondria and endoplasmic reticulum (Figure 4.4).

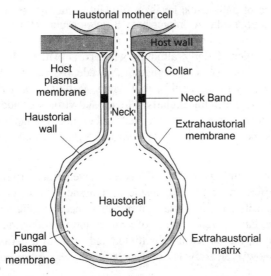

Figure 4.4 Diagrammatic interpretation of haustorial structure.

4.2.4 Infection and Further Developments

Colonization and invasion. Once the infection has taken place, there are variations in the extent and pattern of colonization of host tissues depending upon the nature of parasitic relationship and host reactions during invasion (Figure 4.5). Broadly, two main patterns of colonization are reported, viz. **localized** or **systemic**. Within these two categories, there are numerous subtle variations in pathogen behaviour, which determine the ultimate extent of damage to the host. Different patterns of pathogenic invasion include sub-cuticular, epiphytic with haustoria intracellular, intercellular with haustoria and vascular. Many pathogens grow preferentially in certain host tissues (tissue specificity). Biotrophs grow selectively within certain well-defined host tissues while less specialized necrotrophic pathogens tend to spread indiscriminately through plant organs.

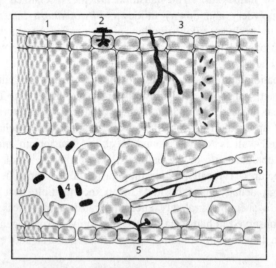

Figure 4.5 Some patterns of pathogenic invasion of plant tissues. 1. subcuticular 2. epiphytic with haustoria 3. intracellular 4. intercellular 5. intercellular with haustoria and 6. vascular.

Bacteria invade tissues intercellularly, although when parts of the cell walls dissolve, they also grow intracellularly. Most plant parasitic nematodes invade tissues intercellularly but some can invade intracellularly as well. Viruses, viroids, mollecutes, fastidious bacteria, and protozoa invade tissues by moving from cell to cell intracellularly. Viruses and viroids invade all types of living plant cells, mollecutes and protozoa invade phloem sieve tubes and perhaps a few adjacent phloem parenchyma cells whereas most fastidious bacteria invade xylem vessels and a few invade phloem sieve tubes.

Growth and reproduction. During process of disease development (infection, colonization and invasion) the pathogen grows and reproduce inside host tissue. The method by which the host is invaded, colonized and parasitized is essentially different in necrotrophic and biotrophic pathogens. Viruses, as plant pathogen, have unique system of growth and reproduction inside living host cells. In case of bacterial infection, the bacterial cells divide and grow to a definite size to divide again. Fungal plant pathogens show typical cycles of vegetative growth followed by reproductive phase (Plate 4.5).

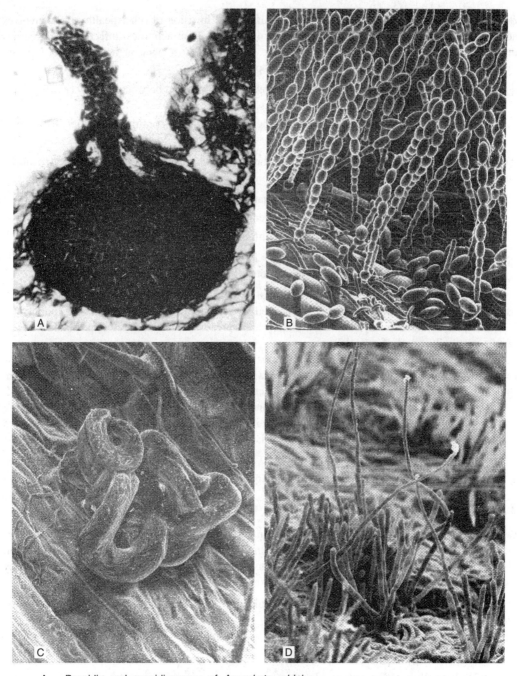

A = Pycnidia and pycnidiospores of *Ascochyta rabiei*
B = Conidiophores and conidia of *Blumaria graminis (powdery mildew fungus)*
C = Cirrhus or spore horn of conidia of *Septoria tritici* erupting from pycnidium
D = Conidiophores and conidia of *Cercospora* spp.

Plate 4.5 Production and dispersal of spores.

Exit of pathogen. Colonization of infected host tissue and invasion of other healthy parts involves rapid growth and reproduction of pathogen (Plate 4.5). With these activities, infection chain comes to an end either due to end of crop season or due to death of host plant or host organ. To ensure the recurrence of disease the pathogen has two options:

- survive with the infected plant debris to bridge the time gap between two successive crops, (details about survival are given in next section)
- come out of host tissue and exploit the alternatives to continue activities with other hosts/vectors.

Plant pathogens adopt various means to leave the "exploited/exhausted" host plants, depending upon the following:

- Nature of pathogen (facultative or obligate parasites).
- Dependence on dispersal/transmitting agents (air, water, vectors).
- Location of pathogen in host tissues (surface, xylem, or phloem).
- Nature of host-plant (seasonal/annual or perennial).
- Type of plant tissue infected (leaves, roots, fruits, seed).

Most viruses, some bacterial and few fungal pathogens are dependent on vector for exit, transportation and inoculation. This is also referred as **transmission**. Thus, the nature, population size and behaviour of vector is vital for initiation and spread of such diseases (e.g. potato viruses, Stewart's corn wilt, ergot of cereals).

Wind currents can carry easily the enormous amount of rusts and powdery/downy mildew conidia by sweeping the infected host surface, without any effort or involvement of pathogen. Similarly, raindrops or splashes can disperse the bacterial inoculum present, as ooze, on host surface. Rust and smut fungi produce inoculum, in abundance, beneath the epidermis or thin host covering (covered smuts). Different physical or mechanical forces break open these covering layers and facilitate the exit of pathogenic propagules for dispersal by various agencies.

4.3 PATHOGEN INDUCED CHANGES

4.3.1 Changes at Biochemical Level

Role of enzymes. One characteristic feature of many phyto-pathogenic organisms is their ability to produce an array of enzymes capable of degrading the complex polysaccharides of the plant cell wall and membrane constituents. These enzymes usually are produced inductively. Generally, they are extra cellular, highly stable and present in infected host tissues.

Cell wall degrading enzymes. The enzyme **cellulase** produced by most microorganisms consists of at least four components:

C_1 releases chains from microfibrils.

C_2 breaks cellulose fibrils to short fibres.

C_x hydrolyses the chains to cellobiose.

Cellobiase, hydrolyses cellobiose to glucose.

Not much is known of the **hemicellulases** produced by plant pathogens. Many parasitic and saprophytic microorganisms produce the enzymes hemicellulases for hydrolysis of these polysaccharides into simple sugars. Certain components of hemicelluloses are degraded by cellulolytic enzymes also. Reports implicating hemicellulases in plant disease are few. Xylanase and arabinase have been found in the hypocotyls of sunflower attacked by *S. sclerotiorum*. *S. fructigena* is known to produce arabinofuranosidase in cultures. Similarly, *Sclerotium rofsii* produces exogalactanase, endomannase, galactosidase and endoxylanase in cultures.

Good amount of work has been done on role of **pectinases** in degradation of pectic substances by plant pathogens. The nature and properties of the enzymes involved have been elucidated. The following classification is based on that of Bateman and Miller (1966):

Group/class	Name of enzyme	Action
Pectin methyl esterase		Removes the methoxy group of pectins and/or pactinic acid.
Pectic glycosidase	**exo-polymethylgalacturonase**	**Terminal cleavage:** Pectin attacked in preference to pectic acid.
	exo-polygalacturonase	**Terminal cleavage:** Pectic acid attacked in preference to pectin.
	endo-polymethylgalacturonase	**Random cleavage:** Pectin attacked in preference to pectic acid.
	endo-polygalacturonase	**Random cleavage:** Pectic acid attacked in preference to pectin.
Pectic lyase	**exo-pectin methyl transeliminase**	**Terminal cleavage:** Pectin attacked in preference to pectic acid.
	exo-polygalacturonate transeliminase	**Terminal cleavage:** Pectic acid attacked in preference to pectin.
	endo-pectin methyl transeliminase	**Random cleavage:** Pectin attacked in preference to pectic acid.
	endo-polygalacturonate transeliminase	**Random cleavage:** Pectic acid attacked in preference to pectin.

Tissue maceration. In many plant diseases, particularly the soft rots, tissue maceration is a prominent and characteristic symptom. This process involves the separation of cells from each other within a tissue system.

Necrosis of host tissues. Host cells are killed by necrotrophic pathogens as an integral part of pathogenesis and local death of host cell occurs when resistant reactions to biotrophic (and some necrotrophic) pathogens are produced. Previously it was considered that the cell death results from the loss of ability to plasmolyse and deplasmolyse, implying the lack of intact plasmallemna. Later this phenomena was explained on the basis of increase in permeability of the cell membrane and loss of electrolytes. However, cell death may also be brought about as a result of physiological disturbances in other parts of the plant.

Role of toxins. Gaumann (1954) claimed that microorganisms are pathogenic only if they are toxigenic. **Toxins** can be defined as *low molecular weight, non-enzymatic microbial products toxic to higher plants*. In recent classification, toxins are divided into two categories: The first is **host-**

non-specific (non-selective) which may affect many unrelated plant species in addition to main host of the pathogen producing toxin; it includes **phytotoxin** and **vivotoxin**. The second is **host-specific** (selective) which affects only the specific host of the pathogen; it includes **pathotoxins**. Toxin in general, interact with cell membrane or organelles (mitochondria or chloroplast) and alter their permeability. Host specific and major host-non-specific toxins are listed in Tables 4.2 and 4.3, respectively.

Table 4.2 Some Important Host-non-specific Toxins

Toxin	Pathogen	Disease	Chemical nature
Alternaric acid/ Zinniol/Alternariol	*Alternaria* sp.	Leaf spot diseases of various crops	Hemiquinone derivatives
Cercosporin	*Cercospora* spp.	-do-	Benzoperyline derivatives
Cerato-ulmin	*Ceratocystis ulmi*	Dutch elm disease	Large M, Carbohydrate
Fumaric acid	*Rhizopus* spp.	Almond hull rot disease	Fumaric acid
Fusicocein	*Fusicoccam amygadali*	Twig blight of almond and peach	—
Fusaric acid and lycomarsmin	*F. oxysporum*	Wilts of tomato and other crops	5-n-butylpicolinic acid and amino acid derivatives
Oxalic acid	*Sclerotium* and *Sclerotinia* spp.	Rots in various crop	Oxalic acid
Diaporthin	*Cryphonectria parasitica*	Chestnut blight	Isocoumarin
Ophiobolins	*Cochliobolus* spp.	Diseases of grain crops	—
Pyricularin	*Pyricularia grisae*	Blast of Rice	Nitrogen containing compounds and picolinic acid
Ten toxin	*Alternaria alternata* (*A. tenuis*)	Chlorosis of seedlings in many plants	Cyclic tetrapeptide
Tabtoxin	*Pseudomonas syringae* pv. *tabaci*	Wild of fire of tobacco	Dipeptide composed of threonine and tabtoxinine
Phaseolotoxin	*Ps. syringae* pv. *phaseolicola*	Holoblight of bean	Modified or nithine alanine-arginine tripeptide carrying a phosphoselfinyl group
Coronatine	*Ps. syringae* pv. *atropuspurea*	Infected soyabean and grasses	—
Syringomycin	*Ps. syringae* pv. *syringe*	Leaf spots of many crops	—
Syringotoxin	*Ps. syringae* pv. *syringe*	Citrus plant	—

(*Source:* Chaube and Singh, 1990; Singh, 2002)

Table 4.3 A List of Host-specific Toxins

S.No.	Disease	Pathogen species/ Pathotype (previous name)	Toxin (synonymous designation)	Host range (susceptible cultivar)	Genetic background of host genes for disease reaction (dominance)	Target site	Chemical structure	Cloning of gene for toxin biosynthesis
1	Alternaria blotch of apple	Alternaria alternata/ Apple pathotype (A. mali)	AM-toxin I, II & III	Apple (Red gold, Starking)	Multiple genes (susceptible)	Chloroplast and plasma membrane	Cyclic depsipeptide	In progress
2	Alternaria leaf spot of pigeonpea	A. tenuissima	ATC-toxin	Pigeonpea	—	—	—	—
3	Alternaria stem canker of tomato	A. alternata/ Tomato pathotype (A. alternata f. sp. lycopersici)	AL (or AAL)- toxin (I, and or Ta & Tb)	Tomato (Earlypak7, First)	Single (homo) gene (resistant)	Sphingolipid & ethanolamine metabolism	Ester of propanetricarbo- xylic acid and aminodimethylhe- ptad ecapentol	In progress
4	Black leaf spot of brassica	A. brassicicola	AB-toxin	Brassica spp.	—	—	Protein (sequence not determined)	—
5	Black leaf spot of strawberry	A. alternata/ Strawberry pathotype	AF-toxin I, II & III	Strawberry (Morioka-16)	Single (hetero) gene (susceptible)	Plasma membrane	Ester of amino acid and epoxydecatrienoic acid	In progress
6	Black spot of Japanese pear	A. alternata/ Japanese pear pathotype (A. kikuchiana)	AK-toxin I & II	Japanese pear (Nijisseiki)	Single (hetero) gene (susceptible)	Plasma membrane	Ester of amino acid and epoxydecatrienoic acid	In progress
7	Black spot of rapeseed	A. brassicae	Destruxin B	Brassica campestris, B. napus	—	—	Cyclicdepsipeptide	Cloned

(Contd.)

Table 4.3 A List of Host-specific Toxins (*Contd.*)

S. No.	Disease	Pathogen species/ Pathotype (previous name)	Toxin (synonymous designation)	Host range (susceptible cultivar)	Genetic background of host genes for disease reaction (dominance)	Target site	Chemical structure	Cloning of gene for toxin biosynthesis
8	Brown spot of rough lemon	A. alternaria Rough lemon pathotype (A. citri)	ACR (L)-toxin I	Rough lemon	—	Mitochondrion	Polyhydroxyalkenyl dehydropyrone	—
9	Brown spot of tangerine	A. alternaria Tangerine pathotype (A. citri)	ACT-toxin I & II ACTG-toxin A&B	Tangerine (Dancy)	—	Plasma membrane	Ester of amino acid and epoxydecatrienoic acid	In progress
10	Brown spot of tobacco	A. alternaria Tobacco pathotype (A. longipes)	AT-toxin	Tobacco	—	Mitochondrion	—	—
11	Eye spot of sugarcane	Bipolaris sacchari (Helminthosporium sacchari)	HS-toxin A, B & C	Sugarcane (51-NG97)	—	Plasma membrane	Sesquiterpene glucoside	—
12	Milo disease of sorghum	Periconia circinata	PC-toxin (Peritoxin A & B)	Grain sorghum (Giant milo)	Single gene (susceptible)	Plasma membrane	Unusual peptide containing chlorine atom	—
13	Northern leaf spot of maize	Cochliobolus carbonum (B. carbonum) race 1	HC-toxin I, II & III	Maize (K-44, K-61)	Multiple gene (resistant) Cloned HMI & HM2	Plasma membrane (histone deacetyalase)	Cyclic tetrapeptide	Cloned

(*Contd.*)

Table 4.3 A List of Host-specific Toxins (*Contd.*)

S. No	Disease	Pathogen species/ Pathotype (previous name)	Toxin (synonymous designation)	Host range (susceptible cultivar)	Genetic background of host genes for disease reaction (dominance)	Target site	Chemical structure	Cloning of gene for toxin biosynthesis
14	Southern leaf spot of maize	*C. heterotrophus* (*B. maydis*) race T	HMT-toxin band 1,2,3 & 1' (T-toxin)	Maize (Tms cytoplasm)	Cytoplasmic cloned *Urf13-T*	Mitochondrion	Linear polyketols	Cloned
15	Target leaf spot of tomato	*Corynespora cassiicola*	CC-toxin	Tomato (Ife no. 1)	—	—	—	—
16	Tan spot of wheat.	*Pyrenophora tritici-repentis*	Ptr-toxin Ptr chlorosis toxin	Wheat (TAM 105)	Single gene	Chloroplast (Photosynthesis) 14 KD protein	14 KD protein	Cloned (*Ptr-A*)
17	Victoria blights of oat	*Cochliobolus victoriae* (*B. victoriae*)	HV-toxin (victorin C)	Oats (Victoria)	Single (hetero) gene (susceptible)	Plasma membrane (glycine decarboxylase)	Unusual oligopeptide containing chlorine atoms	In progress
18	Yellow leaf blight of maize	*Phyllosticta maydis*	PM-toxin A, B, C & D	Maize (Tms cytoplasm)	Cytoplasmic	Mitochondrion	Linear polydetols	In progress
19	Brown spot of European pear	*Stemphylium vesicarium*	SV-toxin	European Pears (Le Lectier, Allaxandrine doulard)		Plasma membrane	In progress	—

(*Source:* Graniti, 1989; Singh, et al., 1994; Walton and Panaccione, 1993; Singh, 2002)

Role of growth regulators. Alteration in concentration of growth regulators like cytokinins, auxins, gibberellins, ethylene and abscisic acid have been found associated with several plant diseases, particularly in those resulting in abnormal plant/ organ/ cell growth like tumors, galls, knots, stunting, epinasty, curling, hypertrophy, and hyperplasia. Increased level of a growth regulator may be either due to its induced production (by pathogen or host) or slow degradation. Decrease in concentration is due to the enhanced degradation by the host's or pathogen's enzymes. Biotrophs like powdery mildews employ these hormones to draw their nutrients from the host cells.

Alteration in the level of growth regulators seems to be a consequence of pathogenesis. However, at least in three diseases hormones have been demonstrated to be determinant of pathogenicity. These are **crown gall** caused by *Agrobacterium tumefaciens* (cytokinin and auxin), **oleander and olive knot** caused by *Pseudomonas syringae* f. sp. *savastanoi* (auxin), and **fesciation disease** caused by *Corynebacterium fascians* (cytokinin). In all these three bacterial pathogens, genes responsible for hormone production have been identified and cloned (Shaw, 1988). Deletion of these genes results in conversion of virulent strain into avirulent.

Changes at physiological level. Disease is a sum total of the altered and induced biochemical reactions in a system of plant or plant part brought about by causal entity(s) leading to malfunctioning of its physiological processes. Major physiological processes involved in plants are respiration, transpiration, photosynthesis, translocation, growth and development. Any one or more of these processes have been documented to be altered /modified depending upon nature of host-pathogen interaction.

Respiration. Respiration is an enzymatically controlled oxidation process in which the burning (oxidation) of carbohydrates and fatty acids liberate energy for proper functioning of various cellular processes. In general, it has been reported that respiration increases once parasitic relationships is established. Uncoupling of oxidative phosphorylation, at least in part, has been found to cause increased rate of respiration in diseased plants. The energy required by the cell for its vital process is then produced through other, less efficient ways including pentose pathway and fermentation

The increased respiration in diseased plants can also be explained as a result of increased metabolism. In many plant diseases, growth is at first stimulated, protoplasmic streaming increases, and defence related materials are synthesized, translocated and accumulated in diseased areas. A major increase, in case of fungal infection coincides with sporulation by the fungus. At this stage fungus draws major nutrients from the host. The energy required for these activities is derived from ATP produced through respiration. The ATP is utilized, the more ADP is produced which stimulates respiration. There is another possibility as well. The infected plant utilizes energy less efficiently than a healthy plant. Because of the waste of part of energy, an increase in respiration is induced.

Glycolytic pathway (glycolysis) is by far most common way through which plant cells obtain energy. Part of energy is produced via the pentose phosphate pathway. This appears to be an alternate pathway of energy production to which plants resort under conditions of stress. Infected plants tend, in general, to activate the pentose phosphate pathway (Figure 4.6) also. Since this pathway is not directly linked to ATP production, the increased respiration through this pathway fails to produce as much utilizable energy as the glycolysis can and is, therefore, a less efficient source of energy for the functions of diseased plants. The pentose phosphate pathway provides vital intermediates for synthesis of important materials, including nucleic acids and defense related macromolecules. Based on the evidences suggested in literature, Lucas (1998) proposed following pathway pertaining to stimulation of respiration in diseased plants.

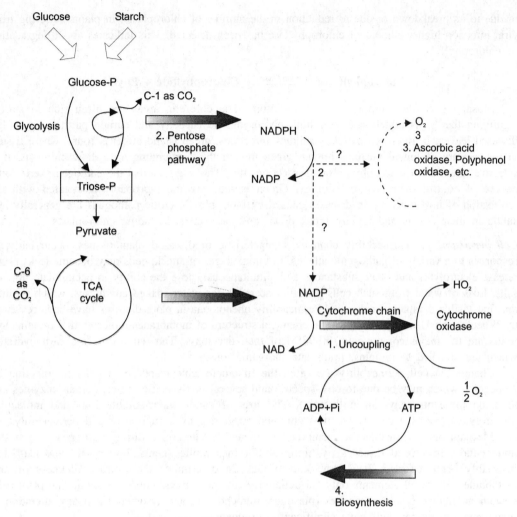

Figure 4.6 The pentose phosphate pathway.

Photosynthesis. Photosynthesis is the most unique feature of green plants where CO_2 from atmosphere and water from soil are brought together in the chloroplast in the presence of light which react to form glucose with concurrent release of oxygen. The pathogens that infect green aerial tissues (Photosynthetic tissues) are most likely to affect plant's productivity. The pathogen, once established in host tissue (fungal colony or virus particles), redirects the host nutrients for their own use, thus very correctly being called **metabolic sink**. This idea has been supported by radioisotope tracer experiments. In diseases like late blight of potato, in the event of a serious outbreak, the entire crop is defoliated while leaf spots cause localized necrosis of the tissues. These comparable examples testify that one major result of pathogen invasion is a reduction in the photosynthetic capacity of the plant by destroying green tissues and hence reduced interception of solar radiation. Chlorosis is a common symptom of plant diseases and this is an indication of reduction of chlorophyll in green tissues. This condition arises either due to inhibition of chlorophyll synthesis or due to its breakdown or due to reduction in the number of chloroplasts. In plants suffering from viral infection higher amount of chlorophyllase has been detected. This indicates about degradation of chlorophyll:

$$\textbf{Chlorophyll} \xrightarrow{\textit{Chlorophyllase}} \textbf{Chlorophyllide + Phytol}$$

Mosaic is another important viral symptom. The chloretic areas are often rich in starch, signifying that virus infection affects both photosynthetic capacity and carbon partitioning within diseased leaves. In rusts and powdery mildew infections, green island effect is found where tissues in the vicinity of fungal pustules remain green though the surrounding area show chlorosis. It is selective retention of chlorophyll around infection sites. This suggests that the pathogen exerts some degree of control over host physiology. Green islands are most probably associated with the redirection of host nutrients in diseases caused by biotrophs. Necrotic pathogens are generally less subtle in their effects and rapidly break down host organelles, including chloroplasts.

Cell permeability. Permeability changes, characteristic of diseased plant tissues, occur early, in responses to a variety of pathogenic attacks. In initial stages of attack, cells may become leaky. They release electrolytes and other substances and simultaneously lose the ability to accumulate mineral salts. Loss of water from such cells probably accounts for water-soaked conditions, which is often the first visible symptom of disease. Permeability phenomena in plant diseases have been reviewed by Wheeler and Hanchey in 1968. The chemical structure of membranes indicates that proteins and lipids are the major components (90-98%) of total dry mass. The remainders are carbohydrates, which are attached to proteins, lipids and inorganic ions.

Changes in cell permeability are often the first detectable response of cells to infection by pathogens, which may be due to host-specific and several non-specific toxins, certain enzymes and to some toxicants (e.g., air pollutants). The loss of small water-soluble ions and molecules (electrolytes) from the cell is the most common effect due to disruption of cell permeability.

Mechanisms responsible for membrane permeability alterations during pathogenesis are still under study. In several diseases by biotic and/or mesobiotic agents, loss of K^+ and Ca^{++} has invariably been reported. It is now known that Ca determines the overall thickness of unit membrane; and of all elements only Ca deficiency results in membrane disruption. The plant cells contain membrane bound organelles (plasmids, mitochondria and lysosome) and any alteration in membrane functioning will have significant consequences.

Absorption and translocation. Plants require water and nutrients (organic/inorganic) to carry out various cellular and physiological activities. Plants absorb water and minerals from soil through their root system, which are generally translocated upward through the xylem vessels into the vascular bundles of leaf veins. The minerals and a part of water are utilized for synthesis of plant substances but most of the water diffuses into the atmosphere through stomatal pores. Any disturbance to these channels will cause abnormality leading to sickness.

The absorption. There are several soil-borne root diseases caused by fungi, bacteria and nematodes, in which the roots or the root systems are damaged to varying extents. This results in poor functioning of roots and therefore poor absorption of water and minerals. Altered permeability of root cells also decreases absorptive capacity of roots.

Translocation through xylem. In several parasitic diseases such as wilts, damping-off, root rots, cankers, etc., the pathogens colonizes xylem vessels in the areas of infection. The infected vessels may also be filled with pathogen propagules or with substances secreted/excreted by the invaders or by the host in response to the pathogen and may become clogged. All this creates condition that reduce translocation through xylem. In several diseases like root knot, club root, crown gall , etc., the cell enlarge and proliferate, such cells in the vicinity of xylem bundles may crush them or may dislocate them, resulting in impairment of their efficiency and function. This aspect is well studied in wilt diseases caused by *Ceratocystis, Ophiostoma, Fusarium oxysporum* and bacterial pathogens *Pseudomones*, and *Erwinia*. In wilts dysfunction of xylem is well recognized. In most diseases the water flow through xylem is reduced to a mere 2 to 4% of that flowing through stems of healthy plants. Though pathogen is the initiator of this "disease syndrome" but host response is equally important. In Figure 4.7 several factors that contribute to wilting are shown:

Translocation through phloem. Organic nutrients are produced in leaf cells and finally reaching living protoplasm of non-photosynthetic cells for utilization and development of storage organs. Phloem elements play most important part. Any damage to plasmodesmata, phloem elements, phloem sieve tubes affect movement of nutrients. In diseases particularly by biotrophs Green Island develop around infected areas.

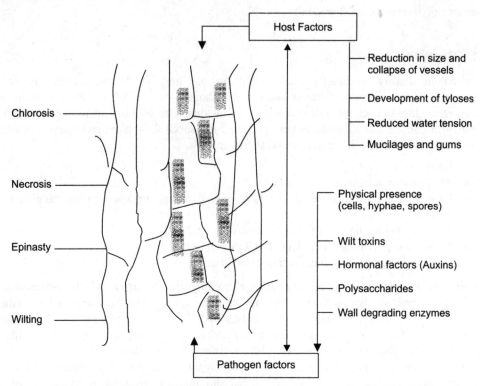

Figure 4.7 Factors that contribute in development of wilt diseases.

Effect on transpiration. In diseased plants particularly in foliage diseases, transpiration is usually increased. This is the result of damage to cuticle, increased leaf cells permeability and dysfunction of stomata. In foliage diseases like rust, mildews, and scab, cuticular and epidermal parts of leaves are damaged up to varying extents. This causes almost uncontrolled loss of water from the infected areas. Eventually, the loss of turgor and wilting of plants are observed as the absorption and translocation of water fail to match the excessive loss of water from plants.

4.4 RECURRENCE OF PLANT DISEASES

Plant diseases are recurring menace. In any particular location they appear with certain periodicity. The infection chain (pathogenesis) that is initiated by primary inoculum comes to natural end, at the end of crop season or death of the host, with production of various types of pathogenic propagules. These propagules must find some way to bridge time gap, between crop seasons, to ensure continuity of infection chain. Thus **survival of plant pathogens** is an important phase in disease cycle/life cycle of any successful pathogen. **Dissemination of pathogen** is another important phenomena in recurrence and epidemiology of plant diseases. Effective dispersal/dissemination of pathogenic propagules (primary or secondary inoculum) is vital for initiation of infection chain and further progress of disease in time and space. These two aspects will be discussed to give readers true picture of recurrence of disease.

4.4.1 Survival

The inoculum density eventually encountered by the host is determined by the survival characteristics of the organism. Thus, a successful pathogen must bridge the discontinuities in the infection chain/disease cycle occurring due to gaps in time. The adoption of high input production technology in commercial agriculture, has facilitated the survival of plant pathogens. Some of the practices that have helped increased survivability include

- Intensive cultivation
- Adoption of minimum or no tillage
- De-emphasis on the practices like fallowing, flooding, organic farming, burning of crop residues, etc.
- Mono-cropping, unscientific crop sequences and rotations
- Crop genetic homogeneity, (reduced biodiversity)
- Improved storage and transportation facilities.

Longevity and survivability. Longevity and survivability are the terms, which complement each other. As mentioned, survival is the basic feature of the organism, but the extent and magnitude of survival depend on longevity under natural conditions. The precise information of survival and longevity carry a lot of practical significance particularly in devising cultural practices like crop rotation, fallowing, flooding, etc. Estimates of the extent of survival of pathogens in soil depend upon the species, strains/isolates/pathotypes, soil types, environment, cropping history, and cultivation practices. Garrett (1956) has pointed out that survivability is the result of many interacting variables such as resistance to deleterious agents, competitive saprophytic ability, disseminability, responsiveness and mutational capacity.

Modes of survival. The modes of survival of plant pathogens are outlined in the following flowchart:

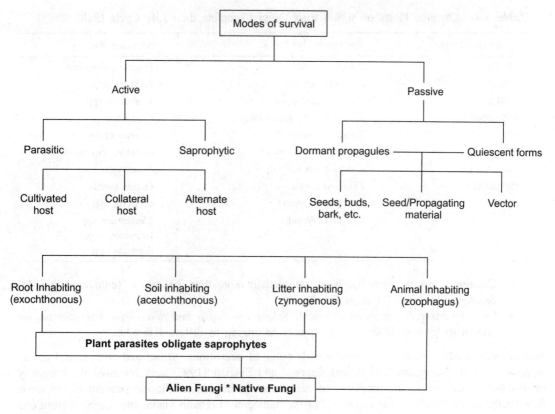

Parasitic survival. Organisms, parasitic on perennial plants (fruits, plantation and forest trees) survive in or on their hosts actively or passively depending on the environmental conditions. Bacterial pathogens such as *X. campestris* pv. *citri*, pv. *juglandis*, pv. *pruni*, *Pseudumonas syringae* pv. *morsprunorum* and *E. amylovora*, are known to be carried perennially in hold over cankers or blighted twigs. Several parasitic fungi, causing anthracnose of mango, powdery mildew of mango and apple, canker and blotch of apple, survive on infected organs. In some areas, a crop is grown twice or thrice per year or in some countries, because of different agro-climatic zones the same crop is grown at different locations at different time. These conciliations provide enough ground for extended parasitic phase of plant pathogens.

Along with cultivated hosts, several undesirable plants (weeds, etc.), both annual and perennial grow independently in nature. Such plants which belongs to the same botanical family to which cultivated host belongs is called **collateral host**. Some important examples include the survival of three *Puccinia* spp. causing wheat rusts in Indian subcontinent. These fungi survive in active sporulating stage on wild species of *Triticum*, *Aegilops*, *Hordeum*, and *Agropyron repens*. Similarly, rice Tungro virus survive actively on *Oryza* spp., *Echinocloa* spp. and *Leersia hexandra*.

Heteroecious rust fungi require two kinds of host plants to complete their life cycle. The other host does not belong to the botanical family of cultivated host, is referred to as **alternate host**. A list of some weeds and wild plants that serve as alternate hosts for rust is given in Table 4.4.

Table 4.4   Alternate Hosts on which Rust Fungi Complete their Life Cycle (Palti, 1981)

Cultivated hosts	Rust fungus	Alternate host
Barley	*Puccinia hordei*	*Ornithogalum* spp.
Cherry	*Puccinia cerasi*	*Eranthis* spp.
Cotton	*Puccinia stakmanii*	*Boutelova* spp.
Gooseberry	*P. caricis* var. *grossulariata*	*Carex* spp.
Oat	*Puccinia coronata*	*Rhamnus* spp.
Plum	*Tranzschelia discolor*	*Anemone coronaria*
Red currant	*Cronarticum ribicola*	*Pinus* spp.
Sorghum	*Puccinia sorghi*	*Oxalis stricta*
Wheat	*Puccinia graminis*	*Berberis* spp.
	Puccinia recondita	*Thalictrum* spp.
		Isopyrum spp.
		Anchusa spp.

- Cucumber mosaic virus has been recorded in more than 700 hosts (cultivated & wild) belonging to some 80 plant families.
- Fungal pathogens *Rhizoctonia solani*, *Sclerotium rolfsii* and *Sclerotinia sclerotiorum* are known to have wide host range (plants belonging to different families).

Survival with seeds.   Seed can harbour a wide range of microflora, viruses and other causal agents of plant diseases. Neergaard (1979), and Agarwal and Sinclair (1997) have reviewed the longevity of seed borne pathogens. The longevity of seed borne pathogens can be independent of the seeds they inhabit and depends on the capability of the pathogen to remain viable and infective from one season to the next, in or on the seeds. Pathogens even may live longer than the seeds they colonize. For example, *Colletotrichum lindemuthianum* remained active even after the bean seeds it colonized lost their viability (Medina, 1970). Flax seeds retained germinability for 18 to 24 months, whereas *Botrytis cinerea, Colletotrichum linicola*, and *Aureobasidium lini* survived for more than 4 years in seeds (Agarwal and Sinclair, 1997). The tobacco ring-spot virus remained viable in soyabean seeds for 5 years at 16 to 32°C, even when most seeds failed to germinate (Laviolette and Athow, 1971). In such situations, a pathogen would be a parasite while the seed would be viable and behave as a saprophyte after the death of seed. Bacterial pathogens that infect bean and other legume seeds serve as excellent examples of bacterial survival in seeds beyond seed viability. *C. flaccumfaciens* pv. *flaccumfaciens* remained viable for 5 to 24 years (Mathur and Ahmad, 1964). Schuster and Sayre (1975) isolated *X. compestris* pv. *phaseoli* from 15 years old bean seeds and *C. flaccumfaciens* pv. *flaccumfaciens* from 8 years old bean seeds stored at 10°C.

Pathogens may not survive seed development and drying stages. In maize seeds, the hyphae of *Peronosclerospora sorghi, Sclerospora sacchari*, and *Sclerophthora rayssiae* var. *zeae* were inactivated when seeds were dried to below 15% moisture content (Chang, 1970; Mikoshiba, 1979). The International Board for Plant Genetic Resources recommended –180°C for long-term storage of seeds (Hewett, 1987). A number of seed borne pathogenic fungi have been found to remain viable when stored dry at –20°C for periods up to 14 years without loss of pathogenicity. Several factors influence longevity of pathogens in seeds. They include host genotypes, amount of inoculum per seed, the location of inoculum in the seeds, the type of survival propagule, seed storage containers, storage environment, storage period and presence of antagonistic microflora.

Survival through vectors. Few fungi, some bacteria, and many viruses exploit their association with insect vectors for survival also. Some vectors such as aphids, and mites carry non-persistent viruses externally on or near the mouthparts (period for which the vectors remain infective for few hours) while in the case of semi-persistent viruses, infectivity is longer. However, in case of persistent (circulative, propagative or non-propagative) viruses the vectors remain infective much longer, some times throughout life or even infectivity is passed to next generation. This provides an opportunity to virus to manage continuity of infection cycle. Viruses are known to persist between crops within vectors, which are themselves inactive. Tobacco rattle virus in dormant nematodes for about a year and barley yellow mosaic virus can persist up to ten years in resting spores of its vector (*Polymyxa graminis*). Stewart's corn wilt pathogen, *Erwinia stewarti* survives in the body of its vector, *Chetocnema pulicaria*. The vector is sensitive to low winter temperature; this relationship has been exploited for developing disease forecasting system for the disease. Nematode play vital role in survival and dispersal of many important plant viruses.

Saprophytic survival. In the absence of the living hosts, the hemibiotrophs and necrotrophs survive as saprophytes. Species of *Pythium, Sclerotium,* etc. survive in soil in absence of their hosts for considerable length of time. Although during this survival, resting structures like oospores, sclerotia, etc. play major role, the ability of fungi to attack and colonize the dead plant materials enables them to remain active as saprophytes for sometime and develop the vegetative structures and more resting spores. Saprophytic survival of such fungi is dependent on pre-colonization of the substrate. Antagonists existing in soil may influence the saprophytic activity of pathogenic fungi as former have strong competitive saprophytic ability (fast and aggressive growth, profuse sporulation and propagule germinability, enzymatic complement and potential, ability to produce antibiotics as well as capacity to tolerate antibiotics produced by others). Usually these fungi sooner or later form dormant structures, which remain so due to existence of widespread natural fungistasis in soil.

Another category of saprophytic survival is of those fungi that are relatively more tolerant to antagonism and usually dominate in rhizosphere. This zone is occupied by a large number of microflora, some of which may be pathogens but do not necessarily infect the plant. These pathogens are restricted to pioneer colonization of dead substrates and are tolerant to competition by other soil microflora. The third category of saprophytic survival in soil is of those pathogens that have low competitive saprophytic survival ability and survive saprophytically for only a short time, these are described as **root inhabiting fungi**. They are defined as having a declining saprophytic phase, which limits their survival in soil. These pathogens remain in active saprophytic phase only so long as the host tissue is not completely decomposed. Many wilt causing species of *Fusarium, Verticillium* spp., and the root rot pathogen *Phymatotrichum omnivorum* fall in this category. After the host roots have completely decomposed, these pathogens are displaced by more aggressive soil saprophytes, and they live only as dormant resting structures. Soil structure, moisture, organic matter, soil reaction, antagonism of indigenous microflora, etc. affect the active saprophytic survival in soil.

Plant pathogenic bacterial genera have been grouped in relation to soil as (i) transient visitors, (ii) resident visitors and (iii) saprophytes. Crosse (1968) subsequently proposed a modified scheme consisting of four groups:

- with permanent soil phase, e.g. *Agrobacterium tumifaciens* and *Erwinia carotovora* pv. *carotovora,*
- with protracted soil phase, e.g. *Pseudomonas solanacearum* and *Agrobacterium rhizogenes,*

- with transitory soil phase, e.g. *Xanthomonas*, and *Pseudomonas*,
- with no soil phase, e.g. *Xanthomonas stewertii*.

Survival through dormant structures. Dormancy is the *reversible interruption of phenotypic development of an organism.* It is an adaptation on part of biological organisms to ensure their survival. Dormant structures, due to less nutrient requirements and hardy structures, have better chance of survival under unfavourable conditions. Fungi, nematodes and phanerogams survive through their resting and/or dormant structures; phanerogams produce seeds, which can live in dormant stage, sometimes for years. Majority of phytophagous nematodes, survive though their dormant structures (eggs, cysts, galls). Plant parasitic fungi produce a variety of resting/dormant structures such as thickened hyphae, chlamydospores, sclerotial bodies, oospores, perithecia, cleistothecia, and so forth.

Viewed in this way, dormancy can be of two types: **induced** (exogenous) **dormancy,** a condition where in development is delayed because of unfavourable physical or chemical conditions of the environment. On the other hand, **inherent** (constitutive) **dormancy** is a condition where in the development is delayed due to an innate property of the dormant structure, such as a barrier to the penetration of nutrients, a metabolic block or self-inhibitory substance produced by the spores.

Fungistasis is another survival mechanism to withstand highly competitive environment in soil. The biotic as well as abiotic factors are responsible for induction, maintenance and termination of fungistasis, though their precise role is not properly understood. Fungistasis has been studied in detail, Dobbs and Hinson, (1953) described it as *failure of propagules to germinate and grow even if necessary physical conditions for germination are favourable.*

Thus, the asexual spores (conidia, chlamydospores), sexually produced spores (oospores, ascospores, teliospores), fruiting bodies (acervuli, pycnidia, sporodochia, cleistothecia, perithecia), and other dormant structure like thickened hyphae, sclerotia, rhizomorphs, etc. are the main dormant structures for survival. When hemi-biotrophs/facultative saprophytes fail to continue as saprophytes in soil or in host crop debris, they produce resting structures. Plant pathogenic bacteria do not form resting structures. They live in or on the host tissues in living or decaying state.

4.4.2 Dissemination of Plant Pathogens

Knowledge about modes by which pathogens are dispersed is helpful for devising suitable and effective disease management practices. Several terms such as **distribution, dissemination, dispersal, spread** and **transmission** have been used by pathologists rather loosely. A outline of the modes of dispersal of plant pathogens are shown in the following flowchart:

With seeds and propagating units. Dispersal of inoculum through **seeds** is accomplished either as

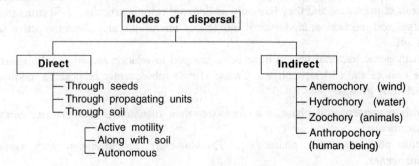

mixture and contaminant dormant structure of pathogens (e.g., sclerotia, galls, cysts, and smut sori), or through presence of propagules on the seed coat (externally seed borne; covered smut of barley) or as dormant mycelium in the seed (internally seed borne; loose smut of wheat). Agarwal and Sinclair (1997) have made a thorough review of seed-borne pathogens causing diseases of major crops.

Transmission of a large number of plant pathogens takes place through the **vegetative parts** of the plants used as planting materials, such as tubers, cuttings, runners, rhizomes, grafts, etc. Over 40% of the bacterial plant pathogens are transmitted on vegetatively propagated materials. Among the pertinent examples are *X. campestris* pv. *citri* (citrus canker), *A. tumifaciens* (crown gall) and pathogens of potato, such as *E. carotovora* and spp. *atroseptica*, *R. solanacearum*, etc. Viruses and related agents are invariably transmitted by vegetative propagules; hence virus diseases are particularly serious in horticultural crops, normally vegetatively propagated.

With soil. A large number of plant pathogens survive in soil. Thus, soil as such becomes an important means for their short or long distance dispersal. Zoosporic fungi, flagellate bacteria and nematodes are capable of limited active mobility. Several others are passively transported.

Active motility. Hickman and Ho (1966) observed that zoospores of *P. aphanidermatum* moved at speeds up to 14.4 cm/h over short period of chemotactically directed movement. However, Lacey (1967) noted that zoospores of *P. infestans* moved about 1.3 cm in 2 weeks in wet soil. Active movement of plant parasitic nematodes has also been studied. According to Wallace (1978) speed of 0.1 to 0.5 cm/d in soil appear to be reasonable approximation for nematodes. *Pratylenchus zeae* moved about 0.1 cm/d in sandy loam soil and *Globodera rostochiensis* at about 0.3 cm/d. Tarjan (1971) found that *Radopholus similes*, *Pratylenchus coffeae* and *Tylenchulus semipenetrans* moved at about 0.4, 0.2, and 0.1 cm/d, respectively. The average speed of *Pratylenchus penetrans* in soil under optimum conditions was about 0.3 cm/d. *Ditylenchus dipsaci* moved at 0.5 to 1.0 cm/d and *Tylenchulus semipenetrans*, 0.1 cm/day.

Along with soil. Pathogens perpetuating in soil either saprophytically on crop debris or in dormant stages are transported from one place to another within a field (redistribution) or from one field to another or even from one area to another area. Irrigation or rainwater, wind with high velocity and hail storms also transport soil and plant debris from one location to another and thus short or long distance dispersal of pathogen propagules takes place in nature.

Autonomous dispersal. Autonomous dispersal takes place by active growth of hyphae or hyphal strands. *Phytophthora cinnamomi* is reported to move at least 4.5 m uphill in 22 months. According to Shipton (1972) runner hyphae of *Gaeumannomyces graminis* grow for a radius of 1.5 m in a growing season. The rate of spread of *Rhizoctonia solani* has been estimated to be 2.5 cm/d, 21.2 cm in 23 days and 25 cm/month. The rhizomorphs of *Armillaria mellea* grow through field soil at about 1 m/year. The rate of such growth/spread in *Phymatotrichum omnivorum* (root rot of cotton) is estimated as 2 to 8 ft per month and 3 to 30 ft. per season in alfalfa crop. *Gonoderma, Polyporus, Sclerotium*, etc. also grow independently.

With wind. Gaumann (1950) has termed this type of spread as **Anemochory**. Some plant pathogenic bacteria, seeds of angiospermic plant parasites and most fungi which produce sporophores and spores on the host surface, downy mildews, powdery mildews, rusts, smuts, and leaf spot/blight causing pathogens, sooty molds, etc. are disseminated by the wind (Plate 4.6). More information on wind dispersal is discussed in section pertaining to epidemiology.

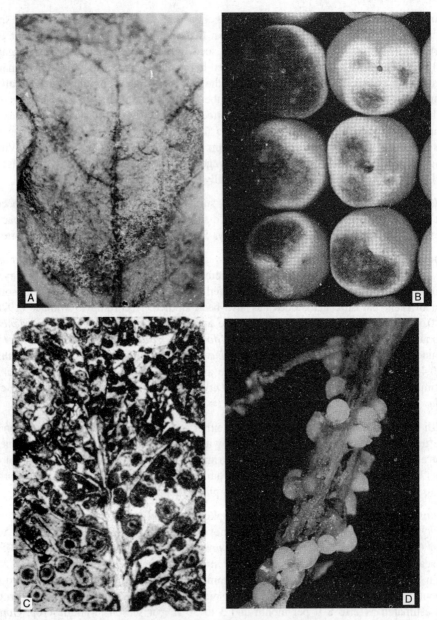

A = Sporangiophores and sporagia of *Phytophthora infestans*
B = Post harvest disease-growth of causal organism
C = Leaf spot fungus – *Alternaria* sp.
D = Nematode-cyst on root surface

Plate 4.6 Growth of pathogen and production of inoculum on host surface.

With water. Water as an agent of dissemination appears to be relatively less important as compared to wind. Water helps in pathogen dissemination in three ways: (i) pathogens (fungal spores, fructifications, sclerotia, bacterial cells, eggs and cysts of nematodes) that are present in or on the soil are dispersed by rain or irrigation/flood water that moves on the surface or through the soil, (ii) most bacteria and spores of many fungi are extruded in gelatinous tendrils that may have hardened when dry, depend on rain or overhead irrigation water which either washes them downward or splashes them in all directions, (iii) the splashing and spattering of water during heavy rains may result in distributing inoculum to plant parts near the soil and may distribute bacterial cells and fungal spores to different parts of the same plant or to neighbouring plants.

With animals

Insects. Insects, particularly aphids, whiteflies and leafhoppers are by far more important vectors of viruses and phytoplasmas. These insects while sucking the plant sap ingest the virus particles also, and while feeding on healthy plants, transfer the viruses into the healthy juice.

The order **Homoptera**, which includes the aphides (**Aphidieae**), leaf hoppers (**Cicadellidae**) and the plant hoppers (**Delphacidae**) contain by far the largest number of important insects that transmit plant viruses. The white flies (**Aleurodidae**) transmit usually several geminiviruses. The mealy bugs (**Coccoidae**) and certain tree hoppers (**Membrtacidae**) also transmit important viruses. A few vectors of plant viruses belong to other orders such as the true bugs (**Hemiptera**), the thrips (**Thysanoptera**) and the beetles (**Coleptera**). Grasshoppers (**Orthoptera**) occasionally transmit a few viruses also. The most important virus vectors are the aphids, leafhoppers and whiteflies. The insect may be a mechanical carrier of bacteria on their body and in some cases there may be a mutualistic relationship between the insect and the bacteria. The bacteria may survive in the hibernating insects in the absence of susceptible hosts or during adverse environmental conditions. The bacterial pathogens, which have some kind of association with insects for dissemination, are listed in Table 4.5.

Table 4.5 Insect Transmission of Plant Parasitic Bacteria

Disease/Pathogen	Insects associated	Nature of association
Fire blight of Apple (*E. amylovora*)	*Drosophila melanogaster, Musca domestica, Lucilia sericata*	General
Walnut blight (*X. juglandis*)	*Eriophyes tristriatus* var. *erinea*	General
Holoblight of beans (*Ps. medicaginis* var. *phaseolicola*)	*Heliothrips femoralis*	General
Bacterial rot of apple (*Ps. melophthora*)	*Rhagoletis pomonella*	General
Citrus canker (*X. campestris* pv. *citri*)	*Phyllocnistic citrella*	General
Bacterial wilt of cucurbits (*Erwinia trachiphila*)	*Diabrotica vittata*, D. *doudecimpunctata*	Specialized, required for inoculation, dissemination and over wintering
Bacterial wilt of corn and stewart's leaf blight (*X. stewartii*)	*Chaetocneme pulicara, C. denticulate*	Specialized, required for dissemination and over wintering
Black leg of potato (*E. carotovora*)	*Hylemyia cilicrura*	Specialized, mutualistic symbiosis.
Oliverknot (*Ps. savastonoi*)	*Dacus oleae*	-do-

(*Source:* Narayanasamy, P., 1997)

The role played by insects in transmission of fungal pathogens is relatively less important except in a few cases. The fungi, which are adapted to dissemination by insects, produce sticky spores in masses, which attract the insects. The fungal-insect associations leading to transmission and infection by the fungal pathogens are presented in Table 4.6.

Table 4.6 Insect Transmission of Fungal Pathogens

Disease and pathogen	Insects associated	Nature of association
Fig endosepsis (*F. moniliforme* var. *fici*)	*Beastophage psenes*	Incidental to pollination
Azalea flowerspot (*Ovulinia azaleae*)	*Heterothrips azaleae*	Through wounds produced by insects
Feeding on fungal masses Ergot of cereals (*Claviceps purpurea*)	*Sciara thomae*	Through communication
Anthracnose of cucumber (*Colletotrichum lagenarium*)	*Diabrotica undecimpunctata howar*	Through feeding wounds
Boll rot of cotton (*F. moniliforme*) (*Alternaria tenuis*)	*Anthonomus grandis, Heliothis zeae, Lygus lineolaris*	Through feeding and oviposition wounds
Red rot of sugar cane (*C. falcatum*)	*Diatraea saccharalis, Anacentrinus subnudus*	Through feeding wounds
Brown rot of apple (*S. fructigena*)	*Forficula auricularia*	Through feeding injuries
Dieback of cocoa (*Calonectria rigidiscula*)	*Sahlbergella singularis Distantiella theobroma*	Through feeding wounds
Downy mildew of maize and sorghum (*Sclerospora sorghi*)	*Rhopalosiphon maidis, Schizaphis graminum*	Through feeding punctures
Pine burn blight (*Diplodia pinea*)	*Aphrophora parallela*	-do-
Internal boll disease of cotton (*Namatospora gossypii*)	*Dysdercus* spp.	Through feeding punctures
Bean rot of coffee (*Nematospora* spp.)	*Antestia lineaticollis*	-do-
Soyabean yeas spot (*Nematospora corylii*)	*Acrosternum hilare*	-do-
Rice grain discolouration (*Nematospora corylii*)	*Oebalus pugnax*	-do-
Apple fruit rot and canker (*Gloeosporium perennans*)	*Eriosoma lanigerum*	Symbiotic
Oat wilt (*Ceratocystis fagacearum*)	Many species belonging to nitidulidae, scolytidae and drosophiladae	Spermatization and transmission
Dutchelm (*Ceratostomella ulmi*)	*Hylurgopinus rufipes, Scolytus multistriatus*	Transmission

(*Source:* Narayanaswamy, P., 1997)

Mites. The mites belong to the class *Arachinida* and are the only non-insect arthropod vectors of plant viruses. The ability to transmit virus is restricted to a few species of eriophyd mites (family– *Eriophyidae*). Diseases transmitted by Eryophid mites include Agropyron mosaic, cherry leaf mottle, current reversion, fig mosaic, rye grass mosaic, peach mosaic and sterility mosaic of pegionpea, wheat spot mosaic and wheat streak mosaic.

Nematodes. Since the first report of transmission of a plant virus by a nematode (Hewitt, et al., 1958), quite a number of plant viruses have been found out to be carried by this group of vector. Members of genera *Longidorus* and *Xiphinema* (family–*Trichodoridae*) transmit polyhedral **nepoviruses** such as the grapevine fanleaf, Arabis mosaic, tomato ring spot. *Trichodorus* and *Paratrichodorus* (family–*Trichodoridae*) transmit the straight tubular tobraviruses (**netuviruses**) such as tobacco rattle and pea early browning.

With fungal vectors. A number of soil borne fungi of the groups of Chytridiomycetes and Plasmodiophoromycetes transmit viruses. Viruses transmitted by soil borne fungi are listed in Table 4.7.

Table 4.7 Plant Viruses Transmitted by Fungi

Fungal vector	Virus diseases
Olpidium brassicae	Lettuce big vein and tobacco necrosis on tobacco, bean, potatoes and tulip.
Olpidium cucurbitacearum	Cucumber necrosis
Polymyxa betae	Beat necrotic yellow vein
Polymyxa graminis	Beet yellow dwarf mosaic, oat mosaic, rice necrosis, wheat spindle, streak mosaic, wheat soil borne mosaic
Pythium ultimum	Pea false leaf roll
Spongospora subterranean	Potato mop top
Synchytrium endobioticum	Potato virus X

With dodder. Many plant viruses are transmitted from one plant to another through establishment of parasitic relationship between two plants by the twining stems of parasitic plant dodder (*Cuscuta* spp). Some important plant viruses transmitted by dodder are summarized in Table 4.8.

Table 4.8 Plant Viruses Transmitted by Dodder

Virus	*Cuscuta* spp
Arabis mosaic	*C. subinclusa* and *C. californica* frequently and *C. campestris* occassionally
Barley yellow dwarf	*C. campestris*
Citrus tristeza	*C. americana*
Citrus exocurtis viroid	*C. subinclusa*
Potato leaf roll	*C. subinclusa*
Tobacco etch virus	*C. californica* *C. lupilofermis*

Dissemination by humans. As the domesticator and cultivator of crops, human activities happen to be an important source for dissemination of plant pathogens. In the process of raising the crops, the growers get closely associated with the crops and the operational equipment employed for various cultural operations. Thus, a contact is invariably established between diseased and healthy individuals/populations. This results in transmission and spread of several infectious/contagious pathogens. Exchange of genetic material (germplasm) and seed is one of the important activities responsible for 'transport' of various pathogens. Various groups of vectors are involved in transmission of plant viruses. The nature of vector involved in transmission and the relationship between the virus and the vector has been studied for the majority of plant viruses and phytoplasmas (Carter, 1973; Harris, 1979; Harris and Maramorosch, 1977).

REFERENCES

Agarwal, V.K. and Sinclair, J.B., 1997, *Principles of Seed Pathology*, Lewis Publishers/CRC Press, Boca Raton, Florida, USA.

Agrios, G.N., 1997, *Plant Pathology*, 4th edition, Academic Press, New York.

Bateman, D.F. and Basham, H.G., 1976, Degradation of plant cell walls and membranes by microbial enzymes, *In: Physiological Plant Pathology* Heitefuss, R. and Williams, P.H. Eds. Spinger-Verlag, Berlin.

Carter, W., 1973, *Insects in Relation to Plant Diseases*, John Wiley & Sons, New York.

Chang, Ho. Y. and Hickman, C.J., 1970, Some factors involved in the accumulation of Phycomycete zoospores on plant roots, *In:* Toussoun, T.A., et al., (Eds), *Root Diseases and Soil Borne Pathogens.* University of California Press, Berkeley, pp. 103-108.

Chaube , H.S. and Singh, R.A., 1984, Survival of plant pathogenic bacteria, in *Progress in Microbial Ecology*, Mukerjee, K.G., Agnihotri, V.P. and Singh, R.P., Eds., Print House (India), Lucknow, p. 653.

Chaube, H.S. and Singh, U.S., 1990, *Plant Disease Management: Principles and Practices,* CRC Press, Boca Raton, USA.

Chaube, H.S., Studies on ascochyta blight of chickpea, Expt. St. Res. Bull. G.B. Pant Univ. of Agric. & Techn., Pantnagar, India, 109.

Cole, G.T. and Hoch, H.C., 1991, *The Fungal Spore and Disease Initiation in Plants and Animals,* Plenum Press, New York.

Crosse, J.E., 1968, Plant pathogenic bacteria in soil, In: *Ecology of Soil-Bacteria*, Gray, T.R.C. and Parkinson, D., Eds., Liverpool Univ. Press, Liverpool, 522.

Dobbs, C.G. and Hinson, W.H., 1953, A widespread fungistasis in soil, *Nature*, 172: 197,

Durbin, R.D., 1981, *Toxins in Plant Disease,* Academic Press, New York.

Goodman, R.N., et al., 1986, *The Biochemistry and Physiology of Plant Diseases*, Univ. of Missouri Press, Columbia Mo.

Graniti, A., et al., Eds., 1989, *Phytotoxins and Plant Pathogenesis*, Springer-Verlag, Berlin.

Harris, K.F., 1979, Leaf hoppers and aphids as biological vectors: Vector-virus relationships, In: *Leaf Hopper Vector and Plant Disease Agents,* K. Maramorosch and Harris K.F. (Eds.) Academic Press, New York.

Harris, K.F. and Maramorosch, K., 1977, *Aphids as virus vectors,* Academic Press, New York.

Hewitt, W.B., Raski, D.J. and Goheen, A.C., 1958, Nematode vectors of soil-borne fanleaf virus of grapevines, *Phytopathology,* 48:86.

Hickman, C.J. and Ho, H.H., 1966, Behaviour of Zoospores in Plant-Pathogenic Phycomycetes, *Annu. Rev. Phytopathol,* 4:105.

Lacey, J., 1967, The role of water in spread of phytophthora infestans in the potato crop, *Annal. Apple, Biol.,* 50:245.

S. Laviolette, F.A., and Athow, K.L., 1971, Longevity of tobacco ringspot virus in soyabean seed, *Phytopatholgy,* 61:755

Lucas, J.A., 1998, *Plant Pathology and Plant Pathogens,* 3rd ed., Blackwell, Science.

Mathur, R.S. and Ahmad, Z.U., 1964, Longevity of *Corynebacterium tritici* causing tundu disease of wheat, *Proc. Nal, Acad. Sci, India.,* 34:335.

Mims, C.A., 1995, *The Pathogenesis of Infectious Diseases,* 5th ed., Academic Press, London.

Neergaard, P., 1979, *Seed Pathology,* The Macmillan Press, London.

Nicole, M., and Gianninazi-Person, V., 1996, *Histology, Ultrastructure* and *Molecular Cytology of Plant Microbe Interactions*, Kluwer Academic, Publisher Dordrecht.

Palti, J., 1981, *Cultural Practices and Infectious Plant Diseases,* Springer-Verlag, Berlin.

Shipton, P.J., 1972, Take-all in spring-sown cereals under continuous cultivation, Disease progress and decline in relation to crop succession and nitrogen, *Annal. Appl. Biol.,* 71:33.

Singh, R.S., 2002, *Introduction to Principles of Plant Pathology,* 4th ed., Oxford & IBH Publishing Co. Pvt. Ltd., New Delhi.

Singh, R.S., 1984, *Introduction to Principle of Plant Patholgy,* 3rd ed., Oxford and IBH Publishing Co., New Delhi, 534.

Singh, U.S. et al., 1994, *Pathogenesis and Host Specificity in Plant Diseases: Histopathological, Biochemical, Genetic and Molecular Bases*, Vols. 1-3, Pergamon/Elsevier, Tarrytown, New York.

Tarjan, A.C., 1971, Migration of three pathogenic citrus nematodes through two florida soils, *Soil Crop Sci. Soc. Fla. Proc.,* 31:253.

Teakle, D.S., 1980, Fungi, in vectors of plant pathogens, Harris, K.F. and Maramorosch, K., Eds., Academic Press, New York, 417.

Wallace, H.R., 1978, Dispersal in time and space: Soil pathogens, In *Plant Disease: An Advanced Treatise,* vol. 2, Horsfall, J.G. and Cowling, E.B., Eds., Academic Press, New York, 181.

Walton, J.P. and Panaccione, D.G., 1993, Host selective toxins and disease specificity: perspectives and progress, *Annu. Rev. Phytopathol.* 31:275

Zentmyer, G.A., 1970, Tactic response of zoospore of *Phytophthora,* In: Toussoun, T.A., et al. (Eds.), *Root Diseases and Soil-Borne Pathogens*, Univ. of California Press, Berkeley, pp. 109-111.

5

Mechanism of Host Defence

Host-parasite interactions seem more of a war where both host and pathogen try to eliminate each other. In plant system, host-parasite interaction involves management of pathogen by restricting its damaging effects. Adjustment is one of the natural laws.

—Singh, R.S., 2002

5.1 INTRODUCTION

Adjustment is, probably, one of the most important virtue of a system that ensures its survival, be it host or parasite. On planet earth, the green plants (autotrophs) constitute the only biological system capable of converting solar energy (electro-magnetic radiations) into chemical energy. Various forms of visitors, including men, pests and pathogens, try to get their share of stored food material for their sustenance. Plants as a biological system **resist** this exploitation, at all levels and by all means. The co-evolution, forced by co-existence with pathogen, has led to development of **defence mechanism in plants**. Thus, resistance against any 'deleterious act' has become a natural and universal response of plant system. **The resistance against parasites/pathogens is the heritable trait of plants by virtue of which they resist attack by parasites/pathogens or their activities.** The defence mechanism(s) has ensured the survival of plants in spite of living amongst some of the potentially devastating pathogens, in addition to abiotic stresses. **Plants have also developed ability to resist/tolerate various abiotic stress(s).** In this chapter we will see how does a plant system defend itself against pathogenic and non-pathogenic agents.

5.2 PHILOSOPHY OF DEFENCE IN PLANTS

All biological organism, plants or animals, have developed system for their defence against various undesirable agents/activities. These defence systems have been fashioned depending upon the basic structural framework of the organism and their needs. Plants and animals differ significantly on both these accounts. Thus the basic philosophy of defence in plants is altogether different from that of animals. Table 5.1 compares and contrasts the defence systems in plants and animals.

Table 5.1 Comparison of Plants and Animals Defence Systems

Defence system—Plants	*Defence system—Animals*
Since plants cannot move, they have to resist or tolerate the pathogen standing on the same site.	Animals can move and can protect themselves by changing their positions if there is a threat.
Plants have developed very strong preformed defence system in the form of structural and toxic barriers.	Animals have developed active/induced defence mechanism. The body can be immunized to face the predicted 'enemies'.
Plants cannot eliminate but can only limit (contain) the invaders.	Animals can fight and eliminate the invaders from the body.
Plants can tolerate greater drain of nutrients. Often they sacrifice some of the tissues to restrict the pathogen.	Animals cannot tolerate much drain on their energy system.
Division of labour is not that developed, hence, every cell has to perform functions including defence.	Animals have well developed division of labour and specialized cells to fight the invaders.
Plant cells contain anti-microbial substances in compartments, which help the cell to defend it.	Not much is known about animal cells.
Plant metabolism is influenced by environmental conditions, and in turn the defence mechanism is influenced.	Animals can regulate their environment, and can keep the pathogens at disadvantage.
Vascular system in plants is not efficient, movement through apoplast is passive while loading in symplast is very selective (toxic molecules cannot be transported).	Circulatory system in animals is very efficient; all the cells of body are connected. Defence related materials could move throughout body, basically centralized defence system.
Every individual plant has its own defence system. Nothing operates at population or community level.	To fight against disease agents lot of efforts are made at community level to protect the populations.
Primitive system akin to animal immunity system is likely to operate; common antigenicity in compatible host-pathogen interactions reported.	Animals have pronounced immunity system, which makes the core of defence system.

There are some interesting parallels emerging between the plant defence responses and selected cellular defence of mammals (Hutchenson, 1998). The bacterial elicitation of programmed cell death involves hrp-encoded protein translocation complexes that are nearly identical to those of their mammalian counterparts. Even some of the proteins secreted by mammalian pathogens are similar to known avr gene products of plant pathogenic bacteria.

5.3 PATHOGENESIS AND HOST RESPONSE

Analysis of most of the host-parasite relationships reveals that on the pattern of pathogenesis, the plants, on their part, do exhibit defence mechanisms (structural and chemical) as soon as challenged by the pathogen (Vidhyasekaran, 1998). The moment pathogen propagules come in contact with host surface, the plants due to hereditary characters have several naturally occurring physical and chemical barriers (*pre-existing*) resisting penetration, and if at all the penetration occurs, the host reacts by different means resulting in formation of physical and chemical barriers. These two conditions are discussed in Figure 5.1.

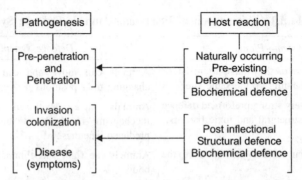

Figure 5.1 Pathogenesis and host defence reactions.

5.4 DEFENCE MECHANISMS: PRE-EXISTING OR PASSIVE

5.4.1 A Pre-existing Structural Defences

The first line of defence in plants is present on its surface. Several characters of the plants surface function as barriers to penetration which pathogen must breach to enter the host. The pathogens enter the plant host by penetrating the epidermis (mechanical-enzymatic) or through wounds or natural openings. The structure of epidermis along with cuticle and cuticular wax and number of natural openings existing before the onset of pathogenesis can obstruct penetration.

If pathogen succeeds in penetration; it encounters pre-existing internal structural barriers. The external and internal structural barriers existing before pathogen attack are also called **Pre-existing defence structures** *or passive/static or anti-infection structures* (Singh, 2002). Starting from periphery, the following barriers occurring in different host plants are described:

Wax and cuticle. The cuticle covers the epidermal cells of plants and consists of pectin layer, a cutinized layer and a wax layer. Cutin is composed of fatty acids. Waxes are mixture of long chain aliphatic compounds, which prevent the retention of water on plant surface essential for spore germination. A negative charge usually develops on leaf surfaces due to fatty acids. This condition repels air-borne spores/propagules. Only few pathogens are known to dissolve cutin enzymatically. Examples: *Monilinia fructicola* penetrates cuticle of cherry leaves but not of *Gingko biloba* leaves; the latter contains abundant cutin than the former. *F. solani* f sp. *pisi* produces the enzyme cutinase production by specific antibodies and inhibitors.

Epidermal layer. Epidermis is the first layer of living host cells that comes in contact with attacking microbes. The toughness of epidermis is due to the polymers of cellulose, hemicellulose, lignin, mineral substances, polymerized organic compounds, suberin, etc. Potato tubers resistant to *Pythium debaryanum* contain higher fibre. Silicon accumulation in epidermal walls provides resistance against fungal attack. Suberization of epidermis confers protection against plant pathogens.

Natural openings. Many pathogens enter plants through natural openings, like stomata, hydathodes, lenticels, nectarines, etc. **Stomata** are large enough for active penetration by germ tubes of zoosporic fungi, as well as for the passive entrance of bacterial cells and fungal spores in water droplets. Resistance or susceptibility to some of these pathogens has been related to numbers, spatial arrangement, structure and time of opening and closing of stomata. Mandarin orange is resistant to

Xanthomonas axonopodis pv. *citri* because of broad cuticular lips covering the stomata. A functional defence mechanism has been observed in some wheat varieties (cv-Hope) in which stomata open late in the day when moisture on leaf surface has dried and the infection tubes have become non-functional. A correlation between the number of stomata open at the time of inoculation and the amount of disease has been found in the infection of hop leaves by zoospores of *Pseudoperonospora humuli* (Singh, 2002).

Hydathodes are natural openings on the edges of leaves and serve to excrete excess water from the interior. They are easy entry points of bacterial pathogens such as *X. campestris* pv. *campestris* (black rot of cabbage). Similar to hydathodes are the **nectarthodes** in inflorescence of many plants. They secrete sugary nectar and this serves as barrier to those organisms that cannot tolerate high osmotic pressure. *Erwinia amylovora* (fire blight of apple and pear) can tolerate this condition and thus, can enter through nectarines. Leaf hairs on leaves and on nectarines also resist entry of pathogens. High hairiness of leaves and pods in chickpea is resistant character against *Ascochyta rabei*. Groundnut varieties showing resistance to Cercospora leaf spots have thick epidermis-cum cuticle and compact palisade layer, fewer and smaller stomata and high frequency of trichomes on the abaxial surface of leaf (Kaur and Dhillon, 1988; Mayee and Suryavanshi, 1995).

Lenticels are openings in outer walls involved in gaseous exchange. They are weak points in defence unless the cork cells within them are suberized. After suberization and periderm formation, lenticels are more resistant to invasion by pathogens (e.g. *streptomyces scabies*).

Internal structures. The thickness and toughness of **cell walls** of internal tissues is important in invasion by some pathogens. For example, the sclerenchyma tissues are made up of thick and tough-walled cells. The amount and distribution of these tissues varies in different species and varieties of plants. In wheat varieties containing these tissues in relatively high proportion in stem possess certain degree of resistance to *Puccinia graminis* f. sp. *tritici. Pythium* spp. invade only juvenile tissues, seedlings become resistant as they advance in age and secondary thickenings are formed. Biochemical factors may also be involved in this age-based resistance. Lignifications, suberization, deposition of carbohydrates, etc. to strengthen the internal tissues are also mechanical barriers to infection.

5.4.2 Pre-existing Biochemical Defence

Plants liberate different chemicals, which interfere with activities of the pathogen and pathogenesis, thereby preventing or reduce infection. These chemicals and the biochemical conditions that develop may act either directly through toxic or lytic effect on the invader or indirectly through stimulating antagonistic plant surface microflora. Bell (1981) called the compounds pre-existing in plants as **constitutive antibiotics** and those, which are formed in response to wounds as **wounds antibiotics**.

Release of anti-microbial compounds. Plants while growing and developing release gases as well as organic substances, from leaves and roots (leaf and root exudates), containing sugars, amino acids, organic acids, enzymes, glycosides, etc. These materials have profound effect on the nature of surrounding environment, particularly the phyllosphere, rhizosphere microflora and fauna. Although these substances are ideal nutrients for microbes and help in germination and growth of several saprophytes and parasites, a number of inhibitory substances are also present in these exudates. Theses inhibitory substances directly affect the microorganism, or encourage certain groups to dominate the environment and function as antagonists of the pathogen. According to Kalita, et al. (1996) there are numerous examples of resident microflora enhanced by exudates, which are potential biocontrol agents. The root exudates favour development of plant growth promoting rhizobacteria (PGPR), which suppresses the plant pathogens and induces resistance in the plant (Weller, 1988). Root exudates contain compounds that are directly toxic to pathogens. For instance, certain varieties of linseed (flax) resist infection by *F. oxysporum* f. sp. *lini* because of the presence of hydro cyanides (HCN) in their root exudates; in addition, HCN does not affect the development of fungal antagonists—*Trichoderma* species. Thus, HCN encourages biological control of disease. Presence of HCN in roots of maize and sorghum is also reported. HCN in sorghum root exudates might be responsible for reduction of pigeon pea wilt caused by *Fusarium udum* in plots where sorghum is grown as mixed crop with pegionpea.

Tomato leaves are known to exude chemicals that checks attack of *Botrytis cinerea*. Similarly, cowpea leaves, resistant to Cercospora leaf spots, possess toxic substances that inhibit conidial germination. Certain powdery mildew resistant varieties of apple exude three toxic waxes on leaf surface, which prevent germination of conidia of *Podosphaera leucotricha*. Red scales of onion (red varieties) contain protocatechuic acid and catechol, which may exude in drops and impart resistance to attack of *Colletotrichum circinans* (onion smudge disease).

Inhibitors present in plant cells.   In many host-parasite interactions, pre-existing toxic substances in the cells form the basis of resistance. In resistant variety these substances are in abundance while in susceptible variety they may be less or completely absent. Several *phenolic compounds, tannins,* and some fatty acid like compounds such as ***dienes*** pre-existing in high concentrations in cells have been implicated for the resistance of young tissues to parasitic fungi such as *Botrytis*. Many such compounds are potent inhibitors of many hydrolytic enzymes. Several other types of preformed compounds, such as **saponins** (glycosylated steroidal or triterpenoid compounds) **tomatine** in tomato, and **avenacin** in oats, have antifungal membranolytic activity. The fungal pathogens, which lack enzymes (saponinases) that breakdown the saponins, are prevented from infecting the host. Several preformed plant proteins have been reported to act as inhibitors of pathogen proteinases or of hydrolytic enzymes. Similarly, *lactins* (proteins that bind to certain sugars) cause lyses and growth inhibition of many fungi. Plants surface cells also contain variable amounts of hydrolytic enzymes such as *glucanases* and chitinases, which may cause breakdown of pathogen cell wall components.

Lack of essential factors

Recognition factors.   The first step in infection process is the cell-to-cell communication between host and pathogens. Plants of species or varieties may not be infected by a pathogen if their surface cells lack specific recognition factors (specific molecules or structures). If the pathogen does not recognize the plant as one of its hosts it may not adhere to the host surface or it may not produce infection substances such as enzymes, or structures (appresoria, haustoria). These recognition molecules are of various types of oligosaccharides and polysaccharides and glycoproteins.

Host receptors and sites for toxins.   In many host parasite interactions, the pathogen produces host specific toxins, which are responsible for symptoms and disease development. The molecules of toxin are supposed to attach to specific sensitive sites or receptors in the cell. Only the plants that have such sensitive sites become diseased.

Essential nutrients and growth factors.   The fact that many facultative saprophytes and most of the obligate parasites are host specific and sometimes are so specialized that they can grow and reproduce only on certain varieties of those species suggests that for these pathogens the essential nutrients and growth factors are available only in these hosts. Absence of these nutrients and stimulus make the other varieties and species unsuitable hosts. If the pre-existing substances cannot be utilized by the pathogen or become unavailable due to reactions taking place after infection, the pathogen will fail to grow. For example, in seedling diseases of several crops caused by *Rhizoctonia solani*, successful infection depends on formation of infection cushions from which infection-peg develops and causes penetration. Formation of these cushions is induced by certain essential nutrients in the host. In resistant plants, lack of such nutrients results in resistance to *R. solani*. In the apple scab disease, the pathogen *Venturia inaequalis* has genetically controlled requirement for a growth factor in order to become pathogenic. Certain mutants of the pathogen cease to be pathogenic in absence of their ability to synthesize this factor. They can be induced to establish infection by external application of the growth factor.

5.5 DEFENCE MECHANISM: INDUCED OR ACTIVE

Plants, like **medieval castle,** have to face the wide variety of pathogens (enemies) standing at a place. Thus we see a strategically designed pre-existing (structural and biochemical) defence mechanism in plants. The real value of this system has not been critically examined. It appears that these pre-existing defence mechanisms help plants in warding-off most of microbes as non-pathogens. But it does not seem to be sufficient. Hutchenson (1998) observed that **plants are not passive host** to constant onslaught of microorganisms with which they interact in their environment. The plants also have induced defence like most other eukaryotic organism described as **active defence** as they are **a response to pathogen** attack and they require **expenditure of energy** by plants. The induced/active defence mechanism in plants may operate at different levels:

- Biochemical defence
- Defence at cellular level
- Defences at tissue level

Dixon (1994) proposed a multistructural and biochemical component defence response. The activation or induction of defence mechanism may be both specific (race × cultivar interaction) and non-specific type (non-host response). Several structural changes (development and modifications) are known to be induced by a range of biotic or abiotic elicitors. These dynamic defence mechanisms prevent further colonization or spread of pathogen. Following are the post-infectional (induced) structural barriers that may resist the advances of invading pathogens. Active defence in plants involve cellular defence that rely upon preformed surveillance systems to detect and respond to invading pathogens during primary interaction. These surveillance systems are encoded by resistance genes (gene products are receptors). The receptor-proteins are strategically located in cell membranes to detect the pathogen or factors translocated by pathogens. The ability of plant to mount an active defence response (timing being crucial) is again under genomic control.

Disease occurs when

1. Pre-existing defence mechanisms are not enough to check the entry of pathogen (pathogen has devised means to breach the host defence lines).
2. A pathogen avoids timely eliciting active defence system in plant tissue or inhibits active defence responses by secreting metabolic toxins.

5.5.1 Induced Structural Defence

Induced histological defence.   Even after the establishment of infection in plant cells, the host defence system tries to create barriers for further colonization of tissues. These may be at various levels:

Lignifications. Lignified cell wall provide effective barrier to hyphal penetration. They also act as impermeable barrier for free movement of nutrient causing starvation of pathogen (Plate 5.1).

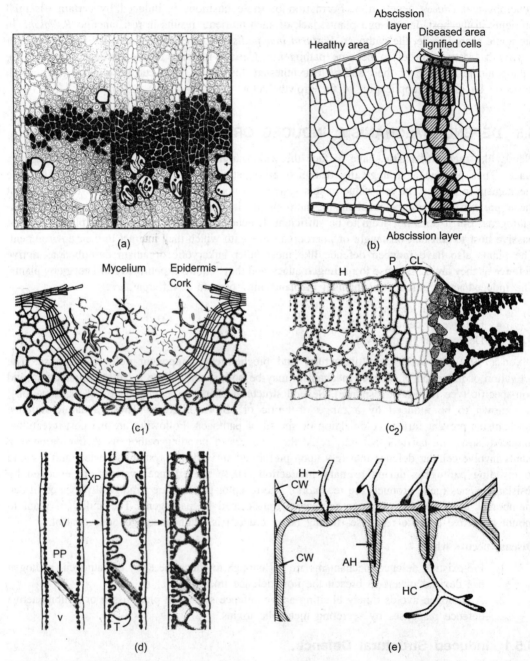

Plate 5.1 Mechanism of host resistance a = Lignification, b = Abscission layer formation, c₁ & c₂ = Cork layer formation, d = Tyloses formation and e = Sheathing of infection threads (After Agrios, G.N., 1997).

Following are examples:

Radish: *Peronospora parasitica*
Alternaria japonica
Potato: *Phytophthora infestans*
Wheat: *Septoria nodorum*
Cucumber: *Cladosporium cucumerium*
Colletotrichum lagenarium
Carrot: *Botrytis cineria*

Suberization. In several plants the infected cells are surrounded by suberized cells. Thus, isolating them from healthy tissue. Corky layer formation is a part of natural healing system of plants [Plate 5.1 (c_1 & c_2)]. e.g. common scab of potato (*streptemyces scabis*) and *Rhizopus* rot of sweet potato are good examples.

Abscission layers. It is a gap between host cell layers and devices for dropping-off older leaves and mature fruits. Plant may use this for defence mechanism also, i.e. to drop-off infected or invaded plant tissues or parts, along with pathogen [Plate 5.1(b)]. Shot holes in leaves of fruit trees is a common feature.

Tyloses. The tyloses are formed by protrusion of xylem paranchymatous cell walls, through pits, into xylem vessels [Plate 5.1(d)]. The size and number of the tyloses physically block the vessel. The tyloses are inductively formed much ahead of infection, thus blocking the spread of pathogen. It suggests biochemical elicitors and movement of tyloses inducing factor (TIF) up the stem, e.g. sweet potato: *Fusarium oxysporum* f. sp. *batatas.*

Gum deposition. The gums and vascular gels quickly accumulate and fill the intercellular spaces (apoplast) or within the cell surrounding the infection thread and haustoria, which may starve or die.

Induced cellular defence. The cellular defence structures, i.e. changes in cell walls, have only a limited role in defence. Following types are commonly observed:

1. Carbohydrate apposition (synthesis of secondary walls and papillae formation).
2. Callose deposition (hyphal sheathing just outside plasma lemma around the haustorium, which delays contact of pathogen (*Phytophthora infestans*) with host cells.
3. Structural proteins.
4. Induced cytoplasmic defence that presents last line of host defence and may be effective against slow growing pathogens, weak parasites or some symbiotic relationships.

Hypersensitivity. H.M. Ward in 1902 discovered strong correlation between hypersensitivity and disease resistance. E.C. Stakman (1915) introduced the term **hypersensitivity.** It is a phenomena commonly occurring in wide variety of plants. Initial work was confined to biotrophs and viruses where it was believed that plants used the **suicide cell strategy** to check growth, multiplication and colonization by obligate parasite by isolating them from living cell cytoplasm, thus starving them. Later the phenomenon was reported from non-obligate fungi, bacteria and nematodes. Hypersensitive response or **necrogenous reaction** of plant tissue to invading pathogen involve rapid metabolic and cytological changes leading to cell death, browning of tissues and accumulation of toxic chemical. It may provide both structural and physiological defence. Gilchrist (1998) advocated the theory that some host cells die to save others; the host cells are programmed to die

(**Programmed cell death or Pcd**) in response to attack of pathogen and the process starts just after contact of host cells with pathogen (cell membranes).

Programmed cell death (Pcd). The invaded host cells or just adjacent cells frequently react in a form of programmed cell death (Pcd). This suicidal approach is an active process resulting from specific recognition event controlled by protein-protein interaction. This is more common in gene for gene interactions but also observed during non-host interactions. Hypersensitive response is macroscopic manifestation of pathogen induced Pcd (Hutchenson, 1998). The pathogen induced Pcd is a rapid process, often completed in less than 6 h and begins with a series of membrane aberrations: Lipid per-oxidation, K^+ efflux and Ca^{++} influx. This is followed by an oxidative burst in early stages. The changes in cell morphology include condensation and vacuolarization of cytoplasm, endonuclease degrading both DNA and RNA (cleavage of chromosomal DNA in to large fragments is also observed). Other biochemical manifestation during Pcd includes enhanced expression of phenyl propanoid metabolism and pathogenesis related proteins (β-1, 3 glucanose and chitinase). Hutchenson (1998) considers these gene expressions in Pcd responding plant cell as primary responses and suggests that signal molecules produced by pathogen induced Pcd may be responsible for secondary responses (a similar system works in case of activation of defence mechanism in mammals against viruses). Hutchenson (1998) categorized active defence response in following three groups:

1. **Primary responses** are localized to the cell in contact with pathogen, in very close proximity. It involves the recognition of specific signal molecules and outcome is commonly **programmed cell death** (Pcd).
2. **Secondary responses** are induced in adjacent cells, surrounding the initial infection site. The diffusible signal molecules play important role.
3. **Systemically acquired resistance** is hormonally induced and is noticed at distant places from site of infection, probably throughout the plant.

Pcd is a normal but important process of host plant development. It offers following advantages to plants:

1. The sacrifice of 'some' host cells will isolate the pathogen (obligate parasite) from nutritional sources in plant tissue.
2. Disruption of flow of nutrient to pathogen will abolish metabolic process necessary for survival of pathogen (virus replication).
3. The nucleases formed in early part of Pcd could degrade viral genome in host cell undergoing Pcd. Although the facultative parasites may not be affected according to the nutrient disruption theory, these exhibit reduced growth or multiplication in cells undergoing Pcd. This is indicative of some alternate mechanism operating such as induction of an oxidative burst in affected cells (demonstrated in *Arabidopsis*).

5.5.2 Induced Biochemical Changes

The induced biochemical changes in host plants are the last line of host defence. This may condition a plant or plant tissue from susceptible to resistant to immune status as per their genetic potential. Singh (2002) suggested that to establish the role of a biochemical factor in host defence it must possess the four attributes and match the following "Koch's postulates" for pathogenicity (modified).

1. The substance is associated with protection against disease at the site where protection occurs.
2. The substance can be isolated from the host showing protection against the disease.
3. Introduction of isolated substance to the appropriate susceptible host confers protection.
4. The nature of protection so induced resembles that of the natural agents of a resistant plant.

Toxic substances produced. Rapid production/suitable modifications and/or accumulation of chemicals toxic to pathogens up to effective concentrations is an important component of overall active defence strategy of plants. Slow production or accumulation or low levels of similar chemicals have been reported in susceptible host plants also (compatible interactions). In fact, this created confusion among workers and put a question mark on role of these toxic chemicals induced to protect the plants tissues against invading pathogens.

Role of phenolic compounds. The phenolic compounds, viz. chlorogenic acid, caffeic acid and oxidation products of floretin, hydroquinone hydroxyquinones and phytoalexins are main toxic chemicals produced to inhibit pathogen or its activities (Nicholson, et al., 1992). Some of these are preformed toxic chemicals while others may be *de novo* synthesized or modified to more toxic forms (conversion/oxidation of phenols to more toxic quinones). The enzymes involved in chemical pathways are present in host cell (pre-existing). That is indicative of genetic potential of plant to defend itself, (phenol-oxidizing enzymes: Phenolases, Phenoleoxidases, Poly phenol oxidases and complex poly phenols (tannins and lignins).

Role of phytoalexins. Most common response of plants to stress, biotic (pathogens/insects) or abiotic (wounding), is the production and accumulation of substrates that can inhibit the growth and activities of the biotic factors or may help in healing process. Nicholson and Hammerschmidt, (1992) reported that in plants continuous irritation by pathogen is essential for production of effective amount of these phenolic compounds. Muller and Borger proposed the concept of **phytoalexins** in their study on hypersensitive reaction of potato to avirulent *P. infestans* strains. Tomiyama, et al., (1968) characterized phytoalexins, rishtin, (a non-sequiterpene alcohol). Kuc (1972) defined Phytoalexins as *antibiotics produced in plant-pathogens interactions or as result response to injury or other physiological stimulation.* Wide variety of toxic chemicals was reported to increase in concentration in response to infection, thus phytoalexins are now considered as **low molecular weight anti-microbial compounds produced** *de novo* **in plants as a result of infection or abiotic stress.** This excludes the pre-existing common phenols, e.g. chlorogenic acid, caffeic acid and scopoletin, etc. Table 5.2 and Plate 5.2 give information on chemical structures of some of the common phytoalexins reported. The phytoalexins have been demonstrated in wide variety of plants belonging to families *Gramineae* (oats, rice, sorghum, sugarcane), *Solanaceae, Leguminaceae, Chenopodiceae, Convolulaceae, Compositae, Malvaceae* and *Umbellifera.* Members of family *Orchidaceae* are known for production of phytoalexins.

Table. 5.2 Common Phytoalexins Reported in Host-pathogen Interactions

Phytoalexin	Host	Fungal pathogen
Capsidol	*Nicotiana clvelandi, N. tabacum*	Tobacco necrosis virus, Capsicum (Papper)
Pisatin	Pea (endocarp) pods, leaves	*Monilinia fructicola* (non-pathogen)
Glutinosone	*Nicotina glutinosa*	T.M.V.

(Contd.)

Table. 5.2 Common Phytoalexins Reported in Host-pathogen Interactions. (*Contd.*)

Phytoalexin	Host	Fungal pathogen
Phaseollin	French bean (*Phaseolus vulgaris Phaseolus lunatus, P. radiatus. P. leucanthus, Viguna sinensis*)	*Sclerolinia fructigena, Phytophthora infestans Colletrotiruchum liudemuthianum Pseudomonas savastonvi* pv. *phaseolicola*
Ipomeamarone	Sweet potato	*Ceratocystis fimbriata*
Medicarpin	*Medicago lupulina* (alfalfa) (*Phaseolus vulgaris, Cicer arietinum Medicago sativa, Trifolium pratense, T. repens*	*Helmithosporium turcium, Colletotrichum phomoides, Stemphyllium loti*
Triflorrhizin	*Trifolium pratense*	*Monilia fructicola*
Maackiain	*Trifolium Pratense* and Pea, *Cicer arietinum Fusarium solani* f. sp. phaseoli	
Wyerone	Pea	*Botrytis fabae*
Glyceollin	Soyabean	*Phytophthora megasperma* var. *sojae*
Orcinol and Hircinol	Orchids-mycorrhizal fungi	

Other phytoalexins reported include: rishitin, phytuberin, capsidol and glutinosone (Solanceae). sativan (alfalfa), vestitol (*Lotus corniculatus*) isocoumarin (carrot), vergosin and hemigossypal (cotton), safynol and dehydrosafynol (sunflower) avenalumin I, II, and II (barley–*Puccinia coronata* f.sp. *avenae*)

In spite of work done on phytoalexins and good amount of evidences presented, there are certain questions to be satisfied before establishing direct role of phytoalexins *in vivo* containment of pathogen. The following points should be considered:

1. Phytoalexins are not produced by all plants (more than 100 plants belonging to 21 families (Singh, 2002).
2. Phytoalexins have been demonstrated only against avirulent races/strains of pathogen (mostly weak pathogens).
3. Most of the work is confined to fungal pathogen (some of them non-pathogenic on the plant or even saprophytes).
4. Wide range of elicitors can induce phytoalexins production

These issues require attention of researchers but they do not reduce the value of a potential component of natural plant defence mechanism, i.e. phytoalexins.

Role of new proteins synthesized. Post-infectional changes in host cells involve production and modification of large number of proteins (structural and enzymatic), which have important role in defence mechanism. The enzymes are required for various synthetic pathways (normal or modified) for production of resistance related substances. In addition, phenol-oxidizing enzymes have vital role. The influence of these changes may be confined to infection site or near by cells. Increased synthesis and activity of phenyl ammonia lyase (PAL) has been reported in several bacterial and viral pathogens in resistant reaction. PAL plays key role in synthesis of phenols, phytoalexins and lignin. The effectiveness of resistance depends on speed and amount of synthesized products and their movement to neighbouring healthy tissues to create defensive barriers.

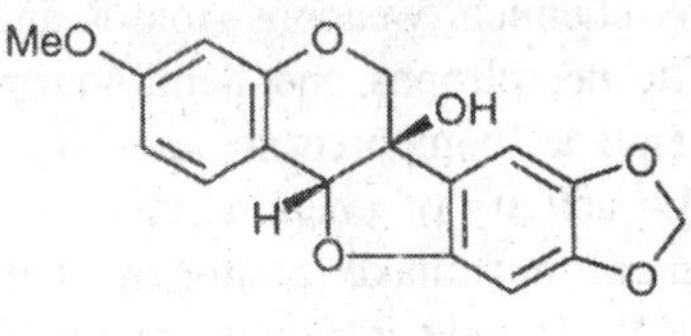

Pisatin (Pea)

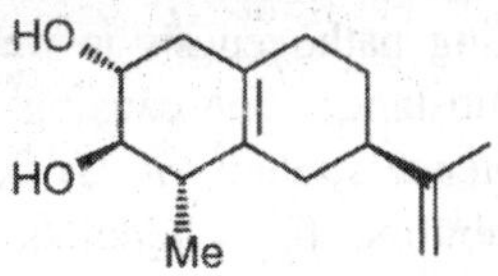

Rishitin (Potato)

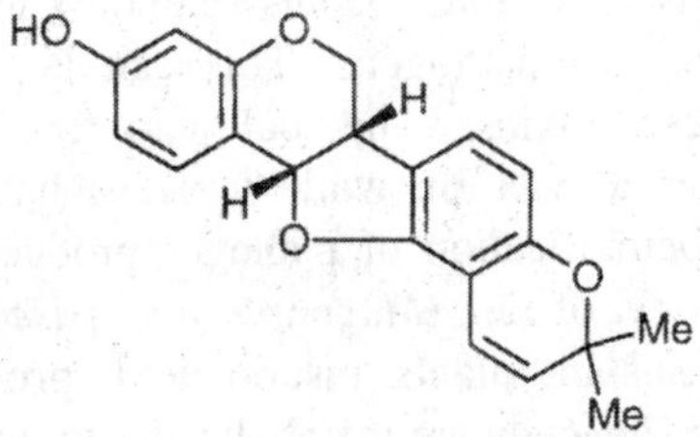

Phaseollin (*Phaseolus* bean)

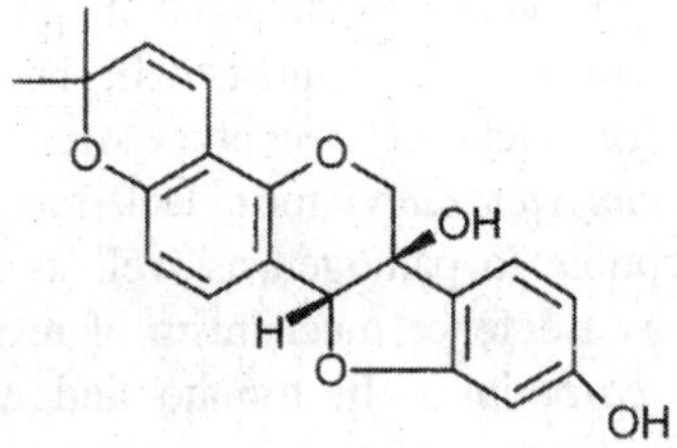

Glyceollin (Soyabean)

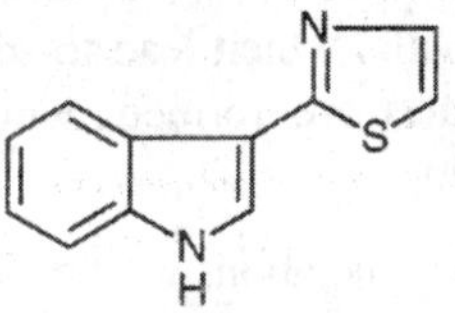

Camalexin (*Arabidopsis*)

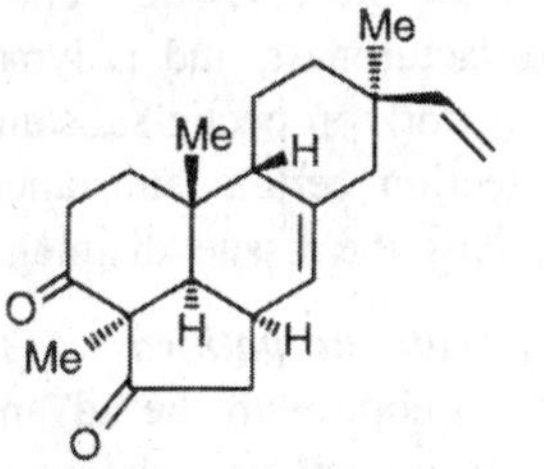

Momilactone A (Rice)

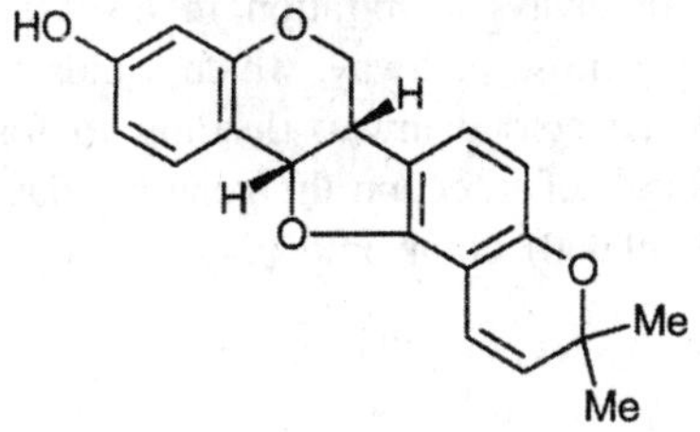

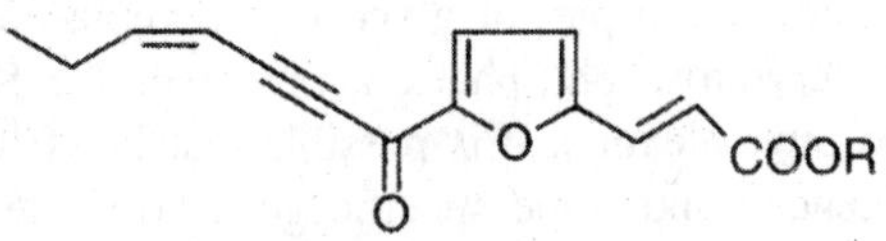

Wyerone acid R = H
Wyerone R = CH₃
(*Vicia* bean)

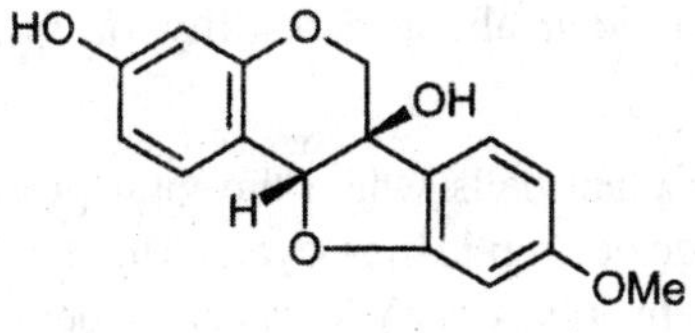

Phaseollin
(*Phaseolus* bean)

Isoflavonoid phytoalexins

Medicarpin
(Alfalfa)

Plate 5.2 Structures of some common phytoalexins.

Inactivation of enzymes and toxins. The role played by chemical weapons (toxins and enzymes) of pathogens during pathogenesis is well established. The necrotrophs and hemibiotrophs employ more of these substances for causing host tissue damage as compared to specialized obligate parasites. The defence strategy of resistant plants, through activity of phenols, tannins and protein as enzymes inhibitors, the phenolics are not anti-fungal but make pathogen ineffective by neutralizing their enzymes. In immature grape fruits catechol-tannin is known to inhibit enzymes produced by *Botrytis cinerea*.

Toxins are known to be involved in pathogenesis to various extents (pathotoxins/vivotoxins). The resistance to toxins, in host, will be resistance to pathogens. This can be achieved by detoxification or lack of receptor sites for these toxins. The oat varieties resistant to *Helminthosporium victorae*/victorin lack receptor sites to victorin while varieties having receptor sites are susceptible to pathogen as well as toxin. Detoxification of pathogen-produced toxin has been reported as a defence mechanism of resistant in cv. of rice (*Magnaporthae grisea*) and maize (*Cochliobalus carbonum*). In tomato and cotton resistant plants fusaric acid, produced by *F. oxysporum* f. sp. *lycopersici* and *F. oxysporum* f. sp. *vasinfectum* are metabolized into non-toxic form (N-methyl fusaric acid amide). Plant pathogens employ variety of enzymes for breakdown of structural integrity of host tissue. The pectinolytic enzyme pectin methyl esterase, pectin glycosidase, polygalacturonase and polymethyl gatacluronase, commonly produced by fungal and bacterial pathogens, work on pectic substances in middle lamella, which lead to softening of tissues. In response to infection certain substances (calcium pectate) are formed, which is resistant to enzymatic action, thus the tissue disintegration is prevented.

Role of altered biosynthetic pathways. The post infectional metabolism of host tissue is altered (stress physiology) to cope with the advancing activities of pathogen. New enzymes (proteins) are produced in an effort to synthesize defence related substances. Most of these compounds are formed through Shikmic acid pathway and modified acetate pathway. Respiration in diseased tissue is invariably increased; a part of glycolysis is replaced by pentose pathway, which yields four carbon compounds (erythrose phosphate, a precursor for Shikmic acid pathway (leading to formation of phenols and phytoalexins). It is possible that in early stages of infection the gene regulation of host cell is influenced and some specific genes (resistance related) come into play.

5.5.3 Active Defence to Pathogens

Induction of host resistance, structural or biochemical seems to be universal in plants. Active defence responses have been reported against all classes of pathogens (fungi, bacteria, viruses and nematodes). Active defence response may lead to incompatible host-pathogen interaction. Following situations are described for the readers, to give an idea about versatility of induced defence mechanism.

Viral infections. The intact virus particles enter the plant cells where the viral proteins are likely to be recognized as "stimulus' in host cell at early stages of replication cycle. This leads to induction or activation of defence mechanism in resistant host. In tobacco-TMV system where gene-for-gene system has been established, the host and pathogen proteins have been demonstrated to act as avirulence determinants. These included TMV-replicase and the movement protein of TMV.

Bacterial infections. It has been predicted that in bacterial infections the product of **avr gene** (proteins) play vital role in incompatible interactions with resistant host plants. Genes from

Pseudomonas syringae and *Xanthomonas* strains have been cloned and sequenced. The structural features of bacterial proteins have been identified to elicit the defence response. It has also been reported that in soyabean—Ps. *syringae* incompatible systems the **hrp gene** products are capable of inducing plant defence while same gene product, is essential for pathogenicity in susceptible hosts. The adsorption of one bacterial cell is enough to elicit a response in single plant cell.

Fungal infections. Plant pathogenic fungi interact with host plants in many different ways. The pathogenesis in tomato—*Cladosporium fulvum* system has been worked out in detail. **Avr 9 gene** product, a protein, was first to be isolated from infected tomato leaves in compatible interaction. The isolated protein, 28 amino acid peptide, was also responsible for eliciting response in tomato cultivars carrying **CF9** resistant gene. It has been established that specific three-dimensional space of protein is important for recognition. The role of other specific genes like barley—*Rhynchosporium secalis* (Rrs1), Rice—*Magnaporthe grisea* (AVR2-YAMO), Flax—*Melamposra lini* (L6 and M gene), *Arabidopsis-Peronospora parasitica* (RPP5), Tomato—*Fusarium oxysporium* f. sp. *lycopersici* race 2 (12 c-1) has also been studied, in host-pathogen interactions.

Nematode infection. Sugar beet cyst nematode and root knot nematode have been studied in detail. It has been established that resistance to nematode infections operate in similar fashion. In sugar beet cyst nematode (Hs1 pro^1) gene is responsible for induction of host resistance. The gene has been cloned and sequenced. The gene product is same as Cf family of resistant genes. The nematodes are capable of introducing several proteins into host cell and some of them may be crucial for recognition/induction of host defence. Intense induced metabolic activities take place during formation of giant cells (syncitium), which decide the fate of nematode infection.

5.6 SUMMARY OF INDUCED BIOCHEMICAL DEFENCE REACTIONS

Singh (2002) summarized the induced/active biochemical defence in following manner:

1. On entry of the pathogen, a temporary increase in cellular metabolic activities occurs in the host. Due to stress caused by increased metabolic activity the cells die rapidly (Pcd), showing hypersensitive reaction. Rapid death of cells is correlated with increased degree of resistance in most diseased systems.
2. When the infected tissues are reaching the necrotic stage, metabolism of neighbouring tissues is also increased and phenolics and other compounds are accumulated. In this process, the synthesized compounds move from healthy to diseased tissues.
3. The reactions expressed by hypersensitivity form common phenols, phytoalexins, and other abnormal substances. The oxidized products of phenolics may detoxify the toxins or inactivate other 'weapons' of the pathogen.
4. When spread of the pathogen is checked, the neighbouring healthy tissues with accelerated metabolic activities try to isolate the damaged parts by forming new tissues and eliminate the disease/pathogen.

Host defence, pre-existing or induced, is a multi-component strategy where several factors work together to fashion the final outcome. Figure 5.2 presents a case where more than one factors are responsible to condition resistance in immature grape berries against *Botrytis cinerea.*

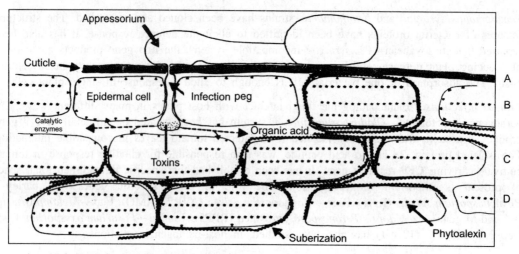

A = High density and thickness of cuticle
B = Inactivation of macerating enzyme by tannins
C = Formation of phytoalexins
D = Suberization of cell walls

Figure 5.2   Multi-component defence mechanism in young grapevine berries against *Botrytis cinerea.*

5.7 SYSTEMIC ACQUIRED RESISTANCE

Induced resistance (cross protection) in plants is a phenomenon of significance, which has not been properly exploited for plant disease management, probably because of our poor understanding. Induced resistance, localized or systemic, may be specific (between related stains of virus) or non-specific (triggered by non-pathogens or by certain abiotic factors). Kuc (1995) discussed systemic acquired resistance in detail. The signal molecules, that propagates the resistance to distant places are vital in systemic induced resistance (Van Loon, et al., 1998). The resistance is induced in a manner comparable to immunization in mammals but the mechanism differs (Sticher, et al., 1997). The resistance may be induced due to any of the following:

- Accumulation of PR proteins
- Activation of lignin synthesis
- Enhanced peroxidase activity
- Suitable changes in plant metabolism

Principle of induced resistance. Induced resistance is a phenomena where a leaf treated with certain chemicals or inoculated with pathogen's avirulent strain produce a signal compound that is transported systemically throughout the plant and activates its defense mechanism (making the entire plant resistant to subsequent infection) without its own physical presence at the site. Figure 5.3(c) illustrates a hypothetical model to explain induction of SAR.

Characteristics of SAR

Following features are associated with SAR:

1. Resistance is expressed against broad spectrum of organism.

2. It confers quantitative molecules.
3. Time needed for establishment of SAR depend on both the plant and type of inducing factor.
4. Dependence on salicylic acid and pathogenesis related protein.
5. Necrosis is involved,
6. Involvement of avirulent/virulent strain of pathogen or chemicals.

Role of PR proteins in acquired resistance have been emphasized (Sticher, et al., 1997). More PR proteins accumulate in diseased parts (intercellular spaces) as compared to healthy parts. Figures 5.3(a) and (b) give the diagrammatic representation of local and systemic SAR.

Signal compounds. Following are some of the candidate molecules for vital role of transferring induced signal in SAR. Table 5.3 and Figure 5.3 give more information on chemical structure and mode of action of these candidate molecules.

Table 5.3 Candidate Molecules for Signal Transfer in SAR

Candidate molecule	Mode of action
Salicylic acid, endogenous signal, widespread occurrence in plant system.	Binds to and inhibit several hem containing enzymes such as catalase, ascorbonate or ascotinase by its affinity for iron.
H_2O_2, second messenger of salicylic acid	Induces the accumulation of PR-1, inhibits hem containing enzymes, direct anti-microbial effect and reinforces reactive O_2 species.
Jasmonates	Induces proteiase inhibitors.
Systemin	Induces proteiase inhibitors.
Ethylene	Induces some PR proteins, structural reinforcement of cell wall.
Inorganic compounds (Phosphate salts).	
Natural organic acids (Arachidenic acid, linolenic acid and oleic acid).	
Synthetic compounds (Propenozole).	

The positive aspects of SAR. Plant immunization for control of plant diseases has following positive features over established method of disease control:

1. It is broad spectrum, thus effective against viral, bacterial and fungal pathogens.
2. It depends on activation of several different mechanisms and therefore is stable.
3. Its ability to immunize susceptible plants implies that genetic potential for resistance is in all types of plants.
4. The significant practical aspects of SAR is the discovery of chemical inducers of plant defence.
5. Dichloro isonicatinic acid (DCINA) provides systemic protection, as provided by biotic agents.
6. This ability of chemicals to induce SAR is being exploited for development of new generation of fungicide, which act as a plant defence system, rather than killing pathogen.
7. ICGA-245 704, a benzothiadiazole compound (plant activator) switches on SAR in host plant.
8. Foliar sprays of phosphate and carbonate salts reduce the intensity of grapevine powdery mildew (Reuvini and Reuvini, 1998).

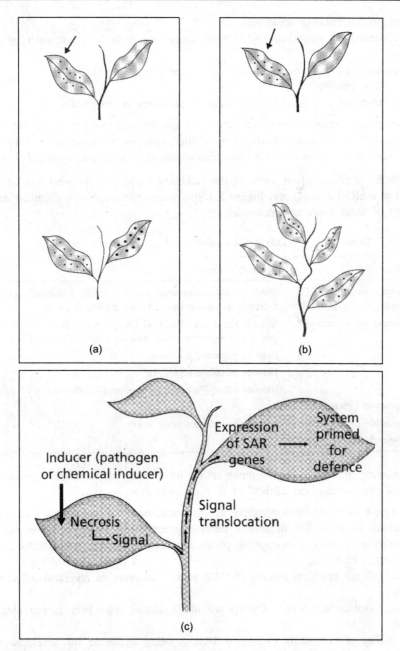

Figure 5.3 Representation of acquired resistance (a) local, (b) systemic and (c) presents a model explaining SAR.

The negative aspects of SAR. SAR has not been very widely used to control plant diseases in fields except some reports of effectiveness in laboratory and green house. Following are factors which prevent wider utilization of SAR:

1. Accumulation of undesirable secondary metabolites, e.g. solanine, protease inhibitors in potato leaves, which may make foliage undesirable for consumption by cattle.

2. Low molecular weight elicitors are not available and high molecular weight compound cannot diffuse readily across the plant cell wall, the best approach would be to characterize the smallest segment of elicitor that is biologically active.
3. Induced resistance may cause substantial losses in yield because it is energy demanding process.

REFERENCES

Bell, A.A., 1981, Biochemical mechanisms of disease resistance, *Annu. Rev. Plant Physiol*, 32:31.

Dixon, R.A., Harrison, M.J., and Lamb, C.J., 1994, Early events in the activations of plant defence responses, *Annu. Rev. Phytopathol*, 32: 479.

Gilchrist, D.G., 1998, Programmed cell death in plant disease: the purpose and promise of cellular suicide, *Annu. Rev. Phytopathol.,* 36:393

Hutchenson, S.W., 1998, Current concepts of active defence in plants, *Annu. Rev. Phytopathol.,* 36:59.

Kalita, P., Bora, L.C., and Bhagbati, K.N., 1996, Phylloplane microorganism of citrus and their role in management of citrus canker, *Indian Phytopath.,* 49:234.

Kaur, J. and Dhillon, M., 1988, Pre-infectional anatomical defence mechanism of groundnut leaf against *Cercosporidium personatum. Indian Phytopath.,* 41:376.

Mayee, C.D. and Suryavanshi, A.P., 1995, Structural defence mechanisms in groundnut to lat leaf spot pathogen, *Indian Phytopath.,* 48:160.

Nicholson, R.L. and Hammerschmidt, R., 1992, Phenolic compounds and their role in disease resistance, *Annu. Rev. Phytopathol.,* 30:369.

Reuvini, R. and Reuvini, M., 1998, Foliar-fertilizer therapy, a concept in integrated management, *Crop. Prot.,* 17:111.

Shaykh, M., C. Soliday and Kalattukudy, P.E., 1977, Proof for the production of cutinase by *Fusarium solani* f. sp. *pisi durin* penetration into its host *Pisum sativum, Plant Physiol.,* 60:170.

Singh, R.S., 2002, *Introduction to Principles of Plant Pathology*, 4th ed., Oxford & IBH Publ., New Delhi.

Sticher, L., Mauch-Mani, B., and Metraux J.P., 1997, Systemic acquired resistance, *Annu. Rev. Phytopathol.,* 35: 235.

Tomiyama, K., Sakuma, T., Ishazaka, N., Sato, N., Katsui, N., Takasugi, M., and Masamura, T., 1968, A new antifungal substance isolates from resistant potato tuber tissue infected by pathogen, *Phytopathology,* 58:115.

Van Loon, L.C., Bakker, P.A.H.M., and Pieterse, C.M.J., 1998, Systemic resistance induced by rhizosphere bacteria, *Annu. Rev. Phytopathol,* 36:453.

Vander Plank, J.E., 1984, *Disease Resistant in Plants,* 2nd ed., Academic Press,

Vidhyasekaran, P., 1998, Molecular biology of pathogenesis and induced systemic resistance, *Indian Phytopathology,* 1(2), 111.

6 Genetics of Host Pathogen Interaction

Indeed, disease resistance of one kind or other occurs throughout the plant kingdom, hand in hand with parasitism.

—Day, P.R., 1974

6.1 INTRODUCTION

Host-pathogen-environment interaction had been the focus of pathologists' attention over a century. In early stages, Stakman, et al. (1930) and Flor (1942-46) made significant contributions in this area. Dichotomies were visualized and terms like pathogenic/non-pathogenic, virulent/avirulent and host/non-host were used freely and firmly. Further development in our understanding about plant diseases and notable contributions made by molecular biology and biotechnology helped in redefining the terms. Let us understand some of the terms, frequently used in host-pathogen interaction, before discussing the Genetics of host-pathogen interaction.

Pathogenicity.   Capability to cause disease, a genetic trait.

Non-pathogenic.   Lack of pathogenicity.

Virulence.   Genetic ability of pathogenic race to overcome host resistance, which may be effective against other races of pathogen.

Avirulence.   Antonym of virulence, specific inability to establish compatible interaction in host cv. in which other races may establish compatibility.
  (Virulence and avirulence are phenotypes of genetic trait, pathogenicity).

Aggressiveness.   Descriptive of relative rate at which the disease develops. Measure of reproductive fitness of pathogen while growing in/on the host.

Resistance.   Genetic ability to prevent, check or slow down (**resist**) the activities of a known pathogen of the plant species.

Susceptible.   Lack of resistance.

Tolerance.   Genetic ability to tolerate pathogen and its activities, without showing significant yield losses, at a given level of disease severity.

Basic compatibility.   The ability of a microbial population to successfully reproduce and maintain itself in a parasitic mode on any member of a plant species (host).

Basic incompatibility.   The absence of basic compatibility.

6.2 GENES AND PLANT DISEASE

The discovery of deoxy-ribonucleic acid (DNA) as the genetic material, in eukaryotic cells, revolutionized the biological science. The initial discovery of transforming principle by Avery, McLeod and McCarty (1944) and experimental evidence of Hershey and Chase (1952) established that DNA, the hereditary material, is transmitted between parents and offspring. Although, Mendel, father of genetics, used the term *Mermal* to denote dominant and recessive alternatives in his experiments on peas, Johansen's term *gene* is widely accepted as basic unit of heredity. The genes occupy specific positions (locus/loci) on chromosomes, largely made up of nucleoproteins. Except for some viruses, where RNA does the function, the genetic information about attributes of an organism (structure and behaviour) is encoded in DNA.

In eukaryotic cells the chromosomes are present in nucleus while in prokaryotes (bacteria and mollecutes) a single circular chromosome is present in cell cytoplasm (membrane bound nucleus lacking). The eukaryotic cells exhibit presence of extranuclear DNA, in chloroplast and in mitochondria [Figure 6.1(a)]. The bacterial cells also possess extra-chromosomal DNA *(plasmogenes)* located in plasmids, self-replicating circular bodies present in cytoplasm [Figure 6.1(b)]. The extra-chromosomal DNA in prokaryotes as well as eukaryotic cells is responsible for *cytoplasmic* or *maternal inheritance*, which does not follow the Mendelian laws of inheritance.

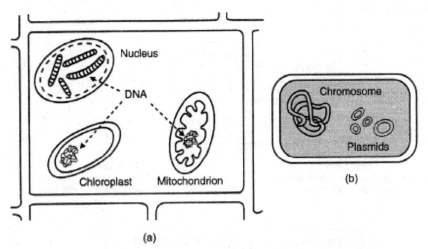

(a)

Figure 6.1 Extra chromosomal genetic material (a) Eukaryotic cell; (b) Prokaryotic cell. (*Source:* Agrios, G.N., 1997)

Gene regulation. The organism does not require all the genetic information, encoded in genetic material, all the time. This is supported by the fact that plants or animals at different growth stages, have to perform different functions, thus different genes express at required time. The genes may be turned on or off as and when required. Every cell is provided with inbuilt mechanism of *gene regulation*. This includes, in addition to proper structural gene, the inducers/promoter or terminator, which act through certain signals. These signals may sometime be extracellular also, even produced by other organisms or provided by environment. *Elicitors*, produced by avirulent gene of microbes or the wounding induces certain specified changes (e.g. phytoalexin production) by activating certain genes in plant cells.

6.3 HOST PATHOGEN INTERACTION

Host-pathogen interaction is a component of the bigger game plan, struggle for survival, operating in nature. The survival of either host or pathogen is at stake, the pathogens survive by 'exploiting' the plant resources and the resulting damage may threaten the existence of plants. The strategies employed by host and pathogens are complex and very often counter-productive. The host plant develops devices to defend against attack by pathogen(s). On the other hand pathogen evolves new virulences to attack the host plant to ensure its parasitic mode of life. The co-existence and co-evolution of host and pathogen initiated an unending 'race' where each tries to have the upper edge. This race must go on because the *alternative to co-existence is elimination* of either of them.

6.3.1 Levels of Host-Pathogen Interactions

All microbes are not pathogens, as they are unable to incite disease. Thus, the world of microbes can be divided into pathogens or non-pathogens (Figure 6.2). Any pathogen can cause disease to one or few plant species (host range). *Phytophthora infestans* can infect potato and tomato (host plants) but not wheat or apple (non-host plants). Races of *P. infestans* may infect some cultivars of potato or tomato (virulent) while on some other cultivars same races may not cause infection (avirulent). Table 6.1(a) shows some of the levels of host-pathogen interaction where disease may (+) or may not (–) develop.

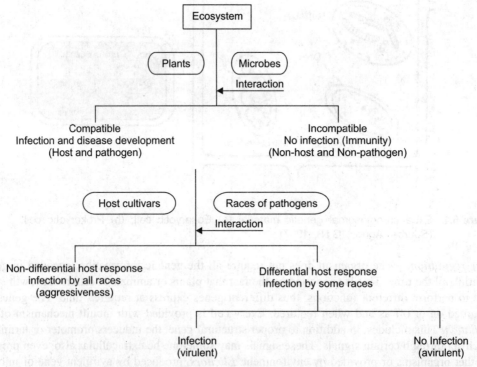

Figure 6.2 Different levels of host-pathogen interactions and specificity exhibited in plant-microbe interaction. Different mechanisms are believed to operate and influence the outcome of interaction.

Table 6.1(a)   Specificity in Host-pathogen Interactions (Crop species)

Microorganism	Host Plant		
	Potato	Tomato	Apple
P. infestans	+	+	–
Synchytrium endobioticum	+	–	–
Venturia inaequalis	–	–	+
Colletotrichum	–	+	–
	Wheat	Barley	Oats
Puccinia graminis	+	+	+
P. graminis tritici*	+	–	–
P. graminis hordei	–	+	–
P. graminis avenae	–	–	+

* within *P. graminis tritici* population, the races differ for their virulence on different wheat cultivars. The races are identified based on the reaction on set of differential hosts.

+ / – indicate presence or absence of disease.

6.3.2 Host-Pathogen Specificity

Host-pathogen specificity is exhibited in nature at different levels. Specificity is one of the most intriguing phenomenon in nature, so vital but poorly understood. In biological world, animals exhibit the specificity as they breed only within the biological species. The pollen-stigma interaction, the stock-scion grafting and plant-pathogen interactions are other examples where specificity is observed. Another level of specificity, a very unique type, exhibited by pathogen is at the tissues or organ levels. Plant pathogens are known as foliar pathogens, fruit pathogens, vascular or root pathogens depending upon the tissues they generally invade. Tables 6.1(b) and 6.1(c) show the tissue/organ specificity in host-pathogen interaction. Kohmoto, et al. (1995) discussed pathogenesis and specificity in plant pathogenic fungi and nematodes.

Table 6.1(b)   Different Levels of Specificity in Host-pathogen Interaction (Plant Parts)

Pathogens/Plant Parts	Leaves	Fruits	Roots
Venturia inaequalis	+	+	–
Pythium	+	+	+
Synchytrium endobioticum	–	–	+ (tubers)
Ustilago segetum tritici	–	+ (grains)	–
Plasmodiophora brassicae	–	–	+
Meloidogyne javanica	–	–	+
Puccinia recondita	+	–	–

Table 6.1(c) Different Levels of Specificity in Host-pathogen Interaction (Tissue Specificity)

Pathogen	Types of Host Tissues				
	Epidermis	Periderm	Cortex	Cambium	Vascular Tissue
Fusarium oxysporum	–	–	–	–	+
Clytocybe sp.	–	–	–	+	–
Colletotrichum sp.	–	–	+	–	–
Helicobasidium sp.	–	+	–	–	–
Synchytrium	+	–	–	–	–

6.4 GENETICS OF RESISTANCE

Although, Theophrastus (327–286 BC) recorded in his observations that "all plants do not get equally diseased, even under similar conditions." Knight (1799) was probably the first to report resistance in wheat to leaf blight (probably caused by *Puccini striformis*) in England. Later Darwin (1868) mentioned differences in reactions of onion (*Colletotrichum circinans*), grapes (*Uncinula nector*) and strawberries (*Sphaerotheca humuli*) due to varietal resistance. Breeding efforts in every economically important crop have given high hopes, but sometimes the resistance has failed in spectacular way (Southern corn leaf blight epidemic in USA, 1970). Major breakthrough came when Biffens (1905) demonstrated that resistance to yellow rust (*Puccinia striiformis)* in wheat was governed by single recessive gene and obeyed Mendel's laws of inheritance. In the same year, Orton (1905) made significant contribution by selecting wilt-resistant plants of cotton, cowpea and watermelon in his varietal trials. Plant breeders, geneticists and plant pathologist have to understand genetics of resistance, nature and inheritance of genes responsible for proper utilization.

6.4.1 Types of Resistance

Host resistance, a natural trait, by virtue of which host tries to prevent, checks or slows down (resist) the pathogen or its activities has been studied by scientist from different point of view. It may be described under preformed or induced resistance, as structural or biochemical resistance, as mono/oligo genic (qualitative trait) or polygenic (quantitative trait) or cytoplasmic and passive or active resistance. Vanderplank (1963) introduced *vertical* and *horizontal resistance* to describe two distinct classes of resistance differing in mechanism of operation and their epidemiological consequences.

Apparent resistance. In nature, plants show variability in amount of disease suffered. Due to certain circumstances some plants appear healthy while others become diseased. Although genetically susceptible, somehow these plants remain free from diseases and 'appear resistant'. This apparent resistance may be due to chance escape or tolerance.

Disease escape. For normal disease development suitable combination of four elements of disease pyramid is required. Suitable growth stage of susceptible plant should come in contact with active phase of virulent pathogen and this interaction should continue for certain duration under favourable environmental conditions. If any one or more of these conditions do not coincide, disease may not develop. Following situations may explain the disease escape.

- Short duration or early maturing variety may escape serious disease attack. (potato late blight and wheat rust).
- Fast germination of seed and growth of seedling may escape attack by damping-off pathogens (soil borne).
- Plants may escape due to patchy distribution of soil inoculum.
- Sensitive growth stage of host may not coincide with favourable condition for disease development (*Alternaria* and *Botrytis* are more severe on old senescing plants).
- Chance dispersal of inoculum may be responsible for escape.
- Environmental conditions (temperature, moisture, wind and rain) play vital role in escape of disease. Good planning and modification of cultural practices may help to reduce the damage caused by diseases. Strategists have mostly neglected this potential area.

Disease tolerance. Tolerance is defined as an act or capacity of enduring, other usage of the word include an intermediate level of observable resistance between immunity and susceptibility. Cladwell and coworkers (1958) gave elaborate definition of tolerance to diseases as *the inherent ability or a required capacity of a plant to endure the effects of levels of parasitic infection and disease which if occurred at equivalent levels in other plants of the same or similar species would cause greater impairment/reduction in growth or yield.* Mussell (1980) discussed various aspects of tolerance to disease.

Components of tolerance

(a) **Tolerance to parasite**: The relative ability of plant to tolerate the physical presence of a developing parasite or an accumulation of a metabolite produced by parasite. It has been demonstrated in case of vascular wilts where plants can do even when pathogen blocks some of the vessels.

(b) **Tolerance of disease**: Situations are known where virus multiply and spread normally through the plant but produces mild or negligible symptoms. Tolerance is evaluated by estimating parasite biomass, measuring amount of disease (area under disease progress curve) or affect on host growth and yield potential reduced.

Mechanisms of tolerance

(a) In case of vascular wilts, plants may develop alternate roots for translocation where some vessels are blocked by the pathogens.

(b) Developing parasite acts as additional sink (metabolic sink) and may induce increased rate of photosynthesis to cope with increasing demand.

(c) Compensation effect: Unaffected plant parts compensate for the damaged or lost plant parts. The maize plants develop additional roots when some roots are damaged by pathogen. "Green Island" in powdery mildew affected barley leaves have faster rate of photosynthesis.

Merits of tolerance

(a) Tolerance starts where resistance ends.
(b) Tolerance is a polygenic character like HR, thus stable.
(c) Tolerance gives reasonable yields without putting selection pressure.

Demerits of tolerance

(a) Tolerant plants become a site for pathogen multiplication and provide secondary inoculum to adjoining fields.

    (b) Growth and reproduction of pathogen may facilitate variability in pathogen population.
    (c) Identification and breeding for tolerance is not easy (polygenic).
    (d) Tolerance is a passive process.

True resistance. Occurrence of some form of resistance is universal in plant communities; otherwise co-existence with pathogens would have eliminated them. It is beyond doubt that resistance/susceptibility in plants, like any other phenotypic characters, are governed by genes. But main question is about nature of these genes involved and how they provide resistance in various forms and at different levels?

Non-host resistance. It is the most common and most effective form of plant defence, which renders most of microbes incapable of attacking plants. They are termed as **non-pathogen** and the plant as **non-host**. The plant is totally exempt from infection and phenomenon is called **immunity**. Unfortunately not much is known about a phenomenon of such vital importance. Probably nature wants to keep this treasure hidden and undisturbed. Decoding and exploitation of this would have created ecological imbalances.

Oligogenic or vertical resistance. Vanderplank (1963) coined the term, *vertical resistance (VR)*, to describe the differential or discriminatory response of host genotypes to different races of pathogen. The host cultivars possessing VR show high degree of resistance to some races of pathogen while it is susceptible to some other races of the pathogen (Figure 6.3). Host reaction is qualitative, i.e. resistant or susceptible (present/absent) while the pathogenic races are termed as **avirulent** and **virulent**, respectively. Since VR works by discriminating among the pathogenic races, it acts like as selective filter and as a result of discrimination it reduces the amount of effective initial inoculum, which initiates the infection. Thus in true sense, vertical resistance is the resistance to infection but does not operate in subsequent infection cycles, in case of multiple cycle diseases. It operates by reducing initial inoculum, *sanitation sensu* Vanderplank (1963).

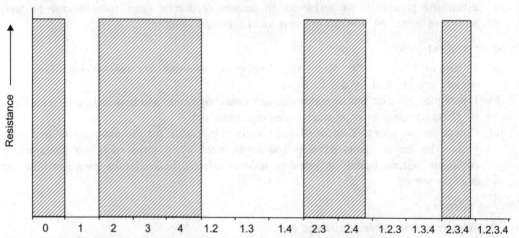

Figure 6.3 Differential reactions of potato cultivar Kennebec (R_1) to different races of *P. infestans*. The resistance to races (0), (2), (3), (4) (2.3) (2.4) (2.3.4) is represented by vertical bars **(vertical resistance)**. The cultivar Kennebec, does not confer resistance to race (1), (1.2), (1.3), (1.4), (1.2.3), (1.3.4) and (1.2.3.4).

The **'R' genes** are responsible, in certain varieties, for recognition of specific virulences to offer complete resistance at infection level. Various models have been proposed to explain this phenomenon. R genes are rather rare in genetically heterogeneous natural plant population. However, in cultivated plants (crops) R genes have been frequently used in plant improvement (Table 6.2). Gene Hm^1 that provides resistance to maize against Race 1 of *Bipolaris/ Helminthosporium carbonum* was the first R gene reported. The gene coded for a protein (enzyme) HC-toxin reductase in resistant cultivars, which was able to detoxify the pathogenicity factor (HC-Toxin) produced by pathogen. Thus the pathogen became avirulent.

Table 6.2 The R genes Reported in Different Host-pathogen Interactions and Probable Function of the R genes

R gene	Host	Pathogen	Function
Hm^1	Corn	*Cochliobolus carbonum*	Encodes protein; detoxifying enzyme
PTO	Tomato	*Pseudomonas* syringae pv. *tomato*	Encodes protein signals transducing kinase.
Cf2,Cf4,Cf9	Tomato	*Cladosporium fulvum*	Encodes receptor protein; that reacts with avr gene product (elicitor)
L6	Flax	*Melampsora lini*	Encodes nucleotide binding protein; transmits signal
X221	Rice	*Xanthomonas campestris* pv. *oryzae*	Encodes receptor protein

Sources of oligogenic resistance. Host resistance is one of the best (economical, environment-friendly and easy for growers) options for plant disease management, particularly in developing countries. We have also realized that deployment of host resistance genes (particularly oligogenic type) is not permanent solution and running out of varieties is common to all economically important crops. Thus, there is need to introduce newer genes, to replace old and defeated ones. Nature is the treasure house for resistant genes, which are mostly found in wild types or related species of economic plants. Vavilov (1949), a person interested in Phytogeography, after his vast and prolonged expeditions concluded that

- Variability in cultivated crop plants is geographically unevenly spread.
- Bulk of genetic diversity, in important agricultural crops, is geographically confined to relatively few restricted areas.

He originally called these areas as *centres of diversity* which exhibited more variability, in genetic terms, as compared to other parts where economic plants were introduced by migrants and travellers (Zohary, 1970). Considering suggestions from Schiemann (1943), Vavilov modified them in to primary centres (places where domestication of wild relatives originated; Middle East for wheat) and secondary centres (where crop plants were taken after domestication; Ethiopia for wheat). Later these centres were recognized as sources of disease resistance (Leppik, 1970), and are the places hunted when new genes are wanted.

Field characteristics of VR. Due to its discriminatory or specific behaviour VR exhibits following field characteristics:

- As it reduces the initial inoculum, it delays the onset of epidemic.
- VR is resistance against infection. But once infection is established, disease develops as in normal susceptible host plant.
- As an oligogenic trait, it is easy to identify and breed.

- VR operates through specific host genes, thus gains from heterogeneity.
- In long-term perspective VR promotes build up of specific inoculum (directional selection), experimentally demonstrated by Black (1960) in potato-*Phytophthora infestans* system.

VR gains from heterogeneity. Since VR is specific by nature and promotes specific racial inoculum; its advantages are proportional to degree of heterogeneity in host population (for R genes). Inoculum produced on one particular host genotype (having specific VR genes) will be ineffective on other host genotype having different VR genes. Thus, in heterogeneous host population lot of inoculum is rendered ineffective (Figure 6.4). This is considered as advantage of VR genes. This also explains why VR is at its best in breeder's nursery.

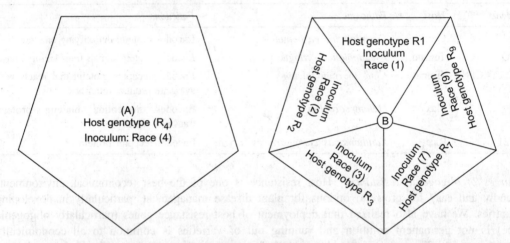

Figure 6.4 Hypothetical plan for potato cultivars, **plot (B)** having VR genes (R_1, R_2, R_3, R_7 and R_9) will produce inoculum of races (1), (2), (3), (4) and (9), respectively. Inoculum produced in any of the triangular fields will be ineffective on host genotypes in any other plots. This demonstrates the advantages of heterogeneous population as compared to **plot (A)** where homogenous population of host genotype (R_4) is planted, inoculum produced will be Race (4) which will be effective all over the plot (A) leading to development of disease.

VR losses by popularity. The popularity of VR based crop cultivars is self-destructive or advantages of VR are diluted/lost as cultivars become more popular. Once a new VR gene is introduced in an area, the cultivar looks attractive and becomes popular among farmers. The popularity of VR genes put selection pressure on pathogen population, which strikes back, sooner or later, by developing suitable/matching virulence. As a result the whole area under that particular host genotype becomes dramatically susceptible. Thus popularity of VR becomes self-destructive. This is also described in literature as *boom and burst cycle*. There are several classical cases reported in literature. First rust resistant wheat var. Eureka (Sr6) was introduced in Australia in 1938 and in 1941 a new matching race of *P. graminis tritici* (Race 6) was recorded. Figure 6.5(a) depicts the popularity of wheat variety Eureka overtime. The figure also illustrates the appearance, increase and decline in Race 6 population over corresponding years. In 1955 race 6 was not observed, due to discontinuity of Eureka, but as Eureka was reintroduced in 1961, the race 6 reappeared in 1963. To manage rust situation in Australia, new series of wheat cultivars (Gabo, Charter, Kendee and

Yelta), all having Sr_{11}, were introduced in 1946, these were in turn replaced by next series having VR genes Sr_{9b}, Sr_{17}, etc. Figure 6.5(b). This clearly illustrates the boom and burst cycle due to popularity of a particular VR based host genotype.

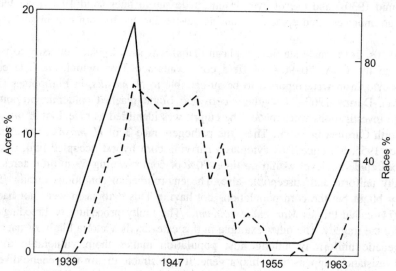

Figure 6.5(a)   Popularity of wheat variety Eureka (Sr6), solid line, and virulent races of *P. graminis tritici* (broken line) expressed as percentage of total wheat acreage/rust isolates identified (from Vanderplank, 1984: data of Watson and Luig, 1963).

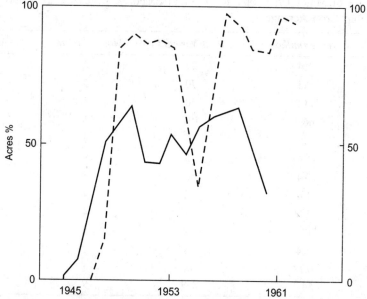

Figure 6.5(b)   Popularity of wheat variety Gobo (Sr11), solid line, and virulent races of *P. graminis tritici* (broken line) expressed as percentage of total wheat acreage/rust isolates identified (from Vanderplank, 1984: data of Watson and Luig, 1963).

Uniformity of VR makes plants vulnerable.   We have seen that vertical resistance being race specific is best in breeder's nursery (due to heterogeneous population). But once the resistant cultivar becomes popular, the 'fate' of resistance is questioned. *Helminthosporium maydis*, the cause of southern corn leaf blight, was a minor pathogen in US for many years. The introduction of hybrid corn in US (mid 1930s) and use of cytoplasmic male sterile lines (mid 1940s) created a situation, which led to an unprecedented epidemic, causing severe damage to corn belt in southeastern region of the USA

During 1950s, Texas male sterile cytoplasm (Tms) was used by seed industry to the extent that by 1969–70, in the USA, 70–90% of field corn contained Tms cytoplasm. The corn cultivars carrying Tms cytoplasm were reported to be susceptible to *H. maydis*, in Philippines (Mercado and Lantican 1961). During 1969–70 southern corn leaf blight reached epidemic proportions. Lot of discussion and investigations were made. The culprit was identified as race T of *H. maydis* (reported to exist in North Carolina in 1955). Thus, the pathogen, race T of *H. maydis*, pre-existed as minor pathogen since 1955, but once Tms cytoplasm carrying corn hybrid occupied bulk of corn belt, the disease reached epidemic level within no time. 70% of corn covering 69 million acres in USA was cytoplasmically uniform and susceptible also. The environmental conditions during 1969–70 were favourable for blight but the corn populations not having Tms cytoplasm were not badly damaged.

Day (1974) called this as *Man made epidemic*. The faulty procedure or breeding strategy was responsible for the tragedy. The other example in this category is Victoria blight of oats (1946). High degree of genetic uniformity among host population makes them vulnerable to catastrophic epidemics, if resistance happens to be major gene. It is desirable to aim for genetic diversity, at least for resistance genes. Table 6.3 gives the idea about the extent of genetic uniformity created due to various reasons. The important lesson to be learned from such cases is that *the genetic uniformity is a cause for concern* and it should be avoided for stabilizing crop yields.

Table 6.3   Acreage of Major US Crops in 1969 and Extent to which Small Numbers of Cultivars Made-up Crop Acreage

Crop	*Acreage (millions)*	*Total Varieties*	*Major Varieties*	*Acreage (%)*
Bean, dry	1.4	25	2	60
Bean, snap	0.3	70	3	76
Cotton	11.2	50	3	53
Corn	66.3	197	6	71
Millet	2		3	100
Peanut	1.4	15	9	95
Peas	0.4	50	3	96
Potato	1.4	82	4	72
Rice	1.8	14	4	65
Soyabean	42.4	62	6	56
Sugar beet	1.4	16	2	42
Sweet potato	0.13	48	1	69
Wheat	44.3	269	9	50

(*Source:* Horsfall, et al., 1972)

Value of vertical resistance in agriculture. Vertical resistance has been a major tool in efforts to manage diseases of economically important crops (wheat rust and late blight of potato). But dramatically 'break down' has put a question mark on fate of VR. VR has certain inbuilt weaknesses. Due to oligogenic or major gene trait it is easy for pathogen to match or overcome the genes, the resistance becomes ineffective. It is also known as **unstable resistance** or **doomed to failure**. Robinson (1971) examined the uses of VR and drawn up the following set of rules:

- VR will be more useful in single cycle diseases as compared to multiple cycle diseases.
- VR will not be useful in vegetatively propagated crops.
- VR will be useful against pathogens with low chances of variability.
- VR will be of low value in perennial crops or crops where breeding new *var.* is difficult and time consuming.
- VR will be useful if stabilizing pressure can be exploited.
- VR will be of no use if the crop is grown round the year.
- Crop and plant patterns (time and space) are important for VR. As it gains from heterogeneity, thus mosaics/mixed planting, multiline or genes zones can help in containing disease.
- VR is valuable for pathogens, which do not survive locally (wheat rust in India, USA and Canada).
- Legislative measures can enhance values of VR.

Vertical resistance and fitness of race. VR being specific in nature dictates the pathogen population and decides which race will infect, multiply and survive. If a pathogenic race does not have the required matching genes it becomes avirulent and a negative selection pressure (stabilizing pressure) operates in population. Sooner or later such avirulent race will disappear from population. If VR genes are withdrawn from cultivation, the matching virulent genes are no more wanted and become unnecessary or extra. Stabilizing pressure operates against extra gene(s) and pathogenic races with optimum number of genes are favoured. The extra genes for virulence becomes unwanted genetic load and reduce the fitness of race, stabilizing pressure can be exploited for plant disease management also. Effectiveness of stabilizing pressure in pathogen population is determined by relative strength of VR genes (strong or weak) in host. Strength of VR genes in turn is defined in terms of strength with which stabilizing selection acts against complementary race. Fitness of a race is measured by race's ability to maintain itself as the major constituent of pathogen population.

Polygenic or Horizontal Resistance (HR). Vanderplank identified non-differential resistance of potato cultivars Maritta, against *P. infestans*, as horizontal or general resistance (Figure 6.6). The mechanism of operation of HR is by *reducing the infection rate*, which permits only slow development of disease. Being polygenic or minor gene character HR seems to be stable/durable resistance. As HR does not put any specific selection pressure on pathogenic population, it is not liable to be overcome or 'broken' by pathogenic population. Being intermediate (quantitative) it allows the growth and multiplication of pathogen. Robinson (1973) and Nelson (1978) reviewed information on HR while Johnson (1984) discussed critical analysis of durable resistance.

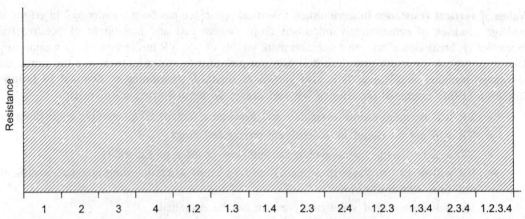

Figure 6.6   Non-differential/uniform reaction of Maritta to all races of *P. infestans* as represented by horizontal bar (horizontal resistance).

Mechanism of operation of HR.   The mechanism of operation of HR is more complex as compared to VR, since HR is non-discriminatory or uniform in behaviour, it allows all the races of pathogen to cause infection and permits disease development to certain level. The HR provides resistance to infection, growth, colonization of host tissues and reproduction of pathogen. As compared to susceptible cultivars the HR *slows down the progress of disease* but uniformly against all the races of pathogen. Slow down of disease progress or reduction in rate of infection can be brought about by the following factors:

(a)   HR cultivars allow less infection efficiency of pathogenic races, as compared to susceptible host.

(b)   On HR cultivars the incubation and latent periods are longer, as compared to susceptible interactions. This increases the duration of infection cycle, thereby reduces the number of repeating cycles in crop season.

(c)   HR operates by restricting growth and colonization of the host.

(d)   HR reduces the amount of sporulation and duration of sporulation (infectious period). Thus, the secondary inoculum is reduced.

(e)   HR operates on each infection cycle, throughout the course of disease development.

Field characteristics of horizontal resistance.   HR is known as **rate reducing and partial resistance**. These terms explain the main attributes of polygenic resistance, which is also known as **stable** or **durable resistance**. Durability, in terms of time duration for which HR remains effective, is the significant attraction over its counterpart VR, which is liable to break down more easily and quickly. Since HR is polygenic, effect is cumulative of several minor genes, it is difficult for the pathogen to adopt to match or overcome the host genes responsible for HR. Tables 6.4 and 6.5 give the performance of three potato cultivars Eigenheimer, Binje and Voran under field conditions, against late blight pathogen *P. infestans*, over a long period (1933–1968). In the initial years of introduction the inoculum to Voran came from neighbouring fields of Eigenheimer, but by 1950, Voran became popular and was self-contained for inoculum, still resistance survived. Later it occupied about 80% of potato area (40,000 h) but the host reaction remained unchanged. Had it been vertical/major gene resistance the fate would have been 'boom and burst' at much early stage?

Table 6.4 The Performances of Three Potato Cultivars Eigenheimer, Binje and Voran under Field Conditions, against Late Blight Pathogen *P. infestans*, over a Long Period (1933–1968).

Cultivars/Year of Introduction	Disease Rating 1938	Disease Rating 1968	Category of Resistance	Rate of Infection
Eigenheimer (1893)	4	5	Intermediate	0.21
Binje (1910)	3	3	Low	0.42
Voran (1936)	7	7	High	0.16

Table 6.5 The Reaction (resistance rating for foliage and tubers) of Potato Cultivar Voran to *P. infestans*, which remained Unchanged over 30 years of Cultivation Depicts Stability of HR

Plant reaction	1937	38	42	46	50	52	57	60	68	70	Scale
Foliage	6	7	8	8	8	8	7	7	7	7	3 very susceptible
Tubers	7	7	7	7	7	7	6.6	6.5	6.5	6.5	10 very resistant

Vertical vs Horizontal Resistance. Before we close discussion on vertical and horizontal resistance, let us compare the attributes of these two types of resistance as given in Table 6.6.

Table 6.6 Comparative Features of VR and HR

Vertical Resistance (VR)	*Horizontal Resistance (HR)*
Oligogenic and major gene trait.	Polygenic and minor gene trait.
Resists the first infection cycle.	Resists in all of infection cycles.
Effective against primary inoculum.	Effective against primary as well as secondary inoculum.
Reduces primary inoculum and delays the on set of epidemic.	Reduces rate of infection and slows down progress of disease.
Effective against some races of pathogen (discriminatory).	Effective against all races of pathogen (non-discriminatory).
More attractive in heterogeneous host population (breeder's nursery).	More effective under field conditions.
Benefits are lost with increased popularity (Boom and burst cycle).	Benefits increase with increased popularity.
Easy to identify and breed (qualitative character).	Difficult to identify and breed (quantitative character).
Not effective for long duration (unstable resistance).	Effective for long duration (stable resistance).
Promotes directional selection (race specific), strong stabilizing pressure operates.	Does not promote specific virulence, not much role for stabilizing pressure.
More effective for single cycle diseases.	More effective for polycyclic disease.
Not advisable for vegetatively propagated and perennial crops.	Advisable for any crop.
Known as specific, differential, major gene oligogenic.	Known as general, uniform, field, rate reducing, minor gene/polygenic.

6.4.2 Cytoplasmic Resistance

In eukaryotic cells, extra-chromosomal genetic material is present in organelles in cytoplasm. This is responsible for cytoplasmic or maternal inheritance. Disease resistance/susceptibility, like other phenotypic characters, has been reported to be cytoplasmically determined. The phenomenon was established after study of the southern corn leaf blight epidemic, USA, 1970. The susceptibility of hybrid corn was cytoplasmically governed. It was reported that all corn hybrid plants carrying cytoplasm (used for male sterility) were highly susceptible to race T of *H. maydis*.

6.4.3 Gene for Susceptibility

During mid 19th century *P. infestans* was established in Europe and repeatedly damaged the potato crops (*Solanum tuberosum*). Sincere efforts were made and in 1920s, breeders were able to introduce resistant gene R_1 from *S. demissum*. The progeny of resistant and susceptible parents segregated roughly in 1 : 1 ratio (R/S), resistant gene R_1 and its allele, *gene for susceptibility*, r_1 were recognized. Evidences suggest that r_1 was present in *S. tuberosum* in Europe before 1920, as potatoes were universally susceptible to *P. infestans*. It is now believed that what we call as '*gene for susceptibility' is a plant gene, not just a host plant gene* (not a gene to welcome pathogen). It has some primary role in healthy plants, and secondary role in parasitism has been thrust upon by parasite. It is an essential plant gene with certain primary role to perform irrespective of whether there is pathogen or not. Thus the gene for susceptibility has two roles, i.e. some primary role/ essential function for plant and a secondary role of serving some purpose of pathogen.

Very popular wheat cultivars in USA and Canada, Marquis, carried universally and homozygous alleles 'for susceptibility' (Sr_9, SR_{11}, Sr_{12}, Sr_{13}, Sr_{14}, Sr_{17} and recently recognized alleles SR_{24}, Sr_{25}, SR_{26} and Sr_{27}). This indicates that Sr genes were necessary part of Marquis genomes. The great bulk of world's wheat has low ratio of Sr to sr alleles. At most relevant loci susceptibility is universal in wheat population. The situation is even more marked with Lr and lr alleles for resistance or susceptibility to wheat rust pathogen *Puccinia recondita*. Had these genes for susceptibility been harmful or problem gene for host, they would have been deleted during evolution; higher plants are well equipped to remove unwanted genes. Parasite has selected a gene or gene product, for its association, realizing the importance of gene that will not be deleted by plants.

Vavilov (1949) postulated certain geographical areas as 'centres of origin' for crop plants. These gene centres are also the places to locate the genes for resistance to various pests and pathogens. It is therefore surprising that when plants 'left' their centre of origin; they preferably took with them the genes for 'susceptibility' and left more useful resistant genes, at the centre of origin. Despite many years of breeding for resistance to pests and pathogens, genes for susceptibility still predominate numerically. Possibly the gene for susceptibility are the genes needed to cope with stress. In case of wounding or attack by pest or pathogen, these genes may be required to maintain the vital life process during critical phase. The genes for susceptibility are abundantly replicated.

6.4.4 Resistance to Abiotic Stresses

Phenotypic performance of a plant is determined by its genotype and environment (G × E) interaction. When any factor of the environment interferes with the complete expression of genotypic potential, it is called **stress**. Depending on their nature the stresses are classified as *biotic* and *abiotic*. Abiotic stresses results due to moisture, temperature (high/low), minerals (deficiency/toxicity), salinity, soil pH, air pollution, etc. These determine the geographical/regional distribution of crops and their pathogens. They are the primary sources of yield losses. Drought (water stress) is the main abiotic factor as it affects 26% of the arable area (Table 6.7). Drought is defined as *inadequacy of water availability, including precipitations and soil moisture storage capacity, in quantity and distribution during the life cycle of a crop to restrict expression of its full genetic yield potential.*

Table 6.7 The Fraction of World's Arable Land Subject to an Abiotic Stress.

Abiotic Stress	Fraction (%) of Arable Land
Drought	26
Minerals (toxicity/deficiency)	20
Freezing	15
No stress	10

Specific features of abiotic stress

1. The relative importance of stresses is mainly region/location specific.
2. A given abiotic factor may increase/decrease the level of another stress, e.g. in saline soil, moisture stress enhances salinity stress.
3. The occurrence and the degree of some stresses are highly unpredictable.
4. Different varieties of a crop show large differences in their ability to tolerate/resist abiotic stresses.
5. The degree of some stresses is likely to vary during the crop season.

Genetics of drought resistance. Drought resistance can be defined as *the mechanisms causing minimum loss of yield in a drought environment relative to the maximum yield in a constraint free,* i.e., optimal environment of the crop. The following mechanisms are involved:

Drought escape. It is the ability of the phenotype to complete its development including the reproductive cycle, before severe water deficit occurs. Early maturity is an important attribute of the drought escape.

Drought avoidance. It is the ability of plant to maintain higher level of water status under the conditions of drought. This is achieved either by reducing transpiration (water savers) or increased water uptake (water spenders).

Drought tolerance. It is the ability of a plant to withstand water stress as measured by the degree and duration of low plant water potential.

Water deficit and the predisposition to disease. Water deficiency is known to predispose plants to diseases. A decrease in the photosynthetic activity due to water stress predisposes plants to disease. Another important effect is the decrease in protein synthesis in dehydrated tissues that might contribute to increased host susceptibility by preventing the synthesis of important enzymes for disease resistance in the host plant. In the dehydrated host, decrease in xylem water potential alter part of the gradient and deprive the outlying cells of water for growth. The reasons for pathogen growth while the host fails to grow during water deficit are basically unknown but probably are related to those changes affecting the host metabolism. Boyer (1995) discussed biochemical and biophysical aspects of water deficit and the predisposition to diseases.

6.5 GENETICS OF PATHOGENICITY

Like resistance in host plants, pathogenicity in pathogen is a heritable trait and roles played by both chromosomal as well as cytoplasmic genes are well known. The study of host resistance, its field behaviour and durability (particularly vertical type) are greatly influenced by genetic makeup of pathogenic population. Stackman, et al. (1918) indicated that any change in host genotype (for resistance) is likely to be responded by pathogen population. In later years it was realized that effectiveness of host resistance is basically determined by the genetic status of pathogenicity. As in the case of host resistance, the pathogenicity in parasites is dependent on polygenes, genetic background and the environment. *The virulence and aggressiveness are phenotypes of genetic trait, pathogenicity.* Virulence and aggressiveness are used to identify and evaluate host resistance in terms of host response. Aggressiveness, the quantitative disease causing capacity of pathogenic races, is a relative strength, which may enhance the chances of epidemic development.

6.5.1 Virulence and Aggressiveness

Vanderplank (1984) suggested that greater virulence is not associated with greater aggressiveness. It has been reported that simple race(s) with one or few virulence genes are more aggressive than complex races having higher number of virulence genes, suggesting a negative correlation between virulence and aggressiveness (Roy, 2000). Simple race(s) with suitable matching virulent genes are more aggressive and fit to survive as compared to complex races.

6.5.2 Mechanism of Variability

The characteristics of individuals within biological species are not fixed because the members of a population may be similar but not identical. The progenies produced involving sexual reproduction will differ among themselves as well as from the parents. In addition to sexual reproduction organisms employ other means of multiplication, which also provide some mechanism for promoting variability among the population. We will see the causes and consequences of variability in pathotypes. Mutation and recombination are common mechanism employed by various organisms, in addition, fungi and bacteria have some specialized methods of generating variability.

Fungal pathogens. Fungal cells, like other eukaryotic, have a membrane bound nucleus, which contain most of the genetic material on the chromosomes. The mitosis in fungi occurs rapidly (completed in 5–6 minutes). In multinucleate hyphae, a wave of mitosis travels the length of hypha from the tip cell, in 5–10 minutes. Fungal populations are genetically flexible. Stackman called them 'shifty enemies'. Various mechanisms operate in different groups of fungal pathogen and are responsible for developing variability in phenotypic characters including virulence. Let us see various mechanisms operating in fungi for creating variability, due to their ability to adapt to changing environment including host genotypes.

Mutation. It is a universal mechanism of creating alternations in genetic material of a living organism. Mutations occur due to sudden change in genetic material (DNA or RNA), which is stable and inherited by the progeny. In nature mutations occur spontaneously, but they can be induced also (using physical and chemical mutagens). Frequency of spontaneous mutation is very low about 10^{-7} to 10^{-4}. Mutations are brought about by any change in base sequence in genetic material,

DNA/RNA, which may be effected due to addition, deletion or substitution of one or more base pairs. Insertion of transpogenes and inversion of a DNA segments are other causes of mutations.

Once a change in genetic material is brought about by mutation, it will enter the sexual or asexual reproduction cycle to add variability in population for affected phenotypic character (including pathogenicity/virulence). The immediate expression or identification of altered trait depends on ploidy level of the organism. Mutation in dominant trait will express irrespective of ploidy status but for expression of a recessive character, the organism should be either haploid or homozygous for recessive condition. Mutations in extra chromosomal DNA are also known. The frequency of mutation for virulence is same as for other phenotypic character. But the enormous amount of progeny produced makes it possible that large number of individuals differ in virulence. The survival and fitness of a new virulence is more important for it to become a threat to crop plants.

Recombination. The fusion of two haploid nuclei results in formation of zygote, the first diploid state of life cycle. During further division of zygote there are chances of crossover of parts of chromatids. This results in exchanges of genetic material and formation of recombinants. Recombination is most potent tool for creation of variability in pathogen population. Variations for a specific character (virulence) once created, by any mechanism, is further amplified and maintained by the process of recombination.

Heterokaryosis. A fungal cell containing two genetically different nuclei in the same cytoplasm is known as **heterokaryon**, which may arise due to fertilization or anastomosis between genetically different cells or due to mutation in one of the nucleus of bi/multinucleate cell. Heterokaryosis is a unique feature of fungi and provides a mechanism for creation of variability in Basidiomycotina (rust and smut fungi). Heterokaryon is important for causing infection also. Heterokaryosis is common in pathogen as rusts, smuts, *Alternaria solani*, *Rhizoctonia solani*, *Verticillium albo-atrum* *Phytophthora infestans* and *Botritis cineria*.

Parasexuality. Certain fungi enjoy the benefits of recombination without undergoing normal sexual cycle. No coordination or sequence in fertilization, segregation and recombination is observed. Occasional fusion of two nuclei and formation of diploid zygote followed by several divisions, including crossing over at certain stage results in formation of recombinants. The chances of variability created through parasexuality are great as it may originate heterokaryon. Parasexuality is expected to be means of variability in fungi where sexual reproduction is not known.

Heteroploidy. Spores or cells of the same fungus may contain variable number of chromosomes depending upon the nuclear status. They may be other than normal haploid number for that organism. There may be triploids or tetraploids or aneuploids (having one, two or more extra or missing chromosomes than normal euploid number). Heteroploidy in fungi may play role in creation of variability for several characters including pathogenicity.

Bacterial pathogens. In bacteria and probably in mollecutes, following sexual like process are responsible for creating variability for various characters:

Conjugation. Two bacterial cells come in contact and genetic material (a portion of chromosome or plasmids) is transferred from one bacterial cell to another, through a conjugation bridge called **pilus** (Figure 6.7a). Once this 'alien/foreign' DNA is inside recipient cell, it may result in formation of recombinant.

Transformation. Bacterial cells absorb genetic material secreted by other, without coming in physical contact, (Figure 6.7b). This genetic material gets integrated in its own genome and may lead to creation of variability for certain characters.

Transduction. This is bacterial virus (bacteriophase) mediated transfer for genetic material from one bacterial cell when the phage particle infects another bacterial cell (Figure 6.7a). This is highly potential tool for horizontal gene transfer. *Agrobacterium* is often used to transmit genetic matter crossing various taxonomic barriers, sometimes across kingdom also.

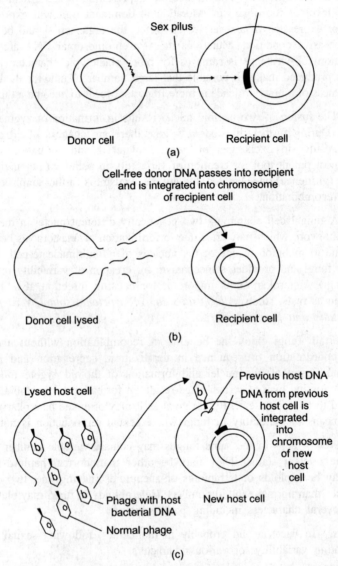

Figure 6.7   Three types of gene transfer from which genetic recombination results. (a) Conjugation, the transfer of genes between cells requires physical contact (perhaps by sex pilus), (b) Transformation, the transfer of genes or 'naked' DNA from one cell to another, (c) Transduction, the transfer of genes between cells is mediated by a bacteriophage.

Viral pathogens.   Viruses are too simple a system to be called 'organisms' but presence of genetic material DNA/RNA gives them versatility to be among the most dangerous pathogens. This also ensures creation of variability through **mutations** (most common method) or recombination. The possibility of recombination, in case of multiparticle virus particles or more than one type of virus particle infecting same host cell, cannot be ruled out. Insect vectors provide another opportunity of coming together for different strains of viruses, if carried simultaneously. Presence of more than 50 strain of TMV tells about extent of variability in viruses. Several strains of cucumber mosaic virus, sugarcane mosaic virus and curly top of sugar beet are known.

6.5.3 Physiologic Specialization

In plant kingdom, within a biological species, the variability is well known, i.e. individuals are similar but not identical. In biology, the race is commonly defined as *group of individuals possessing common features, which distinguish them from other groups of individuals of the same species* (Figure 6.8). Darlington and Mather (1949) considered biological race as "genetically and geographically distinct mating groups within a species".

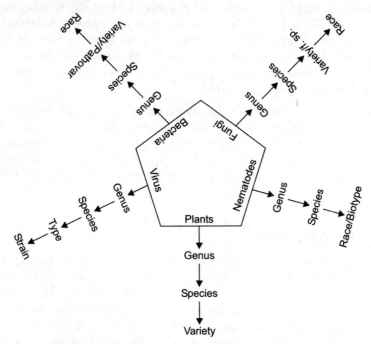

Figure 6.8 Specialization within species of biological systems.

The variability in pathogenic population, within species/variety/*forme specialis*, was reported by Stackman and coworkers in 1918. Stackman and Harrar (1957) defined race as *a biotype or group of biotypes within a species or variety that can be distinguished with reliable certainty and facility by physiological characters including pathogenicity and in some fungi, by growth on artificial media.* In asexually reproducing pathogens, the population of physiologic races will be homogeneous, while the sexual reproduction is likely to add heterogeneity. Hobgood (1970) discussed designation of physiological races of plant pathogens. Physiologic races are identified on the basis of specific pathogenicity. A set of varieties (differential hosts), each having one major dominant gene for resistance, is used to identify the races based on their characteristic reaction (qualitative, +/–, scoring system applied).

Phytophthora infestans as well as potato are believed to have originated, co-existed and thereby co-evolved in central Mexico. This is supported by the extent of variability in both the systems in highlands of Mexico. In 1950s two mating types (A1 and A2) were discovered in Mexico, it was also known that the involvement of the two mating types is required for sexual reproduction of fungus. A1 was universal in distribution while A2 was confined to Mexico till 1984, after which it was reported from Europe, America and later from Asia. The pathogenic variability was first recorded as potato race (produce only small necrotic spots on tomato) while tomato race, equally virulent on both hosts. The R genes, which provided specific (vertical resistance) against *P. infestans*, were transferred to commercial cultivars of potato from a wild relative, *S. demissum*. The potato cultivar × *P. Infestans* race interaction was found to be highly significant, demonstrating presence of physiologic races within isolates of *P. infestans*. Originally breeders identified and used four R genes (R1, R2, R3 and R4), which were dominant and inherited in Mendelian fashion. The race that could only infect potato cultivars without R genes was designated as R_0. Till 1992, the total number of physiologic races identified was 82. In tomato isolates of *P. infestans* some variability has been demonstrated. Physiologic races (0) and (1) are known to attack tomato cultivars having no or Le^1 resistant genes, respectively.

Puccinia graminis tritici. The nature and extent of variability in wheat rust fungus is more complex as compared to *P. infestans* or other pathogenic fungus. The genetic studies of both wheat and dikaryotic phase of *Puccinia graminis tritici* has demonstrated variation in the number of genes (mono/oligogeneric) or the type of genes (dominant/recessive) involved. There are 7200 races of *P. graminis tritici*. The races are known to have biotypes (e.g. 117–117.A–117.A.1 and 15–15B).

6.5.4 Gene for Avirulence

Flor (1942), during his studies on Flax–*M. lini* system, conceived the idea of avirulent gene as alternate form of gene for virulence in pathogen and also as the gene in pathogen that corresponds with gene for resistance in host to determine an incompatible reaction. The induced plant defense response which may ultimately culminate in hypersensitive response. How these factors are induced or operated by avr genes is not clearly understood. However, it is believed that Avr is the gene, which makes a pathogen unable to induce disease on a specific variety of host plant. Thus, Avr genes determine the host range of pathogen, at race-variety level. Leach and White, (1996) discussed various models for avirulent gene function (Figure 6.9)

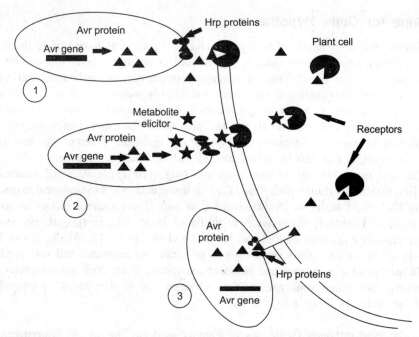

Model (1) (TMV–tobacco, N' gene), the Avr gene product is the elicitor, which is exported from cell via Hrp apparatus and interacts directly with plant receptor (the product of corresponding resistance gene).

Model (2) (*P. syringae* pv. *tomato*–tomato, Rpg 4 gene), Avr directs the synthesis of or modifies a metabolite or protein, which is race specific elicitor.

Model (3) (No examples) Avr is the elicitor, but it is directly delivered to the cytoplasm of plant cell.

Figure 6.9 Models for avirulence gene function in elicitation of plant disease response.

Avr genes and race specificity. The Avr genes are detected in members of a single pathogen species by inoculation set of host differentials. Individual pathogen strain may have multiple Avr genes, and the combinations of Avr genes within a particular strain species are the physiological races of the strain. Thus, Avr genes impose race-specificity on as pathogen, e.g. avr A, the first avirulent gene characterized, was cloned from race-6 strains of soyabean pathogen *Pseudomonas syringae* pv. *glycinea* and when transferred to other races of pathogen conferred ability to elicit a resistance response only on cultivars of soyabean with Rpg 2 gene for resistance.

The most important function of Avr gene is the elicitation of resistance. Either the product of Avr gene itself functions as elicitor or it modify some other protein or metabolite to produce an elicitor (in enzymatic mode of action). Now increasing evidence also implicate Avr genes in roles other than race specificity. Avr proteins may be transported directly into plant cells, where their intended targets are plant cellular process involved in resistance. The first such evidence was found in strains of *X. compertis* pv. *vesicatorie* containing an inactivated avr Bs_2 gene were less aggressive to a susceptible cultivar of pepper than was the wild type strain. Mutant in avr Bs_2 homologous in *X. compestris* pv. *alfalfa* was also reduced in their ability to multiply in alfalfa plants. Therefore, avr Bs_2 appears to be essential for growth of the pathogen in these hosts. A property common to all avr genes is the *geneicity* of the direct or indirect products. These producers allow the pathogen to be recognized by the host. In general, avirulent gene is dominant reversal but it may also be recessive as was reported in *P. graminis*, *tritici*, where the avirulent gene was recessive on one variety but dominant on other.

6.5.5   Gene for Gene Hypothesis

The co-existence and co-evolution of host plants and their pathogens have lead to the development of a complementary system where changes in virulence of pathogen were balanced by changes in host resistance and vice-versa. Thus, a dynamic equilibrium of resistance and virulence is maintained, and both host-pathogen survived. Oort (1944) working with wheat *Ustilago tritici* described the genetic basis of host-pathogen interaction. This, could not become popular probably due to time of publication (World War II) and the language of the paper (Dutch Journal). Flor, H.H. (1946) explained this stepwise evolution of virulence and resistance based on his data from genetic studies on resistance in flax (*Lisum usitatissimum*) and virulence in *Melamposra lini*.

The flax rust fungus *M. lini* is autoecious and long cycle (pycnial, aecial, uredial and telial stages on flax plant). It exhibits high variability as more than 400 physiological races have been identified in USA and Canada on 18 differential host lines. The resistance in flax to rust fungus is dominant while avirulence is dominant over virulence in *M. lini*. In flax–*M. lini* system genes conditioning resistance occur as multiple alleles in 7 loci (K (1), L (12), M (7), N (3), P (4) O (?) and Q (?). In all 36 resistant genes are known (L or l stand for resistance and susceptible alleles at locus L). In pathogen the avirulence and virulence, on corresponding loci, are designated as AL and al, respectively. Flor tested genotypes of flax varieties and *M. lini* races by cross inoculation experiments presented in Table 6.8.

Table 6.8 The Host-pathogen Genotypes of Parents used by Flor in his Experiment, and their Reactions

Flax Varieties	Races of *M. lini*	
	Race 22 ($a_L\,a_L\,A_N\,A_N$)	Race 24 ($A_L\,A_L\,a_N\,a_N$)
Ottawa 770B (LLnn)	S	R
Bombay (llNN)	R	S

Flor made digenic crosses between Ottawa 770 B and Bombay and selfed the F_1. The F_2 progeny was test inoculated by Race 22 and Race 24. Table 6.9 gives the genotypes and phenotypic reactions (R/S) for the crosses. The Analysis of data indicated a **dihybrid ratio (9:3:3:1)**.

Table 6.9 The Reactions of Parental Flax Varieties (Ottawa and Bombay), their F_1 and F_2 Progenies to Race 22 and 24 of *M. lini*.

Race and genes conditioning pathogenicity	Host genes conditioning reactions and type of host reaction						
	Parent varieties		F_1	F_2 plants (total 194)			
	Ottawa LL nn	Bombay ll NN	L- N-	L- N-	L- nn	ll N-	ll nn
Race 22 ($a_L\,a_L\,A_N\,A_N$)	S	R	R	R	S	R	S
Race 24 ($A_L\,A_L\,a_N\,a_N$)	R	S	R	R	R	S	S
Number of plants observed =				110	32	43	9
Number of plants expected = (9:3:3:1)				109	36	36	12

In another experiment, Flor crossed Race 22 and Race 24 of *M. lini*, selfed the F_1 and tested the F_2 progeny on Flax varieties Ottawa 770B and Bombay. The genotypes and phenotypic reactions are given in Table 6.10, a **Digenic ratio (9:3:3:1)** was observed.

Table 6.10 The Reaction of Flax Varieties (Ottawa and Bombay) to two Parental Races 22 and 24 of *M. lini* and their F_1 and F_2 Progenies

Flax Variety and Genotype for Reaction	Pathogen Genes Conditioning Pathogenicity and Types of Host Reaction						
	Race 22 $a_L\,a_L\,A_N\,A_N$	Race 24 $A_L\,A_L\,a_N\,a_N$	F_1 $A_L\text{-}\,A_{N\text{-}}$	F_2 cultures (Total 133)			
				$A_L\,-A_{N\text{-}}$	$a_L\,a_L\,A_{N\text{-}}$	$A_L-a_N\,a_N$	$a_L\,a_L\,a_N\,a_N$
Ottawa LL nn	S	R	R	R	S	R	S
Bombay ll NN	R	S	R	R	R	S	S
Number of cultures observed =				78	27	23	5
Number of cultures expected = (9:3:3:1)				75	25	25	8

Flor found that on flax variety that has one gene for resistance to avirulent parent race, the F_2 cultures of fungus segregated into monofactorial ratio (1:3). On varieties having 2,3 or 4 genes for resistance to avirulent parent race, the F_2 cultures segregated into bi, tri or tetra factorial ratio, respectively. Based on these observations, Flor (1942) proposed gene for gene hypothesis, which states, *for every gene conditioning resistance in host, there is a corresponding gene for avirulence in pathogen*. Gene for gene concept is more common in specialized and obligate parasites and absent in facultative parasites (Table 6.11).

Table 6.11 The Host-pathogen Systems where Gene for Gene Hypothesis has been Demonstrated/ Proposed

Host	Pathogen	Disease
Flax	*Melampsora lini*	Rust
Cotton	*X. axonopodis* pv. *malvacearum*	Cotton blight
Coffee	*Hemileia vastratrix*	Coffee rust
Legumes	Rhizobium	(Symbiosis)
	Bremia lactuceae	Downy mildew
Maize	*Puccinia sorghi*	Rust of maize
	Drechslera turcica	Maize blight
Oats	*Puccinia graminis avenae*	Stem rust
	Ustilago avenae	Oat smut
	Helminthosporium victoriae	Victoria blight
Potato	*Phytophthora infestans*	Late blight
	Synchytrium endobioticum	Potato wart
	Globodera rostochinensis	Cyst nematodes
	Potato virus X	Mild mosaic
Rice	*Magnaporthe grisea*	Blast of rice
Sunflower	*Puccinia helianthi*	Rust of sunflower
	Orobanche	Flowering plant parasite

(Contd.)

Table 6.11 The Host-pathogen Systems where Gene for Gene Hypothesis has been Demonstrated/ Proposed (*Contd.*)

Host	Pathogen	Disease
Tomato	*Cladosporium fulvum*	Leaf mould
	Spotted wilt virus	
	Tobacco mosaic virus	
Wheat	*Puccinia graminis tritici*	Black or stem rust
	Tilletia controversa	Dwarf bunt
	P. striiformis	Yellow or stripe rust
	Puccinia recondita	Brown or leaf rust
	Ustilago segatum tritici	Loose smut of wheat
	Erysiphe graminis tritici	Powdery mildew
	Mayetiola destructor	(insect)
Barley	*Rhyncosporium secalis*	Leaf spots
	Puccinia graminis hordei	Rust
	Ustilago avanae	Smut
Beans	Bean common mosaic virus	
Apple	*Venturia inaequalis*	Apple scab

Vanderplank (1976) suggested that gene for gene type of relationship can exist only in those host-parasite systems where both components are living for a certain critical period of time in order to let their nuclei, translate and subsequently exchange genetic information. He observed that Flor's hypothesis is purely a *hypothesis of identities* and it does not tell anything about gene quality. He also proposed a *second gene for gene hypothesis*, which tells us about the quality of resistant gene. *The quality of resistant gene in the host determines the fitness of the matching virulent gene in parasite to survive, when virulence is unnecessary or the host having resistant gene has been withdrawn.* Reciprocally, the fitness of virulent genes to survive, when it is unnecessary, determines the quality of matching resistant gene in host. Vanderplank (1978) proposed *protein for protein hypothesis* for host pathogen systems where gene for gene is applicable.

Protein for protein hypothesis. Under gene for gene hypothesis, proposed by Flor (1942), host and pathogen recognize each other by their proteins (gene products). Vanderplank (1978) proposed protein for protein hypothesis, for the cases where gene for gene is applied. The two hypotheses differ in their emphasis; the gene for gene hypothesis centres on gene for resistance in host plants while protein for protein hypothesis is concerned primarily, but not exclusively, with susceptible host plants, i.e. with compatible host pathogen interaction. Vanderplank (1978) hypothesized that *in susceptibility the pathogen excretes a protein into the host cell which co-polymerizes with complementary host-protein. This co-polymerization interferes with auto regulation in host genes that codes for the protein used by pathogen as food.* That explains the active parasitism. In resistance, the protein specified by Avr gene and excreted into host cell does not co-polymerize. It steps in host cell as catalyst and induces/elicits (elicitor) the reactions that inactivate the pathogen. The host-protein is not available to pathogen so it is practically starved.

Antigenic relationship between host and pathogen. Once the gene for gene hypothesis was established, it was expected and soon reported that compatible host-pathogen interactions shared more common antigens as compared to incompatible partners in flax–*M.lini* system. The evidences from other system studied, it was observed that compatibility of parasite with host increase with increasing antigenic similarity. It was reported that *Xanthomonas axonopodis* pr. *malvacearum* has more antigenic similarity with host cotton as compared to other Xanthomonas. Although there is no evidence but it has been speculated that the host plant and pathogen might have something similar to immunity system between animals and their parasites. Boubly, et. al. (1960) conducted an experiment on flax–*M. lini* system by taking four varieties of flax (varying in degree of resistance) and four isolates of *M. lini* (varying for virulence). From their serological studies they concluded that for susceptible interaction, the titers of rust antisera against flax antigen were relatively high (1:60 or 1:320) (more common antigens), while in resistant interaction the titers were low (1:20 or 1:40) (less common antigens).

De vay, et al. (1972) has generalized that tolerance of parasite by the host increases with increasing antigenic similarity whereas resistance of host is characterized by increasing disparity. Successful parasitism depended on a substantial quantity of antigen being shared by host pathogen. Antigens common to host and parasite would imply genetic materials common to host and parasite and antigenic disparity would imply genetic disparity. Probably this is the message of gene for gene hypothesis. More the matching of host genes by pathogen more susceptibility will be expected. Maize pathogen, *Ustilago maydis*, shares antigens with oat seedling which it can parasitize. Chakraborty and Purkayastha (1983 and 1998) showed not only antigenic similarity between *Macrophomina phaseolina* and soyabean but also indicated that antigenic patterns are influenced by exogenous application of chemicals.

6.6 RECOGNITION MECHANISM IN HOST-PATHOGEN INTERACTION

Recognition is the masterstroke in plant defense system, which takes place in early stages of pathogenesis when pathogen comes in contact with host. At this stage plant tissues/cells are able to differentiate between self and non-self and it also settles whether the interaction will be compatible (resistant to susceptible) or incompatible (non-host or immune). The microbes, which have developed *basic compatibility* have acquired the capability to establish infection, thus became pathogen and the target plant became suscept. This involves breaching of host's general defense barriers and synchronization of physiological process so as to avoid recognition as non-self and subsequent rejection by the plant. Establishment of basic compatibility is no guarantee that all individuals of pathogenic species will cause disease on all individuals of plant species. There is another level of interaction, *the specificity*, which finally decides the outcome of any interaction. Recognition of self or non-self is probably most important feature of living systems. It helps them to ward-off most of unwanted agents just at the first stage of interaction, i.e. the physical contact.

We have already discussed that *in nature plant disease is exception rather than rule,* in spite of the fact that plants are constantly exposed to millions of microbes, only few are able to cause some level of disease. The genetic information in host (susceptible/resistance) and pathogen (virulence/ avirulence) play vital role in the process where plant and microbes meet each other. Cell to cell contact is the first stage in host pathogen interaction, with exception of plant viruses, which find some way to enter the host-cell. Clarke and Knox (1978) defined cell wall recognition as *the initial event of cell-cell communication which elicited a defined biochemical, physiological or morphological response.* This description established two basic concepts:

- That recognition depends on the informational potential contained in the surface that comes in contact.

- That a response will follow the complementary interaction of the molecules those come in contact.

Basic compatibility. An important element of basic compatibility is the strategy used to overcome general host defenses. There is obvious biochemical specificity in suppression, toleration and detoxification of specific molecular defenses. Gene for gene system evolved as a result of selection pressure on the host population by the pathogen (Heath, 1991). It is basically a hypersensitive type resistance activated by the product of avirulence gene (pathogenic gene). The avirulent gene product, elicitor, binds with specific receptor, the product of resistant gene (Figure 6.10).

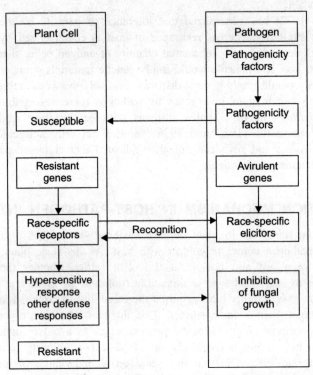

Figure 6.10 Model to illustrate interaction between a fungal pathogen and its host.

6.6.1 Requirements of Successful Pathogens

In order to colonize host tissues and reproduce, a successful parasite must have accumulated the genetic information to eliminate, overcome, avoid or escape all the host defenses encountered. The *lock and key analogy* where the notches on the *parasite key* are those factors required to allow colonization of plant tissue and/or to overcome *host resistance lock* factor. Pathogens of different plants must have different keys depending on the host lock and their relationship with it. A non-specific pathogen such as *Sclerotium rolfsii* has a relatively simple key [Figure 6.11(a)], with notches for the production of pectic enzymes and oxalic acid, the enzymes needed for detoxification or insensitivity to preformed host antibiotic factors and a cell surface coated with melanin or glycoproteins that do not elicit host defense. The notches considered here are concerned with overcoming the general resistance of the host, i.e. establishing basic compatibility. More specialized relationship requires more complex notch pattern [Figure 6.11(b)], the extreme being found in specialized obligate parasites.

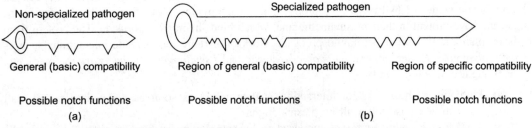

Figure 6.11   Lock and key analogy of microbe's requirements to become pathogen on a plant. Non-specialized parasites have simple requirement, hence few notches (a). The specialized parasites, in addition to basic compatibility notches (to breach general defenses of host) have additional notches required to meet the specificity. Taken as a whole, the notch pattern in specialized (obligate parasites) is more complex (b).

Following are the major points of the lock and key analogy:

- If the parasite lacks one or more of the necessary notches in the basic compatibility region for a certain plant lock, it will not be successful on that plant.
- The more specialized relationship with the host, the more complex must be the parasites notch pattern in the region of general compatibility.
- The growth rate of specialized pathogens in their hosts is the result of molecular interactions occurring primarily in the portion of the key denoted as the region of specific compatibility.

Mechanism of recognition in plant-pathogen system.   Recent information and interpretations have led to the idea that surface molecules modulate recognition in host-pathogen system. Certain surface molecules of pathogen's origin that play a vital role in the process of recognition have been discussed in the following sections.

Viroids and viruses.   Viroids have no protein capsids but consist only of nucleic acid; perhaps for this reason, there are no known resistant genes against viroids in plants (Keen, 1982). Viruses, however, have coat proteins or glycoproteins, and may elicit hypersensitive defense reactions in plants. The actual recognition of system is unknown.

Mycoplasma like organisms.   There are no known resistant genes against phytopathogenic mycoplasmas or spiroplasmas. These organisms lack cell walls and surface carbohydrates. Some may contain protein molecules, e.g. *Spiroplasma citri* contains a major surface membrane protein, spirallin, thought to be important in membrane integrity.

Bacteria.   Gram-positive bacteria differ fundamentally from gram-negative forms in possessing a teichoic acid based surface and peptidoglycan matrix. The gram-negative bacteria have highly developed outer membrane. Although single gene resistance to G +ive plant pathogens is rare but several examples of single gene resistance to G –ive bacteria are known. The highly organized outer membrane of gram-negative bacteria is composed of lipopolysaccharide (LPs); certain proteins, phospholipids and a peptidoglycan backbone. Occurrence of LPs O-antigenic side chains at the cell surface may be prime candidates for a recognition role in plant bacterial interaction.

Fungi. The glycoproteins are predominant surface molecules in fungi. The evidences suggest that cell surface recognition phenomena are mediated through the interaction of carbohydrate containing macromolecules and proteins. The host specific toxin secreted by *H. sacheri* is called Helminthosporoside (2-hydroxy cyclopropyl-α-D-galactopyranoside). Susceptible varieties of sugarcane have protein in their plasmamembrane, which binds helminthosporoside. The protein from resistant plants fails to bind helminthosporoside. Work on certain host parasite interactions such as *P. infestans*-potato, *P. megasperma* var. *sojae*-soyabean and *Pseudomonas solanacearum*-tomato, etc. have brought following points:

(a) Outcome of host parasite interaction is determined as soon as the pathogen cell wall contacts the host cell wall or plasmalemma.

(b) Constitutive components are supposed to be complimentary binding sites present on the surface of the host and the parasite.

(c) Binding sites determining basic compatibility are different from those determining specificity, i.e. susceptibility or resistance.

(d) *Binding at basic compatibility site* will lead to an array of metabolic changes in the host resulting in increased synthesis of bio-molecules and other nutrients required for growth of the pathogen. It will lead to *compatible interaction*.

(e) *Binding at specificity site* along with basic compatibility site will result in resistant response (*incompatibility*) due to one of the following effects:

- Shutting-off of the metabolic changes induced by binding at the basic compatibility sites.
- Induction of metabolic reactions leading to synthesis of compounds toxic to the pathogen such as phytoalexins.
- Binding of the host with parasite at a specific site may cause death of both pathogen as well as the host cells.
- Binding at a specific site may inhibit or slow down advance of the parasite with or without causing death of the host cells.

The nature of host binding sites. The initial contact between the components of two biological surfaces determines, to a large extent, the final outcome of the relationship. In most cases the host cell recognizes some common component of the microorganism on contact and then responds to it in a predictable manner. The transfer of information between the biologically active surfaces on a molecular level is a complex phenomenon. Two concepts considered to explain are: (a) **the glycocalyx concept** and (b) **the lectin concept**.

(a) The **glycocalyx** are surface polysaccharides in the fibrillar mucilaginous membranes or capsular material in cell wall. These surface polysaccharides contain many useful sites for the recognition phenomena through similarities or dissimilarities in the carbohydrates of two surfaces.

(b) **Lectins** are sugar binding proteins or glycoproteins of non-immune origin, which are devoid of enzymatic activity towards sugars to which they bind. Each molecule of a lectin has two or more sites, possibly clefts or grooves, into which complementary molecules of sugars or other oligosaccharides fit.

6.6.2 Molecular Features of Recognition Process

Active defense mechanism, which involves the phenomenon of recognition, basically operates at biochemical level. It was postulated and later established in selected host-pathogen systems that protein products of resistant gene (the receptors) bind specifically with pathogen produced protein (product of Avr gene–the elicitor). This binding stimulates the host cells to initiate the defense mechanism. The binding of a ligand to its receptor is usually reversible. Thus, receptor can bind to several signal molecules, but with different affinity. The specificity of the recognition is proposed to be similar to protein-protein interaction of IgD or IgM molecules on the surface of mammalian B cells with their specific antigens. The three-dimensional structure of protein molecules has vital role to play in specific binding. The plant systems where evidence to support this model exists include Avr Pto-Pto interaction Avr 4/9 interaction with Cf product and flax-rust.

6.6.3 Recognition Models

In most host-pathogen interactions the product of resistant gene, a protein, binds with another specific protein, product of avirulent gene of the pathogen. Thus, gene for gene, proposed by Flor (1946), has been converted into protein for protein hypothesis (Vanderplank, 1978). Various models have been proposed to explain this phenomenon of recognition at molecular level. No single model could satisfactorily explain all the situations. Valuable contributions have been made from fundamental work by biochemists, physiologists and geneticists. The findings have led to conceptualization of certain models proposed to explain the phenomenon of recognition and elicitation of active host defense mechanism. Some of the models are described as follows:

Elicitor–receptor model. It was the first model proposed by Albersheim and Anderson–Prouty (1975) to explain recognition process in plant–pathogen system. The work of physiologists and biochemists contributed immensely in development of this model. The focus is on plant hypersensitive response in incompatible interaction. It is proposed that Avr gene product, glycosyl transferase (enzyme protein), modifies the surface glyco-proteins for their molecular specificity. These glycoproteins bind with host receptor proteins (encoded by R genes). This binding specifically triggers a generalized host defense (hypersensitive response) and the interaction becomes incompatible due to sudden/fast death of host cells. The hypersensitive response (instant death of infected cells) does not support the activity of biotrophs, this also leads to blockade of water/nutrient supply from host cells to the parasite, required for growth and development of the latter. Hence the infection is checked just in the very early stages. The stimulus is transmitted to neighbouring host cells [Figure 6.12(a)].

Evidences to support this model were listed by Keen (1982). Later refinements in the model introduced the concept of endogenous elicitors, i.e., existence of intracellular signalling and amplification mechanisms. *Erwinia caratovora* elicits phytoalexin accumulation by releasing cell wall fragments, endo-polygalacturonic acid lyase. According to this model, elicitation of active defense mechanism, hypersensitive response, is the key element. This makes the vast majority of parasites as non-pathogens.

Dimer model. This model is based on genetic studies on biotrophic interactions in host pathogens where gene for gene system has been established. Ellingboe (1982), proposed a testable physiological model where focus of basic compatibility remains same as proposed in E-R model [Figure 6.12(b)]. There is less emphasis on elicitation of active defense mechanism; rather establishment or disruption of basic compatibility has been emphasized. Dimers are conceived as

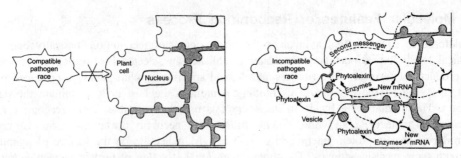

Figure 6.12(a) The Elicitor-Receptor model (Albersheim and Anderson–Prouty (1975)

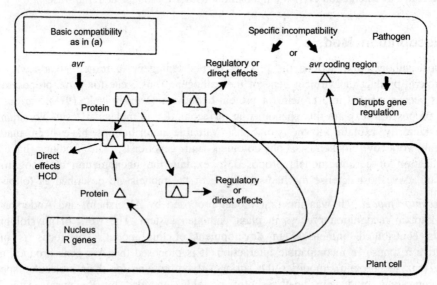

Figure 6.12(b) The Dimer model (Ellingboe, 1982).

being formed by primary products of R genes and avr genes. Two alternatives have been proposed: (a) direct binding (protein-protein) is supported by evidence from Tomato–*Cladosporium fulvum* system where Cf 9 gene product (a peptide of 27 amino acid length) binds with receptor protein which results in incompatibility, alternatively (b) one of the gene products (R or avr protein) may bind the other gene or mRNA transcript and formation of this dimer also leads to incompatibility.

The dimer model explains observed heterologous incompatibility between host plants and microbes due to 'lack of virulence gene' and not due to host defense. According to this model *hypersensitive response is the consequence and not the cause of incompatibility*. There are certain weaknesses associated with this model as discussed by Gabriael (1990). These include lack of evidence of protein-protein or protein-nucleic acid dimer formation. It is also not clearly understood as to how dimer formation will affect incompatibility.

Ion-channel model. Gabriael proposed ion-channel model in 1988, which combines certain features of earlier two models. It agrees with E-R model for recognition of endo and exogenous elicitors. It also emphasizes the ability to recognize the product(s) of avr activity. In elicitor-receptor and Ion-channel models, the R genes are to encode trans-membrane protein receptors. But Ion-channel model differs with elicitor-receptor model for explaining heterogeneous incompatibility with biotrophs. Ion-channel model agrees with dimer model that *hypersensitivity is primarily due to deficiency in microorganism (virulence)* rather than the result of active host defense. Ion-channel model explains homologous incompatibility due to opening of ion-channels, which results from binding of avr gene product (elicitor) with receptors (product of R genes). According to ion-channel model the cell plasmamembrane is equipped with large member of trans-membrane protein receptors capable of being opened into ion-channels [Figure 6.12(c)]. A distinctive feature of ion-channel model is that signal transmission is due to electrolyte fluxes and, in particular, by calcium ions. Thus, it is a testable physiological model. This model also explains the co-dominance and dosage effect based on effective level of expression of R genes, which determines the quantity of receptors present in plant cells (Gabriel and Rolfe, 1990).

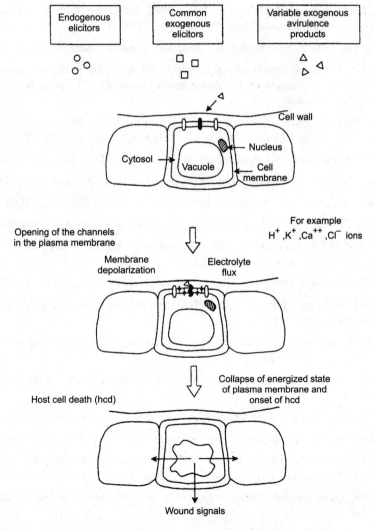

Figure 6.12(c) Ion-channel model (Gabriael, 1988).

REFERENCES

Albersheim, P. and Prouty, A.J., 1975, Carbohydrate, protein, cell surfaces, and the biochemistry of pathogenesis, *Annu. Rev. Plant Physiol.,* 26:31.

Biffen, R.H., 1905, Mendel's laws of inheritance and wheat breeding, *J. Agric. Sci.,* 1:4.

Black, W., 1960, Races of *Phytophthora infestans* and resistance problem in potatoes, *Rept. Soct. Pl. Bred. Stn. Pentl and Field,* Edinburg, UK, p. 29.

Boyer, J.S., 1995, Biochemical biophysical aspects of water deficits and the predisposition to disease, *Annu. Rev. Phytopathol.,* 33:251.

Cladwell, R.M., Schafer, J.F., Compton, L.E. and Patterson, F.L., 1958, Tolerance to cereal leaf rusts, *Science,* 128:714.

Daniels, M.J., Dow, J.M., and Osbourn, A.E., 1988, Molecular genetics of pathogenicity in phytopathogenic bacteria, *Annu. Rev. Phytopathol.,* 26:285.

Day, P.R., 1974, Genetics of host pathogen interaction, *Freeman,* San Francisco, California.

De Wit, P.J.G.M., 1992, Molecular characterization of gene for gene system in plant-fungus interactions and the application of avirulence genes in control of plant pathologens, *Annu. Rev. Phytopathol.,* 30, 391–481.

Ellingboe, A.H., 1982, Genetical aspects of active defense, In: *Active Defense Mechanisms in Plants, Proc. NATO Conf.,* Cape Sounion, Greece, (Ed.), R.K.S. Wood, 179–92, New York, Plenum.

Flor, H.H., 1942, Inheritance of pathogenicity in *Melampsora lini., Phytopathology,* 32:653.

Flor, H.H., 1946, Genetics of pathogenicity in *Melampsora lini., J. Agric. Res.,* 73:335.

Flor, H.H., 1947, Inheritance of reaction to rust in flax, *J. Agric. Res.,* 74:241–62.

Flor, H.H., 1971, Current status of the gene-for-gene concept, *Annu. Rev. Phytopathol,* 9, 275.

Gabriel, D.W., and Rolfe, B.G., 1990, Working models of specific recognition in plant-microbe interactions, *Annu. Rev. Phytopathol.* 28:365.

Groth, J.V., 1976, Multiline and super race: A sample model, *Phytopathol,* 66:937.

Hammond-Kosach, K.E. and Jones, J.D.G., 1997, Plant disease resistance genes, *Annu. Rev. Plant Physio, Plant Mol. Biol.,* 48:575.

Heath, M.C., 1991, The role of gene-for-gene interactions in the determination of host species specificity, *Phytopathology,* 81:127.

Hobgood, R.M., 1970, Designation of physiological races of plant pathogens, *Nature,* 227: 1268–1269.

IAEA/FAO, 1971, Mutation breeding for disease resistance, *Proc. of Panel, IAEA,* Vienna.

Johnson, R., 1984, A critical analysis of durable resistance, *Annu. Rev. Phytopathology,* 32:309.

Keen, N.T., 1982, Specific recognition in gene-for-gene host parasite systems, In: *Advances in Plant Pathology* (D.S. Ingram and P.H. Williams, Eds.), vol. I, p. 35, Academic Press, London.

Kenn, N.T., 1990, Gene-for-gene complementarities in plant pathogen interactions, *Annu. Rev. Genet.,* 24:447.

Kerr, A., 1987, The impact of molecular genetics of plant pathology, *Annu. Rev. Phytopathol.,* 25: 87.

Kiyosawa, S., 1982, Genetics and epidemiological modeling of breakdown of plant disease resistance, *Annu. Rev. Phytopathol.,* 20, 93.

Kohmoto, K. Singh, U.S. and Singh, R.P., 1995, Pathogenesis and host specificity in plant *Pathogenic Fungi and Nematodes, In: Pathogenesis and Host Specificity in Plant Diseases,* Eds. Kohmoto, K., Singh, U.S. and Singh, R.P., Pergamon, Elsevier Science Ltd.

Kue, J. 1995, Phytoalexius, stress metabolism and disease resistance in plants, *Annu. Rev. Phytopathol.,* 33, 275–297.

Leach, J.E. and White, F.F., 1996, Bacterial genes, *Annu Rev. Phytopathol,* 34:153–179.

Leonard, K.J. and Czochor, 1980, Theory of genetic interaction among population of plants and their pathogens, *Annu. Rev. Phytopathology,* 18:237.

Loegering, W.Q., 1966, The relationship between host and pathogen in stem rust of wheat, *Hereditas Suppl.,* 2:167.

Lucas, J.A., 1998, *Plant Pathology and Plant Pathogens,* 3rd edn., Blackwell Science Ltd.

Nelson, R.R., 1978, Genetics of horizontal resistance in plant disease, *Annu. Rev. Phytopathology,* 15:359.

Nelson, R.R., 1978, Genetics of horizontal resistance in plant diseases, *Annu. Rev. Phytopathol.,* 15:359.

Parlevliet, J.E., 1979, Components of resistance that reduce the rate of epidemic development, *Annu. Rev. Phytopathology,* 17:203.

Parlevliet, J.E., 1981, Stabilizing selection in crop pathosystems: an empty concept or reality euphytica, 30:259:269.

Person, C., Groth, J.V. and Mylyk, O.M., 1976, Genetic changes in host-parasite populations, *Annu. Rev. Phytopathology,* 14:177.

Robinson, R.A., 1969, Disease resistance terminology. *Rev. Appl. Mycol.,* 48:593.

Robinson, R.A., 1971, Vertical resistance, *Rev. Plant Pathology,* 50:233.

Robinson, R.A., 1973, Horizontal resistance, *Rev. Plant Pathology,* 52:483.

Roy. D., 2000, Study of host parasite interaction, In: *Plant Breeding, Analysis and Exploitation of Variations,* Narosa Publishing House, New Delhi, 287.

Schuathorst, W.C. and Devay, J.E., 1969, Common antigens in *Xanthomonas malvacearum* and *Gossypium hirsutum* and their possible relationship to host specificity and diseases resistance, *Phytopathology,* 53:1142.

Sidhu, G.S., 1987, Host-parasite genetics, In: *Plant Breeding Reviews,* Ed. J. Janick, 393-432, New York: Van Nostrand Reinhold.

Singh, R.S., 2002, *Introduction to Principles of Plant Pathology,* Oxford and IBH, New Delhi.

Singh, U.S., Singh, R.P. and Kohmoto, K., Eds. 1995, "Pathogenesis and host specificity in Plant Diseases: Histopathological, Biochemical, Genetic and Molecular Bases," Vols. 1-3. Pergamon, Elsevier Science, Tarrytown, New York.

Stackman, E.C. and Harrar, C., 1957, *Principles of Plant Pathology,* Ronald Press, New York.

Vanderplank J.E., 1963, *Plant Diseases: Epidemics and Control,* Academic Press, New York.

Vanderplank, J.E., 1976, Four assays, *Annual Review of Phytopathology,* 14:1.

Vanderplank J.E., 1978, Genetics and molecular basis of plant pathogenesis, Springer, Berlin Heidelberg, New York, 167.

Vanderplank, J.E., 1984, *Host–pathogen Interaction in Plant Diseases,* Academic Press, New York.

Vavilov, N.I., 1949, The Origin, Variation, Immunity and Breeding of Cultivated Plants, Trans. by K. Starr Chester, Waltham, Mass Chronica Botanica., 364.

Wit de, P.J.G.M., 1992, Molecular characterization of gene for gene system in plant fungus interaction and the application of avirulence genes in controlling plant pathogens, *Annual Rev. Phytopath.,* 30:391.

7 Disease Development in Populations

Epidemics of plant diseases have influenced man's food, his health, his social customs and even his ability to wage war. Infact, human sufferings and epidemics of plant diseases have gone hand in hand since the earliest history of man.

—Horsfall, J.G. and Cowling, E.B., 1978

7.1 INTRODUCTION

Plant disease development is a dynamic process, especially when studied at population level. Plant disease epidemics are the outcome of interaction of host and pathogen populations when environment is favourable for onset and spread of disease, for reasonable time. Infact, it was infamous epidemic of late blight of potato *(Phytophthora infestans Mont. de Bary)* during 1840s in Ireland that brought the plant diseases and the science of plant pathology in social limelight. Certain notions have been attached with the word epidemic; it is presumed that epidemic has to be widespread, devastating, severe and sudden outbreak. Like many other scientific words *epidemic* is derived from two Greek words *epi* -(on/among) and *demon* (population). It means any event/ phenomenon affecting most of the individuals of a population at the same time. The Webster's International Dictionary defines the word epidemic as *affecting or intending to affect many individuals within a population, a sudden and rapid growth or development.* Thus, in simple words, plant disease epidemic means, if most of the plants in a population are diseased at the same time and same place. The epidemic may be widespread or may reach severe proportions in short duration. Vanderplank (1963) very aptly defined epidemiology as *the science of disease in population.*

Under agro-ecosystem plant diseases exhibit variability both in occurrence and severity, in time and space. Lucas (1998) stated, *epidemiology seeks to understand the process underlying such temporal and spatial changes in disease incidences.* Epidemiology is a science with purpose, as it aims to identify causes and to provide a rational basis for disease management. The term epiphytotic or botanical epidemiology has been used in literature as an alternative of epizootic. But since epidemic and epidemiology have come long way and are well understood by plant pathologists these words should continue. Horsfall and Cowling (1978) advised to avoid these refinements as unnecessary bits of jargon. If an epidemic is spreading on continental or global scale it is known as ***pandemic***. The classical example is late blight of potato (*P. infestans*). While the diseases that are confined to an area and occur regularly at moderate level are called **endemic**, e.g. wart disease of potato is endemic in Darjeeling area. Some pathogens are monocyclic, as they complete one cycle during one year but these increase over several years with perennial hosts. The *polyetic pathogens* produce enormous amount of inoculum, which is capable to survive between seasons and carry over the infection. Dutch elm disease is monocyclic, if considered over one year but the pathogen

Ophiostoma ulmi is polyetic as it increases exponentially over several years and may result in epidemic situations (USA and Europe, since 1930).

7.2   DEVELOPMENT OF EPIDEMIOLOGY

The development of epidemiology can be conveniently partitioned into pre and post Vanderplank era. The path breaking analytical and quantitative approach given by Vanderplank was a turning point in the study of epidemics. His text "Plant Diseases: Epidemics and Control" published in 1963 presented an entirely different treatment of the subject that popularized epidemiology among the young plant pathologists. The following phases can be identified in development of epidemiology:

Descriptive and comparative phase.   The early approaches in epidemiology were confined to study the factors, mostly environmental, on development of diseases. Influence of temperature and relative humidity on pathogen or host-pathogen interactions, under controlled conditions, dominated the trend. Workers also attempted to compare the well-publicized epidemics that occurred in different times or different places.

Quantitative and analytical phase.   Beginning of Vanderplank era was marked with introduction of mathematical and analytical approach in epidemiology. Vanderplank used simple exponential and logistic growth equations to study the increase of disease in plant population, calculation of infection rates, making of disease progress curves, the patterns of epidemics, calculating area under disease progress curve and relating them to yield losses were major trends. He also introduced new concepts, viz. sanitation as principle, to plant pathology. He, for the first time, emphasized the application of epidemiological principles for plant disease control.

Present phase.   Introduction of mathematical tools in epidemiology and simultaneous development of computers laid the foundation of more innovative and quantitative approaches in plant disease epidemiology. Modelling became the buzzword. Predictive models (disease forecasting), Simulation models (evaluation of strategies for likely benefits), System approach (a holistic treatment of results of isolated studies) and finally Expert system (optimization of management package for specific conditions) are some of the trends in present day epidemiology. From 1980s the term epidemiology has become *applied plant pathology* in true sense, in the service of growers and the mankind.

7.3   PREREQUISITES FOR DEVELOPMENT OF EPIDEMICS

Plant diseases acquire epidemic proportions only when the factors involved in disease development are favourable for infection and spread of pathogen. Following conditions are prerequisite for development of epidemics:

- Population of susceptible **host** (Genetically uniform susceptible host population planted on large area)
- Virulent and aggressive **pathogen** (Effective primary inoculum, fast growth and multiplication)
- **Environmental** conditions remain favourable (For infection, multiplication and effective dispersal of pathogen)
- Host-pathogen-environment interaction is permitted for some **time**

The optimization of all variable factors does not happen frequently, thus *epidemics are rare*. Only few epidemics are known to have influenced human affairs till date (Table 1.2, Chapter 1). Plant disease acquires epidemic proportions only if there is a significant shift in equilibrium of host-pathogen-environment interaction in favour of pathogen/disease.

7.4 ELEMENTS OF EPIDEMICS

Epidemics are structured system. The system (epidemic) can be split into sub-systems or in various elements. Reciprocal cause-effect relationships among these elements may explain the behaviour of epidemics. Host, pathogen, environment and time are identified as four elements of epidemics. Represented by four arms, they form the disease pyramid (Figure 7.1). Disease was earlier represented by disease triangle, formed by three elements, viz. host, pathogen and environment.

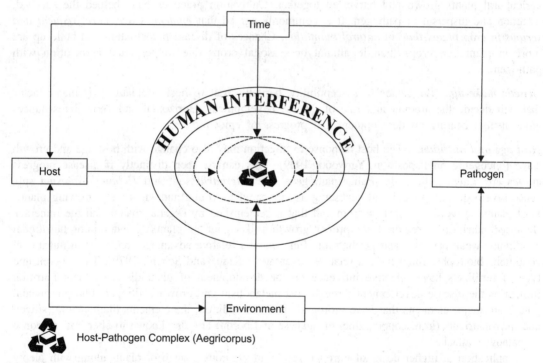

Host-Pathogen Complex (Aegricorpus)

If four elements of epidemic (represented by pyramid's arm length) can be quantified, the volume of pyramid will represent the amount of disease. Representation of disease by *pyramid is superior over triangle* as it accounts for an extra factor "time", which has important bearing on final outcome of interactions.

Figure 7.1 Elements of epidemics and their interactions

In case of plant diseases where vector is involved, situation becomes more complex. The fifth element, **the vector** population, may facilitate the survival and dispersal of inoculum, in addition to inoculation of the host. Vector population is also influenced by environmental factors.

7.4.1 Role of Host Factors in Epidemiology

Autotrophic green plants not only 'host' the microbial parasites/pathogens but also provide them valuable range of habitat required to maintain the ecological niche. The host factors like genetic make-up, age, nutritional status and population structure influence the onset and progress of epidemic. Certain host factors should be considered for their influence on plant diseases, which are as follows:

Type of plant community. Plants make natural vegetation as well as agricultural crops, yet they have different impact on disease development. Natural vegetation is complex in composition and behaviour. Different plant species grow in a mixed stand; even the individuals of same species differ in phenological stages that add further complexity. Natural vegetation has environment of its own, matching to its composition. Infection efficiency and effective dispersal of pathogen is very poor in natural vegetation, due to wastage of inoculum. Crops are single species population of agricultural plants grown and harvested together. Cultivation practices have helped the survival, infection and dispersal of pathogen. It is commonly agreed that *epidemics are more frequent and serious in crop plants than in natural plantation.* Chances of disease perpetuation and build-up are more in plantation crops than in annual or seasonal crops due to perpetual association with pathogen.

Genetic make-up. Resistance or susceptibility, heritable trait of host populations, is major factor that will decide the amount and rate of disease development. Horizontal and vertical resistances have distinct bearing on development and progress of epidemic.

Host age and nutrition. The host response to infection may also change with host age and growth stage (oncogenic predisposition, Yarwood, 1959). This can be seen distinctly if disease progress curves are drawn judiciously. Foliar pathogens like *Alternaria* spp. and *Helminthosporium* spp. cause severe damage to old and senescing as compared to young and vigorously growing plants. Host plants derive their nutrition from soil that is replenished by organic matter and the minerals. Balanced nutrition is required for proper growth and vigour of plants. "Under poor nutritional conditions, weak parasites and perthotropic fungi have a relative advantage; under good nutritional conditions biotrophic fungi have a relative advantage" (Kranz and Schein, 1979). The amount and type of fertilizers have selective influence on the development of plant diseases. Plant nutrition influences the disease development through host metabolism and growth. Nitrogen, phosphorus and potash are major elements that have profound effect, in addition, the elements like calcium; silicon and micronutrients (iron, copper, zinc, manganese and boron) are also known to alter host response to pathogen attack.

Application of higher doses of nitrogen results in vigorous growth of plants along with plenty of succulent and prolonged vegetative growth. Some specialized pathogens, powdery mildew and rust fungi cause more severe damage under these conditions. On the other hand, low nitrogen fertility creates the stressed conditions for host growth and hastens the senescence. These conditions favour infection by pathogens like *Alternaria, Fusarium, Pseudomonas, Sclerotium* and *Pythium*. The forms of nitrogen fertilizer used (nitrate or ammonium) also influence disease development. Diseases caused by *Fusarium* spp., *Plasmodiophora brassicae, Sclerotium rolfsii* increase in severity by use of ammonium fertilizer. The nitrate nitrogen is reported to favour infection by *Gaumenomyces graminis, Phymatotrichum* and *Straptomyces scabis*. The forms of nitrogen are likely to influence diseases/pathogens through effect on soil pH and microbial activity.

Phosphorus and potash fertilizers have been studied in relation to plant diseases. They are known to reduce disease severity by inducing host resistance or accelerating maturity of crop plants.

Calcium fertilizer application (calcium ammonium nitrate—CAN) is known to reduce root and stem diseases caused by *Rhizoctonia, Sclerotium, Botritis, Fusarium oxysporum, Erwinia* spp. and few nematodes. The calcium application may influence the composition of cell wall (middle lamella) thus hampering penetration by pathogens. Application of silicon as soil or foliar spray is reported to reduce cucumber powdery mildew (*Sphaerotheca fuligena*), brown spot (*Bipolaris oryzae*) and blast of rice (*Magnaporthe grisea*). Foliar applications of micronutrients (Fe, Zn, Mn, Bo and Cu) have been reported to reduce severity of several diseases. The micronutrients may correct the deficiency of these vital nutrients and thereby alter the host response.

Host population structure. Crop density, crop sequence and rotations have significant bearing on the type and amount of plant diseases. High crop density or close planting will influence microclimate and will make infection and dispersal of inoculum more effective. Both these factors will help the development of disease.

Type of propagation. Nature of plant propagation affects the development of disease. Chances of disease/pathogen carryover (establishment and spread) are more if plants are vegetatively propagated.

7.4.2 Role of Pathogen Factors

The microorganisms that have developed special faculties to overcome host defense are responsible for initiation and development of disease. There are certain important pathogen factors that affect the course of epidemic:

Virulence and aggressiveness of pathogen. Virulence is the ability of any microbe (qualitative character) to cause successful invasion of a plant species, while the aggressiveness (quantitative trait) relates to sum of all pathogenic activities that decides the amount of disease and/or rate of its progress. The pathogenic variants (races) may vary in virulence (virulent or avirulent) or aggressiveness by causing slow or fast damage to host population.

Survivability of pathogen. Pathogenic propagules have to face the vagaries of environmental conditions before initiating new infections. The ability of inoculum to withstand the hostile environment (physical, chemical and/or biological) decides the survivability, hence the amount of pathogenic propagules (*primary inoculum*) to initiate a new disease cycle. The amount of primary inoculum is of paramount importance in epidemiology of mono as well as polycyclic diseases.

Inoculum potential. Horsfall (1932) introduced the idea of inoculum potential when he equated the inoculum potential with inoculum density. Later Garrett (1956) considered it in wider perspective and defined as *the energy available for colonization of substrate (host) at the surface of the substrate (infection court) to be colonized.* This energy angle in conceptualizing idea of inoculum potential seems reasonable as the success of any army in a war or colonization of host tissue by pathogen depends not only on its number but also on it's capability. The status of energy in infection court will be determined by following two factors:

Inoculum density. The amount of inoculum is a physical quantity and can be measured by counting number of pathogenic propagules per unit volume (air/soil). Inoculum density is the primary determinant of inoculum potential; *more the inoculum density more will be the inoculum potential.* Efficiency of inoculum production may vary in different groups of plant pathogens. In case of viruses and bacteria there is hardly any modification for inoculum production. In contrast, fungal pathogens produce different kind of propagules and show various adaptations depending upon their habitat. Based on the habitat and type of infective propagules produced the fungi can be divided in two main groups:

Fungi with motile cells. These are groups of fungi with common features: aquatic habitat, simple thallus and motile (flagellate) reproductive cells. The Chitridiomycetes and Hypo-chytridiomycetes produce posterior/anteriorly uniflagellate cells. Oomycetes produce spores, which are biflagellate. The members of family Peronosporaceae in addition to producing biflagellate zoospores also produce non-motile spores for aerial dispersal under dry environmental conditions. Zygomycetes shows a gradual transition from sporangia to conidia, which are more suited to terrestrial life. They also show tendency of branched sporangiophores, which further increases, the efficiency of inoculum production.

Fungi without motile cells. Members of Ascomycetes are most adapted to drier and terrestrial habitat. They have completely lost the motile cells. The conidia, typical asexual spores, are produced in exceptional abundance. This may be the reason that *this group of fungi is more successful in producing epidemics.* In some advanced Ascomycetes there is tendency to suppress sexual reproduction; as if fungus is confident to survive only through abundance of asexual spores, conidia. In *Taphraina deformance* the budding of conidia augments the inoculum production efficiency. *Sclerotinia sclerotiorum* can produce about 30 million ascospores in a small cup. The Basidiomycotina, most advanced class of fungi, are a group of 20,000–25,000 spp. *Tilletia caries* carries some 12 million spores per infected grain of wheat. Although the conidiation is not common in Basidiomycetes, but spores in many smut fungi bud indefinitely to increase the inoculum density. The rust and smut fungi produce spores in abundance for long distance dispersal.

The bacteria and viruses multiply by cell division or *de novo* synthesis of particles. The amount of inoculum produced will depend on the "doubling time" (duration required for division of bacterial cell: also known as generation time). If generation time for certain bacterial pathogen is three hours, at the end of six days one bacterial cell will produce a population of 280 billion cells.

Inoculum capacity. The capability of pathogenic propagules is vital for colonizing the host tissue, as the capability of a soldier is to wage the war. Inoculum capacity is a quantitative trait, which is contributed by several factors. The prevailing environmental conditions may also influence the capacity of inoculum. Following are some of the factors that determine the capacity of pathogenic propagules:

- Genetic factors (aggressiveness)
- Biological status (active/dormant state)
- Nature of propagules (motile/non-motile)
- Age of inoculum (young/mature/old)
- Nutritional status (fat conidia/thin conidia)
- Responsiveness to environmental stimulus
- Infection devices used (physical force/enzyme/toxin)

Growth and reproduction. Growth and reproduction of pathogens is essential for development and spread of disease. The diseases can be grouped into two classes: (a) where growth of pathogen is dominantly vegetative or pathogens sporulate only once during crop season, the *spread of disease is linear*—single cycle disease, (b) where many cycles of sporulation are repeated during crop season, the *spread of disease is logarithmic*—multiple cycle disease. Plant pathogenic fungi exhibit varied type of reproduction, e.g. asexual, sexual and parasexual. The asexual mode helps in faster multiplication while sexual reproduction adds the variability to pathogenic population, through genetic recombination. *Both these events have significant epidemiological consequences.* Till recently, *Phytophthora infestans* population outside Mexico, comprised only A1 mating type (a heterothalic fungus), thus the sexual reproduction was not observed in nature and limited variability (races) was reported. After 1970s, A2 mating type has been reported from different parts of the world. It is expected that occurrence of sexual reproduction in nature will result in more variability in population.

Inoculum density-disease relationship. Amount of initial inoculum determines the amount of disease. This applies more to single cycle diseases where the relation between inoculum density and disease is direct. In case of multiple cycle diseases inoculum-disease relationship holds true in the early stages, but the ultimate disease development depends on two other important factors, viz. rate of infection and duration of disease development. Vanderplank (1975) described the inoculum density-disease relationship through an idealized sigmoid curve (Figure 7.2). The curve can be dissected in the following phases:

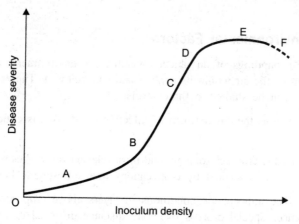

Figure 7.2 The inoculum density disease relation curve showing: Distribution tail (**A**) Log phase (**B**) Synergistic phase (**C**) Transitional phase (**D**) The plateau (**E**) Antagonistic phase (**F**).

Normal distribution tail. The infection courts as well as the infective propagules are normally distributed and propagules act independently, at low inoculum density. At the beginning of the Id-d curve the amount of inoculum is limited, this slows down the progress of disease, depicted by gentle slope of the curve. Vanderplank stated that 'when disease is plotted against inoculum, both on arithmetic scale, the curve starts at the origin (**A**). This is known as *law of origin* and contradicts Gaumann's *concept of inoculum threshold.*

Log phase. As the inoculum density is increased, the Id-d curve moves up gently, depicting increase in amount of resulting disease. There is no limiting factor, unit increase in inoculum density results in proportional increase disease. This is true logarithmic phase (**B**) where the rate of progress is proportional to the quantity itself (inoculum density).

Synergistic phase. During synergistic phase the observed increase in resulting disease is more than the increase in amount of inoculum. It is proposed that pathogenic propagules 'help each other' (synergism) during process of disease development (**C**).

Transitional phase. Further increase in inoculum density leads to a situation where the infection courts become limiting factor. Thus, for unit increase in inoculum, there is less than unit increase in resulting disease. This is transitional slope (**D**) and the Id-d curve slants gradually towards right side.

The plateau. By now all the infection courts have been saturated and any further addition of inoculum will not increase the disease, as no host tissue is available for infection. The Id-d line becomes flat, known as the plateau (**E**).

Antagonistic phase. In certain exceptional cases it has been reported that increase in inoculum density has resulted in decrease in disease intensity. This is depicted by dotted line in Id-d curve (**F**). In case of bean-*Uromyces phaseoli*, increased concentration of uredospores resulted in decrease in disease intensity. Similar observations were recorded in barley powdery mildew (*E. graminis*). Workers have explained this behaviour by assuming that propagules at very high concentration become antagonistic and may have inhibitory effect.

7.4.3 Role of Environmental Factors

The environment. Surroundings of an object constitute its environment; a tree makes its own environment. It influences the air within its canopy and soil below it. The environment, from plant disease point of view, can be studied at three levels:

Microenvironment. This is the environment of infection court. This is critical during early stages of infection process.

Mesoenvironment. This is crop environment and most relevant for studies related with disease and epidemic development. It is delimited by crop canopy and atmospheric layers surrounding it.

Macroenvironment. The atmospheric conditions in layers above crop surface constitute macro-environment. It influences special process like long distance dispersal of fungal spores.

In conventional meteorological descriptions the term microclimate is commonly used which refers to environmental conditions in three-dimensional space occupied by crop and also extends downward into the root zone of soil. Following two factors make microclimate different than the normal environmental conditions recorded:

- Interception of radiant energy by leaf canopy
- Reduced air movement in crop canopy

Elements of environment. Temperature, humidity/moisture, radiation and wind are basic elements of environment. The temperature and moisture regimens below minimum and above maximum create conditions of physical stress, for host, pathogen and vector populations. Agroeco-environment in different parts of the world is highly variable. These can broadly be classified into cool/hot or dry/wet areas. The types of plants grown and the types of diseases reported in different areas are different. The occurrence of plant pathogens and severity of diseases, in time and space, exhibit great variation.

Influence on host. The environmental factors have great influence on the growth and development of host plant or population. The processes that get affected include rate of growth, expansion of foliage, vigour and the maturity (ageing and senesces). The expression of resistance may also be temperature dependent. The vertical resistance in wheat cultivars (Sr 6 gene) is effective against pathogen *Puccinia graminis tritici* below 20°C but not at 25°C.

Influence on pathogen. The pathogen or its activities are influenced by environment directly or indirectly, through host plant or vector population.

Effect of temperature. Plant pathogens like other biological systems are influenced by temperature changes. The plant pathogens differ in their preferential temperature requirements. This explains why certain disease/pathogen is more prevalent in temperate regions while others dominate the tropical areas. Time of appearance of a disease, early or late, is decided by prevailing temperature. Early and late blight of potato come in that sequence due to high and low temperature preferences of *A. solani* and *P. infestans*, respectively. The disease caused by *Monilinia fructicola* (brown rot of stone fruits), *Colletotrichum* spp. (anthracnose) and *Ps. solanacearum* (wilt of solanaceous plants) are more serious in hot areas. In case of viral disease the prevailing temperature influences the establishment and multiplication of virus particles, the type of symptoms and the time taken for expression. The effect of temperature on progress of viral diseases may also be mediated through vector population. Trapero-Casas and Kaiser (1992) studied influence of temperature and wetness periods on infection and development of Ascochyta blight of chickpea. They reported that <5 and 30°C as lower and upper limits (20°C being optimum) for infection and disease development. In Figure 7.3, at a constant temperature of 20°C, minimum incubation and latent period were 4.5 and 5.5 days, respectively. Duration of these periods increased at lower and higher temperatures.

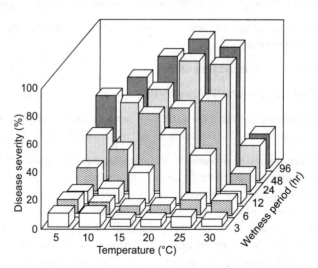

Figure 7.3 Development of Ascochyta blight (*Ascochyta rabei*) at different temperatures and leaf wetness durations (Trapero-Casas and Kaisar, 1992).

Effects of moisture. Relative humidity, dew, rainwater, and irrigation water are some of the forms of moisture that affect initiation, development and spread of plant diseases. Certain important diseases, late blight of potato, apple scab, downy mildews and bacterial blights are more serious in areas having high rainfall/high humidity. The changes in moisture levels for aerial pathogens influence the amount of sporulation, the effective dispersal, spore germination and penetration. The amount of soil moisture influences the soil borne pathogen by affecting survival, reproduction and mobility and infection process. Generally high soil moisture and saturation level favour the pathogen and disease development by *Pythium, Phytophthora, Verticillium, Scelerotium*, Bacteria and Nematodes etc. However, diseases caused by *Fusarium, Streptomyces* etc. are more serious under low moisture conditions. Powdery mildews and vascular wilts are favoured under dry conditions. Soil moisture may also influence the pathogen activities through associated microbiota, including antagonistic bioagents, present in rhizosphere soil. Frequency and amount of rain play important role in dispersal of inoculum present on host surface (powdery and downy mildews, rusts, leaf spotting fungi, canker and scab causing pathogens) and in soil (rain, irrigation and flooding water) may facilitate horizontal movement of pathogens.

Effect of wind.   Wind is an important factor of environment as mixing agent. The air movement influences the changes in temperature and relative humidity in crop canopy. Thus, wind has indirect role in influencing disease development. But primarily wind helps the pathogenic propagules in dispersal to various distances. It may be short, medium or long distance dispersal depending upon direction and speed of wind.

The following terms should be clearly understood by the students:

Absolute Humidity Vapour density of atmosphere (gm/m^3). Actual amount (gm) of water vapours present in unit volume (m^3) of air.

Specific Humidity Actual mass (gm) of water vapours present in unit mass (kg) of air.

Relative Humidity Ratio of actual amount of water vapours present to the amount required to saturate air at a given temperature.

Vapour Pressure Pressure of water vapour in air.

Vapour Pressure Deficit (Saturation VP-Actual VP)

Dew Point Critical temperature at which the saturation level of water vapour is reached. Any further drop in temperature will result in 'condensation of extra moisture' in air and will be seen as dew.

How environment influences plant diseases?   Plant pathogens are found all over the world and attack plants but the occurrence of diseases and their severity, in time and space, exhibit great variation. It is commonly agreed that, in addition to variability in type of plants/cultivars grown, the environmental conditions are the main factor accounting for observed patterns of variability. The prevailing environment influences both host and pathogen, the host also influences its environment but pathogen hardly has any significant bearing on environment. Physical environment can be the modulator of interaction and may tip the balance in the interplay between host and pathogen in favour of host or the pathogen/disease (Figure 7.4). In later case [Figure 7.4(a)], it may lead to epidemic proportions.

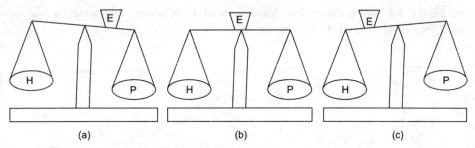

Figure 7.4 Role of environment factors in disease development. It can tip the balance in favour of either host or the pathogen/diseases (modulator).

Kranz and Schein (1979) observed that very often environment have relative rather than absolute effects on epidemics. For understanding the above statement, we should consider the following points:

1. Fluctuations in any one element of environment influence the other elements, e.g. temperature fluctuations affect the relative humidity and vice versa. The wind influences temperature and relative humidity.
2. Favourable or unfavourableness of one element (temperature or, humidity) may compensate for other elements, as explained by hypothesis of compensation (Rotem, 1978).
3. The conditions favourable for disease development are very rightly expressed in terms of range of environmental conditions rather than absolute values.
4. Plant diseases or epidemics are dynamic process accomplished in several steps. Each of these component steps have their own sets of optimal requirements. This is best explained in case of temperature requirement for different stages of late blight pathogen.

Optimum temperature for growth of fungus mycelium 16–18°C
Sporulation occurs at temperature from 9–26°C.
Growth of germ tube is best at 21–24°C.
Sporangia germinate in the range of 2–3 to 21–24°C
Temperature for sporangial germination is 12–13°C (zoospores) and 24°C (germ tube).

Before we close discussion on environmental factors two important terms, weather and climate should be introduced and differentiated. In simplest words weather tells about atmospheric state (temperature, humidity, sunshine, wind, etc.) at a place at a particular time. Weather conditions are highly variable in time and space. In contrast, climate is the aggregate weather. The climatic features of a place and large geographical area, tell about the patterns of temperature, precipitation, sunshine durations and winds over fairly long periods of time, e.g. seasonal and annual patterns. Elements of climate are same as that of weather. Both weather and climate have influence over plant diseases but the operational part; their impact, is different. Climate of a place dictates and shapes the type of vegetation and type of pathogens that will survive and flourish. It will decide the *type of diseases*. The weather will determine the *severity of diseases* prevalent in the area. Daily or seasonal weather fluctuations will influence the severity or intensity of the disease.

Hypothesis of compensation

Distribution of plant diseases is mainly influenced by the climatic conditions of geographical area. But certain pathogens are known to be worldwide in occurrence, though their incidence or severity may vary. Figure 7.5 shows the global distribution of *P. infestans*, indicating its occurrence in temperate, sub-tropical as well as semi-desert locations.

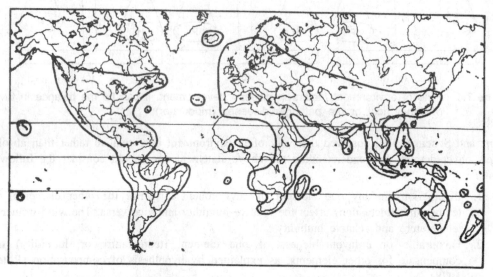

Figure 7.5   Geographical distribution of late blight of potato; note the occurrence of disease in diverse climatic conditions.

This behaviour of disease can be categorized in the following two classes:

- Epidemics of same disease occurring in different climatic area.
- Epidemics by different pathogens, which differ in their requirements, but occur in same climatic region.

Rotem (1978) explained that ability of pathogen to succeed in several differing climatic regions stems from its ability to complete its life cycle regularly in spite of marginal state of one factor. It has been demonstrated that effects of marginal or optimal states of physical or biological factors are relative rather than absolute.

- The first hypothesis of compensation states *A highly favourable (optimum) state of one factor essential for development of a given phase in the life cycle of a pathogen can compensate for the limitations imposed by the simultaneously unfavourable state of another factor.* This explains occurrence of late blight of potato in diverse climates, temperate cool-humid to semi-desert in different locations of world.
- According to second hypothesis, *a specific weakness in a pathogen can be compensated for by a specific strength.* If a pathogen is not able to survive very effectively, this weakness can be compensated by faster multiplication of primary inoculum and/or effective dispersal, which will result in good amount of disease in the season. The sporangia of *P. infestans* are very delicate and require free moisture on leaf surface (weakness), this is compensated by the fact that sporangia very quickly germinate and penetrate inside leaf. Thus, short durations of leaf wetness are exploited by pathogen to cause infection. Rotem (1978) observed, "obviously there are limits beyond which no degree of compensation can overcome the rigours of climate." This explains confinement of same pathogens to specific climatic zone.

7.4.4 Role of Time Factor

Plant pathologists originally recognized role of three factors (host, pathogen and environment) and visualized the disease triangle of unknown origin, to represent disease. Although, disease was recognized as a dynamic process, yet the time factor was not given due attention. Time has great influence on other three variables of disease development, thus affects the rate of progress of disease. This is reflected in all mathematical equations where time is invariably used as a component.

$$X = x_0 (1 + rt) \qquad \text{Monocyclic diseases}$$
$$X = x_0 e^{rt} \qquad \text{Polycyclic diseases}$$

Any practice that can shorten duration of host, pathogen interaction and could avoid occurrence of favourable environment during susceptible growth phase of host, will decrease the amount of disease.

7.5 STRUCTURE AND PATTERNS OF EPIDEMICS

Interactions of host and pathogen factors, under variable environmental conditions, result in various *patterns of epidemics.* The patterns of epidemic exhibit the point of origin, the rate of progress, shape of growth curve and discontinuities, if any.

7.5.1 Disease Progress Curves

Periodic observations on disease severity, in any field or area, when plotted against time on a graph paper (both on arithmetic scale) give curved lines representing progress of disease over time (Figure 7.6). These cumulative disease curves are known as ***Disease Progress Curves*** (DPCs). More frequent the observations the smoother will be DPC. DPCs are highly sensitive indicators; they reflect any fluctuation in factors affecting course of disease development. DPCs, like other biological growth curves, are sigmoid in nature (S-shaped). Figure 7.6 shows an idealized DPC where bold line represents cumulative disease over time and the dotted line represents the rate of progress (infection rate) at different time of disease progress. The straight solid straight line depicts the progress of disease plotted on logarithmic scale. It is the characteristic of any polycyclic disease.

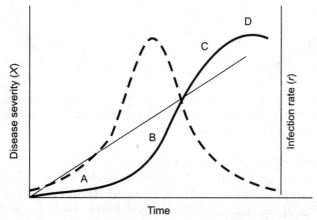

A—Lag phase; B—Log phase; C—Decline phase; D—The plateau

Figure 7.6 Disease progress curves for polycyclic disease.

Baker (1971) analyzed the sigmoid DPC into following four phases:

Lag phase. This initial phase of disease development is characterized by slow development of disease shown in Figure 7.6(A). Amount of primary inoculum is the main limiting factor for slow progress of disease.

Logarithmic or exponential phase. During logarithmic phase also called **exponential phase**, the progress of disease is fast. There are no limiting factors. The inoculum has multiplied, plenty of infection courts are available and environment is not unfavourable. This leads to very fast progress of disease and peak infection rate (**r**) is observed in this phase (B). In exponential phase the *rate of development is proportional to the quantity itself.*

Transitional or decline phase. As the disease (*x*) progresses, the amount of healthy tissue available for infection (1 − *x*) decreases. This results in slowing down of disease progress due to wastage of inoculum for want of infection courts. This results in decline in cumulative disease and infection rate (C).

The plateau. In later stages of disease development, there is no further increase in disease with time, as most of host tissue is already infected and the disease development reaches a saturation point or plateau, represented by flat line (D). There may be production of inoculum on infected host tissues.

These phases in DPC represent biological facets of epidemics. In an idealized DPC for polycyclic diseases (late blight of potato and rusts of wheat), the line representing the infection rate is *bell shaped* [Figure 7.7(b)]. These are called **symmetrical curves**. The variables of host, pathogen and environment may produce *asymmetrical DPCs*. In some situations, the infection rate may be higher in early part of disease progress [*positive skewness*, Figure 7.7(a)] while in others the rate of progress may be higher in later part of disease development [negative skewness, Figure 7.7(c)].

   +ve skewness–apple scab and powdery mildew of rubber

   −ve skewness–slow rusting of wheat

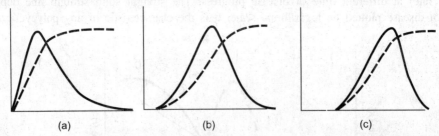

| (a) | (b) | (c) |

Figure 7.7   The symmetrical (b) and asymmetrical (a and c) DPCs. The dotted lines represent the progress of disease and the bold line are for rate of infection. (a) shows +ive skewness and (c) shows −ive skewness.

Asymmetrical *DPCs* may exhibit more than one peak, due to fluctuations in factors related with host (susceptibility with age), pathogen (rate of inoculum production and dispersal), environment (favourableness) and human interference (control measures). These are called **bimodal** [two peaks: rice blast, Figure 7.8(a)] or multi-modal/oscillating [more than two peaks, Figure 7.8(b)]. Fluctuations in environmental conditions may also change the pattern of epidemic.

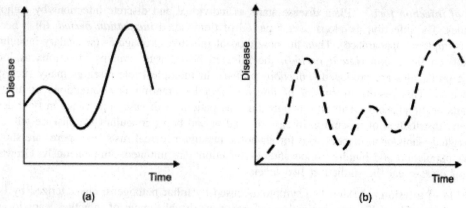

Figure 7.8 Bimodal (a) and oscillating (b) disease progress curves.

7.5.2 Infection Rate

Infection rate is the **increase or decrease in disease per unit time.** If we assume small increase in disease, dx in time dt, then

$$\frac{dx}{dt} \propto x \quad \text{or} \quad \frac{dx}{dt} = r \cdot x$$

Where r represents rate of infection and x is the amount of initial inoculum.

Vanderplank (1963) in his novel treatment of quantitative epidemiology derived the formula for calculation of infection rate,

$$r_l = \frac{2.3}{t_2 - t_1} \log_{10} \frac{x_2}{x_1} \qquad r = \frac{2.3}{t_2 - t_1} \log_{10} \frac{x_2(1 - x_1)}{x_1(1 - x_2)}$$

where

r_l and r are logarithmic and apparent infection rates, respectively.

x_1 and x_2 are disease at time t_1 and t_2, respectively.

Factors affecting the rate of infection. Calculating rate of infection (r) is useful in more than one way. Following factors have direct and significant bearing on rate of infection:

- r is directly proportional to infectious period.
- r is indirectly proportional to latent period.
- r is directly proportional to infection efficiency.
- r is directly proportional to sporulation efficiency.

In case of bacterial pathogens, every single bacterial cell serves as inoculum and a cell divides into two and then into four in a specific time, called **doubling time.** Thus, the rate of development of bacterial diseases will depend on (a) amount of initial inoculum and (b) the doubling time.

Spread of infection foci. Plant disease starts as individual and discrete infections by pathogenic propagules. The infection develops over a period of time called ***incubation period***, till it becomes visible (symptoms appearance). Then the new crop of infective propagules (secondary inoculum) is produced, on the lesion (*latent period*), the infected host tissue remains infectious as long as infective propagules are produced (*infectious period*). In multiple cycle diseases many such cycles are repeated. This results in *spread of infection foci* by creating new infections on the same plant/parts or on adjacent plants in a population. The pattern of disease appearance in field depends on general distribution of inoculum. In case of seed or soil borne inoculum, the disease will appear on individual plants or in patches. But for air-borne inoculum (cereal rusts) the spores are showered on plant population and hundreds/thousands of infections are initiated simultaneously. Growth and spread of disease can be studied at two levels.

Expansion of a lesion. Lesion is a symptom caused by foliar pathogens, characterized by limited necrosis of host tissue due to colonization by pathogen. Establishment of infection leads to growth of pathogen, colonization and invasion of host tissue from the point of infection. This results in *expansion* of *the lesion*. An expanding lesion can be divided into three distinct zones (Figure 7.9).

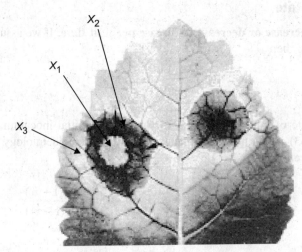

Figure 7.9 Different zones in a expanding lesion, central zone X_1 has passed the latent as well as infectious period, middle zone X_2 has passed latent period, but still in infectious period (actively sporulating), outer zone X_3 has passed the incubation period but not the latent period (not producing secondary inoculum).

The central dark area (X_1) where infection was initiated, has crossed the latent period (p) and infectious period (i). Thus, it has reached, $t > (p + i)$, a stage where it is neither contributing to multiplication nor available for infection. This dead tissue is fit for removal from the total diseased area recorded for quantitative estimation. The middle zone (X_2) represents the host tissue actively involved in pathogen multiplication and the disease development. This diseased tissue has crossed the latent period (p) but is actively producing new infective propagules (still not crossed the infectious period). The outermost zone (X_3) is recorded as diseased tissue, as it has crossed the incubation period (symptoms are visible) but since it is not producing new infective propagules (not crossed the latency period). To sum up the situations the disease tissue (X) recorded as diseased area (brown leaf spot) consists of $X = (X_1 + X_2 + X_3)$. But in reality only (X_2) is producing infective propagules, thus participating in multiplication of pathogen and development of disease. These facts should be taken into account while calculating *basic infection rate* (*R*) (correction for latency) or *corrected basic infection rate* (R_c) (correction for removals).

Expansion of foci. Few early-infected plants in a field create a focus from where infective propagules disperse and disease spreads from such focal points. Expansion of foci has been studied by van den Bosch (1990) who made an analogy of the phenomenon with the waves generated by throwing a stone in a still pond. Host plant distribution plays a role in expansion of foci.

Onset and spread of the epidemic. During summer of 1845 the attack of potato late blight took Europe completely by surprise, the blight damaged potato crops in North America during 1843–44. In Europe late blight was first noticed in Belgium by end of June, 1845 (Figure 7.10). By mid-July it reached Netherlands and France. On July 31, 1845, Abb'e Edouard van den Hecke published an article claiming that late blight was caused by fungus.

Late blight was reported in Paris (France) by mid-August, where C. Montagne described the fungus (*Botrytis infestans*) in proper detail. By this time disease also reached southern England. On 6th September 1845 the outbreak of late blight was reported in Ireland. The disease developed at alarming rate and destruction of potato crop, including tubers, was seen everywhere. By October, the harvest time, the tuber rot was noticed and popular panic spread through the Irish Newspapers. By this time disease also appeared in Scandinavia and Central Europe.

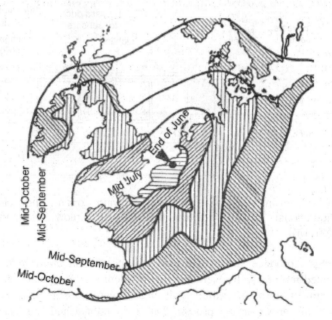

Figure 7.10 Progress of late blight of potato in Europe, as indicated by date of occurrence.

7.6 DISPERSAL OF PLANT PATHOGENS

Dispersal is the phenomena where inoculum is transported from source of production, by means of some agencies and reaches the target, infection court. Dispersal is pivotal to epidemics and without effective dispersal there cannot be spread of disease or progress of epidemic. *Effective dispersal* is the process by which viable and pathogenic propagules reach the suitable infection court and subsequently initiate new infection. Dispersal is a phenomenon of paramount importance in epidemiology, but it has not been attended well. Fitt, et al. (1989) discussed the limitations in the study of dispersal. The aerobiology group at Rothamsted Experimental Station, Harpenden (UK) has created a *rain tower and wind tunnel* facility (Figure 7.11) where dispersal of plant pathogens can be studied under different set of conditions. Readers should refer to Fitt, et al. (1989) for more details about rain tower/wind tunnel complex.

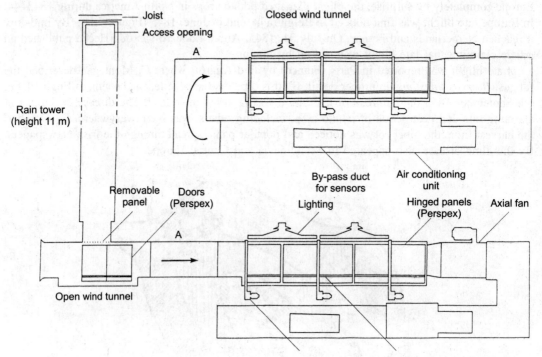

Figure 7.11 Rain tower/wind tunnel complex, showing open and closed wind tunnel configurations; arrows indicate direction of airflow (Rothamsted Experimental Station, UK).

All living beings reproduce and at any place the population build-up may lead to growing competition for limited resources. To overcome this problem the biological organisms have adopted two evolutionary strategies: (a) *Migration:* Advanced organisms (birds, animals and men) have adopted migratory habit, an organized process that is directional and less chances of loss of life during migration, thus organism with low progeny parent ratio adopted it. (b) *Dispersal:* This is the alternative process, adopted by lower organisms, with high progeny parent ratio. Dispersal, a mechanism for movement of propagules, is unorganized and random process.

Among the plant pathogens viruses are transmitted in specialized manner. In addition to mechanical transmission (by contact) most of viruses are transmitted by insect-vectors or planting material (seed as well as vegetative parts). The bacterial pathogens in addition to seed/planting material, are mostly dispersed by water (irrigation or rain splashes) in standing crops. The fungal pathogens can be classified into two groups based on habitat:

1. **Soil borne fungi,** these inhabit in soil for most of their lifetime, the dispersal of propagules is to limited extent, mostly redistributed, during cultural practices. Water is an important agent of dispersal (irrigation/ flood water).
2. **Air borne pathogens,** this is a vast group of fungi, adapted to terrestrial mode of life. They produce enormous amount of inoculum, which is mainly dispersed by wind in addition to rain splash.

7.6.1 Wind Dispersal of Fungal Spores

The process of spore dispersal by wind is purely a passive phenomenon, except active or forced liberation of spores by certain genera of fungi. The distance and direction covered are solely dependent upon carrying agent, the wind. The process of wind dispersal involves the following three phases:

Liberation or removal of propagules. The first stage in dispersal of fungal spores is the detachment of fungal propagules from the parental tissues. In some fungal genera, belonging to Ascomycetes and Basidiomycetes, the fungal spores are actively discharged by the fungal structures (apothecia, perithecia and puff balls), while in majority of cases, the spores are detached by air currents/wind using the physical force. The minimum wind speed required to dislodge or detach spores from the parent tissue is known as *critical wind speed*. It varies greatly in different fungal pathogens. Removal of conidia of powdery mildew fungus (*Erysiphe polygoni*) is accomplished by very gentle breeze, using very little force. In contrast, for removal of spores of *Helminthosporium maydis*, a force of 0.018 dynes is required. It has been reported that the process of liberation of spores in such cases is achieved due to creation of *gusts* which are transitional or intermittent high speed winds created for very short period of time.

Transportation or flight of fungal spores. Fungal spores, once liberated from parental tissues and cross the boundary layers, are suspended in air like any other physical entity (dust particles). They are solely dependent on the speed and direction of wind for transportation. The distance covered by the inoculum (fungal spores) depends on factors like: (a) strength of source of inoculum, (b) vertical height attained by the spores and (c) wind speed.

Deposition of fungal spores. The fungal spores at different vertical heights in air soon start settling down. This involves two processes: (a) *sedimentation*; where in fungal spores gradually sediment under the influence of gravity. (b) *impaction*; which means fungal spores moving with wind currents come across various objects in their way and may stick (impact) to surface due to inertia. The wind speed decides the relative importance of these two means of deposition (sedimentation or impaction).

Spore dispersal gradient. It is generally observed that as we move away from the focus of infection there is reduction in intensity or severity of disease (disease gradient). It has also been reported that fungal spores trapped at different distances from the source are inversely proportional to distance from source. An inclined plain represents dispersal gradient that may be shallow or steep depending upon direction and/or speed of the wind (Figure 7.12). The spore dispersal gradients can help in explaining the disease gradients, provided other conditions remain same.

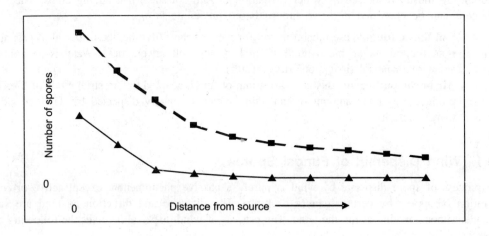

Figure 7.12 Spore dispersal gradients; the - - - - line represents the number of spores collected, at different distance from source, with the wind direction (shallow curve), the ——— line represents the number of spores collected, at different distance from source, against the wind direction (steep curve).

Following mathematical models have been used for studying dispersal gradients:

Power law model (Gregory, 1968). If this model is fitted, number of spores Y is inversely proportional to some power of distance X.

$$Y = aX^{-b}$$

where

Y = number of spores at distance X,

a = number of spores at the source ($X = 0$),

b = dispersal gradient.

Exponential model (Kiyusawa, 1972). If exponential model is fitted, the number of spores Y is inversely proportional to an exponential function of the distance X and the value of Y decreases by half as the distance from source X increases by a constant increment.

$$Y = C \exp. dX$$

where

Y = number of spores at distance X,

C = number of spores at the source $X = 0$,

d = the dispersal gradient.

Rhythms in spore dispersal. The concentration of spores in air does not remain uniform, i.e. at any place the number of spores in air varies with time of day or time of year. It has been observed that spore concentrations in air exhibit certain periodicities or rhythms. These rhythms can be attributed mainly to two factors:

Endogenous or biological. The biological stimulus may be responsible for vegetative and reproductive phases in life cycle of fungal pathogens.

External or abiotic. Certain environmental factors, viz. light, temperature, and humidity are crucial for production and liberation of fungal spores. Daily fluctuations in these factors, during day and night, are responsible for rhythms or periodicity (*diurnal periodicity*) observed at different time of the day. Sharma (1996) and Amita (1999) studied the diurnal periodicity of Alternaria spores in mustard crop (Figure 7.13) and reported that simultaneous increase in temperature and reduction in relative humidity, along with leaf wetness, are responsible for peak liberation of Alternaria spores (at about 11 am). The peak in downy mildew spores is recorded in late night or early morning hours.

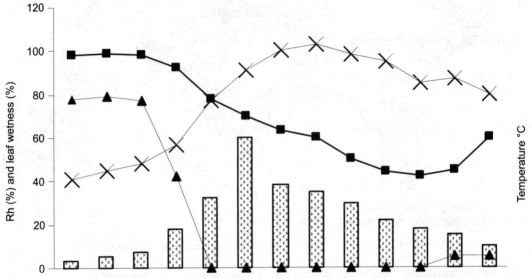

Figure 7.13 The diurnal periodicity observed in mustard fields infected by *Alternaria brassicicola*. The changes in environmental factors like temperature (x- - - -x), relative humidity (■ ■) and leaf wetness (▲ ▲) are used to explain the changes in spore concentration (vertical bars) at different time of the day.

Spore traps. The spore traps are simple devices used for sampling air for presence of fungal spores: the type and amount. The spore traps are useful in the study of aerobiology and spore dispersal of fungal pathogens. The spore traps can be grouped into two major types:

Sticky surfaces. There are mostly vertical or horizontal sticky glass slides or cylindrical rods, used to collect spores. The spores trapped can be viewed under microscope. The efficiency of these devices is low due to limited amount of air coming in contact with sticky surface.

Volumetric or suction spore traps. These are mechanical devices where air is sucked in and allowed to contact the sticky surface, which traps the spores. The efficiency of these spore traps is comparatively high. Some of the volumetric spore traps used include *Hirst's volumetric spore trap, Bournilon's slit sampler, Cascade spore trap, Rotorod spore sampler and Burkard's 7 days volumetric spore trap.*

Long distance dispersal. Long distance dispersal (Ldd) of fungal spores is a unique phenomena, commonly occurring in nature, but not discussed in texts on plant pathology. Nagarajan and Singh (1990) presented an interesting and informative account of Ldd. Dispersal of fungal spores is known as Ldd, *when the distance between source and target areas is few thousand kilometres.* Following are some of the examples under Ldd, also presented in Figure 7.14 and Table 7.1.

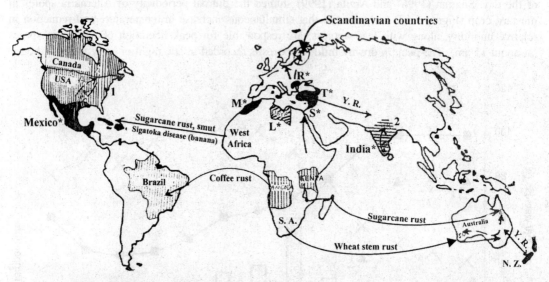

*Self-sustaining centres of rust fungi, Mexico, Morako, Libya, Syria, Turky, Romania, India.

Figure 7.14 Global Highways, depicting long distance dispersal (Ldd).

Table 7.1 Some Ldd Routes Along with the Source and Target Area

Disease and Pathogen	Source	Target Area
Puccinia pathway USA	Mexico	North USA and Canada
Puccinia pathway India	Nilgiri-Palni hills	Indo-Gangetic plains
Trans-Atlantic spread		
Sugarcane rust (*P. melancocephela*)	West Africa	West Indies
Sugarcane smut (*U. Scitaminea*)	West Africa	West Indies
Sigatoka of banana	West Africa	West Indies
Coffee rust (*Hemelis vastatris*)	Angola	Brazil
Wheat stem rust (*P. graminis tritici*)	Queens Land	S-W Australia
Wheat leaf rust (*P. striformis*)	Australia	New Zealand
European Tracks of Rust Movement		
East European arm	Turkey-Romania	Scandinavian Countries
West European arm	Morocco-Libya	Scandinavian Countries

Ldd may help in defining the global movement of plant pathogens, e.g. sugarcane rust pathogen, *Puccinia melancocephela*, has been recorded in Kenya (1941), Madagascar (1962), Reunion Island (1965) and Australia (1978).

The appearance of pathogen in successive years in above places indicate possible route taken by pathogen. Migration of new virulence(s) of yellow rust pathogen, *Puccinia striformis,* was recorded in different locations at different times:

(a) Turkey (1967), Lebanon (1968), Iran (1969), Indo-Pak (1970) and Nepal-Burma (1971).

(b) Syria (1991), Iran (1992), Afghanistan (1993) and Pakistan (1994), India and Nepal.

These facts do suggest a path followed by the pathogen as it reaches far distant places. This information can be effectively utilized in developing strategy for management of wheat rust in India or at global level. Computer based mathematical models (backward trajectory analysis and branching trajectory analysis) can be used to trace the point source of inoculum (origin of epidemic).

7.6.2 Water Dispersal of Spores

Water, besides wind, is the second important factor for dispersal of plant pathogens. Rain showers, trickling drops from infected leaves and twigs, splashes, irrigation and flood water are some of the ways water helps in dispersal of inoculum. The water droplets (>2.5 mm diameter) when allowed to fall from a height of 7.4 m produce about 5000 reflected droplets and thrown up to 100 cm, majority carrying spores . Under natural conditions the drops of heavy showers and dripping from foliage or twigs are effective in splashing of spores from infected host surface. Splash dispersal is essentially a short-range yet very effective method within the plant canopy. The combination of splash with strong wind may spread pathogens over considerable distances, e.g. Papaya fruit rot; *Phytophthora palmivora* and Coffee berry disease *Colletotrichum coffeanum.*

7.7 MODELLING IN PLANT PATHOLOGY

The use of mathematical models in science is probably a search for underlying general principles, so that they can be explained in language of numbers and used for quantitative estimations. The models are important and integral part of science, whether physical or biological, as they have become valuable tools applied for benefit of humanity. Model is not a miniature of some real system. Models are simple representation of otherwise more complex real systems. The models provide opportunity for better understanding and system management. Kranz (1974) stated that a model might be a verbal statement, a hypothesis, a theory or a law. Modelling in Plant Pathology started with pioneering synthesis of Vanderplank (1963) and aerobiology of Gregory (1961). The selection of a suitable model is determined by the purpose and goals which must be defined very precisely. Four types of models have been described in Plant Pathology.

7.7.1 Conceptual Models

The conceptual models were conceived during initial stages of introduction of models in Plant Pathology. They were basically qualitative, without much quantification. The relationships and interactions were displayed in diagrammatic form of flowchart manner. The famous disease pyramid (Figure 7.1) and components of pathogenesis (Figure 3.1) or system approach (Figure 7.15) are good examples of conceptual models. These also included hypothesis or statements about basic features of disease development (gene for gene hypothesis).

7.7.2   Analytical Models

Vanderplank (1963) used differential equations for calculation of pathogen population growth. Equations for single and multiple cycle diseases, threshold theorem and fitting curves to empirical data are common analytical models used in Plant Pathology. Polynomial expressions became valuable tools. Best choice is always the simplest function that gives the best fit to the observed facts (data). Following are few other analytical models studied by various workers include biological control of cereal rust (1980), competition among sensitive and insensitive races of pathogen to fungicide (1982), development of fungicide insensitivity (1983) and relative fitness in plant pathogens (1983).

7.7.3   Predictive Model

These are generally used for estimation of yields and forecasting diseases. Regression and differential equations are generally employed. The value of predictive model is judged by their efficiency of predicting correctly. These are considered a boon to growers for bringing precision in management decisions. Validity and reliability tests are vital particularly for models related with disease forecasting. Several models have established their credibility, e.g. PHYTOPROG in West Germany (Ullrich and Schrober, 1967) and BLITECAST in USA (Krause, et al., 1975) in giving short-term warnings of potato late blight attacks. FAST is the computer model for forecasting early blight and schedulling fungicide applications in tomato (Madden, et al., 1978).

7.7.4   Simulation Models

These models try to simulate or mimic the real life situations under study. Description of system or a part of it representing the underlying mechanism of natural process like disease or epidemic was started in Plant Pathology during mid 20th century. Waggoner and Hosfall, in 1969, developed first simulator EPIDEM: Alternaria blight of potato and tomato during late sixties. Examples of other simulators are:

EPIMAY: Southerncorn leaf blight of maize,
EPIVEN: Apple scab,
CERCOS: Cercospora blight of celery,
MYCOS: Mycospherella blight of chrysanthemum,
EPICORN: Southern corn leaf blight of maize,
EPIVIT: For contact and aphid transmitted virsus of potato,
EPIPRE: Cerial rusts and aphids.

Fry, et al. (1983) modified and evaluated BLITECAST by incorporating host resistance and fungicide weathering. EPIPRE (Zadoks, 1981 and 1984) is most successfully used in Europe for management of cereal rusts and aphids. Several workers have studied root knot nematode population dynamics, the host damage and management. Interest was also shown in coupling of plant disease models with crop models that provide estimates of crop yield (biomass). In management sense, the simulation model allows great experimentation and understanding of the interactive biology of plant-pest system. They allow the manipulation of alternate strategies through probability and risk associated with specific management decision.

Gutierrez, et al. (1983) proposed cotton-Verticillium wilt model that provides an example of coupling of crop and disease model. The model predicts cotton yields (biomass) for different inoculum densities of pathogen *V. dahliae*. Pest and diseases affect both sides of source/sink ratio in plants. Organisms that cause premature abscission of fruits/balls (sink) affect demand side, while those that cause leaf damage and decreased photosynthesis affect source side. Verticillium wilt of cotton comes in second category.

7.8 SYSTEM APPROACH IN PLANT PATHOLOGY

Agriculture is a man made activity, which operates under unnatural, short-term and frequently disturbed agro-ecosystem. Agriculture production requires the management of biological systems, which involve plants, animals (the residues), soil microbes, insects and pathogens. Agro-ecosystem is a complex system, which needs careful analysis and management of resources for optimization of sustainable farm income. System analysis earlier known as operation research has its origin in the areas known for their problem solving abilities, viz. industrial engineering, economics and business management. *A system is a set of components coordinated to accomplish a set of goals*. The system approach can be very conveniently applied in areas of crop health management. System analysis in Plant Pathology has emerged as a sub-discipline of epidemiology where plant disease management is the goal to be achieved through system approach.

7.8.1 Steps Involved in System Approach

Churchman (1968) established five steps in system approach, which can also be utilized for plant disease management. Figure 7.15 outlines the stepwise process of system development, evaluation and optimization.

System objectives. This is initial but very vital step in system approach. The system objectives and measures of performance are to be set by worker(s) before starting the task. The objectives must be clearly defined; for example, control/eradication/management may be the options to be achieved. The objectives should be obtainable within limits of the system resources. The management of disease at sub-economic level should be a reasonable long-term objective.

System design. It involves the detailed description of the problem, including the important factors that influence the system or ultimate output, i.e. the crop yield. The problem, to be solved, must be described in logical and structured manner. The system design may desire the breakup of complex system into sub-systems, components or elements as per the need of the situation. It will involve the study of relationships (cause-effects) among the factors influencing the system and their quantification, if possible.

System model. The system model is the product of system analysis. Once developed, system model is a good tool for experimentation for various presumed situations.

System evaluation. The evaluation of system model is done in accordance with the set objectives and the measures of performance. The system evaluation has to be a continuous process, where feedback based modifications are made. The best evaluation is the one performed by the end user (the growers/community) under their prevailing conditions.

System management. System model, after proper evaluation and validation, becomes a useful tool for growers and further experimentation. It can be conveniently used to compare alternative management strategies or optimization of the system for achieving the modified goals. Plant disease management program is the end product of system analysis, but it may not be the end of the approach. The system analysis has to be an ongoing program, particularly for agriculture production system, considering the frequently changing situation of resources and technology. Plant disease should only be taken as outcome of natural interaction between host-pathogen-environment. It is to be thought, discussed and treated as a system (system thinking) and not as a 'social evil'.

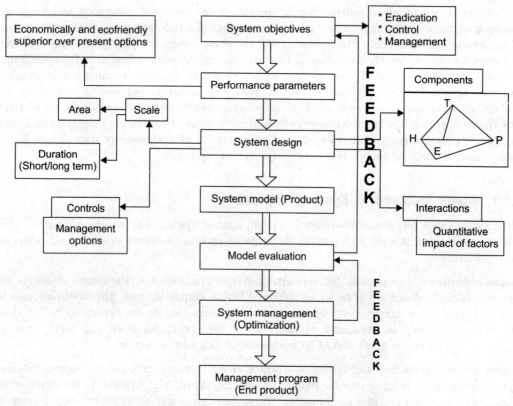

Figure 7.15 Steps involved in system management.

7.9 EXPERT SYSTEMS IN PLANT PATHOLOGY

Expert systems (Es) are the frontiers, which combines and integrate both science of plant pathology and art of diagnosis and disease management. These computer decision support systems were formally introduced in Plant Pathology in 1987. Es are computer programs that emulate the logic and problem solving proficiency of human expert. The computerized disease forecasting systems of 1970s (BLITECAST) and 1980s (*apple scab forecaster*) were the precursors to expert systems. In principle the Es are an artificial intelligence application that uses encoded knowledge from a human expert. Es has the ability to use complete or incomplete data; accordingly it will assign certainty values to the solutions of the problems. The Es are programmed to review a consultation and provide user with an explanation. Three main areas involved in decision-making are pest risk estimation, current threat assessment and pesticide selection. Future development of Es will require more interactive role of experts (pathologists, entomologist, and computer programmers) and growers. Es provide site-specific recommendations for judicious resource utilization for optimum production with least disruption of environment. It will help to satisfy the IPM objectives. Es have decentralized the maiden computer aided grower service (BLITECAST).

7.9.1 Expert System Being Used in Plant Pathology

PLANT/ds. First Es developed (1983) for diagnosis of 17 soyabean diseases (USA)

POMME. Developed to manage diseases and insects on apples. First Es to incorporate decision-making process.

PSACO. Pennstate apple orchard consultant developed for 8 diseases, 17 insects. Es takes into consideration biological, chemical and cultural control options.

POTATOES. Es for late and early blights of potato.

TOMEX. It uses 78 questions, 87 photographs, for diagnosis of 37 diseases of tomato.

Grenmen. This is used for green house disease management.

PRO-PLANT. Es for cereals, potato, sugar beet and vegetables.

More crop. Managerial options for reasonable economical control of rusts and other problems.

EPIPRE. Epidemic Prediction and Prevention (1992) spring and winter wheat.

> Es for diagnosis of potato diseases, Boyd, D.W. and Sun, M.K. (1994)
> EXSYS: Es for flower-bulb diseases, Kramers, M.A., et al. (1997)
> DESSAC: Integrated approach to DSS for Arable Crops, Brooks (1998)
> TomEx-UFV: Es for diagnosis of tomato diseases, Pozza, et al. (1998)
> SIMPHYT III: Es for *P. infestans*, Gutsce, et al. (1999)
> ES for cotton production system, Bie-Shu, et al. (2001)
> DSS for precision agriculture, Chen Li Ping, et al. (2002)

7.10 SANITATION: A PROFITABLE PRACTICE

Adoption of sanitary practices, clean cultivation, was an age-old practice that aimed at reducing inoculum. Vanderplank treated *sanitation as principle* and included all practices that reduce or tend to reduce initial inoculum. He included seed certification and treatment (seed borne inoculum), rouging, prophylactic fungicide spray (air borne inoculum), cultural and chemical methods (soil borne inoculum) and vertical resistance under sanitation. Sanitation is 'buying time', the time taken by pathogen, in plot with sanitation, to multiply up to the level in plots without sanitation (Figure 17.16). Vanderplank developed following mathematical formula for calculating benefit from sanitation (advantage time Δt).

$$\Delta t = \frac{2.3}{r} \log_{10} \frac{x_0}{x_{0s}} \qquad \Delta t \propto \log_{10} \frac{x_0}{x_{0s}}$$

Advantage time (Δt) is proportional to log of sanitation ratio $\left(\dfrac{x_0}{x_{0s}} \right)$

80% sanitation (SR = 5) will give Δt, = 8 days (if r = 20% or 0.2 units/day).

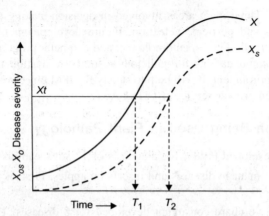

Figure. 7.16   Sanitation and its benefits. The DPC (bold line) for field without sanitation (x_0——x) and DPC (dotted line) for field with sanitation (x_0s — x_s). The same level of disease (xt) is reached at time T_1 in field without sanitation and at time T_2 in field with sanitation. Advantage time (Δt) will be $T_2 - T_1$.

The 90% sanitation gives $\Delta t = 5$ days, 99% sanitation gives $\Delta t = 10$ days while 99.9% sanitation gives $\Delta t = 15$ days. This shows that increasing sanitation by a factor of 10, the increase in Δt is only 5 days. Thus, the law of diminishing returns applies. For better returns the sanitation should be quick and practicable at field level. Efforts to eradicate last traces of pathogen/disease may not yield desired benefits.

Sanitation will be more effective under the following conditions:

- For single cycle disease where secondary infection does not take place, any reduction in amount of initial inoculum will be proportional to reduction in amount of final disease, during log phase.
- In situations where the rate of infection is low, as advantage time is inversely proportional to rate of infection, (halving the r will double the Δt).
- In situations where the duration of disease development is short. For long duration diseases the benefits of sanitation are gradually lost.
- In case of seasonal or annual crops rather than perennials.

Although difficult to demonstrate, the usefulness of sanitation is undisputed. Sanitation can be more effective if supported by reduction in rate of infection. Robinson (1971) discussed situations where vertical resistance would be more useful.

One of the most ambitious sanitation based programmes was barberry eradication in USA. Gigantic human efforts were made to eradicate the barberry bushes where wheat rust fungus, *Puccinia graminis tritici*, was known to survive and breed. The aim was to control wheat rust. It was a logical thinking in two ways: (a) to reduce the chances of survival of pathogen and (b) not providing fungus the opportunity for sexual reproduction, thus reducing chances of development of new strains (races) that pose a constant threat to resistance breeding programme. But the practical limitations in implementation of 'novel thought' put a big question mark on utility and financial justifications of the whole effort. A similar case can be traced from citrus canker eradication programme in USA and later in Australia, which also met the same fate.

7.11 GENETICS OF EPIDEMICS

Day, P.R. (1974), probably for the first time, used the phrase *genetics of epidemics* in his book Genetics of Host Pathogen Interaction. What does this mean? Are epidemics *living systems*? Yes, if not, epidemics are akin to living systems. Plant disease is the outcome of interaction of two living populations (host plant and pathogen), Loegering (1966) recognized plant disease as *aegricorpus*, third organism, a living entity, greater than sum of its components (host and parasite). Basically an epidemic is born when the environment tilts the balance of host-pathogen interaction significantly in favour of pathogen/disease. Further course of epidemic depends on nineteen variables and 361 possible interactions going on continuously and changing over time (Day, 1974). We will see how genetic factors related with host and pathogens influence the onset and progress of epidemic in Chapter 14.

7.12 MAN AND EPIDEMICS

Agriculture is a man made activity where the natural vegetation was gradually replaced by 'cropping systems' for specific needs. The agricultural practices, viz. tillage, sowing, irrigation, fertilizers, weeding, plant protection measures and harvesting, were bound to disturb the delicate ecological balance. The prolonged interference in natural ecosystem led to the development of agro-ecosystem where the disease became more pronounced and epidemics more frequent. Cowling (1978) identified the following areas of human interference that ultimately encouraged plant diseases/epidemics.

Narrowing down the biodiversity. Man knows more than 3000 species of edible plants but human population of more than 6 billions is dependent on only 15 plant species for their Food. In America five varieties of beans and two varieties of peas cover about 93 and 96% area under cultivation, respectively. In Australia two varieties of peanut occupy 99% of peanut growing area (Day, 1974). This type of genetic uniformity makes crop plants more vulnerable to pathogens.

Breeding procedures. Over dependence of breeders on vertical resistance for development of crop varieties has led to frequent destabilization of host pathogen equilibrium. P.R. Day (1974) termed them as **man made epidemics**. More details are discussed in 'Genetics of Epidemics' in Chapter 14.

International trade and exchange of planting material. It has profound impact on global disease situation. The plant pathogens are known to move with planning material/packing material of plant origin crossing political and geographical boundaries. Human interference and modified cultivation practices have modified the macro and microclimate that has favoured the pathogen. Yarwood (1959) described predisposition as *environmentally conditioned susceptibility* or non-genetic conditions acting before infection to affect the susceptibility of plant to disease. Following practices tend to encourage disease development either by predisposing plants and/or favouring pathogen:

1. Modified tillage practices may help in survival/distribution of inoculum.
2. Time and method of planting may selectively favour pathogen/disease.
3. Time/method of harvesting/threshing may affect dispersal/survival.
4. Amount and type of fertilizer applied may influence host response.
5. Amount and type of irrigation used may help in infection and dispersal.

6. Pruning or wounding of fruit trees may expose cut tissues to infections.

7. Cropping patterns, in time (crop sequence and rotation) and space (host population dynamics), have profound effect on behaviour of pathogens.

8. Off-season cultivation has changed the scenario in terms of quantity and quality of pests (summer paddy, off-season vegetables, etc.).

9. Non-judicious use of biocides kills all microbes including beneficial ones while selective biocides will create ecological voids.

Ultimately the crop plants, the microbes and human beings are all components of the ecosystem. We should learn to live together and work for optimizing the system with minimum conflict and competition. Human interference or modified cultural practices have resulted in unintended loss to plant community. Following may be some of the reasons for such human behaviour:

1. Lack of communication between technology developer and technology users the growers may not know the full information about 'new technology', particularly the undesirable side effects.

2. Market demand for 'specific' product (value added product) might motivate growers to take up new ventures with non-scientific and undesirable practices (summer paddy in rice-wheat growing area of north India).

3. Conflicts between short-term and long-term objectives might have not been judiciously settled by scientists and governments to the conviction of the growers and the communities.

Epidemics follow a predicted course and our understanding about the process can make management strategy more effective, economic and eco-friendly.

7.13 EPIDEMIOLOGY AND PLANT DISEASE MANAGEMENT

Chemical industry and plant breeders develop the 'weapons' but the epidemiologists set the strategy.

— Vanderplank, 1963

Methods of plant disease control were developed even before true nature of plant disease was understood. During early stages, 19th and early 20th century, the methods of plant disease control were more a wishful thinking of plant pathologists. Epidemiological studies generate lot of information on different aspects of disease development. This processed data (knowledge) helps in developing appropriate technology for plant disease management. The technology based on epidemiological principles is logical as they are based on facts. The following points do suggest that epidemiology may make plant disease management biologically and economically justified and environmentally safe:

1. The monocyclic diseases (loose smut of wheat and wilts) and polycyclic diseases (rusts, powdery mildews, downy mildews and late blight of potato) should be given different treatment.

2. The information about source of primary inoculum and amount is vital as it can help us in forecasting disease and proper methods can be employed for disease management:

Diseases	Source of Inoculum	Methods Employed
Loose smut of wheat	Internally seed borne	Seed treatment—hot water or systemic fungicides
Wilts, root rots and nematode problem	Soil	Suitable crop rotations and cultural practices
Apple scab	Perithecia on fallen leaves	Destroy the infected leaves from orchard floor, prophylactic spray
Potato viruses	Tuber borne	Pathogen free certified seed
Wheat rust	Air borne	Prophylactic spray/HR
Post harvest decay of fruits and vegetables	Fruit surface	Treatment before transportation or storage

3. Information about potential for variability in pathogen population can help in adopting suitable breeding strategies, e.g. management of late blight of potato or wheat rust, with high chances of new races, should emphasize on development of horizontal resistance.

4. The economic threshold levels, once established, may justify the actions to be taken for disease management.

5. Field management of a disease on resistant crop cultivars will require much less fungicide use as compared to susceptible cultivars.

6. The behaviour of vector populations can be effectively utilized to control plant diseases. This has been demonstrated in case of potato viruses and Stewart's corn wilt).

8. Diseases forecasting can help in adopting the appropriate measures, which can help in reducing pesticides use without risking crop health.

9. Fungicides should be used judiciously for plant disease management. Contact fungicides (manocozeb, copper oxychloride, sulfur dust, etc.) are effective only as prophylactic. The systemic fungicides (metalaxyl, bavistin, tilt etc.) can be used for eradicative and curative action.

10. All possible information about pathogen and disease should be used for developing IPM schedule keeping local conditions in mind.

7.13.1 Use of $X = X_0 e^{rt}$ for Plant Disease Management

Above equation proposed by Vanderplank (1963), for polycyclic diseases, could be used for disease management. This reveals that final amount of disease X depends on (a) amount of initial inoculum (X_0), (b) rate of disease development (r) and (c) duration of disease development (t). Suitable manipulation that can bring any reduction in any one or more of the above three factors will reduce the final disease severity (X).

***Reducing amount of initial inoculum* (X_0).** The practices discussed under sanitation, viz. seed certification, rouging, burning of crop debris and other cultural and chemical methods are popular among the growers. Nurserymen are practicing sanitation. Use of disease/pathogen free seed/ planting material, treating them suitably, changing the beds for raising seedlings and use of polythene as mulch for *soil solarization* is becoming popular as it overall improves the growth and vigour of seedlings.

Reducing rate of infection (r). Repeated sprays of fungicides, horizontal resistance and environment turning unfavourable can slow down the progress of disease, i.e. reduction in infection rate.

Reducing duration of disease development (t). In multiple cycle diseases the duration of disease determines the number of repeating or infection cycles completed by the pathogen. Manipulating time of planting or harvesting, duration of crop maturity and rate of seedling growth can bring about significant reduction in disease severity.

REFERENCES

Agrios, G., 1997, *Plant Pathology*, 4th edn., Academic Press, New York.

Amita, 1999, Epidemiological studies on *Alternaria* blight of Mustard, *Ph.D. Thesis,* p. 79.

Anonymous, 1983, Symposium on estimating yield reduction of manor food crops of the world, [Several papers] *Phytopathology,* 73:1575.

Anonymous, 1995, Epidemiology, crop loss assessment, phytopathometry, A collection of papers, *Can. J. Plant Pathol,* 17:95.

Baker, R., 1971, Analyses involving inoculum density of soil-borne plant pathogen in epidemiology, *Phytopathology,* 61:1280.

Berger, R.D., 1977, Application of epidemiological principles to achieve plant disease control, *Annu. Rev. Phytopathol.,* 15, 165–183.

Bie-Shu, et al., 2001, Cotton production management expert system and its effect in application. *China Cotton,* 28:3, 2–4.

Bolkan, H.A. and Reinert, W.R., 1994, Developing and implementing IPM strategies to assist farmers: An industry approach, *Plant Dis.,* 78:545.

Boyd, D.W. and Sun, M.K., 1994, Prototyping an expert system for diagnosis of potato diseases, *Computers and Electronics in Agriculture,* 10:3, 259–267.

Brooks, D.H., 1998, Decision Support System for Arable Crops (DESSAC): an integrated approach to decision support, In: *Proceeding of an International Conference,* Brighton, UK, vol-1, 16–19, November 1998, 239–246.

Campbell, C.L. and Madeen, L.V., 1990, *Introduction to Plant Disease Epidemiology,* Wiley, New York.

Carefoot, G.L. and Sprott, E.R., 1967, *Famine on the Wind,* Rand McNally, Chicago, Illinois.

Chen Li Ping, et al., 2002, Design and implementation of intelligent decision support system for precision agriculture, *Transactions of the Chinese Society of Agricultural Engineering,* 18:2, 145–148.

Coakley, S.M., 1988, Variation in climate and prediction of disease in plants, *Annu. Rev. Phytopathology,* 26:163.

Day, P.R., 1974, *Genetics of Host Parasite Interaction,* Freeman, San Francisco, California.

Fitt, B.D.L., McCartney, H.A. and Walklate, P.J., 1989, The role of rain in dispersal of pathogen inoculum, *Annu. Review of Phytopathology,* 127:241.

Fry, W.E., Apple, A.E. and Bruhn J.A., 1983, Evaluation of potato late blight forecasts modified to incorporate host resistance and fungicide weathering, *Phytopathology*, 73(7), 1054–1059.

Fry, W.E., Goodwin, S.B. and Dyer, A.T., 1993, Historical and recent migrations of *Phytophthora infestans* Chronology, pathways and implications, *Plant Disease*, 77:653.

Garrett, S.D., 1956, *Biology of Root Infecting Fungi*, Cambridge Univ. Press, London.

Gaunt, R.E., 1995. The relationship between plant disease severity and yield, *Annu. Rev. Phytopathology*, 33:119.

Gutsche, V., et al., 1999, Phytophthora-prognosis with SIMPHYT III. Kartoffelbau, 50:4,128–135.

Horsfall, J.G. and Cowling, E.B., (Eds.), 1977–1980, *Plant Disease*, vols. 1-5, Academic Press, New York.

Kramers, M.A., et al., 1997, EXSYS, an expert system for diagnosing flower bulbs diseases, *Acta Horticulturae,* II: 430, 651–656.

Kranz, J., 1974, Comparison of epidemics, *Annu. Rev. Phytopathology*, 12:355.

Kranz, J. and Schein, R.D., 1979, *Epidemiology and Plant Disease Management,* Oxford University Press, Oxford.

Krause, R.A., Massie, L.B., and Hyre, R.A., 1975, BLITECAST, a computerized forecast of potato late blight, *Plant Dis. Rep.*, 59:95.

Leonard, K.M. and Fry, W.E. (Eds.), 1986, *Plant Disease Epidemiology,* vol. 1: *Population Dynamics and Management*, Macmillan, New York.

Loegering, W.Q., 1966, The relationship between host and pathogen in stem rust of wheat, *Hereditas, suppl.*, 2, 167–177.

Lucas, J.A., 1998, *Plant Pathology and Plant Pathogen*, Blackwell Science, Oxford.

Meredith, D.S., 1973, Significance of spore release and dispersal mechanisms in plant disease epidemiology, *Annu. Rev. Phytopathology,* 11:313.

Nagarajan, S. and Singh, S.V., 1990, Long distance dispersal of rust pathogens, *Annu. Rev. Phytopathology*, 28:137.

Nilsson, H.E., 1995, Remote sensing and image analysis in plant pathology, *Annu. Rev. Phytopathology*, 33:489.

Padmanabhan, S.Y., 1973, The great Bengal famine, *Annu. Rev. Phytopathology*, 11, 11–26.

Pozza, E.A., et al., 1998, Development and evaluation of an expert system for diagnosis of tomato diseases, In: *7th International Conference on Computers in Agriculture*, Orlando, Florida, USA, 26–30, October 1998, 431–437.

Rotem, 1978, In: *Plant Disease–An Advanced Treatise* (Ed.) Horsfall and Cowling, vol. II, p. 317.

Scott, P.R. and Bainbridge, A., (Eds.), 1978, *Plant Disease Epidemiology*, Blackwell, Oxford.

Sharma, J., 1996, Studies on dispersal of *Alternaria* sp. in rapeseed mustard crop, *M.Sc. Thesis*, p. 67.

Somasekhar, N., 1999, CropCare-X1.0, a model expert system for the diagnosis and management of crop pests and diseases, *Pest Management in Horticultural Ecosystems*, 5:1, 54–56.

Tarr, S.A.J., 1972, *The Principles of Plant Pathology*, Winchester Press, New York.

Trapero, A. Casas and Kaiser, W.J., 1992, Influence of temperature, wetness period, plant age and inoculum concentration on infection and development of Ascochyta Blight of Chickpea, *Phytopathology,* 82(5): 589–96.

Travis, J.W. and Latin, R.X., 1991, Development, implementation and adoption of expert systems in plant pathology, *Annu. Rev. Phytopathology,* 29:343.

Vanderplank, J.E., 1963, *Plant Disease: Epidemics and Control,* Academic Press, New York.

——, **1975,** *Principles of Plant Infections,* Academic Press, New York.

Vloutoglou, I., Fitt, B.D. and Lucas, J.A., 1995, Periodicity and gradients in dispersal of *Alternaria linicola* in linseed crops, *European Journal of Plant Pathology,* 101, 639–653.

Waggoner, P.E., Horsfall, J.G. and Lukens, R.J., 1972, EPIMAY, A simulator of southern corn leaf blight, *Conn. Agric. Exp. Stn.,* New Havon, *Bull.,* 729.

Zadoks, J.C., 1984, A quarter century of disease warning, *Plant Dis.* 68, 352–355.

Zadoks, J.C. and Schein, R.D., 1979, *Epidemiology and Plant Disease Management,* Oxford University, Press, Oxford and New York.

8 Disease Measurement and Forecasting

How can we expect practical men to be properly impressed with importance of our work and to vote large sums of money for its support when in place of facts we have only vogue guesses to give and we do not take the trouble to take careful estimates?

—Yaman, G.R., 1914

8.1 DISEASE MEASUREMENT

Plant pathology is all about plant diseases and their effects on plants, men and environment. The plant disease measurement and its impact on crop yield are the crucial areas ignored by plant pathologists for long. Almost a century later the statement of Yaman (1914) seems very timely, even today. In present era of commercial agriculture the estimation of yield losses, due to pests and pathogens, have acquired special significance as they directly or indirectly influence the crop economy. Chester (1959) identified *amount of disease and crop losses as important components of crop economy*. Prediction of crop yield or quality of produce can be useful to growers as well as society in more than one-way. The general work of plan on measurement and yield loss estimation should include the following stages (Large, 1966):

1. The workers should have precise information on normal morphology of crop plants, at growth stages and in different seasons.
2. The workers should know the characteristic symptoms of disease at different stages (syndrome).
3. The disease development should be followed for few years in the area, for drawing general and valid conclusions.
4. All minor details about the crop husbandry, agro-climatic zone and precise weather data during the season should be recorded.

E.C. Lagre (1953) introduced the term *pathometry* or *phyto-pathometry* for disease assessment and/ or disease measurement, which has gained the status of a sub-discipline of plant pathology. Pathometry includes *disease measurement, yield loss estimation, forecasting of plant disease and predicting their impact*. All these activities, closely interlinked, provide vital information to growers, researchers and administration. Mayee and Datar (1986) defined pathometry as *the quantitative study of suffering plant, that involves both qualitative as well as quantitative measurement of plant disease*. Large (1966) published review article on pathometry.

171

8.1.1 The Objectives of Disease Measurement

The information on disease measurement may be important to scientists and growers both as it provides logical and reliable basis for taking the precise decisions in the following areas:

- Development of epidemics in time and space.
- Analyzing the factors that affect disease development.
- Evaluation of control measures, fungicides and host resistance, can be performed only with suitable methods for disease assessment.
- The scientists and administrators can prioritize the allocations of time and money for various problems.
- Growers can take judicious decisions for crop protection by using information on diseases, yield loss and threshold levels.

8.1.2 Disease Parameters

Three parameters have been used for assessments or measurement of plant diseases. Disease incidence or prevalence and disease severity are direct measures of disease while crop yield loss has been used as indirect measure of plant diseases. In addition, amount of initial inoculum may also predict amount of disease, indirectly.

Disease incidence. It is the measure of proportion of plant population diseased at a time and a place. Numbers of infected plants (whole plant) or plant parts (leaves, twigs, stems, fruits, flowers, roots) that are infected are counted and disease incidence is expressed as percent of infected plants in a sample or population. It is a qualitative measure of disease; counting a plant is diseased or not, irrespective of amount of disease. The term *disease prevalence* tells about occurrence of disease on large geographical area, e.g. Barley yellow dwarf virus, which was prevalent in cereal crops throughout UK during 1990s, due to survival of large population of virus carrying aphid vectors through mild winters. Bacterial wilt is prevalent in Kumaon hills and late blight of potato was prevalent in European countries during 19th century. Prevalence is synonym for incidence and used by surveyors and scouts. Chiarappa (1971) and Kranz (1974) introduced the term *frequency* for disease incidence. It has not been popular with plant pathologists. Smuts, wilts, fruit rots are some of the diseases generally expressed as incidence. Disease incidence can be equated to yield loss if 'unit' is completely lost/damaged. Disease incidence (%) can be calculated using following formula:

$$\text{Disease incidence} = \frac{\text{No. of diseased plants} \times 100}{\text{Total no. of plants examined}}$$

Disease severity. It is the measure of sickness of diseased plant. It is a quantitative trait, which measures amount of disease on a plant in terms of intensity of symptoms or damage. Not all plant diseases are simple to measure. Various disease assessment keys have been developed and standardized to ensure uniform measurement at different time and place by various workers. Disease severity (DS) can be calculated by using the formula:

$$\text{Disease severity} = \frac{\text{Area of plant tissue affected}}{\text{Total area}} \times 100$$

Disease index. Chiarappa 1971 equated *disease index* (DI) with total disease having two components, i.e. disease incidence and disease severity. The term disease intensity has also been used in literature as parameter for measuring amount of disease (Horsfall and Cowling, 1978 and Chiarappa, 1971). Mckinney (1923) defined *numerical rating* as severity of disease to visual quantitative estimates. Depending upon the type of disease (symptoms) several other keys have been developed.

$$DI = \frac{0(X_0) + 1(X_1) + 2(X_2) + \cdots + n(X_n)}{X_0 + X_1 + X_2 + \cdots + X_n \text{ (maximum grade)}} \times 100$$

X represents no. of entries within a grade/class and $0–n$ are grades or classes of disease, as per disease rating scale.

8.1.3 Methods for Disease Assessment

Accurate disease assessment allows comparison of disease situations in different experiments/treatments conducted at different times and locations.

Descriptive keys. The descriptive keys are prepared by describing the characteristic symptoms of disease or amount of disease along with description. Late blight of potato assessment key was developed by British Mycology Society (1945) and is still being used by scientists world over (Table 8.1). Intensity of symptoms is only an indicator of host pathogen interaction; sometimes it may be misleading, as certain amount of disturbance/damage to plant may not be expressed. The viral diseases are known to cause relatively more yield loss than the severity of visual symptoms noticed.

Table 8.1 Key for the Assessment of Potato Late Blight caused by *P. infestans*

Blight (%)	Description
0	Not seen on field.
0.1	Only few plants affected here and there; up to 1 or 2 spots in 12 yards' radius.
1	Up to 10 spot per plant, or general light spotting.
5	About 50 sports per plant or up to 1 leaflet in 10 attacked.
25	Nearly every leaflet with lesions, plants still retaining normal form; field may smell of blight but looks green, although every plant is affected.
50	Every plant affected and about ½ of leaf area destroyed by blight; field looks green flecked with brown.
75	About 3/4th of leaf area destroyed by blight; field looks neither predominantly brown nor green.
95	Only a few leaves left green but stems green.
100	All leaves dead, stems dead or dying.

Standard area diagrams. A set of pictures (diagrams, sketches or photographs) having different amount of disease can help in measurement of disease under field conditions. The pictures of different grades are matched with the plant samples for rating disease. Cobb (1892) developed a scale for measurement of wheat rust, where rust severity is scored from 0 to 100% (actual leaf area covered by rust fungus is only 0 to 37%). The idea of Cobb's scale was used by many workers for developing scales for different diseases. Large (1966) and James (1974) reviewed the information on standard area diagrams. Figures 8.1, 8.2 and 8.3 show the disease rating scales for common scab (tubers), black scurf (tubers) and late blight (foliage) of potato for field evaluations.

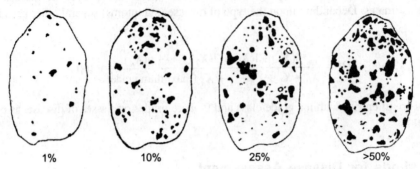

Figure 8.1 Disease assessment key for black-scurf of potato.

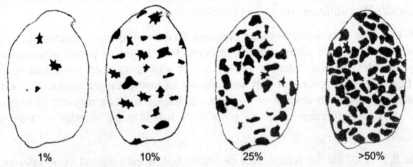

Figure 8.2 Disease assessment key for common scab of potato.

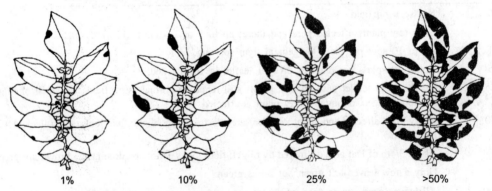

Figure 8.3 Percent leaf area covered in late blight of potato.

Eye as a sensitive visual device has its limitations and according to Weber-Fechner law *visual acuity of eye is proportional to the logarithm of the intensity of stimulus*. Capitalizing on the fact, Horsfall and Barrat (1945) developed grading system with a ratio of two. This system has grades both ways from 50%. The H-B system has been widely used by workers (James, 1974). The proposed grades are as follows:

Upgrades: 0–3%, 3–6%, 6–12%, 12–25% and 25–50%,

Downgrades: 50–75%, 75–85%, 85–94%, 94–97% and 97–100%.

Growth stage keys.   Plant growth stages have significant bearing on development of plant disease and resulting crop yield losses. Growth stage keys are required to describe the developmental stages of the crop. These are usually based on detailed phenological studies of plants and are of immense value to mention the growth stage at which disease severity/intensity is recorded.

8.1.4 Inoculum-disease Relationship

This is an indirect method of assessing plant diseases. It is presumed that surviving primary inoculum will initiate disease if susceptible host crop is planted under suitable environment. The *amount of disease will be proportional to the amount of primary inoculum* present. This is being practiced for diseases caused by nematodes and other soil borne fungi, e.g. *Rhizoctonia solani, Sclerotium rolfsii, Pythium* spp., *Fusarium* spp., etc. Modules have been devised for estimation of cereal rusts based on uredospores count in air (Eversmeyer, et al., 1973). Zadoks, (1972) justified use of inoculum as parameter for measuring plant disease.

8.1.5 Crop Yield Loss-disease Relationship

Plant diseases are important only because they reduce crop yields. Crop yield losses have been used as indirect measure of disease provided other factors are kept under watch. But yield losses give very rough or gross estimate of plant disease. These are used by surveyors or for estimations where precise values are not needed. Production and price forecasts, used by administrators and planners, are made using this relationship. Teng (1983) discussed the relationship between disease intensity and crop losses in commercial crops.

Crop yield losses: the concept.   Assessment of plant disease, diagnosis and measurement, may not interest the growers until it is converted in terms of possible yield losses. The basic requirement is to identify and establish a relationship between the cause (plant disease) and the effect (yield loss). This relationship will depend upon the nature of pathogen, the type of host-pathogen interaction and the plant part affected. During development of plant disease the parasitic and pathogenic activities interfere with normal metabolism of the host plant. Plant, as a biological system, has some flexible limits to tolerate these impairments but beyond those limits (Figure 8.4) *stress* will lead to *injury* (irreversible structural or functional disruptions at cellular or tissue level), which may cause damage (injury of significant nature that affects productivity or survival of host plant).

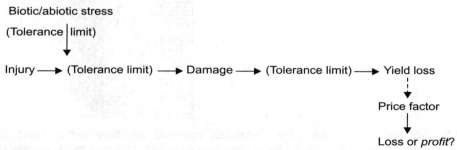

Figure 8.4 The factors affecting the crop performance.

Profit or losses are financial terms that have relative rather than absolute value. Generally, if grower gets less than the expected value for his produce from a field, he considers it as loss. More realistic approach should be to compare the crop produce/value obtained from diseased and healthy (protected) crops, grown under similar conditions. The ultimate profit or loss not only depends on quantity or quality of produce but also on market price (input/output price) which is influenced by several factors including demand-supply situation.

In certain situation, severe pest/pathogen attack may reduce the crop produce or market supply. This may lead to increase in market price and the grower may get more value (profit?) than the normal bigger harvest. Let us examine the following example (all values hypothetical):

- Disease free year: potato yield 300 Q/ha, market price @ Rs 100/Q (income Rs 30,000/ha, expenditure Rs 35,000/ ha, loss? Rs 5,000/ha)
- Epidemic year: potato yield 150 Q/ha, market price @ Rs 400/Q (income Rs 60,000/ha, expenditure Rs 35,000/ ha, profit? Rs 25,000/ha)

Amongst the strategists there may be debate, whether to go for more production or more profit?

Crop yield is the measurable produce of economic value. For any crop cultivar the yield produced under optimum conditions, without biotic and abiotic stress is *potential yield*. The quantum of crop produce that can be obtained at farmer's field, with suitable measures is *attainable yield*. Since some yield losses are unavoidable the potential yield is not attainable, generally *harvested yield* is what farmers harvest at the farm conditions. Figure 8.5 shows the crop yield levels and types of losses.

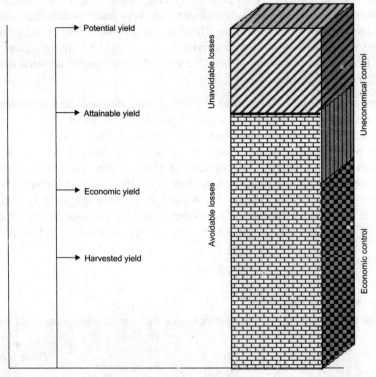

Figure 8.5 Different levels of crop yields (harvested, economic, attainable and potential). On the right side bar types of yield losses and status of plant protection measures are shown.

The gap between attainable and harvested yield can be logically partitioned in two parts; one where the application of plant protection measures is economical at the local market price. There may be some control methods to further enhance the yield, but the extra expenditure may not be economically justified. This partitioning of crop yield losses and the yield targets to be achieved is not only an academic exercise but highlights the following points:

- The growers should accept the diseases as 'natural'.
- Some yield losses are unavoidable and prevention of some is uneconomical.
- Pathologists should consider 'economics' of their recommendations.

Plant disease management combines and integrates the science of disease development and the art of disease management with crop economics. The grower must know when and what practice(s) will give him best financial returns. The study of population dynamics, under different set of conditions, coupled with economics of treatment(s) and financial returns have made it possible to determine the insect/disease levels at which the treatment cost equals the treatment benefits, this is known as **threshold level**. The population level at which the grower has to act, *action threshold* is stage just before damage threshold, defined as *lowest population density that will cause economic damage* (Figure 8.6). The *warning threshold* indicates a possibility of future danger and it precedes the action threshold to allow sometime required for preparations to apply the control measures (chemicals, machines and man power management). It may also help the plant protection trade to get better organized (inventory management, transportation and product positioning).

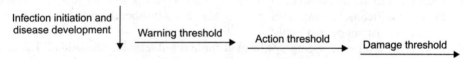

Figure 8.6 Steps involved in crop damage and its management.

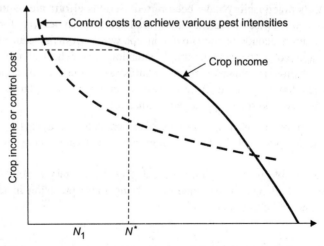

Hypothetical representation of simplified economic threshold (Carlson, 1971). Net crop income (solid line) decreases at an increasing rate as pest density N increases above some crop tolerance levels N_1. The dotted lines represents cost of control measures to achieve at different pest densities. Economic threshold N^* is pest density at which incremental costs of control just equals incremental crop returns

Application of threshold concept. Entomologists conceived the idea and have taken lead in establishing the threshold levels for various pests. This has become a component of integrated pest management programme. Plant pathologists have not been able to make significant breakthrough in this regard. The threatening population levels of some soil borne nematodes and fungi have been reported and actions suggested. Threshold concept, although a difficult proposition in practice, should be the corner stone of any integrated pest management programme.

Some recent contributions in economic threshold (ET) area are:

> Hem, et al. (1997), ET levels for sheath blight and borer to rice.
> Wang, et al. (1998), ET and forecasting of larch needle brown rust.
> Gadoury and Tensvand (1998), PAD as threshold level for apple-*V. inaequlis.*
> Forrer, et al. (1998), Intervention threshold for *Septoris triticina* in wheat.
> Jurecka, D. and Riha, K. (1999), ET values for diseases of cereals.
> Beuve, M., et al. (1999), BDY of cereals and barley.
> Brust, G.E. and Foster, R.E. (1999), ET cucumber bacterial wilt.

Zadoks (1987) discussed following difficulties in practical use of threshold concept for management of plant diseases:

1. Since the sensitivity of crop to injury varies with season or growth stage, the threshold levels must be related to time bound monitoring. EPIPRE applies shifting/dynamic thresholds depending upon developmental stage.
2. Usually under field conditions crops suffer from several pests/pathogen(s) simultaneously, though at different severity levels. In this complex situation, the threshold levels may not be easy to determine and apply.
3. Production level or cropping system will influence threshold calculations. The economic benefits may vary under different situations. This includes variable transportation, processing and storages charges.

Questions about its practicability have been raised. Serious efforts are required to find solutions to practical problems; otherwise the theory may gradually vanish leaving footprints in literature. Zadoks (1987) considered economic threshold concept worth from an educational point of view. However, it can be applied on large-scale simple situations like wheat or rice cultivation (as done in case of EPIPRE) or disease management in orchards, as in the case of apple pest management. Following advantages have emerged from threshold concept. Acceptance of idea of disease management over disease control or pathogen eradication.

- Preference for need based applications over scheduled sprayings.
- Progressive adoption of integrated approach for management of few host-pathogen systems.
- The grower is able to see an immediate expected monetary benefit of recommendations.
- It provides a challenge to the scientist to bring more precision in management tools by applying innovative methods.

8.1.6 Models for Crop Yield Loss Estimation

Depending upon the type of host-pathogen relationship, the nature of damage caused and the method of disease measurement employed, different models have been proposed to predict yield losses. Following are some of these models used in plant pathology:

Critical point model. The disease severity at a *critical point* is used to establish relation with crop yield loss. These models generally use linear regressions where disease is taken as independent variable. These models work satisfactorily for certain diseases if critical stage for disease rating can be identified, e.g. rice blast, wheat stem rust severity at growth stage 11-12 (First-second leaf unfold) and potato cyst nematode (*Globodera rotochiensis*), i.e.,

$$Y = a + bx$$

The major limitation is that the models *do not account for epidemiological factors* that contribute to the progress of disease and the process of yield reduction.

Multiple point model. This is a modified approach over first model as disease is scored at different times, during disease progress, and crop yield losses is computed as sum of disease ratings and regression coefficients. Multiple regression analysis is employed, where Y (% yield loss; dependent variable) depends upon disease increments (X_1), (X_2) and (X_n), independent variables, observed periodically:

$$Y = b_1X_1 + b_2X_2 + b_3X_3 + \dots + b_nX_n$$

Area under disease progress curve (Audpc). Disease progress curves are highly sensitive to fluctuations in epidemiological factors during disease development. The Audpc accounts for all these factors. Since the crop damage/yield loss depends upon severity as well as duration of disease. There may be situations with same Audpc but having varying amount of disease, at critical stages. The yield losses will be different. This is one of the limitations of these models.

Large, E.C. (1952) in his classical studies on late blight of potato developed a system for predicting tuber yields based on progress of disease. Studies on mean bulking curves (MBC) revealed that further tuberization stops once 75% foliage has been damaged (Figure 8.7). However, for certain other cultivars this value was reported to be 40-50%. Disease progress curve, for a location, can give information as when 75% foliage was damaged. This can be read from MBC, to foretell the expected yield or the yield losses.

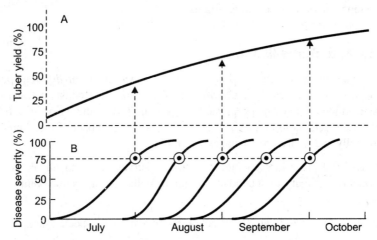

Figure 8.7 Estimation of potato yields by using mean bulking curve (A) and disease progress curves (B). It was reported that further tuberization stops if 75% foliage is damaged.

Recent approaches in crop yield estimation

1. Simulation models for crop growth and yield estimation under different disease/pest pressure have been proposed.
2. Crop yield loss was described as functions of area under disease progress curve. This has been further modified where relative area under disease progress curve multiplied by the effect of disease on bulking rate gives better explanation of yield losses. The model was tested on 53 epidemics and differences between predicted and observed losses were less than 5% in 80% of observations.

8.1.7 Monitoring of Plant Diseases

Plant diseases are dynamic systems. Fluctuations in disease situation in time and space are common observations. Thus, a close watch is required to gather information on changing status of disease. Disease monitoring is most common method employed by government agencies, pesticide industry, crop consultants/scouts. The objectives of monitoring may be:

1. Reporting of occurrence of disease by the scouts.
2. Farmer's should inspect and assess the crops for on-location decisions.
3. The data on patterns and progress of disease are valuable for planners and as well as researchers.
4. For high threat potential diseases the periodical reports/warnings from computer database are issued (late blight of potato).
5. Study of development and spread of epidemics on continental basis (late blight of potato and wheat rust) may help in planning preventive measures against potentially disastrous diseases.
6. Regular monitoring of crops is useful for detecting the following:

   • Appearance of new virulence in pathogen.
   • Development of less sensitive strains.

8.1.8 Survey and Surveillance

Survey means *to view the situation comprehensively and extensively at different periodicity* while surveillance is *vigilant supervision of a situation* (to keep close and constant watch). Plant disease surveys are basic guide to disease progress that help in fixing the priorities. It may serve as forewarning for certain actions to be taken. It also tells about the impact of the changing agricultural technology, especially plant disease management tools.

Survey procedure.   The procedure adopted for disease survey will depend on the objectives and the type of information (primary or secondary) required. Following are some common ways used for disease surveys:

Random sampling.   Area sampling stratified or purposive (only specific area or growers to be covered).

Trap nurseries.   Generally used for detecting new virulence in an area and screening of germplasm.

Mobile units. The mobile plant clinic vans go in different directions, on pre-planned routes, and collect samples at predefined distances to cover large geographic area.

Spore trapping. Spore trapping devices or spore trap nurseries give information about arrival (time and quantity) of air borne inoculum.

Vector population. It is an indirect indicator of pathogen activity and threat potential to the crop in the season. Aphid populations are monitored by the use of suction traps in Europe. This helps in developing *distribution and movement maps* of vector species. For accurate risk assessment, additional information of virus carrying status is required. This can be obtained either by feeding the trapped vectors on susceptible plants or use of molecular methods. Sensitive ELISA tests can detect the presence of virus even in single aphid (sugar beet yellows and potato leaf roll virus).

8.1.9 Remote Sensing and Its Applications

Modern technology has helped the development of all the branches of sciences and plant pathology is no exception. Detection and measurement of disease, on large areas can be done with the help of specialized equipments. Remote sensing camera uses infrared photography to differentiate patches as against uniform picture this is very useful in identifying infection foci, for late blight of potato or banana leaf spot the appearance and their further spread can be followed. Nelsson (1995) wrote an interesting review on remote sensing and image analysis. Remote sensing is a useful tool for disease surveys for plantation crops and forests due to difficult terrain. It is very convenient for crops grown on larger tracts, viz. wheat, rice, banana and other plantation crops (Hatfield, 1990). The satellite technology along with image analyzing technique of computer is proving to be boon for monitoring pest populations on global areas.

8.2 PLANT DISEASE FORECASTING

Plant diseases vary in consistency of occurrence and severity, thus epidemics are irregular feature. The growers are often faced with the dilemma: *whether to spray or to wait?* Agrios (1997) very aptly described epidemics *they resemble hurricanes.* They come, devastate and vanish. Pathologists have been successful in understanding the factors responsible for initiation, buildup and demise of epidemics. Fortunately epidemics follow a predictable course. The understanding about interactions of four elements of epidemics has been exploited for prediction of disease/epidemics. Our ability to predict diseases is an indicative of developments in science of plant pathology. Disease forecasting or warning systems are boon to the growers as it encourages judicious use (need based) of pesticides. This not only saves the money and energy of the growers, without risking crop health, but also avoids the environmental pollution.

Miller and O' Brien (1952) proposed a descriptive definition of disease forecasting that stands valid even today. They stated, *Forecasting involves all the activities in ascertaining and notifying the growers of community that conditions are sufficiently favourable for certain diseases, that application of control measures will result in economic gain or on the other hand, and just as important that the amount expected is unlikely to be enough to justify the expenditure of time, energy and money for control.* The above statement made explicit distinction between *positive forecast* and *negative forecast* and both have value for growers as well as society in general.

Positive forecast. Employs need based chemical sprays, provides adequate protection to crop and reduces damage to environment.

Negative forecast. Avoids unnecessary chemical sprays, no risk to the crop health and no disruption of environment.

8.2.1 Pre-requisites for Developing a Forecast System

Disease forecasting is a complicated, expensive and risky venture as several biotic and abiotic factors influence appearance and development of plant disease. The advancements in science and technology have made *Disease warning system* a working proposition, it requires lot of expenditure in terms of time, money and technical personnel Following points should be considered before starting a project on disease forecasting:

1. The crop must be a cash crop (economic value).
2. The disease must have potential to cause damage (yield losses).
3. The disease should not be a regular feature (uncertainty).
4. Effective and economic control known (options to growers).
5. Reliable means of communication with farmers.
6. Farmer should be adaptive and have purchase power.

8.2.2 Disease Forecasting Systems

Based on the method of development of forecasting system the models may be of two types: *Empirical models* are usually based on experience of growers, the scientists or both. Dutch rules (Van Everdingen, 1926) were developed for late blight forecast based on experience. *Fundamental models* involve research and experimentation for establishing fruitful relationships, identifying critical factor(s) and relating them with appearance (time and amount) of disease. An empirical model can be further refined or modified by experimentation. Forecasting systems may aim on two aspects: *Infection forecasting* which is prediction of initial appearance of disease. It is generally based on amount of primary inoculum and prevailing environmental conditions. In *disease forecasting,* the emphasis is on further development of disease. Amount of secondary inoculum and number of infection cycles are important.

The appearance and buildup of plant disease epidemic depends on suitable crop growth stage (canopy: microclimate) and the establishment of pathogen in the crop. This combination determines the *zero date* before which disease outbreaks are rare or of little significance, and therefore, warrants no control measures. Royle (1993) discussed approaches towards understanding and predicting epidemics by selecting four fungal pathosystems.

8.2.3 Criterion Used for Disease Forecasting

Every plant disease is a unique story and interactions of four variable elements make every situation a case. First disease forecasting system in plant pathology was developed for vine downy mildew (*Plasmopara viticola*) in 1913 (*Muller's incubation calendar*, Germany). For prediction of plant diseases the criteria used are related with survival of inoculum, production and dispersal of primary and secondary inoculum and role of vector population. Following criteria are used for predicting plant diseases:

Weather conditions during non-crop period. The amount of primary inoculum depends on survivability of pathogenic propagules during non-crop period. This relationship has been exploited to predict the Stewart's corn wilt (Stevens, 1934). The pathogen (*Erwinia stewartii*) overwinters in the body of vector, corn flea beetle (*Chaetocnema pulecaria*). Severe winters (low temperature) kill vector population, thereby reducing the initial inoculum for the next season. Forecasting of stewart's corn wilt can be made based on *cumulative winter temperature index (CWTI),* is the sum of mean temperatures of December, January and February. Table 8.2 gives the relationship between CWTI and different phases (wilt phase in early stage and leaf blight phase in mature plant) of the disease.

Table 8.2 Relationship of Cumulative Winter Temperature Index and Different Phases of Stewart's Corn Wilt

CWTI (°F)	80 or below	80–85	85–90	90–100	>100
Wilt phase	Absent	Absent	Absent/rare	Light/severe	Destructive
Leaf blight phase	Only trace	Light to moderate	Moderate/severe	Severe	Severe

The severity of blue mould of tobacco (*Peronospora tabacina*) in southern US is predicted based on winter temperature (January). Above normal temperature means severe and early appearance of disease. Blue mould warning service has been operative in North America by Tobacco Disease Council which keeps the growers and industry aware of location and time of appearance and speed of blue mould to help with the timing and intensity of control.

Amount of initial inoculum. This criterion is more important for monocyclic diseases where the secondary infection does not take place and amount of primary inoculum is related to disease severity and damage. Amount of primary inoculum present in seed, soil or vector can be estimated and disease prediction can be made, without much problem. It is being used in case of loose smut of wheat (*Ustilago tritici*), potato tuber borne inoculum (bacterial and viral pathogens) and soil borne inoculum of *Sclerotium, Verticillium, Rhizoctonia,* nematodes can be estimated and disease can be forecast. Pea root rot (*Aphanomyces euteiches*) can be predicted by conducting winter grow out test in glasshouse. In North America, *Blue mould warning system* is operative since 1980s where based on January temperature the threat to seedbeds is forewarned.

Apple scab forecasting. Apple scab (*Venturia inaequalis*) is one of the most important diseases of quality apples. Plants are exposed to attack by the fungal spores for very long period (bud breaking to fruit maturity). Apple – *V. inaequalis* system was a fit case for development of forecasting system to guide the growers for first (prophylactic spray) and further need based sprays to reduce pesticide usage. Three main criteria were used: (a) quantity of primary inoculum, measured as ascospore dose/ascospore discharge (b) phenological stage of apple trees, time of bud breaking and (c) infection periods. (Mills criteria, discussed in Chapter 2) depends on prevailing weather (temperature, Rh, leaf wetness and rain fall). Apple scab warning services are operating in Germany, Netherlands, England (CEEFAX: computerized programme managed by BBC by subscription) and India (Himachal Pradesh). Thakur and Khosla (1999) tested relevance of Mills infection periods to apple scab prediction and rescheduling fungicide application in Himachal Pradesh (India). They found that at least three sprays could be saved to control the scab disease below the economic threshold. Following systems of apple scab forecasting have helped the growers:

- Gadoury and Mac Hardy developed linear model based on accumulated degree-days.
- Richter-Haussermann invented an electronic scab warning instrument (biomat SWG).

- Apple scab predictor: A battery powered microprocessor based unit, foretells:
    (a) How much time is left for after infection spray?
    (b) What type of fungicides will be used?

Weather conditions during crop season. Prevailing weather conditions have become major criteria for diseases forecasting for polycyclic diseases where in addition to amount of primary inoculum, the multiplication and dispersal of secondary inoculum are weather dependent. Forecasting of early and late blight of potato, anthracnose and Septoira leaf spot of tomato, wheat rusts, apple scab, powdery mildew of cucurbits and downy mildew of grapes are made considering the prevailing weather conditions which determine the amount of disease and damage to the crop. Jhorar et al. (1992) developed a bio-meteorological model for forecasting Karnal bunt disease of wheat (*N. indica*) based on weather conditions in late crop season (heading and anthesis stage). Humidity thermal index (HTI), having highest correlation, was used in the forecasting model.

Forecasting late blight of potato. Late blight of potato had been instrumental in development of various fundamental concepts in plant pathology and disease forecasting is no exception. The potato growers in Europe were wise enough to recognize *blight weather* (Moderate temperature and lots of moisture: rain, dew or humidity) much earlier than Van Everdingen postulated *Dutch rules* in 1926. Following are four conditions related with weather that could foretell about appearance of late blight in Netherlands:

The Dutch Rules

- Night temperature below dew point for atleast 4 hours.
- Minimum temperature of 10°C or slightly above.
- Clouds on the next day.
- Rainfall during next 24 hours of at least 0.1 mm.

Notable contributions in late blight forecasting

Van Everdingen postulated Dutch rules in 1926.
Cook (1947), 7-day moving graph.
Hyre (1954), Blight favourable days.
Wallin (1962), Severity values
Bhattacharya, et al. (1970), 7-day moving precipitation.
Krause, et al. (1975), BLITECAST.
Mac Hardy (1979), Non-computerized model.
Singh, et al. (1980), JHULSACAST for Indo-Gangetic plains.
Fry and Apple (1983), Integrated host resistance and fungicide weathering in BLITECAST.
Dommermuth (1998), Phytoprog I. late blight warning service.
Runno and Kopple (2002), NEGFRY.
Grunwald (2002), Modified and validated SIMCAST.

Major breakthrough in late blight forecasting came when Krause et al. (1975) with a genius stroke designed an adjustable matrix (Table 8.3), using Hyre's (1947) concept of *blight favourable days* and Wallin's (1962) *severity values*. The output of BLITECAST was in the form of recommendations for the grower, tailor made to his own conditions. The growers of Pennsylvania State could send the weather data recorded in potato fields to a computer through a telephone at forecasting centre and get the recommendations. The recommendations to the growers were main attraction of this centralized disease forecasting system.

Table 8.3 Adjustable Matrix Developed by Krause, et al. (1975) using Hyre's Blight Favourable Days and Wallin's Severity Values

Total rain favourable days during last 7 days	Severity values during last 7 days					
		< 3	3	4	5	6	< 6
	< 5	−1	−1	0	1	1	2
	> 4	−1	0	1	2	2	2
	Message numbers					

Message number	Recommendation
−1	No spray
0	Late blight warning
1	7-day schedule
2	5-day schedule

BLITECAST and after. BLITECAST was a success story. Mac Hardy (1979) developed a non-computerized method and Fry and Apple (1983) incorporated factors like host resistance and fungicide withering in BLITECAST. Several computer based decision systems have been developed. Hijmans, et al. (2000) estimated the global severity of potato late blight with geographic information system (GIS)—linked disease forecast models. They used BLITECAST and SIMCAST along with climate database in GIS. They identified zones of high late blight severity, which included the tropical highlands, western Europe, the east coast of Canada, northern USA, south-eastern Brazil, and central-southern China. Major production zones with low late blight severity include the western plains of India, north-central China, and the north-western USA. Grunwald, et al. (2000) evaluated TOMCAST, BLITECAST and SIMCAST for potato late blight management in Toluca Valley (Mexico). They found that SIMCAST was superior over other two systems compared. They also reported that SIMCAST accurately allocated fungicide application for susceptible potato cultivars but needed modifications for resistant cultivars. In 2002 these workers reported field validation of modified SIMCAST for potato cultivars with high field resistance. There was significant reduction in fungicides required on resistant cultivars, without risking crop health. Runno and Koppel (2002) reported NEGFRY—a computer based programme for control of potato late blight. NEGFRY is based on two existing models: (a) model for forecasting risk of primary attack (first spray) and (b) model for timing of subsequent fungicide applications. Hansen, et al. (2000) reported decision support system (PlanteInfo) for the control of late blight via PC-NgFry and internet based information. The success of this system may be due to its regional character.

Prognosis is another term used in literature to describe forecasting or warning of diseases, pests, weeds, etc. (*the noxious organisms*). Prognosis is characterized as the prediction of the outbreak, development and outcome of disease. The objective is to decide in advance whether expected damage is threatening and whether control measures are to be taken (would be economically justified). Prognosis has been attempted at two levels: (a) Date prognosis and (b) Loss prognosis.

(A) Date Prognosis/Infestation Prognosis. Date prognosis basically deals with the prediction of the outbreak of a disease. It may be term or mid-term prognosis depending upon the duration of a generation of damage producing organism. Following two criteria are considered for date prognosis:

    (a) Estimate of initial population of pathogens and their antagonists, if possible.
    (b) Recording weather parameters and their prediction over prognosis time span.

Date prognosis was based on weather necessary meteorological prerequisites for the onset are fulfilled? Ullrich and Schrodter (1966) termed this question as "How long these prerequisite will not be fulfilled? This they called *negative prognosis*, Negative prognosis was very useful in cases like potato *P. infestans* where date of first spray (if needed) can be conveniently decided by negative prognosis i.e. how long the first spray can be delayed? This information has practical value for the growers.

(B) Loss Prognosis. Loss prognosis is based on estimate of expected economic loss, in relation to disease intensity–crop damage, and constitutes the basis or the decision as to spray or not? In loss prognosis in addition to economic aspects, consideration of the biological and eco-toxicological consequences of a plant protection measure are important factor. In recent years the possibilities for working out loss prognosis have improved considerably due to development of computerized models. EPIPRE (EPIdemic – PREdiction –PREvention) in such as system developed in Netherlands by Zadoks, et al. (1984). It is a supervised pest and disease management system which utilizes epidemiological and economical criteria in wheat. It covers yellow rust (*P. striformis*), brown rust (*P. recondite*), powdery mildew (*E. graminis*), leaf spot (*Septoria tritici*), septoria leaf blotch (*S. nodorum*) and aphids. The basic data recorded by growers is to provide central data bank (computer based).

Late blight forecasting in India. Early work on late blight forecasting was initiated by Chaudhury and coworkers in Darjeeling where they developed a 7-day moving graph for predicting late blight appearance in the area. Later Bhattacharya and coworkers at CPRI, Shimla carried further work. The precipitation was taken as major criteria, as temperature is generally favourable. The model developed had two stages of blight forecast in Himachal hills. Singh and coworkers in 1980 developed two-component model for blight forecast in plains (Singh, et al., 1999).

1. Stage 1: 7-day moving precipitation of at least 30 mm with mean temperature of 23.9°C. (blight appearance within three weeks)
2. Stage 2: Hourly temperature between 10–20°C and Rh > 80% for > 18 hr. for two consecutive days. (blight appearance within a week)

Model for Non-Rainy Years: 7-day moving graph.

Rh > 85% for > 50 hr and temp. (7.2 – 26.6°C for > 115 hr)
(if above conditions prevail for 7 consecutive days, blight would appear within 7–10 days)

Model for Rainy Years: 7-day moving graph.

Measurable rain (0.1–0.5 mm) for two consecutive days.
Five-day moving Rh > 85% for > 50 hr,
Five days moving congenial temperature (7.2–26.6°C) for > 100 hr
(if above conditions prevail for five consecutive days, **blight would appear within 7–10 days**)

The rain forecast may not stop rain but can help us to plan our day's work (indoor/outdoor) or use the umbrella. Similarly disease forecast can give grower some advantage: *The goals of our science: to describe essentials in epidemics, and to enable us to manipulate them in the interest of mankind.* Disease forecasting is a challenge, both intellectually stimulating (Agrios, 1997) and socially relevant. It must be taken-up by those serving plant pathology.

8.2.4 Long-range vs. Short-term Forecast

The disease forecasts being made are solely depending on prevailing weather conditions. Our ability to foretell weather is very limited, so the present day disease forecasts are 'short term forecasts'. The farmers get little or no time to protect the crops before the infection sets in (most of conventional fungicides have only protective function). There is urgent need to predict meteorological events in coming days, weeks or months. This may be feasible in future by use of synoptic weather charts, remote sensing devices and satellite gathered data. This may result in long-term weather forecast as well as long-term disease forecasts. The growers will have more sophisticated and commercially useful forecast and sufficient time to modify the agricultural practices that may be more economically acceptable.

REFERENCES

Agrios, G.N., 1997, *Plant Pathology*, 4th ed., Academic Press, New York.

Beuve, M., et al., 1999, Research on an economic threshold for BDY associated with rapid estimation of viruliferous alate populations of Rhopalosiphum padi (L.) captured live in young crops, In: *Proceedings of the Fifth International Conference on Pests in Agriculture,* Part 2, Montpellier, France, 7–9 December, 1999, 441–451.

Bhattacharya, S.K., et al., 1970, Forecasting late blight of potato in Indian hills, In: Nagaich, B.B., et al. (Eds.), *Potato in developing countries,* Indian Potato Assoc., CPRI, Shimla, 20.

Brust, G.E. and Foster, R.E., 1999, New economic threshold for striped cucumber beetle (Coleoptera, Chrysomelidae) in cantaloupe in the Midwest, *Journal of Economic Entomology,* 92: 4, 936–940.

Carlson, G.A. and Main, C.E., 1976, Economics of disease loss management, *Annu. Rev. Phytopathology,* 14: 381.

Carlson, G.K., 1971, Economic aspects of crop loss at farm level, In: *Crop loss Assessment Methods* (L. Chiarappa, Ed.), 2.3/1-2.3/6, FAO, Rome.

Chiarappa, L. (Ed.), 1971, Crop loss terminology, In: *Crop Loss Assessment Methods,* Supp., 3, 117–123.

Chiarappa, L., Chiang, H.C. and Smith, R.F., 1972, Plant pests and disease: assessments of crop losses, *Science,* 174, 769–773.

Cobb, N.A., 1892, Contribution to our economic knowledge of the Australian rust (Uredineae), *Agric. Gaz. N.S., Wales* 3: 60–68.

Cook, H.T., 1947, Forecasting tomato late blight, *Plant Dis. Reptr.*, 31: 245.

Cox, A. and Large, E.C., 1960, Potato blight epidemics throughout the world, US Dept., Agric, *Agric. Handbook,* 174, p. 230.

Eversmeyer, J.G., Burleigh, J.R. and Roelfs, A.P., 1973, Equation for predicting wheat stem rust development, *Phytopathology,* 63, 348–351.

Forrer, H.R., et al., 1998, Intervention thresholds for Septoria tritici in wheat, *Agrarforschung,* 5: 5, 249–252.

Fry, W.E., Apple, A.E. and Bruhn, J.A., 1983, Evaluation of potato late blight forecast modified to incorporate host resistance and fungicide weathering, *Phytopathology,* 73(7), 1054–1059.

Fry, W.E., et al., 1992, Population genetics and intercontinental migration of *P. infestans, Annu. Rev. Phytopathology,* 30, 107–130.

Gadoury, D.M., et al., 1998, Influence of light, relative humidity and maturity of populations on discharge of ascospores of Venturia inaequalis, *Phytopathology,* 88: 9, 902–909.

Hatfield, J.L., 1990, Remote detection of crop stress: application to plant pathology, *Phytopathology,* 80, 37–39.

Hem, et al., 1991, Study on the mixed damage and economic threshold of sheath blight and stem borer to rice, *Acta Phytophylacica Sinica,* 18: 3, 241–246.

Horsfall, J.G. and Cowling, E.B., 1978, How disease develops in populations. In: *Plant disease, An Advanced Treatise,* vol. II, J.G. Horsfall and E.B. Cowling, Academic Press, New York.

Horsfall, J.G. and Barrat, R.W., 1945, An improved growing system for measuring plant disease, *Phytopatho*logy, 35: 655.

Hyre, R.A., 1954, Progress in forecasting late blight of potato and tomato, *Plant Dis. Rep.,* 38, 245.

James, W.C., 1974, Assessment of plant diseases and losses, *Annu. Rev. Phytopathology,* 12, 27–48.

Jurecka, D. and Riha, K., 1999, Occurrence and importance of diseases in cereals, *Metodiky pro Zemedelskou Praxi,* 16: 27.

Kranz, J., 1974, Comparison of epidemics, *ARP,* 12, 355–374.

Krause, R.A. and Massie, L.B., 1975, Predictive systems: modern approaches to disease control, *Annu. Rev. Phytopathology,* 13: 31–47.

Krause, R.A., Massie, L.B. and Hyre, R.A., 1975, Blightcast: a computerized forecast of potato late blight, *Plant Dis. Rep.,* 59: 95–98.

Large, E.C., 1953, Growth stages in cereals, Illustration of the Feekes Scale, *Plant Pathology,* 3: 128–129.

Large, E.C., 1952, The interpretation of progress cumer for potato blight and other plant disease, *Plant Pathology,* 1: 109–117.

————, **1958,** Losses caused by potato blight in England and Wales, *Plant Pathology,* 7: 39–48.

————, **1966,** Measuring plant disease, *Annu. Rev. Phytopathology,* 4: 9–28.

Main, C.E., 1977, Crop destruction—the *raison d'etre* of plant pathology, *In Plant Disease: An Advanced Treatise* (J.G. Horsfall and E.B. Cowling, (Eds.), vol. 1, pp. 55–78, Academic Press, New York.

Mayee, C.D. and Datar, 1986, Phytopathometery, *Technical Bulletin–*1 MAU, Parbhani.

Mckinney, H.H., 1923., Ed., On infection of wheat seedlings by *Helmainthosporium sativum, J. Agric. Res.,* 26: 195–218.

Nelsson, H.E., 1995, Remote sensing and image analysis in plant pathology, *Ann. Rev. Phytopathology,* 33: 489.

Padmanabhan, S.Y., 1973, The great Bengal Famine, *Ann. Rev. Phytopathology,* 11: 11.

Royle, D.J., 1994, Diseased approaches towards underlanding and predicting epidemics by selecting four fungal pathosystems, *Plant Pathology.*

Royle, D.J., 1993, Understanding and predicting epidemics: a commentary based on selected pathosystems, *Plant Pathology,* 43(5): 777–789.

Singh, B.P., Singh P. H. and Bhattacharya, S.K., 1999, Epidemiology, In: *Potato Late Blight in India, CPRI Tech. Bulletin,* No. 27.

Stevens, N.E., 1934, Stewart's disease in relation to winter temperatures, *Plant Dis. Rep.,* 12: 141–149.

Teng, P.S., 1983, Estimating and interpreting disease intensity and loss in commercial fields, *Phytopathology,* 73: 1587–1590.

Waggoner, P.E., 1960, Forecasting epidemics, In: *Plant Pathology: An Advanced Treatise* (J.G. Horsfall and A.E. Dimond, Eds.), vol. 3, 291–312, Academic Press, New York.

Wallin, J.R., 1962, Summary of recent progress in predicting late blight epidemics in the United States of America and Canada, *Amer. Pat. J.,* 39: 306–312.

Wang Yong Min, et al., 1998, The economic threshold and forecasting of larch needle brown rust, *Scientia Silvae Sinicae,* 34: 3, 74–79.

Yarwood, C.E., 1959, Predisposition, In *Plant Pathology: An Advanced Treatise* (J.G. Horsfall and A.D. Dimore, Eds.), vol. 1, 512–562, Academic Press, New York.

Zadoks, J.C., 1972, Methodology of epidemiological research, *Annu. Rev. Phytopathology,* 10, 253.

9 Principles of Plant Disease Management

9.1 INTRODUCTION

Information on etiology, symptoms, pathogenesis and epidemiology of plant diseases are intellectually interesting and scientifically justified, but most important of all, they are useful as they help in formulation of methods developed for successful management of disease and thereby increasing the quantity and improving the quality of plant and plant products. Practices of disease management vary considerably from one disease to another depending upon the type of pathogen, the host and the biotic and abiotic factors involved. Contrary to management of human and animal diseases, where every individual is attended, the plants are generally treated as populations and measures used are preventive rather than curative.

9.2 DISEASE CONTROL vs. DISEASE MANAGEMENT

In the past, plant pathologists always aimed at the impossible task of eradicating pathogen to control diseases. However, diseases really controlled are very few. No plant pathogen has ever been wiped out from the face of the earth. So long as the pathogen survives and its host is cultivated, the chances of disease incidence will persist. It is a different matter that due to some direct or indirect efforts on the part of man the disease-causing agent has been subdued or has been reduced to an innocuous level. These efforts could better be called **management practices** whereby the populations of the pathogen or its disease causing abilities have been kept under check so that it is unable to cause noticeable damage to the crop.

Although **disease control** is an established and widely understood term, there is convincing rationale supporting the substitution of management for control. The word control evokes the notion of finality, the final disposal of problem (Apple, 1977). Management conveys the concept of a continuous process rather than an event accomplished through application of an intrinsic factor. Recommendation for disease control are to be followed almost every year, suggests that these control methods are also a part of continuous process, to manage the disease under certain limits. The plant pathogens strategically are inherent components of the ecosystem, which, must be dealt with on a continuous and strategic basis. Management should be based on the principle of maintaining the damage or loss below and economic injury level or at least minimizing occurrence above that level. This management concept must be clearly known to growers.

9.3 ESSENTIAL CONSIDERATIONS IN DISEASE MANAGEMENT

9.3.1 Economic Potential of Disease

Every plant disease situation, in time and space, may not cause economic damage, thus may not warrant the control measures. The potential of plant pathogen or plant disease, under specific conditions, to cause economic damage must be clearly estimated. The concept of economic threshold must be known clearly to growers. In most cases, these parameters are not known, the grower may waste efforts and resources by suppressing even those diseases of little destructive potential. In contrast, others may allow some destructive disease to develop to intolerable levels before attempting to suppress them. The objective of disease control is to check reduction in economic gain from a crop and if the control measures fail to increase profits, no grower is likely to accept the recommendations.

9.3.2 Disease Management: An Integral Component of Crop Production

Most cultural practices influence disease development. In modern agriculture we manage ecosystem to favour growth of a single plant species. In such cropping and farming systems, the agroecosystem that develops is unstable but persists due to adoption of management practices. Decisions such as choice of crop, crop variety, planting date, planting method, fertilization rates, pesticides, tillage type and frequency, method and frequency of irrigation, harvesting method, crop storage, etc., all influence plant disease development and the subsequent damage done.

According to Fry (1987) two important precepts result from the integral relation between crop production and disease development. The first is that *disease management will be most successful if it is considered during all stages of crop production.* Effective disease management may require several approaches, at different stages during a crop cycle. For example, if a grower relies solely on weekly applications of fungicide to suppress potato late blight, the resulting disease suppression may be inefficient or inadequate or too expensive. If irrigation practices, microenvironment and plant susceptibility favour disease development, even weekly fungicide application may not suppress disease adequately. Conversely, if properly managed, these factors may not favour disease development and weekly fungicide application may not be required. Disease management will be most successful if it is integrated into the crop production system and it employs diverse approaches. The second precept is *any changes in crop production will affect disease management.* For example, replacement of host genotype or modification in cultural practices is likely to alter activities of several pathogens. Disease management must adjust to these changes in host and agro-climatic alterations.

9.3.3 Disease Management and Area Coverage

Disease management cannot be effective in isolation. For success of any management planning, its adoption over a large continuous area is necessary. If one grower in the area rigidly follows recommended practices of disease management in his crop but neighbouring growers neglect them, the effects of a particular treatment will be nullified due to high disease pressure (inoculum) in the neighbouring fields. To avoid this, methods such as spraying of fungicide on standing crop should be followed on cooperative basis over large areas. The chances of success of disease management will be better and the cost of control will be reduced.

9.3.4 Disease Management and Timing of Treatment

A special feature of plant disease, especially of the annual field crops, is that the disease is recognized when damage has already taken place. Plants do not forewarn their sickness. They also have no system of tissue rejuvenation. In plant disease management most of the procedures are preventive rather curative, and therefore, timing of treatment application is vital to check the disease development.

9.3.5 Disease Management Planning for a Crop

Management planning against a major disease (e.g. wheat rusts or late blight of potato) is directed against it without taking into consideration other diseases of the crop. Management of crop health involves a well-knit plan in which all diseases of varying significance are taken into consideration simultaneously. Obviously, the second approach, though difficult, is of more practical value for the grower because he is interested in increasing productivity of the crop, and therefore, prefers a plan that can provide safeguard against all possible disease threats likely to occur in the area.

9.4 RELATIONSHIP BETWEEN FEATURES OF PLANT PATHOGENS, DISEASE CYCLE AND DISEASE CONTROL

The knowledge of cause of the disease, mode of survival, dissemination, cycles of inoculum production, host-parasite relationship and influence of biotic and abiotic factors can help in development and use of effective and economic control measures. The correct diagnosis of problem makes control more effective and reduces the expenses. The knowledge about source of primary inoculum of the pathogen helps in selection of correct control procedure and attacking the pathogen in its most vulnerable stage. The disease cycle of loose smut of wheat indicates that the fungus is internally seed borne. Therefore, suitable seed treatment, which can destroy the internally present fungus, will eliminate the primary inoculum. A study of disease cycle may help in prevention of primary infection or reducing the secondary spread (Chaube and Singh, 1990).

9.5 PRINCIPLES OF DISEASE MANAGEMENT

Methods for plant diseases control were first classified by Whetzel (1929) into *exclusion, eradication, protection* and *immunization*. Further advances in plant pathology leading to development of newer methods, two more principles—*avoidance* and *therapy* were created (NAS, 1968).

9.5.1 Avoidance

It involves avoiding disease by planting at time when, or in areas where, inoculum is absent or ineffective due to environmental conditions. The major aim is to enable the host to avoid contact with the pathogen or to ensure that the susceptible stage of the plant does not coincide with favourable conditions for the pathogen. The main practices under avoidance are choice of geographical areas, selection of the field, choice of sowing/planting time, selection of seed and planting material, short duration/disease escaping varieties and modification of agronomic/cultural practices. The potato cultivation at high altitude is relatively free from viruses, as prevailing environmental conditions do not permit the build-up of vector populations. Similarly, early planting of potato or wheat, in Indo-Gangetic plains, may escape late blight or stem rust damage, respectively.

9.5.2 Exclusion

It means preventing the inoculum from entering or establishing in a field or area where it does not exist. Seed certification, crop inspection, eradication of inoculum and/or insect vectors, and quarantine measures are some of the means of preventing the spread for pathogens. These are discussed in detail in Chapter 11.

9.5.3 Eradication

The process of reducing, inactivating, eliminating or destroying inoculum at the source, either from a region or from an individual plant in which it is already established is termed as eradication. Eradication involves eliminating the pathogen from infested areas; the magnitude of the operation involved may vary considerably. One of the most extensive eradication operations carried out so far was to get rid of the citrus canker (*Xanthomonas axonopodis*) in the USA during 1927–35. *As many as four million citrus trees were cut and burnt at a cost of about 2.5 million dollars to eradicate the pathogen.* The practices invariably employed to achieve eradication of inoculum include eradication of alternate and/or collateral hosts (Barbery eradication in USA), crop rotations, field sanitations, heat or chemical treatments of plant materials or soil, biological control, etc.

9.5.4 Protection

The protection of infection courts against the inoculum of many fast spreading infectious pathogen, A brought by wind from neighbouring fields or any other distant place of survival. Principles of avoidance, exclusion and eradication may not be sufficient to prevent the contact of host with pathogen, thus development of the disease is imminent. Measures are necessary to protect host plant from invading inoculum. It can be achieved by creating a chemical toxic barrier between the plant surface and the inoculum. Methods employed to achieve such results are chemical sprays, dusts, modification of environment, modification of host nutrition, etc.

9.5.5 Host Resistance

It utilizes in-built mechanism to resist various activities of pathogen. The infection or subsequent damage by pathogen can be rendered ineffective through genetic manipulation or by chemotherapy. The host resistance can also be induced by use of certain biotic and abiotic factors. The discovery of Mendelian laws of inheritance and developments in plant breeding techniques have helped in developing crop varieties resistant to specific pathogen or group of pathogens. The classical breeding techniques include selection, mutation and hybridization. Use of biotechnological tools such as tissue culture, genetic engineering and protoplast fusion are being used to develop resistant cultivars of various economically important crops/plants.

9.5.6 Therapy

It is the treatment of infected host plant, which is attempted in case of economically important horticulture plants. As a principle of plant disease control, it provides an opportunity to cure or rejuvenate the diseased host plant by use of physical and/or chemical agents. The first five of these principles are mainly preventive (prophylactic) and constitute the major components of plant disease management. They are applied to the population of plants before infection takes place. Therapy is a curative procedure and is applied to individuals after infection has taken place. Under the concept of disease management these principles have been classified into following five categories (Horsfall and Cowling, 1977):

1. Management of physical environment (cultural control)
2. Management of associated microbiota (biological antagonism)
3. Management of host genes (host resistance)
4. Management with chemicals (chemical control)
5. Management with therapy (physical, chemical, etc.)

The six principles that characterize the modern concept of plant disease management should be viewed from three stand points: (a) reduction in the initial inoculum or the rate of disease development, (b) management of the pathogen population, the cure or induce defense of the suscept or modify the environment as it influences disease and (c) interruption of dispersal, survival or the course of disease development. These interactions originally proposed by Baker (1968) and Roberts and Boothroyd (1972) and subsequently modified for the readers are illustrated in Figure 9.1.

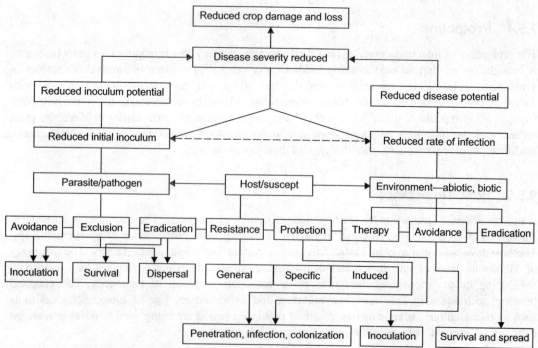

Figure 9.1 The relationship between principles, practices, components of disease pyramid and elements of pathogenesis.

9.6 INTEGRATED DISEASE MANAGEMENT

Major principles and practices of disease management have already been discussed in the preceding pages. The vastness of methods listed suggests that we possess big arsenal of weapons to win the war against the pathogens. The victory in any war, however, does not depend only on quality and quantity of weapons available, success comes from a well-planned strategy, i.e. best use of weapons in a coordinated manner at the right time. To achieve a meaningful management of the pathogen and a substantial degree of disease control, all the four components of disease pyramid are to be managed.

The term *integrated pest management* (IPM) was originally designed for management of insect pest but it is equally applicable to plant diseases also. IPM is an ecosystem-based strategy that focuses on long-term prevention of pests or their damage through a combination of techniques such as biological control, habitat manipulation, modification of cultural practices and use of resistant varieties. Pesticides are used only when monitoring indicates that they are needed and treatments are made with the goal of reducing only target organism. Pest control materials are selected and applied in a manner that minimizes risks to human health, beneficial and non-target organisms and the environment.

This goal can be achieved by the integration of methods directed against the causal agent, in favour of the host and for modification of the environment. This is now known as **IPM** (Figure 9.2). Management of pathogen involves the practices directed to exclude, reduce and/or eradicate inoculum. Management of the host involves the practices directed to improve plant vigour and induce resistance through nutrition, introduction of genetic resistance through breeding and providing need based protection by chemical means. Management of environment involves the practices that modify environment which is not favourable to pathogen and/or disease development and does not predispose host to attack. More details on integrated plant disease management are given in Chapter 16.

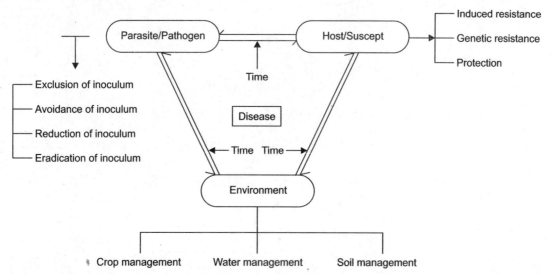

Figure 9.2 Integrated pest (disease) management (IPM).

REFERENCES

Apple, J.L., 1977, The theory of disease management, In: *Plant Pathology: An Advanced Treatise*, vol. I, J.G. Horsfall, and E.B. Cowling, Eds., Academic Press, New York, p. 79.

Baker, R., 1968, Mechanism of biological control of soil-borne plant pathogens, *Annu. Rev. Phytopathology*, 6, 263.

Chaube, H.S. and Singh, U.S., 1990, *Plant Disease Management: Principles and Practices*, CRC Press, Boca Raton , US, p. 319.

Fry, W.E., 1987, *Principles and Practices of Plant Disease Management*, Academic Press, New York, p. 378.

Horsfall, J.G. and Cowling, E.B., 1977, *Plant Disease: An Advanced Treatise*, vol. I, Academic Press, New York, p. 405.

Meloy, O.C., 1993, *Plant Disease Control: Principles and Practices*, John Wiley and Sons, New York.

National Academy of Sciences, 1968, *Plant Disease Development and Control,* NAS, Washington, D.C.

Roberts, D.A. and Boothroyd, C.W., 1972, *Fundamentals of Plant Pathology*, W.H. Freeman and Co., Toppan Company Ltd., Tokyo, p. 402.

Whetzel, H.H., 1929, The terminology of phytopathology, *Int. Congr. Plant Sci. Proc.*, 2: 1204.

10
Physical Methods

10.1 INTRODUCTION

As early as 1832, Sinclair suggested that hot air treatment in an oven might control smuts of oats and barley. Gardeners in Scotland while treating the bulbs of different ornamental plants first employed hot water therapy. However, the credit for conclusively demonstrating the therapeutic nature of heat must go to Jensen, who successfully employed hot water treatment for controlling loose smut of cereal grains and suggested that moisture played some role other than heat transfer. This method was followed in Denmark and was later adopted in US on the recommendation of Swingle in 1892 (Sharvelle, 1979).

10.2 THE PRINCIPLE

The scientific principle involved in heat therapy is that the pathogen present in seed material is selectively inactivated or eliminated at temperatures that are non-lethal to the host tissues. The exact mechanism by which heat inactivates the pathogen is not fully understood. However, it is universally accepted that heat causes inactivation and immobilization of the pathogen. There are two schools of thoughts regarding inactivation of pathogen (viruses) by heat. One holds the opinion that the heat treatment stimulates enzymes that cause the degradation of virus, though according to Benda (1972) this has not been established. The others pursue the idea that heat causes loosening of bonds both in nucleic acid and the protein components of the virus. In nucleic acid, when the bonds are disrupted the linear arrangement of nucleotides is disturbed and thus the virus looses infectivity. In proteins, the bonds holding the chains of amino acids together may be broken, or more likely, the architecture of the folding of the chain may be destroyed. Disruption of bonds causes denaturing of protein molecules which become less soluble in water and finally leads to coagulation. The rate at which the pathogen is inactivated is determined by temperature and the duration of treatment. At constant temperature, the drop in the density of pathogenic inoculum is exponential.

10.3 THE METHODS

Following physical methods are employed for reduction and/or elimination of primary inoculum that may be present in seed, soil, or planting material:

10.3.1 Hot Water Treatment

Hot water treatment is widely used for the control of seed-borne pathogens, especially bacteria and viruses. A list of some important seed-borne diseases, claimed to have been controlled by hot water treatment, is given in Tables 10.1, 10.2 and 10.3.

Table 10.1 Control of Seed-borne Pathogens by Hot Water Treatment of Seed

Crop	Disease	Causal Organism	Treatment
Brassica spp.	Black rot	*X. campestris* pv. *campestris*	50°C for 20 or 30 min
Clusterbean, Guar (*Cyamopsis tetragonoloba*)	Blight	*X. campestris* pv. *cyamopsidis*	56°C for 10 min
Cucumber (*Cucumis sativus*)	Seedling blight	*Ps. syringae* pv. *lachrymans*	50°C and 75% RH for 3 days
Lettuce (*Lactuca sativa*)	Leaf spot	*X.campestris* pv. *vitians*	70°C for 1 to 4 days
Peanut (*Arachis hypogea*)	Testa nematode	*Aphlenchoides arachidis*	60°C for 5 min after soaking for 15 min in cool water
Pearl millet (*Pennisetum typhoides*)	Downy mildew	*Sclerospora graminicola*	55°C for 10 min
Potato (*Solanum tuberosum*)	Potato phyllody	*Phytoplasma*	50°C for 10 min
Rice (*Oryza sativa*)	Udbatta	*Ephelis oryzae*	54°C for 10 min
	White tip	*Aphlenchoides besseyi*	51-53°C for 15 min after dipping for 1 day in cool water
Safflower	Leaf spots	*Alternaria* spp.	50°C for 30 min
Teasel (*Dipsacus* spp.)	Stem nematode	*Ditylenchus dipsaci*	1 hr at 50°C on 48.8°C for 2 h
Tobacco (*Nicotiana tabacum*)	Hollow stalk	*E.carotovora* pv. *carotovora*	50°C for 12 min
Tomato (*Lycopersicon esculentum*)	Black speck	*Ps. syringae* pv. *tomato*	52°C for 1 h

Source: Chaube and Singh, 1990

Table 10.2 Control of Seed-borne Diseases by Hot Water Treatment of Sugarcane Cutting

Disease	Pathogen	Treatment
Downy mildew	*Perenosclerspora sacchari*	54°C for 1 h, dried at room temperature of 1 day and again treated in 52°C for 1 h
Grassy shoot	*Phytoplasma*	54°C for 2 h
Leaf scald	*Xanthomonas albilineans*	Soaking in cold water for 1 day and then treating the cuttings at 50°C for 2-3 h
Mosaic	Virus (potato virus Y group)	20 min treatment each day on 3° successive days at 52° and 57.3°C, respectively.

(Contd.)

Table 10.2 Control of Seed-borne Diseases by Hot Water Treatment of Sugarcane Cutting (*Contd.*)

Disease	Pathogen	Treatment
Ratoon stunting	*Clavibacter xyli* ssp. *Xyli*	50°C for 3 h
Red rot	*Colletotrichum falcatum* (*Physalospora tucumanensis*)	54°C for 8 h
Smut	*Ustilago scitaminea*	55 to 60°C for 10 min
Spike	Virus	52°C for 1 h
White leaf	*Phytoplasma*	54°C for 40 min
Wilt	*Acremonium* sp. *Fusarium moniliforme*	50°C for 2 h

Source: Chaube and Singh, 1990, 2000

Table 10.3 Time and Temperature Recommendations for Hot Water Treatment for Denematizing Planting Stocks

Nematode	Planting Stock	Time (min)	Temp. (°C)
Aphelenchoides ritzemabosi	Chrysanthemum stools	15	47.8
		30	43.0
A. *fragariae*	Easter lily bulbs	60	44.0
Ditylenchus dipsaci	Narcissus bulbs	240	43.0
D. *destructor*	Irish bulbs	180	43.0
Meloidogyne spp.	Cherry root stocks	5–10	50–51.0
	Sweet potatoes	65	45.7
	Peach root stocks	5–10	50–51.1
	Tuberose tubers	60	49.0
	Grapes rooted	10	50.0
	Cuttings	30	47.8
	Begonia	30	48.0
	Tubers	60	45.0
	Caladium tubers	30	50.0
	Yam tubers	30	51.0
	Ginger rhizomes	10	55.0
	Strawberry roots	5	52.8
	Rose roots	60	45.5

Source: Reddy, 1983

10.3.2 Hot Air Treatment

Hot air treatment is less injurious to seed and easy to operate but also less effective than hot water treatment. It has been used against several diseases of sugarcane. Singh (1973) claimed complete control of red rot in varieties Co 527, CoS 510, Bo 3 and Bo 32 by hot air treatment at 54°C for 8 hours. It is used for treating sugarcane stalks on commercial scale in Louisiana (Steiband Forbes, 1958) to control Ratoon-stunting Disease (RSD). It is employed for treating canes which are soft and succulent. Lauden (1953) working in Mainland, US, reported that hot air treatment at 54°C for

8 hours effectively eliminates RSD pathogen without impairing the germination of buds. After 3 years, Steiband and Chilton (1956) confirmed Lauden's findings using thermocouple. Similarly, grassy shoot disease of sugarcane has been controlled by hot air at 54°C for 8 hours (Singh, 1968).

10.3.3   Steam and Aerated Steam

The use of aerated steam is safer than hot water and more effective than hot air in controlling seed-borne infections. The heating capacity of water vapour is about half that of water and 2.5 times that of air. The advantages of this method include easier drying of seeds, low loss in germination, easy temperature control and no damage to seed coat of legumes. Besides its use in controlling sugarcane diseases, it has also been used against citrus greening (Cheema, et al., 1982). Most frequent application of steam and aerated steam has been in greenhouses where steam also provides heat during cold seasons. As a gas, it moves readily through soil, in contrast to the slow, inefficient movement of water. Steam raises temperatures efficiently. As gaseous water molecules (steam) condense into a liquid they release much more latent heat than that given out as warm water cools (540 cal/g relative to 1 cal/g). Aerated steam provides an opportunity to treat soil at temperatures lower than those possible with pure steam.

10.3.4   Refrigeration

It is an accepted fact that the low temperature at or slightly above the freezing point checks the growth and activities of all such pathogens that cause a variety of post harvest diseases of vegetables and fruits. Therefore, most perishable fruits and vegetables should be transported and stored in refrigerated vehicles and stores. 'Cool Chains', refrigerated space from field to consumer's table is becoming very popular. Regular refrigeration is sometimes preceded by a quick hydro-cooling or air-cooling to remove the excess heat carried in them from the field to prevent development of new or latent infections.

10.3.5   Radiation

Electromagnetic radiations such as ultraviolet (UV) light, X-rays and γ-rays, as well as particulate radiations (α particles and β particles) have been studied in relation to management of post harvest diseases of horticultural crops. Findings of experiments revealed that γ-rays controlled post harvest fungal infections in peaches, strawberries and tomatoes but doses of radiation required to kill pathogens, were found injurious to host tissues. More efforts are required in this area as radiations can be very effective in inactivating pathogens in larges stores or handling bulk material that cannot be heated for sterilization. Some plant pathogenic fungi (*Alternaria, Botrytis, Stemphylium*) sporulate only when they receive light in the ultraviolet range (below 360 nm). It has been possible to control diseases on greenhouse vegetables caused by species of these fungi by covering or constructing the greenhouse with a special UV-absorbing vinyl film that blocks transmission of light wavelengths below 390 nm.

10.3.6   Drying Stored Grains and Fruits

In presence of sufficient moisture, a variety of microflora already accompanying harvested grains, nuts, etc. cause decay. Such decay, however, can be avoided if seeds and nuts are harvested when properly mature and then allowed to dry in the air or are exposed to sun. Maize downy mildew pathogen is seed borne. If the maize seeds are properly sun dried, the inoculum gets inactivated. Hot air can be used until the desired moisture is reached (about 12% moisture) before storage. Subsequently, they are stored under conditions of ventilation, which do not allow build-up of moisture. Fleshy fruits (peaches, strawberries) should be harvested later in the day, after the dew is gone, to ensure that the fruits do not carry surface moisture during storage and transit, which could lead to decay by microorganisms.

10.3.7 Burning

Controlled burning may alter the environment and affect plant disease response, providing both a temperature effect and a means of destroying the pathogen (Zentmyer and Bald, 1977). Parmeter and Uhrenholt in 1975 introduced a new aspect of burning by demonstrating that smoke may kill a number of plant pathogens in tissues. According to Hardison (1976, 1980) burning is a single most important practice in grass seed production in the Pacific Northwest. It was initiated to control the blind seed disease of perennial rye grass caused by *Gloeotinia temulenta*. It also effectively controlled *Claviceps purpurea* (ergot of rye), *Anguina agrostis* (seed nematode) and silver top. Fire can be applied to cereals in which inoculum can be destroyed after harvest or pasture grasses which can periodically be freed from inoculum before they make new growth. It has also been realized that the increasing success of non-tillage in some crops and the resultant problems of debris management can make burning an attractive and effective proposition. Diseases that have been successfully managed by burning or flaming crop residue are given in Table 10.4.

Table 10.4 Disease Controlled by Fire and Flame

Pathogen	Disease	Pathogen	Disease
Anguina sp.	Seed nematode of *Lolium rigidum*	*Anguina agrostis*	Seed nematode of *Festuca rubra*
Angullulina tumifaciens	Leaf gall nematode of *cynodon transvalensis*	*Corticium sasaki*	Sheath blight of rice
Claviceps paspali	Ergot of *Paspalum dilatatum*	*Claviceps purpurea*	Ergot of *Lolium perenne*
Cuscuta sp.	Parasite of lucern	*Diaporthe vaccinii*	Die back of low bush blueberry
Drechsler poae	Leaf mould of *Poa pratensis*	*Gaeumannomyces graminis*	Take-all of wheat
Gerlachia nivalis	Snow mould of wheat and barley	*Glueotinia temulenta*	Blind seed of *olium perenne*
Godronia cassandrae	Canker of *Vaccinium* sp.	*Leptosphaeria* sp.	Leaf blight of sugarcane
Phleospora idahoensis	Stress eye spot of *Festuca rubra*	*Leptosphaeria* sp. *Pleiochaeta setosa*	Brown spot of lupin
Pseudocercosporella herpotrichoides	Eye spot of wheat	*Puccinia menthae*	Rust of peppermint
Puccinia asparagi	Asparagus rust	*Puccinia poaenemoralis*	Leaf rust of *Poa pratensis*

(Contd.)

Table 10.4 Disease Controlled by Fire and Flame *(Contd.)*

Pathogen	Disease	Pathogen	Disease
Puccinia graminis	Stem rust of *Poa pratensis*	*Puccinia striformis*	Stripe rust of *Poa pratensis*
Rhynchosporium secalis	Eye blotch of barley	*Sclerotium oryzae*	Stem rot of rice
Septoria avenae	Leaf blotch of oat	*Septoria nodorum, Septoria tritici*	Leaf blotch of wheat
Selenophoma bromigera	Leaf spot of *Bromus inertis*	*Urocystis agropyri*	Flag smut of wheat
Verticillium dahliae	Wilt of potato and peppermint		

(Source: Hardison, 1976; Palti, 1981)

10.3.8 Flooding

Flooding fields and orchards to reduce or eliminate soil-borne inoculum of plant pathogens is an ancient practice. According to Kelman and Cook (1977) flooding has been recognized to be one of the key factors for the low incidence of soil-borne disease in Chinese agriculture. In lower Yangtze and South China, the plots where vegetables are grown, are pre-cultivated with one or two crops of rice or spinach, water chestnut, water bamboo or lotus (William, 1979) for the control of soil-borne pests.

Several explanations of the harmful effects of prolonged flooding on soil-borne pathogens have been suggested. Lack of oxygen may be involved in some cases or, more often perhaps, accumulation of CO_2 in the soil. The survival of *F. oxysporum* f. sp. *cubense* in soil after 2 weeks depends on formation of chlamydospores, since the conidia are not apparently long lived in soil. Newcombe (1960) found that CO_2 and flooded soil both largely inhibited chlamydospores formation whereas at first they stimulated the production of conidia. Consequently the fungus, although able to survive in banana plantation soil containing organic matter, is likely to die out in a fallow, flooded field where organic matter is in short supply. Newcombe (1960) concluded that the main factor in the elimination of the fungus by flooding is a high CO_2 content in the flooded soil combined with a decreased availability of colonizable substrate. In flooded soil, CO_2 stimulates germination of conidia, presumably by overcoming the fungistatic factor present in soil but prevents the formation of chlamydospores so that the fungus dies out when the organic matter is exhausted. A similar situation perhaps holds for other soil borne fungi but few cases have been investigated (Tarr, 1972). A list of plant diseases that have been successfully controlled by flooding fields and orchards is given in Table 10.5.

Table 10.5 Plant Disease Controlled by Flooding

Pathogen	Disease	Pathogen	Disease
Alternaria porri f. sp. *solani*	Alternaria blight of tomato and potato	*Alternaria dauci*	Blight of carrot
Aphelenchoides besseyi	White tip of rice	*F. oxysporum* f. sp. *cubense*	Wilt of banana

(Contd.)

Table 10.5 Plant Disease Controlled by Flooding (*Contd.*)

Pathogen	Disease	Pathogen	Disease
Meloidogyne sp.	Root knot of celery	*Orobanche* spp.	Phanerogamic plant parasite of several crops
Phytophthora parasitica var. *nicotianae*	Black shank of tobacco	*Pyrenophora teres*	Canker and blight of barley
Radopholus similes	Burrowing nematode of banana	*Sclerotinia sclerotiorum*	White mould of vegetables
Trichodorus sp.	Stubby root nematode of celery	*Tylenchorhychus* sp.	Stunt nematode of celery
Verticillium dahliae	Wilt of cotton		

Source: Stover, 1955; Roteim and Palti, 1969; Tarr, 1972; Palti, 1981

REFERENCES

Antoine, R., 1957, Cane Diseases, *Rept. Sug. Res.,* Mauritius, 53.

Benda, G.T.A., 1972, Hot water treatment for mosaic and RSD control, *Sugar J.,* 34: 32.

Chaube, H.S. and Singh Ramji, 2000, *Introductory Plant Pathology,* International Distributors, Lucknow, India, p. 500.

Chaube, H.S. and Singh, U.S., 1990, *Plant Diseases Management: Principles and Practices,* C.R.C. Press, US, p. 319.

Cheema, S.S., Chohan, J.S. and Kapur, S.P., 1982, Effect of moist hot air treatment on citrus greening infected bud wood, *J. Res. Punjab Agric. Univ.,* India, 19: 97.

Hardison, J.R., 1980, Role of fire for disease control in grass seed production, *Plant Dis,* 64: 641.

Haridson, J.R., 1976, Fire and flame for plant disease control, *Annu. Rev. Phytopathology,* 14: 355.

Kelman, A. and Cook, R.J., 1977, Plant Pathology in the People's Republic of China, *Annu. Rev. Phytopathology,* 15: 409.

Lauden, L., 1953, Decision on the control of the stunting disease, *Sugar Bull.,* 31: 382.

Newcombe, M., 1960, Some effects of water and anaerobic condition on *Fusarium oxysporum* f. sp. *cubense* in soil, *Trans. Brit. Mycol. Soc.,* 43: 51.

Palti, J., 1981, *Cultural Practices and Infectious Crop Disease,* Springer Verlag, Berlin, p. 343.

Parmeter, J.R. Jr. and Uhrenholt, B., 1975, Some effects of pine needle or grass smoke of fungi, *Phytopathology,* 65: 28.

Reddy, P.P., 1983, *Plant Nematology,* Agricole Publishing Academy, India, p. 287.

Rotem, J. and Palti, J., 1969, Irrigation and plant diseases, *Annu. Rev. Phytopathology,* 7: 267.

Sharvelle, E.D., 1979, *Plant Disease Control,* AVI Publishing, West Port, Conn., p. 331.

Singh, K., 1968, Hot air therapy against grassy shoot disease of sugarcane, *Curr. Sci.,* 37: 592.

Singh, K., 1973, Hot air therapy against red rot of sugarcane, *Plant Dis. Rep.,* 57: 220.

Steiband, R.J. and Chilton, C.J.P., 1956, Recent studies conducted on the ratoon stunting disease of sugarcane in Louisiana, *Sugar Bull.*, 34: 238.

Steiband, R.J. and Forbes, I.L., 1958, Hot air for control of ratoon stunting disease of sugarcane in Loouisiane, *Phytopathology*, 48: 398.

Stover, R.H., 1954, Flood-fallowing for eradication of *Fusarium oxysporum* f. sp. cubense II, Some factors involved in fungus survival, *Soil Sci.*, 77: 401.

Stover, R.H., 1955, Flood-fallowing for eradication of *Fusarium oxysporum* f. sp. cubense III, Effect of oxygen on fungus survival, *Soil Sci.*, 80: 397.

Tarr, S.A.J., 1972, *Principle of Plant Pathology*, Macmillan Publishers, p. 632.

William, P.M., 1979, Vegetable crop protection in the people's republic of China, *Annu. Rev. Phytopathology,* 17: 311.

Zentmyer, G.A., and Bald, J.G., 1977, Management of the environment, In: *Plant Diseases: An Advanced Treatise*, vol. 1, J.G. Horsfall and E.B. Cowling, Eds., Academic Press, New York, p. 122.

11

Regulatory Methods

11.1 INTRODUCTION

Exclusion is one of the principles of plant disease management. The practices tend to prevent the inoculum from entering or establishing into the field or area where it does not exist. In this commercialized world, through easy and quick means of transportation, there is exchange of not only grains and other foodstuffs between nations but also of germplasms or seeds for crop improvement. Past experiences have revealed that no country or state can afford unrestricted movement of plant and planting materials. Thus, a legally constituted authority enforces in public interest the principle of exclusion of the pests and pathogens.

11.2 PLANT QUARANTINE

11.2.1 Concept and Importance

Quarantine is derived from Latin word *quarantum* meaning forty. It refers to a 40-day period of detention of ships arriving from countries with bubonic plague and cholera in the middle ages. Plant quarantine is an endeavour through which restrictions are imposed by the governments to regulate the introduction and movement of plants and plant materials with a view to prevent introduction of exotic pests/pathogens into uninfested areas. The adoption of Quarantine Regulations and Acts by different countries of the world has been necessitated due to the fact that often extensive damages have been caused by exotic one which have been introduced. Some of the important plant pathogens introduced into different countries of the world where they caused severe losses, are listed in Table 11.1.

Table 11.1 Examples of Plant Pathogens Introduced into Some Countries

Disease and Pathogen	Introduced From	Introduced Into	Year of Introduction
American goose berry mildew (*Sphaerotheca morsuvae*)	N. America	England	1899
Bacterial canker of tomato (*C.michiganense* pv. *michiganense*)	US	UK	1942
Bacterial leaf blight of paddy (*X. campestris* pv. *oryzae*)	Phillipines	India	1959
Black rot of crucifers (*X. campestris* pv. *campestris*)	Java	India	1929

(Contd.)

205

Table 11.1 Examples of Plant Pathogens Introduced into Some Countries (*Contd.*)

Disease and Pathogen	Introduced From	Introduced Into	Year of Introduction
Black shank of tobacco (*Phytophthora nicotianae*)	Holland	India	1938
Blister rust of pines (*Cronartium ribicola*)	Europe	US	1910
Bunchy top of banana (Viral)	Sri Lanka	India	1940
Chestnut blight (*Endothia parasitica*)	Asia	US	1904
Citrus canker (*X. campestris* pv. *citri*)	Asia	US	1907
Powdery mildew of cucurbits (*Erysiphe cichoracearum*)	Sri Lanka	India	1910
Downy mildew of grapes (*Plasmopara viticola*)	US	France	1878
	Europe	India	1910
Downy mildew of maize (*Sclorospora phillipinensis*)	Java	India	1912
Dutch elm (*C. ulmi*)	Holland	US	1928–30
Flag smut of wheat (*Urocystis tritici*)	Australia	India	1906
Fire blight of apple (*E. amylovora*)	N. America	New Zealand	1919
Golden nematode of potato (*G. rostochiensis*)	Europe	US, Mexico	1881
		India	1961
Hairy root of apple (Viral)	England	India	1940
Late blight of potato (*Phytophthora infestans*)	S. America	Europe	1830
	UK	India	1883
Leaf rust of coffee (*Hemileia vastatrix*)	Sri Lanka	India	1879
	Asia, Africa	Brazil	1970
Onion Smut (*Urocystis cepulae*)	Europe	India	1958
Paddy blast (*Pyricularia oryzae*)	SE Asia	India	1918
Peanut rust (*Puccinia arachidis*)	Brunei US	Brazil	–
Powdery mildew of grape (*Uncinula necator*)	North America	England	1845
Powdery mildew of rubber (*Oidium heavea*)	Malaya	India	1938
Rye grass seed infection (*Gleotinia temulenta*)	New Zealand	Oregon	1940
Wart of potato (*Synchytrium endobioticum*)	Netherlands	India	1953
Wheat bunt (*Tilletia caries*)	Australia	California, US	1854
Witches broom of cocoa (*Marasmitus perni*)	Trinidad	S. America	1974–75

11.2.2 Principles, Basis and Justification

All nations of the world are passing through a period of intensive agricultural development in an effort to accelerate and stabilize food production. Introduction of high yielding exotic germplasm is being extensively used as a resource for national programme, even though it carries with it the danger of introducing new pathogens or new biotypes or races unknown in the importing country. Sometimes grains imported for milling purposes find their way into the farmers field, thereby introducing organisms. Thus, international trade with regard to plant and plant products is seen as potential threat for domestic agriculture. This eventually puts great burden on quarantines system all over the world.

Plant quarantines measures promulgated by a government or group of governments, restrict the entry of plants, plant products, soil, culture of living organisms, packing materials and commodities as well as their containers and other means of conveyance and thus, help to protect agriculture and environment from avoidable damages by hazardous alien organisms. However, *quarantines are justified only if the organism has little or no chance of spreading naturally*. Thus, before its formulation and enforcement, detail information about nature of the pathogen, its mode of spread/ transmission, host range and natural barrier should be properly understood. In addition, socio-economic and geopolitical factors likely to work against the interest of exporting and importing countries should not influence the quarantine decisions.

Plant quarantine regulations, in order to be effective, have to be based on the following scientific principles (Mathys and Baker, 1980):

1. The biology and ecology of the organism against which quarantine measure is proposed to be enforced should be known; only those organisms which are supposed to pose threat to major crops and forests should be taken into consideration.
2. In the event of its introduction whether the organism is likely to establish and cause significant damage should be looked into.
3. Regulation is formulated to prevent or control the entry of the organism and not to hinder trade or attainment of other objectives, as quarantine measures are for the crop and not for trade protection.
4. The regulations are derived from adequate legislation and operated solely under the law.
5. The measures can be amended as conditions change or further facts become available.
6. The quarantine regulations are implemented by trained and experienced workers but the public must cooperate for their effective enforcement.

11.2.3 Significance and Risk Analysis

Organisms of quarantine significance may include any pest or pathogen that a government (or inter-government organization) consider to pose a threat to the country's (or region's) agriculture and environment. Such organisms are usually exotic to that country or region but may also include exotic strains or races of domestic organism. For larger countries the definition may also be extended to include foreign isolates of domestic organisms. Some plant pathogens of quarantine significance though not yet reported from India are given in Table 11.2

Table 11.2 Destructive Plant Pathogens of Quarantine Significance (not yet reported from India)

Disease (pathogen)	Principal Host(s)	Geographical Distribution	Remarks
Fungi			
Foot rot/collar rot (*Phoma medicaginis* var. *Pinodella=Ascochyta pinodella*)	Pea	Netherlands, Germany, USA, Canada, Argentina, England, USSR, New Zealand, France, Japan and Israel	Can survive for several years in soil and debris.
Snow mould/brown foot rot (*Fusarium nivale*)	Wheat, barley, rye	Widely distributed in Europe, USSR, Japan, Australia, New Zealand, N.E. and N.W. USA and Canada	Its report from India is doubtful. Crop losses from 5–15% are reported. Fungicide resistant stains are known.
Downy mildew (*Peronospora manshurica*)	Soyabean	Widely distributed in North and South America, Asia, Europe and also reported from Africa	Oospores can survive in soil for several years.
Rust (*Uromyces betae*)	Sugarbeet	Wide spread in Europe, reported from Africa, Asia, Australia, New Zealand, North and South America	Seed-borne rust spores can cause epidemic conditions in new areas.
Ergot (*Claviceps purpurea*)	Wheat, barley, triticale	Widely distributed	In India, the pathogen is multiplied on rye for medicinal purposes. However, in other countries it is reported to cause serious losses on wheat and barley. Can remain viable for more than 10 years.
Black leg/black rot (*Phoma lingam*)	*Brassica* spp.	Widely distributed	Crop losses up to 100% have been reported from USA.
Blue mould/downy mildew (*Peronospora tabacina*)	Tobacco	Europe (widely distributed), Africa, America, Australia, Asia (Iran, Iraq, Burma)	High risk pathogen, capable of spreading very fast. Within four years the pathogen has spread in many parts of Europe from a single source.
Dwarf bunt (*Tilletia contraversa*)	Wheat	Europe (widely distributed), also reported from some places in Africa, Asia, North and South America.	Crop losses up to 95% are reported, can remain viable in soil for several years.

(Contd.)

Table 11.2 Destructive Plant Pathogens of Quarantine Significance (not yet reported from India) (*Contd.*)

Disease (pathogen)	Principal Host(s)	Geographical Distribution	Remarks
Bacteria			
Hairy root (*Agrobacterium* (*Agrobacterium*	Apple, rose	Japan, Australia, Bulgaria, France and USA	High incidence in apple at 75% moisture holding capacity of soil and soil temp. of 28°C.
Bacterial wilt (*Corynebacterium flaccumfaciens* pv. *flaccumfaciens*)	Bean, soyabean	North and Central America, Europe (Bulgaria, Hungary, Yugoslavia) and Australia	Use of seed from disease free area has been recommended.
Fire blight (*Erwinia amylovora*)	Apple, pear	Africa, Asia, New Zealand, Europe, North and Central America.	The disease has occurred in USA in epiphytotic conditions.
Bacterial wilt (*Erwinia tracheiphila*)	Melon, cucumber	Wide spread in USA, Canada, also reported sporadically in South Africa, Congo, Japan China, USSR, Europe	Transmitted by beetles.
Bacterial wilt/Stewart's wilt (*Erwinia stewartii*)	Maize	North and South America, Europe, and Asia	Seed treatment and spraying of plants with fungicides are not effective.
Halo blight (*Pseudomonas syringae* pv. *coronafaciens*)	Oat	North America, South America (Argentina) and Europe	Antibiotics are effective for seed treatment.
Spikelet rot (*Pseudomonas syringae* pv. *atrofaciens*)	Wheat	North America, Europe, South Africa, Australia, New Zealand	—
Gummosis (*Xanthomonas campestris* pv. *vasculorum*)	Sugarcane	Africa, New Guinea, Mexico, Central and South America	Its record from India is doubtful.
Bacterial blight/root scab (*Xanthomonas campestris* pv. *carotae*)	Carrot	North America, Europe, (Hungary, USSR) South Africa, Asia (USSR) and Australia	2% loss is reported from USA. Hot water treatment affective.
Viruses, viroids, Mycoplasma like Organisms (MLO) and rickettsia			
Brown streak virus	Cassava	Africa (East Africa, Malawi, Mozambique, Zimbabwe.	—
Avocado sunblotch viroid	Avocado	Australia, Israel, Peru, South Africa, USA and Venezuela	Seed transmission rate of 80 to 100% has been reported.
Plum pox virus	Plum, peach and apricot	Europe (Especially southeastern Europe) and Turkey	Yield losses in some varieties can be almost 100%.

(Contd.)

Table 11.2   Destructive Plant Pathogens of Quarantine Significance (not yet reported from India)   *(Contd.)*

Disease (pathogen)	Principal Host(s)	Geographical Distribution	Remarks
Chloretic streak virus	Sugarcane	Africa, Asia, Australia and Oceania and America	—
Fiji disease virus	Sugarcane	Australia, Fiji, Madagascar, Papua New Guinea, New Hebrides, Philippines, Malaysia and Thailand	—
Phony peach	Peach	USA	Caused by rickettsia
Swollen shoot virus	Cacao	West Africa, Sri Lanka and Malaysia	In Ghana and Nigeria, millions of trees have been either killed by the virus or uprooted in eradication campaigns; in some areas, the disease is apparently out of control.
Lethal yellowing (MLO)	Coconut	Bahamas, the Cayman Islands, Cuba, Dominican Republic, USA, Jamaica	Palms start showing symptoms from 18 months of age.
Peanut stunt virus	Groundnut	USA and Japan	Two major strains have been reported.
Tomato ring spot virus	Tomato	North America, Japan, USSR, Sweden, UK, Netherlands, Denmark, Yugoslavia, France, Spain, New Zealand	The virus also causes prunus stem pitting and apple union necrosis and decline.

Source: NBPGR, New Delhi

Analysis of pest and pathogen risks is the decision-making process that brings the biological approach into play. The analysis is based on two general precepts (Kahn, 1977) (a) *the benefits must exceed the risk and* (b) *the benefit must exceed the cost*. The benefits include the opportunity to introduce new crops or new varieties of established crops or to introduce new genes to improve existing varieties. When costs are entered into pest risk analysis, the costs of adequate safeguards are taken into account.

In US, estimation of the expected economic impact has been used to establish priority of quarantine activity. Once a pest is established in an area, in all probability, there will be some economic impact. In a report published in 1973, the expected economic impacts of 551 exotic plant pathogens were established and the pests, considered to be most serious economically, were identified (McGregor, 1978). This can be used by the US *Animal and Plant Health Inspection Service* (APHIS) to focus its activities on the most important pests. Thurston (1973) developed descriptions of tropical diseases of global importance and these could aid countries in the tropics to establish priorities for their quarantine efforts. A list of threatening diseases of global importance is given in Table 11.3.

Table 11.3 Threatening Plant Diseases of Global Importance

Disease	Pathogen
Limited threat potential	
American leaf spot of coffee	*Mycena citricolor*
Coconut cadang-cadang	Viroid
Enanisimo of barley, oats, wheat	Etiology unknown
Potato rust	*Puccinia pittieriana*
Intermediate threat potential	
Bunchy top of banana	Virus
Cocoa swollen shoot	Virus (CSSV)
Gummosis of imperial grass	*Xanthomonas axonoperis*
Hoja blanka of rice	Virus (HBV)
Lethal yellowing of coconut	*Phytoplasma*
Monilia pod rot of cocoa	*Monilia roreri*
Red ring of coconut	*Rhadinaphelenchus cocophilus*
Streak disease of maize	Virus
Stunting virus of pangola grass	Virus
High threat potential	
African cassava mosaic	Virus
Bacterial leaf blight of rice	*X. campestris* pv. *oryzae*
Downy mildew of maize	*Sclerospora* spp. *Sclerophthora* spp.
Moko disease of bananas and plantains	*Pseudomonas solanacearum*
South American leaf blight of rubber	*Microcyclus ulei*

11.2.4 Entry and Establishment of Pathogens

An exotic species of pest or pathogen must first gain entry and become established to pose any threat to local plants. It is an extremely difficult proposition to predict accurately whether an exotic organism will become established and become economically important. In a relatively few cases, the patho-geographical approach has led to prediction of the occurrence of pathogens based on knowledge of the life-cycles, distribution of the pathogen and ecological characteristics of the host and pathogen. The assessment revealed that two organisms, the potato wart fungus (*Synchytrium endobioticum*) and the pathogen of citrus scab (*Elsinoe fawcetti*), could not survive unfavourable seasons. The potato wart fungus does not survive in soil where the temperature rises to 30°C in any season. Consequently, it was recommended that quarantine regulations against this pathogen be relaxed in tropical countries. *Soyabean rust pathogen (Phakopsora pahyrhizi) was introduced in India during early 1970s but fail to establish, probably due to unfavourable climatic conditions, as a result occurrence of diseases was not recorded.*

According to Kahn (1977) some factors which affect entry and establishment include: (a) potential compared with natural dispersal, (b) ecological range of the pest as compared with ecological range of its host, (c) weather, (d) ease of colonization, including reproductive potential and (e) agricultural practices including pest management.

11.2.5   Plant Quarantine as a Management Practice

Plant quarantine as a practice covers two basic principles of disease management: *exclusion* and *eradication*. When germplasm movement is regulated by quarantine, the entry of organism is prevented by inspection and treatment or the host is banned or otherwise restricted. According to Kahn (1977) exclusion is a positive-image term that relates to keeping organisms out whereas plant quarantine is a negative image that is related to keeping plants out. This concept has been recognized by the California Department of Agriculture which employs a detection and exclusion officer rather than a plant protection officer.

11.3   PLANT QUARANTINE REGULATIONS

In 1660, France promulgated first quarantine law against barberry. In 1873, an embargo was imposed in Germany to prevent importation of plant and plant products from US to prevent the introduction of the Colorado potato beetle, and in 1877, the United Kingdom Destructive Pests Act prevented the introduction and spread of this beetle. In 1891, the first plant quarantine measure was initiated in US by setting up a seaport inspection station at San Pedro, California, and the first US quarantine law was passed in 1912. The Federal Plant Quarantine Service was established in Australia in 1909 (Mathys and Baker, 1980). In India, a Destructive Insect and Pests Act was passed in 1914. Since then most of the countries have formulated quarantine regulations.

On the global scale, the first International Plant Protection Convention (the Phylloxera Convention) was signed in 1881, with the objective of preventing the spread of severe pests. This convention was amended in 1889, 1929 and 1951. The International Plant Protection Convention (IPPC or Rome convention) under the FAO was established to prevent the international boundaries. This convention provided a model phytosanitary certificate (Rome certificate) to be adopted by member countries. Within this convention, ten regional plant protection organizations have been established on the basis of biogeographical areas (Neergaard, 1990; Singh, 1983).

11.3.1   Plant Quarantine in US

The regulation of plant introduction in US began in 1829, when the US Congress allotted $1000 for import of rare plant and seeds. The office of the US Patent Commissioner was authorized for the introduction of germplasm from 1836 to 1862. With the establishment of US Department of Agriculture (USDA) in 1862, a Commissioner of Agriculture was made responsible for collection, testing and distribution of potentially valuable plant germplasm. A section, Seed and Plant Introduction, was established in 1898. This system was continued with minor changes. Over 465,000 plants or seeds have been introduced since 1898. At present, about 7500 new introductions are made each year. The Plant Protection and Quarantine Program (PPQP) is planned and executed by the Animal and Plant Health Inspection Service (APHIS) of the USDA. At present three quarantine acts are in operation in US.

Plant Quarantine Act of 1912.   The first US federal plant quarantine law, known as the Plant Quarantine Act of 1912, was passed after the establishment of white pine blister rust and chestnut blight fungi and the citrus canker bacterium. The act controls the introduction of exotic pests and the spread of plants new to US and within US as a domestic quarantine (Waterworth, 1993).

Organic Act of 1944.   This act is mainly for pest management strategies but gives an authority for issuance of phytosanitary certificates in accordance with the requirements of the importing states and foreign countries.

Federal Plant Pest Act of 1957. This act authorizes emergency actions to prevent the introduction or interstate movement of plant pests not covered under the act of 1912.

Nearly all imported germplasms fall into one of the three categories: restricted, post-entry or prohibited. Import of some major crop seeds prohibited in US is given in Table 11.4.

Table 11.4 Import of Some Major Crops Seeds Prohibited in US

Crop	Country	Disease
Gossypium spp. (cotton)	All countries	Various diseases
Lens spp. (lentil)	South America	Rust
Oryza sativa (paddy, rice)	All countries	Smuts, viruses and other diseases
Sorghum vulgare (milo, sorghum)	Africa, Asia, Brazil	Smuts
Triticum aestivum (wheat)	Asia, Australia, Eastern Europe	Flag smut
Zea mays (corn, maize)	Africa, Asia	Downy mildews

Post-entry surveillance for the detection and interception of seed-borne pathogens on introduced plants and the production of diseases-free seeds are accomplished at the regional plant introduction stations. These stations are operated by cooperative agreement between the USDA and land-grant colleges and universities. Here, the plants are subjected to inspection, detection, post-entry surveillance and release of seeds.

11.3.2 Plant Quarantine in UK

The plant health legislation in UK was passed as the Destructive Insects Act of 1877 to prevent the entry and establishment of Colorado beetle. Destructive Insects and Pests Act of 1907 was enacted to check the entry of American gooseberry mildew (*Sphaerotheca morsuvae*) and all insects, fungi or other destructive pests of plants. To cover bacteria and viruses as well as invertebrate pests, the act was extended as the Destructive Insects and Pests Act of 1927. These three acts were consolidated and formulated in a Plant Health Act of 1967. This was further amended by the European Committees Act of 1972. The most familiar activity is the inspection of plants or plant produce either before export or after import.

11.3.3 Plant Quarantine in India

Wadhi (1980) has reviewed plant quarantine activities in India. The earlier activities concerned with the introduction of plant pests and diseases with plant material, in early 1900s, included fumigation of all imported cotton bales to prevent introduction of the Mexican boll weevil (*Anthonomus grandis*). In 1914, the Government of India passed the Destructive Insects and Pest Act prohibiting or restricting the import of plant and plant materials, insects, fungi, etc., to India from foreign countries. This comes under *foreign quarantine*. Rules and regulations have been made prohibiting or restricting the movement of certain diseased and pest-infested materials from one state to another in India. This comes under *domestic quarantine*.

The enforcement of plant quarantine regulations is carried out by the technical officers of the Directorate of Plant Protection and Quarantine, Ministry of Agriculture, Government of India, under the overall supervision of Plant Protection Advisor. There are eight quarantine stations at seaports, seven at airports and seven at land frontiers. Research material is examined by three agencies, the National Bureau of Plant Genetic Resources, New Delhi, for agricultural and horticultural crops; the Forest Research Institute, Dehradun, for forest plants and Botanical Survey of India, Calcutta, for all other plants of general economic significance. NBPGR has established two-field stations, at Pantnagar (for tropical plants) and Rani Chauri (for temperate plants) for post entry quarantine checking of imported plant material.

11.4 INTERNATIONAL ORGANIZATIONS

The first successful attempt towards solving a major pest problem on a collaborative basis resulted in the establishment in Europe of the *Phylloxera* convention of 1881. Each contracting government had to guarantee that only American rootstocks were used in vine growing so as to secure containment of *Phylloxera vitifolia*, the root aphid which had been devastating the European vine yards. In 1929, a first world plant protection convention was signed in Rome. In 1945, the United Nations and its specialized agency, the Food and Agriculture Organization (FAO), were established. This provided the best forum for the development of plant protection on a global level. The real breakthrough in this respect occurred with the establishment of the 1951 FAO International Plant Protection Convention. For implementation of various tasks the signatory governments have to make provision for: (a) the establishment of an official plant protection service, mainly in charge of quarantine matters, including plant health certification and surveillance of the phytosanitary situation within the country and controlling harmful organism of major importance, (b) a system securing technology transfer and (c) a research organization. The FAO Plant Protection Convention stipulated that governments needed to cooperate with one another through regional plant protection organizations of the appropriate areas. At present there are eight regional plant protection organization covering different areas of the world (Table 11.5).

The regional organizations, listed in Table 11.5, differ from each other in scope and functions. Some of them dealing with all protection technologies and other specifically with quarantine. However, they all serve as advisory and coordinating bodies to participating governments. They operate as a network to promote concerted action for combating pests of international importance and to propose quarantine measures for preventing the spread of these pests.

Table 11.5 Regional Government Organizations

Region	Organization	Member Government	Establishment
Western hemisphere	Central America (OIRSA)	7	1955
	FAO Caribbean commission	12	1967
	South America: northern part (OBSA)	3	1965
	Southern part (CIPA)	6	1965
West and east palaearctic	EPPO	35	1951
	OFAO Near-East commission	16	1963
Africa	North and Central Africa (IAPSC)	41	1967
	South Africa (SARCCUS)	8	1950
Asia	FAO committee (SEAPPC)	18	1956

11.5 MECHANISM OF PLANT QUARANTINES

If a quarantine law is worth having (scientifically justified), it is worth enforcing and quarantines that cannot adequately and effectively enforced should never be enacted. The method of enforcement varies with the disease problem and the methods of trade.

11.5.1 Embargoes

An embargo prohibits any movement of susceptible or affected plant materials from a quarantined area into protected areas. Example: US doesn't impart cotton and rice from any country. Similarly, import of sorghum, wheat and maize from Asia is prohibited.

11.5.2 Inspection and Certification

Many plant propagating materials entering any region/nation are inspected regularly at the point of entry (land, sea and airports) and allowed entry only after having been declared free of injurious insects and disease. It is done at the point of origin as well as point of destination.

11.5.3 Disinfestations of Imported Material

The plant materials entering new area may require disinfestation treatments, either at the point of origin or at the port of entry.

11.5.4 Special Permits for Imports

Plant and plant products for scientific work, e.g. breeding work, botanical specimens and exotic plant material may be brought after obtaining special permit, even though quarantine prevents commercial shipments of the product.

11.5.5 Unrestricted Shipment

Where no potential pest is involved, plant materials of importance in world trade may be shipped from one country to another without disinfestations, or other restrictions, although they are subject to occasional inspection.

These regulations apply to international shipments and many similar regulations govern the shipment of plant products from one state to another under either state or federal law.

REFERENCES

Chaube, H.S. and Singh, U.S., 1990, *Plant Disease Management: Principles and Practices,* CRC Press, Boca Raton, Florida, 319.

Kahn, R.P., 1977, Plant Quarantine: Principles, Methodology, and suggested approaches. In: *Plant Health and Quarantine in International Transfer of Genetic Resources,* W.B. Hewitt, and Chirappa (Eds.), CRC Press, Cleveland, 289.

Mathys, G. and Baker, E.A., 1980, An appraisal of the effectiveness of Quarantines, *Annu. Rev. Phytopathology*, 18: 85.

McGregor, R.C., 1978, People placed pathogens: The emigrant pests. In: *Plant Diseases. An Advanced Treatise,* vol II, J.G. Horsfall and E.B. Cowling (Eds.), Academic Press, New York, 383.

Neergaard, P.A., 1990, A review on quarantine for seed, In: *Golden Jubilee Commemoration Volume, National Acad. Sci.,* New Delhi.

Singh, G.K., 1983, Regional ASEAN collaborations in plant quarantine, *Seed Sci. Technol.,* 11: 1189.

Thurston, H.D., 1973, Threatening plant diseases, *Annu. Rev. Phytopathology*, 11: 27.

Wadhi, S.R., 1980, *Plant Quarantine Activity at the National Bureau of Plant Genetic Resources,* NBPGR Sc. Mongr, No. 2., National Bureau of Plant Genetic Resources, New Delhi, p. 90.

Waterworth, H.E., 1993, Processing foreign plant germplasm at the National Plant Germplasm Quarantine Centre, *Plant Dis.,* 77: 854.

12

Cultural Practices

12.1 INTRODUCTION

Adjustment in crop management practices to prevent or minimize disease development represent the oldest and most broadly applicable approach to plant disease control (Anonymous, 1968). Cultural practices often offer the opportunity to alter the environment, the condition of the host, and/or the behaviour of the causal agent, to achieve economic management of disease. Most cultural practices used to control plant disease are preventive in nature. Integration of cultural practices, host resistance and pesticides or biocontrol agents may be necessary to provide options for controlling economically important plant diseases (Andrews, 1983; Baker, 1983).

12.2 THE CONCEPT AND APPLICATIONS

Katan (1996) has classified cultural practices into three categories:

- Practices, which are usually applied for agricultural purposes not connected with crop protection, such as fertilization and irrigation. They may or may not have a positive or a negative side-effect on disease incidence.
- Practices that are used solely for disease control, such as sanitation and flooding.
- Practices, which are used for both agricultural purposes and for disease control, such as crop rotation, grafting and composting.

The interest in studying the effect of cultural practices on disease has dual purpose: to develop suitable practices as control methods and to obtain information regarding their impact on diseases when they are used as agricultural practices in order to avoid negative side-effects. Cultural practices may be employed, before or after planting. Deep ploughing and flooding are used before planting while irrigation and fertilization can be applied several times during the crop season for disease management.

12.3 THE PROCEDURES FOR DISEASE MANAGEMENT THROUGH CULTURAL PRACTICES

Singh (2000) has described several procedures for disease control through cultural practices, kept under, three categories Figure 12.1. In today's commercial agriculture where sustainability and integrated approach are the guiding principles, all the methods listed are not very relevant. Only those that contribute to sustainability and concept of integration are being described.

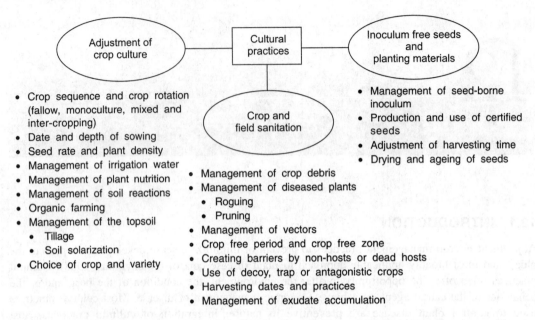

Figure 12.1 Procedures for disease control through cultural practices.

12.4 THE PRACTICES

12.4.1 Inoculum Free Seeds and Planting Materials

A large number of biotic and mesobiotic agents survive and get introduced in the crop or field or an area through true seed or through vegetative planting material such as seed tubers, cuttings, bulbs, grafts, rhizomes, etc. The inoculum is present either as contaminant or admixture (ear cockle of wheat – *Arguina tritici*, cysts of golden nematode of potato – *G. rostochiensis*, oospores of *Albugo candida*, sclerotia of ergot fungi), or as internally seed borne (loose smuts of wheat and barley, ascochyta blight of chickpea, phomopsis blight of brinjal, etc.) or as externally seed borne (covered smut of barley, grain smut of sorghum, covered smut of oats, bunt of cereals, etc.), or through nursery raised planting stocks. Some cultural practices such as cleaning, drying and ageing of seed and proper adjustment of harvesting time are the practices which, if followed, would reduce the introduction, survival and spread of inoculum.

Vegetable seedlings, tree seedlings and grafts raised in infested nurseries when used for transplanting, carry inoculum to main field or orchard. Vegetable seedlings infected in nursery with root knot nematode are an important source of introduction of *Meloidogyne* spp. in clean field. In bacterial canker of tomato (*Clavibacter michiganense* subsp. *michiganense*), bacterium which has caused seedlings infection from the seed is carried in symptomless seedlings and such seedlings are major source of dissemination of the bacterium. Transmission of parasitic fungi (*Pythium*, *Phytophthora*) is common in papaya through seedlings raised in infested soils. According to Naqvi (1994) in citrus seedlings major source of inoculum of Phytophthora root and collar rot is the nursery infected planting stock and infested nurseries. Nursery stock infected with powdery mildew fungus (*Podosphaera leucotricha*) is a major source of introduction of disease in apple orchard.

12.4.2 Crop and Field Sanitation

Sanitation is a major practice of disease management. Regular removal of diseased plants from a population is an important sanitary precaution. It is one of the effective recommendations in the management of viral diseases of field crops. For the control of loose smut of wheat and production of disease free seed, roguing is always recommended in seed plots. Roguing of infected plants is recommended in several other diseases, e.g. smut of sugarcane, red rot of sugarcane, downy mildews of sorghum and maize, wilts of pigeon pea and several viral diseases.

Management of weeds, collateral and volunteer host plants is another important sanitary practice. Plant pathogens usually have wide host-range. These additional hosts ensure carry over of the pathogen from one season to the next, and also provide a base on which inoculum multiplies and reaches epidemic proportions early in the season of main crop. Cucumber mosaic virus, powdery mildew fungi (*Erysiphe* spp.) and root knot nematodes have over 700 plant species as their host (Singh, 2000). Keeping the field free from additional hosts of the pathogen is a major sanitary cultural practice.

The destruction of crop debris especially the roots to reduce source of survival and multiplication of inoculum helps in control of many diseases. The oospores of fungi causing downy mildew of pearl millet, maize, sorghum, pea, grapevines and white rust of crucifers perennate in soil through crop debris. In cooler regions, the fungus causing powdery mildew of wheat and pea also survive through their perithecia in crop refuse and locally produced conidial inoculum on infected hosts for dispersal by wind to distant places. In certain areas, the linseed rust fungus, the rice blast and leaf spotting fungi, and the pathogen causing early blight of potato and tomato also perennate through dormant stages in diseased crop debris. In rice growing areas, paddy straw harbours many pathogens such as true sclerotia of *Ustilaginoidea virens* (false smut), the sheath blight fungus (*R. solani*), the stem rot fungus (*S. oryzae*) and rice bunt fungus (*Neovossia horrida*) as well as spore of leaf smut (*Entyloma oryzae*). In temperate climate, fungus causing late blight of potato besides surviving in seed tubers also survives as mycelium and sporangia in crop debris. In apple scab (*V. inaequalis*) fallen leaves play the major part in providing inoculum in the next spring.

Use of fire and flame has been recommended as one method of destroying infected crop debris (Hardison, 1976). Deep ploughing, especially during summer in the tropics, buries the debris to such depths where the pathogens are automatically destroyed. Fallows also help in the reduction of inoculum through sanitary effects of decomposition of crop debris in absence of a host. The principle of flood fallowing is also a method of cleaning the soil of pathogens.

12.4.3 Adjustment of Crop Culture

Crop rotation, cropping systems and crop sequence. Crop rotation is the growing of economic plants in recurring succession and in definite sequence on the same land (Curl, 1963). Cook and Baker (1983) defined the cropping system as *the sequence or combination of crops grown in a single field*. The term *crop sequence* is to be preferred, according to Palti (1981), since it covers monoculture also. The sequential sowing of crops may or may not include fallow or green manure. The crop rotation programme determines the frequency of growing each crop, the list of crops (and fallow periods) during a defined period (cycle), the order (history) of crops and the agricultural practices which will be employed during the whole cycle (Katan, 1996). Monoculture is the opposite of such a practice and is applied for agroclimatic reasons and economic considerations.

The effectiveness of crop rotation in disease control will depend on the nature of the pathogen and the crop, the agricultural practices involved, soil properties and other biotic and abiotic factors. The factors that reduce effectiveness of crop rotation in controlling soil borne diseases include (a) wide host range of the pathogen, (b) pathogens having effective mechanisms for survival in the absence of host, (c) pathogens producing large inoculum densities as resting structures, (d) crops that are susceptible to several diseases, (e) crops which stimulate formation of resting structures, (f) frequent infestation of soil with pathogen from external sources, (g) soils that are conducive to diseases and (h) poor weed management.

Vegetables are rotated with grain crops such as rice or with highly resistant cultivar of the same vegetable to control pathogens like root knot nematode. When potato is grown in two consecutive seasons in infested soil, there is 35.5% rise in the incidence of common scab (*Streptomyces scabies*) in the first year, and 65.5% in the second year. Keeping two crops of cereals (wheat and rice) or a legume and millet between two potato crops significantly reduces the disease incidence (Singh and Jeswani, 1986). Generally a four-year rotation is recommended against this disease avoiding beet and fleshy rooted crucifers. Long rotations with graminaceous crops between potatoes are a major recommendation against bacterial wilt caused by *Ralstonia solanacearum* (Verma and Shekhawat, 1991). A crop of rice taken after cotton reduces inoculum of *Verticillium dahliae* and that of pea taken after wheat reduces the inoculum of the take-all fungus. Even virus diseases are suppressed by suitable crop rotations and cropping practices (Thresh, 1982; Thomas, et al., 1993).

Monoculture. According to Palti (1981), monoculture is cultivation of a single or closely allied crop species in annual or seasonal succession, with interruption only by fallow or intermittent growing of green manure crop or application of soil amendments, not necessarily after each crop. It is generally agreed that in each agro-ecosystem diversity is a stabilizing factor and prevents excessive pressure on any part of the system. This applies to crop disease system also (Singh, 2000). From the general biological aspects, monoculture is therefore, undoubtedly dangerous because it does not permit diversity. Monoculture may also exert selection pressure on pathogens, resulting in emergence of new pathotypes. There are examples however, when continued monoculture resulted in development of soil suppressiveness (Baker, 1980). Take-all decline of wheat due to monoculture has been extensively studied. One of the suppressive factors which was fostered by wheat monoculture, has been identified as *Pseudomonas fluorescens*. The suppressiveness was gradually lost due to rotation, fumigation or steaming. Three concurrent processes are thought to be responsible for take-all decline: (a) development of specific antagonism, (b) changes in pathogen's population and (c) changes in the microflora which affect the pathogen.

Tillage. This is a major agricultural practice which affects many physical properties of soil such as water infiltration, bulk density, aeration, temperature, moisture, compacting and resistance to root penetration. These affect biological activities in the soil, root growth, pathogen activity and the capacity of the plant to withstand pathogen action (Katan, 1996). In addition, tillage affects the spatial distribution of crop residues in the soil. There are various tillage practices, including deep ploughing, reduced cultivation, subsoiling, chiseling, conservation tillage, minimum tillage and zero or no tillage (Palti, 1981 and Summer, et al., 1981). Deep plouging is practised to reduce the contact between plant roots and pathogen propagules or to expose the propagules to natural heating and desiccation. Minimum tillage practice may increase, decrease or have no effect on plant diseases. Leaving crop debris on the surface or partially buried in the soil may allow numerous pathogens to survive until the next crop is planted but conditions favourable for biological control may also be increased (Katan, 1996). In a long-term study, the intensity of common root rot disease caused by *Cochliobolus sativus* was generally lower under zero than conventional tillage (Tinline and Spurr, 1991). Unfortunately, although some pathogens can be controlled by reduced tillage systems, many others are favoured if the soil is not tilled adequately (Cook and Baker, 1983).

Organic amendment of soil. One of the cheapest hazard-free and ecofriendly effective methods of modifying soil environment is amendment of soil with decomposable organic matter. Sun and Huang (1985) had rightly observed that continuous extensive agricultural practices that depend heavily on use of chemicals have resulted in loss of organic matter, an increase in acidity, and accumulation of toxic elements in cultivated soils creating an environment favourable for development of certain soil borne pathogen. The reduction in common scab of potatoes (*S. scabies*) by green manuring through prevention of the build-up of inoculum was the first report of organic amendments as a means of disease suppression. Since this observation of Sanford (1926), numerous reports have appeared regarding the beneficial effects of organic and inorganic amendments of soil.

The list of soil-borne diseases that have been controlled in glasshouse, microplots or field plots by organic amendment of soil, is quite exhaustive. Some of the important ones are given in Table 12.1.

Table 12.1 Suppression of Soil-Borne Diseases by Organic Amendment of Soil

Pathogen	Crop and Disease
Fungal diseases	
Aphanomyces euteiches	Root rot of peas
Fusarium oxysporum f. sp. *udum*	Wilt of pigeon pea
Fusarium oxysporum f. sp. *cubense*	Wilt of banana
Fusarium oxysporum f. sp. *lini*	Wilt of linseed
Fusarium oxysporum f. sp. *pisi*	Wilt of pea
Fusarium oxysporum f. sp. *corianderi*	Wilt of coriander
Fusarium oxysporum f. sp. *ciceri*	Wilt of chickpea
F. solani f. sp. *phaseoli*	Wilt and root rot of bean
Fusarium coeruleum	Wilt and root rot of guar
Helminthosporium sativum	Root rot of wheat
Macrophomina phaseolina	Root rot of cotton
Ophiobolus graminis	Take-all disease of wheat
Phymatotrichum omnivorum	Root rot of cotton
Phytophthora sp.	Root rot of ornamentals
Phytophthora cinnamomi	Root rot of avocado
Pythium spp.	Browning root rot of wheat
Pythium aphanidermatum	Soft rot of ginger
Pythium ultimum	Seedling blight of alfalfa
Rhizoctonia solani	Black scurf of potato
Sclerotium rolfsii	Wilt of *piper beetle*

(Contd.)

Table 12.1 Suppression of Soil-Borne Diseases by Organic Amendment of Soil (*Contd.*)

Pathogen	Crop and Disease
Sclerotium graminis	Foot rot of wheat
Streptomyces scabies	Common scab of potato
Thielaviopsis spp.	Root rots of ornamentals
Thielaviopsis basicola	Root rot of bean and sesamum
Verticillium albo-atrum	Wilt of potato, tomato and cotton
Diseases caused by nematodes	
Belanolaimus longicaudatus	Sting nematode
Heterodera avenae	Cereal cyst nematode
Heterodera major	Cereal cyst nematode
Heterodera rostochidensis	Potato cyst nematode
Heterodera schachtii	Sugarbeet cyst nematode
H. tabacum	Tobacco cyst nematode
Hoplolaimus indicus	Lance nematode
Hoplolaimus tylenchiformis	Lance nematode
Meloidogyne javanica	Root knot nematode of vegetables
M. incognita	Root knot nematode of vegetables
Pratylenchus penetrans	Lesion nematode
Tylenchulus semipenetrans	Citrus nematode

Source: Singh and Sitaramaiah, 1973

The mechanisms of action of organic amendments leading to plant disease control are not yet fully understood. Different pathogens respond differently to organic amendments. One of the reasons is the difference in *C/N* ratio of decomposing material. The complex nature of soil environments makes it difficult to assess the possible activities occurring in the soil. However, it is generally believed that antagonists play the major role. The manifold increase in the number and variety of microorganism including fungi, bacteria, saprozoic, mycophagous and predatory nematodes is well-established. It appears that disease control in amended soil is the result of not one specific mechanism, but different mechanisms operate at different stages during decomposition of the organic matter. These mechanisms affect disease incidence and severity through their effect on soil, host and the pathogen. Stover (1962) had proposed the following mechanisms:

- Changes in physical environment, such as soil pH and CO_2
- Increased host tolerance or resistance
- Antagonism— (a) plant fungistasis and microbial fungistasis, (b) direct parasitism of the pathogen by microbes or lysis and decomposition of the pathogen induced by microbes, (c) poor competitive ability or antibiosis prevents utilization of nutrients by the pathogen resulting in indirect starvation or there is low level of essential nutrients that causes reduction or cessation of pathogen activity.

More or less similar conclusions were drawn by Singh and Sitaramaiah (1973) and Singh, et al. (1972) in studies on control of root knot (*M. javanica*) of vegetables and organic amendments. They had concluded the following mechanism:

1. Disease avoidance through modification of physico-chemical environments of soil in favour of the host
2. Suppression of the pathogen and disease management through effects of the decomposition products and microbial metabolites on the pathogen and the host
3. Suppression of pathogen through direct antagonism

A modified version of the possible pathways of action of organic amendments against pathogen is shown in Figure 12.2.

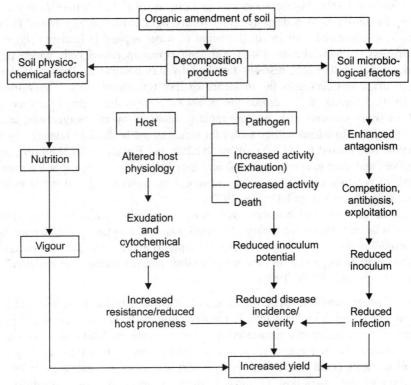

Figure 12.2 Schematic diagram showing mechanism of organic amendment of soil.

Irrigation and water management. Irrigation affects both soil-borne and foliar diseases (Rotem and Palti, 1969). It alters soil's moisture content and consequently influences the aeration and temperature, which in turn affect soil-borne diseases through their actions on biotic and abiotic processes in soil. Irrigation also affects disease incidence indirectly due to change in agricultural regimes such as intensification of cropping, changes in date of sowing and growing seasons (Katan, 1996). Irrigation occasionally makes it possible to avoid diseases by growing crops out of season (Rotem and Palti, 1969). Irrigation water is often a means of transport of inoculum through the field and to adjacent fields in the area. Transfer of conidia and appresoria of *Colletotrichum falcatum*, sporangia of downy mildew fungi, sporangia and zoospores of *Pythium* and *Phytophthora*, cells of bacteria, can be moved in and outside the field through irrigation or running water. The crop debris carrying active or dormant inoculum of pathogens is also transported by irrigation and drainage water in channels through infested field.

Soil moisture is related to many diseases. For example, wet soil favours club root of crucifers, silver scurf of potatoes and *Cercosporella* on wheat while dry soil increases severity of white mould of onion, common scab of potatoes and fusarium diseases of cereals (Colhoun, 1973). Damping-off diseases caused by *Pythium* spp. can be reduced by maintaining a dry soil surface as zoosporic fungi such as *Pythium* and *Phytophthora* depend on soil water for zoospores release and motility. Diseases cased by these fungi have invariably been reported to be favoured by heavy or frequent irrigations. The incidence of root rot of chilli peppers caused by *P. capsici* in plots receiving alternate-row irrigation was significantly less than in plants with irrigation of every row (Biles, et al., 1992). According to Ristaino (1991) Phytophthora root and crown rot in bell pepper were greater in plots irrigated more frequently with a deep system. Weekly light irrigation aggravated *Pythium* rot of groundnut pods, as compared with an equal amount of water applied in heavier irrigation at longer (every two weeks) intervals (Frank, 1967). Growing plants in raised beds which provide good drainage and aeration will reduce diseases favoured by wet conditions. This practice of reducing the number of irrigations decreases the incidence of root rot caused by *S. sclerotiorum* in lettuce (Steadman, 1979). Sclerotia of *S. sclerotiorum, S. minor, S. cepvoirum*, dried for short periods and remoistened results in nutrients leak, and are rapidly colonized by microorganisms, and rot within 3 weeks (Smith, 1972). Irrigation will be useful for management of diseases favoured by water stress such as charcoal rots caused by *M. phaseolina*, (Gaffar and Erwin, 1969). Moisture status of soil affects microflora and their interactions in soil and thus irrigation can be a tool for cultural control. Common scab of potatoes (*S. cabies*) can be managed by maintaining soil water near field level during tuberization (Lapwood and Hering, 1970).

In addition to the amount of irrigation, the timing of irrigation is also important. The principles influencing the relation between the timing of irrigation and its frequency, with disease management include: (a) providing the crop with uniform water supply to avoid water stress or excess, (b) timing of irrigation in relation to periods of host susceptibility and (c) minimizing period of continuous leaf wetness (Chaube and Singh, 1990).

Management of plant nutrition. The plants absorb mineral nutrition from soil and the parasites attacking them take energy from the plants. The macronutrients (N, P, K) are needed in large amounts by plants while the micronutrients are needed in smaller quantities. Maintenance of optimum plant health with sufficient, but not excessive, levels of fertility can be beneficial in crop resistance to infection. Soil nutrients could affect diseases by direct effects on the pathogen or by their effects on the nutrition of the plant host or through their influence on soil microflora particularly antagonists (Figure 12.3).

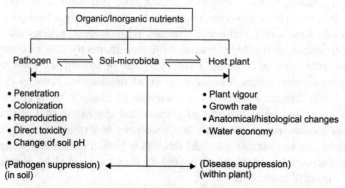

Figure 12.3 Soil fertility and disease management.

Nitrogen. It is one of the major elements for plant growth and markedly affects cell size. The forms of nitrogen may influence the disease severity. Cortical and root diseases caused by *Fusarium, Rhizoctonia, Aphanomyces, Cercosporela, Amillaria,* etc. may be reduced by nitrate nitrogen or increased by ammonical nitrogen, while diseases caused by *Ophiobolus, Diplodia, Pythium,* and *Streptomyces* respond in an opposite manner. Cereal rusts and mildews generally increase with NO_3–N and are reduced with NH_4–N (Huber and Watson, 1974).

Dosages of nitrogen influence plant susceptibility also. Application of dosage make potato high nitrogen nutrition crop canopy dense, which becomes prone to late blight attack. In sheath blight of rice (*R. solani*) higher nitrogen promotes disease. According to Patel, et al. (1992) since there is no difference in yield of crop receiving 100 to 200 kg/ha nitrogen, the low dose of 100 kg/ha is recommended to suppress the disease. Excess of nitrogen predisposes the host to rusts, powdery mildew and Karnal bunt of wheat, tobacco mosaic and potato tubers to soft rot. When nitrogen is deficient, the plant is weak and the maturity is fixed. Pathogen favoured by slow growth of the host are favoured by low nitrogen. This category includes tomato wilt (*F. oxysporum* f. sp. *lycopersicae*), bacterial wilt caused by *Ralstonia solanacearum*, root rot caused by *S. rolfsii* and damping-off caused by *Pythium* spp.

Phosphorus. One of the major elements is phosphorus, largely used in membranes, cell division, nucleic acids and high energy compounds. Its deficiency is second in importance next only to nitrogen, and is likely to affect the development of roots. Leaves tend to be undersized, erect, and somewhat necrotic, and relatively few lateral buds are formed. Foliage may be red or of purple tinge. Phosphate and potassium generally have the tendency to decrease susceptibility. Effects of P on some important disease have been summarized by Palti (1981) and Huber (1980). According to them, diseases such as damping-off of pea (*R. solani*), downy mildews of cabbage and grapes, flag smut of wheat (*U. tritici*), root rot of tobacco (*T. basicola*), root rot of soyabean (*R. solani*), and take-all of wheat (*G. graminis*) decrease as a result of phosphate application.

Potassium. Usually high potassium has been reported to reduce incidence of diseases. The mechanism by which K affects disease differs greatly, and includes both direct and indirect effects (Chaube and Singh, 1990). Direct effects include reduction or stimulation of pathogen penetration, multiplication, survival, aggressiveness and rate of establishment in the host. Indirect effects include promotion of wound healing, increase in resistance to frost injury and delay in maturity in some crops. Among the diseases reported to be reduced include ascochytosis of chickpea, blast of rice, brown spot of rice, downy mildews of lettuce, grapes and cauliflower, early blight of tomato, gray mould of grape, late blight of potatoes, northern blight of corn, powdery mildew of cereals, root rot of pea, pine apple, cotton and jute, rusts of cereals, sheath blight of rice, stalk rot of maize, wilts of cotton, melon and tomato (Palti, 1981; Huber, 1980).

Balanced and imbalanced nutrition. It has invariably been observed that in fields having imbalanced levels of NPK, the plants are predisposed to the attack of pathogens (Sharma and Basuchaudhary, 1985). A balanced dose of NPK (120: 80: 40 kg/ha) was found suitable for reducing wilt and root rot of cauliflower (Sharma and Basuchaudhary, 1985). Incidence of bacterial stalk rot of maize increased with high N applications without P or K but decreased with high doses of P and K (Saxena and Lal, 1981). Practically, application of varying levels of commercial fertilizer in a balanced way helps to maintain the health of plants (Basuchaudhary and Gupta, 1988).

Soil solarization. Soil solarization is an advanced field technology for the control of soil-borne pathogens. This non-chemical control procedure has been adopted by farmers in several parts of the world. The first report on use of solar energy for the control of soil-borne diseases was published by Katan, et al. (1976). Since then hundreds of papers have been published, covering the subject in over 38 countries around the globe (Chaube and Singh, 1990; Tjamon, 1996). Soil solarization is based on trapping solar irradiation by tightly covering the soil, usually with transparent polyethylene sheets. This results in a significant increase (10–15°C above normal temperature) of soil, temperature up to the point where most pathogens are vulnerable to heat effects.

Soil solarization offers multiple pest control (Plates 12.1 and 12.2). It controls parasitic diseases, soil-borne pests, weeds and improves soil suppressiveness and fertility. Major parasitic fungi and diseases managed successfully include damping-off, root rots, stem rots, fruit rots, wilts and blights caused by *Pythium* spp., *Phytophthora* spp., *Fusarium* spp., *S. rolfsii, R. solani, Sclerotinia sclerotiorum, T. basicola* and *Verticillium* spp. (Katan, 1981; Chaube and Singh, 1990; Tjamon, 1996).

(A)

(B)

Plate 12.1   (A) Solarized plots, (B) Solarized plot and non-solarized plot with high weed population.

(A)

(B)

Plate 12.2 (A) Non-solarized plot showing poor seedling stand and growth, (B) Solarized plot showing high plant population and vigorous growth.

Among the nematodes *Ditylenchus dipsci, Globodera rostochiensis, Heterodera* spp., and *Meloidogyne* spp. have been managed successfully. Bacterial canker of tomato caused by *Clavibacter michiganensis* subsp. *michiganensis* successfully controlled by soil solarization for 1-2 months (Tjamon, et al., 1992). In general, most of the annual and many perennial weeds (Plates 12.1 and 12.2) such as *Amaranthus* spp., *Amsickia donglasiana, Anagallis* sp., *Avena fauta, Chaenopodium* spp., *Convolunalus* spp., *Cynodon dactylon, Digitaria sanguinalis, Echinochloa-crus-galli, Eleusine* sp., *Fumaria* sp., *Lactuca* sp. *Lanium amplexicaule, Molueella, Montia, Notabaris* sp., *Phalaris* spp., *Poa* sp., *Portulaca oleraceae, Sisymbrium* sp., *Senecio valgaris, Solanum halpense, Sorghum stellaria,* and *Xanthium pensylvanicum* have been controlled, many graminae are especially sensitive, while others like *Melilotus,* remain unaffected. *Cyperus rotundus* is only partially controlled (Katan, 1987; Chaube and Singh, 1990; Esfahani, 1991; Khulbe, et al., 2001, Chaube, 2002).

Soil solarization has been observed to improve plant growth and yield increase. Increased growth response has been attributed to altered/increased concentrations and availability of macro and micronutrients. Abdel-Rahim, et al. (1988) reported reduction in soil salinity due to solarization. Electrical conductivity increases significantly (Patel and Patel, 1997; Khulbe, 2000; Chaube, 2002). Total soil nitrogen increases significantly (Gruntzweig, et al., 1998; Patel and Patel, 1997; Khulbe, 2000). During solarization, increased amounts of nitrogen (principally ammonical and/or nitrate nitrogen) are liberated (Chauhan, et. al., 1988). Increased levels of phosphorus and potash have also been recorded (Gruntzweig, et al., 1998; Patel and Patel, 1997; Ahmad, et al. 1996; Khulbe, 2000). According to Stapleton and DeVay (1984) solarization increase KCl, extractable NO_3-N, NH_4^+-N, Mg^{2+}, Fe^{2+}, Cl^- and EC. However, solarization did not consistently affect available K, Fe, Mn, Zn, Cu concentrations, soil pH and total organic matter. Nitrogen appears to be one of the major elements whose availability most consistently increased in solarized soil (Stapleton, et al. 1991).

Mechanisms. Reduction in disease incidence occurring in solarized soils, results from the effects exerted on each of the three living components involved in diseases (host, pathogen and soil-microbiota) as well as the physical and chemical environments which, in turn affect the activity and interrelationships of the organisms. Although these processes occur primarily during solarization, they may continue to various extents and in different ways, after the removal of sheets and planting the crops. The most pronounced effect of soil mulching with polythene is a physical one, i.e., an increase in soil temperatures for several hours of the day. However, other accompanying processes such as shift in microbial populations, changes in chemical composition and physical structure of the soil, high moisture levels and changes in gas composition of the soil should also be considered when analyzing mechanisms of disease control. In Figure 12.4, the integrated management of crop health through solarization are explained.

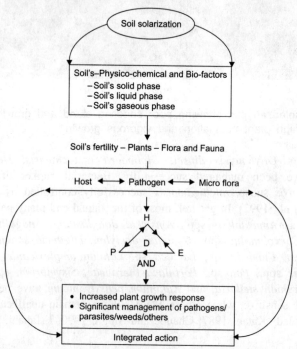

Figure 12.4 A flow chart explaining effects of solarization and integrated management of crop health.

Indirect management of microbial populations. Baker and Cook (1974) in their book on biological control have emphasized the relationship between disease management and biological control. Effective control tactics have involved approaches such as crop rotation, altering soil pH, use of certain fertilizers and organic amendments, tillage methods that modify soil structure, irrigation practices, planting dates, use of trap or inhibitory plants and manipulation of the environment to promote maximum resistance of the host. Table 12.2 lists some of the various methods used to manage diseases.

Table 12.2 Examples of Agricultural Practices that Relate to Biological Control of Diseases

Method	Pathogen Managed	Crop
Crop rotation	*Cephalosporium gramineum, G. graminis* var. *tritici*	Wheat
Crop spacing	*Sclerotinia sclerotiorum*	Dry beans
Decoy crop	*Spongospora subterranea*	Potato
Fallow	*Pseudomonas solanacearum*	Banana
Fertilizer practices	*F. oxysporum* f. sp. *phaseoli*	Dry bean
Flooding	*F. oxysporum* f. sp. *cubense*	Banana
Monoculture	*Streptomyces scabies*	Potato
	G. graminis var. *tritici*	Wheat
Organic amendments	Several parasitic fungi and nematodes	Crops
pH adjustment	*Plasmodiophora brassicae*	Crucifers
	Streptomyces scabies	Potato
Tillage	*Sclerotium rolfsii*	Peanut
Time of planting	*Fusarium roseum 'culmorum', Tilletia controversa*	Wheat
Trap crop	*Meloidogyne* spp.	Crops
Water management	*Phytophthora* spp.	Walnut, Cherry
	Macrophomina phaseolina	Sorghum

Source: Baker and Cook, 1974; Chaube and Singh, 1990

Modern agriculture involves several practices used under different conditions. Every cultural practice should be evaluated as a potential tool for disease management. A thorough familiarity with the ecology and crop husbandry is absolutely necessary; for disease management, appropriate modification or innovations in crop husbandry practices have furnished the foundations for success of all types of crop cultivation (Garrett, 1970).

There are many potential promising methods. The renaissance of CP for disease management is a fact. Our march towards ecologically harmonious and sustainable agriculture has already commenced. We must continue it, CP can and should play an important role in achieving this goal. "The main objective of cultural practices is to plant healthy seed in pathogen free soil or in soil with minimal contamination and obtain healthy stand of the crop" (Katan, 1996).

REFERENCES

Abdel-Rahim, M.F., et al., 1988, Effectiveness of soil solarization in furrow irrigated soils, *Plant Dis.*, 72: 143.

Ahmad, Y., Hameed, A. and Aslam, M., 1996, Effect of soil solarization on corn stalk rot, *Plant and soil*, 179: 17.

Andrews, J.A., 1983, Future strategies for integrated control, Chapter 40, In: *Challenging Problem in Plant Health*, T. Kommedahl and P.H. Williams (Eds.), American Phytopathological Society, St. Paul, Minnesota, p. 538.

Anonymous, 1968, *Plant Disease Development and Control*, vol. I, Principles of plant and animal pest control, Publ. 1596, Nat. Acad. Sci., Washington, DC, p. 250.

Baker, K.E. and Cook, R.J., 1974, Biological control of plant pathogens, Freeman, San Francisco.

Baker, K.F., 1983, The future of biological and cultural control of plant diseases. In: *Challenging Problem in Plant Health*, T. Kommedahl and P.H. Williams (Eds.), American Phytopathological Society (APS) Press, St. Paul, Minnesota, p. 217.

Baker, R., 1980, Pathogen suppressive soils in biocontrol of plant pathogens, *Plant Prot. Bull.* (Taiwan), 22: 183.

Basuchaudhary, K.C. and Gupta, D.K., 1988, Role of fertilizers in plant disease management, In: *Prospectives in Mycology and Plant Pathology*, V.P. Agnihotri, A.K. Sarbhoy and Dinesh Kumar (Eds.), Malhotra Publishing House, New Delhi, p. 84.

Biles, C.L., Lindsey, D.L. and Liddell, C.M., 1992, Control of Phytophthora root rot of chilli peppers by irrigation practices and fungicides. *Crop Protection*, 11:225.

Chaube, H.S., 2002, Soil solarization and management of seedling diseases of horticultural crops, *Technical Bulletin, Directorate of Exp. Sta.*, G.B. Pant University of Agriculture and Technology, Pantnagar, p. 142.

Chaube, H.S. and Singh, U.S., 1990, *Plant Disease Management: Principles and Practices*, CRC Press, New York, p. 329.

Chauhan, Y.S., et. al., 1988, Effect of soil solarization on pigeon pea and chickpea, *Research Bull II. ICRISAI*, Patoncheru, p. 16.

Colhoun, J., 1973, Effect of environmental factors on plant diseases, *Ann. Rev. Phytopathology*, 11: 345.

Cook, R.J. and Baker, K.F., 1983, *The Nature and Practice of Biological Control of Plant Pathogens*, American Phytopathological Society, St. Paul, p. 539.

Curl, E.A., 1963, Control of Plant Diseases by Crop Rotation, *Bot. Rev.*, 29: 413.

Esfahani, Mehdi Naser, 1991, Effect of soil solarization on soil-borne seedling diseases of some vegetable crops, *Ph.D. Thesis*, G.B. Pant Univ. Agric. Tech., Pantnagar.

Frank, Z.R., 1967, Effect of irrigation procedure in *Pythium* rot of groundnut pods, *Plant Dis. Rep.*, 51:414.

Gaffar, A. and Erwin, D.C., 1969, Effect of soil water stress on root rot of cotton caused by *Maenephomina phasoli, Phytopathology*, 59: 795.

Garrett, S.D., 1970, *Pathogenic Root Infecting Fungi*, Cambridge University Press, Cambridge, p. 294.

Gruntzweig, J.M., et al., 1998, The role of mineral nutrients in the increased growth response of tomato plants in solarized soil, *Plant and Soil*, 206: 21.

Hardison, J.R., 1976, Fire and flame for plant disease control, *Annu. Rev. Phytopathol.*, 14: 355.

Huber, D.M., 1980, Role of nutrients in defume, In: *Plant Pathology—An Advanced Treatise.* vol. V, J.G. Horsfall and E.B. Cowling (Eds.), Academic Press, New York, p. 163.

Huber, D.M. and Watson, R.D., 1974, Nitrogen form and plant disease, *Annu. Rev. Phytopathology,* 12: 139.

Katan, J., 1987, Soil solarization, In: *Innovation Approaches to Plant Diseases Control* (I. Chet, Ed.), John Wiley and Sons, New York, p. 77.

Katan, J., 1996, Cultural practices and soil borne disease management, In: *Management of Soil-borne Diseases,* R.S. Utkhde and V.K. Gupta (Eds.), Kalyani Publishers, India, p. 100.

Katan, J., Greenberger, A., Alon, H. and Grinstein, A., 1976, Solar heating by polyethylene mulching for the control of diseases caused by soil-borne pathogens, *Phytopathology,* 66: 683.

Khulbe, D., Chaube, H.S. and Sharma, J., 2001, Soil solarization: An ecofriendly method to raise healthy crops, In: *Microbes and Plants,* A. Sinha (Ed.), Campus Book, p. 158.

Khulbe, D. 2000, Soil solarization: Effect on soil's nutrients, microorganisms and plant growth response, *Ph.D. Thesis,* G.B. Pant Univ. Agric. & Tech., Pantnagar, Uttranchal.

Lapwood, U.H. and Hering, T.F., 1970, Soil moisture and the infection of young potato tubers by *Streptomyces scabies* (common scab) *Potato Res.,* 13: 296.

Miller, D.E. and Burkey, D.W., 1985, Effect of soil physical factors on resistance in beans to fusarium root rot, *Plant Dis.,* 69: 324.

Miller, D.E. and Burkey, D.M., 1975, Effect of soil aeration on Fusarium root rot of beans, *Phytopathology,* 65: 519.

Naqui, S.M., 1994, Effect of some fungicides in control of Phytophthora diseases of Nagpur mandarin in central India, *Indian Phytopathology,* 47: 430.

Nawaz, R.M.S. and Narayanaswamy, P., 1983, Influence of host nutrition on powdery mildew disease development in black gram, *Madras Agric. J.,* 70: 57.

Palti, J., 1981, *Cultural Practices and Infection Crop Diseases,* Springer-Verlag, Berlin, p. 243.

Patel, B.K. and Patel, H.R., 1997, Effect of nematicides, soil solarization, rabbing, green manuring on some physical and chemical properties of soil in nematode infested bidi tobacco nursery, *Tobacco Research,* 23: 19.

Patel, K.V., Vala, D.G., Mehta, B.P. and Patel, T.C., 1992, Effect of nitrogen doses on incidence of false smut of rice, *Ind. J. Mycol. Pl. Pathology,* 22: 250.

Ristaino, J.B., 1991, Influence of rainfall, drip irrigation and inoculum density on the development of Phytophthora root and crown rot epidemic and yield in bell pepper, *Phytopathology,* 81: 922.

Rotem, J. and Palti, J., 1969, Irrigation and plant diseases, *Annu. Rev. Phytopathology,* 7: 267.

Saxena, S.C. and Lal, S., 1981, Effect of fertilizer application on the incidence of bacterial stalk rot of maize, *Indian J. Myco. Plant Pathology,* 11: 164.

Sharma, Y. and Basuchaudhary, K.C., 1985, Effect of inorganic fertilizers on the incidence of wilt and root rot of cauliflower, *Indian J. Plant Pathology,* 3: 259.

Singh, B.P. and Jeswani, M.D., 1986, Managing common scab of potato through chemicals and cultural practices, *Indian Phytopathology,* 39: 152.

Singh, R.S., 2000, *Plant Disease Management,* Oxford & IBH, New Delhi.

Singh, R.S., and Sitaramaiah, K., 1973, Control of plant parasitic nematodes with organic amendments of soil, *Exp. Sta. Res. Bull. No-6,* G.B. Pant Univ. Agric. & Tech, Pantnagar (Uttranchal).

Singh, R.S., Chaube, H.S. and Singh, N., 1972, Studies on the control of black scurf disease of potato, *Indian Phytopathlogy,* 25: 343.

Smith, A.M., 1972, Biological control of fungal sclerotia in soil, S*oil Biol. Biochem.,* 4: 131.

Stapleton, J.J. and DeVay, J.E., 1984, Thermal components of soil solarization as related to changes in soil and root microflora and increased plant growth response, *Phytopathology,* 74:255.

Stapleton, J.J., Quick, J. and DeVay, J.E, 1991, Soil solarization: effect on soil properties, crop fertilization and plant growth, *Soil Biol. Biochem.,* 17: 369.

Steadman, J.R., 1979, Control of plant disease caused by Sclerotinia disease, *Phytopathology,* 69: 904.

Stover, R.H., 1962, Fusarial wilt (Panama diseases) of bananas and other *Mussa* species, Phytopathological paper No. 4, CMI, Surrey (UK), p. 117.

Summer, D.R., Doupink, B. Jr. and Boodalis, M.G., 1981, Effect of reduced tillage and multiple cropping on plant diseases, *Annu. Rev., Phytopathology,* 17: 167.

Sun, S.K. and Huang, J.W., 1985, Formulated soil amendment for controlling Fusarium wilt and other soil-borne diseases, *Plant Dis.,* 69: 917.

Thomas, P.E., et al., 1993, Potential role of winter rapeseed culture on the epidemiology of potato leaf role disease, *Plant Dis.,* 77: 420.

Thresh, J.M., 1982, Cropping practices and virus spread, *Annu. Rev. Phytopathology,* 20: 193.

Tinline, R.D. and Spurr, D.T., 1991, Agronomic practices and common root rot in spring wheat: Effect of tillage on disease and inoculum density of *Cochliobolus sativus* in soil, *Can. Pl. Pathology,* 13: 258.

Tjamon, E.C., 1996, Chemical treatment and soil solarization for management of soil-borne Diseases, In: *Management of soil-borne Diseases,* R.S. Utkhede and V.K. Gupta (Eds.), Kalyani Publishers, New Delhi, p. 261.

Tjamon, E.C., Antonou, P. and Panago Pulos, C.G., 1992, Control of bacterial canker of tomato by application of soil solarization, *Phytopathology,* 82(10): 1076 (Abst.)

Verma, R.K. and Shekhawat, G.S., 1991, Effect of crop rotation and chemical soil treatment on bacterial wilt of potato, *Indian Phytopathology,* 44: 5.

13
Biological Control

Advance is made by the study of cases, which can not be embraced by a general principle, by the possession of an eye to detect expectations and of a mind willing to examine them instead of putting them aside because they are not in harmony with preconceived ideas.

— Sir Richard Gregory, 1916

13.1 INTRODUCTION

Biological control has been practised through cultural practices such as crop rotations and green manuring, in agriculture through ages though the term was used in scientific literature in 1914 by G.F. Von Tabuef, a German plant pathologist. The first experiments in biological control with antagonists were conducted by G.B. Sanford in Canada. His paper (1926) dealt with factors affecting the pathogenicity of the potato scab organism. He launched a new phase of studies in microbial ecology. Sanford attributed the control to increase in population density of certain saprophytic bacteria antagonistic to *Streptomyces* (*Actinomyces*) *scabies*, multiplying upon the decomposing crop residues. The biological control, thus, entered in phytopathological research in a simple way, but later it showed the complexities that made it difficult even though rewarding (Dubey, 2001).

13.2 DEFINING THE DOMAIN

Garrett (1965) defined biological control *as the practice in which or the process whereby the undesirable effects of an organism are reduced through the agency of another organism that is not the host plant, the pest or pathogen or man.* On the other hand, some scientists have adopted an extremely broad view of biological control. Baker and Cook (1974), defined biological control as *the reduction of inoculum density or disease producing activities of a pathogen or parasite in its active or dormant state, by one or more organisms, accomplished naturally or through manipulation of the environment, host or antagonist or by mass introduction of one or more antagonist.*

An attempt was made to determine the degree of acceptance of the various concepts of what constitutes biological control. Response to survey by 138 members of American Phytopathological Society working with soil-borne pathogens indicated 49% preferred Baker and Cook's (1974) definition, 34% preferred Garret's (1965) whereas 17% felt that a good definition had not been published. It is obvious that scientists engaged in this area do not have uniform concepts. To provide a working definition for use in delimiting discussion at USDA Interdisciplinary Biological Control Conference held at Las Vegas in 1983, an ad-hoc group developed a definition (Baker, 1983) based on *pest suppression with biotic agents, excluding the process of breeding for resistance to pests, sterility techniques and chemicals modifying pest behaviours.* This is close, if not identical, to Garrett's (1965) concept.

Lupton (1984) in his presidential address to the Association of Applied Biologists in Great Britain entitled Biological Control—The Plant Breeder's Objective, emphasized the role of introducing resistant genes by conventional methods or by recombinant DNA technology in Biological Control. The current trend is in favour of including gene manipulations in host as a part of biological control. Lupton (1984) has perhaps stated it best: *accelerating or diverting evolutionary processes in order to obtain genotypes adaptable to [Men's] needs are a most important example of the application of biological control to agricultural and horticultural crop.* Cook (1987) has in his report of the Research Briefing Panel on Biological Control in Managed Ecosystems defined biological control as *the use of natural or modified organisms, gene or gene products to reduce the effects of undesirable organisms (pests) and to favour desirable organisms such as crop, trees, animals and beneficial insects and microorganisms.*

13.3 THE SCIENTIFIC FRAMEWORK

The scientific framework of biological control can be studied by discussing the strategies, agents and methods involved.

13.3.1 The Strategies

The scientific framework proposes three broad strategies for achieving biological control (Figure 13.1):

1. Regulation of pest population (classical approach) at or below economic threshold. This is the only accepted strategy for many insect pests, plant parasitic nematodes, rodents and weeds.
2. Exclusionary system of defense, such as rhizosphere or phyllosphere microflora colonizing infection courts and giving protection. For instance, *A. radiobacter* K84 (Kerr, 1980) colonizes infection court and excludes *A. tumifaciens* causing crown gall; potection of conifer stumps from *Heterobasidium (Fomes) annosum* by *Peniophora gigantean* (Risbeth, 1963; 1979), or protection from post-harvest damage of fruits by fruit rotters by treating with non-pathogenic antifungal bacteria instead of fungicides (Wilson and Pusey, 1985).
3. Systems of self-defense through resistance to disease and pests achieved genetically. It may be enhanced by cultural practices, induced by inoculation of plants with avirulent or mild strains of the pathogen or by expression of genes for biological control mechanisms in transgenic plants.

13.3.2 The Agents

The agents (Figure 13.1) of biocontrol, as follows, can be used in any of the above strategies:

The pest or disease agent itself. The ice-minus strain of *Pseudomonas syringae* are used to exclude ice nucleation strains of *Ps. syringae* from foliage of frost sensitive plants (Strategy 2; Lindow, 1983). Cross protection provided by inoculation with mild strain against virulent strains provides control by inducing self-defense (Strategy 3). Now transgenic tobacco and tomato plants containing genes for TMV protein coat are available that provide biological control against TMV.

Antagonists or natural enemies. The antagonists are the classical biocontrol agents, which have made success story in control of weeds by reducing the weed population (Strategy 1). Antagonists are applied to prunning wounds to provide protection against *Fomes* and *Armillaria* (Strategy 2; Rishbeth, 1979). Induced systemic resistance by rhizobacteria is an example of biocontrol by initiating self-defense in host (Strategy 3).

The manipulated plants or populations. The plants can be used as trap to regulate the population of plant parasitic nematodes (Strategy 1) e.g. *Crotalaria specteabilis* is used as a cover crop in peach orchards to reduce the population of root knot nematodes. The dense sowing of cereal crops prevents growth of weeds (Strategy 2). In Strategy 3, hosts are manipulated genetically to boost up biochemical disease resistance.

	Biological Control		
A	Regulate the pest population	Exclusionary defense system	Self defense
Pest used against itself	Sterile males	*A. radiobacter*	Cross-protection
Natural enemies; antagonists	Parasitoids	Protection of fruits	Induced-resistance
Plant or animal that benefits	Trap/cover crop	Dense sowing of cereals	Host plant resistance
B			
Pest used against itself	Genetically modified vector	Ice-minus *P. syringae*	Tobacco mosaic virus coat protein gene
Natural enemies; antagonists	Bt gene in *B. thuringiensis*	Bt gene in *P. fluorescens*	Bt gene in tobacco
Plant or animal that benefits	Trap plants	Modified growth habit	Genetically engineered plants

Figure 13.1 Examples of biological pest control categorized according to strategy and biocontrol agent. (A) mainly traditional examples, most of which are used commercially, (B) mainly experimental, involving research and development.

13.3.3 The Methods

Figure 13.2 Illustrates the methods used in biological control.

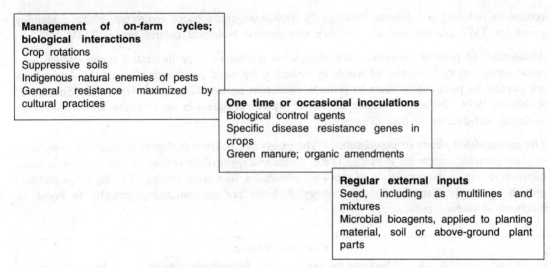

Figure 13.2 Methods of biological control.

13.3.4 The Antagonists

Antagonism is a phenomenon in which the activity of an organism (antagonist) inhibits, limits or harms the activity of other participants of an ecological association of a particular habitat. A large number of such microorganisms have been identified and exploited as biocontrol agents. Among fungal antagonists, *Trichoderma*, *Gliocladium*, *Aspergillus* and saprophytic Fusaria as well as fluorescent *Pseudomonas* and *Bacillus* species of bacteria have been widely recommended for the management of several soil borne plant pathogens. In Table 13.1, biocontrol agents commonly used for the management of plant diseases are listed.

Table 13.1 Biocontrol Agents Commonly used for the Management of Plant Diseases

Antagonistic Genus	Common Species	Type of Pathogens
1	2	3
Fungi		
Ampelomyces	A. quisqualis	Sphaerotheca fuliginia,
Arthobotrys	A. dactyloides	Nematodes
	A. oligospora	Ditylenchus myceliophagous, Meloidogyne spp.
Ascocoryne	A. sarcoides	Coniophora puteana, Polysporus tomentosus, Heterobasidium annosum
Candelabrella	C. javanica, C. musiformis	Nematodes
Catenaria	C. auxilaris, C. anguillulae	Nematodes Heterodera schachtii, H. avenae
Chaetomium	C. globosum, C. cochliodes	F. roseum Helminthosporium victoriae, Penicillium, Mucor, Venturia inequalis
Cladosporium	C. herbaraum, C. cladosporiodes	F. roseum, B. cinerea, N. galligena, V. inequalis

(Contd.)

Table 13.1 Biocontrol Agents Commonly used for the Management of Plant Diseases (*Contd.*)

Antagonistic Genus	Common Species	Type of Pathogens
1	2	3
Coniothyrium	C. minitans	S. sclerotiorum, S. trifolirum, S. cepivorum, B. cineria, B. fabae, Claviceps purpurea, S. rolfsii
Dactylaria	D. vermicola	Various nematodes in soil
Dactylella	D. oviparasitica D. doedycoides D. lobata	Nematodes, Heterodera schachtii Trichodorous semipenetrans Acrobeloides spp. Meloidogyne
Fusarium	F. roseum F. lateritium F. oxysporum	Fusarium spp.
Gliocladium	G. virens G. roseum G. catenulatum	Ceratocytis fimbriata Helminthosporium sativum, Trichothecium, R. solani, S. sclerotiourum, Fusarium, Pythium
Nematophthora	N. gynophila	Nematodes, H. avenae, H. carotae, H. cruciferae, etc.
Penicillum	P. liliacium P. nigricans P. frequentens P. oxalicum P. chrysogenum	S. cepivorum, Pythium, R. solani, Verticillium alboatrum, P. ultimum, Cephalosporium
Pythium	P. oligandrum	F. roseum f. sp. cerealis, F. nivale, G. graminis.
Trichoderma	T. viride T. harzianum T. polysorum T. koningii	R. solani, S. sclerotiorum, Pythium, Armillaria, Phytophthora, S. rolfsii, Heterobasidium annosum
Tubercularia	T. maxima	C. rebicola, C. quercuum f. sp. fusiforme
Verticillium	V. chlamydosporium V. lecanii V. bigttatum V. nigrescens	V. dahliae, Heterodera avenae, Uromyces dianthi
Bacteria		
Agrobacterium	A. radiobactor	A. radiobactor pv. tumefaciens
Bacillus	B. subtilis B. cereus B. penetrans	Phythium, R. solani, P. cinnamoni, S. cepivorum, F. roseum
Bdellovibrio	B. bacteriovorous	P. syringae pv. glycinea
Erwinia	E. herbicola E. uredovora	E. amylovora
Pseudomonas	P. fluorescens P. cepacia P. putida	Guanomyces graminis, Fusarium oxysporum (f. sp.) R. solani, S. rolfsii, Pythium, etc.
Streptomyces	S. griseus S. praecox S. lavendulae	Phomopsis, Fusarium, Gaeuanomyces

Source: Singh, U.S., et al., 2001

13.4 THE MECHANISM

Management of the associated microbiota provides a major opportunity for biological control of plant diseases. Cook (1987) has discussed five elements, which may contribute in biocontrol mechanism. The theory behind this type of disease management is to encourage the soil microbiota to perform the same job as the man does for suppression of plant pathogens and for helping the plant to resist attack of pathogens.

13.4.1 Reduction of Inoculum Density

Inoculum density can be reduced by destroying propagules or by preventing their formation. Crop rotation adds chemically different plant residues to soil. It may also starve the pathogen due to absence of host and/or weakens it to the extent that it is more rapidly destroyed by antagonistic microflora. There is evidence that with increased organic matter content in soil, perforations appear in the walls of resting structures due to activity of some organisms. Microbes enter the structure through these perforations and destroy them. To achieve good results it is desirable that resting structures should be first induced to germinate under hostile environment. Decomposing organic matter releases substances, which stimulate germination of sclerotia, chlamydospores or conidia as well as induces activity of saprophytic microflora. In such situations germination is followed by lysis.

13.4.2 Suppression of Germination and Growth of Pathogen

This form of biological control has two aspects: (a) reduction or prevention of germination (soil fungistasis) and (b) slowing down of growth of germlings due to starvation, antibiotics, bacteriocin, mycoviruses, etc. The phenomenon of fungistasis has been discussed separately.

13.4.3 Displacing the Pathogen from Host Residues

This approach applies to those pathogens that depend for survival on occupancy of the host remains (crop debris) during absence of host. The pathogens use the residues both as shelter and as a food base. This gives them the advantage of pioneer colonization. The system of residue possession by root pathogens is *passive*, *active* or both. *Pythium* spp., that attack succulent roots exemplify *passive possession*. Utilization of the substrate is slow and the pathogen persistently defends the substrate against saprophytes. Normally the active possessor does not retreat into a dormant structure, *Cephalosporium germineum* is a typical example. *Gaeumannomyces graminis* and *Fusarium graminearum* have some characteristics of active possessors. *F. oxysporum*, *F. solani* and *F. culmorum* are both active as well as passive possessors. They also need displacement for control through cultural practices.

13.4.4 Protection of an Infection Court

This approach aims at encouraging the soil microflora in or on the infection court, which slow or prevent infection by the particular pathogen. Such protection mainly includes conditions where a weak pathogen or non-pathogenic organism takes possession of the sites of infection on the host.

The mechanisms by which these precolonizers may protect the infection courts include (a) prior use of essential nutrients or oxygen needed by the pathogen, (b) modification of the rhizosphere pH, redox potential, other environmental factors that places the pathogen at a competitive disadvantages, (c) production of antibiotics, (d) hyperparasitism or exploitation of the pathogen and (e) modification of the host resistance.

13.4.5 Stimulation of Resistance Response of the Host

This includes cross protection provided by a weak avirulent or hypovirulent, strain of the same pathogen or by another pathogen. Tomato variety resistant to *F. oxysporum* f. sp. *lycopersici*, if inoculated with that pathogen, becomes resistant to *Verticillium dahliae*. Mint is resistant to *V. dahliae* if inoculated first with *V. nigrescens*. Take-all of wheat (*Gaeumannomyces graminis* var. *tritici*) is reduced if the roots are precolonized by *Phialophora radicicolia*.

13.5 FUNGISTASIS

Soil fungistasis, a phenomenon of inhibition of the spore germination in soils, is an ecologically important mechanism in maintaining the biological balance in soil. Three decade of investigations on the nature of fungistasis have attributed it to the involvement of chemical substances of non-volatile and volatile nature of either biotic or abiotic origin, nutrient status of the soil and kind of fungal propagules. Nevertheless, it is accepted that generally more than one factor is responsible for the widespread occurrence of fungistasis in soil. The term fungistasis, originally proposed by Dobbs and Hinson (1953), describes the phenomenon whereby *viable propagules, not under the influence of endogenous or constitutive dormancy, do not germinate in the soil in conditions of temperature and moisture favourable for germination.*

Watson and Ford (1972) proposed a theoretical explanation for the dynamic phenomenon of soil fungistasis, that there are three stages in fungistasis, namely, induction, maintenance and release of fungistasis. These stages are controlled by "a complex balance of stimulators and inhibitors" present in soil microenvironments. The stimulators are of biotic origin and may act as nutrients while inhibitors are both biotic and abiotic origin.

The organic substances present in root exudates have important role to play. The sclerotia of *Sclerotim cepivorum* were freed from fungistasis by volatiles associated with the root of *Allium* species. These substances have been identified as allyl sulfides from allyl cystein sulfoxides originating from *Allium* roots. Similarly, the volatile compounds like alcohols and aldehydes with low molecular weights released from plant residues were also found to be stimulatory to soil fungi. Freeing the fungal propagules from soil fungistasis and allowing a spore germination and lysis are important aspects for those using soil fungistasis as a tool in controlling soil-borne pathogens.

13.5.1 Soil Fungistasis and Biological Control

The reviewers have suggested the possibility of using soil fungistasis in controlling plant diseases caused by soil-borne plant pathogens. Fungistasis in natural soil is usually nullified by enriching the soil with energy sources or organic matter. The manipulation of the soil environment by organic amendment to enhance the liberation of volatile fungistatic substances is useful for the biological control. The enhanced production of ammonia was reported from soil amended with chitin, organic matters of crucifers and soyabean, linseed and cotton seed meals, and it was found that ammonia was suppressive to some of the soil-borne fungal pathogens like *Fusarium oxysporum* and *F. solani*, *F. solani* f. sp. *cucurbitae*, *Macrophomina phaseolina*, and *Phytophthora cinnamomi* (Chaube and Singh, 1990).

13.6 SUPPRESSIVE SOILS: THE NATURAL BIOLOGICAL CONTROL

The inhospitality of certain soils to some pathogens is such that either the pathogens cannot establish themselves or they are established but fail to cause disease or they diminish in severity with continued culture of the crop (Table 13.2). Thus, suppressive soil is an umbrella term encompassing fungistasis, competitive saprophytic ability and other disease and pathogen interactions where the defined relationship of reduced disease in the presence of the pathogen and susceptible host exist. The term, which is used in this chapter, is suppressive soils and its opposite, conducive soils.

Table 13.2 Examples of Pathogen/Disease-suppressive Soils

Pathogen	Disease(s) Caused	Pathogen	Disease(s) Caused
Armillaria mellea	Root rot of conifers	*Cephalosporium graminearum*	Stripe of wheat
Didymella lycopersici	Stem rot of tomato	*Fusarium avenaceum*	Root rot of many crops
F. oxysporum f. sp. *batatos*	Wilt of sweet potatoes	*F. oxysporum* f.sp. *cubense*	Wilt of banana
F. oxysporum f. sp. *dianthi*	Wilt of carnation	*F. oxysporum* f. sp. *lini*	Wilt of flax
F. oxysporum f. sp. *lycopersici*	Wilt of tomato	*F. oxysporum* f. sp. *melonis*	Wilt of melon
F. oxysporum f. sp. *pisi*	Wilt of pea	*F. oxysporum* f. sp. *raphani*	Wilt of radish
Fusarium udum	Wilt of pigeon pea	*Fusarium solani*	Root rot of bean
Gaeumannomyces graminis	Take all of wheat	*Heterodera avenae*	Cereal cyst nematode
Olpidium brassicae		*Phomopsis sclerotoides*	Root rot of cucurbits
Phytophthora cinnamomi	Root rot of various crops	*Poria weirii*	Root rot of conifers
Pseudocercosporella herpotrichoides	Root rot of cereals	*Pseudomonas solanacearum*	Soft rots
Pythium aphanidermatum	Root rot of radish	*Pythium ultimum*	Root rots
Pythium spp.	Root rots	*Rhizoctonia solani*	Root rots of many crops
Sclerotium rolfsii	Root rot of tomato	*Sclerotium cepivorum*	Wilt of onion
Streptomyces scabies	Scab of potatoes	*Verticillium alboatrum*	Wilt of potatoes

Source: Chaube, 1989

13.6.1 Characteristics of Suppressive Soils

Examples of suppressive and/or conducive soil are summarized in Table 13.3.

Table 13.3 Physical and Chemical Properties of Suppressive and Conducive Soils

Disease(s)	Soil Properties
Where the pathogen does not get established	
Fusarium wilt of banana	Sandy soil (C), Clay soil(S)
Fusarium wilt of cotton	Acidic soil (C)
Fusarium wilt of peas	Heavy clay soil (S)
Fusarium root rot of wheat	Sandy soil, low organic matter and low rainfall, (C) Fine textured, high organic matter and high rainfall (S)
Fusarium root rot of bean	Loessial (C) Lacustrine (S)
Aphanomyces root rot of peas	Aluminium ions (S)
Phymatortichum root rot of cotton	Alkaline soils (C)
Pine root rot	Light soil (C) Heavy soil (C)
Verticillium wilt of sunflower	Aluminium ions (S)
Pathogen established but fail to cause disease	
Aphanomyces root rot of peas	Compact soil (C)
Fusarium root rot of beans	Compact soil (C)
Phytophthora root rot of avocado	High organic matter, high exchangeable calcium (S)
Phytophthora root rot of avocado	Abiotic fungistatic factors (S)
Verticillium wilt of cotton	Copper induced fungistasis (S)
Pathogen established, produces disease for a while but then declines	
Fusarium root rot of bean	Continuous crop (S)
Phymatootrichum root rot of cotton	High exchangeable sodium (S)
Scab of potato	Continuous potatoes (S) in rotation with sugar beat, oats and maize (C)
Rhizoctonia damping off of radish	Continuous crop (S)
Note: C = conducive,	S = suppressive.

(*Source:* Schneider, 1982, Chaube 1989)

13.7 MECHANISMS OF ANTAGONISM

Mechanisms of action of different fungal antagonists against plant pathogens/diseases has been summarized in Table 13.4 and Figure 13.3. Following are five important components of mechanisms of antagonism.

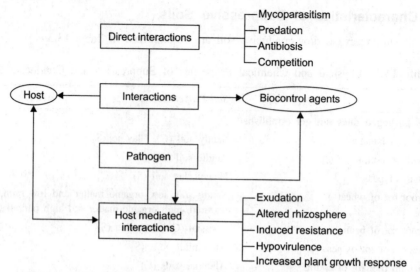

Figure 13.3 Modes of action of bioagents (Chaube, et al., 2002).

Table 13.4 Mechanism of Action of Fungal Biocontrol Agents Against Plant Pathogens

Antagonists	Pathogens	Mechanism of Action
Aspergillus flavus, A. niger, A. nudulans	*Meloidogyne incognita, M. phaseolina, Xantomonas oryzae* pv. *oryzae, Sclerotium rolfsii, Glomerella cingulata, R. solani, F. oxysporum*	Non-volatile compounds of culture filtrate, Antibiosis, Mycoparasitism, induced systemic resistance and production of siderophores
Acremonium obclavatum	*Puccinia arachidis*	Hyperparasitism
Chaetomium globosum	*Alternaria alternata F. moniliformae*	Antibiosis
Epicoccum purpurascens	*M. phaseolina*	Antibiosis
Gliocladium roseum, Gliocladium sp.	*Sclerotinia sclerotiorum, Sarocladium oryzae*	Mycoparasitism and antibiosis
Gigaspora margarita	*Heterodera cajani, F. udum*	Antibiosis
Glomus claroidium, G. mosseae, G. etunicatum, G. fasciculatum G. vessiforme	*M. phaseolina F. oxysporum* f. sp. *lycopersici, S. rolfsii, Meloidogyne incognita, R. solani, R. bataticola, Sclerotium oryzae*	Changes in population of micro-organisms in rhizosphere, alternation in root exudation, antibiosis, thickening of cell wall by lignification and production of polysaccharides
Paecilomyces lilacinus	*Rotylenchulus reniformis M. incognita, R. solani*	Antibiosis
Pencillium citrinum, P. oxalicum, P. simplicissimum, P. funiculasum, P. conylophilum,	*Collectotrichum gloeosporioides, Xanthomonas campestris, M. phaseolina, Sarocladium oryzae, Alternaria brassicicola, f. oxysporum* f. sp. *ciceri,*	Parasitism and antibiosis

(Contd.)

Table 13.4 Mechanism of Action of Fungal Biocontrol Agents against Plant Pathogens (*Contd.*)

Antagonists	Pathogens	Mechanism of Action
P. islandicum, P. pinophilum, P. pinophilum, P. purpurescens	Mycosphaerella arachidis, R. solani, Ralstonia solanacearum, Ustilago scitaminea	
Trichoderma aureoviride, T. hamatum, T. harzianum, T. viride, T. koningii, T. lignorum, T. longibrachiantum, T. virens	R. solani, Meloidogyne javanica, M. phaseolina, Sclerotium rolfsii, F. oxy. f. sp. zingiberi, F. oxy, f. sp. vasinfectum, Cerocospora monicola, F. solani, Ustilago segetum tritici, Pythium aphanidermatum, Claviceps fusiformis, Phytophthora cinnamomi, P. cactorum, P. nicotianeae, P. fragariae, Sclerotinia americana, Aspergillus flavus, Collectotrichum, gloeosporioides, Neovossia indica, Drechslera sorokiniana, Botrytis alli, Sarocladium oryzae, F. moniliforme	Parasitization on mycelium and sclerotia, direct parasitization of second juvenile larva and eggs of nematode, induction of systemic resistance, competition.

Source: Chaube, et al., 2002

13.7.1 Mycoparasitism

Parasitism of pathogenic fungi by other fungi is generally termed as **mycoparasitism.** There are at least 50 species of fungi, which are known to parasitize other fungi. Some of these mycoparasites, such as *Trichoderma* spp. have very broad host-range while others, such as Chytrids are host-specific. At molecular level, phenomenon involving *Trichoderma* spp. has received most of the attention (Plates 13.1–13.4). When a mycoparasite is grown with its host in dual culture, hyphae may coil around the host; an event of considerable interest but not fully understood. Hooklike structures (appresoria) are formed. At this stage, recognition phenomena involving agglutinin (lectin) from the host binds to carbohydrate residues, on the cell walls of *Trichoderma* spp. Fluorescent indicators and enzyme studies provided evidence for enzymatic activity leading to penetration of host hyphal cell by mycoparasites. Mycoparasites (such as *Trichoderma* spp. and *P. nunn*) produce hydrolytic enzymes, β-1, 3-gluconase, cellulase and chitinase and predictably, different combinations of enzymes are produced that are appropriate to the cell wall substrate (Plates 13.1–13.4).

Involvement of numerous separate genes and gene products has been proposed in mycoparasitic interactions. Harman, et al. (1989) tested the involvement of chitinase and β-1, 3-gluconase in *Trichoderma* mediated biocontrol. Lorito, et al., (1996) listed 10 separate chitinolytic enzymes alone. Practical application of mycoparasites for biological control has yet to be exploited. Mycoparasitism has the potential for eradication of pathogens and remains an attractive stratagem in biological control.

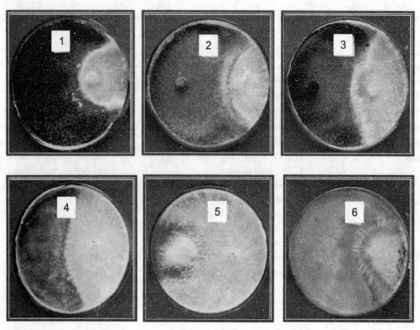

1. *R. solani* + *T. harzianum*
2. *R. solani* + *T. harzianum*
3. *R. solani* + *T. harzianum*
4. *R. solani* + *T. harzianum*
5. *R. solani* + *V. lecanii*
6. *R. solani* + *Bacillius* sp.

Plate 13.1 Antagonism between *R. solani* and bioagents.

13.7.2 Antibiosis

It was demonstrated that many soil microbes produced inhibitory metabolic products *in vitro* and this raised the existing possibility of enhancing the activity of antibiotic producing organisms in soil to induce suppression of plant pathogens. Many antibiotics have been isolated and characterized from bacterial and fungal bioagents. These include gliotoxin and glyoviridin from *T. Virens*; *Viridin alkalye pyrones, isonitriles, polyketides, peptaibols, diketopiperazines, susquiterpenes* and some *steroids* form *Trichoderma* spp.; compounds of *hydroxamate* and *cotecholate group*, e.g. *trans-* and *cis-4- (3-acetoxy-6-methoxy-2-hydroxyphenyl)-2-methoxy butanolide* from *Aspergillus* spp. (Chaube, et al., 2002). These antibiotics are effective against a large number of plant pathogens.

The optimism that antibiotic producing organisms in soil will induce suppression of pathogens, was questioned when experiments revealed that antibiotic production in soil is primarily a defensive strategy for exclusion of other saprophytes from the microsites. The factors limiting antibiosis in soil systems are known. The production of antibiotics usually requires relatively large amounts of carbon while other environmental parameters (e.g., matric potential, soil reaction) in substrate microsites influence metabolism. Once produced, antibiotics can be immobilized by soil colloids. Other microorganisms may utilize antibiotics as carbon substrates. Clearly reasoned strategies must

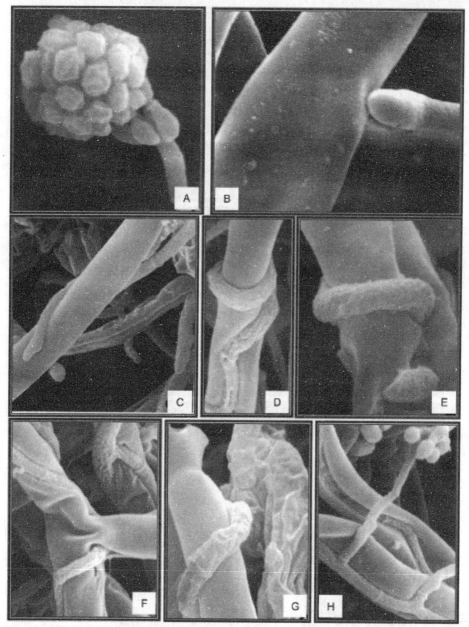

(A) Phialids bearing conidia of *G. virens* (× 3540); (B) Hyphal growth of *G. virens* towards *R. solani* hypha (× 5000); (C) Initial stage of coiling of *G. virens* around *R. solani* and formation of pseudoappresorium (× 2400); (D) Coiling of *G. virens* around *R. solani* hypha and ramification of the hyphal tip of the antagonist (× 2500); (E) Coiling of *G. virens* around *R. solani* hypha (× 4780); (F) Shrinkage in *R. solani* hypha as a result of mycoparasitism by *G. virens* (× 2500); (G) Lysis of *R. solani* hypha (× 2500); (H) Depression in *R. solani* hypha in contact with the mycoparasite (× 2500)

Plate 13.2 Scanning electron microphotographs of the hyphal interaction between *G. virens* and *R. solani*. (Courtsey: U.S. Singh)

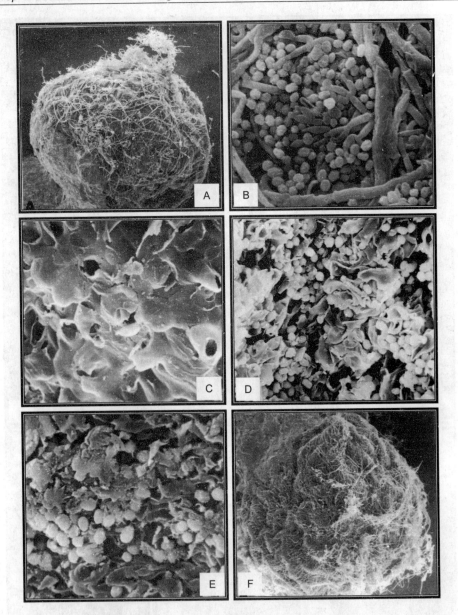

(A) Sclerotium of *S. rolfsii* colonized by *G. virens* (x 68.5)

(B) Growth and sporulation of *G. virens* on surface of parasitized sclerotium (x 1200)

(C) Penetration holes on the surface of parasitized sclerotium (x 1850)

(D) and (E) Profused sporulation of *G. virens* inside the parasitized sclerotium (x 1100 and x 1620, respectively)

(F) Mummified sclerotium of *S. rolfsii* (x 63)

Plate 13.3 Scanning electron microphotographs of parasitism of sclerotia of *Sclerotium rolfsii* by *G. virens* (Courtsey: U.S. Singh).

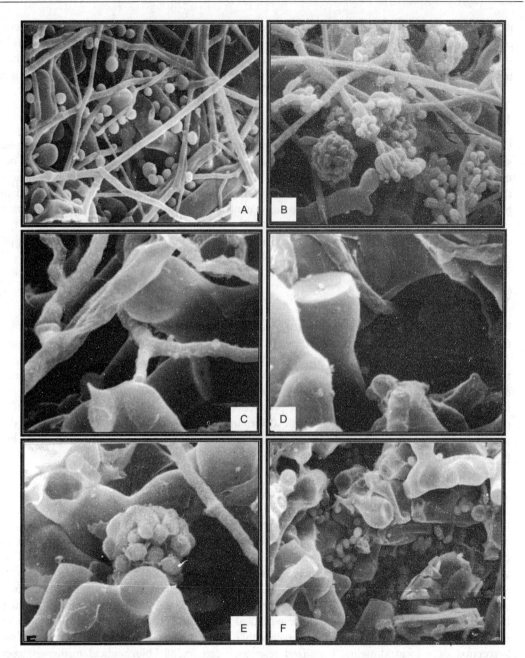

(A) and (B) Growth and sporulation of *G. virens* on the sclerotia of *R. solani* (x 1250 and x 1150, respectively); (C) and (D) Mycelial growth of *G. virens* inside the parasitized sclerorium (x 3860); (E) Typical spore ball of *G. virens* formed inside the parasitized sclerotium (x 2500); (F) Profused sporulation of *G. virens* inside the parasitized sclerotium and disintegration of sclerotial hyphae (x 1100)

Plate 13.4 Antagonism between *R. solani* and bioagents (Courtsey: U.S. Singh)

therefore be employed for successful application of antibiotics-producing bioagents for the control of soil borne plant pathogens. Another habitat where antibiotic-producing fungi could operate is in the rhizosphere. Even though substrates are available, especially at root tips where many pathogens penetrate, nutrient concentration at these locations are not so high as around seeds or organic matter.

13.7.3 Competition

Clark (1965) defined competition in the narrow sense of active demand in excess of the immediate supply of material or condition on the part of two or more organisms. Competition may be the mechanism most prevalent in natural systems. Competition among microorganisms in soil and the rhizosphere is primarily for nutrients. One of the examples of competition as mechanism of biocontrol is the use of *Peniophora gigantea* to control root rot of pine caused by *Heterobasidium annosum*. Conidia of the antagonist, ***P. gigantean,*** are applied usually in chain saw oil, to freshly cut stumps. Although the primary mechanism is competition for space by physical exclusion of the pathogen, the antagonist also produces an antibiotic like substance against *H. annosum*.

13.7.4 Hypovirulence

Chestnut blight (*Cryphonectria parasitica*) was accidentally introduced from the Orient and has destroyed every mature chestnut tree in eastern North America. As studies of this disease progressed, abnormal isolates of *C. parasitica*, which did not kill the trees, were observed. The presence of this factor was associated with reduced virulence (hypovirulence), as well as pigment differences, abnormal growth and reduced sporulation of the fungus. The introduction of hypovirulent strains in Italy and France has enabled chestnut production to occur in orchard previously infested with pathogen (Griffin, 1986). The cytoplasmic determinants responsible for hypovirulence are double stranded (ds) RNA. It has been demonstrated that transfer of ds RNA to virulent isolates by hyphal anastomosis induces hypovirulence.

13.7.5 Induced Resistance

It is believed that all plants, whether resistant or susceptible, have the inherent ability to respond in a defensive manner following pathogen attack, with the timing and magnitude of response being critical (Kuc, 1985). In theory, if the natural defense machinery of a plant can be switched on by an attenuated or avirulent pathogen, it is possible to prevent disease development from subsequent attack by bonafide pathogen. The induced resistance depends on recognition between host and pathogen. Induction of the resistance response is brought about by the interaction of products of both host and parasite. Such responses include local events that occur within the immediate vicinity of the invading organism and systemic events that move throughout the plant in response to the perception of a local stimulus. Localized responses can include biochemical responses, such as induction of phytoalexin biosynthesis in cells and physical responses, such as formation of callus or suberin or lignin as structural barriers around a lesion.

Systemic resistance develops at sites at a distance from the area of initial interaction of plant and pathogen. Changes associated with this response include lignifications, chitinase induction, involvement of protein inhibitors, and pathogenesis related proteins. These factors, which are synthesized *de novo* following challenge, presumably enable the plant to cope with general stress.

There are reports describing field control of cucumber anthracnose and tobacco blue mould by prior inoculation with specific but weakly virulent pathogens. It has been shown that stem injection with spore suspensions provided increased growth and protection of tobacco in the field against *Peronospora tabacina*.

13.7.6 Growth Promotion

Biocontrol agents are reported to induce the growth of various crops (Table 13.5). These responses may be due to: (a) suppression of deleterious root flora including those not causing obvious disease, (b) production of growth stimulating factors (hormones or growth factors), and (c) increased nutrient uptake through solubilization and sequestration of nutrients and/or enhanced root growth. Enhanced root development is also helpful in tolerating the biotic and abiotic stresses by the plants.

Table 13.5 Plant Growth Promotion by Fungal Biocontrol Agents

Crop	Biocontrol Agents	Special Features
Aonla	*A. niger*	Increase in growth of plant
Bean	*T. harzianum*	Increase in size and weight of plants
Brinjal	*T. harzianum, A. niger*	Promotion of shoot and root length
Cauliflower	*T. harzianum, A. niger*	Increase in root and shoot growth
Chickpea	*T. harzianum*	Increase in root and shoot growth
Cucumber	*T. harzianum*	Increase in plant growth
Chrysanthemum	*T. harzianum*	Increase in plant height and no. of flowers
Lentil	*T. harzianum, T. virens*	Increase in plant growth
Muskmelon	*A. niger*	Increase in growth of plant
Pigeon pea	*T. harzianum*	Increase in root and shoot growth
Potato	*A. niger*	Increase in shoot and root length as well as total biomass of plant
Radish	*T. harzianum*	Increased vigour and emergence of seedlings
Rice	*T. virens, T. longibrachiatum, T. harzianum, A. niger*	Increase in plant growth
Safflower	*A. niger*	Increase in growth of plant
Sorghum	*A. niger*	Increase in growth of plant
Tomato	*T. harzianum, Glomus* sp.	Promotion of shoot and root length

Source: Chaube, et al., 2002

13.8 IMPROVING THE BIOAGENT

To improve efficacy of biocontrol agents for desirable characteristics like better antagonistic ability, wider host-range, tolerance to pesticides, survival ability in the environment, rhizosphere-competence, tolerance to adverse environmental conditions, vigorous growth and long shelf-life, the methods used are as follows:

13.8.1 Mutation

Mutations are employed to generate variability in populations, which give an opportunity to select the desirable type. Criteria are defined for selecting a particular phenotype from the population. N-methyl-N-nitro-nitrosoguanidine (*NTG*) has been the most widely used chemical for inducing mutations in fungal bioagents. By exposing the conidia of *Trichoderma* spp, to NTG, Ahmad and Baker (1990) generated mutants that were rhizosphere competent and superior to wild-types in respect of controlling *Pythium ultimum*. These mutants were insensitive to up to 100 μg/ml of benomyl. Liu (1988) used several chemicals (diethyl sulfate, ethyl methane sulfonate, sodium nitrate) to induce benomyl resistant mutants of *T. koningii* without decreased mycoparasitic ability. Mukherjee et al., (1997) developed benomyl-tolerant mutants of *Trichoderma viride* through chemical mutagenesis.

Several genetic variants of fungal bio-agents have also been developed by using radiations. Troutman and Matejka (1978) induced benomyl tolerant strains of *T. viride* by exposing the conidia to gamma radiation. The application of ultraviolet (UV) radiations for this purpose has been most extensive. By exposing conidia of *T. virens* to UV-radiation, Howell and Stripanovic (1983) generated mutants, one deficient for antibiosis against *P. ultimum* and the other with increased antibiosis. Howell (1987) generated mycoparasitic deficient mutants of *T. virens* to study the relevance of mycoparasitism in *T. virens-R. solani* interaction in cotton. Mukherjee and Mukhopadhyay (1993) developed seven stable mutants of *T. virens* by exposing the cultures to 125 k rad of gamma radiation. The mutants differed from the wild type strains in phenotype, growth rate, sporulation and antagonistic potential. One of the mutants (M-7) that produced profuse chlamydospores but no conidia was more aggressive than the wild type in antagonizing *Sclerotium rolfsii* and *Fusarium oxysporum* f. sp. *ciceri*. Selvakumar and co-worker (2000) developed carboxin tolerant mutants of *Trichoderma viride* by exposing the culture to UV-light and ethyl methane sulfonate. Triazole (tebuconazole) tolerant biotypes of *T. viride* developed by UV-irradiation showed wide variation in enzyme activity especially β-1, 3-glucanase, β-1, 4-endoglucanase and chitinase (Kumar and Gupta, 2000).

13.8.2 Protoplast Fusion

Trichoderma is well known as a producer of chitinases, glucanases, cellulases and various other mycolytic enzymes. Combination of these desirable traits from different species/strains can give rise to superior strains. The strain improvement of bioagents by protoplast fusion is one of the ways. The advantage of protoplast fusion is that the possibility to obtain recombinants is higher, which also allows testing of a large number of recombinants in a short time. Sundaram (1996) developed fusants of two isolates of *Trichoderma barzianum* (Th-1 and Th-3), among them, some showed morphological characteristics intermediate between Th-1 and Th-3. In majority of the fusants, dominance of characteristics of Th-1 over Th-3 was observed. When *T. harzianum* (Th-3) was fused with *T. virens,* many fusants were developed and few of them exhibited improved biocontrol potential over parent isolates (Ghose, 1996). Protoplast fusants developed by taking 10 isolates of *Trichoderma* spp., *T. harzianum* and *T. longibrachiatum* as parent strains exhibited an enhanced antagonistic potential against *Rhizoctonia solani, Fusarium oxysporum* f. sp. *lycopersici, Venturia inaequalis. Curvularia lunata* and *Cochliobolus miyabeanus* (Lalithakumari, 2000).

13.8.3 Genetic Engineering

The biosynthesis of cell wall degrading enzymes like chitinases, glucanase and proteases which are involved in mycoparasitism, is controlled mainly at transcriptional level and responsible genes are present as single copy genes. To overproduce these enzymes, their gene copy number has been increased by transformation (Harman and Bjoorjman, 1998). Transformants overproducing these enzymes are more efficient as biocontrol agents. Biocontrol efficiency of *Trichoderma* has been improved by transformation with genes *prbl* (basic protease), *egll* (β-1, 4-glucanase) and *chit* 33 (chitinase). Lo, et al., (1998) developed transformant of *T. harzianum* strain 1295-22 by integrating β-glucuronidase (GUS) and hygromycin B (hygB) phospho-transferase genes, that exhibited increased biocontrol activity against *R. solani* as compared with the wild type.

13.9 COMMERCIALIZATION OF BIOCONTROL AGENTS

In recent years, many small and large entrepreneurs have entered into commercial production of biocontrol agents resulting in development of several products into world market. Commercialization of biopesticides is a multi-step process involving a wide range of activities illustrated in (Figure 13.4).

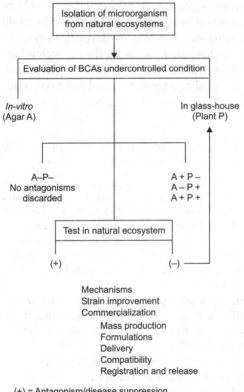

Figure 13.4 Components and sequences of assays in screening for biocontrol activity.

13.9.1 Discovery

Development of a bioagent begins with discovery of a useful naturally occurring organism. The search involves extensive screening of natural soil isolates for strains having the desired traits.

Isolates are then screened for activity against the pathogen in laboratory assay and green house condition. Once an isolate with desirable traits is obtained, it is evaluated under field condition. Many of the promising soil isolates in recent years have been obtained in the university laboratories. In India, a collection of large number of antagonistic strains of *Trichoderma* and *Pseudomonas* are being maintained at Project Directorate of Biological Control, Bangalore and biocontrol laboratory G.B. Pant University of Agriculture and Technology, Pantnagar.

13.9.2 Mass Production

One of the greatest obstacles to biological control by introduced antagonists has been the lack or scarcity of methods for mass culturing and delivering the biocontrol agents. The problems in developing bio-pesticides, a living system, are during the process of formulation and short shelf-life. The most widely used fungal antagonist, *Trichoderma* spp. have been grown on solid substrates like sorghum grain, wheat straw, wheat bran, spent tea leaf waste, coffee husk, wheat bran-saw dust, diatomaceous earth granules impregnated with molasses, and so forth for their mass multiplication (Table 13.6). Papavizas, et al., (1984) produced biomass of fungal antagonists by liquid fermentation consisting of molasses and brewer's yeast. Montealegre, et al., (1993) proposed liquid fermentation method consisting of molasses, wheat bran and yeast for large-scale production of *T. harzianum*. The bacterial biocontrol agent *Pseudomonas* has been used as cell-suspension for experimental purpose. For commercial production of these antagonists, different technologies have been adopted on industrial scale. Fermented biomass of *Trichoderma* consisted mainly of chlamydospores and conidia with some amount of mycelial fragments. Air-dried mats were ground and mixed with a commercially available carrier (Table 13.6). The formulation thus developed, contained 10^8 to 10^9 propagules/g.

Table 13.6 Base Materials/Carriers Used for Mass Production of Fungal Biocontrol Agents

Biocontrol Agent	Base Material(s)	Form of Formulation
T. harzianum	Black gram shell, shelled maize cob, coir-pith, peat, gypsum, coffee fruit skin + biogas slurry, coffee husk, coffee-cherry husk, fruit skin and berry mucilage, molases-yeast, molases-soy, molases-NaNO$_3$, molases-KNO$_3$, mushroom-grown waste, poultry manure, soil, sorghum grain, spent tea leaf waste, sugarcane straw, wheat bran + biogas manure(1:1), wheat-bran + kaolin	Powder, pellets
T. viride	Barley grains, black gram shell, shelled maize cob, coir-pith, peat, gypsum, coffee husk, coffee-cherry husk, fruit skin and berry mucilage, mushroom grown waste, mustard oil cake, neem cake + cow dung, poultry manure, spent tea leaf waste, sugarcane straw, talc, vermiculite + wheat bran + HCl	Pellets
T. virens	Barley grains, coffee husk, coffee-cherry husk, fruit skin and berry mucilage, mushroom-grown waste, neem cake + cow dung, poultry manure, soil, sorghum grains, talc, wheat bran saw dust	Pellets
T. longibrachiatum	Talc, wheat bran + saw dust	Powder
A. niger	Citrus pomae (waste from canning industry), talc + cmc	Pellets, powder
A. terreus	Maize-meal + sand	Powder

(*Source:* Chaube, et al., 2002)

13.9.3 Formulation

Developing a safe, easy to use, cost-effective formulation that will keep the microorganism alive is one of the most important steps in developing a biological product. Formulation is the blending of active ingredients such as fungal spores with inert carriers such as diluents and surfactants in order to improve the physical characteristics. A final formulation must have a long shelf-life, at room temperature, be easy to handle, insensitive to abuse and must be stable over a range of –5 to 35°C. Failure to meet these rigid standards, however, should not stop the commercialization of biologicals. What is needed urgently is the development of drying techniques, which allows retention of maximum number of viable propagules in dried product. At PDBC, Bangalore, three carrier materials namely talc, kaolin and bentonite were tested for their effect on shelf-life of *T. harzianum*. Kaolin and talc were identified as better carriers of *T. harzianum* (Prasad and Rangshwaran, 2000).

13.9.4 Shelf-life

One of the critical obstacles to commercialization of a biopesticidal preparation is the loss of viability of the biocontrol agents over time. A talc based preparation of *T. virens* conidia retained 82% viability at 5°C in refrigerator after 6 months while at room temperature (25-35°C) same level of viability was observed only up to 3 months. Shelf-life was same, when *T. virens* treated chickpea or soyabean seeds were stored at room temperature. Viability was better for CMC based formulations (Tewari, 1996). Conidia of *Trichoderma* in pyrophyllite survived better than fermenter biomass propagules alone at –5 to 30°C. The most suitable temperature to prolong shelf-life of conidia and fermenter biomass propagules in pyrophyllite were –5°C to 5°C (Mukherjee, 1991).

Chlamydospores based formulations of *Trichoderma* sp. exhibited longer shelf-life (80% viability for 9 months) than conidia based formulations (80% viability for 4 months) at room temperature. A preparation of *T. virens* (mainly in the form of chlamydospores was from peat moss czapeks broth culture) stored at 25°C for six months without loss of viability. Commercial formulations of *Aspergillus niger* AN-27 showed an extraordinary long shelf-life of more than two years at room temperature (15-35°C) when packed in polyethylene bags and stored under less than 80% relative humidity (Sen, 2000). Seed coating with biocontrol agents has emerged as a feasible way of delivering the antagonist, i.e. supplying the coated seeds to the farmers directly by the seed companies/agencies. The time gap between coating seeds and sowing such seeds by farmers is critical. Mukherjee (1991) quantitatively assessed the viability of *T. virens* on coated chickpea seeds when the seeds were stored at low temperature (5°C) and at room temperature (15-35°C), 88% of the propagules remained viable for up to 4 months.

13.9.5 Green House and Field Testing

Testing of bioagents usually begins in growth chambers or green houses. Although green house testing often provide a useful preliminary screening for selecting candidate microorganisms for further testing, it is very difficult to mimic true farming conditions. Therefore, well-designed field trials are necessary to establish the efficacy of any bioproduct. Once promising results are obtained they are tested under field conditions. It is important that field tests ultimately be conducted at several locations to prove efficacy under varying climatic conditions.

13.9.6   Regulation and Registration

As current legislation stands, there are certain categories of biocontrol agents that have an easier and quicker passage for registration. Indigenous microorganisms that are never recorded as being plant, animal or human pathogens and which are specific to a defined group of target have a comparatively straightforward progress. Under the Section of 9(3) of Pesticide Act of India (1968), information required for registration of any bio-pesticides includes:

- systemic name and common name
- natural occurrence and morphological descriptions
- detail of manufacturing process (active and inert ingredients of formulation)
- mammalian toxicity
- environmental toxicity and residue analysis

13.9.7   Commercialization Efforts

The efforts made to commercialize a biocontrol agent can be grouped into three categories:

·   The first group, which follows the lead of Rishbeth and Kerr is to apply the antagonist directly and precisely to the infection court when and where needed. This group also exemplifies the strategy based on an innundative application, where the antagonist is applied at an instantly high and timely population with the intent to preempt or swamp the pathogen. This includes examples of seed applied antagonists for protection of germinating seeds against damping off, to fruits against fruit decay in storage and ice-minus bacteria to frost injury. Nearly all bioagents commercialized till date fall into this group (Table 13.7).

- The second group includes antagonists applied at one place, e.g. on seeds, with the intent that they will spread and protect the plant at one or more distant places. Plant growth promoting rhizobacteria (PGPR) fall into this category.
- The third category of antagonists includes cases that would exemplify the strategy of effective biological control following a one time or occasional inoculative release.

Table 13.7   List of Commercial Bioagents Produced

Products	Biocontrol Agents	Name of the Manufacturer/ Distributor
Aq10 biofungicide	*Ampelomyces quisqualis* isolateM-10	Ecogen, Inc. Israel
Biofungus	*Trichoderma* spp.	Groundortsmettingen deCuester n. v., Belgium
Aspire	*Candida oleophila* I-182	Ecogen, Inc. Israel
Binab T	*Trichoderma harzianum* (ATCC 20476) and *Trichoderma polysporum* (ATCC 20475)	Bio-innovation AB, UK
Bioderma	*Trichoderma viride/T. harzianum*	Biotech International Ltd., India
Biofox C	*Fusarium oxysporum* (Non-pathogenic)	S.I.A.P.A., Italy

(Contd.)

Table 13.7 List of Commercial Bioagents Produced (*Contd.*)

Products	Biocontrol Agents	Name of the Manufacturer/ Distributor
Biosave 100, Biosave 1000	*Pseudomonas syringae* ESC-10	EcoScience Corp., Orlando, USA
Biosave 110	*Pseudomonas syringae* ESC-11	EcoScience Corp., Orlando, USA
Blight ban A 506	*Pseudomonas fluorescens* A 506	Plant Health Technologies, USA
Conquer	*Pseudomonas fluorescens*	Mauri Foods, Australia
Contans	*Coniothyrium sclerotiorum*	Prophyta Biologischer Pflanzenschutz GmbH', Germany
Deny	*Burkholderia cepacia*, *Pseudomonas cepacia* type Wisconsin	Stine Microbial Products, Sthwanee, KS
Epic	*Bacillus subtillis*	Gustafson Inc., USA
Fusaclean	*Fusarium oxysporum* (Non-pathogenic)	Natural Plant Protection, France
Galltrol-A	*Agrobacterium radiobacter* strain 84	Agbiochem Inc., USA
Intercept	*Pseudomonas cepacia*	Soil Technological Corp., USA
Kodiak, Kodiak HB, Kodiak At	*Bacillus subtillis*	Gustafson Inc., USA
KONI	*Coniothyrium minitans*	Bioved Ltd., Hungary
Mycostop	*Streptomyces griseoviridis* strain K61	Kemiro Agro. Oy, Finland
Nogall diegall	*Agrobacterium radiobacter*	Bio-Care Technology, Pvt. Ltd., Australia
Norbac 84C	*Agrobacterium radiobacter* strain K84	New Bioproducts Inc., USA
Phagus	*Bacteriophage*	Natural Plant Protection, France
Polygandron	*Pythium oligandrum*	Vyskummy Ustav Rastlinnej, Slovakia
Prestop, Primastop	*Gliocladium catenulatum*	Kemiro Agro. Oy, Finland
PSSOL	*Pseudomonas solanacearum* (Non-pathogenic)	Natural Plant Protection, France
Rhizo-plus, Rhizo-plus Konz	*Bacillus subtilis* FZB 24	KFGB Biotechnik GMBh, Germany
Root shield	*Trichoderma harzianum Rifai* strain KRL-AG (T-22)	Bioworks Inc., USA
Rotstop, P.g. Suspension	*Phlebia gigantea*	Kemiro Agro. Oy, Finland
Serenade	*Bacillus subtilis*	AgraQuest. Inc., USA
Soil gard	*Gliocladium virens* strain GL-21	Thermo Trilogy, USA
Supreivit	*Trichoderma harzianum*	Borregaard and Reitzel, Czech Republic

(*Contd.*)

Table 13.7 List of Commercial Bioagents Produced (*Contd.*)

Products	Biocontrol Agents	Name of the Manufacturer/ Distributor
System 3	*Bacillus subtilis* GBO3 and chemical pesticides	Helena Chemical Company, USA
T-22 G, T-22 planter box	*Trichoderma harzianum* strain KRL-AG2	Bioworks, Inc., USA
Trichodex, Trichopel	*Trichoderma harzianum*	Makhteshim Chemical Works Ltd., USA
Trichoject, Trichodowels, Trichoseal	*Trichoderma viride*	Agrimm Technologies Ltd., New Zealand
Trichoderma 2000	*Trichoderma* sp.	Mycontrol Ltd., Israel
Victus	*Pseudomonas fluorescens* strain NUB 12089	Sylvan Spawn Laboratory, USA
Kali sena	*Aspergillus niger*	Cadilla Pharma., India
Tri-control	*Trichoderma* spp.	Jeypee biotechs, India
Ecofit	*T. viride*	Hoechst Schering Afgro Evo Ltd., India
Bas derma	*T. viride*	Basarass Biocontrol Res. Lab., India

Source: Singh, U.S., et al., 2001

13.10 RHIZOBACTERIA AND BIOLOGICAL CONTROL

The rhizosphere bacteria that can colonize the plant roots have been termed as **rhizobacteria** by Kloepper and Schroth (1978) and Suslow, et al. (1979). The rhizobacteria that are strains of *Pseudomonas fluorescens* Migula and *Pseudomonas putida* (Trevisan) Migula, have been regarded to have co-evolved with their host plants. The term rhizobacteria has been used to accentuate their intimate association with root (Suslow, 1982). These naturally occurring, non-pathogenic, root colonizing bacteria, may be harmful or beneficial for growth of plants are called **deleterious rhizobacteria (DRB)** and **plant growth-promoting rhizobacteria (PGPR)**, respectively. PGPR, fall under genera *Pseudomonas, Achromobacter, Arthrobacter, Bacillus, Citrobacter, Enterobacter* and *Flavobacterium* (Dubey, 2001).

The PGPR besides enhancing growth and yields, are also potential biocontrol agents and are usually isolated from suppressive soils. Most of the PGPR are fluorescent pseudomonas (*P. fluorescens* and *P. putida*) but also include non-fluorescent *Pseudomonas* sp., *Bacillus subtilis* and *Serratia* spp.

13.10.1 Fluorescent Pseudomonas

Pseudomonas fluorescens and *P. putida* are reported to suppress several major plant pathogens. The former is well known for its usefulness in the biocontrol of take-all of wheat caused by *G. graminis* var. *tritici*. The suppression depends on the ability of the bacterium to colonize the roots and production of an antibiotic phenazine-1-carboxylic acid, a siderophore called pyoverdin, and an antifungal factor. Iron-regulated, non-siderophore antibiotics may also be frequently produced by fluorescent pseudomonas (Thomashow and Weller, 1990).

Mechanisms of disease suppression. The rhizobacteria can reduce plant disease by antagonizing soil-borne pathogenic fungi through production of antibiotics and/or lytic enzymes (Chitinase) and through competition for ecological niche and nutrients as well as by inducing systemic resistance.

Competition for iron. In oxygenated and weakly acidic, neutral or alkaline soils, iron (Fe^{3+}) is found as insoluble iron complexes, $Fe(OH)_3$, and it becomes unavailable and a limiting factor for growth. To sequester the scarcely available iron, microorganisms produce low molecular weight (>1000 dalton) compounds called *siderophores*. Siderophores producing ability gives a competitive edge to the organisms. The ability of strains to utilize siderophores produced by other strains increases their competitiveness in the rhizosphere (Bakker, et al., 1993). Schippers, et al., (1987) proposed a hypothesis that growth promotion of potato plants in response to seed bacterization in soil was due to siderophore-mediated suppression of microbial cyanide production. The hypothetical interactions (Schippers, 1988) are believed to take place as shown in Figure 13.5.

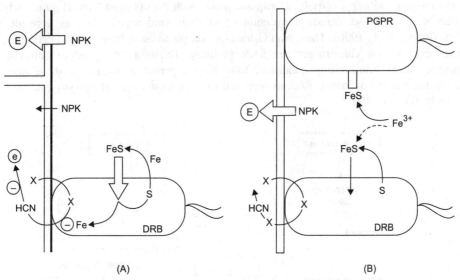

(A)   (B)

Figure 13.5 Interaction between PGPR, DRB and the plant root cell. (A) Inhibition of potato root cell function by hydrocyanide producing DRB. The uptake of iron by siderophores of DRB(s) from the soil enhances their HCN production from root exudate component "X". HCN inhibits the energy metabolism (e) of the root cell and thus decreases uptake of NPK. (B) Competition for iron by siderophores of a PGPR inhibits the HCN production by DRB, cell for uptake of NPK (Schippers, 1988).

Production of antibiotics. Fluorescent pseudomonas produce secondary metabolites with antibiotic activities some of these (phenazine-1-carboxylicacid (PCA), 2,4,-diacetylphlroglucinol (DAPG), oomycin-A, pyocyanine, pyoluteorin and pyrrolnitrin) have been implicated in suppression of soil borne diseases (Thomashow and Weller, 1996). Gene loci involved have been cloned and used to enhance the biological properties of *Pseudomonas* spp. by either over expressing the genes and hence increasing antibiotic production. HCN, a volatile inhibitor, inhibits activities of harmful organisms and reduces plant growth. Transfer of the HCN biosynthetic gene clusters to non-HCN producing strains of *Pseudomonas* increased their biocontrol activity against black root rot, as well as against the foliage pathogens *Septoria tritici* and *Puccinia graminis* in wheat (Flaishman, et al., 1996).

Production of lytic enzymes. Some bacteria can parasitize fungi and kill them by secreting lytic enzymes like chitinase, B-1, 3-glucanases, proteases and lipases. Chitinase produced by *Serratia marcescens* have been associated with biocontrol of fungal disease of pea and bean. The chiA gene was cloned and expressed constitutively in *P. putida*. The chiA + recombinant provided increased protection of radish against *F. oxysporum* f. sp. *redolens* (Dubey, 2001).

Induced systemic resistance. The rhizobacteria can suppress the disease caused by foliar pathogens by trigerring plant mediated resistance mechanism called **induced systemic resistance** (ISR). This is evident when biocontrol bacteria and pathogens are applied at spatially separated locations on the plant. ISR is similar to pathogen induced systemic acquired resistance (SAR) as both provide enhanced resistance against challenge pathogen. ISR has been demonstrated against fungi, bacteria and viruses in several crops. SAR and ISR differ in their signalling pathways (Figure 13.6). SAR is dependent on the synthesis of salicylic acid by the plant that acts as an inducer signal and is associated with the accumulation of novel pathogenesis related proteins, some of which have been shown to possess antifungal activity. Transgenic plants with Nah G gene from *P. putida* which codes for salicylic hydroxylase, causes conversion of salicylic acid to catechol, as a result, no SAR develops (Ryals, et al., 1996). Thus, Nah G-transformed plants have been used to determine whether ISR-inducing bacteria can trigger the SAR pathway. Bacteria that produce salicylic acid as siderophore, under iron-limiting condition, have been reported to induce SAR. *P. aeruginosa* 7 NSK2 has been found to induce SAR in bean and tobacco plants against *Botrytis cinerea* and TMV, respectively (Dubey, 2001).

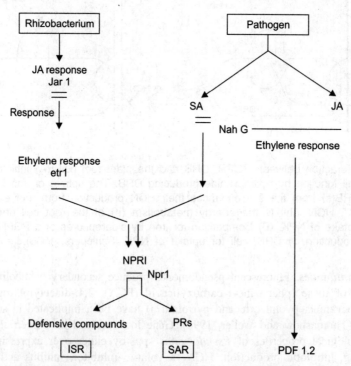

Figure 13.6 Proposed model for the non-pathogenic rhizobacteria mediated ISR signalling pathway as part of the network of pathways controlling biologically induced systemic resistance.

Rhizobacteria mediated ISR signalling pathways does not involve salicylic acid or PRs. Rather it requires jasmonate and ethylene response, and like the SAR, depends on the regulatory protein NPRI (Figure 13.6). Thus, NPRI differentially regulates ISR and SAR-related gene expression depending on the pathway that is activated. The jasmonate and ethylene dependency of ISR is based on enhanced sensitivity of these hormones, rather than on the increase in their production.

Although the extent of induced resistance attained is similar in both SAR and ISR, the latter usually is less effective. It is not yet clear whether ISR is as broad spectrum as SAR is, and no evidence is available that these bacteria stimulate the plant to produce antimicrobial compound such as phytoalexins.

13.11 USE OF VA MYCORRHIZAL FUNGI

Vesicular-arbuscular (VA) mycorrhizal fungi are symbiotic fungi forming associations with plant roots (Mosse, 1973). These are probably the most common of all soil fungi with approximately 90–95% vascular plants capable of becoming mycorrhizal. Some benefits accruing to plants by this relationship are, improved growth and yield as a result of increased uptake of nutrients such as phosphorus, zinc, copper and water. The VA mycorrhizal fungi develop an extensive network of external hyphae, which increase the absorbing capacity of plant roots by exploring a greater volume of soil normally inaccessible to the plant (Figure 13.7). Another significant benefit to many plants is the suppression of plant disease. There are numerous studies on the interactions between VA mycorrhizal fungi and soil-borne plant pathogens (Table 13.8).

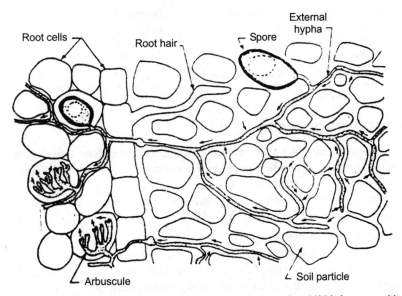

Figure 13.7 A diagrammatic representation of the association of a VAM fungus with a root. Small arrows indicate the flow of nutrients such as phosphorus, zinc, and copper into the root cells. (Boyetchko and Tewari, 1996)

Table 13.8 Influence of VA Mycorrhizal Fungi on Soil-borne Pathogens

Host	Pathogen	Effect on Disease
Alfalfa	*Fusarium oxysporum* f. sp. *medicaginis*	Decreased
	Phytophthora megasperma	Increased
	Pythium paroecandrum	Decreased
	Verticillium albo-atrum	Decreased
Barley	*Bipolaris sorokiniana*	Decreased
Citrus	*Phytophthora parasitica*	Decreased
	Thielaviopsis basicola	No effect
Cotton	*T. basicola*	Decreased
	Verticillium dahliae	Increased
Onion	*Pyrenochaeta terrestris*	Decreased
Pea	*Aphanomyces euteiches*	Decreased
Peanut	*Sclerotium rolfsii*	Decreased
Poinsettia	*Pythium ultimum*	Decreased
	Rhizoctonia solani	Decreased
Soyabean	*Fusarium solani*	Decreased
	Macrophomina phaseolina	Decreased
	P. megasperma	Decreased
	R. solani	Decreased
Strawberry	*Phytophthora fragriae*	No effect
Tobacco	*T. basicola*	*Decreased*
Tomato	*F. oxysporurm* f. sp. *lycopersici*	Decreased
	Pseudomonas solanacearum	Decreased
	P. syriangae	Decreased
	V. albo-atrum	No effect
Wheat	*Gaeumannomyces graminis* var. *tritici*	Decreased

Source: Boyetchko and Tewari, 1996

13.12 FUTURE PROSPECTS

Realistically, biocontrol may not totally replace chemicals in immediate future. However, judicious use of biocontrol agents can significantly reduce amount of pesticides and thereby contribute to sustainable development of agriculture.

The biocontrol has yet to become an integral part of protection technology. Areas awaiting attention of scientists and policy makers include:

1. Biodiversity in biocontrol agents.
2. Improvement of biocontrol agents by using molecular tools.
3. Improvement in mass multiplication, formulation, shelf-life and delivery system.
4. Integration of biocontrol with other management practices.
5. Bio-priming of seeds with biocontrol agents, biofertilizers and/or micronutrients must be explored and exploited.
6. There is need to select strains, which are not only good antagonists but also inducers of good growth and plant defense.

REFERENCES

Ahmad, J.S. and Baker, R., 1987, Rhizosphere competence of *Trichoderma harzianum, Phytopathology*, 77: 182.

Ahmad, J.S. and Baker, R., 1988, Implications of rhizosphere competence of *Trichoderma harzianum, Can. J. Mirobiology*, 34: 229.

Baker, R., 1990, An overview of current and future strategies and models for biological control, In: *Biological Control of Soil Borne Plant Pathogens,* D. Hornby (Ed.), 375, CAB International Wallingford, United Kingdom.

Baker, K.F., 1987, Evolving concepts of biological control of plant pathogens, *Annu. Rev. Phytopathology,* 25: 67.

Baker, K.F. and Cook, R.J., 1974, *Biological Control of Plant Pathogens,* W.H. Freeman and Co, San Francisco, California, 433. (Book, reprinted in 1982, *Amer. Phytopathology Soc.*, St. Paul, Minnesota).

Baker, R., 1983, State of the art: Plant diseases, pp. 14, In: *Processing of the National Interdisciplinary Biological Control Conference,* 15-17 February 1983, S.L. Battenfield (Ed.), Las Vegas, Ny., CSRS/USDA, Washington, DC.

Boyetchko, S.M. and Tewari, J.P., 1961, Use of VA mycorrhizal fungi in soil borne disease management, In: *Management of Soil borne Disease*, R.S. Utkhede and V.K. Gupta (Eds.), Kalyani Publishers, New Delhi, p. 354.

Campbell, R., 1989, *Biological Control of Microbial Plant Pathogens*, Cambridge Univ. Press, Cambridge.

Chaube, H. and Singh, U.S., 1991, *Plant Disease Mangement: Principles and Practices*, Boca Raton, CRC Press.

Chaube, H.S., 1989, Pathogen suppressive soils, In: *Perspectives of Phytopathology,* V.P. Agnitre, et al. (Eds.), Today and Tomorrow Printer, New Delhi.

Chaube, H.S., Mishra, D.S., Varshney, S. and Singh, U.S., 2002, Biological control of plant pathogens by fungal antagonists: Historical background, present status and future prospects, *Annu. Rev. Plant Pathology*, vol. II, *Ind. Soc. Mycol. Pl. Pathalogy.*

Chet, I., 1987, *Innovative Approaches to Plant Disease Control*, John Wiley & Sons, New York.

Cook, R.J., 1987, Research Briefing Panel on Biological Control in Managed Ecosystems, Committee on Science, Engineering, and Public Policy, National Academy of Sciences, National Academy of Engineering and Institute of Medicine, National Academy Press, Washington, DC p. 12.

Cook, R.J. and Baker, K.F., 1983, *The Nature and Practices of Biological Control of Plant Pathogens,* APS Books, St. Paul, Minnesota, USA, p. 599.

Dubey, H.C., 2001, Rhizobacteria in biological control and plant growth promotion, *J. Mycol. Pl. Pathology,* 31: 9.

Flaishman M.A.Z., Eyal, A. Zilberstein, C. Voisard and D. Haas, 1996, Suppression of *Septoria tritici* blotch and leaf rust of wheat by recombinant cyanide-producing strains of *Pseudomonas putida. Mol. Plant-Microbe Interact.*, 9: 642.

Fravel, D.R., 1988, The role of antibiosis in biocontrol of plant diseases, *Annu. Rev. Phytopathol.*, 26: 75.

Garrett, S.D., 1965, Toward biological control of soil-borne plant pathogens, 4-17, In: *Ecology of Soil-borne Plant Pathogens*, K.F. Baker and W.C. Snyder (Eds.), Univ. Calif. Press, Berkeley.

Ghosh, S., 1996, Biocontrol characterization of *Trichoderma harzianum Rifai*, isolate-3 and its protoplast fusion with *Gliocladium virens* Miller, et al., M.Sc., Thesis, G.B. Pant University of Agric. and Tech., Pantnagar, p. 75.

Griffin, G.J., 1986, Chestnut blight and its control, *Hortic. Rev.*, 8: 291.

Harman, G.E., Taylor A.G., and Stasz T.E., 1989, Combining strains of *Trichoderma harzianum* and solid matrix priming to improve biological seed treatments, *Plant Dis.*, 73: 631.

Harman, G.E. and Bjoorjman, T., 1998, Potential and existing uses of *Trichoderma* and *Gliocladium* for plant disease control and plant growth enhancement, In: *Trichoderma* and *Gliocladium*, vol. II, G.E. Harman and C.K. Kubicek, (Eds.), 229, London: Tayor and Francis Ltd.

Harman, G.E., 2000, Myths and dogmas of Biocontrol: Changes in the perceptions derived from research on *Trichoderma harzianum* T-22, *Plant dis.*, 84: 377.

Hornby, D., 1983, Suppressive soils, *Annu. Rev. Phytopathology*, 21: 65.

Hornby, D., 1990, *Biological Control of Soil Borne Plant Pathogens*, CAB International, Willeingford.

Howell, C.R. and Stripanovic, R.D., 1983, Gliovirin, a new antibiotic from *Gliocladium virens* and its role in the biological control of *Pythium ultimum*, *Can. J. Microbiology*, 29: 321.

Kerr, A., 1980, Biological control of crown gall through production of agrocin 84, *Plant Dis.*, 64: 25.

Kloepper, J.W. and Schroth, M.N., 1978, Plant growth promoting rhizobacteria on radishes. In: *Proc. Int. Conf. Plant Pathology Bact.*, Angers, France, p. 879.

Kuc, J. 1985, Expression of latent genetic information for diseases resistance in plants, In: *Cellular and Molecular Biology of Plant Stress*, J.L. Key and T. Kosuge (Eds.), Alan R. Liss, New York, p. 303.

Kumar, A. and Gupta, J.P., 2000, Variation in the enzymatic activity of tebuconazole tolerant biotupes of *Trichoderma viride*, In: *Proceeding of Indian Phytopathological Society*, Golden Jubilee, International Conference on Integrated Plant Diseases Management for Sustainable Agriculture, p. 391.

Lalithakumari, D., 2000, Development of effective technology for strain improvement of *Trichoderma* spp., In: *Proceeding of Indian Phytopathological Society*, Golden Jubilee, International Conference on Integrated Plant Disease Management for Sustainable Agriculture, p. 851.

Lindow, S.W., 1983, Methods of preventing frost injury caused by epiphytic ice nucleation active bacteria, *Plant Dis.*, 67: 327.

Liu, S.D., 1988, The use of Benomyl resistance mutant of *Trichoderma koningii* as a biocontrol agent against root rot diseases of chrysanthemum and adjuki bean, *Trichoderma News Letter*, 4: 5 (Abstr.).

Lo, C.T., Nelson, E.B, Hayes C.K and Harman, G.E., 1998, Ecological studies of *Trichoderma harzianum stain* 1295-22 in the rhizosphere and on the phylloplane of creeping bentgrass, *Phytopathology*, 88: 129.

Lorito, M., et al., 1996, *Mol. Plant Microbe. Interac.*, 9: 206.

Lupton, F.G.H., 1984, Biological control: The plant breeder's objective, *Ann. Appl. Biol.*, 104:1.

Mishra, D.S., 2002, Development of mixed formulation of fungal (*Trichoderma*) and bacterial (*Pseudomonas*) biocontrol agents for management of plant disease, Ph.D. Thesis submitted to G.B. Pant Univ. of Agriculture and Technology, Pantnagar, 185.

Montealegre, J., Varnero, M.T. and Sepulveda, C., 1993, A method for biomass production of *Trichoderma harzianum* strain V: growth evaluation, *Fitopathol.*, 28: 99.

Mosse, B., 1973, Advances in the study of Vesicular-arvuscular mycorrhizas, *Annu. Rev. Phytopathology*, 11: 171.

Mukherjee, P.K., Haware, M.P. and Raghu, P., 1997, Induction and evaluation of benomyl-tolerant mutants of *Trichoderma viride* for biological control of Botrytis gray mould of chickpea, *Indian Phytopathology*, 50: 485.

Mukherjee, P.K., 1991, Biological control of chickpea wilt complex. Ph.D. Thesis, G.B. Pant University of Agric. & Tech. Pantnagar, p. 188.

Pandey, V.S., 1996, Studies on population dynamics, plant growth promotion activities and antagonistic potential of fluorescent *Pseudomonas* isolated from rhizosphere soil of wheat and chickpea, Ph.D. Thesis, G.B. Pant University of Agric. and Tech., Pantnagar, 360.

Papavizas, G.C., Dunn, Mt. Lewis, J.A., and Beagle-Ristaino, J.E., 1984, Liquid fermentation technology for experimental production of biocontrol fungi, *Phytopathology*, 74: 1171.

Prasad, R.D. and Ranjeshwaran, R., 2000, Shelf-life and bioefficacy of *Trichoderma harzianum* formulated in various carrier materials, *Plant Dis. Res.*, 15: 38.

Rishbeth, J., 1979, Modern aspects of biological control of *Fomes* and *Armillaria*, *Eur. J. For. Pathology*, 9: 331.

————, **1963,** Stump protection against *Fomes annosum*, 111, Inoculation with *Peniophorea gigantean, Ann. Appl. Biology*, 52: 63.

Ryals, J.A., et al., 1996, Systemic acquired resistance, *Plant Cell*, 8: 1809.

Schippers, B.A., et al., 1987, Interaction of deleterious a beneficial rhizosphere microorganism and the effect of cropping practices, *Annu. Rev. Phytopath.*, 25: 339.

Schippers, B., et al., 1986, Plant growth-inhibiting and stimulating rhizosphere microorganism, In: *Microbial Communities in Soil,* V. Jensen, A. Kjoller, L.H. Sorensen (Eds.), p. 35, London/ New York, Elsevier Scientific.

Schneider, R.W., 1982, *Suppressive Soils and Plant Disease*, Am. Phytopathol. Soc., St. Paul, Minnesota.

Selvakumar, R., et al., 2000, Studies on development of *Trichoderma viride* mutants and their effect on *Ustilago segetum tritici, Indian Phytopath.*, 53: 185.

Sen, B., 2000, Biological control: A success story, *Indian Phytopath.*, 53: 243.

Sequeira, L., 1983, *Cryphonectria parasitica,* cause of chestnut blight, In: *Advances in Plant Pathology,* vol. 6, G.S. Sidhu (Ed.) Academic Press, New York, 123–136.

Sequeira, L., 1987, Biological control of plant pathogens: Present status and future prospects, In. *Integrated Pest Management,* V. Delucchi, (Ed.), Parasitis, Geneva, p. 289.

Singh, U.S., Mishra, D.S., Prasad, R.D. and Chaube, H.S., 2001, Biological control of plant pathogens in India: Historical perspectives, present status and future prospects, In: *Hundred Years of Biological Control in India,* S.P. Singh (Ed.), ICAR, New Delhi (In Press).

Sundaram, R.M., 1996, Biocontrol characterization of *Trichoderma harzianum* Rifai, isolate-1 and its protoplast fusion with *Trichoderma harzianum* Rifai, isolate-3, M.S.C. Thesis, G.B. Pant University of Agric. and Tech., Pantnagar, p. 91.

Suslow, T.V., 1982, Role of Root-colonizing bacteria in plant growth, In: *Phytopathogenic Prokaryotes,* vol. I., M.S. Mount and G.H. Lacy (Eds), Academic Press, New York/London, p. 187.

Suslow, T.V., et al., 1979, Beneficial bacteria enhance plant growth, *Calif. Agric.,* 33: 15.

Tewari, A.K., 1996, Biological Control of chickpea wilt-complex using different formulations of Gkiocladium virens through seed treatment, Ph.D. Thesis, G.B. Pant University of Agric. & Tech., Pantnagar, India, 167.

Thomashow, L.S. and Weller, D.M., 1996, Current concepts in the use of introduced bacteria for biological disease control: mechanism and antifungal metabolites. In: *Plant-Microbe Interactoins,* vol. I., G. Stacey, N. Keen (Eds.), Chapman & Hall, New York.

Thomashow, L.S. and Weller, D.M., 1990, Role of antibiotics and siderophores in biological control with mycoherbicides, *Rev. Weed Sci.,* 2: 1.

Troutman, J.L. and Matezka, J.C., 1978, Induced tolerance of *Trichoderma viride* to benomyl, *Phytopathology,* News 12: 131 (Abstr.)

Varshney, S. and Chaube, H.S., 2001, Mycorrhizal-Rhizobacterial and fungal antagonists: Interactions, In: *Microbes and Plants,* Asha Sinha (Ed.), Campus Books International, New Delhi, p. 226.

Wilson, C.L. and Pusey, P.L., 1985, Potential for the biocontrol of postharvest plant disease, *Plant Dis.,* 69: 375.

14 Management Through Host Genes

The history of breeding for resistance is a success story. No field research and development has a more favourable ratio between input and return, especially when calculated on the basis of all socio-economic effects.

—Nogenboon, N.G., 1993

14.1 INTRODUCTION

Undoubtedly host resistance has been the best aid in our fight against the menace of deadly pathogens causing rusts, blights, mildews and wilts. Breeding for disease resistant varieties is not only cost effective but also grower and consumer friendly. Breeding for disease resistance is an ongoing and cumulative process. The sources are exploited and new genes are added to the gene pool for need-based utilization. Resistance in plants, pre-existing or induced, is the natural trait developed during course of co-evolution over millions of years. Thus, disease management through host resistance genes should be considered most natural way to counter the threat posed to plants. Swaminathan, M.S., noted Indian agriculture scientist, stated *undoubtedly the most attractive form of defence is provided by disease resistance, for as long as it remains effective it provides protection at no cost to the farmer or the community.* The duration for which resistance remains effective is the practical problems, which puts a question mark on reliability of disease resistance. The role of resistant genes in plant disease management should be assessed subject to the following conditions:

Easy availability of resistant genes.　Availability of known sources of resistant genes may be one of the limitations. Recently the biotechnologists are using diverse type of genes to provide or induce resistance in crop plants.

Easy transfer of genes in crop cultivars.　Breeders used conventional breeding methods, hybridization/backcrossing and recurrent selection for obtaining desirable plant type. The biotechnologists have made things easier and faster by more precise gene transfer by using novel techniques. They have also overcome compatibility barrier (genus/kingdom) faced in conventional breeding. Production and insertion of *resistance cassette* in any plant genome, as per need, has been proposed.

Deployment of resistant genes.　Resistant genes are among the most valuable treasure provided by nature and these must be used very carefully. Lot of thinking by breeders and pathologists has led to development of various strategies for gene deployment for deriving maximum benefits, discussed under Gene deployment (14.4).

14.2 DISEASE RESISTANCE: A HISTORICAL PERSPECTIVE

The present day agriculture was started, some 10,000 years ago, by the wanderer and hunter man when he decided to 'settle down' on a patch of fertile land, probably near a water source. It must have begun with 'selection of vigorous, good looking and healthy plants', thereby the selection for quality, yield and disease resistance has gone in, probably unintentionally. Co-evolution of host and pathogen, natural selection and the efforts of plant breeders have contributed in the development of present day scenario where it is possible to feed more than 6 billion people on the planet; earth. The long course of development can be broadly divided in the following phases:

Pre-mendelian era. Mostly the crop improvement was through mass selection of desirable plants or plant population by agricultural scientists or the grower himself. Rediscovery of Mendelian genetics enthused plant breeders to take up crop improvement, including host resistance, in more systemic manner. Zadoks opined that 'natural and strong negative selection pressure for pathogen has been operative since beginning' and the process was further accelerated, in recent past, by the positive mass selection for the host resistance by the breeders.

R-gene era. Biffen (1905) discovered that resistant genes in wheat to rust fungus, *Puccinia striiformis*, were inherited in Mendelian fashion. Later monogenic dominant genes(s) in *Solanum demissum* were shown to provide 'complete' resistance against most dreaded fungus, *Phytophthora infestans* (Miederhausev, et al., 1954). The attractive oligogenic resistance caught eye of both scientific community and growers. Soon much wanted vertical resistance was shown to be prone to 'break down'. This put a question mark on the future utility of oligogenic resistance. Vanderplank in sixties and Johanson in seventies advocated replacement of specific resistance with polygenic (non-differential) resistance, particularly in developing countries where the replacement of outgoing vertical cultivars was not easy. Robinson (1971) reassessed the value of vertical resistance in agriculture. The breeders tried to promote tolerance as well as multilane cultivars but without much success. Some limited acceptability of tolerant cultivars against viral diseases was reported in sugarcane (sugarcane mosaic virus) and maize (African streak mosaic virus).

Recent era. The shortlived/non-durable specific resistance gave way to non-specific and durable polygenic resistance. Breeders got success in potato-late blight and wheat-rusts, two dominant patho-systems, at global level. But non-differential/durable resistance was a polygenic and quantitative trait, thus difficult to identify, measure and breed. Disease resistance has been recognized as single most important component of any integrated pest management programme. In EPIPRE, (Zadoks, 1984) proposed that R gene resistance should be suitably supported by pesticides to check the buildup of pathogen levels at critical periods. Biotechnology, during later part of 20th century, opened new opportunities in plant improvement. The transgenics were developed in major cash crops with traits like herbicide tolerance, pest resistance, tolerance to abiotic stress and value addition in terms of commercial and industrial use. The potential seems to be unlimited but risks are there. The golden word is caution and 'case by case' approach should be adopted (Pattanayak and Kumar, 2000).

14.3 BREEDING FOR DISEASE RESISTANCE

The importance of host resistance in plant disease management and the risk of its failures have made breeding for disease resistance a continuous process with focus on following points:

14.3.1 Sources of Resistance

For a successful and efficient resistance-breeding programme search for sources of resistance is the pre-requisite step. Importance was realized early and Vavilov (1949) made significant contribution in this regard. Zhukovski (1970) suggested 'micro-centres' (the restricted geographical area with primary gene centres) and 'mega-centres' (several micro-centres are united). Leppik (1970) proposed that gene centres of cultivated plants (for resistance genes) could be located by following distribution pattern of variability in specialized parasites of the crop. Central highlands of Mexico are known to house maximum variability in *P. infestans* as well as resistance genes in potatoes.

At international level serious efforts in the area of exploration, collection, evaluation, maintenance and exchange of germplasm of cultivated plants have been made. The International Bureau of Plant Genetic Resources (IBPGR) was established in 1973. The national chapter in the form of National Bureau of Plant Genetic Resource (NBPGR) was initiated in 1976 with headquarter in New Delhi. To support the fieldwork on plants in different regions three out centres were created, with suitable gene bank facilities, located at Hyderabad, Bhawali and Pantnagar.

Variability is the law of nature. Natural plant populations exhibit variability for various characters including resistance to pests and pathogens. Genetic variability has been reported and exploited in different crop improvement programmes. The sources of resistance can be located in any of the following forms:

- Land races/cultivated plants
- Wild/alien species
- Cytoplasm as source of resistance (Grogan, 1971 proposed use of 'multiplasm' against mono-plasm)
- Induced/created variability through mutations

14.3.2 Methods for Resistance Breeding

Breeding for disease resistance is an activity where man tries to speed up the things that nature is doing in slow but consistent and systematic manner, without disturbing the ecological balance. For plant breeders' resistance to pests and pathogens is just like any other trait but in this case two biologically interacting systems are involved. The success or failure of product (host resistance) depends on behaviour of both populations. Depending upon nature of reproductive process in plants, self or cross- pollinated crops, different breeding methods have been devised by plant breeders for plant improvement. Singh (1986) described the details of methods used or resistance breeding for self as well as cross-pollinated crops. He emphasized role of mutation breeding, especially in situation where reliable sources of resistance genes are not available under natural conditions. He described a scheme of mutation breeding in self pollinated crops, (Figures 14.1 and 14.2). Same procedure can be adopted in other crop with suitable modifications.

Figure 14.1 Desirable plant type (resistant to MBYMV) developed by mutation breeding. No natural source of resistance was known. (Courtesy, D.P. Singh, Pantnagar)

Exposure/treatment of seeds with physical/chemical mutagen.

↓

Each M_1 plant is selfed. Screening of dominant mutations, if any may be carried out. Seed from individual plant/spike/tiller may be harvested separately

↓

M_2 plant progenies are grown. Selection of individual plants with moderate to high degree of resistance is carried under epiphytotic conditions.

↓

M_3 plant progenies of selected M_2 plants are grown. Selection of plants/progenies under epiphytotic conditions.

↓

M_4 generation consists of progenies of individual selected M_3 plants and selected progenies. Preliminary yield trial of selected progenies along with parental variety and standard checks are conducted.

↓

Multi-location trial of the high yielding and disease resistant progenies alongwith checks.

↓

Release and seed multiplication of superior progeny.

Figure 14.2 General outline of a mutation breeding procedure in autogamous crop plant.

14.3.3 Testing of Resistance in Plants

Suitable methods for reliable and reproducible testing of resistant genes in plants make backbone of any breeding for disease resistance programme. This vital screening, against target pest or pathogen, is used at two stages: (a) rigorous testing of parents used in breeding programme and (b) reasonable screening of improved plant populations before release for cultivation by the growers. Screening methods will differ for different diseases, as every host-pathogen interaction is a special case. The inoculation methods should be as natural as possible but without leaving any chance of escape for the plants. Dhingra and Sinclair (1986) gave a critical treatment to the methods of screening against various pathogens. For screening of germplasm mixed inoculations, with different pathogen, have also been suggested, to save time and space. It may be required also to get proper host response, as in soil-born pathogen (nematodes and wilt causing fungi and bacteria). Efforts are also made for *in-vitro* screening of large number of germplasms against pathogen/pathogen produced toxins. This not only saves time and energy but can also be performed without waiting for the season. For screening plant resistance against viruses the role of insect vector should be critically evaluated, as non-preferential feeding on certain plants may give them freedom from viral pathogen(s) transmitted by the insect vector.

14.4 GENE DEPLOYMENT

Running out of cultivars due to 'break down' of resistance is a common phenomenon in modern agriculture. As discussed in Chapter 6 the 'break down' of resistance is a misnomer. Johnson (1984), while discussing strategic use of disease resistance stated, "differences in the degree of inherent durability of the disease resistance of different cultivars are demonstrable." Following two specific cases can be cited in support of this statement:

1. Resistance in cabbage against *Fusarium conglutinans* has been found operative and effective over seventy years in North US.
2. The resistance in barley (Ml-g and Ml-La) against powdery mildew fungus, *Erysiphae graminis* f. sp. *hordei*, was effective for many years when used on small scale. Once the cultivars became popular, selection pressure increased and pathogenic race developed rendering it ineffective (boom and burst cycle).

Gene deployment is a well-planned strategy for utilization of resistant genes for maximum benefits on long-term basis. It requires special consideration for specific or major genes, which are inherently unstable. The strategy may be adopted at following levels:

14.4.1 Development of Suitable Cultivar

Gene pyramiding. Vertical resistance governed by one or few genes is always liable to pathogenic adaptability once exposed to field conditions on large scale. It has been proposed that suitable number of specific/major genes be accumulated in host cultivars. This will not only enhance durability of resistance but also give certain epidemiological advantages like restricted/ineffective dispersal of specific races of pathogen, resulting in wastage of inoculum. Gene pyramiding is the stacking of R genes in cultivars or simultaneous introduction of more major genes in host cultivars. The purpose of combining genes, in host plant, is to create a situation where pathogen could not develop matching genotype. Thus the specific resistance becomes durable also.

Mutation is the means to counter R genes in host populations by pathogen. The probability of mutation to multiple virulences is equal to the product of rates of mutation for each avirulence/ virulence locus (Roy, 2000). He further stated, "considering mutation rates, 4 or 5 genes for resistance might provide stable resistance for centuries.' It has also been speculated that pathogenic races with multiple virulence (complex races) will suffer from reduced fitness, in terms of establishment and survival. Nelson (1972) considered pyramiding approach superior to mutilines programme, but pyramiding too has problems.

- Combining many major genes in a cultivar may pose breeding challenges.
- Allelic or linked nature of genes may pose problem for desirable result.
- Though hypothetical, there is threat of development of super race.

Higher the number of resistant genes (gene pyramid), greater would be the longevity of resistance provided. The genes should be of non-allelic type, governing resistance to major virulences present in a given area. Flor and Comstock (1971) developed flax cultivars with multiple rust conditioning genes by using back crossing gene lines carrying five genes (Sr5, Sr6, Sr8, Sr9 and Sr11). It has been postulated that chance development of matching complex virulence in pathogen will make all major genes ineffective used alone or in combinations. However, it appears to be speculative rather than real threat.

Combination of VR and HR. It has been proposed that a combination of quantitative/horizontal resistance, (potentially durable) and qualitative/vertical resistance, (inherently unstable but complete), in a cultivar may improve utility of both. This may be due to reduced probability of selection of the pathogen genotype able to match both types of resistance simultaneously (Figure 14.3).

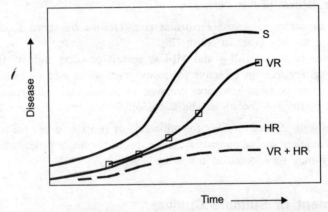

Figure 14.3 Hypothetical representation of epidemiological consequences of different types of resistance under field conditions. The DPCs for susceptible (S), vertical resistance (VR), Horizontal resistance (HR) and a combination of vertical plus horizontal resistance. The (VR + HR) is likely to have advantages of both, under field conditions.

Tolerance to pathogen/disease. We have discussed the concept of tolerance, its merits and demerits in Chapter 6. The term *tolerance* in relation to plant disease and their management has been used widely and loosely since the time of Cladwell, et al., (1958) who defined it as *quality of susceptible plant to endure severe attack by pathogen without sustaining severe losses in yields.*

It attracted the scientists as an alternative strategy to resistance. Theoretically tolerance is an attractive concept due to more stability and less selection pressure on pathogen population, but in practice following are limitations in using tolerance as a means of plant disease management:

- Tolerance has been reported to be specific, in case of yellow rust of wheat (*P. striiformis*), Johnson and Bowyer (1974).
- Due to presence of disease, difficult to identify and evaluate.
- Not suitable for potentially 'epidemic' pathogens, the fields with tolerant cultivars will become 'storehouse' of inoculum for the area. This will increase the chances of new mutants. There are contrasting opinion, on large-scale adoption of tolerance, whether it will suppress or promote epidemics.
- Farmers do not appreciate the look of the fields; this may be the last choice, in case resistance is not available.
- Tolerance may be, as a choice, between moderate resistance and moderate susceptibility, as shown in Figure 14.4 (Browning, et al., 1977).

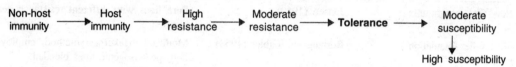

Figure 14.4 Different host responses to pathogens, as observed in nature.

Simons (1965) developed a technique for indexing oat genotypes for tolerance by calculating ratio of productiveness in paired plots of oat cultivars, one with rust and one without rust (Table 14.1).

$$\text{Tolerance index} = \frac{\text{Grain yield in plot with rus}}{\text{Grain yield in plot without rus}}$$

Table 14.1 Rust Reaction and Tolerance Index of Four Oat Cultivars to Different Races or Mixtures of Races of Crown Rust Fungus (*Puccinia coronata*)

Cultivar	Rust Races (203 + 216)		Rust Race 290	
	Reaction	*Tolerance index*	*Reaction*	*Tolerance index*
Clint land	R	0.86	S	0.67
Cherokee	S	0.81	S	0.83
Benton	S	0.74	S	0.74
Clinton	S	0.65	S	0.70

R = Resistant, S = Susceptible

Cherokee is known for its tolerance for more than 25 years. Selection for tolerance to rust should be done in absence of genes for vertical resistance.

Multiline cultivars. Genetic uniformity makes crop plants vulnerable, if resistance happens to be major gene/vertical type and several cases of boom and burst cycle have been documented in literature (Chapter 6). For specific resistance heterogeneity is desirable, which can be achieved through development of multiline cultivars. Mutilines are basically 'synthetic resistance' where each component line (isoline) has a particular or resistant gene effective against a specific different race of the pathogen. Generally, 8-16 isolines are blended into a phenotypically uniform multiline cultivar. The isolines are developed by modified conventional backcross breeding method. The number of isolines in a multiline cultivar is variable (3-4 to 8-16) depending upon racial composition.

Two approaches proposed for mutilines: *clean crop approach* (Marshall, 1977) and *dirty crop approach* (Jensen, 1952, Borlaug, 1958, Browning and Frey, 1969) are employed to extend the useful life of strong resistant genes, including those, which were defeated earlier. Initially multiline approach appeared promising, at least theoretically, but at practical level it was agronomically conservative and the variability in plant produce could never found favour with both growers and consumers, except in processing industry. Table 14.2 describes the features of major multiline programmes.

Table 14.2 The Features of Some Multiline Programmes

The Programme	Workers	Product/Features
New York programme	Jensen (1952)	Pure lines with different resistance genes blended.
Rockefeller foundation Programme	Borlaug and Gibler (1958)	Modified backcross method employed, 8-16 near isogenic lines blended. Borlaug (1965) proposed multiline hybrids.
Iowa programme	Browning, et al., 1962	Multilines E68, E69 and E70 (early multiline M68, M69 and M70 (mid season) were released in oats against crown rust.
Indian programme		Four multiline varieties of Kalyan Sona (KSML-1, KSML-2, KSML-3 and KSML-4) and three vars. of Pv-18 (PVML-1, PVML-2, PVML-3). Multiline also developed for Sonalika (RR-21).

First multiline cultivar (Miramar 63) was released from Colombian programme (Rockefeller foundation, 1963–1964). It was mechanical mixture of 10 isolines with resistance to leaf and stem rust fungi. Within two years, rust fungus infected two component lines, which were dropped and four new were added form reserve of 600 lines.

14.4.2 Filed Level Deployment of Genes

Mixed cultivars and varietal mixture cultivations. This is a practical compromise, which has following advantages:

- diversification at farm level
- can compensate for breeders limitation of combining too many genes in any one cultivar
- mixtures have less than average level of disease compared with component cultivars grown as pure stand
- may also work for multiple disease resistance
- other epidemiological advantages

Cultivar mixtures have been successfully exploited in barley for management of powdery mildew for processing purpose. These are one step ahead of multiline cultivars. These provide greater genetic heterogeneity to host population. They are also developed on the same principle as that of multiline but they provide greater buffering capacity and more effective against more than one pathogen. The component variety may be replaced whenever their resistance run out. The limitations are same as in case of multilines. The varietal mixtures were adopted only in course grains where grain quality or uniformity was not the primary concern.

Inter or mixed cropping. This is probably the last stage in creating heterogeneous plant population to slow down the progress of disease/pathogen. The growers plant simultaneously more than one plant species such as cereals (wheat + barley), cereals + legumes (wheat + chick pea or sorghum + pigeon pea), wheat + oilseed (mustard), certain intercroppings are popular among growers like sugarcane + potato, sugarcane + mustard, potato + mustard for reasons other than disease management. This may be planted in rows (intercropping: potato-mustard) or as mixed stand (mixed cropping: wheat + mustard).

14.4.3 Regional Deployment of Resistant Genes

Gene recycling. Major genes provide complete resistance to crop plants and put selection pressure on pathogen population. The pathogen may respond by selecting a new and matching virulence. The host resistance becomes ineffective (break down?). But as soon as the host genes are withdrawn from cultivation, the new virulence is no more wanted and the stabilizing forces tend to bring the situation back to original, and the new virulence vanishes soon. This phenomenon (stabilizing pressure) has been exploited in the form of gene recycling/gene rotation or sequential release of major genes to prolong their effective life. Under this scheme major genes are released, in host cultivars, and once they are 'defeated', they are withdrawn and replaced by new major genes (Figure 14.5). The defeated or withdrawn genes are conserved for future use, after long gap (when matching virulence has disappeared). This approach was adopted to control stem rust of wheat in Australia between 1938–1950 (Watson and Luig, 1963) and oat rust 1942–54 (Figure 14.5).

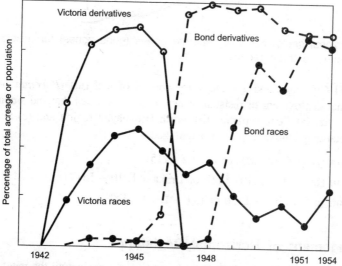

Figure 14.5 Relationship of resistance in oat cultivars and composition of *P. coronata* population (Victoria or Bond races).

Creation of gene zones. Vertical resistance, governed by major genes, is more effective in heterogeneous host populations, where inoculum produced on one host genotype is ineffective on other host cultivar (carrying different resistance gene). This principle has been suggested for creation of gene zones (geographical areas planted with cultivars having particular resistant gene(s)) for management of rust pathogens (Nelson, 1972). Frey, et al., (1973) proposed regional deployment of suitable host genotypes for effective management of crown rust of oats (*Puccinia coronata*) in Iowa state (Figure 14.6).

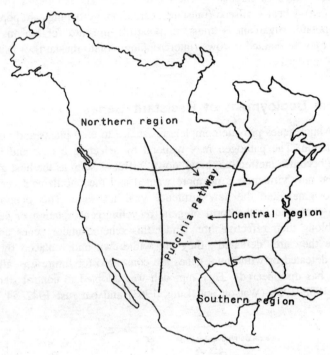

Figure 14.6 Regional deployments of separate genes (gene zones) for resistance to crown rust in oats in three regions.

Reddy and Rao (1979) suggested a strategy for control of leaf rust (*Puccinia recondita*) of wheat in India by regional deployment of resistant genes. It was proposed that India could be divided into three gene zones, viz. (a) Central plains, (b) North Himalayan region and (c) Southern Nilgiri and Palani hills by planting cultivars with resistant genes

> **Region (a)** (Lr9 or Lr19 or Lr10 + Lr15)
>
> **Region (b)** (Lr1 + Lr107 Lr1b or Lr3ka + Lr10 + Lr17)
>
> **Region (c)** (Lr3ka + Lr20 or Lr1 + Lr10 + Lr17)

14.4.4 Management of Horizontal Resistance

Horizontal resistance, *sensu* Vanderplank is uniformly spread against all the races of pathogen. Since it is a polygenic character (minor genes with additive effects), the resistance provided is fairly stable.

Nelson (1978) emphasized reduction of apparent infection rate as the main criteria to define HR. The components of HR include smaller pustules, low infection percentage, less sporulation and/or longer latent period. Kuhn et al., (1980) suggested that if these characters are under separate genetic control, there is possibility of selecting these characters in segregating population, and development of host genotype having assembly of these components to provide higher level and more stable HR. Components in HR should be critically evaluated so that the judicious selection should be made. He further reported heritability for components of slow leaf rusting against *P. recondita* in wheat. The higher heritability of latent period (49%) will be more effective as compared to pustule size (heritability; 27%).

Vertifolia effect. HR and VR, as defined by Vanderplank 1963, differ in their behaviour and mechanism (Chapter 5). All plant cultivars have some level of HR, to provide general resistance, irrespective of presence or absence of VR. Vanderplank defined vertifolia effect as the *loss of horizontal resistance while breeding for vertical resistance*. The phenomenon is named after the potato variety Vertifolia, having R_3 and R_4 genes, which gave resistance against blight pathogen *P. infestans*. It was observed that once infection starts on Vertifolia (VR is matched) the rate of infection was very high. This was interpreted as loss of HR (rate reducing resistance). The breeders while selecting for VR (R_3 and R_4 genes) did not care for the level of HR or the genes responsible for it. Table 14.3 gives performance of six potato cultivars with VR and six without VR, in a study conducted by Kirste (1958). This is important aspect of breeding for disease resistance and all care should be taken to monitor the HR levels, during breeding process, so that vertifolia effect is not repeated.

Table 14.3 Progress of Late Blight of Potato

Potato Cultivars	Diseases Rating Observed				
	Rating 1 on		Rating 3 on	Disease duration	Comparative (r)
5 cvs with VR	15 Aug	(08days)*	30 Aug	15 days	26/15 (1.733)
Vertifolia ($R_3 R_4$)	22 Aug	(15 days)*	29 Aug	06 days	26/6 (4.333)
6 cvs without VR	07 Aug	(00 days)*	02 Sept	26 days	1

*Δ' Advantage time, delay in onset of disease due to vertical resistance.

14.5 USE OF RESISTANCE TO PATHOGEN VECTORS

Role of pathogen vectors in epidemiology is well established (Chapter 7). We have also emphasized this while discussing epidemiology in relation to plant disease management. Use of vector resistant cultivars is an attractive proposition, especially in case of viral diseases, but it is not easy to develop them. Johnes (1976) reported resistance in red raspberries to aphids (*Amphorphora rubi*), which effectively suppressed several diseases transmitted by aphids (Figure 14.7). Aphid resistant and aphid susceptible plants may be equally susceptible to virus infection, when mechanically inoculated. Fry (1982) observed that plant resistance to pathogen vector might not always suppress epidemic development. He further explained that resistance to vector might result in more frequent visit by vectors to different plants (since resistant plants are poor hosts). These more frequent visits may help in more inoculations, particularly in case of mechanically transmitted/stylet borne viruses.

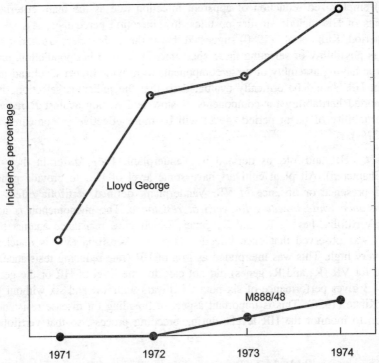

Figure 14.7 Incidence of virus in plots of aphid resistant (M888/49) and aphid susceptible (Lloyd George) red raspberry cultivars.

14.6 ROLE OF BIOTECHNOLOGY IN DISEASE MANAGEMENT

Man selected suitable plants and animals, from nature, and domesticated them for his sustenance through agriculture. Plant breeding improved the plant genotypes and enhanced crop yields. But it has certain limitations, incompatibility being major one. Biotechnology came to the rescue during late 20th century (transgenic microbes in late 1970s and transgenic plants and animals in 1980s). It has helped to further increase the productivity and production without compromising ecological balance. Biotechnology has provided techniques to incorporate foreign genes (**transgenes**) into plants with precision and reliability. Pattanayak and Kumar (2000) described three broad areas in biotechnology;

- **Plant genetic engineering** deals with basic molecular biology, isolation of genes and their introduction.

- **Molecular breeding** encompasses the utilization of molecular tools in breeding programmes (character tagging, marker-assisted selection and map-based cloning of genes).

- **Genomics** deals with the structural and functional dimensions of plant/crop genetic material.

The technological advancements have been put to maximum use for generating novel plant type that can resist the biotic stress (pathogens and insect pest) and minimize the yield losses (average

30–40% on global basis). We will discuss some of the significant achievements made in the field of plant resistance against different plant pathogens.

14.6.1 Resistance against Viruses

Viruses cause significant damage to most of cash crops, viz. potato, tomato, tobacco, apple, grapes, sugarbeet, sugarcane, citrus, coconut, etc. Though very simple in structure and function, controlling viruses is a difficult task, especially due to non-availability of 'viricides'. Biotechnology has facilitated use of pathogen-derived resistance (PDR) as well as host-derived resistance (HDR). Transgenic tobacco plant expressing TMV coat protein gene was developed (Powell-Abel et al., 1986). Coat protein gene approach was employed against several plant viruses (Table 14.4). The other genes used were RNA dependent RNA polymerase, defective viral movement protein (Cooper, et al., 1995) and inhibition of long distance transport of potyviruses (Cronin, et al., 1995). Synthesis of antibodies, against viral proteins has been used to induce resistance in crop plants (Tavladoraki, et al., 1993). Ogawa, et al., (1996) used a novel approach of virus induced cell death in transgenic tobacco against cucumber mosaic virus.

About 150 Gemini viruses are known to cause serious damage to plants. Researchers found a gene whose truncated version, when introduced into plants, stopped replication of Gemini viruses, thus making plant resistant to number of potential pathogens. In mid 1980s, work started on improving resistance in papaya against ring spot virus, a pathogen for which no natural resistance was available. By 1992, ring spot became serious problem in widespread area of Hawaii. Transgenic papaya plants, resistant to ring spot virus, were developed and within few years 60% papaya in Hawaii were protected by the use of transgenic papaya.

Table 14.4 Transgenic Plants Generated in Various Crops for Viral Resistance

Gene	Transgene Product	Stage of Infection Cycle	Mode of Action	Virus	Transgenic Plant
Structural	Coat protein	Uncoating	Competition of RNA	TMV/PEMV	Tobacco, Pea
Replicase protein	Replication	Competition for enzyme	PVY Potato	PSbM VRYMV	Pea Rice
	Movement protein	Transport	Interference with	TMV	Potato & Tobacco
			transport PLRV, PVX	PVY	
	Viral protease	Replication	Polyprotein processing	PVY	Potato
Others	Helper component	Transport	Interference with transport	TEV	Tobacco
Antisense RNA		Translation	Blocks viral RNA and prevents translation	PLRV	Potato
	Ribozyme	Translation	Cleaves viral RNA	CEVd	Tomato
	Statellite RNA	Assembly	Competes for capsids	CMV	Tobacco
Antiviral protein	Ribonuclease	—	Degrades ds-RNA (Viroids)	PSTV	Potato

(Contd.)

Table 14.4 Transgenic Plants Generated in Various Crops for Viral Resistance (*Contd.*)

Gene	Transgene Product	Stage of Infection Cycle	Mode of Action	Virus	Transgenic Plant
	Pokeweed antiviral Protein	Translation	Inhibits rRNA of 60S Subunit	TMV PVX	Tobacco
	2', 5'-oligoadenylate	Replication ds-RNA	Degrades	CMV	Tobacco
	System ferritin	—	Sequester iron and oxdative damage	TNV	Tobacco
	Antibody	Assembly	Competes for viral protein against which it is generated	AMCV	Tobacco

14.6.2 Resistance against Fungi

Management of fungal diseases is mostly dependent on application of fungicides, which have obvious problems related with environmental pollution and human health. Breeding for fungal resistance has limitations, biotechnology has helped to overcome some of these problems. In several cases (Table 14.5) success has been achieved where antifungal transgenes have been introduced in plants.

Chitinase and glucanase genes have been engineered into transgenic plants (Brolie, et al., 1991, Lin, et al., 1995). The combination of chitinase and glucanase has also been reported in Alfalfa-*Cercospora nicotianae* and in barley-*R. solani* system (Jach, et al., 1995).

Disease resistance in transgenic plants has been improved by insertion of a chitinase gene from biocontrol fungus, *Trichoderma harzianum*. The gene encoding strongly anti-fungal endochitinase was transferred in tobacco and potato, which became highly tolerant or completely resistant to foliar pathogens, viz. *Alternaria alternata, A. solani, Botrytis cineria* and soil borne fungus *Rhizoctonia solani* (Matteo Lorito, et al., 1998). Constitutive expression of PR-1 gene and osmotin gene in tobacco has provided effective resistance against *P. infestans*. Expression of ribosome inactivating protein (RIP) gene in tobacco provided resistance against *R. solani* (Logemann, et al., 1992).

Strittmatter and co-workers (1998) successfully employed genetic engineering to induce hypersensitive cell death in potato plants in response to fungal attack. Under this strategy, a bacterial ribonuclease gene (barnase) and an inhibitor of barnase (barstar) were introduced into potato under the control of fungal infection specific (prp 1-1) promoter and CaMV 35 S promoter, respectively. It is believed that level of barstar (inhibitor) is exceeded by the level of barnase only in cells close to infection sites, which leads to cell death.

Table 14.5 Transgenic Plants Generated in Various Crops for Fungal Resistance

Plant	Gene/Protein	Target Pathogen
PR protein		
Tobacco	Chitinase from *Serratia marcescens*	*Alternaria longipes*
	Chitinase from bean	*Rhizoctonia solani*
	Chitinase from *N. tabacum*	*Rhizoctonia solani*
	PR-1-a gene from tobacco	*Phytophthora parasitica*

(*Contd.*)

Table 14.5 Transgenic Plants Generated in Various Crops for Fungal Resistance (*Contd.*)

Plant	Gene/Protein	Target Pathogen
Rice	Chitinase from rice	*Rhizoctonia solani*
Cucumber	Chitinase from rice	*Botrytis cinerea*
Tobacco	Glucanase from alfalfa and chitinase from rice	*Cercospora nicotianae*
	Chitinase and glucanase from barley	*Rhizoctonia solani*
Brassica napus	Bean chitinase	*Rhizoctonia solani*
	Chimeric endochitinase by fusion of tomato and tobacco chitinase gene	*Cylindrosporium concentricum, Sclerotinia sclerotiorum, Phoma lingam*
Potato	β-1,3-endoglucanase from soyabean	*Phytophthora infestans*
Kiwifruit	β-1,3-endoglucanse from soyabean	*Botrytis cinerea*
Tobacco	Barley RIP	*Rhizoctonia solani*
	Rs AFP-2 from radish	*Alternaria longipes*
Potato	Osmotin from tobacco	*Phytophthora infestans*
Antifungal compounds		
Tobacco	Stillbene synthase from grapevine	*Botrytis cinerea*
Genes/proteins that induce artificial cell death		
Potato	Barnase and barstar	*Phytophthora infestans*
Potato	Glucose oxidase from *Aspergillus niger*	*Phytophthora infestans*
Tobacco	Nettle agglutinin	*Botrytis cinerea*
Tobacco	Cryptogein from *Phytophthora cryptogea*	*Erysiphe cichoracearum, Botrytis cineraea*

14.6.3 Resistance to Bacterial Pathogens

Transgenic plants of important crops like tobacco, apple, potato, sugarcane, bean and rice have been developed to counter the damage done by bacterial pathogens. Pattanayak and Kumar (2000) listed following strategies employed for developing transgenic plants resistant to bacteria:

Production of antibacterial proteins of non-plants origin. Include lytic peptides, lysozymes and iron sequestering glycoprotiens. Cercopins, causes pores in bacterial membrane, have been expressed in potato and tobacco (Mourgue, et al., 1998) and atachins in apple plants. Lysozymes, enzymes with specific hydrolytic activities against bacterial cell-wall peptido-glycan, have been used in tobacco and potato (Nakajima, et al., 1997).

Inhibition of bacterial pathogenicity/virulence factors. Transgenic tobacco and bean plants have been developed by introducing **ttr gene** whose product inactivates tab-toxin produced by *Pseudomonas syringae* (Table 14.6). Similar approach has been successfully used for producing transgenic sugarcane plants expressing an albincidin detoxifying gene (**alb**) providing resistance to *Xanthomonas albilineans* [(Table 14.6). Zhang, et al., (1999)].

Enhancement of natural plant defence mechanism. In transgenic potato, expression of pectinolytic enzyme known to release cell-wall sugar oligomers (elicitors) made plants less susceptible to *E. carutovora* (Wegener, et al., 1996).

Induced programmed cell death (pcd). Induction of naturally occurring phenomena of pcd can help to manage the pathogen eliciting hypersensitive reaction. Barnase and barstar genes have been used in potato. This approach is likely to provide generalized (non-specific) resistance against wide variety of pathogen.

Table 14.6 Some Examples of Transgenic Plants with Bacterial Resistance

Plant	Gene/Protein	Origin	Target
Potato	Lysozyme	T4 bacteriophage	*E. carotovora*
Sugarcane albilineans	Albicidin detoxifying gene	*Pantoea dispersa*	*Xanthomonas*
Tobacco	Tabtoxin resistant protein (Tabtoxin acetyl transferase)	*P. Syringae* pv. *tabaci*	*P. syringae*
Bean (Phaseolicola)	Phaseolotoxin insensitive	*P. syringae* pv. phaseolicola ornithine carbamoyl	*P. syringae* pv.
Potato	Pectate lyase	*E. carotovora*	*E. carotovora*
Potato	Glucose oxidase	*Aspergillus niger*	*E. carotovora*
Tobacco	Bacterio-opsin	*Halobacterium halobium*	*P. syringae* pv. *tabaci*

14.6.4 Resistance against Nematodes

Root knot nematode (*Meloidogyne* spp.) and cyst nematode (*Heterodera* and *Globodera* spp.) are important not only as pathogens, causing damage to plants, but also because they are difficult to manage, once introduced in soil. Limited success has been achieved in use of biotechnology for development of nematodes resisting plants. Cowpea trypsin inhibitor (CptI) when introduced in potato helped in management of *Meloidogyne spp.* (reduced fecundity) and *Globodera pallida* (population shift: more males than females, Atkinson, et al., 1995). Nematode inducible transmembrane pore protein in root cells have been identified and related gene have been cloned from tobacco. It is expected that expression of such genes in host will provide wide spectrum resistance against nematode attack.

14.6.5 Resistance to Abiotic Stresses

Concept and significance of tolerance/resistance to abiotic factors have been discussed in Chapter 6. These environmental stresses, viz. drought, salinity, heat, freezing and flooding have been the scourge of agriculture since ages, bringing with them poor harvests. With likelihood of increasing environmental hazards (global warming and likely shift of seasons?) has made the policy makers and scientists to recognize the importance of abiotic stresses and crop resistance.

Biotechnology can help in transfer of genes encoding for protective proteins or enzymes from various sources. This may involve alteration in membrane systems to achieve the objectives. The accumulation of low molecular mass osmoprotectants and osmolytes is considered to be an important strategy to overcome environmental stress. Holmberg and Bulow (1998) introduced cholive dehydrogenase gene (*E. coli:* bet A gene) in tobacco and potato resulted in development of salt and freezing tolerance in transgenic plants, respectively. In Table 14.7, some more cases where biotechnology has helped to develop desired levels of tolerance/resistance in plants are given. One interesting area of cold and water stress tolerance has been explored by transferring DREB genes (dehydration responsive transcription factor) in tobacco (Smirnoff and Bryant, 1999). Transfer of barley HVAI gene encoding a group 3LEA (Late-embryogenesis abundant) protein to rice conferred improved osmotic stress tolerance to the transgenic lines.

Abiotic stresses are often the cause for formation of reactive oxygen species, which damage membranes and macro-molecules. Genes coding for superoxide dismutase, peroxidase, catalase and glutathione reductase, are being transferred in transgenic plants.

Water logging may lead to anoxia or hypoxia (complete or partial deprivation of oxygen) for plant roots. This leads to collapse of membranes and production of toxic oxidant products. Constitutive expression of non-symbiotic haemoglobin gene from barley (HB) and the bacteria vitreoscilla (vhb) in maize (Sowa, et al., 1998) and tobacco, respectively has improved the plant performance under anaerobic conditions.

Table 14.7 Some Important Examples of Plant Genetic Engineering for Developing Tolerance to Abiotic Stresses

Stress	Gene/Enzyme	Source Plant	Transgenic
Drought, salinity and freezing	Dehydration response element-binding protein (DREBIA)	*Arabidopsis*	*Arabidopsis*
Osmotic	D-pyrroline-5-carboxylate synthetase (p5cs)	Moth bean (*Vigna aconitifolia*)	Tobacco
Drought and salinity	Mannitol-1-phosphate dehydrogenase (mltd)	*E. coli*	Tobacco
Cold and salinity	Choline oxidase (cod A) glabiformis	Arthrobacter	*Arabidopsis*
Salinity	Glyoxalase 1	*Brassica juncea*	Tobacco
Salinity	Na$^+$/H$^+$ antiport	*Arabidopsis*	*Arabidopsis*
Salinity	Choline dehydrogenase (Bet A)	*E. coli*	Tobacco
Cold	O-3-fatty acid desaturase (Fad 7)	*Arabidopsis*	Tobacco
Cold	Δ 9-desaturase (Des9)	*Anacystis nidulans*	Tobacco
Drought	Trehalose-6-phosphate synthase (TPS 1)	*Bacillus subtilis*	Tobacco
Drought	Levan sucrase (Sac B)	*Bacillus subtilis*	Tobacco
Salinity and drought	Lea protein (HvA 1)	Barley	Rice
Oxidative and chilling	Cu/Zn super oxide dismultase (Cu/Zn SOD)	Rice	Tobacco
Oxidative	Fe SOD	*Arabidopsis*	Maize
Chilling	ω-3-fattyacid desaturase (Des 9)	*Anacystis nidulans*	Tobacco
Freezing	Antifreezing protein (Afp) (fish)	Winter flounder	Tobacco
Oxidative	Mn-superoxide dismutase(Mn-Sod)	*N. plumbaginifolia*	Tobacco Alfalfa
Hypoxia and anoxia	Non-symbiotic haemoglobin (vhb)	*Vitreoscilla stercoraria*	Tobacco
Hypoxia	Non-symbiotic haemoglobin (hb)	Barley	Maize
Cadmium	Metallothionein-I(MT)	*N. glutinosa L.*	Tobacco

14.6.6 Future Prospects and Limitations

Increasing pressure for healthy food and healthy environment is likely to put the host resistance in the central place. The other methods will have a need based supporting role in overall strategy of plant diseased management. The rapid progress made in the fields of molecular biology and genetic engineering is indicative that in near future mystery of host-pathogen and plant-non-pathogen recognition and response systems may be revealed. This may start a new era, with more options (genes/system) for wider and more stable host defence. Horizontal gene transfer is already being utilized in different genetic backgrounds, thereby giving more option to plant breeders. There will be a possibility to synthesize a desirable gene or protein or modified receptor, which may interfere at different stages of infection.

Lucas (1998) visualized, "a modified receptor would bind a widely conserved molecular 'signature', such as a common component of the fungal or bacterial cell wall, thereby switching on defence on contact with a whole range of pathogens." The role of avr genes or the elicitors produced is likely to be exploited more to induce programmed cell death. The possibility to introduce alien/foreign genes in plant may provide great opportunities. The plantibodies thus produced may have uses other than protecting plant health.

Monsanto has developed a transgenic potato line having 7 genes imparting resistances to Colorado potato beetle, viral diseases, *Verticillium,* bruising resisting and altered carbohydrate metabolism. Monsanto has also developed corn and wheat/transgenic having CBI (confidential business information) which enhances the photosynthetic efficiency. Miffin (2000) has described crop improvement in 21st century highlighting commercial implication of second-generation transgenic plants, which may be designed for industrial needs, pharmaceuticals, therapeutics and environmental health. New avenues can be used to handle abiotic stress tolerance, photosynthetic capacity, nutrient utilization efficiency and biological nitrogen fixation. Gene therapy/chimeric oligonucleotide dependent mismatch repair (cdMMR) has been used in tobacco and maize (Hohn and Puchta, 1999).

Limitations. During last two decades plant biotechnology has made significant contribution, particularly in fields of herbicides, insect pests and virus resistance (first generation crops). In spite of early experimental success and great hopes, there are certain limitations in use of biotechnology in plant improvement. The following are some points that need consideration:

- Only small amount of genetic material can be introduced in any plant genome.
- The other limitation is devising a proper vector for desired gene(s).
- 'Boom and Bust' applies both for resistance and selective fungicides.
- Field success of transgenics still remains to be established with mate testing which is to be done by the growers in field laboratory.
- Gene silencing, due to multiple copies and methylation of introduced gene is a limitation faced by plant breeders.
- Extending host range of virus by transgenes encoded coat protein from another virus (recombination between an infecting virus and viral sequences present on plant chromosome) is a hypothetical but dangerous proposition.
- Great caution need to be exercised for bio-safety and risk assessment.

14.7 RESISTANCE AS A COMPONENT OF IPM

During last decade of the 20th century, it was realized that the host resistance, although potential and desirable means of disease management, has its own limitations. Main problem is the durability or effectiveness of gene(s) once exposed to field conditions. This was more pertinent to vertical resistance, which is more prone to 'breakdown' due to inherent mono/oligogenic basis. It was also reported that resistance lasts longer if disease (pathogen X environment interaction) does not put excessive pressure on host. All this led to the idea that with suitable management practices the life of resistance genes (VR/HR) can be prolonged. Resistance can serve for longer period provided it is supported by other measures of diseases management, which keep pathogen/disease pressure under control. It gave sound logic to develop a strategy.

In integrated pest management (IPM) philosophy, it is accepted fact that no single method of pest control, howsoever effective, should be used alone, in long-term interest. In IPM various options of control are integrated to develop a package which may be location specific (fine tuning to address the specific problems of the area). The host resistance, to one or more major pests, becomes the major focal point around which the IPM strategy is developed. For example, in potato and wheat, IPM has to start with selection of varieties resistant to late blight and wheat rust, respectively. The minor problems of these crops can be managed by other means of disease control. This is the first stage of integration of host resistance in IPM. The next stage logical approach is the *judicious use of fungicides* to bring down the initial level of inoculum from which disease/infection starts (sanitation *sensu* Vanderplank). This prophylactic spray of fungicide will reduce the initial disease severity and slow down its progress. By adopting this we can take a lot of pressure from host resistance, which will perform efficiently and for longer time. Fry (1983) made significant contribution in management of late blight of potato by *integrating host resistance with fungicide application*, which work in synergistic manner. Two important points emerged:

- Fungicide requirement of resistant cultivars is significantly reduced (avoiding unnecessary pesticide use).
- Host cultivars not fully resistant can perform reasonably well, if initial fungicide protection is provided.

Another important component of this philosophy is the role of quarantine or legislative methods may play vital role as introduction and establishment of new virulence from outside might risk the host resistance. Similarly, introduction of plant germplasm into a new geographical area should be planned with great care, taking into account the racial population of the new area where plant genotype is to be introduced. The generation of scientific information on behaviour of host, pathogen, environment and their interaction has enriched our knowledge. With logical thinking this knowledge should be put to use. The consideration is for a long-term planning for disease management where host resistance is effectively and economically utilized, as a component of IPM strategy, along with other supporting component.

REFERENCES

Atkins, D., et al., 1995, The expression of antisense antiribozyme genes targetting citrus exocortis viroids transgenic plants, *J. Gen. Virol.,* 16: 1781–1790.

Atkinson, H.J., Urwin, P.E., Hansen, E. and McPherson M.J., 1995, Design for engineered resistance to root parasitic nematode, *Trends Biotech*, 13: 369–374.

Biffen, R.H., 1905, Mendel's laws of inheritance and wheat breeding, *J. Agric. Sci.,* 1:4.

Borlaug, N.E., 1958, The use of multilineal or composite varieties to control air borne epidemic diseases of self-pollinated crop plants., In: *Proc Symp 1st Int Wheat Genet*, Winnipeg, 12–27.

Broglie, K., et al., 1991, Transgenic plant with enhanced resistance to the fungal pathogen *Rhizoctonia solani, Science,* 254:1194–1197.

Browning, J.A., Simons, M.D. and Torres, E., 1977, Managing host genes, Epidemiology and genetic concepts, In: *Plant Disease: An Advanced Treatise*, J.G. Horsfall and E.B., Cowling, (Eds.), vol. I, 191–212, Academic Press, NY.

Browning, J.A. and Frey, K.J., 1969, Multilines cultivars as a means of disease control, *Annu. Rev. Phytopathlogy,* 7:355–382.

Cooper, B., et al., 1995, A defective movement protein of TMV in transgenic plants confers resistance to multiple viruses whereas the functional analog increases susceptibility, *Virology*, 206: 307–313.

Cronin, S., et al., 1995, Long-distance movement factor: A transport function of the potyvirus helper component proteinase, *Plant Cell,* 7:549–559.

Dhingra, O.D. and Sinclair, J.B., 1986, *Basic Plant Pathology Methods,* CRC Press Inc., Boca Raton, Florida, p. 280–339.

Frey, K.J. and Browning, J.A., 1971, Breeding crop plants for disease resistance, In: *Proc Symp Mutat Breed Dis. Resist. Int At Energy Ag*, Vienna, 45–54.

Fry, W.E., 1982, *Principles of Plant Disease Management*, 220–234, Academic Press, NY.

Fry, W.E., Apple A.E., and Bruhn, 1983, Evaluation of potato late blight forecasts modified to incorporate host resistance and fungicide weathering, *Phytopathalogy,* 73(7):1054–1059.

Grogan, C.O., 1971, Multiplasm a proposed method for the utilization of cytoplasms in pest control, *Plant Dis. Rep,* 55:400–401.

Harlan, J.R., 1975, Our vanishing genetic resources, *Science,* 188:618–621.

Hohn, B. and Puchta, H., 1999, Gene therapy in plants, *Proc. Natl. Acad. Sci.* USA, 832–833.

Holmberg, N. and Bulov, L., 1998, Improving stress tolerance in plants by gene transfer, *Trends Plant Sci.,* 3, 61–66.

Jach, G., et al., 1995, Enhanced quantitative resistance against fungal disease by combinatorial expression of different barley antifungal proteins in transgenic tobacco, *Plant J.,* 8: 97–109.

Johnson, R., 1984, A critical analysis of durable resistance, *Annu. Rev. Phytopathology*, 32:309.

Kirste, 1958, Ergebnisse von Krautfaule-Spritzversuchen, *Kartoffelbau,* 9: 114, 115.

Leppik, E.E., 1970, Gene centres of plants as sources of disease resistance, *Annu. Rev. Phytopathology*, 8:323–344.

Lin, W., et al., 1995, Genetic engineering of rice for resistance to sheath blight, *Bio/Technol,* 13:686–691.

Lomonossof, G.P., 1995, Pathogen-derived resistance to plant viruses, *Annu. Rev. Phytopath.,* 33: 323–343.

Longmann, J., Jach, G. and Shell, J., 1992, Expression of barley ribosome inactivating protein leads to increased fungal protection in transgenic tobacco plants, *Bio/Techol.,* 10:305–308.

Lucas, J.A., 1998, Plant Pathology and Plant Pathogens, 3rd edn., Blackwell Science Ltd.,

Miffin, B.J., 2000, Crop improvement in 21st century, *J. Expt. Bot.* 51:1–8.

Mourgues, F., Brisset, M.N. and Chevreau, E., 1998, Strategies to improve plant resistance to bacterial disease through genetic engineering, *Trends Biotechnol*, 16:203–210.

Nakajima, H., et al., 1997, Fungal and bacterial resistance in transgenic plants expressing human lysozyme, *Plant Cell Rep.*, 16:674–679.

Nelson, R.R., 1972, Stabilizing racial populations of plant pathogens by use of resistance genes, *J. Environ. Qual.*, 1:220–227.

Nogenboon, N.G., 1993, *Durability of Disease Resistance*, T.H. Jacobs and J.E. Parleviet (Eds.), 1993, Kluwer Academic Pub. London.

Norelli, J.L., et al., 1996. Increasing the resistance of apple rootstocks to fire blight by genetic engineering: a progress report, *Acta Hortic.*, 411:409.

Ogawa, T., Hori, T. and Ishida, I., 1996, Virus induced cell death in plants expressing the mammalian 2^l, 5^l oligoadenylate system, *Nat. Biotech,* 14:1566–1569.

Pattanayak, D. and P. Anand Kumar, 2000, Plant biotechnology: Current advances and future prospectives, *Proc. Indian Natn. Sci. Acad. (PINSA)* B66 No. (2000).

Powell-Abel P., et al., 1986, Delay of disease development in transgenic plants that express the tobacco mosaic virus coat protein gene., *Science* 232:138–143.

Reddy, M.S.S. and Rao, M.V., 1979, Resistance genes and their deployment for control of leaf rust of wheat, Ind. J. *Genet Plant Breed* 39:359–365.

Roy, D., 2000, *Plant Breeding: Analysis and Exploitation of Variance,* Narosa Publication, New Delhi.

Roy, D., 2000, Study of host parasite interaction, In: *Plant Breeding, Analysis and Exploitation of Variations*, Narosa Publishing House, New Delhi, 287.

Shirnoff, N. and Bryant, J.A., 1999, DREB takes the stress out of rowing up, *Mat. Biotechnol.*, 17:229–230.

Singh, D.P., 1986, Breeding for resistance to disease and insect pests, Crop Protection Monograph, Cpringer-Verlog, Berlin.

Sowa, A.W., Daff, S.M.G., Guy, P.A. and Hill, R.D., 1998, Altering haemoglobin levels changes energy status in maize cells under hypoxia, *Proc. Natl. Acad. Sci.*, USA, 95:10317–10321.

Strittmatter, G., Goethals, K. and Van Montagu, M., 1998, Strategies to engineered plants resistant to bacterial and fungal disease; In: *Subcellular Biochemistry,* vol. 29, 191–213, B.B. Biswas and H.K. Das (Eds.), Plenum Press, New York.

Tavladoraki, P., et al., 1993, Transgenic plants expressing a functional single chain FV antibody are specifically protected from virus attack, *Nature,* 366:469–472.

Vavilov, N.I., 1951, Phytogeographic basis of plant breeding, The origin, variation, immunity and breeding of cultivated plants, *Chronica Bot.,* 13:1–366.

Watson, I.A. and Luig, N.H., 1963. Classification of *Puccinia graminis* var. *Tritici* in relation to breeding resistance varieties, *Proc. Linn Soc.* NSW, 88:235–258.

Wegener, C., et al., 1996, Pactate lyase in transgenic potatoes confers preactivation of defense against *Erwinia carotovora, Physiol. Mol. Plant Pathol.*, 49:359–376.

Zhang, L., Ku J. and Birch, R.G., 1999, Engineered detoxification confers resistance against a pathogenic bacterium, *Nat. Biotechnol.*, 17:1021–1024.

Zhukovskij, P.M., 1965, Main gene centres of cultivated plants and wild relatives within the territory of the USSR, *Euphytica*, 14:177–188.

15 Chemical Control

15.1 INTRODUCTION

Toxic chemicals were put to logical use by man against pest and pathogens, much earlier than scientific discovery of pesticides. Presently, the word pesticide refers to *any substance that is intended for preventing, destroying, attracting, repelling or controlling any pest during production, storage, transport, distribution and processing of food, agricultural commodities or animal feed.* The term pesticide, includes substances intended for use as plant growth regulator, defoliant, desiccant, fruit thinning agent or sprouting inhibitors and those applied to crops either before or after harvest, to protect the commodity from deterioration during storage and transport (Mukhopadhyaya, 2003).

The word fungicide has originated from two Latin words, viz. *fungus* and *caedo* (to kill). So literally speaking, a fungicide would be any agency (physical or chemical), which has ability to kill a fungus. However, the word is restricted to chemicals. Hence, the word *fungicide* should mean *a chemical capable of killing fungus*. However, there are a number of compounds, which do not kill the fungus. They simply inhibit fungal growth or spore germination temporarily, and if fungus is freed from such substances, it would revive. Such a chemical is called a **fungistat** and the phenomenon of temporary inhibition of growth is called **fungistasis**. Certain chemicals, like phenanthrene derivatives and Bordeaux mixture, may inhibit spore production without affecting the growth of vegetative hyphae. These are called **antisporulants**. There are other groups of chemicals which exhibit very poor or no antifungal activity *in vitro* condition, but provide protection to the plants against the disease either by inhibiting the penetration of host surface by the fungi or by inducing the host defense system. The former types of chemicals are termed as **antipenetrants** and later as **antipathic agents**.

Even though fungistats, antisporulants, antipenetrants and antipathic agents do not kill fungi, they are included under the broad term fungicide because by common usage, the word fungicide has been defined as a chemical substance, which has ability to prevent damage caused by fungi to plants and their products. Fungicide, which is effective only if applied prior to fungal infection, is called **protectant**. On the other hand, fungicide, which is capable of eradicating a fungus after it has caused infection, and thereby curing the plant, is called **therapeutant**. Most of the non-systemic fungicides, like dodine, organomercurials, etc. which, due to their limited ability to penetrate host surface, can eradicated the fungal pathogens upto some extent from infected area. These compounds are called as **eradicants**. However, this classification does not hold much ground as compounds listed, as eradicants are basically effective in plant disease control only when used as a protectant.

15.2 CHARACTERISTICS OF GOOD FUNGICIDE

Application of fungicides is a common and effective technique to manage plant diseases but at the same time it has now become controversial because of the rising cost involved and its polluting effect on the environment. Nevertheless, fungicides will continue to be an important component for plant disease management. An ideal fungicide should have the characteristics listed in Table 15.1, although it would be unrealistic to think of having all the features in a single product.

Table 15.1 Characteristic of a Good Fungicide

(A) Biological factors
    (1) High and consistent field performance
        (a) Inherent fungitoxicity
        (b) Availability of the active constituent
        (c) Good and prolonged coverage of the host surface
    (2) Low or non-phytotoxic
    (3) No adverse effect on other components of the crop ecosystem

(B) Formulation factors
    (1) Stable and safe to store and transport
    (2) Simple to apply at a precise dosage level
    (3) Formulation should increase its efficiency
    (4) Stability after dilution to spray strength

(C) Toxicological factors
    (1) Non-hazardous during application
    (2) No residual toxicity to consumers

(D) Economic factor
    (1) Financial return should exceed the cost of application.

15.3 FORMULATIONS

Formulation is an art, which is mainly concerned with method of presenting the active ingredient (active/toxic fungicidal compounds), in most effective physical form. Effective, is with regard to storage, application and ultimate biological activity. Actually the amount of fungicide that is biologically effective at the plant surface is so small that for economic use the chemical must be diluted, either with a solid (dust, powder, etc.) or liquid (concentrates, emulsion, suspension, etc.), before application. Water provides a cheap and effective dilution medium, and with few exceptions, is used as the carrier for agricultural sprays. As majority of the fungicides are of very low water solubility, they must be formulated to make them compatible with water, hence surface-active agents are required to prepare water-dispersible powders, stock emulsions or emulsifiable concentrates. In addition, surface-active agents may be needed to improve the suspending, spreading and wetting properties of the sprays. Other supplements that may be incorporated with sprays include stickers to improve the weather resistance of the deposit, and materials to improve storage stability, deposition on plant surface and penetration of plant surfaces and/or fungal cells. The type of formulation chosen for a fungicide is determined by a variety of factor of which cost and biological efficiency are the most important. Wettable powder, dusts, emulsifiable concentrates, granules, solutions and suspensions or slurries are some of the common formulations of the fungicides in the market.

15.4 AUXILIARY SPRAY MATERIALS (ADJUVANT)

Some relatively inert materials are added to a fungicide to improve physical characteristics of the toxicant and active agents and therefore cause a variation in either surface tension or interfacial tension. Various adjuvants used are:

Wetting agents. Materials which reduce surface tension of particles and ensure that there will be no air layer between a solid and a liquid, are referred to as wetting agents. Wetting agents used are invariably esters of fatty acids, polyethylene oxide condensate and flour.

Spreaders. Wetting and spreading are closely related phenomena. Wetting must precede spreading. Spreaders such as soap are used to facilitate uniform spreading of the toxicants so that coverage of the treated plant surface is maximum and uniform.

Stickers (Adhesives). Stickers are added to fungicide formulations to increase tenacity and residual action. Fish oil, linseed oil, gelatine, milk casein, polyethylene and polysulfides are mostly used.

Deflocculating agents. Materials which keep particles away from each other to prevent flocculation, to ensure dispersion, and to check settling down of a solid within a liquid are called **deflocculating agents**. These check sedimentation. Examples are gelatine, plant gums and milk products.

15.5 SYSTEMECITY OF FUNGICIDES

A fungicide when applied may remain on the plant surface (non-systemic) or absorbed by the plant system. The latter may remain there in treated plant part (*locosystemic*); may move in the direction of evapotraspiration stream (*apoplastic*) or may move with photosynthates to sink (*symplastic*) or in both directions (*ambimobile*) (Table 15.2). The symplast is the living space of the plant which is enclosed by membranes, i.e., protoplasts and plasmodesmata, including the phloem sieve cells. Long-distance transport in phloem is symplastic. The apoplast is the non-living part of the plant, i.e., intercellular cell walls and cuticle, including xylem vessels and tracheids. Long distance movement in the transpiration stream is apoplastic.

Table 15.2 Terms Related with Transport of Fungicides in Plants

	Transport in tissues
Apoplastic:	Transport in apoplast, the coherent network of free space, cell walls and non-living cells
Symplastic:	Transport in the symplast, the coherent network of protoplasts connected by plasmodesmata
	Long distance transport
Xylem-mobile (apoplastic):	Apoplastic transport in vessels and tracheids of xylem by means of the transpiration stream (xylem-systemic)
Phloem-mobile (symplastic):	Symplastic transport in the sieve tubes of phloem by means of the mass flow from source to sink (phloem-systemic)
Ambimobile:	Transport in xylem and phloem (ambisystemic)
Locally mobile	Transport within the organ of application (locosystemic)
A mobile	No long-distance transport from site of application (non-systemic)

Source: Jacob and Neumann, 1987; Singh and Tripathi, 1982.

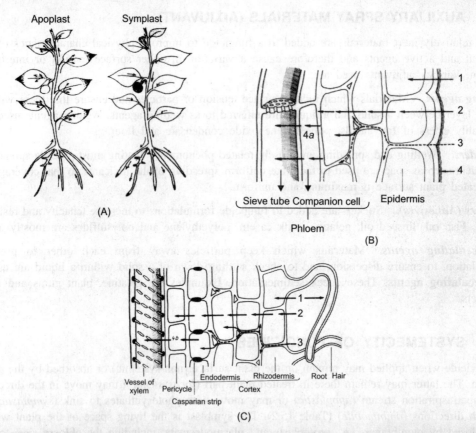

Plate 15.1 **(A)** Translocation pattern in the apoplast and symplast. Arrows indicate direction of transport, black area indicates accumulation of systemic chemicals, stippling indicates areas of lesser accumulation (*Source:* Edgington and Peterson 1977) **(B)** the pathway of fungicide movement in plant tissue by penetrating the leaf **(c)** The pathway of fungicide movement in plant tissue by penetrating the root surface. **1.** uptake in outer cells, **2** symplastic transport, **3** apoplastic transport, **4a** absorption in sieve tubes, **4b** transfer to vessels, **5** absorption in cuticular layers (*Source:* Jacob and Neumann, 1987).

15.5.1 Apoplastic Translocation

Apoplastic translocation, within the plant, is usually directly form roots to transpiring areas, especially leaves (Plate 15.1). Fungicides are absorbed by the roots, mainly in root hair zone, along with water. Root absorption is usually a passive phenomenon, and does not involve expenditure of metabolic energy. Radial movement through the cortex zone occurs either symplastically or apoplastically (Plate 15.1). Symplastically moving substances cross the plasmalemma and are transported via protoplast and plasmodesmata of cortex cells and then through the endodermis cells to the vessels of the xylem (Plate 15.1). Apoplstic movement is supposed to be accomplished in the free space of the cell walls. Since this route is blocked by lipophilic (suberized) incrustations of the casparian stripes at the endodermis level, fungicide should enter the symplast at this site to be transferred to xylem. Entrance into the symplast requires lipophilic properties therefore, extremely hydrophilic compounds (log P<0.5) are retained in the free space of the cortex and are usually not translocated in the long distance stream of the xylem to the leaves. Partioning into the xylem or transpirational stream (transpirational stream concentration factor, TSCF) (Table 15.2), is favoured by water solubility. Once the fungicides enter the roots, systemic movement occurs over the range of log P values form – 0.5 to 3.5. (Plate 15.1).

Peterson and Edington, 1975 listed following properties of fungicides with typical apoplastic translocation:

(i) Upward movement within the plant following seed, root or stem application.

(ii) Movement into various plant organs is dependent on their transpiration rate.

For fungicides, particularly ambimobile, which enters the cytoplasm, intraleaf distribution, depends on venation of leaves. In monocotyledons, where venation is convergent, palmate parallel type, metalaxyl is drawn much strongly through veins resulting in its accumulation at tips and margins. In dicotyledons because of reticulate venation, driving forces toward the periphery get drastically reduced, thereby, allowing metalaxyl to enter the cytoplasm. In such cases metalaxyl is either uniformly distributed in entire lamina (e.g., pea) or accumulation at margin is quite delayed (e.g., pegion pea, cowpea, French bean). In cowpea, when applied through roots or seeds, metalaxyl exhibits delayed accumulation at margin of primary leaves but remained uniformly distributed in trifoliate. However, majority of the fungicides with typical apoplastic translocation are accumulated at tips and margins of the leaves irrespective of the plant species involved (Plate 15.1). Lack of downward translocation means that chemical applied to above ground parts of the plant does not move to the roots. Plant organs (e.g., fruits and flowers) which normally have a negligible amount of transpiration are largely bypassed by fungicides moving in the xylem.

15.5.2 Symplastic Translocation

Mode of the symplastic translocation is well worked out for the sugars, which are actively loaded into the phloem (i.e., sieve tube-companion cell complex) in plants. It is generally agreed that accumulation of sugars results in water influx and subsequent hydrostatic pressure, which move the phloem, assimilates (including sugars) to sinks. Fully expanded photosynthesizing leaves serve as a source and roots, flowers, young growing leaves and fruits serve as a sink. A fungicide with symplastic translocation, after entry into the phloem follows the same source to sink pathways as followed by the phloem assimilates (Plate 15.1).

Metalaxyl in photosynthesizing leaves gets loaded inside the phloem as indicated by its accumulation in minor veins. After phloem loading metalaxyl moves from source to sink with respect to sugar. Since in majority of the ambimobile fungicides, except fosteyl-Al predominant mode of translocation is apoplastic, they cannot be expected to provide protection to the roots on foliar application. However, due to their better redistribution inside the plant, they provide protection to the young growing host tissues, thereby minimizing the number of sprays required to protect the crop.

15.6 SELECTIVITY OF FUNGICIDES

No single fungicide can be used to control all fungal diseases. Except strong biocidal agent like mercury compounds, no fungicide can kill all fungi. In true sense every fungicide shows some degree of selectivity. Nevertheless, there are fungicide which are effective against a wide spectrum of fungi (e.g., dithiocarbamates, phthalimdies, etc.) while others exhibit moderate (e.g., benzimidazoles) to high degree of selectivity (e.g., melanin biosynthesis inhibitors) are used only against *Pyricularia oryzae*; Phenylamides are effective only against oomycetes. Selectivity to fungicide is probably regulated by biochemical factors, these include: (a) differences in the accumulation of a fungicide in the cell, (b) different structure of receptor or target site, (c) differences in ability to toxify (conversion from inactive to active form) a compound, (d) differences in ability to detoxify a compound, and (e) difference in importance of a receptor or target site for survival of the fungus (Lyr, 1987).

15.7 CLASSIFICATION OF FUNGICIDES

Ever since the introduction of systemic fungicides, systemecity has been the most popular criterion for the broad classification of the fungicides. They were classified as: (a) non-systemic and (b) systemic. However, in this book selectivity has been preferred over systemecity and based on that fungicides are broadly classified as non-selective and selective. Selectivity is the prime requirement for systemecity. All the systemic fungicides are selective but all the selective fungicides are not systemic.

15.8 NON-SELECTIVE FUNGICIDES

15.8.1 Sulfur Fungicides

Elemental sulfur has probably been employed longer than any other chemical for the control of plant diseases. Wettable sulfur is still a very effective fungicide for control of powdery mildews, notably on fruits, and has the merit of being a cheap, and safe chemical. It is, however, easily washed-off the leaf surface and therefore, frequent applications are necessary. Following uptake, *elemental sulfur possibly affects electrons transport in the respiratory system of sensitive fungi.*

The *organosulfur* compounds, in terms of tonnage, are most extensively used fungicide in the world. Many of these fungicides are derivatives of *dithiocarbamic acid* (Figure 15.1). When reacted with another acid or with some metal, stable and highly fungitoxic dithiocarbamates are obtained. The first to be commercially exploited as a fungicide was tetramethyl thiuram disulfide or *thiram*. It is sold under the trade names of Thiram, Thiride, Arasan, Arasan SF, Thylate, Tersam 75, Spottrete, Nomersan, Panoram 75, and Fermide. It is a broad spectrum fungicide most intensively used for seed treatment @ 250 g/quintal seed. In some diseases soil application @ 15–25 kg/ha had been recommended. Thiram has also some antibacterial activity.

The metallic dithiocarbamates such as *ferbam* and *ziram* are obtained by the reaction of methylated dithiocarbamic acid molecules with iron and zinc, respectively. Ferbam is ferric dimethyl dithiocarbamate. It has broad spectrum and sold under the trade name of Ferbam, Fermate, Fermocide, Ferberk or Coromet. Normally it is used as foliar spray against downy mildew of chillies, anthracnose of citrus, blast of rice, early blight of tomato and diseases caused by *Botrytis* and *Rhizoctonia*. Ziram is zinc dimethyl dithiocarbamate and is sold as Ziram, Karbam white, Corozate, Cuman, Methasan, Vancide 51Z. It is effective against anthracnose of cucurbits, ripe fruit rot of chilllies, early blight of solanaceous crops, Alternaria blight of wheat and cercospora leaf spot of beet.

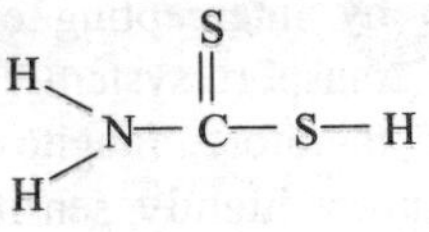

Dithiocarbamic acid

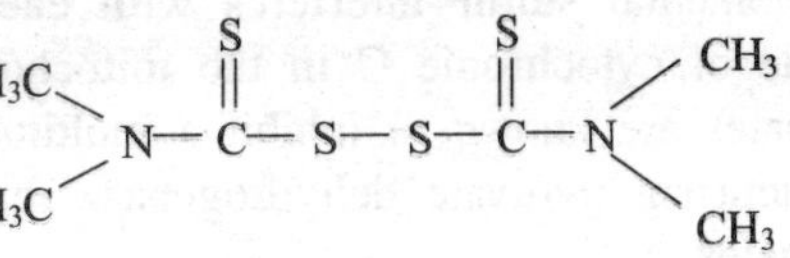

Thiram

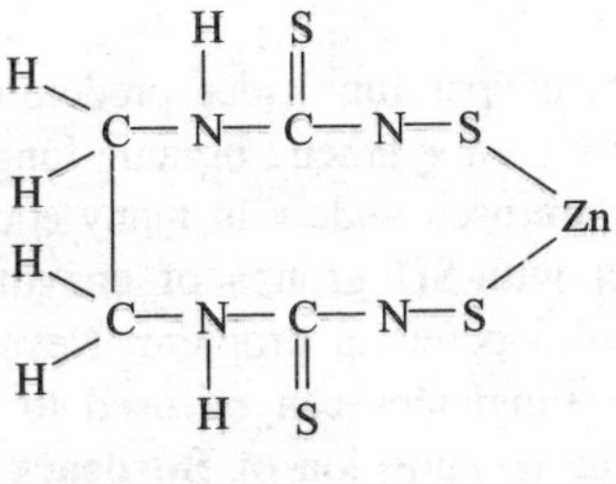

Zineb

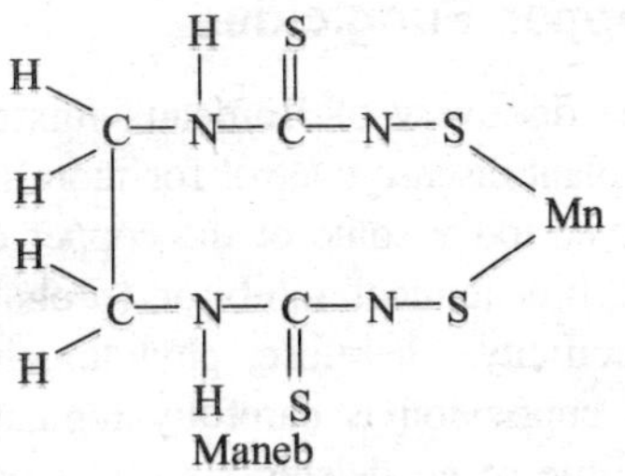

Maneb

Figure 15.1 Chemical structures of some dithiocarbamates.

In 1943, fungicidal properties of sodium ethylene-bisdithiocarbamates were discovered, which initiated the development of the most widely used organic fungicides known as **ethylene bisdithiocarbamates** (EBDC), such as *nabam, zineb, maneb* and *mancozeb*. The sodium salt **nabam** (Sodium ethylene bisdithiocarbamate) was the first in this group. It is sold as Dithane D-14, Dithane A-40, Parzate liquid, etc. It is unstable and water-soluble hence it has phytotoxicity. It is effective against early and late blight of tomato and potato, and seedling blight caused by *Pythium, Fusarium* and *Rhizoctonia*. However, it is especially recommended to be used as soil drench.

Zinc and manganese salts of ethylene bisdithiocarbamates are relatively water insoluble and not phytotoxic, as they do not enter host cells. **Zineb** (zinc ethylene bisdithiocarbamate) is sold as Dithane Z-78, Lonacol, Parzate, etc. It had been one of the most popular spray fungicides intensively used against late and early blight of tomato and potato, blast of rice, helminthosporoside of rice, anthracnose and ripe fruit rot of chillies, leaf blight and downy mildew of maize and certain rusts. The tenacity of zineb is low.

Maneb is manganese ethylene bisdithiocarbamate and is sold as Dithane M-22 or Manzate. This fungicide also has low tenacity with slight phytotoxicity. Maneb was improved by adding zinc to form **mancozeb** (Dithane M-45 or Indofil M-45), which is not phytotoxic. In many diseases maneb and mancozeb have proved more effective and economical than zineb. With nickel added to maneb, *Dithane S-31* is formed. It contains 2 parts maneb and one part nickel sulfate hexahydrate. Maneb and mancozeb are especially used as spray materials in vegetable crops. Anthracnose caused by *Colletotrichum* spp. in bean, cucurbits, jute, spinach, tomato, tobacco, downy mildews of bean, cucurbits, lettuce, peas, spinach, beet, rusts of pea and wheat, leaf sports and blight caused by *Alternaria, Phytophthora* and *Cercospora* on crops like potato, tomato, cauliflower, cabbage, cucurbits, beet, etc., and leaf blight of maize have been successfully managed by maneb and mancozeb. The dosage of the dithiocarbamates varies from 2 to 3 kg/ha.

Another member of dithiocarbamate group is **Vapam** (Sodium methyl dithiocarbamate or SMDC) which is available in liquid form. It is soluble in water and is used for soil treatment. It is effective against many fungi, nematodes and certain weeds.

All sulfur fungicides are non-systemic, and except lime sulfur, are non-phytotoxic (excluding sulfur shy varieties) and compatible with most of the pesticides. As far as their mode of action is concerned elemental sulfur interferes with energy production by intercepting electron of the substrate side of cytochrome C in the mitochondrial electron transport system. The dialkyleyl dithiocarbamates are known to inhibit a multitude of enzymes; therefore, fungitoxicity probably involves concurrent pyruvate dehydrogenase reaction is particulary hightly sensitive to dialkyl dithiocarbamates.

15.8.2 Copper Fungicides

Ever since the discovery of Bordeaux mixture in 1885, copper fungicides predominated the field of fungicidal plant disease control for more than 50 years until synthetic organic fungicides invaded the market. Even today some of the copper compounds are used widely in many countries. Copper is a multisite biochemical inhibitor (probably interact with-SH groups of enzymes) with little biological specificity. Therefore, phytotoxicity is always a potential problem. Nevertheless, when the dissolved cupric ion is carefully regulated, copper fungicides can be used to control fungal disease with little or no deleterious effect on plants. The composition of **Bordearx mixture** is 4-4-50 or 5-5-50, i.e., 1.5 kg $CuSO_4$ and 1.5 kg lime in 200 litres of water, or 2.0 kg each of these in 200 litres of water. The chemical reaction involved in Bordeaux mixture is as follows:

$$CuSO_4 + Ca\,(OH)_2 = Cu(OH)_2 + CaSO_4$$

It was discovered for the control of downy mildew of grapevines but was soon extensively used to control late blight of potato. Even now it is one of the most effective fungicides for the control of foliar diseases if prepared correctly. *Bordeaux paste, burgundy mixture, and chestnut compound* are other copper based homemade fungicides. Copper oxychloride is important compound in this group. Its chemical formula is $CuCl_2.3Cu(OH)_2$ and has no phytotoxicity problem. It is available in trade names, blitox-50, blue copper, cupramar, esso-fungicide, fungimar copper, fytolan (all having 50% active ingredient), fycol 8 (oil based 72% a.i.), fycol 8E (oil and water based), fycol 40A, etc.

15.8.3 Quinone Fungicides

Chloranil (2,3,5,6-tetrachloro-1,4, benzoquinone), one of the quinone derivatives, was introduced as a fungicide as early as in 1940. However, now it has been replaced by **dichlone**. Quinone fungicides are multisital in their mode of action. The two mechanisms which are thought to be likely for dichlone and chloronil are: (a) binding of the quinone nucleus to –SH and –NH_2 groups in fungal cell and (b) interference with the electron transport system. Only dichlone (phygon) is still used for seed treatment against externally seed borne pathogen.

15.8.4 Heterocyclic Compounds

This group has some very effective fungicides also known as **phthalamides** and dicarboximides, such as captan, captafol, dyrene, glyodin, iprodione and vinclozolin. Most (Figure 15.2) of them inhibit production of essential compounds containing –NH_2 and –SH groups (amino compounds and enzymes).

Captan sold under the trade name of captan, orthocide, vancide etc., is an excellent fungicide for control of leaf spots, blights and fruit rots on fruit crops, vegetables, ornamentals and turf. It is also used as seed protectant for agronomic crops, vegetables, flowers and grasses. Folpet is closely related to captan and is sold as phaltan, orthophaltan, etc. In addition to diseases controlled by captan, this fungicide is effective against powdery mildews and some rusts. Captafol is sold as difolatan, difosan and sanspor. It is a foliar spray and seed treatment fungicide and controls downy mildew also. It has high resistance to weathering and has been used to control apple scab, late blight of potato and tomato and several other foliar diseases. Iprodione is sold as rovral or chipko-26019. It is a broad spectrum, foliage contact fungicide. It has been effectively used against diseases caused by *Botytis, Monilinia, Sclerotinia, Alternaria, Helminthosporium,* and *Rhizoctonia.* Vinclozolin sold as ornalin, ronilan or vorlan, is a contact protective.

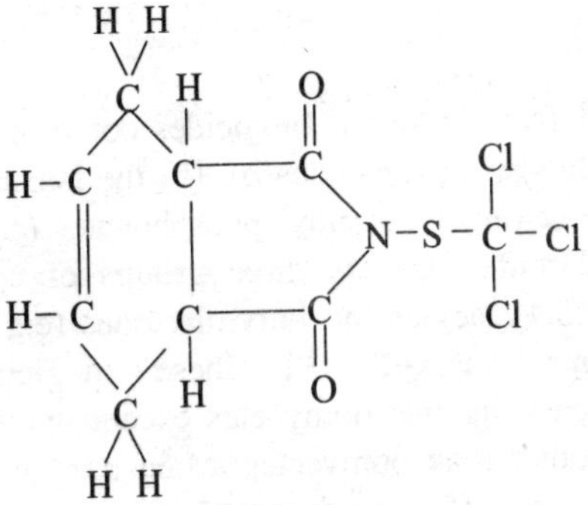

Captan 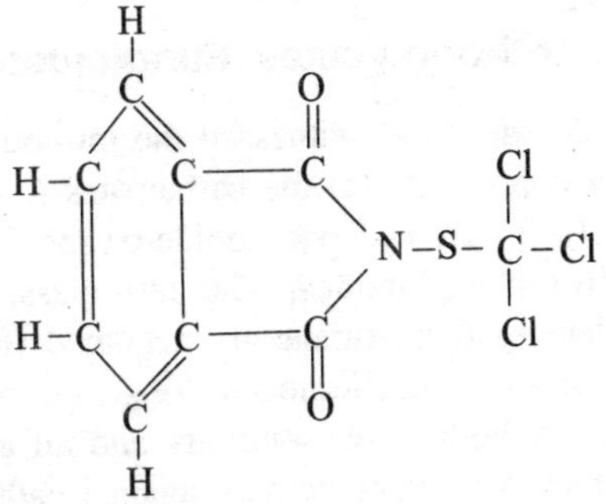   Folpet

Figure 15.2 Chemical structures of some heterocyclic fungicides.

15.9 SELECTIVE FUNGICIDES

15.9.1 Aromatic Hydrocarbon Fungicides

Aromatic hydrocarbon fungicides (AHF) are a heterogeneous group of compounds which have been in use since long. The group was actually formed after the general cross resistance between these fungicides was recognized, which is indicative of their common mode of action. Although AHFs are reported to affect several metabolic processes in fungal cell, the primary toxic effect is on induced lipid peroxidation. The development of AHFs was stimulated by their relatively simple structure, low production cost and low mammalian toxicity combined with good but selective antifungal activity. The AHFs have gained more popularity as soil fungicides because of their high volatility, low UV light stability and high activity against some soil-borne fungi. They are also used against seed borne pathogen and post-harvest decay fungi.

Chlorothalonil (tetrachloro-isophthalonitrile) is sold as daconil, brano, and termil and is a broad spectrum fungicide used against a wide variety of fungal disease of field, vegetables and fruits trees (Figure 15.3). Diazoben (dimethyl amino benzeneidiazo-sodium sulfonate) sold as dexon is used as seed and soil treatment fungicide for the control of damping-off and root rots caused by *Pythium* spp. and *Phytophthora* spp. Dichloran (dichloronitroalanin) sold as botran (Figure 15.3) is used against fruit and vegetable diseases as spray and soil treatment. It is effective against sclerotial fungi. Dinocap (methyl heptyl dinitrophenyl crotonate) is sold as karathane, mildex, arathane, and crotothane. It is an effective fungicide for the control of powdery mildews of field crops and fruit trees.

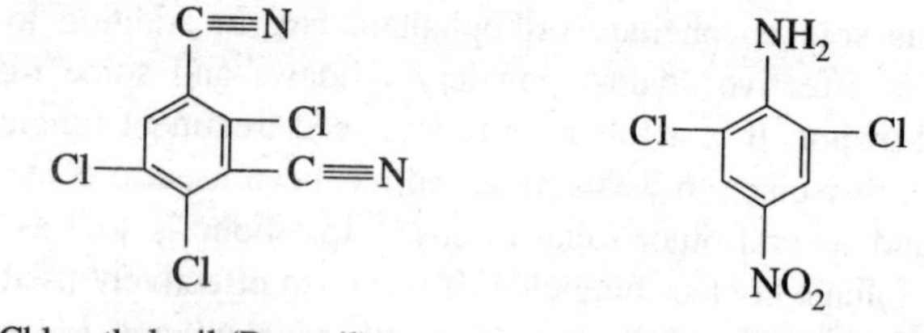

Chlorothalonil (Daconil)   Dichloran (Botranl)

Figure 15.3 Chemical structure of some aromatic hydrocarbon fungicides.

15.9.2 Anti-oomycetes Fungicides

The past decades have witnessed the introduction of five classes of fungicides controlling diseases caused by oomycetes: (a) the carbamates (e.g., prothiocarb, propamocarb), (b) the isoxazoles (e.g., hymexazol), (c) the cyanoacetamide-oximes (e.g., cymoxanil), (d) ethyl phosphonates (e.g., fosetyl-Al) and (e) phenylamides. The last class, phenylamides, covers three groups of compounds: (1) acylalanines (e.g., furalaxyl, metalaxyl (Figure 15.4), acylamino butyrolactones (e.g., ofurace), and acylamino-oxazolidinones (e.g., cyprofuram, oxadixyl). All these fungicides show comparatively high water solubility and all are selective against oomycetes except hymexazol and fosetyl which also show activity against pathogens other than oomycetes. Main uses and mode of application of these fungicides are listed in Tables 15.3 and 15.4. So far metalaxyl is the most active, versatile and widely used compound of this class. Its main biological features can be summarized as: (a) high inherent fungitoxicity, (b) protective and curative activity against all peronosporales, (c) rapid uptake, high acropetal and limited basipetal systemicity, (d) protection of new growth, (e) good persistence in plant tissue (extended spray interval), (f) control of systemic seed and soil-borne diseases.

Phenylamides interfere with the activity of RNA polymerase I. Hymexazol and cymoxanil also inhibit RNA synthesis but exact site of action is not yet clear. Not much information is available regarding mode of action of other fungicides. Of all the antioomycetes fungicides, only phenylamides have met with serious resistance problems in the field and resistance development was due to altered target site. Field resistance to phenylamides has developed shortly after their introduction in cases of intensive, continuous and exclusive use of the product, against *Phytophthora infestans*, *Plasmopara viticola* and *Peronospora tabacina*. Cross resistance exists among phenylamides even though the resistance factors may vary in some strains. Parasite fitness of metalaxyl resistant strains is as good as wild type strains. Cymoxanil, fosetyl-Al and a number of protectant fungicides are used in mixture with phenylamides to control resistance problem. Cymoxanil is reported to act synergistically with metalaxyl.

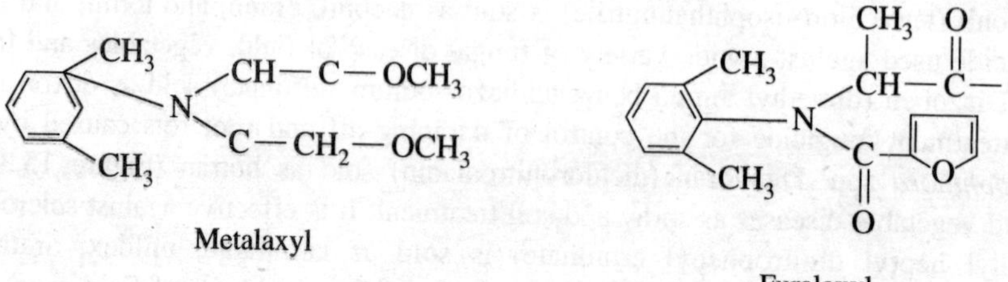

Metalaxyl   Furalaxyl

Figure 15.4 Chemical structure of metalaxyl and furalaxyl.

Table 15.3 Activity Spectrum of Antioomycetes Fungicides

Common name	Pathogen on root/stem	Foliar pathogen	Additional activity against non-oomycete pathogen
Hymexazol	Aphanomyces, Pythium		Corticium sasaki, Fusarium spp.
Propamocarb/ Prothiocarb	Aphanomyces, Pythium, Phytophthora,	Bremia Peronospora Pseudoperonospora	
Cymoxanil	—	Phytophothra Plasmopara Peronospora Pseudoperonospora	
Fosetyl-Al	Phytophthora, Pythium	Bremia Plasmopara Psedoperonospora	Phomopsis viticola Guignardia bidwellii Psedopeziza tracheiphila
Phenylamides	Peronosclerospora Phytophthora Pythium Sclerospora Sclerophthora	Albugo Bremia Peronospora Peronosclerospora Phytophthora Plasmopara Pseudoperonospora Sclerospora Sclerophthora	

Source: Schwinn and Staub, 1987.

Table 15.4 Uses of Antioomycetes Fungicides

Compounds	Main uses against	Main crop	Application method
Prothiocarb/propanocarb	Diseases of root and stem	Ornamentals vegetables	Drench
Hymexazol	Diseases of root and stem in seedling stage	Rice, sugarbeets carnations	Drench, seed dressing, dust
Furalaxyl	Diseases of root and stem in seedling stage	Rice, sugarbeets carnations	Drench, seed dressing, dust
Cymoxanil	Foliar disease	Grapes, potato	Spray
Fosetyl Al	Foliar, stem and root diseases	Grapes, avocado, pineapple, citrus, ornamentals	Spray, drench, dip, injection
Metalaxyl and related compounds	Foliar, stem and root disease	Grapes, potatoes, avocado, pineapples, citrus, tobacco, hops,	Spray, drench, dip, injection

15.9.3 Oxathiins

Carboxin and oxycarboxin (Figure 15.5) were first systemic fungicides to be discovered and introduced for plant disease control. These fungicides are readily absorbed by the seeds, roots and leaves and translocated apoplastically in the plant. They are very effective against smuts, bunts and rusts of cereals, and soil fungus-*Rhizoconia solani* (Table 15.5). The treatment of seeds or plant with these chemicals results in higher yield of crops not only because of disease control but also because of growth stimulation. Both carboxin and oxycarboxin have low animal toxicity and are quickly degraded in soil, and leave no residue. Their mode of action is very specific. They interact with succinat-eubiquinone reductase complex (complex II) resulting in inhibition of oxidation of succinate via electron transport chain. So far, no widespread development of resistance of fungal pathogens to carboxin and oxycarboxin has been observed in the field.

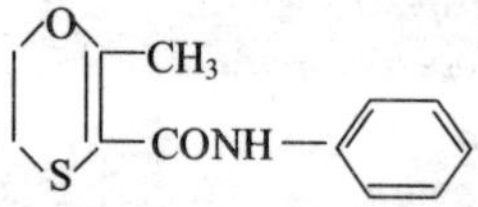

Carboxin (Vitax) 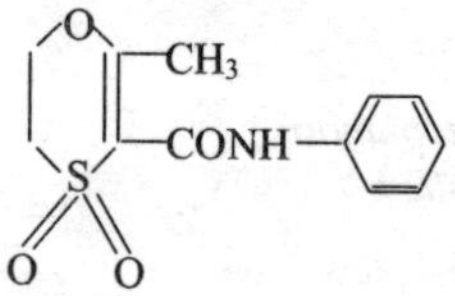   Oxycarboxin (Plantvax)

Figure. 15.5 Chemical structures of some oxathiins.

15.9.4 Organophosphate Fungicides

The organophosphate fungicides include primarily Fosetyl-Al sold as Aliette, highly effective against root, stem and foliage diseases caused by members of Peronosporales in a variety of crops. It is applied as foliar spray, soil drench, root dip, and post harvest dip. Fosetyl-Al has been reported to induce defense reactions and synthesis of phytoalexins against oomycetes. Three other compounds included are: Kitazin (IBP) and Edifenphos (Hinosan), both effective against rice blast and several other disease and Pyrazophos (Afugan) which is effective against powdery mildews and *Bipolaris* and *Drechslera* diseases on various crops.

15.9.5 Benzimidazoles and Related Fungicides

Benzimidazoles (Figure 15.6) and thiophanates, which are transformed to benzimidazoles, represent a group of highly effective broad spectrum systemic fungicides (Table 15.6). These are widely used for efficient plant disease control. Most ascomycetes, some of the basidiomyctes and deuteromycets, but none of the phycomycetes are sensitive to these fungicides (Table 15.6). Their mild cytokinin-like effects on some plants tend to retain chlorophyll and in some cases increase yield and delay senescence. Benzimidazoles are readily absorbed by different plant parts and exhibit typical apoplastic translocation inside the plant. Their translocation is poor in woody plants due to strong binding with root and stem lignins. Major limitation of these compounds is high resistance risk. Exclusive use of these fungicides have resulted in serious control failures in fields in several cases due to development of resistant strains, and show cross resistance to all benzimidazole and thiophanate fungicides. In order to tackle the resistance problem, these fungicides are now being used in various combinations with other fungicides (Table 15.7). Compatibility of benzimidazole wettable powder formulation with most other agricultural chemical is good except with highly alkaline pesticides such as bordeaux mixture or lime sulfur.

Table 15.5 Carboxin and Related Fungicides in Commercial Use

Common name	Chemical name	Year of introduction (by)	Used against	Formulations
Carboxin	5, 6-dihydro-2, -methyl-1, 4-oxathi-ine-3-carboxanilide	1966 (Uniroyal)	Seed treatment of cereals against bunts and smuts; against *Rhizoctonia* spp. on cotton, groundnut and vegetables; *Exobasidium vexans* (tea), *E. vaccinii* (blueberry): *Helminthosporium* spp. (barley); combination product with other fungicides for most other seed-borne seedling diseases	'Vitaflow', FS (400 g/l); WP or SC; 'Vitavax', WP (750 g/kg), Ls (340 g/l), dust (100 g/kg)
Oxycarboxin	5, 6, dihydro-2-methyl-1, 4-oxathiine-3-carboxanilide 4,4-dioxide	1966 (Uniroyal)	Rust diseases of cereals, ornamentals, vegetables, coffee, sunflower, bean, safflower, flax	'Plantvax' EC (200 g/l), WP (750 g/kg)
Pyracarbolid	3, 4-dihydro-6-methyl-2 H-pyran-5-carboxanilide	1970 (Hoechst)	Effective against rusts, smuts and *Rhizoctonia solani*, blister blight of tea.; currently not much in commercial use	'Sicarol', WP (500 g/kg)
Benodanil	2-iodobenzanilide	1974 (BASF)	*Puccinia striiformis* (wheat and barley), *P. hordei* (barley), rust diseases of coffee, ornamental and vegetables	'Calirus', WP (500 g/kg)
Flutolanil	α, α, α-trifluoro-3¹-isopropoxy-o-toluanilide	1982 (Nihon Nohyaku)	Some basidiomycetes	'Moncut'
Mepronil	3¹-isopropoxy-o-toluanilide	1981 (Kumiai)	Basidiomycetes, foliar application *Rhizoctonia solani* (rice), *Gymnosporangium fus icim* (pears) and *Puccinia chrysanthemi* (chrysanthemums); soil or seed treatment- *Thanatephorus cucumeris* (potato) and *R. solani* (vegetable)	'Basitac', WP (750 g/kg), DP (30 g/kg), SC (400 g/kg)
Fenfuram	2-methyl-3-furanlide	1974 (Shell Research Ltd.)	As seed dressing against smuts and bunts of temperate cereals	'Pano-ram', DS, LS Mixtures: with guazatine acetates ('Panoctina Super', LS), guazatine acetate + imazalil ('Panoctine Universal', LS), guazatine acetate +imazalil +gamma- HCH ('Panoctine AT Universal') or imazalil + anthraquinone + gamma-HCH
Furmecyclox	Methyl N-cyclohexyl-2, 5-dimethylfuran-3-carbohydroxamate	1977 (BASF)	Seed treatment for cereals, cotton (against *Rhizoctonia solani*), potato and other crops; also to protect wood against fungal decay	'Campogran', 'Xyligen B', wet treatment (500 g/l)

Benzimidazoles bind with β-tubulin subunit of the microtubules of sensitive fungi and thereby inhibit formation of spindle and subsequently chromosomal separation during nuclear division. β-tubulins of resistant strains show less affinity for binding.

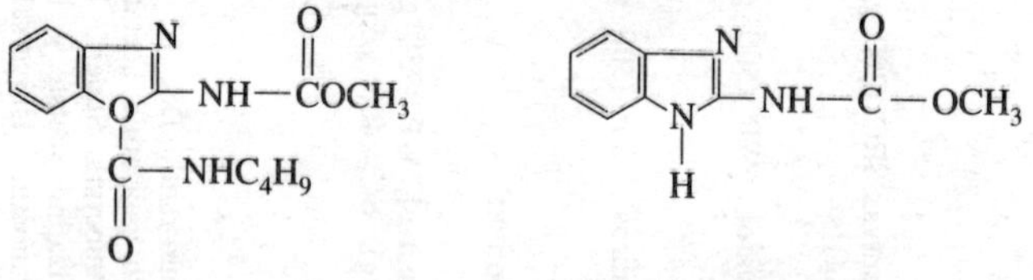

Benomyl (Benlate) MBC (Bavistin)

Figure. 15.6 Chemical structure of some benzimidazoles.

Table 15.6 Benzimidazoles and Related Fungicides

Common name	Chemical name	Year of introduction (by)	Formulations
Benomyl	Methyl 1-(butylcarbamoyl) benzimidazol-2-ylcarbamate	1966 (du Pont)	'Benlate', WP (500 g/kg), 'Tersan' 1991 turf fungicide (500 g/kg)Mixture: 'Benlate T', WP (200 g benomyl + 200 g thiram/kg)
Carbendazim	Methyl benzimidazol-2-ylcarbamate	1967 (BASF, Hoechst, du Pont)	'Battal FL', 'Bavistin FL', SC (500 g/l); 'Bavistin' WP 'Agrozim', WP (500 g/kg); 'Carbate', 'Derosal', WP (594 g/kg), SC (188 g/l); 'Derroprene FL', 'Focal', 'Maxim', SC (510 g/l); 'Stempor DG', WG (500 g/kg); 'Supercarb', 'Fungicide BLP' SL (7g Carbendazim phosphate/l) Mixture: with maneb ('Bavistin M', 'Delsene M', 'Septal', WP), triadimefon ('Bayleton Bm', 'Bayleton total'), triadimefon + captafol ('Bayleton triple'), and with several other fungicide like Sulfur, triforine, chlorothalonil, fenpropimorph, fenarimol, mancozeb, diclobutrazol, propiconazole, flutriafol, etc.
Fuberidazol	2-(2-furyl) benzimidazole	1968(Bayer)	'Voronit' seed treatment Mixtures: for seed treatment with triadimenol ('Bayten'), triadimenol + imazalil hydrogen sulfate ('Baytan IM'), nabam ('New-Voronit'), quintozene ('Voronit special') and anthraquinone
Thiabendazole	2-(1,3-thiazol-4-yl) benzimidazole	1968 (Merck)	'Mertect', 'Tecto' , 'Storite' WP (400, 600 or 900 g/kg); SC (450 g/l); FT (7 ga.i.). Mixture: two-or-three-way mixtures with several fungicides like fosetyl-AL, Captan, metalaxyl, carboxin, ethirimol, flutriafol, tecnazene, thiram, bendiocarb, etc.
Thiophanate	Diethyl 4,4-(O-phenylene) bis (3-thioallphanate)	1970 (Nippon Soda)	'Topsin', 'Cercobin', 'Nemafax', WP (500 g/kg)
Thiophanate-methyl	Dimethyl 4, 4-(o-phenylene) bis (3-thioallophanate)	1970 (Nippon Soda)	'Topsin M', 'Cercobin M', 'MIldothane', 'Cytosin' WP (500 or 700 g/kg) Mixture: with etridiazole ('Ban-rot'), thiram ('Homai'), maneb ('Labilit') and imazalil ('Mist-O-Matic Muridal') (all WP)

Table 15.7 Major Practical Application of Benzimidazoles and Related Fungicides

Crops	Pathogens
Almond (*Prunus*)	*Monilinia* spp.
Banana (*Musa*)	*Colletotrichum musae, Fusarium* spp., *Mycosphaerella musicola, M. fijiensis var. difformis* and *Penicillium* spp.
Beans (*Phaseolus*)	*Botrytis cinerea, Colletrotrichum* spp., *Sclerotinia sclerotiorum* and *Cercospora* spp.
Carrot (*Daucus*)	*Cercospora carota*
Chestnut (*Castanea*)	*Colletotrichum castanea*
Citrus	*Botrytis cinerea, Colletotrichum gloeosporioides, Diplodia natalensis, Guignardia citricarpa, Mycosphaerella citri, Penicillium* spp., *Phomopsis citri,* and *Oidium tingitaninum*
Clove (*Eugenia*)	*Cylindrocladium quinqueseptatum*
Coffee	*Cercospora coffeicola, Colletotrichum coffeanum* and *Pellicularia*
Cole crops, canola or rape (*Brassica*)	*Fusarium oxysporum, Mycosphaerella brassicola, Phoma lingam* and *Sclerotinia sclerotiorum*
Cucurbits and melons (*Cucumis*)	*Cladosporium cucumerinum, Colletotrichum gossypii, Colletotrichum lagenarium, Erysiphe cichoracearum, Fusarium* spp., *Mycospaerella citrullina, Oidium* spp., *Rhizoctonia solani* and *Sclerotinia sclerotiorum*
Grape (*Vitis*)	*Botrytis cinerea, Gloeosporium ampelophagum, Guignardia bidwellii, Melanconium fuligenum, Pseudopeziza* spp. and *Uncinula necator*
Lettuce (*Lactuca*)	*Botrytis cinerea* and *Sclerotinia sclerotiorum*
Mango (*Mangifera*)	*Colletotrichum gloeosporioides* and *Oidium*
Mulberry (*Morus*)	*Phyllactinia* spp.
Olive (*olea*) onion (*Allium*), ornamentals and trees	*Cycloconium oleaginum* *Botrytis allii, Colletotrichum gloeosporiodes* and *Fusarium, Ascochyta, Botrytis cinerea, Ceratocystis* spp., *Cercospora* spp., *Cylindrocladium, Oidium* spp., *Penicillium* spp., *Phomopsis* spp., *Phyllostictina* spp., *Ramularia* spp., *Rhizoctonia* spp., *Sclerotinia* spp., *Sphaerotheca pannosa*
Papaya (*Carica*)	*Oidium caricae*
Peanut (*Arachis*)	*Ascochyta* spp., *Aspergillus* spp., *Cercospora arachidicola, Cerocosporidium personatum* and *Mycosphaerella arachidicola*
Pea (*Pisum*)	*Mycosphaerella pinoides* and *Oidium* spp.
Pepper (*Capsicum*)	*Botrytis cinerea, Fusarium piperi* and *Fusarium solani*
Pineapple (*Ananas*)	*Fusarium moniliforme, Rhizoctonia* spp. and *Teielaviopsis paradixa*
Pome fruit (*Malus and Pyrus*)	*Botrytis cinerea, Cladosporium* spp, *Gloeodes pomigena, Gymnosporangium* spp., *Marssonina mali, Microthyriella rubi, Mycosphaerella pomi, Penicillium* spp., *Phyllactinia pyri, Physalospora* spp., *Podosphaera leucotricha, Rosellinia necatrix, Valsa ceratosperma,* and *Venturia* spp.

(Contd.)

Table 15.7 Major practical application of Benzimidazoles and Related Fungicides (*Contd.*)

Crops	Pathogens
Potato (*Solanum*)	*Fusarium solani, Oospora* spp., *Phoma* spp. and *Rhizoctonia solani*
Rice(*Oryza*)	*Acrocylindrium oryzae, Cercospora oryzae, Gibberella fujkuroi, Pyricularia oryzae, Thanatephorus cucumeris* and *Rhizoctonia solani* (*stem rot*)
Rubber (*Hevea*)	*Ceratocystis fimbriata, Microcyclus ulei* and *Mycosphaerella* spp.
Soyabean (*Glycine*)	*Cercospora kikuchii, C. sojina, Colletotrichum truncatum, Diaporthe* spp., *Phomopsis sojae* and *Septoria glycinea*
Stone fruit (*Prunus*)	*Cladosporium carpophilum, Coccomyces hiemalis, Cytospora leucostoma, Fusarium* spp., *Monilinia* spp., *Oidium* spp., *Phomopsis persicae* and *Sphaerotheca pannosa*
Strawberry (*Fragaria*)	*Botrytis cinerea, Cercospora* spp., *Fusarium oxysporum, Mycosphaerella fragariae, Odium* spp., *Sphaerotheca humuli* and *Verticillium* spp.
Sugarbeet (*Beta*)	*Cercospora beticola*
Sugarcane (*Saccharum*)	*Ceratocystis paradoxa* and *Cercospora* spp.
Tea (*Thea*)	*Gloeosporium theae-sinensis, Elsinoe leucospila* and *Rosellinia necatrix*
Tobacco (*Nicotiana*)	*Ascochyta nicotianae, Cerospora nicotianae, Helicobasidium mompa* and *Pellicularia filamentosa*
Tomato (*Lycopersicon*)	*Botrytis cinerea, Cercospora* spp., *Cladosporium* spp., *Colletotrichum phomoides, Corynespora melongenae, Fusarium oxysporum, Odium* spp., *Phoma destructiva, Sclerotinia sclerotiorum* and *Septoria lycopersici*
Wheat (*Titicum*)	*Erysiphe graminis, Fusarium* spp., *Pseudocercosporella herpotrichoides, Rhynechosporium* sp. *Septoria acenae, Ustilago tritici*

15.9.6 Sterol Biosynthesis Inhibiting Fungicides

Pyrimidines. The pyrimidines include diamethirimol (Milcurb), ethirimil (Milstem) and dupirimate (Nimrod), all effective against powdery mildews of various crops. Fenarimol (Rubigan) and nuarimol (Trimidol) are effective against powdery mildew and also several other leaf spots, rust and smut fungi.

Triazoles. This group includes some of the best systemic fungicides as triadimefon (Figure 15.7) (Bayleton), triadimenol (Bayton), bitertanol (Bacor), boutrizol (Indar or RH-124), propiconazole (Tilt), etaconazole (Vanguard), myclobutanil (Eagle, Nova, Rally, Prothane, Enzone and Systhane), difenoconazole, cyproconazole, tubuconazole and fluquiconazole. These are basically spray fungicides but also used as seed and soil treatments. These fungicides show long term protective and curative activity thus facilitating fewer applications and longer intervals between sprays. Bayleton has been used against cereal rusts, karnal bunt and powdery mildews in India. It is effective against ergot (*Claviceps*) also. Tilt is very effective against cereal rusts even with one spray. Boutrizol has been highly successful chemical against leaf rust (*P. recondita*) and stripe rust (*P. striiformis*) in several countries. Myclobutanil and flusilazole can control apple scab with only four sprays. Cyproconazole and tebuconazole are very effective against leaf spot as well as against soil borne diseases caused by *Rhizoctonia* and *Sclerotium*.

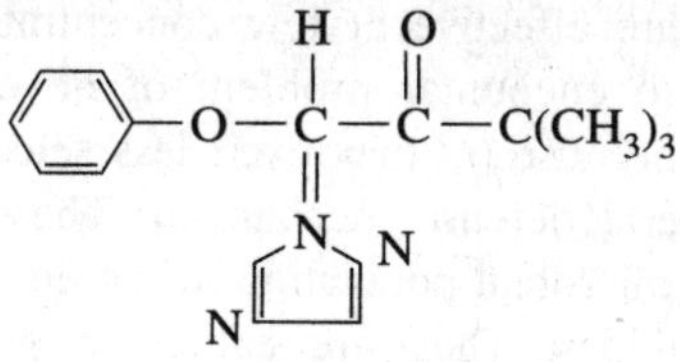

Triadimifon

Figure 15.7 Chemical structure of bayleton.

Morpholines. Morpholines include the fungicides dodemorph (Meltatox) and tridemorph (Calixin) (Figure 15.8). Both are preventive and eradicant foliar fungicides effective against powdery mildews and leaf spots on cereals. Calixin has been commercially used against apple scab. It is also effective against cereal stripe rust, sigatoka of banana and pink disease of rubber and other plantation crops. Triforine (Piparazine) is a foliar fungicide sold as Saprol, Sella or Funginex and used against powdery mildews, leaf and fruit rots and anthracnose.

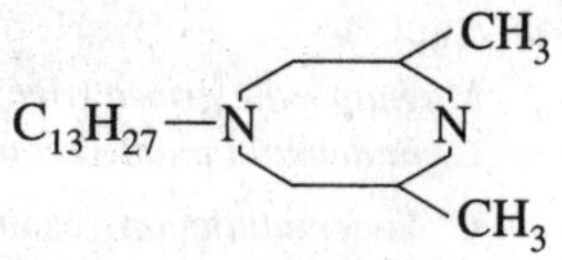

Tridemorph

Figure 15.8 Chemical structure of tridemorph (Calixin).

15.9.7 Miscellaneous Systemic Fungicides

Pyracarbolid is closely related to oxathiins and is more effective than the latter. It conrols rusts, smuts and *Rhizoctonia solani*. Chloroneb (Demosan) is used as seed and soil fungicide. Ehazol (Turban, Terrazole, Kaban) is another seed and soil fungicide effective against damping-off, seed and stem rot caused by *Phythium* and *Phytophthora*. Imazalil (Fungaflor) has excellent curative and protective properties and is effective against powdery mildew, leaf spot, vascular wilts and fruit rots causd by ascomycetous and imperfect fungi. Cycprodinil belongs to the anilopyrimidine group and was developed in 1994 against a variety of diseases caused by ascosporic and imperfect fungi. It is recommended against apple scab, powdery mildew of apple and disease caused by *Botrytis cinerea*. Carpropomid, a new generation carboximide fungicide, is a melanin biosynthesis inhibitor and controls rice blast by preventing melanization of appresoria of *Pyricularia grisea*. Strobilurins are a new class of fungicides derived from natural antibiotic found in the symbiotic fungus *Strobilurus tenacellus*. They have protective and curative actions against fungi in all taxonomic groups.

15.9.8 Non-fungitoxic Compounds with Indirect Mode of Action

Recent generation of plant disease molecules for control consists of those compounds, which are not fungicidal, as they exhibit little or no fungitoxicity *in vitro* condition. They manage the disease by their novel mode of action either by interference with processes involved in fungal penetration into the plants (antipenetrants) or by enhancing host defense resistance (defense activators/inducers)

(Table 15.8). These compounds are effective at low concentration. Compounds that trigger host defense activity are less likely to encounter problem of development of resistant strains than conventional systemic fungicides because (a) they exert less selection pressure on the pathogen, (b) they act by inducing hosts' general defense mechanism. These compounds are potentially very valuable since the side effects on microbial population in the environment are less severe than those produced by conventional fungicides. They are called as **green chemicals** because of their environmental friendliness. In the recent past, a number of antipenetrant compounds have been introduced and some of these are being used at field scale for diseases caused by parasitic fungi, on the other hand, a number of host defense inducing compounds have been identified. They have shown effectiveness against plant diseases under green house conditions or in some cases even under field conditions (Rohilla et al., 2001) (Table 15.8).

Table 15.8 Some Non-fungitoxic Compounds with Indirect Mode of Action

Compounds	Pathogens (host)
ANTIPENETRANTS	
Melanin biosynthesis inhibitors (MBIs)	
Tricyclazole	*Magnaporthe grisea* (rice); *Collectotrichum lagenarium* (cucumber); *C. lindemuthianum* (bean)
Pyroquilon	*C. lindemuthianum* (bean), *M. grisea* (rice)
Carpropamid	*M. grisea* (rice); *C. lagenarium* (cucumber)
Pentachloro benzyl alcohol	*M. grisea*
Phthalide	*M. grisea*
Probenthiazone	*M. grisea*
Chlobenthiazone	*M. grisea*
PP 389	*C. lindemuthianum* (bean); *M. grisea* (rice)
Cerulenin	*C. lagenarium* (rice); *M. grisea* (rice)
Pentachloro aniline	*M. grisea* (rice)
Pentachloro nitrobenzene	*M. grisea* (rice)
CUTINASE INHIBITORS	
IBP	*C. gloeosporioides* (papaya), *Fusarium solani* (pea), *M. grisea* (rice)
Edifenphos	*C. gloeosporioides* (papaya), *F. solani* (pea)
Inezin	*C. gloeosporioides* (papaya)
Benomyl	*C. gloeosporioides* (papaya); *F. solani* (pea)
Phenylthiourea	*M. grisea* (rice)
Butyl isocyanate	*F. solani*
(transient fungitoxic product of benomyl)	
Phosphate salts	*C. gloeosporioides* (papaya)
HOST DEFENSE INDUCERS	
Salicylic acid	*Albugo candida* (rapeseed), *Alternaria brassicae* (sicklepod), *A parasitica* (brassica), *A. solani* (tomato), *Cladosporium cucumerinum* (cucumber), *Peronospora parasitica* (rapeseed), *V. inaequalis* (apple)

(Contd.)

Table 15.8 Some Non-fungitoxic Compounds with Indirect Mode of Action (*Contd.*)

Compounds	*Pathogens (host)*
Jasmonic acid and its methyl ester	*Alternaria parasitica* (brassica), *Erysiphae graminis* f. sp. *hordei* (barley), *P. parasitica* (brassica), *Phytophthora infestans* (potato and tomato), *Verticillium dahliae* (cotton)
Isonicotinic acid (INA)	*Cercospora beticola* (sugarbeet), *Collefotrichum lagenarium* (cucumber), *C. lindemuthianum* (bean); *E. graminis* (barley), *Erwinia amylovora* (Pear), *M. grisea* (rice), *P. parasitica* (Arabidopsis), *Peronospora tabacina* (tobacco), *Pseudomonas lacrymans* (cucumber), Tobacco mosaic virus (tobacco), *Uromyces appendiculatus* (bean), *V. inaequalis* (apple), *X. vasicatoria* (pepper)
β-amino butyric acid (BABA)	*Aphanomyces eutechies* (Pea), *E. graminis* f. sp. *tritici*, (wheat), *F. oxysporum* f. sp. *lycopersici* (tomato), *F. oxysporum* f. sp *melonis* (melon), *F. oxysporum* f. sp. *niveum* (watermelon), *F. oxysporum* f. sp. *vasinfactum* (cotton), *F. oxysporum moniliforme* (corn), *P. tabacina* (tobacco), *P. parasitica* and *Alternaria brassicicola* (broccoli and cauliflower), *P. infestans* (potato and tomato), *Pseudoperenospora cubensis* (cucumber and melon), *Plasmopara viticola* (grapevine), *P. halstedii* (sunflower), *Puccinia tritici* (wheat), *V. dahliae* (cotton)
2, 2 dichloro 3, 3-dimethyl cyclopropane carboxylic acid (DCP)	*M. grisea* (rice)
Probenazole	*M. grisea* (rice), *X. oryzae* (rice)
Benzothiadiazole	*A. candida* (rapeseed), *A. brassicae* (rapeseed), *Cercospora nicotianae* (tobacco), *Cladosporium cucumerinum* (cucumber), *Erwinia carotovora* (tobacco), *E. graminis* f. sp. *tritici* (barley, wheat), *P. parasitica* (rapeseed and arabidopsis), *Phytophthora parasitica* (tobacco), *Ps. syringae* (tobacco, Arabidopsis), *Ps. tabacina* (tobacco), *Rhizoctonia solani* (rice, brassica), TMV (tobacco), turnip crinkle virus (Arabidopsis)
Fosetyl –Al	*P. viticola* (grapevine), *Phytophthora capsici* (tomato), *P. cinnamomi* (*Persea indica*)
Phenylthiourea	*Cladosporium cucumerinum* (cucumber)
Phosphate salts	*C. lagenarium* (cucumber), *Puccinia sorghai* (maize)
SiO$_2$	*Pythyium* spp, (cucumber)
Oxalates	*C. lagenarium* (cucumber)
Unsaturated fatty acid	*P. infestans* (potato)
Trimethyl L-lysine	*Uromyces phaseoli* (beans)
Nutrients (Micronutrients/Fertilizers)	*Brassicae* (Oilseed rape), *Exserohilum turcicum* (maize), *Puccinia sorghai* (maize). *Spaerotheca fulginia* (cucumber).

Source: Rohilla, et al., 2001.

15.10 ANTIBIOTICS

Antibiotics have systemic action in plants moving in both directions (ambimobile). They are not only eradicants but also protectants providing temporary resistance in the host. Phytotoxicity is one major disadvantage with antibiotics and has limited their large scale use. The other disadvantage is their narrow spectrum of antipathogen action.

The antibiotics used in plant disease control mainly belong to groups known as *streptomycin, tetracyclines, polyenes, cycloheximide* and *griseofulvin*. Streptomycin was the first antibiotic used in plant diseases control. It was used against fire blight of pear (*Erwinia amylovora*) in 1953. Streptomycin formulations are available under the name Agrimycin, Phytomycin, Orthostreptomycin, Streptocycline, etc. Agrimycin and Streptocycline are mixed preparation of streptomycin and tetracycline. Maximum use of streptomycin as streptomycin sulfate has been against bacterial diseases of fruit trees such as fire blight of apple and pear and citrus canker. Streptomycin and Agrimycin have been used against bacterial blight of cotton. Streptocycline is used in combination with copper oxychloride for the control of bacterial leaf blight of rice.

Antibiotics in the tetracycline groups are tetracycline (Acromycin), oxytetracycline (Terramycin) and chloretetracycline (Aureomycin). These antibiotics are bacteriostatic and bactericidal. The sensitive groups include the fastidious bacteria, spiroplasma and MLOs.

Cycloheximide (Actidione, Actispray, Actidione RZ) was a very strong antifungal antibiotic but because of its phytotoxicity it could not become popular: Aureofungin, a heptane antifungal antibiotic, is recommended for the control of rice leaf spot, rice blast, barley stripe disease and covered smut of barley through seed treatment and against powdery mildew, anthraconose and downy mildew of grapes, powdery mildew of apple, leaf rust of wheat and citrus gummosis through foliar sprays. Post-harvest decay of mango and guava fruits is also checked by fruit dip in aureofungin.

Griseofulvin had been found very effective against *Botrytis cinerea, Sphaerotheca pannosa, Pseudoperonospora cubensis* and many other common plant pathogens.

15.11 NEMATICIDES

Nematicides belong to two groups: volatile soil fumigants and non-fumigants (contact and systemic nematicides). The fumigants consist of compounds belonging to halogenated hydrocarbons and isothiocyanate groups while the non-fumigants are mostly organophosphorus and carbamates. The former directly kills the nematode larvae while the latter do not cause direct kill. Eggs protected in cysts or crop debris are generally not affected by nematicides.

The soil fumigants such as *methyl bromide, ethylene dibromide (EDB), D-D mixture and methyl isothiocyanate* possess high vapour pressure, get dissolved in soil moisture in concentrations high enough to kill nematode larvae and disperse through the soil pores. They are non-selective and can kill even beneficial bacteria in the soil. The method of application involves injection of the fumigants into the soil with the help of suitable equipment, make the soil compact or provide water seal and let the fumigant act for 2-3 weeks before planting the crop. The halogenated hydrocarbon group includes methyl bromide, ethylene dibromide, toluene, D-D mixture, DBCP (Nemagon) and chloropicrin. The isothiocyanate group includes fumigants that release methyl cyanate such as Vapam, Dazomet, Mylone or Basamid.

The non-fumigant nematicides have gradually replaced the fumigants. They are available in granular form and can be applied at the time of planting or to soil around the standing trees. The contact non-fumigants include fensulphothion (Dasanit or Terracur P), thionazin (Nemafos, Zinophos), diazinon (Basudin) and ethoprop or ethoprofos (Mocap). The systemic nematicides in this group are phenamiphos (Nemacur), phorate (Thimet), aldicarb (Temik) and carbofuran (Furadan).

15.12 FUNGICIDE RESISTANCE

Development of resistant strains of target fungi is one of the major problems with selective fungicides. Some important cases of field resistance are listed in Table 15.9.

Table 15.9 Occurrence of Fungicide Resistance in Crops

Date first observed (approx)	Fungicide or fungicide class	After years of commercial use, before resistance observed (approx.)	Main crop disease and pathogen affected
1960	Aromatic hydrocarbons	20	Citrus storage rots, *Penicillium* spp.
1964	Organomercurials	40	Cereal leaf spot and stripe, *Pyrenophora* spp.
1969	Dodine	10	Apple scab *Venturia inaequalis*
1970	Benzimidazoles	2	Many target diseases and pathogens
1971	2-Amino-pyrimidines	2	Cucumber and barley powdery mildews, *Sphaerotheca fuliginea and Erysiphe graminis*
1971	Kasugamycin	6	Rice blast, *Magnaporthe grisea*
1976	Phosphorothiolates	9	Rice blast, *Magnaporthe grisea*
1977	Triphenyltins	13	Sugarbeet leaf-spot, *Cercospora betae*
1980	Phenylamides	2	Potato blight and grape downy mildew, *Phytophthora infestans and Plasmopara viticola*
1982	Dicarboximides	5	Grape grey mould,*Botrytis cinerea*
1982	Sterol demethylation inhibitors (DMIs)	7	Cucubit and barley powdery mildews, *Sphaerotheca fuliginea and Erysiphe graminis*
1985	Carboxanilides	15	Barley loose smut, *Ustilage nuda*

Source: Brent, 1995

15.12.1 Definitions

A guideline of fungicide resistance terminology was proposed in 1985. According to this proposal, *resistance should be used only to define a stable and heritable adjustment by a fungus to a fungicide resulting in less than normal sensitivity to that fungicide.* It is different from adaptation of a fungal pathogen to a fungicide. Adaptations are neither heritable nor stable and are not expected to cause serious problems. Furthermore, insufficient field performance of a fungicide is not necessarily related to the presence of resistant strains in field. Thus, the term field resistance should be used only when decreased fungicide efficacy is correlated with increased frequency of resistant strains (Kollar and Scheinpflug, 1987).

15.12.2 Mechanism of Fungicide Resistance

Resistant strains of fungus may arise either due to physiological adaptation or gene mutation. Since resistance due to physiological adaptation is unstable and disappears when organism is no longer exposed to the fungicide, gene mutation is the main mechanism for the origin of stable, inheritable resistance. Gene mutation is a spontaneous phenomenon. The fungicide itself does not induce resistance but acts solely as a selecting agent.

Most of the non-selective conventional fungicides interfere with several metabolic processes in the fungal cell, hence, are called *multisite inhibitors*. On the contrary, selective fungicides are site specific. Their primary site of action is restricted to only one, mono-or oligogene regulated metabolic activity. Even a single gene mutation may result in the development of resistant strains against a specific-site fungicide. Thus, the resistance problem is far more common and severe in selective fungicides as compared to non-selective one.

Selective fungitoxicity generally stems from site specific binding of fungicides either to an enzyme involved with respiration, with biosynthetic processes in fungi (e.g., synthesis of nucleic acids, proteins, ergosterol, chitin), or with structural proteins associated with membrane structure or nuclear function. Development of resistance to such specific-site inhibitors is mostly due to single gene mutation resulting in slightly altered target site, with reduced affinity to the fungicide (Table 15.10). Apart from alteration in target site, there are other ways also by which a fungus may develop the resistance not only against selective fungicides but also sometimes against multisite conventional fungicides. These are: (a) non-accumulation of a fungicide inside the fungal cell to a toxic level. This may happen by reduced uptake, increased efflux, conversion of a fungicide into non-fungitoxic compound(s) or lack of conversion of an itself non-fungitoxic compound into a fungioxic form. (Table 15.10)

Genetic studies on fungicide resistance in plant pathogenic fungi are limited due to lack of methods to generate recombinant progeny. Resistance to fungicides is controlled by nuclear genes, which may be major or minor in nature. Major gene controlled resistance may develop in one step as a result of mutation of one gene which has major effect on the phenotype. Occasionally, action of each gene may be influenced by unrelated modifer genes or may itself exert effects on other genes. Usually resistance against benzimidazoles, phenylamides, carboximides and aromatic hydrocarbons is controlled by major gene(s). Minor genes (polygenes) controlled resistance are reported for dodine, ergosterol biosynthesis inhibitors and cycloheximides.

Table 15.10 Some Mechanism of Fungicide Resistance

Fungicide	Site of action	Mode of action	Mechanism of resistance	Comments
Carbendazin	B-tubulin	Inhibition of assembly of microtubules to form spindle, (mitosis inhibited)	Altered site of action	Decreased affinity of tubulin to bind carbendazim
Kasugamycin	Ribosomes	Inhibition of protein synthesis	Altered site of action	Reduced affinity of ribosome towards antibiotic
Metalaxyl	RNA polymerase	Inhibion of RNA synthesis	Altered site of action	Insensitivity of enzyme to metalaxyl
Carboxin	Succinate-ubiquinone reductase complex	Inhibition of electron transport	Altered site of action	Decreased affinity of complex II to carboxin
Polyoxin B	Chitin synthetase	Inhibition of chitin synthesis	Reduced uptake	Alteration in membrane resulting in reduced uptake
Imazalil Fenarimol Triazoles	Microsomal Cytochrome P-450	Inhibition of sterol biosynthesis	Reduced uptake	Increased efflux, of fungicide (low intracellular concentration)
IBP Edifenphos		Inhibition of phospholipids biosynthesis	Metabolism/detoxification	Conversion of fungicide into non-fungi toxic derivatives
Pyrazophos		Inhibition of phospholipids biosynthesis and accumulation of free fatty acids	Non-conversion to fungi toxic form	Non-conversion of pyrazophos into the actural toxic principle
Fenpropimoph	Sterol 14 Reductase	Inhibition of sterol biosynthesis	Utilization of intermediates	Unusual sterols accumulate and are used in membranes

15.12.3 Management of Resistance

The fungicide resistance management tactics are primarily aimed to avoid or delay the development of resistance. Once a major fraction of the pathogen population has become resistant, the most sensible approach is to change to other fungicides with a different mode of action or to non-chemical control measures, if available. Different strategies which could be adopted, to manage the fungicide resistance problem are briefly described as follows:

Prediction and monitoring. While working with new fungicide-pathogen combination, it is desirable to obtain some information about the associated resistance risk like *in vitro* frequency of emergence of resistant strains, and parasite fitness of resistant strains. Based on these information and those available on epidemiology and disease cycle, a model is simulated for the prediction of resistance risk under field condition. While fungicide is in use, monitoring is desirable to keep track of level of resistance.

Reduction of selection pressure. Plant pathogens are biological organisms and they develop resistant strains only when under pressure, by use of pesticides. Different tactics which could, reduce the selection pressure by the high-risk fungicides are: (a) apply minimum possible required number of sprays and quantity of fungicide, (b) avoid using the same type of chemical for treatment of seed or plant material, spraying of the crop and post harvest treatment, (c) avoid treatment of a crop in very large area, with the same type of chemical and (d) avoid exclusively curative use of the fungicide. A very thorough treatment of the crop will increase the selection pressure, favour the build-up of resistance.

Combination and alternation of fungicides. The most widely advocated method to tackle the resistance problem is the use of resistance prone fungicide in a mixture with a low risk multisite conventional fungicides, sufficient theoretical and experimental data are now available to support the view that fungicide mixtures can delay or even reverse the development and spread of resistance. Use of mancozeb and phthalimides has been advocated to prolong life of specific-site fungicides, phenylamides and fenarimol, respectively. Resistance to fenarimil depends on an energy-dependent efflux, and this efflux is inhibited by captan or its degradation products.

Samoucha and Gisi (1987) advocated the use of three-way mixtures (oxadixyl/mancozeb/cymoxanil) to control phenylamide sensitive and resistant strains of *Phytophthora infestans* on tomato or potato and *Plasmopara viticola* on grape particularly under condition when proportion of resistant population is quite high. They demonstrated that as compared to two way mixtures, three way mixtures are more flexible in their use under difficult disease situation; they not only minimize the build-up of resistance, but also contribute to control resistant populations.

In recent years several prepacked mixtures of specific-site and contact fungicides have been introduced by different manufacturers. Theoretically the use of prepacked mixtures offer several advantages: (a) the protectant component should control the resistant isolates, (b) the dose of the systemic component may be reduced to additive or synergistic levels, (c) reduced concentration of systemic component should reduce the selection pressure for resistance, (d) multiple disease control and most importantly and (e) the use of prepacked mixtures is an enforceable strategy.

Alternate use of systemic-contact (S-C) or systemic-systemic (S-S) (with different mode of action) fungicides is another approach proposed to check or lower down the build-up of resistant strains. This approach may be specially useful for disease-fungicide combinations when the basic mixture is judged too risky to be used throughout the season.

Use of antipathic agents. These are the compounds which are not directly fungitoxic but provide protection against the disease by inducing general host defense system. Since these compounds do not directly attack the pathogen, selection pressure should be low. At the same time induced general defense system of the host involve physical barriers like lignin and/or chemical barriers like phytoalexins, which are multisital in their mode of action. So theoretically such compounds should face low resistance risk. Unfortunately at present only few such compounds are known, they too are specific to only few diseases.

15.13 FACTORS AFFECTING EFFICACY OF FUNGICIDES IN NATURE

The efficacy of fungicides depends on a number of factors operating independently or jointly. Fungicides are usually finely ground powders with low solubility. They are either dusted or sprayed on the plants. In order to settle on the plants, the particles must have enough momentum to nullify repulsive forces. Also, the high velocity air streams used to propel dusts and sprays tend to glide around plant surfaces. Therefore, the particles carried by them must have enough momentum to stick the plant surfaces. It has invariably been reported that dust particles should be of about 20 µ diameter for satisfactory deposit build-up. However, the particles of such diameters are easily dislodged by wind and rain. It is because of this that dusting with fungicides has not been a satisfactory method for protecting the crops. Such disadvantages are reduced in case of spraying as the small primary particles are encapsulated in larger liquid droplets that provide enough momentum to penetrate the barrier immediately surrounding the foliage. The amount of fungicides deposited on plant surfaces should be directly proportional to its concentrations in the suspension. However, variations in droplet size and run-off disturb this relationship. For effective control, a good surface coverage is essential. Often the droplets coalesce and run-off occurs, leaving different amount of fungicides on the tips and mid veins of leaves than on edges and interiors of the blades.

After the fungicides are deposited on plant surfaces, their tenacity is governed by London-Vander Waal's forces, electrostatic attraction, capillary or some combination of these effects. The physical factors which influence the tenacity of spray deposits to plants include (a) particle size and shape, (b) the presence of aggregates, (c) distribution on the plant surface, (d) nature of the compounds and (e) the intensity and duration of weathering.

Among the chemical factors affecting the performance of fungicides are photolysis, hydrolysis, phytotoxicity (Figure 15.9) and atmospheric interactions. In the presence of sunlight some chemicals undergo changes due to absorption of energy sufficient to cause dissociation of the molecules into fragments possessing unpaired electrons. For example, quinine fungicides are photosensitive. In solution, p-benzoquinone yields hydroquinone and another product when exposed to a wavelength of less than 5770 Å. Fungicides like captan and folpet having active halogen atoms get hydrolysed in aqueous suspensions. Fungicides are subjected to oxidation as well. Some may lose their fungitoxicity while others may get activated. CO_2 is another component of air which possibly reacts with certain fungicides. For instance, the excess lime of bordeaux mixture in presence of CO_2 gets converted to calcium carbonate. Often a chemical may be phytotoxic. Such chemicals may react with protoplasm of the plant cells or may chelate essential metals.

Fungicides applied in soil, which is an extremely complex combination of physical-chemical-biological system of interactants, are affected in various ways. Ratios of silt, sand and clay, moisture status, organic matter content and microbiological properties of soil do affect the efficacy of the fungicides. For instance, fungicides are more active/mobile in wet soil while fumigants are more effective in dry soil. All organic molecules would be subjected to attack by some microbes in soil. For example, *Aspergillus, Trichoderma, Mucor, Penicillium,* etc. degrade PCNB.

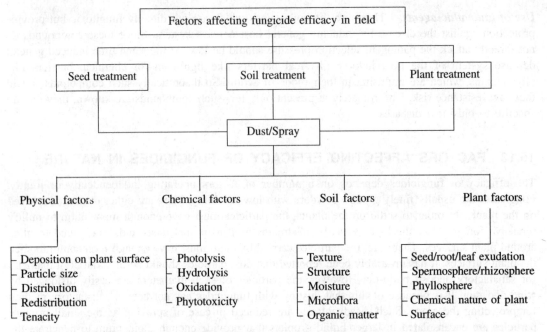

Figure 15.9   Factors affecting efficacy of fungicides under field conditions.

15.14 RELIANCE ON PESTICIDES

In the last two decades, there have been numerous discussions to formulate strategies with respect to role of pesticides in human and plant health. It cannot be disputed that pesticides did play a vital and significant role in increasing and stabilizing food grains production of the world. In fact, the success of green revolution depended much on chemicalization of agriculture. However, indiscriminate/non-judicious use of pesticides led to several environmental, ecological, social and economical problems, and they warranted the attention. The debate started whether to ban pesticides, to continue their use or popularize need based/judicious use of pesticide, all the three options deserve serious considerations and their merits and demerits must be thoroughly known to reach some definite conclusions.

Pesticides have caused health hazards, death/suicides, environmental pollution, recurrence/resurgence/resistance in pests/pathogens, soil health problem and so forth. But the questions arise as to why these hazards and mishaps occurred and what are the real reasons behind such happenings. The analysis of the facts reveal that pesticides as such are not the main culprits. It is their continuous, indiscriminate and unscientific use that have created that problem, everyone including administration, marketing focus and the farmers are responsible for such happenings.

We can not avoid the use of pesticides in the coming decades because

1. food grains production must continue to rise to feed ever growing human populations,
2. intensive cultivation does not allow management through cultural practices and plant genotypes having high input response must be protected,
3. over 30% losses to plants and their products being caused globally by pests must be contained,

4. no better options to manage the pest damage are available. Factually speaking we do not have any other appropriate/adequate options to deal with the pests. The farmers require immediate action and, at present the pesticides remain the only relief.

There are several additional advantages associated with pesticides. They include:

1. Most pesticides are degradable and only a few have a long persistence in the ecosystem.
2. The Rs. 30,000 million Indian agrochemical markets have close to 80 players in the organized sector and more than 500 players in the unorganized sector. Insecticides (73%) dominate the market, followed by herbicide (14%) and fungicides (11%). Pesticide industry provides employment to large number of people.
3. The industry has major hand in the forex earnings. The size of the global agrochemical market was placed at US $32 bn in 1999 and is likely to grow at 5% per annum.
4. Pesticides save the time of the growers and also have quick knockdown effect.
5. They are economic and save labour, easy to handle as compared to other alternatives.

Alternatives to pesticides

- Cultural practices are safe and eco-friendly but not feasible due to intensive cultivation.
- Bioagents–effective, eco-friendly but action very slow and affected by ecology and environment. They may not work against fast developing diseases.
- Host resistance is academically best but not always available in commercial cultivars and frequent breakdown due to development of new biotypes/races.
- Indian export of pesticides Rs. 1500 crore and import Rs. 150 crores during 1999–2000.

Based on above discussions the following conclusions can be drawn:

- Problem is not the pesticide but its non-judicious use and the laws are not being implemented strictly.
- Farmers should be educated about judicious/need based application as part of integrated pest management.
- Even though India has a large capacity in terms of pesticide production, it accounts for less than 2.5% of the world market in value terms. Consumption is also low in India at 600 g/ha compared 10000 gm per hectare in developed countries.

In view of the current status of pesticides and its intense level of utilization, it is unrealistic to think of banning the pesticides. Use of pesticides will continue but emphasis should be on need based judicious use that too under IPM umbrella.

REFERENCES

Backman, P.A., 1978, Fungicide formulations: relationship to biological activity, *Annu. Rev. Phytopathology*, 16:211.

Baldwin, B.C. and Rathwell., W.G., 1988, Evolution of concepts for chemical control of plant disease, *Annu. Rev. Phytopathology*, 26:265.

Brent, K.J., 1995, Fungicide Resistance in Crop Pathogens: How can it be Managed, FRAC. Mongr. I, GIFAD, Brussels, 48.

Chaube, H.S., Singh, U.S. and Razdan, V.K., 1987, Studies on uptake, translocation and distribution of C-metalaxyl in pigeon pea, *Indian Phytopath.*, 40:507.

Cohen, Y. and Coffey, M.D., 1983, Systemic fungicides and the control of oomycetes. *Annu. Rev. Phytopathology*, 24: 311.

Davidse, L.C., 1986, Benzimidazole fungicides: mechanism of action and biological impact, *Annu. Rev. Phytopathology*, 24: 43.

Delp, C.J. and Dekker, J., 1985, Fungicide resistance: definitions and use of terms, *EPPO Bull.*, 15:333.

Delp, C.J., 1987, Benzimidaxsole and related fungicides, In: *Modern Selective Fungicide-Properties, Applications, Mechanism of Action,* H. Lyr, (Ed.), Longman Group UK Ltd., London and VEB Gustav Fisher Verlag Jena, Chap. 15.

Delp, G.J. (Ed.), 1988, Fungicide Resistance in North America, APS, St. Paul, Minn.

Dewaard, M.A., et al., 1993, Chemical control of plant diseases—problems and prospects. *Annu. Rev. Phytopathology*, 31: 403-421.

Dixon, G.K., Copping, L.G. and Hollomon, D.W. (Eds.), 1995, *Antifungal Agents*: *Discovery and Mode of Action,* Bios. Scientific Publishers, Oxford.

Edgington, L.V. and Peterson, C.A., 1977, Systemic fungicides: theory, uptake, and translocat In: *Antifungal Compounds,* vol. 2, M.R. Siegel and H.D., Sisler (Eds.), Dekker, New York, 51.

Elad, Y., Yunis, H. and Katan, T., 1992, Multiple fungicide resistance to benzimidazoles, dicarboximides and diethofencarb in field isolates of *Botrytis cinerea* from Israel, *Plant Pathology*, 41: 41–46.

Geogopoulos, S.G., 1982, Genetical and biochemical background of *Fungicide Resistance in Crop Protection,* J. Dekker and S.G. Geogopoulos (Eds.), Pudoc, Wageningen, 46.

Georgopoulos, S.G. and Skylakakis, G., 1986, Genetic variability in the fungi and the problem of fungicide resistance, *Crop Protection*, 5:299-305.

Georgopoulos, S.G., 1987, The genetics of fungicide resistance, In: *Modern Selective Fungicides—Properties, Applications, Mechanisms of Action,* H. Lyr (Ed.), Longman Group UK Ltd., London, and VEB Gustav Fisher Verlag, Jena.

Jacob, F. and Neumann, S.T., 1987, Principle of uptake and systemic transport of fungicides within the plant, In: *Modern Selective Fungicides—Properties, Applications, Mechanism of Action,* Longman Group UK Ltd., London and VEB Gustav Fisher Verlag, Jena, Chap. 1.

Knight, S.C., et al., 1997, Rationale and perspectives on the development of fungicides, *Annu. Rev. Phytopathology*, 35:349.

Koller, W. 1992, *Target Cites of Fungicidal Action,* CRC Press.

Koller, W. and Scheinpflug, H., 1987, Fungal resistance to sterol biosynthesis inhibitors, a new challenge, *Plant Dis.*, 71:1066.

Lyr, H. (Ed.), 1995, *Modern Selective Fungicides,* 2nd ed., Gustav Fisher Verlag, Jena.

Lyr, H., 1977, Mechanism of action of fungicides, In: *Plant Disease,* vol. I, J.G. Horsfall and E.B. Cowling, (Eds.), Academic Press, New York, 239.

Lyr, H., 1987, Selectivity in modern systemic fungicides, In: *Modern Selective Fungicides-Properties, Applications, Mechanism of Action,* H. Lyr (Ed.), Longman Group UK Ltd., London, VEB Gustav Fischer Verlag, Jena, Chap. 2.

Lyr, H., 1987, Aromatic hydrocarbon fungicides, In: *Modern Selective Fungicides—Applications, Mechanisms of Action,* H. Lyr (Ed.), Longman Group UK Ltd., London, and VEB Gustav Fischer Verlag, Jena, Chap. 5.

Lyr, H., Russell, P.E. and Sisler, H.D. (Eds.), 1993, *Modern Fungicides and Antifungal Compounds,* Intercept, Andover.

Mukhopadhyay, A.N., 2003, *Pesticide Usage Scenario in India and Viable Alternatives,* VHAI, Press, New Delhi.

Nene, Y.L. and Thapliyal, P.N., 1979, *Fungicides in Plant Disease Control,* 2nd ed., Oxford and IBH Publishing Co., New Delhi, 507.

Peterson, C.A. and Edgington, L.V., 1975, Factors influencing apoplastic transport in plants, In: *Systemic Fungicides,* Academic—Verlag, Berlin, 287.

Rihilla, R., et al., 2001, Recent advances in the management of plant diseases using chemicals, *Indian J. Plant Path,* 19:1.

Samoucha, Y. and Gishi, U., 1987, Use of two and three-way mixtures to prevent buildup of resistance to phenylamide fungicides in *Phytophthora* and *Plasmopar, Phytopathology,* 77, 1405.

Scheinpflug, H. and Kuch, K.H., 1987, Sterol biosynthesis inhibiting piperazine, pyridine, pyrimidine and azole fungicides, In: *Modern Selective Fungicides—Properties, Application, Mechanism of Action,* H. Lyr (Ed.), Longman Group UK Ltd., London, VEB Gustav Fischer Verlag, Jena, Chap. 13.

Schwinn, E.J. and Staub, T., 1987, Phenylamides and other fungicides against oomycetes. In: *Modern Selective Fungicides—Properties, Applications, Mechanisms of Action,* H. Lyr. (Ed.), Longman Group UK Ltd, London, 17.

Singh, U.S. 1989, Studies on the systemicity of C-Metalaxyl in cowpea (*Vigna unguiculata* (l) Walp.), *Pestic. Sci.,* 25:145.

Singh, U.S. and Tripathi, R.K., 1987, Physico-chemical and biological properties of Metalaxyl, I., Octanol number, absorption spectrum and effect of different physico-chemical factors on stability of Metalaxyl, *Indian J. Mycol. Plant Pathol.,* 12, 287.

Singh, U.S. and Tripathi, R.K., 1982, Physico-chemical and biologic properties of Metalaxyl, II, Absorption by excised maize roots, *Indian J. Mycol. Plant Pathol.,* 12, 295.

Singh, U.S., 1987, Uptake, translocation, distribution and persistence of C-Metalaxyl in maize (*Zea mays*), Z. Pflanzenkr. Pflanzenszchutz, 94:498.

Sisler, H.D. and Ragsdale, N.N., 1987, Disease control by non-fungitoxic compounds, In: *Modern Selective Fungicides—Properties, Application, Mechanisms of Action,* H. Lyr (Ed.), Longman Group UK Ltd., London, and VEB Gustav Fisher Verlag, Jena, Chap. 23.

Staub, T., 1991, Fungicide resistance: practical experience with antiresistance strategies and the role of integrated use, *Annu. Rev. of Phytopathology,* 29, 421-442.

Staub, T. and Sozzi, D., 1984, Fungicide resistance: a continuing challenge, *Plant Dis.,* 68: 1026.

16 Integrated Plant Disease Management

16.1 INTRODUCTION

The publication of classic book *Silent Springs* by Rachel Carson essentially brought two issues into sharp focus: (a) chemical pesticides can be dangerous to human being as well as the environment and should be used as the last resort, (b) there are biologically based more safe alternatives to synthetic pesticides, and these eco-friendly methods need to be studied and exploited. The message though reasonable, when first introduced whipped up reactions particularly by the people who had vested interests in chemical industry. But the indiscriminate use of pesticides brought home the message of Carson, and recent policy makers are seriously concerned. Thus, the policy adopted by the World Bank since 1980s is to finance projects that do not seriously compromise on public health or cause irreversible environmental deterioration. The World Bank objective is focused on the IPM approach for sustainable agriculture.

16.2 THE CONCEPT

Several definitions of sustainable agriculture are available. No definition is perfect but the one adopted by the Technical Advisory Committee (TAC) of the CGIAR seems satisfactory. It reads *sustainable agriculture should involve the successful management of resources for agriculture to satisfy changing human needs while maintaining or enhancing the quality of the environment and conserving natural resources* (TAC, 1989).

The term, pest management was first envisaged at the beginning of the 1950s as a concept of integrating the use of biological and other methods of pest control. This was later broadened to include the coordinated use of available biological, cultural and chemical methods. Subsequently, various authors advocated a total system approach incorporating pest management practices together with the increased production objectives. This approach needs to be a part of an overall crop production system. The present IPM thesis is a composite of disease management and integrated crop management (ICM) (Figure 16.1).

16.3 THE TOTAL SYSTEM APPROACH

Essentially the IPM paradigm is: (a) eradication should not necessarily be the goal, but only application of minimal level of control that will maintain the pest below economic damage threshold, (b) it accepts multiple techniques in preference to following only the pest eradication

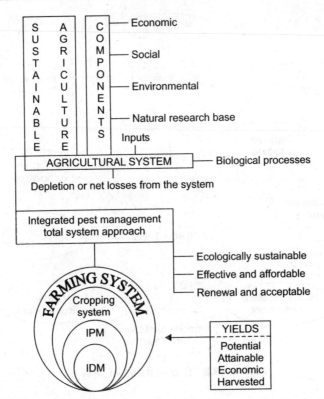

Figure 16.1 Components, processes and levels of various systems of sustainable agriculture and IPM.

strategy, (c) the no-option goal in reducing the levels of pesticide use and least or no damage to the non-target organisms and ecosystem and (d) the need for indigenous knowledge of agricultural system and pest life-cycles. IPM may thus be an excellent choice for industrial agriculture but its transfer to resource poor farmers is problematic. Furthermore, IPM programme so far operated only to limit pest populations. There is need for more simple solutions to determine the economic threshold for each crop location set up. The terms pest control or pest management or crop management prefixed with the word 'Integrated' endorse a need for a total system approach wherein there is a meeting of minds, materials and methods.

16.3.1 Sub-systems of IPM

The IPM system is ecologically safe, as it emphasizes judicious use of pesticides along with non-chemical methods like cultural practices and biological control (Figure 16.2). Various sub-systems and approaches for development and recommendation of IPM modules include surveillance, forecasting, habitat analysis, crop husbandry, impact analysis, technology transfer, human resource besides conservation of parasites, predators, parasitoids, etc. (Figure 16.2).

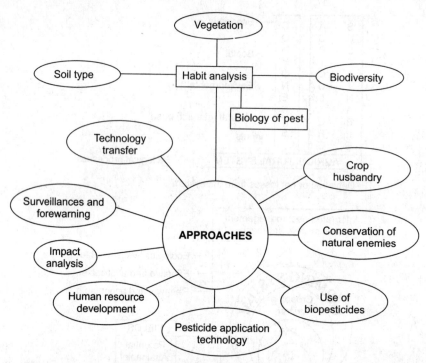

Figure 16.2 Sub-systems of IPM.

16.3.2 IPM Strategy

To achieve ecofriendly and sustainable management of plant disease, the inputs of both productions as well as protection technologies are to be applied appropriately (Figure 16.3). For healthy crop the management practices that reduce inoculum potential (sanitation, removal of weeds, ploughing, etc.) and avoid the conditions that predispose host are selected. In protection technology, practices that reduce inoculum load and slow down the disease progress are invariably adopted.

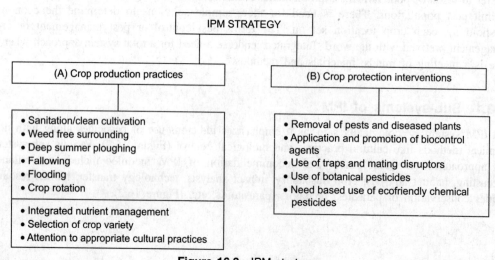

Figure 16.3 IPM strategy.

16.3.3 Integration of Practices

The variety of methods for management of plant diseases listed in the preceding chapters suggests that there exists a big 'arsenal of weapons' to combat the pathogens. However, there is a need of well planned strategy making best use of the 'weapons' in a co-coordinated/integrated manner with proper application technology. In order to achieve this, there will have to be integration of methods directed against the pathogen, in favour of the host and for modification of the environment. This is known as **integrated disease management**.

16.3.4 Benefits and Limitations

IPM embodies an ecological approach to the pest problem with the objective of minimizing use of chemical pesticides while sustaining production levels. The gains are reduction in costs of production, more economic access of food and conservation of the resilience and integrity of the ecosystem. The modules developed and validated have to be either crop or location specific (Figure 16.4) and therefore, lack universal application.

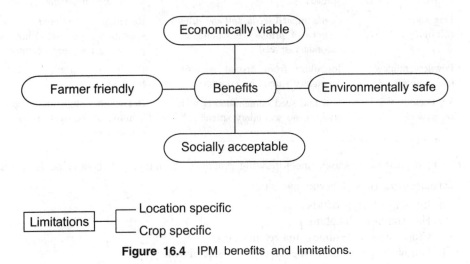

Figure 16.4 IPM benefits and limitations.

16.4 INTEGRATED MANAGEMENT OF WHEAT DISEASES

Wheat is grown throughout the subtropical and temperate regions of the world. Although several diseases caused by fungi, bacteria, nematodes and viruses are known to infect wheat, all are not equally important in every locality. Major diseases of wheat, their mode of carryover, secondary spread and control measures are summarized in Table 16.1.

Table 16.1 Important Diseases of Wheat

Sl. No.	Disease/causal agent	Primary inoculum and secondary inoculum	Management practices
1.	Black/stem rust (*P. graminis*) Brown/leaf rust (*P. recondita*) Yellow/stripe rust (*P. striiformis*)	Inoculum form distant sources, secondary spread through urediniospores	Resistant varieties and spray of the fungicides
2.	Loose smut (*U. segatum*)	Internally seed-borne, infection of ovaries in standing crop	Rouging and seed treatment (physical or chemical)
3.	Karnal bunt (*T. indica*)	Soil/seed borne inoculum, secondary spread through sporidia	Crop rotation, healthy seeds, treatment with fungicides, spray of fungicides at ear emergence
4.	Hill bunt (*T. tritici, T. laevis*)	Seed and soil borne, no secondary spread	Crop rotation, healthy seeds/ certified seeds, seed treatment
5.	Flag smut (*U. agropyri*)	Contaminated seeds, soil and straw sources of primary inoculum, no secondary spread	Resistant varieties, rotation, sanitation, rouging, hot weather ploughing and seed treatment
6.	Powdery mildew (*B. graminis*)	Inoculum from distant sources, secondary spread by conidia	Resistant varieties, spray of fungicides
7.	Ear cockles (*A. tritici*)	Soil and seed contamination with cockles, no secondary spread	Hot weather ploughing, crop rotation, healthy seeds, soil treatment with nematicides

In order to manage these diseases, the following practices are integrated to develop IDM module:

1. Management of soil borne inoculum
   (a) Burning of crop debris
   (b) Hot summer ploughing
   (c) Crop rotation (legumes, maize, mustard)
   (d) Fallow or green manuring or organic amendment

   Note: Except for rusts, powdery mildew and loose smut, the remaining diseases are managed.

2. Reduction of seed borne inoculum
   (a) Use of clean/healthy/certified seeds of resistant or tolerant varieties
   (b) Seed treatment with systemic fungicide (vitavax) in combination with protectant fungicide (thiram)

   Note: Except for rusts and powdery mildew all other diseases are managed.

3. Reduction of secondary spread
   (a) Use of resistant/tolerant varieties against most damaging pathogen
   (b) Select varieties of different maturity durations
   (c) Prophylactic sprays of fungicides

   Note: All diseases managed; particularly rusts, powdery mildew and karnal bunt.

16.5 INTEGRATED MANAGEMENT OF NURSERY DISEASES

Most horticultural crops (fruits and vegetables) are first raised in nurseries and thereafter the seedlings are transplanted. Several soil-borne fungal pathogens such as *Pythium, Phytophthora, Fusarium, R. solani, S. rolfsii* cause seed rot and damping-off. Soil-borne insects, mites, nematodes also damage the seedlings raised in infested soil. Very often the weeds also affect the crop health. To ensure optimum production both population and health of the seedlings are of prime importance. In the following flow chart, the practices that provide desired population and sound health are exhibited.

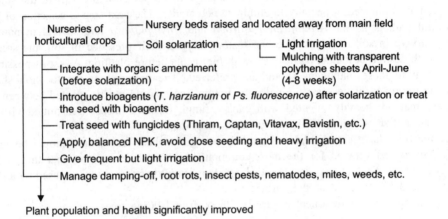

16.6 INTEGRATED MANAGEMENT OF POTATO DISEASES

As mentioned earlier, all the recorded diseases of a single crop do not occur simultaneously in any locality. However, the possibility of occurrence of any one or more of them in the field does exist. IDM in potato crop is discussed here. Wherever the crop is grown, late and early blight diseases black scurf/stem canker, bacterial wilt and brown rot, root knot, mosaic and leaf curl are quite common diseases of this crop. Due to vegetative propagation, all the pathogens are mainly seed (tuber) borne while some of them are soil borne also. Spread by soil, insects, water and wind is common. Therefore, improvement of quality and quantity of the yield can be brought about by adopting following schedule:

1. The field with record of serious incidence of soil-borne diseases in the near past should be avoided. The land must have proper drainage and high fertility level.
2. The certified seed from reliable agency should be used for planting. Additional precaution should be taken by treating seed tubers with 3% boric acid. This may help in eradication of residual inoculum from the seeds and protects during germination and emergence.
3. The date of planting should be decided according to prevailing soil temperature and moisture.
4. Protective steps to prevent secondary infection are essential. One prophylactic spray of Mancozeb @ 0.2% or copper oxychloride @ 0.3% should be given at 30-40 days after planting.
5. Plants showing viral infection are properly removed and the crop is sprayed with metasystox or other insecticides when there is build-up of population of aphid vectors.

6. In addition, need based spraying with fungicides such as zineb, metalaxyl mancozeb, copper oxychloride, etc. is continued to check early and late blight, pathogens.

16.7 IDM IN ORCHARDS (PERENNIAL CROP)

In an integrated disease management program of an orchard like apple, mango, peach, citrus, etc., one must first consider the nursery stock to be used and the location where it is to be planted. The nursery stock (both the root stock and scion) must be free from biotic and mesobiotic agents. Even after obtaining them from a nursery where the saplings are inspected and certified, the stock must be appropriately fumigated, especially to eliminate nematodes. The next step is selection of planting sites. Several pathogens like *Armillaria*, *Fusarium* and *Phytophthora* and several nematodes are known to survive in soil. If experience and history suggest their presence in soil, the soil should be treated with desired pesticide, particularly with fumigants before planting. As far as possible root-stock resistant to these pathogens should be preferred. The drainage of the location should be checked and improved, if necessary. Finally the young trees should not be planted between or next to old trees that are heavily infected with canker fungi, bacteria, insect transmitted viruses and phytoplasmas, pollen transmitted viruses or with other pathogens.

Once the trees have established and until they begin to bear fruits, they should be fertilized, irrigated, pruned and sprayed for the most common insects and diseases so that they will grow vigorously and free of infections. Any tree that develops symptoms of a disease caused by a systemic pathogen, should be removed at the earliest.

The following line of treatment ensure health of fruit bearing trees:

1. Removal through pruning and destruction of dead twigs, branches, and fruits.
2. Pruning equipment should be disinfested before moving to new trees.
3. A dormant spray containing a fungicide-bactericide (Bordeaux mixture) or a plain fungicide plus an acaricide/insecticide is applied before the buds break.
4. After the buds open, blossoms and leaves must be protected with sprays containing a fungicide and/or a bactericide and, an insecticide (that do not harm bees).
5. Young fruits should be protected by appropriate chemical sprays.
6. Wounding of fruits during harvesting and handling must be avoided.
7. Proper post harvest care (transit and storage) is required for profitable marketing of perishable produce.

REFERENCES

Agrios, G.N., 1997, *Plant Pathology*, Academic Press, New York.

Allen, G.E. and Bath, J.E., 1980, The conceptual and institutional aspects of integrated pest management, *Bioscience*, 30: 658.

Bolkan, H.A. and Reinert, W.R., 1994, Developing and implementing IPM strategies to assist farmers: An industry approach, *Plant Dis.*, 78:545.

Chaube, H.S. and Singh, U.S., 1990, *Plant Disease Management: Principles and Practices*, CRC, Press, Boca, Raton, USA.

Eversmeyer, M.G. and Kramer, C.L., 1987, Components and techniques of integrated pest management threshold determination for pathogens, *Plant Dis.*, 71:456.

Ferris, H., 1987, Components and techniques of integrated pest management threshold determination for soil borne pathogens, *Plant Dis.,* 71:452.

Gliessman, S.R., 1995, Sustainable Agriculture: An agroecological prospectives, *Advances in Plant Pathology,* 11:45.

Singh, R.S., 2000, *Plant Disease Management,* Oxford and IBH Publishing Co. Pvt. Ltd., New Delhi.

Thurston, H.D., 1991, *Sustainable Practices for Plant Disease Management in Traditional Farming Systems,* Westview, Boulder, Colorado.

Van Bruggen, A.H.C., 1995, Plant disease severity in high input compared to reduced input and organic farming systems, *Plant Diseases,* 79:976.

17

Kingdom: Fungi

17.1 INTRODUCTION

Man's interest in fungi started with the observation of umbrella-shaped mushrooms and toadstools growing naturally on soils. Since these grew attached to the soil like plants, they were regarded as plants. The word **mycology** derived from the Greek words (*Gr. mykes* = mushroom + logos = discourse). Although mushrooms attracted the attention of naturalists but it was only in the 17th century after the invention of the microscope that the actual systematic study of the fungi began. It is difficult to define the exact limits of this group, the fungi constitute most fascinating group comprising more than 1,00,000 species (Ainsworth and Bisby, 1983).

17.2 THE PLACE OF MICROORGANISMS IN NATURE

Until the last century, living organisms were classified as animals or plants due to obvious differences in form and constitution. These differences can be explained by the basic differences in their body composition and modes of nutrition. In accord with their entirely nutritional mode, plants (carbon-autotrophs) are constructed on a completely different plan. They synthesize the substances needed for growth and maintenance from inorganic materials and utilize sunlight as a source of energy. Other general differences between plants and animals concern the presence of cell walls, the capacity for active movement and change of position and ability to synthesize various substances.

It was easy to make distinctions between plant and animal kingdoms as long as little was known about microorganisms. The fungi, due to many properties in common with higher plants, were included in the plant kingdom despite their generally heterotrophic nutrition. The taxonomists faced more difficulty in assigning bacteria, slime moulds and other unicellular organisms to one of the two kingdoms. **Protista** was established by Haeckel (1866), as third kingdom of living organisms based on selection and evolutionary theory of Charles Darwin (1859). Haeckel unified the then known genera and species of plants and animals from the viewpoint of their possible evolutionary development. In fact, several authors are in favour of a five kingdom classification (Figure 17.1).

The kingdom Protista contains those organisms that are differentiated from plants and animals by their lack of morphological specialization, most of them being unicellular. The protists can be further subdivided into two clearly differentiated groups on the basis of their cellular characteristics. The higher protists (**eukaryotes**) resemble plants and animals in their cell composition; this group includes algae, fungi and protozoa. The lower protists (**prokaryotes**) include bacteria and cyanobacteria (blue-green algae). The viruses lack cellular organization. They are different from all other organisms as they are not capable of independent life and can proliferate only in the living cells. (Figure 17.1)

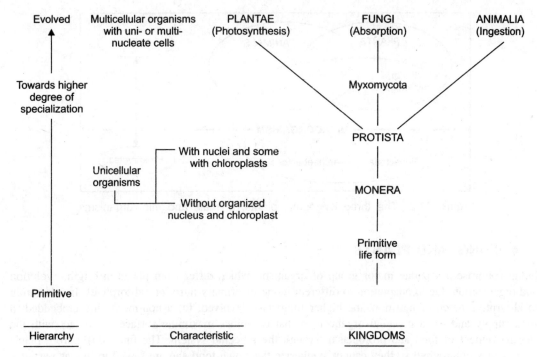

Figure 17.1 A five-kingdom classification of living organisms based on the mode of nutrition, degree of cellular and physiological organization. The kingdoms—Fungi, Plantae and Animalia—assume equal importance. The Myxomycota share both fungal and animal characteristics but are more primitive than both.

17.3 PROKARYOTES AND EUKARYOTES

The cell is the structural and functional unit of life in all the organisms with common material composition; DNA, RNA, proteins, lipids and phospholipids as fundamental components. However, investigations of the details of the composition and fine structures of different cell types have revealed significant differences between bacteria and cyanobacteria on the one hand, and animals and plants on the other. These differences are so fundamental that the two groups are sharply differentiated as prokaryotes and eukaryotes. The prokaryotes are regarded as relics from the earliest time of biological evolution, and the development of eukaryotes represents the greatest discontinuity in the evolution of living organisms. The division of living organisms into the above three main groups, and the distinctions between the two great divisions of prokaryotes and eukaryotes are shown schematically in Figure 17.2.

The eukaryotes possess true membrane bound nucleus (Karyon), which contains the major part of the genome distributed on a set of chromosomes. In chromosomes, DNA is associated with histones (basic proteins). The eukaryotic cell also contains organelles such as mitochondria and chloroplasts (in plants) that contain a small portion of the genome in the form of closed circular DNA. The ribosomes of eukaryotes are relatively large (80S). The prokaryotes lack true membrane bounded nucleus. DNA exists as a closed circular molecule in cytoplasm. This single 'bacterial chromosome' contains all the information necessary for reproduction. In addition, there may be one or more small, circular DNA molecules, called **plasmids**; these are usually dispersible for reproduction but may encode some metabolic functions. Prokaryotic ribosomes are relatively small (70S).

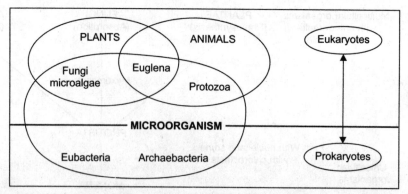

Figure 17.2 The three kingdoms: plants, animals and microorganisms.

17.4 FUNGI AND PLANTS

Fungi comprise a separate major group of organism, which differ from plants in origin, evolution and organization due to adaptation to different mode of primary nutrition (absorptive). In adaptation to absorptive mode of nutrition, the higher fungi have evolved: (a) a non-motile life embedded in food supply and (b) a mycelial organization that combines maximum surface of contact with the free movement of food and protoplasm through the mycelial system. The fungi differ from plants as they lack chlorophyll so they cannot synthesize their own food and are forced to live as parasites or saprophytes. Although fungi resemble green plants in having their protoplasts encased in cell walls, they do not possess differentiated body (stems, roots and leaves) and vascular system. Another feature that separates fungi from the plants is the fact that their primary carbohydrate storage product is glycogen rather than starch.

17.5 DYNAMICS AND SPECTRUM OF ACTIVITIES

Fungi occur in almost all types of habitats. Dynamics and spectrum of their activities are summarized in Figure 17.3.

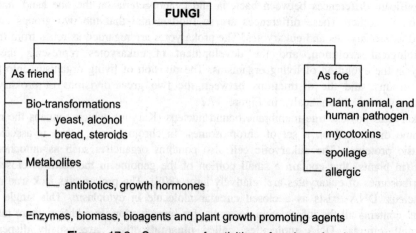

Figure 17.3 Summary of activities of various fungi.

17.6 GENERAL FEATURES OF FUNGI

Fungi are too diverse to be easily defined. The main characteristics are summarized in Table 17.1

Table 17.1 Characteristics of Fungi

Characters	Remarks
Distribution	Cosmopolitan
Habitat	Ubiquitous as saprobes, symbionts, parasites, hyperparasites
Sporocarps	Macroscopic, microscopic, showing limited tissue differentiations
Nutrition	Heterotrophic, absorptive
Thallus	Plasmodial, pseudoplasmodial, pseudomycelial or mycelial
Cell wall	Well defined, typically cutinized but cellulose in oomycetous fungi
Nuclear status	Eukaryotic, multinucleate, homo or heterokaryotic, haploid, diploid
Life cycle	Simple to complex
Reproduction	Asexual, sexual or parasexual

17.7 SOMATIC STRUCTURES

Somatic (*Gr. Soma* = body) refers to the assimilative phase in fungi; a structure or function as distinguished from the reproductive. It is also referred to as vegetative. Somatic/vegetative structures in fungi are very simple. Salient features are as follows:

17.7.1 The Thallus

Thallus (*pl.* thalli; *Gr. thallos* = shoot) is a relatively simple plant body devoid of stems, roots and leaves. Following are types of fungal thalli:

- **Plasmodium** (*pl.* plasmodia, *Gr. plasma* = a moulded object) is naked, multinucleate mass of protoplasm that moves and feeds in an amoeboid fashion such as the somatic phase of Myxomycota (slime moulds).

- **Pseudoplasmodium** (*Gr. pseudo* = false + plasmodium) is a sausage-shaped structure consisting of many amoebae aggregation in the cellular slime moulds (*Dictyosteliomycota* or *Acrasiomycota*).

- **Pseudomycelium** (*pl. pseudomycelia*; *Gr. pseudo* = false + *mycelium*) is a series of cells adhering end to end due to incomplete wall separation after budding in some yeast. It differs from true mycelium in which compartment or cells are formed by septum formation just behind the apex of an extending hyphal tip.

- **Mycelium** (*pl.* mycelia; *Gr. mykes* = mushroom, fungus) is the mass of hyphae constituting the body (thallus) of a fungus.

The most simple type of thallus is wholly converted into reproductive cells and is termed **holocarpic** (*Gr. holos* = entire + *karpos* = fruit). In majority of fungi, however, only parts of the thallus become reproductive forming differentiated or undifferentiated reproductive cells. Such thalli are **eucarpic** (*Gr. eu* = good + *karpos* = fruit). *In relation to host, the thalli may be* **epibiotic** (*Gr. epi* = on + *bios* = life) *or* **endobiotic** (*Gr. endos* = inside + *bios* = life). In fungi with epibiotic thalli, the reproductive organs are formed on the surface of the substratum, but with part or all of the soma within the substrate. An organism that lives within its substrate, usually the cells of its host is referred as *endobiotic.* Further a thallus that produces a single reproductive organ is called **monocentric** (*Gr. monos* = single + *kentron* = centre) while those with many centres at which reproductive organs are formed is referred as **polycentric** (*Gr. poly* = much, many + *kentron*).

17.7.2 The Hyphae

Fungi reproduce by means of spores (Plate 17.1). Under favourable environment spore germinates by sending one or more germ tubes that elongate and become filamentous. Each filament is called a **hypha** (*pl. hyphae, Gr. hyphe* = web). The mass of hyphae, which constitute the fungus thallus, is termed as **mycelium** (*pl. mycelia, Gr. mykes* = mushroom). The thin and plastic hyphal tip,

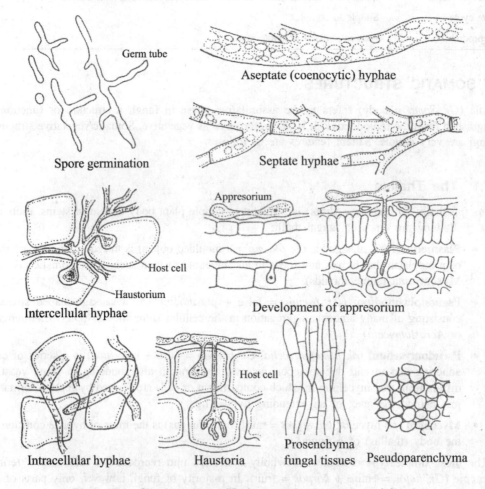

Plate 17.1 Simple and modified vegetative structures of fungi.

50–100 μ in the apical region is the zone of elongation and is filled with protoplasm. The hypha may be **septate** or **aseptate** depending on presence or absence of septa (cross wall). In aseptate hyphae the protoplasm flows uninterruptedly through the filaments and the hyphae are known as **coenocytic** (*Gr. koinos* = common + kytos = *a hollow vessel*). Many fungi while parasitizing host plants grow superficially. Such growth is **ectophytic** while others grow inside the host tissues and are referred to as **endophytic**. In plant tissues hyphae may be **inter-cellular** (lying in between the cells) or **intra-cellular** (lying in the lumen of the cell) (Plate 17.1).

17.7.3 Specialized Somatic Structures

They consist of the following:

Rhizoids. (*Gr. Rhiza* = root + *oeides* = like) A short, root like filamentous out growth of the thallus at the base of thalli/sporophores, serving as an anchoring /attachment organ and also absorption of nutrients from the substrate.

Rhizomycelium. (*Gr. Rhiza* + mycelium) A rhizoidal system extensive enough to resemble mycelium superficially.

Appresorium. (*pl.* appresoria) L = *appremere* = to press against} A flattened, hyphal, pressing organ, from which a minute infection peg usually grows and enters the epidermal cell of the host. (Plate 17.1)

Haustorium. (*pl.* Haustoria) *L. Haustor* = Drinker] An absorbing organ originating on a hypha and penetrating into cells of the host (Plate 17.1).

17.7.4 Hyphal Aggregations and Tissues

Rhizomorph. (*Gr. Rhiza* = root, *morph* = shape) The hyphae become root like or string like and attain great length. The mycelium aggregates to form thick strands in which hyphae lose their individuality and the entire strand acts as a unit.

False tissues. The mycelium of fungi is made up of loosely interwoven hyphae which may be organized in various ways. These are:

Plectenchyma. (*Gr. pleko*= I weave, *enchyma* = infusion) Mycelium of many fungi organizes into a loosely or compactly woven tissue. It may be of two types:

Prosenchyma. (*Gr. pros* = towards + *enchyma* = infusion) A type of plectenchyma in which the component hyphae lie parallel to one another and are easily recognized as such (Plate 17.1).

Pseudoparenchyma. [(*pl.* pseudoparenchymata) *Gr. pseudo* false + *parenchyma* = a type of plant tissue] A type of plectenchyma consisting of oval or isodiametric cells, the component hyphae having lost their individuality (Plate 17.1).

Stroma [*pl.* stromata) *Gr. stroma* = mattress] a compact stomatic structure, much like a matrix, on which or in which fructifications are usually formed.

Sclerotium (*pl.* sclerotia; *Gr. skleron* = hard) It is another modified form of plectenchyma and forms a resting body. These are filled with food materials and the wall either remains thin or becomes thick forming a protective rind, which may be brown or black in colour.

17.7.5 The Fungal Cell

Except for a few primitive fungi, the vegetative cells of all other fungi are enclosed in a cell wall. The cell wall is a dynamic structure that is subject to change and modification at different stages in the life of a fungus (Peberdy, 1990). It is composed basically of a skeleton or microfibrillar component located to the inner side of the wall and usually embedded in an amorphous matrix material that extends to the outer surface of the wall. The skeleton component consists of highly crystalline, water insoluble materials that include β-linked glucans and chitin while the matrix consists mainly of polysaccharides that are mostly water-soluble. Cellulose is a characteristic component of the walls of the stramenopiles, including oomycetous fungi.

It has been known since the beginning that hyphae grow at their tips. How this growth occurs is still not understood fully. The steady-state hypothesis (Wessels, 1986,1988) suggests that the hyphal apex is inherently viscoelastic and expandable and that the newly synthesized wall at the apex consists of a mixture of non-crystalline chitin and β-glucan. As a result of subsequent cross linking of the polymers of the wall the viscoelastic mixture then gradually develops rigidity. The other hypothesis (Bartnicki-Garcia, 1973) suggests that the wall is inherently rigid and that for growth to occur, there must be a permanent delicate balance between the lyses of the wall followed by synthesis of wall polymers and the pushing out and mending of the wall. In either of these two hypotheses, it is clear that the sub-apical region of growing hyphae provides the energy, enzymes, wall precursors and membranes necessary for hyphal tip growth.

17.7.6 Fungal Organelles

The fungal hyphae may invariably contain one or more nuclei. The typical fungal nucleus usually contains a prominent centrally positioned nucleolus. Aside from nuclei other prominent fungal organelle is mitochondria (the power house of cell). Other cytoplasmic components of fungi include ribosomes, strands of endoplasmic reticulum, vacuoles, lipid bodies, glycogen storage particles, microbodies, golgi bodies, filasomes, multivesicular bodies and the microtubules and microfilaments that comprise the fungal cytoskeleton. Spherical structures known as **woronin bodies** are also present in certain fungi (Figure 17.4).

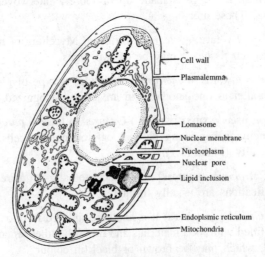

Figure 17.4 A fungus cell.

17.7.7 The Septa

Septa are formed either to cut-off reproductive cells from rest of the hypha or to separate off the damaged parts or to divide hyphae into compartments or cells. The septum is an annulus of cell wall material which vaginates the plasma lemma and grows from all round (in acropetal manner) inward completely or partially closing the passage of cytoplasm in the hypha.

17.8 REPRODUCTION

17.8.1 Asexual Reproduction

Fungi multiply by producing propagules that are capable of growing into new thallus. In most fungi these propagules are differentiated as spores, which are basic units of reproduction. The simple or branched spore bearing hyphae are known as **sporophores** (*Gr. sporos* = seed, spore + *phoreus* = bearer). The sporophores may be simple or compound. *Simple or filamentous sporophores* are branches of the somatic hyphae, which give rise to sporogenous cells and spores. The spore bearing branches usually arise vertically and may bear sporangia (**sporangiophore**) or conidia (**conidiophore**) (refer Plate 17.2). *Compound sporophores* are the aggregation of hyphae form stromatic or semistromatic structures which grow into compound sporophores.

Spores. Spore is any small propagative, reproductive or survival unit which separates from a hypha or sporogenous cell and can grow independently into a new individual. Thus, it is a nucleate portion delimited from the thallus, characterized by cessation of cytoplasmic movement. The spores may be grouped into two categories: **endogenous** or **exogenous.**

Endogenous spores. These are formed within a swollen sac like spore producing structure called **sporangium** (*pl.* sporangia; *Gr. sporos* + *angeion* = vessel) which may be terminal or intercalary in position. The entire contents or a part of the sporangium is converted into spores known as **sporangiospores** (Plate 17.2). The spores may be motile or non-motile. Motile spores are called **zoospores** (*Gr. Zoon* = animal + *sporos* = seed, spore) and the non-motile aplanospores. The zoospores are naked reniform or pyriform or amoeboid, uninucleated, haploid spores equipped with one or two flagella, i.e. uniflagellate or biflagellate. (Sing. *flagellum*; L. *flagellum*= whip). The flagella, are of two types, the whiplash and the tinsel. In whiplash flagellum, the structure resembles the whip. In tinsel, the entire flagellum is covered by hairy projections and looks like a comb. The released zoospores may encyst and thereafter germinate by germ tube.

Exogenous spores. All asexually produced spores except sporangiospores are called **conidia** (sing. conidium; *Gr. konis* = dust + *idion* – suffix). They are formed on branched or unbranched hyphal tips termed as **conidiophores**. In some fungi, conidia may be formed by transformation of existing cells of the thallus and are set free when the parent hyphae decay. They are referred as **thallospores**. They are of two kinds: *Arthrospores or oidia* (*Gr. arthron*= joint + *sporos* = spore), produced by fragmentation of hyphae from apex to base. Each cell rounds off and separates as a spore (Plate 17.2). *Chlamydospores:* (*Gr. chlamys* = mantle + *sporos* = spore) formed by rounding off and enlargement of terminal or intercalary cells of hyphae. These can be single or formed in chains (Plate 17.2).

The **conidia** are formed either as buds from the somatic cells of a hypha (blastospores) or produced by the inflation of the apex of the conidiophores (aleuriospores) or cut off from flask shaped, cylindrical phialides (phialospores). The shape, colour and septation of conidia (Plate 17.3) serve as the basis for identification and description of the fungal species. Following are the sections proposed by Saccardo (1899):

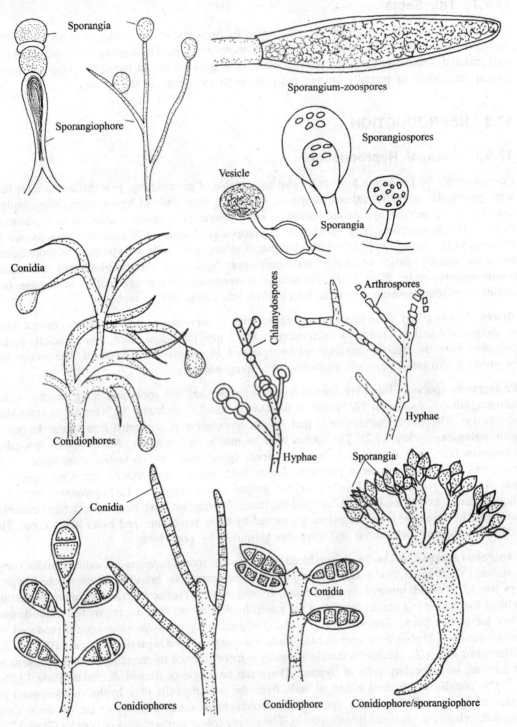

Sporangia

Sporangiophore

Sporangium-zoospores

Sporangiospores

Vesicle

Sporangia

Conidia

Chlamydospores

Arthrospores

Hyphae

Conidiophores

Hyphae

Sporangia

Conidia

Conidia

Conidiophores

Conidiophore

Conidiophore/sporangiophore

Plate 17.2 Asexual reproductive organs of fungi.

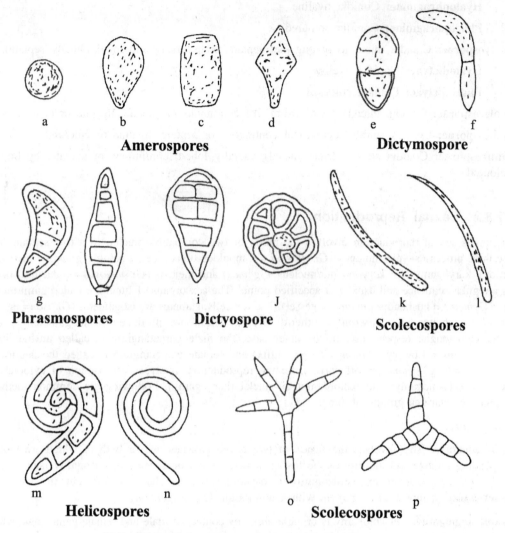

a   b   c   d   e   f

Amerospores   **Dictymospore**

g   h   i   J   k   l

Phrasmospores   **Dictyospore**   **Scolecospores**

m   n   o   p

Helicospores   **Scolecospores**

Plate 17.3 Various types of asexual fungal spores.

Amerosporae: Conidia continuous, spherical, ovoid to elongated or short cylindric

Allantosporae: Conidia cylindric, curved (allantoid), hyaline to pale

    Hyalosporae: Conidia hyaline

    Phaeosporae: Conidia coloured

Didymosporae: Conidia ovoid to oblong, one septate

    Hyalodidymae: Conidia hyaline

    Phaeodidymae: Conidia coloured

Phragmosporae: Conidia oblong, two to many-septate (transversely septate)

Hyalophragmiae: Conidia hyaline

Phaeophragmiae: Conidia coloured

Dictyosporae: Conidia ovoid to oblong, net septate (transversely and longitudinally septate).

Hyalodictyae: Conidia hyaline

Phaeodictyae: Conidia coloured

Scolecosporae: Conidia thread like to worm like continuous or septate, hyaline or pale

Helicosporae: Conidia spirally cylindrical continuous or septate, hyaline or coloured

Staurosporae: Conidia stellate (Star-shaped), radially lobed, continuous or septate, hyaline or coloured.

17.8.2 Sexual Reproduction

In fungus sexual reproduction involves the union of two compatible nuclei. In a true sexual cycle the three processes—plasmogamy (*Gr. plasma* = a moulded object, i.e., a being + *gamos* = marriage/union), karyogamy (*Gr. karyon*= nut/nucleus + *gamos*) and meiosis (*Gr. meiosis* = reduction) occur in a regular sequence and usually at specified points. The sex organs of fungi are called **gamatengia** (*Gr. Gametes* = husband + *angeion* = vessel). The sex cells, gametes are isogametes (*Gr. ison*= equal), or heterogametes (*Gr. heteron* = other/different). These are produced in isogametengia and heterogametengia, respectively. In the latter case, the male gametangium is called **antheridium** (*Gr. antheros* = flowery + *idion* = dimin, suffix) and female gametangium is called the **oogonium** (*Gr. oon* = egg + *gonos* = off spring). Sexual reproduction involves fusion/union of cytoplasmic contents (plasmogamy) and fusion/union of nuclei (karyogamy). Following are common methods adopted by various groups of fungi:

Plasmogamy

Gametogamy. This involves the fusion of two naked gametes one or both of which are motile. Depending on size and motility of the fusing gametes, the process may be—**isogamy** (same shape and size, i.e., isogametes), **anisogamy** (morphologically similar but different in size), and **heterogamy** (a motile male gamete with a non-motile female gamete).

Gametangiogamy. Plasmogamy is brought about by contact of male and female gametangia where both the gametes are non-motile. The male gametic nucleus (or nuclei) migrates into the oogonium either through a pore formed at the point of the contact or through a fertilization tube developed for the purpose by antheridium. The two gametangia do not fuse and retain their identify. The oogonium undergoes post-copulation changes while the antheridium usually disintegrates. The zygote formed is called **oospore** (*Gr. oon* = egg + spores = spore) (Plate 17.4).

Gamentital copulation. The entire contents of the two gametangia fuse, which occurs in two ways: (a) Direct fusion of gametangia: The two gametangia fuse and become one cell, e.g., ***Mucor***. (b) Migration of entire protoplasm of one gametangium into the other through a pore. The recipient gametangium is called female (oogonium) while the donor gametangium is male (antheridium) e.g., *Rhizophidium*.

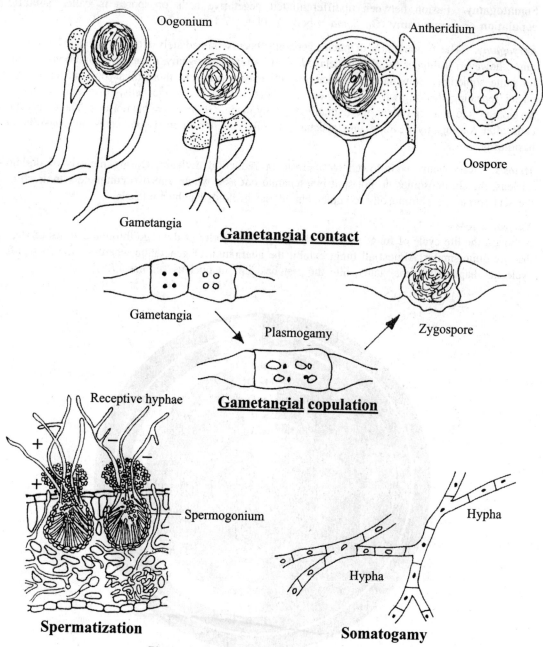

Plate 17.4 Sexual reproduction in fungi.

Spermatization. **Spermatia** (*Gr. spermation* = little seed) are non-motile, uninucleate, spore like male structures which empty their contents into receptive female structure during plasmogamy. They are produced in **spermogonia**.

Somatogamy. Fusion between undifferentiated vegetative cells or spores is called **somatic copulation** or **somatogamy** (*Gr. Soma* = body) (Plate 17.4).

Karyogamy. The fusion/union of nuclei generally occurs immediately after plasmogamy in lower fungi, however, in higher fungi it is delayed where after plasmogamy, dikaryotic conditions prevail for quite sometime. Sometimes the dikaryon cell may divide into more dikaryons and each time nuclei repeating the original pair. Sometimes hypae having dikaryotic cells, form definite tissue developing into a special layer, the hymanium (*pl.* hymania, *Gr. hymen* = membrane). The dikaryotic cells after karyogamy develop into specialized cells called **asci** in ascomycetes and **basidia** in basidiomycetes.

Meiosis. Karyogamy is followed by meiosis or reduction division. During meiosis of diploid nucleus, the chromosomes do not split but separate out as a whole into two complete sets. Each of the sets forms the chromosome complement of the haploid daughter nucleus.

Nuclear Cycle
Although the life cycle of fungi vary greatly, the great majority of them go through a series of steps that are quite similar. Almost all fungi exhibit the alternation of generation where some part of life cycle has haploid nucleus state while the rest has diploid nucleus (Figure 17.5).

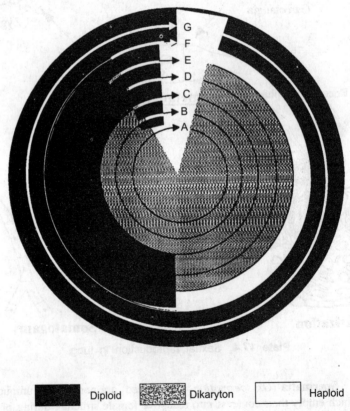

Figure 17.5 Diagrammatic representation of nuclear cycle.

On the basis of sex, most fungi may be classified into three categories:

Monoecious. The thallus that bears both male and female organs may or may not be compatible.

Dioecious. The thallus in some cases bears only male or female organs.

Sexually undifferentiated. Functional structures produced are morphologically indistinguishable as male or female.

Fungi in the categories outlined above belong to one of the following three groups on the basis of compatibility:

Homothallic fungi. Those in which every thallus is sexually self-fertile.

Heterothallic fungi. Those in which every thallus is sexually self sterile and requires another compatible thallus of a different mating type for sexual reproduction.

Secondary homothallic fungi. In some heterothallic fungi an interesting mechanism operates during spore formation whereby two nuclei of opposite mating type are incorporated regularly into each spore or at least in some spores. Germlings arising from these spores are therefore self-fertile and behave as if they are homothallic when in reality they are actually heterothallic.

Heterothallism may be bipolar (unifactorial) (mating controlled by one pair of *loci*) or tetra polar (bifactorial) (mating is controlled by more than one pair of *loci,* located on different chromosomes).

Heterokaryosis. All fungal cells do not necessarily have the same number and kind of nuclei. The phenomenon of the existence of different kinds of nuclei in the individual cell is called **heterokaryosis** (*Gr. heteros* = different + *karyon* = nut, nucleus) and the individuals that exhibit it are heterokaryon. Heterokaryons may originate in various ways:

1. Germination of a heterokaryotic spore
2. Introduction of genetically different nucleus into a cell
3. Mutation in multinucleate, homokaryotic structure
4. Fusion of some nuclei in a haploid homokaryon

Parasexuality. Some fungi do not undergo a true sexual cycle. They may derive the benefits of sexual recombination through a process known as **parasexuality** (*Gr. para* = besides + sex). In this process, plasmogamy, karyogamy and meiosis take place but not at specified points in the thallus or the life cycle. The parasexual cycle may involve the following steps:

1. Formation of heterokaryotic mycelium
2. Nuclear fusion and multiplication of the diploid nuclei
3. Mitotic crossing over during the division of the diploid cells
4. Sorting out of the diploid strains
5. Haploidization

17.8.3 Fructifications and Fruit Bodies

Fructification is a fungal structure that contains or bears spores. They may be asexual or sexual in nature. In lower fungi, the asexual spores are usually enclosed in a simple sac called **sporangia** or **zoosporangia**. In higher forms of fungi, however, there is a tendency to organise complex aggregates of spore bearing hyphae. Some of these are described as follows: (Plate 17.5).

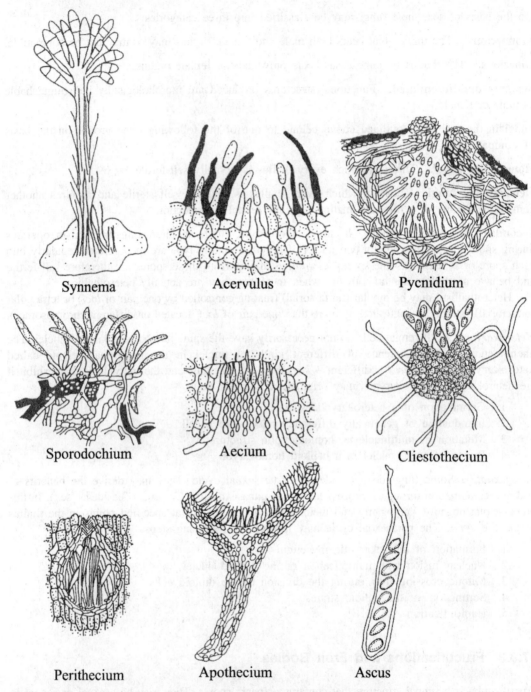

Synnema Acervulus Pycnidium

Sporodochium Aecium Cliestothecium

Perithecium Apothecium Ascus

Plate 17.5 Spore fruits (fructifications).

Synnema. (*pl.* synnemata; *Gr. syn* = together + *nema* = *yarn*) A group of conidiophores cemented together and forming an elongated spore bearing structure.

Acervulus. (*pl.* acervuli; *L. acervus* = heap, dimin, form) A mat of hyphae giving rise to short conidiophores closely packed together forming a bed like mass.

Sporodochium. (*pl.* sporodochia; *Gr. sporos* = seed/spore + *docheion* = container) A cushion shaped stroma covered with conidiophores.

Pycnidium. (*pl.* pycnidia; *Gr. pyknon* = concentrated + *idion* dimin/suffix) An asexual, hollow fruiting body, lined inside with conidiophores.

Perithecium. (*pl.* perithecia; *Gr. Peri* = around + *theka* = a case) A closed ascocarp with a pore at the top, a true ostiole, on a wall of its own.

Apothecium. (*pl.* apothecia; *Gr. apotheka* = store house). An open ascocarp (*Gr. askos* = sac + *karpos* = fruit), a fruiting body containing asci and ascospores.

Cleistothecium. (*pl.* cleistothecia; *Gr. kleistos* = closed + *theke* = case) a completely closed ascocarp.

Spermagonium. (*pl.* spermagonia; *Gr. sperma* = seed, sperm + gennao = I give birth). A structure resembling a pycnidia and containing spermatiophores and spermatia.

Aecium. (*pl.* aecia; *Gr. aikia* = injury) A structure consisting of binucleate hyphae cells, with or without peridium, which produce spore chains consisting of aeciospores alternating with disjunctor cells; by the successive conjugate division of nuclei.

17.9 CLASSIFICATION OF FUNGI

Since the beginning of the study of fungi, many systems of classification have been proposed but still there is none that can satisfy situations. The classification of fungi described here is based on the findings of Anisworth and Bisby (1995).

17.9.1 The Ever Changing Attempts

Persoon (1801) classified fungi into classes, orders and families and published his work in "Synopsis Methodica Fungorum".

Fries (1821–1929) classified fungi and published his work in "Systema Mycologium".

Eicher (1866) divided Thallophyta into Algae and Fungi. The fungi included Schizomycetes, Eumycetes and Lichens.

Saccardo (1822–1931) wrote "Sylloge Fungorum": in 25 volumes and classified fungi into 6 classes.

Schroeter (1897) classified fungi into Phycomycetes, Eumycetes and Fungi-imperfectii.

Gaumann and Dodge (1928) created five classes.

Fitzpatrick (1930) divided Thallophyta into two groups—Myxothallophyta and Euthallophyta.

Tippo (1942) divided Thallophyta into three phyla—Schizomycophyta (bacteria), Myxomycophyta (slime moulds) and Eumycophyta (fungi).

Martin (1950) classified fungi into four classes—Phycomycetes (two sub-classes and 12 orders), Ascomycetes (two sub-classes and 16 order), Basidiomycetes (2 sub-classes and 11 orders), an fungi –imperfectii (four orders).

Smith (1955) divided fungi into two phyla—Myxomycophyta (3 classes) and Eumycophyta with classes, sub-classes and orders.

Alexopoulos (1962) created division mycota with two sub-divisions Myxomycotina and Eumycotina. Myxomycotina included class Myxomycetes with two sub-classes and six orders. Subdivision Eumycotina included nine classes, sub-classes, series and orders.

Ainsworth (1966) classified fungi (Kingdom—mycota) into two divisions—myxomycota and Eumycota. Eumycota was further divided into 5 subdivision—Mastigomycota (4 classes), zygomycotina (2 classes), Ascomycotina (6 classes), Basidiomycotina (3 classes) and Deuteromycotina (3 classes).

Alexopoulos (1979) modified his previous classification and divided fungi into 3 divisions (Gymnomycota, Mastigomycota and Amastigomycota).

17.9.2 Recent Classification (Ainsworth and Bisby—1995)

(A) Kingdom—**Protozoa** are predominantly unicellular, plasmodial or colonial phagotrophic eukaryotes, which lack walls in their trophic phase and mitochondria contain tubular cristae. Ciliary hairs are never rigid and tubular and haptonemes are absent.

(a) Phylum—Acrasiomycota—one class—*Acrasiomycetes*. Trophic phase is amoeboid with lobose pseudopodia; sporocarps are sessile, and multispored, flagellate cells usually absent, sexual reproduction unknown.

(b) Phylum—Dictyosteliomycota—one class—*Dictyosteliomycetes*. Trophic phase amoeboid with filose pseudopodia; sporocarps stalked, multispored; flagellated cells absent; sexual reproduction in some species.

(c) Phylum—Myxomycota can be classified into two categories:

- *Protosteliomycetes* consists of protostelids and the ceratiomyxids. Trophic-phase is simple amoebae or a plasmodium; flagellate cells present or absent; sporulation not preceded by aggregation of myxamoebae; sporocarps stalked one to several spores; or the spores borne singly at tips of fine stalks on surface of sporophore and spore germination resulting in eight haploid swarm spores.

- *Myxomycetes*—the true slime moulds. Trophic phase is free–living, multinucleate, coenocytic, saprobic plasmodia; spores develop in masses with a persistent or evanescent peridium; flagellate cells present; sexual reproduction unusual.

(d) Phylum—Plasmodiophoromycota—one class *Plasmodiophoromycetes* and the order— Plasmodiophorales. Obligate parasites of plants; trophic phase is a minute intracellular plasmodium. Parasitic fungi are *Plasmodiophora brassicae*, *Polymyxa graminis*, *Spongospora subterranean*.

(B) Kingdom—**Chromista** (Heterokonta, straminopila)—including '3 fungal' phyla; largely photosynthetic eukaryotes uniquely defined by the presence of an anterior cilium bearing rigid tubular ciliary hairs or mastigonemes.

(a) **Phylum**—Hypochytridiomycota—one class—*Hypochytridiomycetes*—zoospores with an anterior tinsel flagellum, parasitic on fresh water and marine algae, aquatic mastigomycotina and saprobic; wide-spread. Order—*Hypochytriales* (only one order recognized).

(b) **Phylum**—Labrinthulomycota—one class—*Labrinthulomycetes*—the labrinthulas and thaustochytrids. Trophic phase an ectoplasmic net.

(c) **Phylum**—Oomycota—one class—*oomycetes*—zoospores with two equal flagella, a tinsel flagellum directed forward and a whiplash flagellum directed backwards. Typically aquatic, saprobic or parasitic, some terrestrial (of which a few are obligate parasites of higher plants); cosmopolitan. Oospores (occasionally absent) and biflagellate zoospores (absent in some terrestrial species where the vegetative spore functions like a conidium). Thallus unicellular to mycelial (coenocytic), mainly aseptate. Orders: (i) Leptomitales (ii) Myzocytiopsidales (iii) Olpidiopsidales (iv) Peronosporales (v) Pythiales (vi) Rhipidiales (vii) Salilagenidales and (viii) Saprolegniales.

(C) Kingdom—Fungi are non-phagotrophic unicellular or multicellular or mycelial eukaryotes, which have plate-like cristae in the mitochondria; cell walls are typically chitinous in the trophic phase.

(a) **Phylum**—Chytridiomycota—One class *Chytridiomycetes*—zoospores with one posterior whiplash flagellum. Mainly microscopic parasites of fresh water algae and animals (some are hyperparasites) or saprobes of organic debris; a few are marine; cosmopolitan. Thallus coenocytic, holocarpic or eucarpic, monocentric/polycentric or mycelial; cell wall frequently chitinous; zoospores posteriorly monoflagellate; zygote farming an encysted structure or a diploid thallus. Orders—(i) Blastocladiales (ii) Chytridiales (iii) Monoblepharidales and (iv) Neocallimastigales.

(b) **Phylum**—Zygomycota. The thallus is mycelial and typically aseptate; sexual reproduction resulting in a resting spore (zygospore); motile cells absent. There are two classes:
   • *Zygomycetes*–saprobes or parasites (especially of arthropods) Orders: (i) Mucorales (ii) Zoopagales (iii) Endogonales (iv) Entomophthorales (v) Dimargaritales (vi) Kickxellales and (vii) Glomales.
   • *Trichomycetes*–Parasites or commensals within the digestive tracts of living arthropods, or ectozoic Orders :(i) Harpellales (ii) Asellariales (iii) Amoebidales and (iv) Eccrinales

(c) **Phylum**—Ascomycota. Thallus mycelial and septate or, rarely, unicellular; sexual reproduction by ascospores developing endogenously in asci. There is one class—*Ascomycetes*. This class is further divided into 46 orders. The plant parasitic fungi belonging to Orders—Diaporthales, Dothidiales, Erysiphales, Hypocreales, Microscales, Ophiostomatales, Phyllochorales, Protomycetales, Rhytismatales, Taphrinales and Xsylariales will form part of description with diseases caused by them.

(d) **Phylum**—Basidiomycota—Thallus mycelial and septate, clamp connections are characterstic; sexual reproduction by basidiospores borne exogenously on basidia. There are 3 classes:
   • *Teliomycetes*—Karyogamy by spermatia; clamp connections absent but hyphae with dolipore septum. Orders—(i) Septobasidiales (ii) Uredinales.
   • *Ustomycetes*—Facultative plant parasites; spores in sori; frequently with yeast-like and saprobic; septa generally lacking a dolipore. Orders—(i) Cryptobasidiales

(ii) Cryptomyeocolacales (iii) Exobasidiales (iv) Platygloeales (v) Sporidiales (vi) Tilletiales and (vii) Ustilaginales.

- *Basidiomycetes*—Basidiomata typically gymnocarpous or semi-angiocarpous; basidiospores ballistospores. It is divided into two sub-classes:

1. *Phragmobasidiomycetidae*—Basidiospores generally germinate by replication, or by budding, or by formation of conidia; basidium or sterigmata modified, often either transversely or vertically septate
   Order (i) Agricostilbales (ii) Atractiellales (iii) Auriculariales (iv) Heterogastridiales, and (v) Tremellales.
2. *Holobasidiomycetidae*—Basidiospores forming a mycelium directly or rarely replicating; basidium lacking internal septation. This subclass is further divided into 27 orders.

(e) Deuteromycetes are characterized by the absence of a teleomorph (perfect or sexual state). Most are anamorphs of ascomycetes but a few have affinities with basidiomycetes. For some the teleomorph is known, for some it is still undescribed or unrecognized (unconnected) whilst for others sexuality appears to have been lost and its functions are sometimes replaced by such mechanisms as the parasexual cycle. They are not formally included in the classification of the fungi. The name of the holomorph, the whole fungus in all its states, is that of the teleomorph although separate names for the different states of pleomorphic fungi is permitted. Two form classes are recognized:

- *Hyphomycetes*—Mycelial forms which are sterile or bear conidia on septate hyphae or aggregation of hyphae, as synnematous or sporodochial conidiomata but not within discrete conidiomata.
- *Coelomycetes*—Forms producing conidia in pycnidial, pycnothyrial, acervular, cupulate or stromatic conidiomata.

REFERENCES

Ainsworth, G.C., 1966, A general purpose classification of fungi: *Bibliography Systematic Mycology*, 1-4, Commonwealth Mycol. Inst. Kew, Survey.

Ainsworth, G.C., 1983, *Ainsworth's & Bisby's Dictionary of Fungi*, 7th ed., Commonwealth Mycological Institute, Kew, Survey.

Ainsworth, G.C., Sparrow, F.K. and Sussman, A.S., 1973, *The fungi: An Advance Treatise*, Academic Press, New York.

Alexopoulos, C.J. 1962, *Introductory Mycology*, 2nd ed., John Wiley and Sons, Inc., New York.

Alexopoulos, C.J. and Mims, C.W., 1979, *Introductory Mycology*. 3rd ed., John Wiley and Sons, Inc. New York.

Alexopoulos, C.J. Mims, C.W. and Blackwell, M., 1996, *Introductory Mycology*, 4th edn., John Wiley and Sons Inc., New York.

Bartinicki-Garcia, S., 1973, Fundamental aspects of hyphal morphogenesis, 245-26, In: *Microbial Differentiations*. J.M. Ashworth and J.E. Smith (Eds.), Cambridge University Press, London.

Hawksworth, D.L., Kirk, P.M,. Sutton, B.C., and Pegler, D.N., 1995, *Ainsworth and Brisby's Dictionary of Fungi,* 8th ed., International Mycol Inst., CAB, International.

Peberdy, J.F., 1990, Fungal cell walls: a review, In: *Biochemistry of Cell Walls and Membranes in Fungi*, P.J. Kuhn, A.P.J. Trinci, M.J. Jung, M.W. Goosey and L.G. Coping (Eds.). Springer-Verlag, Berlin, 5-30.

Wessels, J.G.H., 1986, Cell wall synthesis in apical hyphal growth, *Inst. Rev. Cytol,* 104:37.

Wessels, J.G.H., 1988, A steady state model for apical wall growth, *Acta Bot. Neerl,* 37:3.

Whittaker, R.H., 1969, New concepts of kingdoms of organisms, *Science,* 163:150.

18 Kingdom: Protozoa and Plant Diseases

18.1 INTRODUCTION

The members of the phylum Plasmodiophoromycota are usually necrotrophic endoparasites of vascular plants. They cause abnormal enlargement of host cells. Only a few species are of real economic importance: *Plasmodiophora brassicae* is the cause of club root or finger and toe disease of cabbage and related crucifers and *Spongospora subterranea* is the causal agent of powdery scab of potatoes. Various species of plasmodiophorids may also serve as vectors of many plant viruses. The phylum contains single class *Plasmodiophoromycetes* with the single order *Plamodiophorales* and the single family *Plasmodiophoraceae*. Dylewski (1990) has recognized a total of 29 species in 10 genera, including *Plasmodiophora*, *Spongospoa*, *Sorosphaera*, *Sorodiscus*, *Octomyxa*, *Polymyxa* and *Woronina*.

18.2 CLUB ROOT OF CRUCIFERS

18.2.1 Symptoms

Infected plants at first show pale green to yellowish leaves. Later, such plants show wilting with flagging of leaves during hot, sunny days. The characteristic symptoms are seen only on underground parts, after uprooting the plants. Spindle like, spherical, knobby or club shaped swellings are visible on roots. Both tap and lateral roots may be affected (Plate 18.1).

18.2.2 The Pathogen and Disease Cycle

The disease is caused by *Plasmodiophora brassicae*. The thallus is a plasmodium, which gives rise to zoosporangia or resting spores. There are two phases in the life cycle of the pathogen: (a) primary phase which occurs in the root hairs and (b) secondary phase occurring in the cortical cells of the root (Plate 18.1).

(a) Primary phase. Each resting spore germinates to produce a single zoospore with two flagella of unequal length, both whiplash, a short one attached to anterior and the longer one to posterior side. The primary zoospore attaches to the wall of a root hair. Eventually the flagella become inactive, the axonemes are retracted and the zoospore encysted. Finally the protoplast of the encysted zoospore enters the cell. Cruciform mitotic divisions occur and the proplast enlarges to form primary or sporangial plasmodium. After the primary plasmodium reaches a certain size, it cleaves into segments that develop into zoosporangia. Each zoosporangium contains

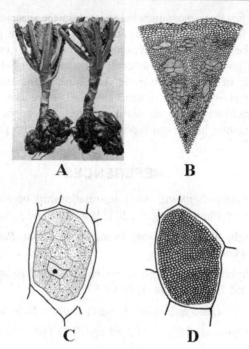

Plate 18.1 (a) Clubroot of cabbage, affected roots; (B) Clubroot of cabbage, cross section of affected root; (C) Clubroot of cabbage, affected root cell containing plasmodia of *Plasmodiophora brassicae;* (D) Clubroot of cabbage, affected root cell containing spores of *Plasmodiophora brassicae.*

4-8 uninucleate zoospores. The mature zoosporangium becomes attached to the host cell wall and a pore further develops at this point through which the zoospores escape in the soil. Further behaviour of the released zoospores is not fully known. However, it is believed that they function as gametes and fuse in pairs to form quadriflagellate, binucleate zoospores. Karyogamy does not follow plasmogamy.

(b) Secondary phase. The binucleate quadriflagellate zoospores are believed to re-infect the root to form binucleate plasmodium, which penetrates the root cortex. Plasmodium enlarges, repeated nuclear divisions take place and the host cells become **hypertrophied**. Plasmodia are then transformed into masses of resting spores. Prior to resting spore formation, karyogamy occurs to give diploid zygote nuclei and meiosis is presumed to follow quickly. Thus, resting spores, cleaved from the plasmodial cytoplasm is haploid. They become surrounded by a thin cell wall and are closely packed together inside the host cell. These are released into the soil as the roots decay. The pathogen survives as resting spores lying freely in soil or in crop debris. In the field, the disease spread by drainage water, farm implements, transport of soil, etc. Resting spores may remain viable for as long as 10 years.

18.2.3 Disease Management

Eradication of cruciferous weeds (collateral hosts), use of well drained pathogen free plots, use of seedlings raised in pathogen free soil/plots, and a very long crop rotation with non-cruciferous crops are some of the cultural practices recommended to contain the disease. Modification of soil pH to 7.0 or above by adding line @ 10-20 ton/ha, about 6 weeks before planting, gives good control. Similar results can also be obtained with gypsum (calcium sulfate) or sodium carbonate. Workers in Taiwan have reported good control by amending the soil with S-H mixture (@ 0.5 to 1% by weight of soil) consisting of sugarcane bagasse, rice husk, oyster shell powder, urea, potassium nitrate and calcium super phosphate and mineral ash. Soil fumigation with volatile chemicals such as Vapam and methyl bromides reduce the resting spores. Soil application of PCNB formulations like Terraclor, and Quintozone have been reported to suppress the pathogen.

REFERENCES

Buczacki, S.T., 1983, *Plasmodiophora*: An Inter-relationship between biological and practical problems, In: *Zoosporic Plant Pathogens*, S.T. Buczacki (Ed.), Academic Press, London, 161.

Chaube, H.S. and Singh, Ram Ji, 2000, *Introduction Plant Pathology*, International Book Distributing Co., Lucknow.

Dylewski, D.P., 1990, Phylum *Plasmodiophoromycota*, In: *Hand Book of Protoctista*, L. Margulis, et al., (Eds.) Jones and Bartlett, Boston, MA., 399.

Karling, J.S., 1968, The *Plasmodiophorales,* 2nd ed., Hafner, New York.

Singh, R.S., 1998, *Plant Disease*, 7th ed., Oxford and IBH Pub. Co. Pvt. Ltd., New Delhi.

19 Kingdom: Chromista (Oomycota) and Plant Diseases

19.1 INTRODUCTION

The organisms included in phylum *Oomycota* have been recognized as significantly different from the organisms included in Fungi. However, there has been a tendency to classify *Oomycota* with true fungi. In recent years, mycologists have invariably excluded oomycetous fungi from true fungi as they have no close phylogenetic relationships with fungi though they are morphologically similar and exhibit absorptive nutrition. The evidences suggest that oomycetes are related to heterokont algae. The oomycetes have been treated in several ways in grouping of heterokont organisms such as the subdivision *Pseudofungi*, phylum *Heterokonta* of the kingdom *Chromista* or the subdivision *Heterokontimycotina* of the kingdom *heterokonta* (Alexopoulos, et al., 1996)

19.1.1 Vegetative Structures

Oomycota includes both unicellular, holocarpic forms and eucarpic, filamentous species composed of profusely branched and coenocytic hyphae. The hyphae grow either intercellularly (with haustoria) or intracellularly. Cell wall composition has been an important characteristic that has been used to separate *oomycota* from fungi. The cell wall of oomycetes is composed predominately of β-1, 3- and β-1, 6-glucans and cellulose rather than chitin, as is the case in the true fungi. The aminoacid hydroxyl proline also has been reported in the walls of oomycetes, an additional characteristic that separates these organisms from those of fungi.

19.1.2 Life Cycle

Most oomycetes reproduce asexually, primarily by means of heterokont zoospores. Two morphologically distinct types of biflagellate zoospores are produced in the oomycetes, although not by all species. The **primary zoospore**, which is pear shaped (pyriform) with the flagellum attached at the anterior end of the spore. The other zoospore is called **secondary zoospores**, is produced by all zoosporic oomycetes. It is kidney or bean shaped (reniform) structure with the flagella attached laterally in the groove on the spore surface (Figure 19.1).

Sexual reproduction is almost always heterogametangia. Developing antheridia are attracted to oogonia by hormones and give rise to fertilization tube only after they have become closely appressed to the surfaces of the oogonia. The haploid nucleus from antheridium is introduced in the oosphere via the fertilization tube and fuses with the nucleus of the oosphere. Following fertilization, an oosphere develops into an oospore that matures in the oogonium. Oospores are thick-walled, resistant structures capable of surviving adverse conditions. The mature oospore wall consists of

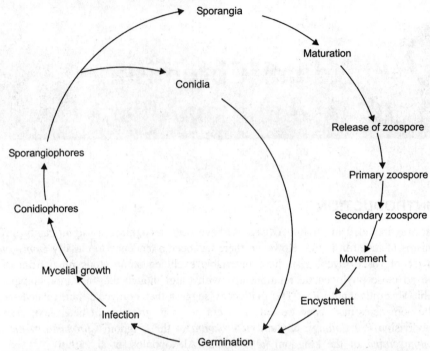

Figure 19.1 Sequence and events in asexual cycle of Peronosporales.

three layers. These include an *exospore layer* derived from residual periplasm, an epispore layer or zygote wall, and an *endospore* layer that functions, at least in part, as a carbohydrate reserve that is used or redistributed at germination. The oospore on germination gives rise to a diploid thallus.

19.1.3 The Classification

Dick (1990) recognized six orders *Leptomitales*, *Rhipidiales*, *Sclerosporales*, *Pythiales*, *Peronosporales* and *Saprolegniales*. However, in this book we are following old classification. Among them the order *Peronosporales* is most important, as the members of this group are important plant pathogens.

19.2 ORDER: PERONOSPORALES

The fungal pathogens causing damping off, white rusts and the downy mildews belong to this order. The three well-defined families—*Pythiaceae*, *Albuginaceae* and *Peronosporaceae* are delimitated on the basis of morphology of their asexual reproductive structures.

19.2.1 Family: Pythiaceae

Members generally bear their sporangia directly on the somatic hyphae. The more specialized species of *Pythiaceae* produce recognizable sporangiophores that are of indeterminate growth. The type of germination appears to be governed by environmental conditions. Dick (1990) included seven genera in the family. The most common of these genera are *Pythium* and *Phytophthora*.

Genus Pythium and plant diseases. Much of what we know about the biology of *Pythium* species has been discussed by Hendrix and Campbell (1983) and Martin (1992). The genus contains over 120 species, most of which are soil-inhabitants. The sporangia are globose to oval and are either terminal or intercalary on the somatic hyphae (Plates 19.1 and 19.2). The differentiation of zoospores takes place in the vesicle. After a short period of swimming the zoospores come to rest, encyst and germinate by germ tubes. In *P. aphanidermatum*, specific sugar residues are involved in the recognition of root surfaces by zoospores.

Most *Pythium* spp. are homothallic. In *P. debaryenum* oogonia and antheridia develop in close proximity, often on the same hypha. All steps of gametangial contact and plasmogamy leads to development of oospores. At high temperature (28°C), the oospore germinates by a germ tube, which develops into mycelium, however, at lower temperature (10–17°C) forms a vesicle in which zoospores develop (Plates 19.1 and 19.2).

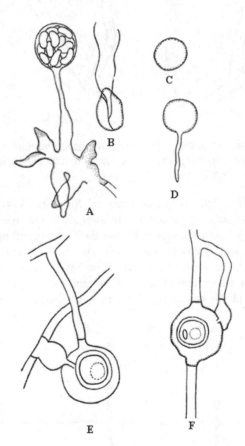

Plate 19.1 Reproductive structures of *Pythium aphanidermatum* (A) inflated filamentous zoosporangium with vesicle, (B) zoospore, (C) encysted zoospore, (D) encysted zoospore producing germ tube, (E) oogonium with intercalary antheridium and (F) oogonium with terminal antheridium.

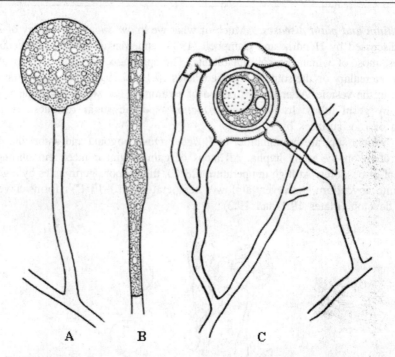

Plate 19.2 Reproductive structure of *Pythium debaryenum*. (A) terminal sporangium, (B) intercalary sporangium, (C) oogonium and atheridia and formation of oospore following fertilization.

Damping-off of seedlings. This is major problem for various horticultural crops (vegetable nurseries). In the early stages of germination the swelling seeds may be invaded by damping-off organisms and destroyed without sprouting. Before the young seedling out of soil line the radical and the plumule undergo seed decay (Figure 19.2). The most obvious symptom of damping-off is the toppling over and death of the seedlings after they have emerged from the soil. Soft, succulent seedlings usually show a water soaked zone at the soil level; this soon becomes, necrotic and shrunken (constriction) and the seedlings falls over, often before it wilts (Figure 19.2).

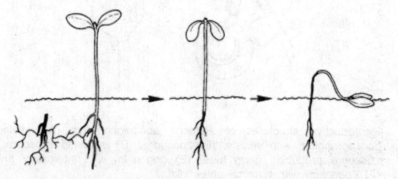

Figure 19.2 Stages in damping-off of seedling.

Damping-off may be caused by any one of the followings:

- *Pythium aphanidermatum, P. debaryanum, P. ultimum, P. irregulare* and certain species of *Phytophthora.*
- The sclerotial fungi e.g., *Rhizoctonia solani* and *Sclerotium rolfsii.*
- *Fusarium moniiliforme* and other *Fusarium* species, *Botrytis* species.
- *Macrophomina phaseoli*, a black sporeless, imperfect soil fungus.

Stem or foot rot of papaya. This is the most destructive disease of papaya, since the entire plantation of the crop can be destroyed during a growing season under congenial conditions. Besides stem rot, the disease also appears in nurseries causing damping-off of seedlings. Though younger plants in nursery may be attacked, typical stem rot symptoms, commonly develop on two to three years old plants. The disease manifests as water soaked lesions on the stem near the ground level. As a result, the terminal leaves turn yellow, droop, wilt and fall-off. The immature young fruits also drop down. In severe attack, the basal portion of the stem disintegrates completely and entire plant dies and topples down. Infected roots may also disintegrate. If fruits are formed, they shrivel and drop. Several species of *Pythium* are responsible for the disease. However, in India *Pythium aphanidermatum* is more common.

Rhizome rot of ginger. The disease is very common in India, Pakistan, Bangladesh, Sri Lanka, Japan and Fiji islands. It is particularly destructive in southern region like Kerala and Tamil Nadu. Besides fields, the pathogen attacks the rhizomes during storage also. Young shoots developing from infected rhizomes topple down due to post-emergence damping-off. Pseudostems of the plants infected after emergence withers and die, resulting in poor stands of crop. The tips of leaves turn yellow and chlorosis extends downwards resulting in the withering and final death of leaves. The base of the stem also becomes translucent, discoloured, soft and watery at the ground level. The pathogen may advance further to the rhizomes below ground. Ginger is known to be attacked by some eight species of *Pythium*. Of these, the most common species are *P. aphanidermatum* and *P. myriotylum.*

Diseases cycle and management of *Pythium*. As described in the preceding pages, the species of *Pythium* are basically soil inhabitants. The major means of survival are the oospores and limited saprophytic colonization of dead plant materials. Another possibility that help survival of *Pythium* species is their wide host range. The entire sequence/events in disease cycle caused by are shown in Figure 19.3.

To achieve economic, ecofriendly and effective management of diseases caused by *Pythium*, the major emphasis should be directed towards reduction/suppression/elimination of primary inoculum, therefore, soil sanitization and the practices that offer soil disinfestations should be part of protection strategies. Proper drainage, raised seedbeds, light sandy soils, light but frequent irrigations are recommended. Avoid high plant density, only healthy/certified seeds should be used. Recommended doses of NPK should be used. Organic amendment of soil with decomposable material like straws, oil cakes farm yard manure, compost, sawdust, green manures, etc. have been reported to reduce diseases like root rots caused by *Pythium*. Soil solarization (as discussed in chapter 12 cultural control) is the ecofriendly recommendation for raising healthy nurseries. It can be integrated with chemicals, bioagents, organic matter, cultural methods, etc. Fungicides like Thiram, Zineb, Maneb, Captan, Fytolan, Difolatan, Metalaxyl, Metalaxyl-Mancozeb, etc. have been used for seed treatment. Bioagents such as *Trichoderma harzianum, Gliocladium virens, Pseudomonas fluorescens* and *Bacillus subtilis* now available in commercial formulations should be used for seed and soil treatment for effective control.

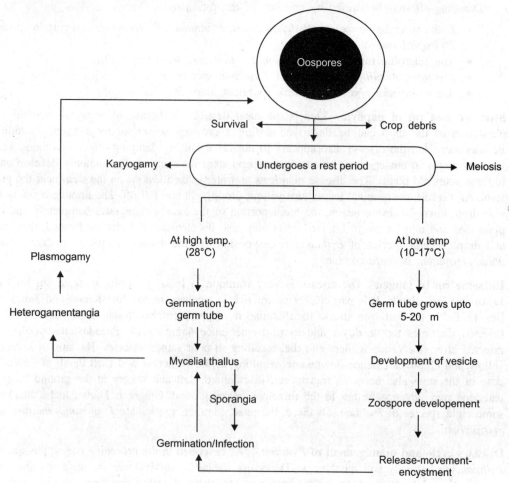

Figure 19.3 Events in disease-cycle of disease caused by *Pythium* spp.

Compost, pre-colonized by bioagents is being used by the growers for mass introduction of bioagents

Genus: Phytophthora and plant diseases. The systematics of the genus *Phytophthora* is based largely on morphological criteria of zoosporangia, gametangia and oospores. About 50 species are currently recognized together with a few varieties and *formae specialis*. *Phytophthora* species cause wide variety of disease on a large number of hosts, including both herbaceous and woody species. The best known species is *P. infestans*, the cause of late blight of potatoes and tomatoes but several other species cause destructive diseases on their hosts. *P. cactorum, P. cambivora, P. cinnamomi, P. citrophthora, P. fragariae, P. palmivora, P. capsici, P. cryptogea, P. megasperma,* and *P. parasitica* cause root, stem and fruit rots, twig blights and fruit rots of wood ornamentals and forest trees as well as of vegetables and fruit crops.

Asexual reproduction takes place by sporangia and chlamydospores. The chlamydospores are produced as additional asexual bodies. They germinate and each germ tube bears sporangia on its tips. The sporangiophores (Plate 19.3) in *Phytophthora* may be of following types:

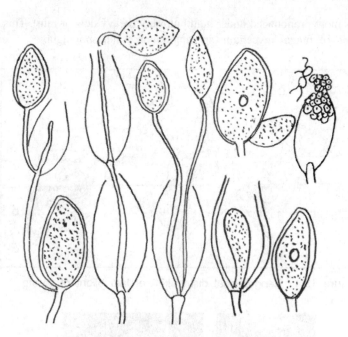

Plate 19.3 The sporangiophores in *Phytophthora* spp.

1. Compound with ultimate sporangium bearing branch a monochasial sympodium (*P. infestans* and *P. phaseoli*).
2. Simple sporangium, a single monochasial sympodium (*P. cactorum*).
3. Proliferating sporangium (*P. megasperma*).

The mode of germination of sporangia in *Phytophthora* varies depending upon environmental conditions. They may germinate directly by germ tube and/or indirectly by zoospores. The zoospores, formed within the zoosporangium, escape through apical papilla. In rare cases they pass into a vesicle and then escape by rupturing its wall.

Sexual reproduction is of *oogamous* type. The species may be homothallic (*P. cactorum* and *P. erythroseptica*) or heterothallic (*P. infestans*, *P. palmivora*, *P. arecae*). On the basis of arrangement of oogonium and antheridium, the species of *Phytophthora* have been classified into two categories: *amphigynous* and *paragynous*. The oospores germinate by the cracking of the outer wall and the inner wall forms a tube, which bears sporangium at the tip. It is believed that before germination of oospore, nuclear fusion might have occurred and the fused nucleus might have divided several times. The oospores of *P. infestans* are not common.

Late blight of potato: In recent Commonwealth Mycological Institute reports (Figure 19.4), late blight distribution is global and coincident with the distribution of potato cultivations. The disease is more severe in areas with cool, moist climatic conditions during potato growing season. Late blight of potato was responsible for historical Irish Famine, which brought the plant diseases and the science of Plant Pathology in to social recognition due to its impact on human affairs. On the leaves, lesions can be observed on the upper surface; more often near the edge or tip of the leaf with a water-soaked appearance. The lesions turn dark brown, dry and brittle after the infected leaf tissues die. On the underside of infected leaves, the edges of the lesions show a fluffy white growth

(Plate 19.4), which is more pronounced under high humidity (heavy dew or rain). This downy growth (mildew) is composed of fungal mycelium, sporangiophores and sporangia.

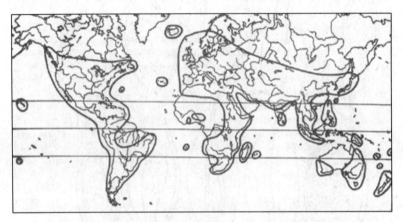

Figure 19.4 Geographical distribution of late blight of potato.

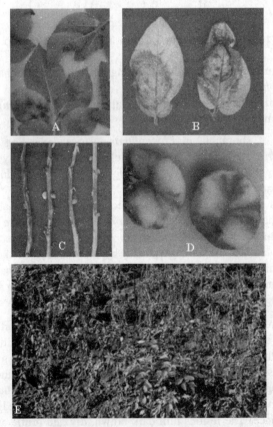

Plate 19.4 Late blight of potato, (A and B) symptoms on leaves, (C) infected stems, (D) infected tubers, (E) field view of the diseased crop.

The lesions on the stems are often black strips along the length of the stem. The infected tuber surface shows small to large, irregularly shaped purplish-brown coloured areas. Beneath the affected skin, the tuber tissue has a granular, brownish-red, dry rot that penetrates a short distance into the interior of the tuber.

The pathogen. Potato late blight is caused by the fungus *Phytophthora infestans* (Mont.) de Bary. The elongated sporangiophores are often branched and have swollen bases where sporangia are attached. Sporangia germinate at temperatures from 1.5°C to 24°C, either directly by producing germ tubes (above 15°C) or indirectly by means of zoospores (up to 15°C), which produce penetration hyphae that enter directly through the cuticle. **Sexual reproduction** in *Phytophthora infestans* is not common. In 1950s two mating types (A1 and A2) were discovered in Mexico. Sexual reproduction involves two different mating types of the fungus. In recent years, the occurrence of the A2 mating type in potatoes grown in Switzerland, Scotland, England and Asia has been reported. In addition to the mating types, the fungus population exhibits variability identified as 'races'. About 20 races have been identified on various potato genotypes. Recently, different strains of the fungus have also been detected based on their resistance or susceptibility to the biochemical action of certain fungicides. The impact of the findings of A2 in new areas, occurrence of selfing and the recent experience of formation of fungicide-tolerant strains is being explored.

The disease cycle. The disease cycle of late blight of potato is summarized in Figure 19.5. The fungal mycelium surviving with infected mother tubers, kept in cold storage, is responsible for

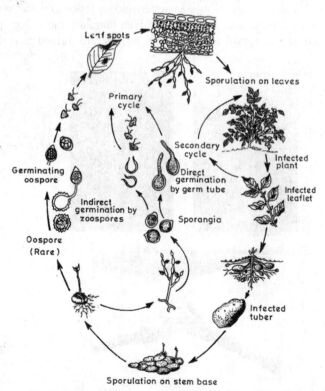

Figure 19.5 Disease cycle of late blight of potato.

initiation of disease in new season. The mycelium of the fungus grows between the plant cells and produces haustoria that invade the cells. Sporangiophores and sporangia produced in large numbers are carried by wind and water to new infection sites. Sporangia and zoospores can also move down to tubers and cause infection of tubers in soil. These infected tubers are a source of sporangia and initiate disease in next season when planted or when in cull piles. Late blight forecasting was the first disease forecasting system, it has very important role in management of disease. Late blight forecasting system has been discussed in Chapter 8.

The disease management. The integrated disease management strategy combines and integrates various options available and their need based utilization. Following steps may be involved:

- Selection of suitable resistant cultivars, viz. K. Badshah, K. Satluj, K. Jawahar, K. Pukhraj, K. Giriraj, Chipsona-1 and Chipsona-2.
- Selection of seed tubers from reliable source (only certified seed). Preferably, early date of planting as the crop can escape late blight damage.
- Need based fungicide spray depends upon prevailing weather or availability of forecasting service. The fungicides commonly recommended for prophylactic spray include mancozeb @ 0.2% or copper oxychloride @ 0.3%. If late blight attack is early in the season and weather conditions are favourable, one spray of metalaxyl + mancozeb @ 0.2% may be given.

Stem blight of pigeon pea. In 1966, the stem blight, stem canker, stem rot or Phytophthora blight joined the list of serious diseases of pigeon pea. The disease affects the crop at any growth stage. The symptoms on infected seedlings are visible as water-soaked lesions on the leaves and within 3 days the lesions become necrotic. Under conditions of high humidity the foliage gives a blighted appearance (Plate 19.5). On stems, brown to dark brown lesions, are formed near the ground level

Plate 19.5 Symptoms of Phytophthora blight of pigeon pea (A) plants leaf showing infection in field, (B) plant showing stem blight, (C & D) gall formation on basal part of stem.

or up the stem. They enlarge in size and girdle the stem/ branches (on a leaf scar or site of branch initiation). Portion of the plant above the lesions wilt. Swelling of the stem at ground level is also common (Plate 19.5). The stem lesions later develop into cankerous structures at the edges. The roots of diseased plants remain healthy although in a similar disease caused by *Phytophthora parasitica* in Australia, there is serious root rot also.

The pathogen and disease cycle. The pigeon pea blight is caused by *Phytophthora drechsleri* f. sp. *cajaini.* The sporangiophores are usually hypha-like except for the swollen tip, which develops into sporangia. Zoospores mature within the sporangia.. The thick walled oospores are spherical to globose. Chlamydospores (intercalary as well as terminal) are also formed. (Plate 19.6).

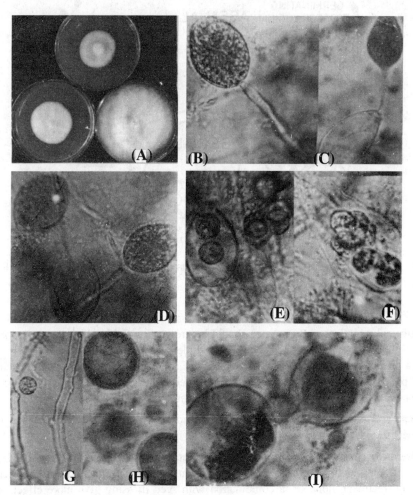

Plate 19.6   Asexual and sexual structures of *P. drechsleri* f. *sp. cajani.* (A) growth on culture media, (B, C and D) sporangiophores and sporangia, (E and F) development and release of zoospores, (G) Encysted zoospore, (H) oogonia, (I) developieng oospores.

The pathogen is capable of surviving in soil (infected debris) for at least one year. Oospores and chlamydospores are the main structures of survival. At the onset of rainy season, oospores germinate by sporangia and on germ tube causes infection of young seedlings. Events and sequences in disease cycle are shown in Figure 19.6.

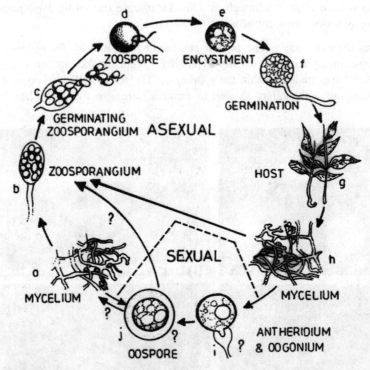

Figure 19.6   Disease cycle of *P. drechsleri* f. sp. *cajani*. (*Source:* Plant Diseases of International Importance, vol. I).

Disease Management

(a) **Cultural practices.**   Pigeon pea should be grown in a field, which has no record of blight in the past. Low lying fields should be avoided. In disease prone areas, sowing of pigeon pea on ridges has been an effective method. Crop rotation, wide inter-row spacing and use of potassium fertilizers are other recommended cultural practices. Intercropping of pigeon pea with low height legumes such as urad and moong has been suggested.

(b) **Host resistance.**   ICRISAT has identified sources of resistance. Resistance is unstable when tested against different isolates of the pathogen.

(c) **Chemical control.**   Seed treatment with Metalaxyl + Mancozeb (Ridomil MZ) provides effective protection upto 15 days after sowing. Seed dressing alone is not effective but spray treatment alone or in combination with seed dressing give more effective chemical control of the disease.

(d) **Biological control.**   *Trichoderma viride*, *T. hamatum*, strains of *Pseudomonas fluorescens* and *Bacillus subitilis* are potential antagonists of *P. drechsleri* f. sp. *cajani*. They are also compatible with recommended fungicides (Metalaxyl, Captan, Captafol, Thiram and Carbendazim). Coating pigeon pea seeds with an antagonist in the presence of a compatible fungicide has also been attempted.

Buckeye rot of tomato. The hot and humid conditions, during growing season, not only favour the luxuriant growth of tomato crop but also favours the development of various diseases, of which buckeye rot (*Phytophthora nicotianae* var. *parasitica*) is the most destructive. In India, losses from this disease range from 35–40 per cent. The pathogen has been reported to attack the plants at all the growth stages, causing damping-off, collar rot and stem canker, blossom blight and buckeye fruit rot. The symptoms appear as water soaked light brown discoloured spots. These spots increase readily showing concentric dark brown rings slightly resembling the markings on a buckeye nut (horse chestnut) (Figure 19.7). The lesions rapidly enlarge and in 3–4 days, whole of the fruit surface turn dark brown and feel soft to touch. White flocculent superficial growth of the fungus consisting of sporangia develops profusely on the diseased fruits in warm and humid weather. Immature green fruits in contact with soil or near to soil level are most vulnerable.

Figure 19.7 Symptom buckeye rot of tomato.

The mycelium of the pathogen *P. nicotianae* var *parasitica* is hyaline; the sporangiophores arise from hyphal threads and produce sporangia, which germinate by releasing 8–16 zoospores Chlamydospores and oospores are produced at different stages of disease cycle. The pathogen over-winter in the soil as oospores and/or chlamydospores and can remain viable till next season. The fungus has also been reported to be internally seed borne and remains viable for more than one and half year.

With the onset of monsoon rains, the oospores and chlamydospores produce mycelium and sporangia (Figure 19.8). The sporangia in turn produce zoospores the source of primary infection. Figure 19.8 explains the steps that follow in disease cycle. Sharma, *et al.*, (1978) developed a short term forecasting method. The disease is not expected at or below 20°C but 22.5°C or above with slight rainfall (10 mm) will result in its appearance. The disease is not expected to be serious above 25°C.

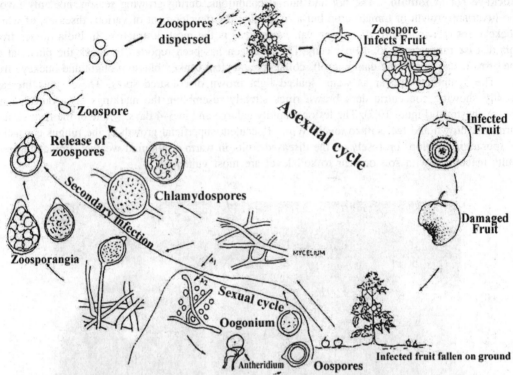

Figure 19.8 Disease cycle of Buckeye rot of tomato (*P. nicotianae* var *parasitica*).

Disease management. Sprays of dithane M-45 or bordeaux mixture or captafol along with staking and removal of infected foliage and fruits have been effective and economical (Sharma, 1992). Integration of fungicide (Indofil M-45, 0.25%) sprays, cultural practices like periodical clipping of lower leaves (15-20 cm), weeding, mulching with white polythene sheet and removal of affected fruits regularly not only reduced disease incidence drastically but also increase fruit yields appreciably.

Phytophthora diseases of citrus. *Phytophthora* spp. cause the most serious soil borne diseases of citrus. Losses occur due to attack at different stages, e.g., damping-off of seedlings, root and crown rot in nurseries, and from foot rot, fibrous root rot and brown rot of fruits in orchards. The typical symptom results when the soil or seed borne fungus penetrates the stem just above the soil line and cause seedlings to topple. *Phytophthora* spp. also cause seed rot and pre-emergence rot. Foot rot results from an infection of the scion near the ground level, producing lesions, which extend down to the bud union on resistant rootstocks. Crown root rot or gummosis may refer to rotting of the bark anywhere on the scion of the tree. From the infected part abundant gum exudation occurs. Lesions spread around the circumference of the trunk, slowly girdling the tree. Badly affected trees have pale green leaves with yellow veins, a typical girdling effect (Figure 19.9). *Phytophthora* spp. infect the root cortex and cause decay of fibrous roots. Later the cortex turns soft, becomes discoloured, and appears water soaked. The fibrous roots slough their cortex leaving only the white, thread-like stele, which gives the root system a stringy appearance (Figure 19.10). *Phytophthora* infection of fruits produce a decay in which the affected area is light brown, leathery and not sunken compared to the adjacent rind. White mycelium forms on the rind surface under humid conditions.

Figure 19.9 *Phytophthora* induced foot rot lesion. (*Source:* Graham and Timmer, 1992, Plant diseases of international importance, vol. III).

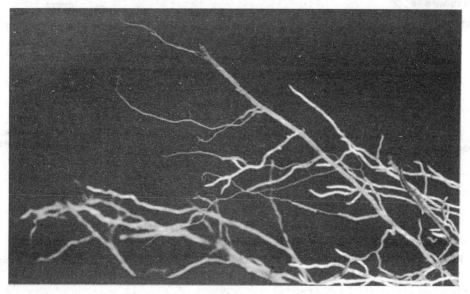

Figure 19.10 Fibrous root rot of citrus caused by *Phytophthora parasitica.* The roots slough their cortex leaving only the white, thread-like stele, which gives the root system a stringy appearance. (*Source:* Graham and Timmer, 1992, Plant diseases of international importance, vol. III).

The pathogen and disease cycle. The most widespread and important *Phytophthora* spp. are *P. parasitica* Dast. and *P. citrophthora* (R.E. Sm and E.H. Sm.) Leonian. *P. Parasitica* is more common in subtropical areas and causes foot rot, gummosis and root rot but usually does not infect above the ground parts. *P. citrophthora* causes gummosis and root rot in mediterranean climates. It attacks aerial parts of the trunk and is most commonly the cause of brown rot. *P. hibernalis* Carne and *P. syringae* Kleb attack citrus fruit to a limited extent in areas with cool moist winters. *P. palmivora* (Butler) Butler and *P. citricola* Saw.are reported to attack citrus in some tropical areas.

Phytophthora spp. are widespread in most citrus orchards. The disease cycle as it occurs under most conditions are portrayed in Figure 19.11. In case of *P. parasitica*, the fungus most likely survives unfavourable periods in root debris. The rotted cortex is sloughed and the fungus produces chlamydospores, which may persist in soil for long periods. When favourable conditions return, chlamydospores germinate indirectly to produce sporangia and zoospores or directly to produce mycelium. When both mating types are present, oospores may also be produced and aid in survival of the fungus. With *P. citrophthora*, which often does not produce chlamydospores or oospores the mechanism of survival is uncertain. However, both species may persist as mycelium or as sporangia in infected living roots.

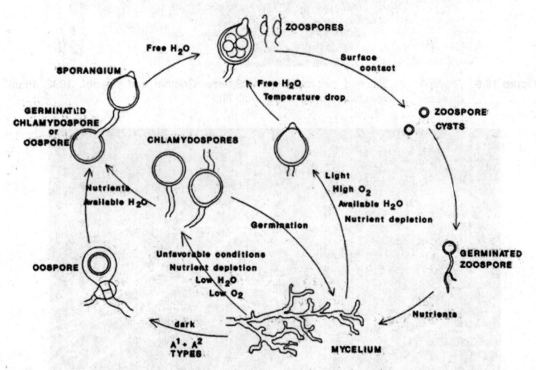

Figure 19.11 Life cycle of *P. parasitica*. (*Source:* Graham and Timmer, 1992, Plant diseases of international importance, vol. III).

Disease management. Citrus nurseries should be maintained free of *Phytophthora* spp. to avoid dissemination of the pathogen to new orchard. The citrus nurseries should be solarized or fumigated. Certain phytosanitary practices should also be followed to keep the inoculum levels under check.

Planting materials should be used from sources known to be free of the disease. Care must be taken not to allow run-off-water from contaminated areas to enter disease free zones. The systemic fungicides, metalaxyl and fosetyl-Al, are highly effective against *Phytophthora* spp.

Budding the root stock seedlings well above the soil line will help reduce foot rot incidence. Where foot rot incidence is high, it may be necessary to apply soil treatments of metalaxyl or foliar sprays of fosetyl-Al to protect healthy trees. Brown rot losses can be reduced by avoiding sprinklers used for irrigation. Copper fungicides or captan applied are usually quite effective. Post-harvest applications of the systemic fungicides fosetyl-AL and metalaxyl to the canopy provide effective control of brown rot.

Phytophthora root rot of avocado.   Phytophthora root rot of avocado (*Persea amercana* Mill.) is caused by *Phytophthora cinnamomi* Rands. The disease is widespread and occurs in most avocados growing countries (Figure 19.12). It is a major limiting factor in production of this fruit crop. Gradual decline or dieback of the foliage followed by progressive defoliation gives a sparse appearance to the trees. The leaves are smaller and pale. Early symptoms of root rot are often detectable at the top of the tree, where the first signs of branch dieback may be visible. Eventually, the tree may be totally defoliated and die. Below ground, the symptoms consist of a distinct absence of healthy feeder roots, many of the smaller feeder roots are black and brittle.

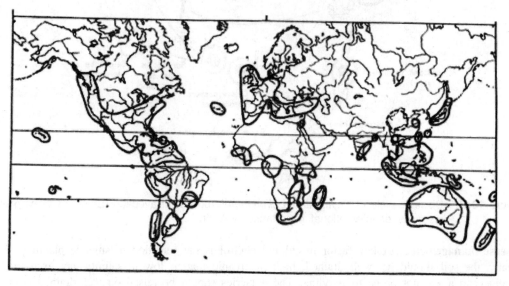

Figure 19.12 Distribution of Phytophthora cinnamomi.

The pathogen and disease cycle.   The pathogen, *Phytophthora cinnamomi* Rands, produces non-papillate sporangia and is heterothallic with two compatible types designated A1 and A2. The fungus survives primarily as chlamydospores in decaying feeder roots. They germinate by producing several germ tubes. Sporangia germinate indirectly by releasing 10 to 30 zoospores. The role of oospores in survival is less certain. (Figure 19.13).

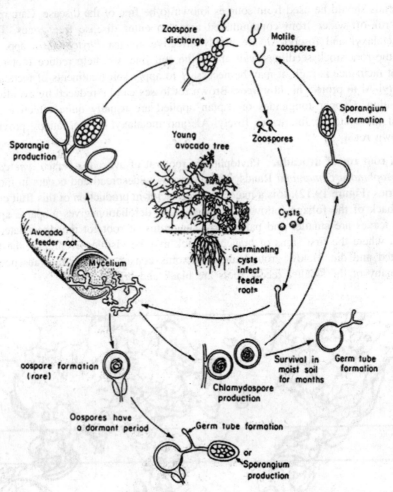

Figure 19.13 Disease cycle of *Phytophthora cinnamomi*, root rot of avocado (Source: Coffey, plant diseases of international importance, vol. III).

Disease management. A key factor in cultural control is the selection of suitable planting site. Ideally, the soil should be, well drained, high in organic matter, low in salinity, not excessively alkaline and a site not prone to flooding. The nurseries should be raised on well-drained potting mixture. The mixture should be fumigated or alternately subjected to thermal treatment, either steamed at 100°C for 30 min or steamed at 60°C for 30 min. Soil solarized for about 4-8 weeks will also be good source to prepare the mix and the technique is cheap, easy, economical and effective. The movement of water from contaminated/infested area must be appropriately regulated. In recent years, two existing classes of fungicides—phenylamides, notable metalaxyl and the phosphonate, especially potassium phosphonate and fosetyl aluminium have given good control of the disease.

19.2.2 Family: Peronosporaceae

Fungal genera belonging to family **Peronosporaceae** are among most important plant pathogens. This is the most advanced family of the order Peronosporales. All the species are obligate parasites of vascular plants, causing diseases called **downy mildews**. Life histories of all species follow the same general pattern, which is similar to that of *Pythium* and *Phytophthora* explained in Figures 19.3 and 19.5.

Identification of Important Genera (Plate 19.7)

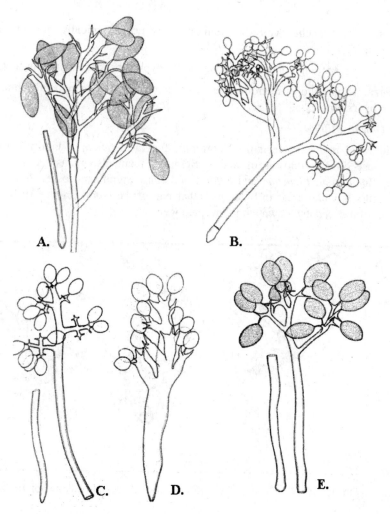

Plate 19.7 Sporophores and spores of some downy mildew fungi. (A) *Perenospora*, (B) *Bremia*, (C) *Plasmopara*, (D) *Sclerospora*, (E). *Pseudospernospora*.

Basidiophora. The sporangiophores are club shaped with swollen head over which the sporangia are borne on minute sterigmata.

Bremia. Similar to *Peronospora* except that the tips of the branches are expanded into cup shaped apophyses with four sterigmata each, bearing sporangia.

Bremiella. It differs from *Bremia* in having the tips of its branches inflated into bulbous apophyses on which sterigmata bearing sporangia are produced.

Peronospora. The sporangiophores are dichotomously branched at acute angles and taper to gracefully curve pointed tips on which spores are borne.

Peronosclerospora. The genus *Sclerospora* was divided into two subgenera, *Eusclerospora* and *Peronosclerospora*, which are differentiated by the formation of sporangia in the former and conidia in the latter.

Plasmopara. The branches and their subdivisions occur typically at right angles and are irregularly spaced.

Sclerospora. The sporangiophore is a long, stout hypha, bearing sporangia at the tips.

Sclerophthora. Sporophores micronemous, short unbranched or sympodially branched, sporangia germinating by zoospores.

Important Downy Mildews

Downy mildew of maize. Specialized biotrophic fungal members of family Peronosporaceae are known to cause downy mildews of maize. Some of them also parasitize species of *Sorghum*, *Saccharum*, *Pennisetum*, *Eleucine*, and *Setaria* and cause significant losses. Maize downy mildew, *P. sorghi*, occurs in wider areas in India and other part of the world (Figure 19.14). Varied types of symptoms are produced by downy mildew pathogens:

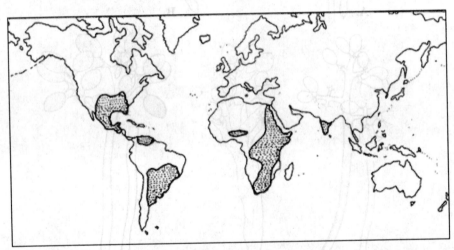

Figure 19.14 Geographical distribution of downy mildew of maize.

- *Sclerophthora rayssiae* var. *zeae* causes local infections (Plate 19.8) in the form of chlorotic to yellow streaks. They turn purplish with age. Severe infections result into blighting of the foliage. Malformation of plants and shredding of leaves does not occur.
- *P. phillipinensis* principally causes systemic infections. Long, light yellow stripes become conspicuous first in the basal regions of the young and newly developed leaves. Systemically infected plants are severely stunted. Tassels may become variously malformed.

Plate 19.8   Symptoms of downy mildews of maize showing downy growth (A and B), chlorotic stripes (C and D), and crazy top (E).

- *S. microspora* induces varied types of symptoms, the earliest symptoms include excessive tillering and rolling and twisting of the upper leaves and distortion of the plants.
- In plants systemically infected with *P. sorghi*, yellowing develops from the basal region of leaves. Plants produce smaller cobs and malformed tassels. *P. sacchari* like *P. phillipinensis*, develops chlorotic stripes supporting conspicuous white growth on down surface of maize leaves.

The pathogen.   Eleven different fungal species belonging to three genera of *Peronosporaceae* are reported to cause downy mildew of maize. Eight of the species belong to the genus *Peronosclerospora*, two to *Sclerophthora* and one to *Sclerospora*. The present binomials of *Sclerospora*, their synonyms, and the common names of downy mildews caused are given in Table 19.1.

Table 19.1 Binomials and Symptoms of Maize Downy Mildew Pathogens and Common Names of Downy Mildew caused by them.

Present Binomial	Synonyms	Common name
Peronosclerospora maydis (Racib.) C.G. Shaw	Peronospora maydis Racib. Sclerospora maydis (Racib.) Butl.Sclerospora javanica (Palm)	Java downy mildew
Peronosclerospora miscanthi (Maiyake) C.G. Shaw	Sclerospora miscanthi Miyake	Leaf-splitting downy mildew
Peronosclerospora phillippinensis (Weston) C.G. Shaw	Sclerospora philippinensis Weston Sclerospora indica Butl.	Philippine downy mildew
Peronosclerospora sorghi (Weston and Uppal) C.G. Shaw	Sclerospora graminicola (Sacc.) de By. Sclerospora graminicola var. andropotgonis-sorghi Kulkarni Sclerospora sorghi Weston & Uppal Sclerospora andropogonis-sorghi (Kulkarni) Mundkur Sclerospora-vulgaris (Kulkarni) Mundkur	Sorghum downy mildew
Peronosclerospora spontanea (Weston) C.G. Shaw	Sclerospora spontanea Weston	Spontaneum downy mildew
Peronosclerospora sacchari (Miyake) Sharai and K. Hara	Sclerospora sacchari Miyake	Sugarcane downy mildew
Peronosclerospora heteropogoni Siradhana, et al.	Sclerospore sorghi Weston & Uppal	Rajasthan downy mildew
Peronosclerospora sp. Nov. Prabhu et al.	—	—
Sclerospora graminicola (Saac.) de Bary.	Protomyces graminicola Sacc. Peronospora graminicola Sacc. Peronospora setariae Pass. Ustilago(?) urbani Magnus	Graminicola downy mildew
Sclerophthora macrospora (Sacc.) Thirum. Shaw & Naras.	Scleroerospora macrospora Sacc. Phytophthora macrospora (Sacc.) Ito & Tanaka Sclerospora kriegeriana Magnus Sclerospora aryzae Brizi Nozenia macrospora (Sacc.) Tsugi	Crazy top downy mildew
Sclerophthora rayssiae var. zeae (Payak & Renfro)	—	Brown stripe downy mildew (BSDM)

An evolutionary trend is traceable within the genera *Sclerophthora*, *Sclerospora* and *Peronosclerospora*. This, alongwith their possible relationship with other members of *Peronosporaceae*, is presented in Figure 19.15.

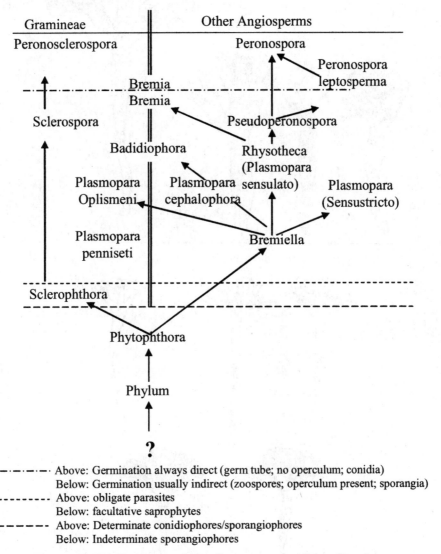

Figure 19.15 Phylogeny of the Peronosporales (from Shaw).

In asexual state of *Bremia* an operculum is present, and thus a sporangium is produced. Although liberation of zoospores has been reported, most workers report germ tube germination. One species of *Basidiophora* and *Bremia* each and two species of *Plasmopara* are reported on *Gramineae*.

Asexual phase. The informations pertaining to asexual structures are summarized in (Table 19.2) Plate 19.9.

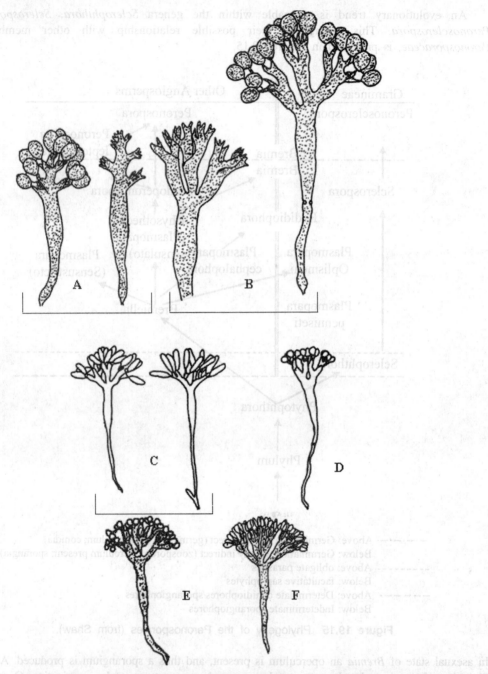

Plate 19.9 Comparative morphology of Sporangiophores of *Sclerospora graminicola.* (A); conidiophores of *Perenosclerospora sorghi* (B); conidiophores of *Perenosclerospora spontanea* (C); *P. sorghi* (D): *P. maydis* (E), and *P. philippinensis (F)*. (From: Weston and Uppal, 1973; Titatarn and Syamananda, 1978).

Table 19.2 Morphological Characteristics of Asexual Spores of Different Maize Downy Mildew Pathogens

Pathogen	Nature of spore	Shape of spore	Size of spore (μm)	Size of sporangiophores (μm)
P. sorghi	Conidia	Globose, ovoid-round	15–29 × 15–27	180–300
P. heteropogoni	Conidia	Globose, ovoid-round	17.7 × 16.2	87.2–142.8
Peronosclerospora spp.	Conidia	Round	15.6 – 18.7	—
P. maydis	Conidia	Round	18–45 × 16–22	150–200
P. sacchari	Conidia	Long, cylindrical-ovoid	24–35 × 11–23	190–280
P. miscanthi	Conidia	Long, cylindrical-ovoid	31–48 × 14–23	97–300
P. philippinensis	Conidia	Long, cylindrical-ovoid	14–44 × 11–27	150–400
P. spontanea	Conidia	Long, cylindrical-ovoid	25–65 × 11–21 (39–45 × 15–17)	350–500
S. graminicola	Sporangia	Globose, ovoid-round	19–21 × 12–21	100
S. macrospora	Sporangia	Elongated, apex truncate or rounded poroid	60–100 × 43–64	—
S. rayssiae var. zeae	Sporangia	Elongated, apex truncate or rounded poroid	29–66.5 × 18–26	—

Sexual phase. Species of *Sclerophthora*, *Sclerospora* and *Peronospora*, with the exception of *P. maydis*, are reported to develop oospores in maize tissues. The mode of oospore germination varies with the organism and the conditions available. Oospores of *S. macrospora* germinate to develop a sporangiophore with a terminal sporangium. Oospores of *Peronosclerospora* form coenocytic germ tubes or *S. graminicola* germinate directly by putting out a germ tube or a germ sporangium.

Disease cycle and management. Several collateral and overwintering host contribute to survival of downy mildew pathogens. *H. contorths*, a wild host, supporting conidia and oospores of *P. sorghi*, and *P. heteropogoni* provides inocula of these pathogens in India (Figure 19.16). *P. Phillipinensis* parasitizes *S. spontaneum* in North India. The continuity of cultivation of maize in different months of the year helps to maintain inoculum of *P. Phillipinensis* across the crop season in the Philippines. The presence of mycelia of *P. maydis*, *P. phillipinsis*, *P. sacchari*, *P. sorghi*, *S. rayssial* var. *Zeae* and *S. macrospora* in maize seeds has been reported.

Three approaches to the management of downy mildew of maize are: (a) cultural practices, (b) use of fungicides and (c) planting of resistant varieties. The cultural practices aim at prevention of infection.

- Collateral/wild hosts and diseased crop debris must be destroyed and suitable long rotations should be adopted.
- Several fungicides have been recommended for use as seed treatment as well as foliar sprays. Four to six sprays of dithane M-45 (0.3%), Dithane M-22 (0.3%), Blitox-50 and Dithane Z-78 (0.3%) have given good control. Seed treatment with Demonsan, rogueing of diseased young plants alongwith single spray of neem oil has been found effective. Seed treatment with metalaxyl (Ridomil 25 WP) @ 4 g/kg seed is effective. Single spray of Ridomil MZ @ 6 g/litre is very useful.

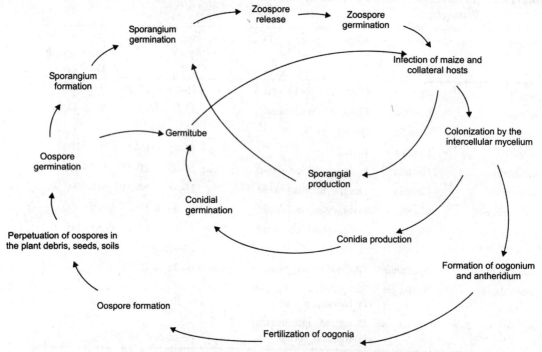

Figure 19.16 Disease cycle of downy mildew of maize.

Downy mildew (Blue mould) of tobacco. First reported in Australia in 1891, the disease has since been reported in USA, Canada, Brazil, Argentina, Chile and Cuba (Figure 19.17). Losses can be very heavy, as in 1979, when more than 90% of the tobacco crop in Cuba was destroyed by blue mould.

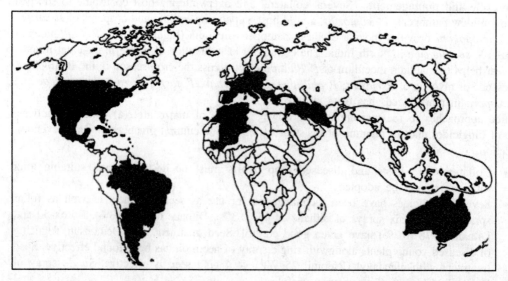

Figure 19.17 Area of blue mould infestation (Black) and areas free of blue mould (Circled).

On young seedlings symptoms may be confused with cold injury or damping-off. Young plants, less than a month old, are very susceptible and may be killed outright. Seedlings show clear round yellow spots on the upper surface with corresponding grey or bluish downy mould on the lower surface of the leaf (blue mould). Infection may also become systemic. In the field, infection begins on the lower leaves (Plate 19.10), with a typical purplish to grayish sporulation on the lower surface.

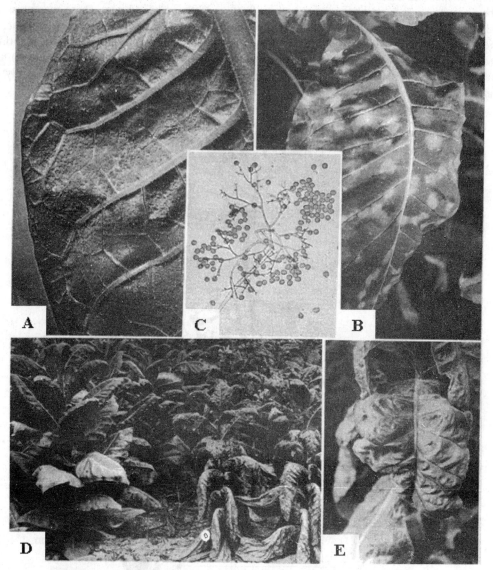

Plate 19.10 (A) Blue mould symptoms on mature leaf, (B) fructification (downy growth) on the lower side of a leaf, (C) conidiophore and conidia of *P. tabacina,* (D) comparison between a resistant (left) and a susceptible cultivar (right), (E) systemic symptoms of blue mould on a leaf. (*Source:* Delon and Schiltz, Plant diseases of internatinal importance, vol. IV).

The pathogen, disease cycle and management. The pathogen can survive as mycelium and over winter in the host tissues of volunteer crops. Under suitable conditions, the fungus grows and subsequently sporulates on the leaves constituting the primary source of infection (Figure 19.18). The pathogen may also be maintained from one season to another through wild species (e.g., *N. repanda* in US and *N. glauca* in Europe). Simple and economic measures to reduce carry over of inoculum include the destruction of host such as ornamental tobacco or crop residues, the burning of tobacco remains and the choice of inoculum free seedbeds and field site. These measures are nevertheless not sufficient in themselves to control the disease. Sources of resistance to *P. tabacina* are present in the genus *Nicotiana*. After initial success of dithiocarbamates and copper-oxychloride, applied before the disease appearance, the introduction of anti-oomycetes fungicide (Metalaxyl) has invariably been recommended for better and longer protection. Metalaxyl should be used only in mixtures with a protectant fungicide.

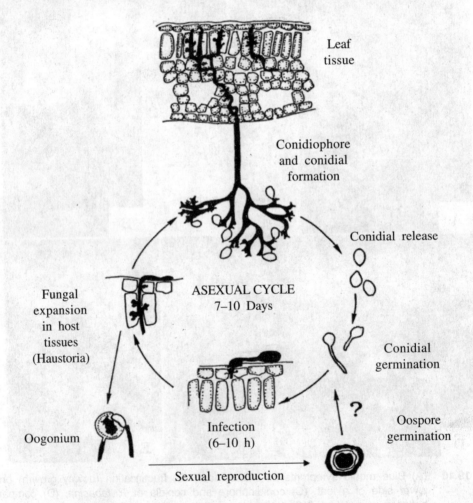

Figure 19.18 Life cycle of *P. tabacina*. (*Source:* Delon and Schiltz, Plant diseases of international importance, vol. IV).

Downy mildew of grapes. Downy mildew is one of the destructive fungal disease of grapevines. It has been reported in 91 countries, from temperate zones to the tropics (Figure 19.19). Most economic losses are associated with cluster destruction and loss of vine foliage. Symptoms of the disease appear on all aerial and tender parts of the vine, they are more pronounced on leaves, young shoots and immature berries. On upper surface of leaves, irregular light yellow spots are seen (Figure 19.20). On the down surface, below these spots, downy growth of the fungus is present (Figure 19.20), which becomes dirty gray. Diseased shoots remain stunted, and due to hypertrophy, may become swollen.

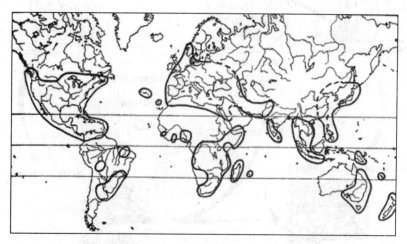

Figure 19.19 Geographical distribution of downy mildew of grape.

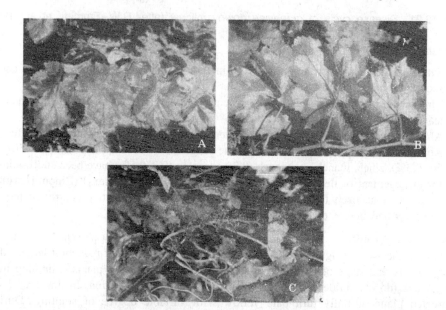

Figure 19.20 Symptoms of downy mildew of grape (A) spots on upper surface of leaves, (B) spots on under side of leaves, (C) bunch-rot.

The pathogen and disease cycle. The disease is caused by *Plasmopara viticola* (B & C) Berl. and de T. Oospores formed in infected leaves during late summer and autumn and survive in leaf debris for at least two years in or on the soil surface (Figure 19.21). When mature, they germinate to produce a sporangium that release zoospores. Inoculum for primary infection arises from either airborne sporangia or splash-dispersed.

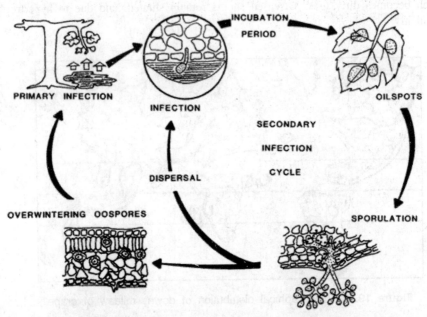

Figure 19.21 Disease cycle of grapevine downy mildew (after R.W. Emmett, et al., 1992).

Disease management

- Sanitation can play very important role in disease management. Fallen leaves and twigs should be collected and burnt.
- Vines should be planted with proper spacing and should be trained in such a manner that leaves are not near the soil surface.
- Among resistant varieties are: Amber Queen, Champion, Cardinal, Champa and Red Sultan.
- Application of copper and dithiocarbamate fungicides. Bordeaux mixture (4: 4:50), Blitox, 50 (0.3%), zineb, maneb, mancozeb (0.2%), captan (0.2–0.5%) have been successfully used for management of disease. Since mid 1970s, mixture of metalaxyl (Ridomil) with either copper or mancozeb fungicides have been found to give effective control of the disease when applied before or after infection.

Downy mildew pearl millet. Downy mildew of pearl millet is widely present in temperate and tropical areas of the world (Figure 19.22). The magnitude of grain yield reduction largely depends on disease severity and stage of crop infection. Total loss may occur in plants exhibiting infection in seedling stage (downy mildew) and green ear during ear head infection. In the downy mildew phase, infected plants initially turn pale yellow with variable degree of stunting. During the advanced stage, the entire foliage becomes white due to presence of fungal growth. In a majority of the cases, chlorotic streaks with downy growth of the fungus appear on the undersurface of the

The pathogen. The *Albugo candida* produces short and club shaped sporangiophores in close proximity to one another in solid layers or beds immediately below the host epidermis. Each sporangiophore gives rise to several sporangia that it produces in succession, (oldest at the tip and the youngest at the base) (Plate 19.13). Oogonium and antheridium are formed within the host tissues. The oospore germinates to form zoospores that eventually encyst and germinate by germ tubes to complete the life cycle.

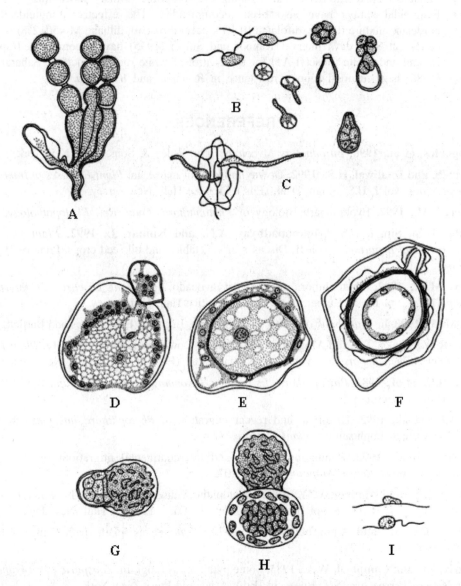

Plate 19.13 Stages in life cycle of *Albugo candida*. (A) sporangiophores and sporangia, (B) release, encystment and gemination of zoospores, (C) stomatal penetration, (D and F) formation of oospores, (G and I) germination of oospore.

Disease cycle and management. The pathogen perpetuates through the oospores formed in disease host tissues lying in the soil or moving with diseased plant pieces along with the seed. Weed host constantly present in the nature may also serve as a source of primary inoculum.

- Since the source of primary inoculum is the oospores lodged in the soil or with the seeds, therefore use of clean, healthy and certified seed should be given priority.
- The weeds that are suspected to harbour the pathogen should be destroyed.
- Suitable crop rotation helps in avoiding the soil-borne primary inoculum.
- Fungicidal sprays have also been recommended. The effective fungicides include bordeaux mixture (0.8%), difolatan (0.3%), daconil (0.1%), dithane M-45(0.2%) or ridomil (0.1%) at 8-10 days interval Kapoor and Suhan (1995) have recommended sprays of ridomil and aliette (Fosetyl A1) for the control of white rust of crucifers. Saharan, et al., (1988) have reported sources resistance in *B. napus* and *B. juncea.*

REFERENCES

Alexopoulos, et al., 1996, *Introductory Mycology*, John Wiley & Sons, INC, New York.

Bains, S.S. and Dhaliwal, H.S., 1992, Downy mildews of maize, In: *Plant Diseases of International Importance,* vol I, U.S. Singh, et al. (Eds.), Prentice Hall, New Jersey.

Brasier, C.M., 1992, Evolutionary Biology of *Phytophthora, Annu. Rev. Phytopathology*, 30:153.

Chaube, H.S., Singh, U.S., Mukhopadhyay, A.N. and Kumar, J., 1992, *Plant Diseases of International Importance*, vol. II, Diseases of vegetables and oil seed crops, Prentice Hall, New Jersey.

Coffey, M.D., 1992, Phytophthora root rot of avocado, In: *Plant Diseases of International Importance*, vol III, J., Kumar, et al. (Eds.), Prentice Hall, New Jersey.

Dick, M.W., 1990, In: *Handbook of Protoctista Margulis*, L. et al., (Eds.), Jones and Bartlett, Boston.

Emett, R.W., Wicks, T.J. and Magarrey, P.A., 1992, Downy mildew of grape, In: *Plant Diseases of International Importance,* vol III, J. Kumar, et al. (Eds.), Prentice Hall, New Jersey.

Erwin, D.C., et al., 1983, *Phytophthora*: *Its Biology, Taxonomy, Ecology and Pathology*, APS Press, St. Paul, Minnesota.

Fry, W.E., et al., 1993, Historical and recent migration of *Phytophthora infestans*: chronology, pathways, and implications, *Plant Disease*, 77:633.

Fry, W.E., et al., 1993, Population genetics and intercontinental migrations of *Phytophthora infestans*, *Annu. Rev. Phytopathology,* 30:107.

Graham, J.H., and Timmer, L.W., 1992, Phytophthora diseases of citrus, In: *Plant Diseases of International Importance,* vol III, Kumar, J., et al. (Eds.), Prentice Hall, New Jersey.

Hendrix, F.F. Jr. and Campbell, W.A., 1973, *Pythium* as plant pathogens, *Annu. Rev. Phytopathology*, 11:77.

Hendrix, F.F. and Campbell, W.A., 1983, Some pythiaceous fungi, In: *Zoosporic Plant Pathogens— A Modern Perspective*, S.T. Buezachi (Ed.), Academic Press, New York.

Hooker, W.J., 1981, Compendium of potato diseases, *Amer. Phytopath. Soc.,* Minnesota, 125.

Ko, W.H., 1992, Phytophthora root rot of papaya, In: *Plant Diseases of International Importance*, vol III, J. Kumar, et al. (Eds.), Prentice Hall, New Jersey.

Kumar, J., Chaube, H.S., Singh, U.S., and Mukhopadhyay, A.N., 1992, Diseases of fruit crops, *Plant Diseases of International Importance*, vol III, Prentice Hall, New Jersey.

Martin, F.N., 1992, Pythium, In: *Methods for Research on Soil Borne Phytopathogenic Fungi*. L.L. Singleton, et al. (Eds.), APS Press, St. Paul., Minnesota.

Mckeen, W.E. (Ed.), 1989, *Blue Mould of Tobacco*, APS Press, St. Paul, Minnesota.

Platt, H.W., (Bud) 1992, Potato late blight, In: *Plant Diseases of International Importance*, vol. II, H.S. Chaube, et al. (Eds.), Prentice Hall, New Jersey.

Sharma, A.K., 1992, Integrated management of Buckeye rot of summer tomatoes in the hills, *Indian J. Mycol. Pl. Pathol.*, 22:287.

Sharma, S.L., et al., 1978, Epidemiology and forecasting of tomato buckeye rot, *Indian Phytopat.*, 31:424.

Singh, R.S., 1998, *Plant Disease*, 7th ed., Oxford and IBH Publishing Co. Pvt. Ltd., New Delhi.

Singh, R.S., 2000, *Diseases of Fruit Crops*, Science Publishers, Inc., Enfield (NH) USA, Plymonth, UK.

Singh, U.P. and Chauhan, V.B., 1992, Phytophthora blight of pigeon pea, In: *Plant Diseases of International Importance*, vol. I, U.S. Singh, et al. (Eds.), Prentice Hall, New Jersey.

Singh, U.S., Mukhopadhyay, A.N., Kumar, J. and Chaube, H.S., 1992, *Plant Diseases of International Importance*, vol. I, Diseases of cereals and pulses: Prentice Hall, New Jersey.

Spencer, D.M. (Ed.), 1981, *The Downy Mildews*, Academic Press, New York.

Thakur, D.P., 1992, Downy mildew of pearl millet, In: *Plant Diseases of International Importance*, vol. I, U.S. Singh, et al. (Eds.), Prentice Hall, New Jersey.

Waterhouse, G.M., 1968, The Genus *Pythium*, *Mycol. Pap.*, 110:1–7

Waterhouse, G.M., 1973, *Peronosporales*, In: *The Fungi, an Advanced Treatise,* G.C. Ainsworth, et al., (Eds.), Academic Press, New York.

20 Phylum: Chytridiomycota and Plant Diseases

20.1 INTRODUCTION

The phylum contains the single class Chytridiomycetes. These are the only members of kingdom Fungi that produce motile cells at some stage in their life cycle. Except for a few species with polyflagellate cells, (zoospores and gametes), most possess a single posteriorly directed whiplash flagellum. There are a number of chytrids that are of some direct importance to humans. Plant pathogenic species include *Synchytrium endobioticum*, *Olpidium brassicae*, *Physoderma maydis*, and *Urophlyctis alfalfae*. The latter two species cause minor diseases known respectively, as brown spot of maize and crown wart of alfalfa. *S. endobioticum* causes black wart of potatoes while *O. brasicae*, a parasite of cabbage roots, is an important vector for a number of plant viruses. The class Chytridiomyates is divided into four orders Chytridiales, Spizellomycetales, Blastocladiales and Monoblepharidales (Barr, 1980, 1983).

20.2 ORDER: CHYTRIDIALES

This order is defined on the basis of zoospore ultra structure. The zoospores are characterized by a constellation of characters. One or more mitochondria are included in the microbody lipid globule complex (**MLC**) of the zoospore and the nucleus appears to occupy the space not taken by microbody lipid globule complex (**MLC**) and the ribosomes. The nucleus is not connected to the kinetosome. The ribosome do not occur dispersed throughout the cell but rather, are packed by a double membrane in the central part of the cell. Rootlet microtubules typically extend from the side of the kinetosome into the cytoplasm (Alexopoulos, *et al.*, 1996). Most members of this order are water-or soil inhabiting fungi. Some of the better-known genera are *Chytridium*, *Chytridiomyces*, *Polyphagus*, *Rhizophydium*, *Endochytrium*, *Synchytium*, *Cladochytrium*, and *Nowakowskiella*. Only a few species in the entire order are economically important. *S. endobioticum* causes black wart of potatoes and is widely distributed in the potato growing regions of the world and is perhaps most destructive.

20.3 GENUS: SYNCHYTRIUM

This genus consists of more than 100 species that are parasitic on flowering plants. These are endobiotic, holocarpic fungi with inoperculate sporangia. The thallus is colonial (exogenous polycentric) and divides into several reproductive organs (sporangia or gametangia) that are enveloped in a common membrane and form a sorus. According to Curtis (1921), lack of water at a certain period in the development of *S. endobioticum* requires maturation period between formation and release that is necessary for the development of gametes (Figure 20.1). If the motile cells are released immediately after their formation, they behave as zoospores. The cell in which they develop functions as zoosporangium or gametangium, depending on the behaviour of the motile cells released. Whether the motile cells will be asexual zoospores or sex cells (gametes) is said to depend on the presence or absence of sufficient water at a critical point in their development. In nature, more zoospores are formed at the beginning than at the end of the season, and the reverse is true for gametes. It is possible that meiosis occurs at the time the resting sporangium germinates (Alexopoulos, et al., 1996).

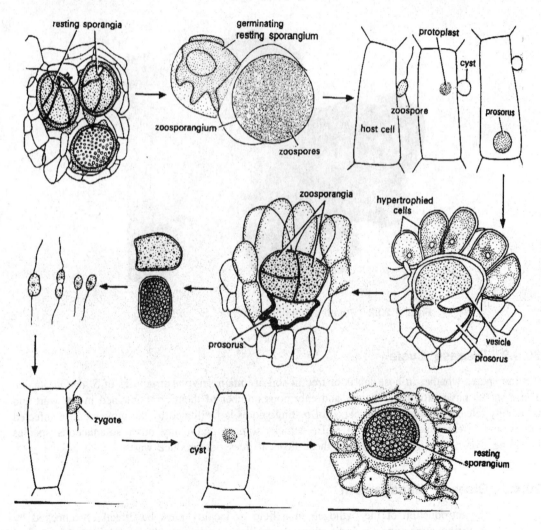

Figure 20.1 Disease cycle of wart of potato caused by *S. endobioticum.*

20.4 BLACK WART DISEASE OF POTATO

20.4.1 Symptoms

Buds on underground stems, stolen and tubers are the centres from where abnormal growth activity starts and lead to development of warts. On the tubers the warts are more typical and conspicuous, sometimes covering the whole tuber and larger than the tuber itself (Figure 20.2). In advanced stages the warts are darker in colour, sometimes black, and undergo putrefaction due to attack of saprophytes. Morphologically the wart consists of distorted, proliferated branched structures growing together into a mass of hyperplastic tissue.

Figure 20.2 Potato tuber infected with *S. endobioticum.*

20.4.2 Disease Cycle

Resting spores whether in host debris or free in soil are main survival structures of *S. endobioticum.* These spores have extreme longevity and enormous number of them are contained in the wart and ultimately released in soil. The dispersal of resting spores is facilitated by the movement of infected tubers and infested soil. The fungus also attacks tomato and many other solanaceous species including *Datura* and *Physalis* but on these hosts it does not produce warts.

20.4.3 Disease Management

1. The introduction of the pathogen in a field or locality must be effectively checked by practising quarantine. In India, through application of quarantine regulation, this disease has so far been confined to Darjeeling hills.

2. The only practical and effective control measure is to cultivate immune or highly resistant varieties. Kufri Muthu, Kufri Sheetman, Kufri Sherpa, Kufri Khasi Garo, Kufri Bahar, Kufri Kumar and Kufri Kanchan are some of the potato varieties that have shown high resistance and therefore should be cultivated.

REFERENCES

Alexopoulos, J.E., et al., 1996, *Introductory Plant Pathology,* John Wiley and Sons, Inc., New York.

Barr, D.J.S., 1980, An outline for the reclassification of the Chytrichales and for a new order–the *spizelomycetales, Can. J. Bot.,* 58:2380.

Barr, D.J.S., 1983, The zoosporic grouping of plant pathogens: entity or non-entity, In: *Zoosporic Plant Pathogen, A Modern Perspective,* S.T. Buczacki, (Ed.), Academic, London.

Barr, D.J.S., 1992, Evolution and kingdoms of organisms from the perspective of a mycologist, *mycologia,* 84:1.

Curtis, K.M., 1921, The life–history and cytology of *Synchytrium endobioticum* (schilb) Pers, the cause of wart disease of potato, *Trans. Roy. Soc. London.* Ser: B, 210:409.

Kole, A.P., 1965, Resting spore germination in *Synchytrium endobioticum, Neth. J. Pl. Path,* 71:72.

Mehrotra, R.S., 1980, *Plant Pathology,* Tata McGraw-Hill. Publ. Comp. Ltd., New Delhi.

21 Phylum: Ascomycota and Plant Diseases

21.1 INTRODUCTION

The distinguishing characteristic feature of ascomycetous fungi is the presence of ascus (*pl.* asci, *Gr. Askos* = goat skin, sac), a sac like structure-containing ascospores (*Gr. Askos* + spora = spore), which is formed after karyogamy and meiosis. Eight ascospores are typically formed within the ascus but this number may vary from one to over a thousand according to the species. The somatic stages of ascomycetes may be single celled, mycelial or dimorphic. A large proportion of the cell walls of filamentous ascomycetes is chitin. Hyphae are divided into compartments by septa that form the hyphal periphery and advance towards the centre, thus invaginating the plasmamembrane. Asexual reproduction in ascomycetes may be carried out by fission, fragmentation, thallospores or conidia formation in different species and factors concerning nutrition and environment. In sexual reproduction, two unlike but compatible nuclei are brought together in the same cell by one of several methods described in Chapter 17.

21.2 LIFE CYCLE PATTERN

The sexual stage/perfect stage is called **teleomorph** and the conidial stage is the **anamorph** or asexual stage. The ascus in most ascomycetes is formed as a result of fertilization of the female sex cell, called an **ascogonium,** by either an antheridium or a minute male sex spore called **spermatium** (Figure 21.1). Upon contact between the two sex organs, the nuclei pass from antheridium to ascogonium via a tubular hair like structure called **trichogyne.** After the entry of the antheridial cytoplasm and nuclei, the compatible nuclei from both organs get paired, but no fusion, and move towards the periphery of ascogonium. The ascogonial wall becomes elastic and ultimately assumes hyphal structures particularly in areas where paired nuclei are located. The hyphal structures that are formed are termed as **ascogenous hyphae.** In these structures, the nuclei move in pairs. The tip cell is invariably binucleate (one nucleus being male and the other female). This cell may directly form crozier (Figure 21.1). The two nuclei in this bent portion divide in such a way that their spindles lie parallel to each other. Two septa divide the hook into three cells. The tip and the basal cells, which are lying side by side, contain one nucleus each, one male and the other female. Meanwhile, the middle cell, which is at the tip of hook now contains two nuclei (a male and another female) become the ascus mother cell. The untied tip and basal cells, now forming a single cell with two nuclei repeat the process. In this way, a large number of ascus mother cells may be produced by the same ascogenous hypha. Karyogamy occurs in ascus mother cell. The fused (diploid) nucleus undergoes meiosis forming four haploid nuclei, which after mitotic division form eight nuclei around which cytoplasm accumulates to form eight ascospores.

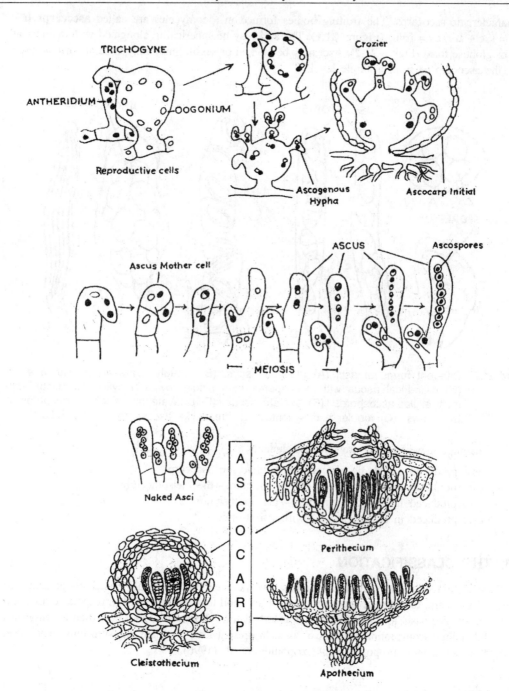

Figure 21.1 Development of ascus, ascospore and ascocarp in ascomycetes fungi.

The above process may occur in ascocarp primordium or the basal portion or cells of ascogonium stalk may produce branches. The sterile hyphae grow around the ascogonium to form the characteristic ascocarps. The fruiting bodies formed in ascomycetes are called **ascocarps** (*Gr. Askos* = sac + *karpos* = fruit) (Figure. 21.1). The asci may be spherical to elongated with cylindrical, ovoid or globose form (Figure 21.2). Asci may be stalked or sessile; they may arise at various levels within the ascocarp or from a single level.

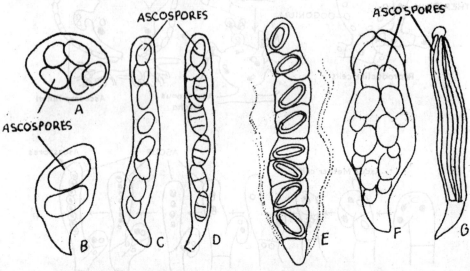

Figure 21.2   Different forms of asci (A) globose ascus, (B) broadly ovate ascus with a stalk, (C) cylindrical ascus with ascospores in a single row, (D) cylindrical ascus with multicellular ascospores, (E) septate ascus, (F) cleavate ascus with ascospores in two rows, (G) tubular ascus containing thread like ascospores in a bundle.

The manners in which asci are borne include:

- asci produced naked, no ascogenous hyphae, no ascocarp
- asci produced in a completely closed structure—the cleisothecium
- asci produced in an open structure—the apothecium
- asci produced in cavity (*locule*) within a stroma

21.3 THE CLASSIFICATION

The classification of ascomycetous fungi has always been controversial. Based on presence or absence of ascocarp, the type of ascocarp, type of asci and their arrangement in respective ascocarp has been the major basis for classification of ascomycetes. Ainsworth (1966) classified ascomycetes under subdivision ascomycotina with six classes. In present text, the plant parasitic fungi have been classified as per scheme proposed by Alexopoulos, et al. (1996).

21.3.1 Class: Archiascomycetes

The fungi in this class are a diverse group including saprophytic and parasitic forms that have been grouped primarily on the basis of rDNA sequence analysis. Two plant parasitic genera belonging to order Taphrinales, families Taphrinaceae and Protomycetaceae, are *Taphrina*, and *Protomyces*, respectively.

Order: Taphrinales, **Family:** *Taphrinaceae*

21.3.2 Class: Pyrenomycetes (ascomycetes with Perithecia)

Members are characterized by (a) perithecial or, occasionally, cleistothecial ascocarps that may be formed in a stroma, (b) ovoid to cylindrical unitunicate asci, usually formed from ascogenous hyphae and croziers in a hymanium or becoming secondarily scattered throughout the ascocarp, (c) persistent asci that have forcible discharge of ascospores through an ascal tip apparatus or evanescent asci with passive discharge, (d) hamathecia that may consist of one or more types of sterile hyphae and pseudoparenchymatous tissue, (e) one to several celled ascospores of various shapes and (f) diverse and often complex anamorphs and related conidial species, which do not reproduce sexually (Alexopoulos, *et al.*, 1996). Important plant parasitic fungi with their taxonomic position are summarizd below:

1. **Order:** Hypocreales, (i) **Family**: Hypocreaceae, **Genera**: *Hypocrea,* (anamorphs *Trichoderma* and *Glioladium;* fungal antagonists). (ii) **Family:** Nectriaceae, **Genus:** *Nectria*, *N. galligena* (canker of hardwood trees; apple and pear), *N. cinnabarina*, *Gibberella zeae* (anamorph: *F. graminearum*-ear rot of maize) *G.* fayikoroi (*F. moniliforme* source of gibberellic acid, foolish disease of rice). (iii) **Family:** Clavicipataceae, **Genus:** *Claviceps C. perpurea* (ergot of grains and grasses), *C. fusiformis* (ergot of pearl millet)
2. **Order:** Melanosporales, **Genus:** *Melanospora* (anamorphs—*Phialophora* and *Ganato-botyrys*)
3. **Order:** Microscales, **Family:** Ceratocystidaceae, **Genus:** *Ceratocystis, C. fagacearum* (Oak wilt); *C. fambriata* (Cankers in stone fruit)
4. **Order:** Phyllochorales **Genus:** *Glomerella G. cingulata,* (anamorph: *Colletotrichum gloeosporioides* anthraconose diseases)
5. **Order:** Ophiostomatales, **Genus:** *Ophiostoma, O. ulmi* (formely *Ceratocystis ulmi*, Dutch elm disease), anamorphs: *Sporothrixaro graphium*
6. **Order:** Diaporthales **Genera:** *Diaporthe* (anamorph: *Phomopsis;* fruit rot of egg plant) *Gaeumannnomyces graminis*: take-all disease of cereals *Magnaporthe* (anamorph: *P. oryzae;* blast of paddy). *Cryphonectria* (formely *Endothia parasitica* chestnut blight)
7. **Order:** Xylariales, **Families:** Xylariaceae and Diatrypaceae **Genus:** *Rosellinia necatria, root of grapevines* and *Hypoxylon mammatum*, canker of trembling

21.3.3 Class: Loculoascomycetes (ascomycetes with ascostromata)

Loculoascomycetes are characterized morphologically by the production of asci within locules in a preformed ascocarp. Ascostroma may be monolocular (pseudothecium) or multilocular. Asci are bitunicate.

1. **Order:** Dothidiales, **Family:** Dothidiaceae, **Genera:** *Mycosphaerella, M. musicola* (sigatoka leaf spots of banana), Anamorphs: *Cercospora, Septoria, Ramularia* and *Ovularia*
2. **Order:** Myriangiales, **Family:** Elsinoaceae, **Genus:** *Elsinoe ampilina,* grape anthracnose (anamorph: *Sphaceloma*)

3. **Order:** Pleosporales, (i) **Family:** *Pleosporaceae*

Table 21.1 Telemorph-anamorph connections in Pleosporaceae

Telemorph	Disease	Anamorph
Pleospora	Black mould rot of tomato	*Stemphylium*
Lewia	Leaf spots	*Alternaria*
Pyrenophora	Leaf spots on cereals and grasses	*Drechslera*
Setosphaera	Leaf spots on cereals and grasses	*Exserohilum*
Cochliobolus	Leaf spots and root rots	*Bipolaris*, *curvularia*

(ii) **Family:** Leptosphaeriaceae, **Genus:** *Leptospharia maculans*; black leg of brassicas. (anamorphs: *Phoma Septoria* and *Coniothyrium*)

(iii) **Family:** Venturiaceae, **Genus:** *Venturia V. inaequalis;* apple scab and *V. pyrina*; pea scab

(iv) **Family:** Botryosphaeriaceae, **Genus** *Guinardia bidwelli*, (anamorph: *Phphyllosticta ampelicida*; black rot of grapes.

21.3.4 Class: Discomycetes (filamentous ascomycetes with apothecia)

Discomycetes are characterized by the ascocarps known as **apothecia**. Apothecial ascocarps produce an exposed hymanium at maturity and ascospores are discharged forcibly from cylindrical to ovoid asci.

Order: Rhytismales, **Genera:** Lophodermium, Rhytisma, Rhabdocline
Order: Helotiales, **Genera:** *Monolinia fructicola* (brown rot of stone fruits), *Sclerotinia sclerotiorum* (foot/stem rot of many crops)

21.3.5 Other Filamentous Ascomycetes (Powdery mildew fungi)

Order: Erysiphales: The fungi belonging to Erysiphales are obligate biotrophs that cause a major group of plant diseases commonly known as **powdery mildews**. These diseases are named because of white appearance due to presence of conidiophores and tremendous number of conidia they produce. Economically important hosts include cereal grains, cucurbits, mango, apples and grapes as well as various ornamentals.

- *Uncinula necator* (powdery mildew of grapes)
- *Sphaerotheca pannosa* (powdery mildew of roses)
- *Podosphaera leucotricha* (powdery mildew of apples)
- *Erysipha cichoracearum* (powdery mildew cucurbits)
- *Erysipha ploygoni* (powdery mildew peas)
- *Blumeria graminis* (powdery mildew of cereals)

Identification of powdery mildew genera. According to Zheng (1985), about six to seven genera of *Erysiphales* have been accepted universally. Yarwood (1973) recognized seven genera. On the other hand, Hawksworth, *et al.,* (1983) recognized some 28 genera while Brawn (1987) recognized some 19 genera. If ascocarps are present, identification of these fungi at generic level is easy. However, in absence of ascocarps, identification of these fungi is very difficult.

The mature ascocarps of most species of Erysiphales are provided with characteristic appendages that vary considerably and that together with the number of asci produced, form the basis of generic separation (Figure 21.3).

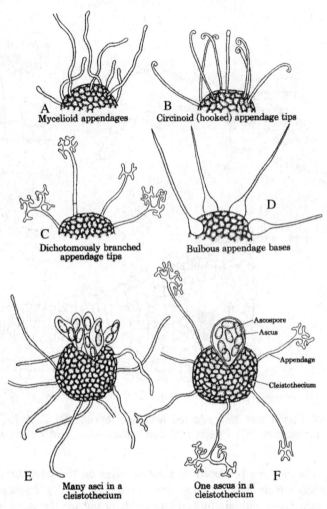

Figure 21.3 Taxonomic characters of *Erysiphales*. (A–D) Types of appendages on ascocarps. (E,F) Variation in number of asci within ascocarp. (*Source:* C.J. Alexopoulos, et al., 1996)

21.4 PLANT DISEASES CAUSED BY ASCOMYCOTA

21.4.1 Peach Leaf Curl: *Taphrina deformans*

Species of *Taphrina* cause leaf, flower and fruit deformation on several stone fruits and forest trees, such as peach leaf curl, plum pockets on plums, leaf curl and witches' broom on cherries and leaf blister of oak. Peach leaf curl is a widespread disease and causes defoliation and distortion of leaf thus reducing the life span of the tree.

Symptoms. Soon after the leaves emerge out of the bud, some of them appear twisted, thickened, puckered, curled downwards and often greatly distorted (Figure 21.4). In the beginning affected leaves are pale green or yellowish but finally they change to reddish purple tint. Young shoots attacked by the fungus are swollen and distorted. Even flowers and fruits are some times attacked.

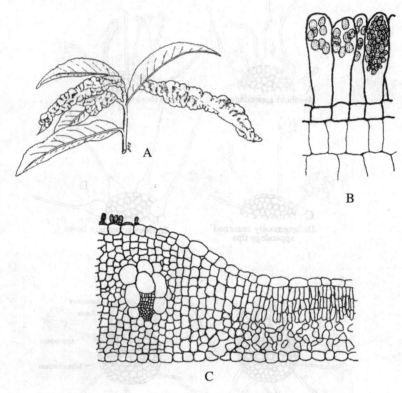

Figure 21.4 (A) Peach leaf curl, affected twig and leaves, (B) *Taphrina deformans*, asci and ascospores, (C) Peach leaf curl, cross-section of diseased leaf.

The pathogen. The asci are produced in a naked layer on the host surface. The mycelial cells contain two nuclei, which may develop into an ascus, usually containing eight uninucleate ascospores. The ascospores multiply by budding inside or outside the ascus, producing conidia. The latter may bud again to produce more conidia or may germinate to produce mycelium (Figure 21.4).

Disease cycle. The asci and sprout conidia remain viable for long periods. These propagules persist during winter on twigs, buds and scales and serve as primary inoculum. During rains these propagules may be washed down and carried to other host plant parts. In early spring, when the buds are opening in cool humid weather, these conidia germinate. The fertilization of the haploid conidia or the binucleate hyphae has taken place by this time.

Disease management. Tree and orchard sanitation is important. The tree should be kept free from diseased leaves. All fallen and diseased leaves twigs etc. should be destroyed. A number of fungicides, viz. perenox, fytolon, blitox-50, bavistin, captan, maneb, topsin, baycor, bayleton, calexin, etc. have been recommended. The disease can easily be controlled by a single spray preferable in late fall or early spring before the leaf bud swells. The fungicides most commonly used are bordeaux mixture (8:8:100) and chlorothalonil; the later controls the disease if applied twice, in late fall and early spring.

21.4.2 Leaf Spot of Turmeric: *Taphraina maculans*

This is a common disease of turmeric (*curcuma longa*) throughout India. Considerable damage to crop, particularly in Northern India, Gujarat, and Tamil Nadu, A.P., Orissa have been reported. The characteristic symptoms are seen as large number of spots that develop on both surfaces of leaves, though more prominent on upper surface. Infected leaves turn to reddish-brown and then become yellow. There is no hypertrophy/hyperplasia in the attacked leaves. No distortion occurs (Plate 21.1).

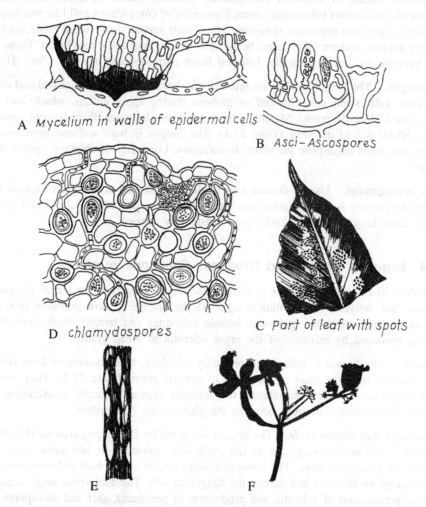

A *Mycelium in walls of epidermal cells*

B *Asci–Ascospores*

D *chlamydospores*

C *Part of leaf with spots*

E F

Plate 21.1 (A–C) leaf spot of turmeric (*T. maculans*), and (D-F) stem gall of coriander (*P. macrosporus*).

The fungal mycelium is present between the cuticle and epidermis and also inside the epidermal cells. Branched or lobed haustoria grow within the host cells. The asci are cylindrical to clavate, each with usually eight ascospores. Ascospores are ovoid, hyaline and unicellular. The ascospores multiply within the ascus itself to form secondary spores (Plate 21.1). The dormant mycelium in the rhizomes and infected dried leaves lying in the field serve as source of primary inoculum for next crop.

Disease management. Field sanitation, sprays of fungicides (Bordeaux mixture, perenox, fytolon, blitox-50 and zineb) and host resistance (cultivars "china" and "javelin") have been recommended.

21.4.3 Stem Gall of Coriander: *Protomyces macrosporus*

An important disease of coriander (*Coriandrum sativum*) occurs in almost all coriander growing areas. The disease causes substantial losses. Formation of conspicuous gall like swellings on all parts of the plant is the most important symptom. These galls appear glossy when intact but become rough when they rupture, and are fairly large, being upto 15 mm long and 4 mm broad. These galls develop due to hypertrophy and hyperplasia. Infected floral parts become massive (Plate 21.1).

The pathogen. The fungal hyphae are intercellular, broad, irregularly branched and closely septate. The hyphal, cells swell into ellipsoid or globose resting spore initials, which later develop into resting spore (chlamydospores). Mature resting spores develop thick, three layered, smooth walls and measure 50–60 μm in diameter (Plate 21.1). The fungus is both soil and seed borne. High soil moisture and shade predispose the plants to infection. Longevity of chlamydospores decreases with their age.

Disease management. Use of disease free seeds, field sanitation and crop rotation are helpful in reducing the primary source of inoculum. Seed treatment with thiram (0.25%) and treatment of soil with the same fungicide @ 20 kg/ha give satisfactory control.

21.4.4 Ergot of Grains and Grasses: *Cleviceps purpurea*

Long before its recognition as fungus disease, the ergots have been known as the cause of human pestilence, the "holyfire" of the middle ages. As the disease is most prevalent in rye, we read in European literature of many epidemics, human sufferings and terrible death from the gangrenous poisoning produced by mixtures of the ergot sclerotia in bread grains.

Symptoms. The disease is recognized primarily by black, hard, banana or horn shaped sclerotia, which protrude from the head in the place of normal grains (Plate 21.2). They usually occur as individual spikelets of the head. Before the sclerotia appear, a careful examination will reveal a sticky secretion oozing out from between the glumes, the "honeydew".

The pathogen and disease cycle. The disease is caused by *Claviceps purpurea* (Fr) Tul. The fungus shows three well-marked stages in its life cycle—the sphacelia or honeydew stage, the sclerotial stage and the ascigerous stage. The honeydew stage occurs on the host inflorescence. The sclerotial stage develops on the host and carries the fungus to soil. The ascigerous stage occurs outside the host after germination of sclerotia and production of perithecia, asci and ascospores. In temperate climate areas the life cycle and development of disease in cereal hosts starts from this ascigerous stage (Plate 21.3).

Plate 21.2   Symptoms of ergot of grains and grasses.

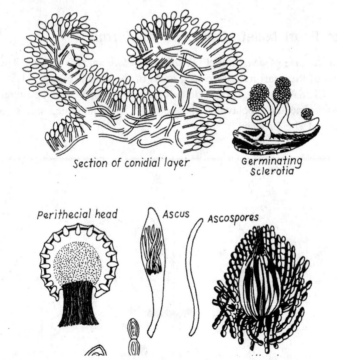

Section of conidial layer   Germinating Sclerotia

Perithecial head   Ascus   Ascospores

Plate 21.3   Reproductive structure of *Claviceps purpurea.*

The ascospores are violently ejected out of the perithecia and are carried by wind to healthy flower at the time of blossoming. After reaching the stigma of the flowers these spores germinate and send out an infection thread which grows down the style and reaches the ovary. The infection of ovary gives rise to honeydew or sphacelia stage. The embryo is attacked, destroyed and replaced by yellowish white mycelium. Subsequently sporogenous hyphae arise from the mycelium on the surface of the ovary. These hyphae function as conidiophores. Conidiophores bear small, oval, unicellular conidia in succession. Later on, honeydew is produced which attracts insects, which acts as carriers of conidia causing secondary infection of fresh ovaries. When the ovary is exhausted or totally replaced by the fungal hyphae, the repeated inter-winning of hyphae produces a compact, hard structure the sclerotium.

The sclerotia (ergots) fall down on the ground or are carried with the seed only to return to the soil at the next sowing time. Thus, the sclerotia serve as resting structures during the off-season. They germinate when the crop is growing in the next season giving rise to ascigerous stage. The ascospores that finally develop in asci formed in perithecia are slender, filiform and hyaline. The cap of the ascus is burst open and the ascospores are discharged with force above the ground level where they are caught in air currents and disseminated.

Management

1. Use clean seed or seed that has been freed from ergot. Sclerotia may be removed from seed manually/mechanically or floating-off sclerotia in a solution of about 18 kg salt in 100 litres of water.
2. Deep ploughing or crop rotation with non-host helps eliminate the pathogen from infested fields. Wild grasses in or around the field too should be removed.

21.4.5 Ergot of Pearl Millet: *Claviceps fusiformis*

Ergot is an important disease of pearl millet (*Pennisetum glancum* (L.) R. Br.). The disease is known to occur in most parts of the pearl millet growing areas of the world (Figure. 21.5). Ergot is a double-edged problem. At ICRISAT centre, grain yield losses of 55–65% were estimated. Ergot of pearl millet contains agroclavine, elymoclavine, chanoclavine, penniclavine, and setoclavine alkaloids, which lowers quality of the produce.

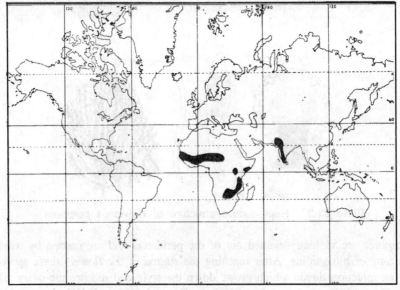

Figure 21.5 Geographical distribution of ergot disease (*C. fusiformis*) of pearl millet.

Symptoms of ergot first appear as a viscous, turbid fluid oozing out from the infected florets of pearl millet panicles (Figure 21.6). Within 10 days of honeydew initiation, sclerotia become visible in infected florets, instead of seeds. Sclerotia are initially whitish, elongated and larger than seed, become hard and brown within 10–15 days (Figure 21.6).

Figure 21.6 Symptoms of ergot of pearl millet, (A) honeydew stage, (B and C) sclerotial stage.

The pathogen. The causal fungus of ergot in pearl millet was known as *Claviceps microcephala* (Waller.) Tul., until 1968 when Loveless (1976) proposed a new name, *Claviceps fusiformis* Loveless. Conidia are hyaline, unicellular, fusiform, broadly fulcate and measure 13–18 × 8–4 μm. The sexual phase initiates with sclerotial germination by producing one to several fleshy, purplish stripes that bear light to dark brown globular capitula, which have numerous perithecial projections

(Figure 21.7). Asci are interspersed with paraphyses in perithecia and emerge through ostioles. Asci are long and hyaline with apical pores and narrow ends. Ascospores are filiform, hyaline, non-septate, and measure 103–176 × 0.5–0.7 μm. The ergot pathogen follows similar disease cycle as described in case of ergot of grains (Figure 21.8).

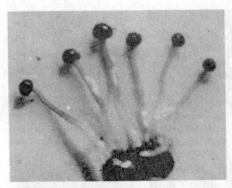

Figure 21.7 Germinated ergot sclerotium showing elongated stipes which bear globular capitula containing perithecia.

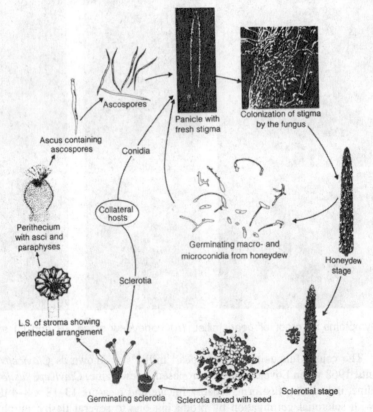

Figure 21.8 Disease cycle of ergot of pearl millet.

Disease management. Various cultural practices reported to the disease are deep ploughing, adjustment of sowing dates, balanced soil fertilization, intercropping, and planting sclerotia free seed. Late sown crops are usually more infected than early sown crops. A balanced application of 80 kg N, and 20 kg P or 40 kg K/ha is reported effective in keeping low levels of disease. Bajra is sometimes intercropped with mungbean, which reduces disease incidence. The use of clean, sclerotia free seed reduces primary inoculum. The best means of managing this disease is through the use of resistant varieties. Several spray fungicides such as ziram, copper oxychloride + zineb, cosan-80, cuman L, difolatan, bavistin, benlate, etc. are reported to provide satisfactory control. Ergot has been controlled by using hyperparasites such as *Fusarium roseum, F. sambucinum, F. heterosporum, F. semitectum* var. *majus* and *Cerebella andropogonis.*

21.4.6 Red Rot of Sugarcane: *Colletotrichum falcatum*

Red rot of sugarcane (*Saccharum* spp.) is prevalent in all sugarcane growing areas (Figure 21.9). It becomes devastating in certain years.

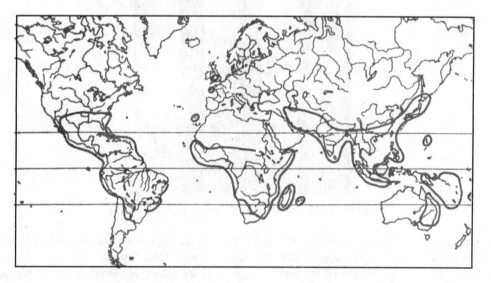

Figure 21.9 Geographical distribution of red rot of sugarcane.

Symptoms. The disease is easily detected during the rainy season or the following period. While foliage is still green and stalks plumpy, root primordia located at the nodal region of the stalks tend to convert into abundant acervuli with profuse sporulation. Drying of third or fourth leaf at the tip and along the margin or the whole leaf is usually the first indication of the disease. In severe cases, the whole crown dries off. On splitting open the diseased stalk, characteristic symptoms are observed at the internodal tissues. The tissues become dull red, interrupted by transverse white patches (Figure 21.10). Affected tissues emit a characteristic odour of vinegar. At harvesting stage, the shrunken stalk displays a longitudinal cavity filled with mycelium and drops of deep brown liquid. Numerous acervuli develop on the ring of the dried stalk.

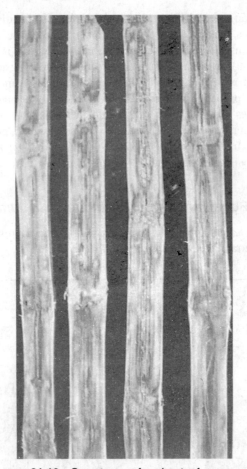

Figure 21.10 Symptoms of red rot of sugarcane.

The pathogen. *Colletotrichum falcatum* Went is the asexual stage. Conidia are produced either in acervuli or directly on hyphal tips. Conidia are hyaline, one celled, falcate, and sometimes fusoid. Von Arx and Muller (1954) placed the perfect stage under the genus *Glomerella tcumanensis* (Speg.) Arx and Muller. The asci are clavate, slightly thickened at the apex, and measures 70 to 90 μm by 13 to 18 μm. The ascospores are hyaline, straight to slightly fusoid, one celled and measure 18 to 22 μm by 7 to 8 μm. The fungus is homothallic.

Disease cycle. The disease starts with the planting of infected sets. The disease cycle is illustrated in Figure 21.11. Most of the infected seed pieces (sets) have dormant mycelium in the bud scales, the leaf scars, and the nodal and inter nodal tissues. Various forms of inoculum are usually present in the soil. The germinating buds are infected by the soil inoculum. The pathogen has a number of collateral hosts, e.g. *Sorghum vulgare, S. halepense, Saccharum spontaneum, Leptochloa filiformis* and *Miscanthus* sp. On the latter two hosts, the perfect stage is also reported to occur. Irrigation water, rainwater and the movement of seed cane are important mean of dissemination.

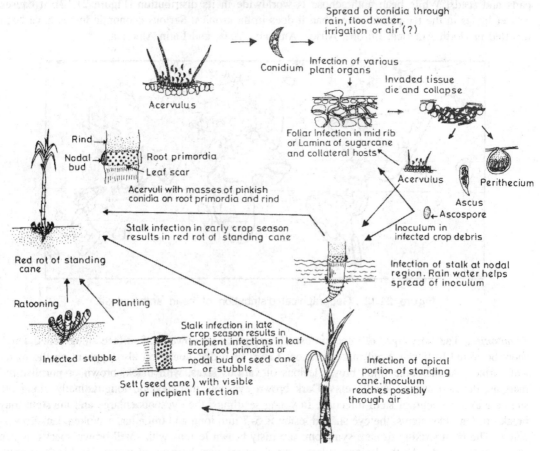

Figure 21.11 Disease cycle of red rot of sugarcane.

Disease management

1. Practices such as field sanitation, seed selection, and crop rotation and field drainage help in reduction of disease incidence.
2. Set treatments with benomyl (0.25%) and carboxin (0.05%) have been found to improve germination and minimize red rot incidence.
3. Hot air treatment of canes at 54°C for 8 hrs has been reported effective. Aerated stem and moist hot air have been observed to be effective in eradicating red rot inoculum from seed material. By aerated steam, canes are treated at 52°C for 4-5 hrs and by moist air at 54°C for 2 hrs.
4. Several inter-specific crosses of *Saccharum officinarum* and *S. spontaneum* and inter hybrid crosses have yielded resistant to moderately resistant varieties (e.g. CO 449, CO 527, CO 658, CO 1148, CO 1261, CO 1336, CO 62101, CO 62399, CO L9, and COC 671).

21.4.7 Bean Anthracnose: *Colletotrichum lindemuthianum*

Bean anthracnose is a disease of the common bean (*Phaseolus vulgaris* L.) affecting all vegetative parts and seeds. While bean anthracnose is worldwide in its distribution (Figure 21.12), it causes greater losses in the temperate zones than it does in the tropics. Serious economic losses have been reported in North America, Europe, Africa, Australia, Asia, and Latin America.

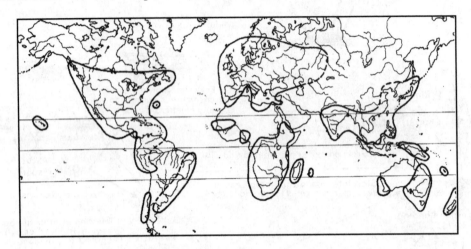

Figure 21.12 Geographical distribution of bean anthracnose.

Symptoms. The early signs of infection usually appear on the lower leaf surface along veins, which show brick red to purplish-red discolouration. Later, such discolouration also appears on the upper leaf surface. At the same time, brown lesions of various sizes, with black, brown or purplish-red margins, develop around small veins. Dark brown eyespots that develop longitudinally along the stem are an early sign of stem infection. In young seedlings, the eyespots enlarge and the stem may break off. On older stems, the eye-shaped lesion is 5–7 mm long and often has a sunken cankerous— centre. The most striking disease symptoms are rusty brown lesions with small brown specks, which appear on the pods. As the lesions enlarge, their centres turn brown and many tiny black acervuli appear randomly on the area, replacing the brown specks (Figure 21.13). Seeds from infected pods may show brown to light-chocolate-coloured sunken cankers on the seed coats (Figure 21.13).

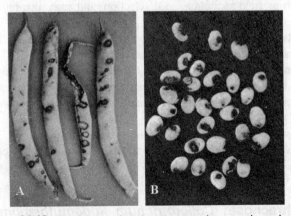

Figure 21.13 Symptoms of anthracnose on bean pods and seeds.

The pathogen. *Colletotrichum lindemuthianum* (Sacc. and Magn.) Briosi. and Cav. is the imperfect stage of the causal fungus. Most isolates do not produce sexual reproductive structures. Some hyphae aggregate to form stromata, which produce conidiophores and setae. Unicellular hyaline conidia, which measure 4-5 × 13-22 μm, are produced on the conidiophores. Conidiophores are hyaline, erect, short, and unbranched, 40-60 μm in length. Setae may appear in culture among the conidiophores or on the host at the margin of a stroma. They are pointed and stiff, with septate brown hairs 30–100 m long.

The fungus was originally named *Glomerella lindemuthiana* Shear but recently it has been renamed *G. cingulata*. The fungus produces perithecia, which are 120 to 210 μm in diameter. Perithecia contain hyaline, filiform paraphyses, asci. The asci, which measure 8 × 48-68 μm, also disappear after 27 to 30 days. Each ascus contains eight ascospores, which may be allantoid (6.5 × 20 μm) or ellipsoid (4 × 10 μm) in shape. Ascospores are ejected from the tip of the ascus.

Disease cycle and management. The fungus overseasons in infected seeds and in plant debris. It can remain viable in infected seeds for several years. The perfect stage of the fungus is rarely formed in nature. Steps in disease cycle are shown in Figure 21.14.

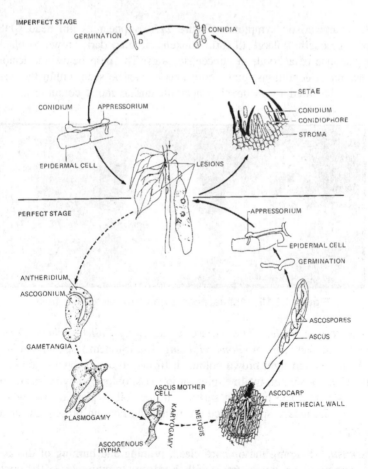

Figure 21.14 Disease cycle of anthracnose of bean.

1. Seed free from anthracnose infection should be used. Before sowing seeds should be treated with ferbam, ziram or thiram @ 0.5 g/100 g seeds. Two formulations IF Plus (captan 25%, diazinon 12.5%, benomyl 17.5%) and DCT (diazinon 6%, captan 18%, thiophanate methyl 14%) have been found effective in reducing seed borne inoculum (Tu, 1992).
2. Many protectant or systemic fungicides such as maneb and zineb @ 3.5 g/L, benomyl @ 0.55 g/L, captafol @ 3.5 kg/ha, carbendazim at 0.5 kg/ha have been used to control anthracnose. Spraying foliage at flower initiation, late flower and pod filling have been recommended for good control (Tu, 1992).
3. Genetic resistance is the most effective control measures and has been used extensively in US and Europe in major cultivars.

21.4.8 Anthracnose of Guava: *Colletotrichum gloeosporioides*

The disease is of common occurrence in all the guava growing regions. The disease appears mostly during rainy season and results in maximum damage during high humidity and moderate temperature.

Symptoms. The characteristic symptoms (Figure 21.15) appear as pin head spots on the unripe fruits. These spots gradually enlarge to form sunken, circular, dark brown to black lesions. These lesions show appearance of acervuli in concentric rings. The pulp below the lesions becomes soft and brown. Under moist conditions, pink spore masses can be seen within the acervulus. Dieback phase also occurs. The dried twigs develop acervuli during moist conditions.

Figure 21.15 Anthracnose symptoms on guava fruits.

The pathogen and disease cycle. The disease is caused by *Colletotrichum gloeosporioides* Penz. (=*C. psidii* Curzi.) imperfect stage of *Glomerella cingulata* (Stonem.) Spauld and Schrenk. Mycelium is intercellular, branched and light brown coloured. Brown to dark brown coloured acervuli develop on infected parts. Conidia are sub-hyaline, pinkish in mass, oblong to cylindrical, obtuse at the apex, 1-celled, 9-24 × 3-4.5 μm. The pathogen survives in the soil in plant debris, which is the primary source of inoculum. Secondary spread occurs through the conidia present in air and also through splashing raindrops.

Disease management. Keeping the orchard clean, pruning and burning of diseased twigs reduces inoculum load. Spraying the guava trees with bordeaux mixture (3:3:50), copper oxychloride, cuprous oxide, captafol and zineb has been recommended. Sprays of benomyl and triforine are also useful. Post harvest dip in benlate, thiabendazole, aureofungin and mineral oil is quite helpful.

21.4.9 Anthracnose of Chillies: *Colletotrichum capsici*

The disease is also known as **dieback blight or ripe rot**. The disease is prevalent wherever the crop is grown. Yield losses in the range of 10 to 60 per cent have been reported. The **symptoms** are observed in two phases, i.e., on twigs as dieback and on ripened fruits as ripe rot. Ripe rot symptoms first appear on mature fruits as small, water soaked, sunken lesions that rapidly expand. Fully developed lesions are sunken and range from dark red to light tan with varying amounts of visible dark acervuli of the fungus. The fungus invades seed cavity, seeds are covered with mycelium (Plate 21.4). Pre and post-emergence damping-off and leaf spots are also reported in some geographical areas. Shoot necrosis or dieback symptoms are also observed. In advanced stages; the entire plant is withered, producing poor quality and less number of fruits.

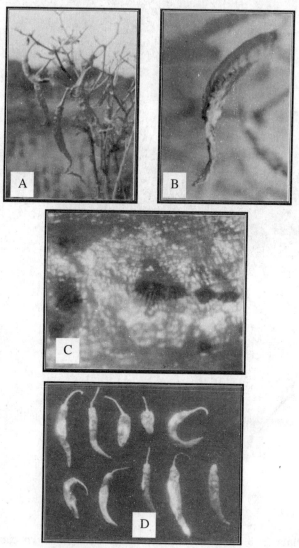

Plate 21.4 Symptoms of dieback and anthracnose of chillies.

The pathogen and disease cycle. The disease is caused by *Colletotrichum capsici* (Syd.) Butler and Bisby [Tel: *Glomerella cingulata* (Stonem.)] Spauld and Schrenk. The acervuli are formed on infected plant parts. The conidia are non-septate, hyaline, uninucleate, falcate with acute apices and narrow truncated base (Plate 21.5).

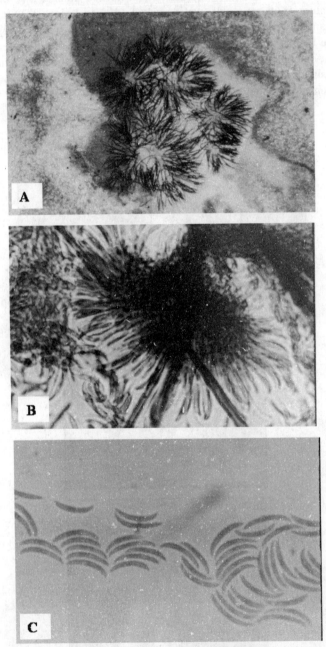

Plate 21.5 Acervuli and conidia of *Colletotrichum capsici.*

The disease cycle is summarized as follows.

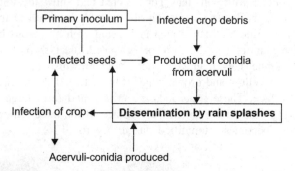

Disease management

1. Crop rotation with non-host, eradication of weed hosts and cultivation in well-drained soils are helpful in minimizing/preventing the disease.
2. Sprays of chemicals such as captan, carbendazim, benomyl, nabam, zineb, captafol and mancozeb, at 10-15 days intervals after transplanting have been recommended (Singh, 2002).
3. Seeds should be obtained from certified agencies and must be treated with fungicides.
4. Kolte. *et al.*, (1994) have reported biological control of the disease with *Azospirillum* sp. and *Azotobacter* sp.

Table 2.2 Some Anthracnose Diseases of Minor Importance

Crop	*Pathogen*	*Primary inoculum*
Mango	*C. gloeosporioides (G. cingulata)*	Diseased plant parts
Papaya	*C. gloeosporioides (G. cingula.)*	Diseased plant parts
Citrus	*C. gloeosporioides* and *Gloeosporium*	Diseased plant parts

21.4.10 Phomopsis Blight and Fruit Rot of Egg Plant: *Phomopsis vexans*

In most of the tropical and subtropical areas, phomopsis blight and fruit rot is considered to be a serious disease (Figure 21.16). The disease initially starts as foliar blight. The most destructive phase of the disease is fruit rot, which results in heavy damages both in the field as well as during the transit and transport.

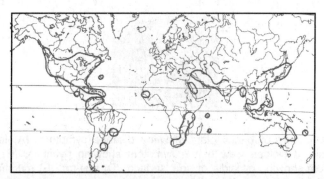

Figure 21.16 Geographical distribution of phomopsis blight and fruit rot of egg plant.

Symptoms. Damping-off of seedlings results the infection of the stem just above the soil surface. The leaves coming in contact with soil, may get infected and show the initial disease symptoms. The lesions on petiole or at the lower part of midrib result in the death of the entire leaf. Affected leaves drop prematurely and the blightened area is covered with numerous black pycnidial bodies. On the stem, the disease manifests in the form of elongated, blackish-brown lesions. On the fruits the disease appears as minute sunken grayish spots, with brownish halo, which later enlarge and produce concentric rings of yellow and brown zones (Plate 21.6). The outermost rings get separated from the healthy fruit surface. These spots increase in size and form large rotten areas on which pycnidia develop, covering most of the rotten fruit surface. If the infection enters the fruits through the calyx, the whole fruit becomes mummified due to dry rot.

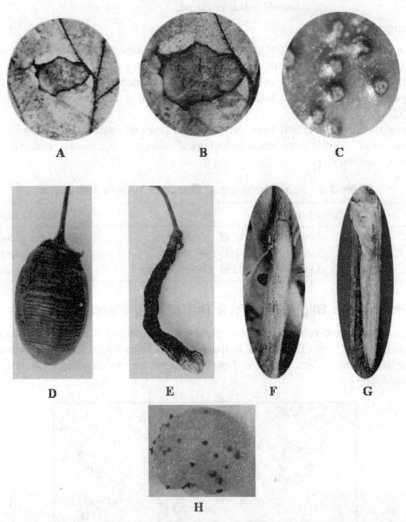

Plate 21.6 Different parts of brinjal plant showing disease symptom, (A) leaf showing typical necrosis, (B) close view of the symptom showing pycnidia, (C) close view of the symptom showing pycnidia on fruit surface, (D) fruit-rot, (E) mummificaiton, (F and G) stem canker, (H) infected seed showing pycnidia.

The pathogen. The disease is caused by *P. vexans* (Sacc. and Syd.) Harter. *Diaporthe vexans* Gratz, is the perfect stage of the pathogen. However, the sexual or perithecial stage of the fungus has not been seen in nature. The conidiophores in the pycnidium are hyaline, simple or branched, sometimes septate, 10 to 16 m long. Pycnidiospores (condidia) are hyaline, one-celled, subcylindrical, 5-9 × 2.0-2.8 μm in size. Another form of conidia, the stylospores, are filiform curved, hyaline and septate. These spores do not germinate. They are 20-30 × 0.5-10.0 μm in size (Plate 21.7). Asci are clavate, sessile and contain eight spores, each measuring 28-44 × 5-12 μm in size. Ascospores are hyaline, narrowly ellipsoid to bluntly fusoid, with one septate, the constricted at the septum. They measure 9-12 × 3-4.4 μm in size.

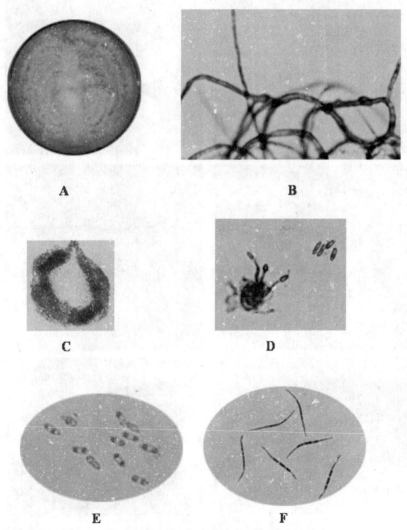

Plate 21.7 Morphology of *P. vexans,* (A) growth on medium in culture plate, (B) mycelium, (C) pycnidium bearing conidia, (D) conidia on conidiophore, (E) alpha conidia and (F) beta conidia (stylospores).

Disease cycle. The fungus is seed borne. The histopathology of infected seeds has revealed that the inoculum is localized as profused, branched and septate mycelium, and aggregated (Figure 21.17) in the seed coat, between the seed coat and endosperm, and in the endosperm as well as the embryo region of the seed. The pycnidia off fungus has also been observed in the seed coat, between the seed coat and endosperm, and in the endosperm tissue. The fungus also survives on diseased crop debris (Figure 21.18) during off-season in the field. The fungus is disseminated by raindrop splashes. Tools and insects can also disseminate them.

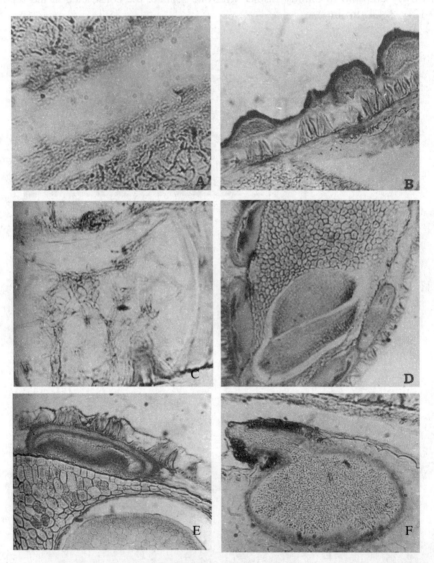

Figure 21.17   Location of *P. vexans* in brinjal seed, (A) mycelium in seed coat, (B) mycelium in between seed coat and endosperm, (C) mycelium in embryo region, (D) pycnidia on seed surface, (E) pycnidia in between seed coat and endosprem, (F) pycnidia in endosperm. (*Courtesy:* Vishunavat, 1992).

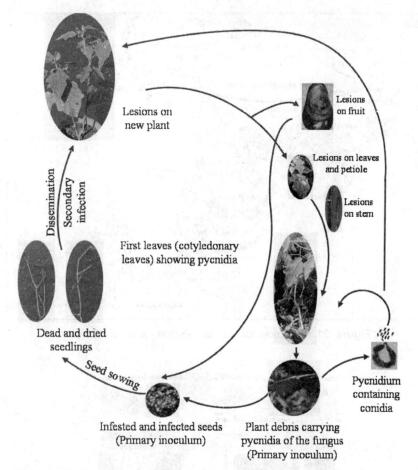

Figure 21.18 Disease cycle of phomopsis blight and fruit rot of brinjal.

Disease management. Burning crop debris and three years of crop rotation may be effective to reduce the disease incidence. Only disease-free seeds should be used. Sprays of dithiocarbamates, copper-oxychloride, captan, captafol, carbendaxim, etc. have been recommended.

21.4.11 Blast of Rice: *Pyricularia grisea*

This serious disease of rice is widely distributed in rice growing areas (Figure 21.19). In India, the disease may cause damage up to 75 per cent. The typical symptoms appear on the leaf sheath, rachis, nodes (culm joints) and even the glumes. The lesions on leaves are small, bluish, water-soaked flecks of about 1-3 mm in diameter. These lesions rapidly enlarge and the centre of the spots appears pale green or dull greyish green changing to grey, and the periphery has a dark brown band with a yellow halo around the lesion. More or less similar spots also develop on leaf sheath. Nodal infection is usually observed after heading, when sheath rots and turns blackish and culm may break at the infected node. Lesions may also develop on internodes in severe infection. As the flowers emerge, the pathogen attacks the peduncles, which are engirdled and the lesion becomes brownish-black. This stage is commonly referred to as rotten neck or neck rot or neck blast or panicle blast (Plate 21.8).

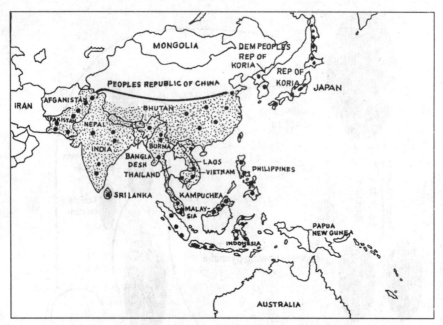

Figure 21.19 Geographical distribution of blast of rice.

Plate 21.8 Symptoms of blast disease of rice (A) leaf, (B) stem and (C) neck infection.

The pathogen. The disease is caused by *Pyricularia grisea*, earlier named as *Trichothecium griseum*, *Pyricularia oryzae* and *Dactylaria oryzae*. The perfect state is *Magnaporthe grisea* (Plate 21.9). Conidiophores are simple or rarely branched, 2-4 septate, single or in fascicles emerging through stomata, olive to fuliginous, swollen at base, tapering towards lighter coloured tip. A single conidium develops at the tip of each conidiophore. Conidia are pyriform to obclavate, lightly pigmented, mostly 2-septate, rarely 1-3 septate and measure 19.2-27.3 × 8.7-10.3 μm, with a distinctly protruding basal hilum.

Perfect state, *Magnaporthe grisea*, also named *Ceratosphaeria grisea* or *Phragmoporthe grisea*, are gregarious, without stoma, base spherical to subspherical, mostly 100-180 μm in diameter, dark brown to black, glabrous, neck long, cylindrical up to 1,100 μm long, with ostiole and periphyses. Asci are hyaline, cylindrical to clavate mostly 60-90 × 10-12 μm, unitunicate, with paraphyses, eight-spored. Ascospores are biseriate, hyaline, fusiform, curved, rounded at both ends mostly 18-23 × 5-7 μm, 3-septate (sometimes 1-, 2- or 4-septate), slightly constricted at septa, extruded in a gelatinous mass.

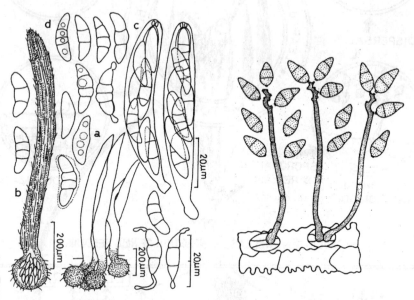

Plate 21.9 Perfect stage *Magnaporthe grisea,* (A–B) perithecia, (C) asci, (D) ascospores, (E) conidiophores and conidia of *P. grisea.*

Disease cycle. In temperate regions, sources of primary inoculum are rice straw residues, seed and weed host and perhaps also teleomorph (perfect state), rice grown at distant locations, and sclerotia and chlamydospores. The pathogen overwinters as mycelium and conidia on diseased straw and seed. In tropical areas, including India airborne conidia, available throughout the year are the source of primary infection (Figure 21.20). In hilly areas of India, the fungus overwinters within straw pile or in straw covered with winter snow, and sporulates in April. The mature conidia are wind disseminated. They are lodged on leaves and germinate in presence of a thin water film (rain, dew, guttation, drops, etc.) by a germ tube. Germination occurs between 10° and 33°C, optimum being 25°C to 28°C. Germ tube develops into an appressorium and the infection peg developing from it penetrates the cuticle or epidermis or enters through stomata.

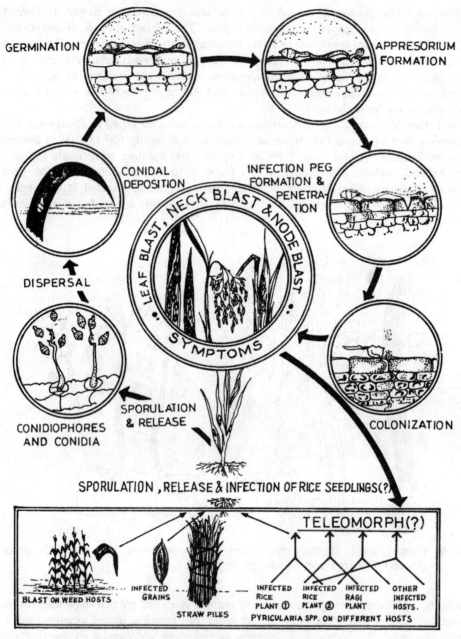

GERMINATION

APPRESORIUM
FORMATION

CONIDAL
DEPOSITION

INFECTION PEG
FORMATION &
PENETRA-
TION

LEAF BLAST, NECK BLAST & NODE BLAST

SYMPTOMS

DISPERSAL

CONIDIOPHORES
AND CONIDIA

SPORULATION
& RELEASE

COLONIZATION

SPORULATION, RELEASE & INFECTION OF RICE SEEDLINGS(?)

TELEOMORPH(?)

BLAST ON WEED HOSTS

INFECTED
GRAINS

STRAW PILES

INFECTED
RICE
PLANT ①

INFECTED
RICE
PLANT ②

INFECTED
RAGI
PLANT

OTHER
INFECTED
HOSTS.

PYRICULARIA SPP. ON DIFFERENT HOSTS

Figure 21.20 Disease cycle of blast of rice.

Disease management

1. Field sanitation, destruction of collateral hosts and other cultural practices help in reducing the disease.
2. Proper adjustments in nitrogen fertilizers and sowing dates could reduce the disease.

3. Fungicidal spray of copper compounds like bordeaux mixture, copper oxychloride, cuprous oxide, sandoz copper, etc. and oragnosulfur compounds like mancozeb and zineb also give good control. Among the organophosphous fungicides, Hinosan (edifenphos) and Kitazin (IBP) are very effective. Benzimidazole and related fungicides are another group of highly effective fungicides that have been widely used for management of disease. More recently, new class of fungicides (melanin biosynthesis inhibitors) and antipenetrants have also been found effective. A number of resistance varieties of rice have also been developed. In India, some resistant cultivars developed for the disease are Co 4, TKM-1, Co 29, Co 30, T-603, T-141, A-67, A-90, A-200, A-249, IR-579 and Bala late-6

21.4.12 Cercospora Leaf Spots of Peanut: *Cercospora arachidicola*

Early and late leaf spots are widely distributed wherever *Arachis hypogaea* L. is cultivated. Geographical distribution is shown in Figure 21.21. Symptoms of diseases are illustrated in Figure 21.22. Lesions are first visible as small chlorotic areas. Early leaf spot lesions are subcircular and usually range from 1 to 10 mm in diameter. Lesions are commonly dark brown on the upper leaf surface and light brown on the lower leaf surface. A chlorotic halo is commonly observed around early leaf spot lesions. Late leaf spot lesions are usually smaller and more nearly circular. Late leaf spot lesions, on the lower leaf surface, are commonly dark gray or black. Concentric rings of conidia on the lower leaf surface are macroscopically visible. Symptoms of early and late leaf spots occur on petioles, stipules, stems and pegs as well.

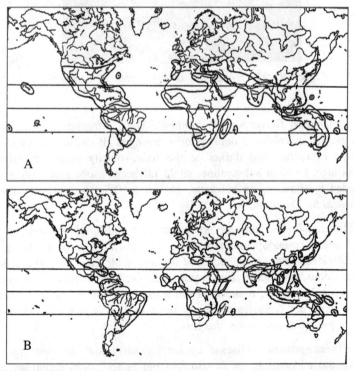

Figure 21.21 Geographical distribution of *Cercospora arachidicola* (A) and (B) *Cercosporidium personatum*.

Figure 21.22 Symptoms of leaf spots of groundnut.

The pathogen

Early leaf spot. (anamorph *Cercospora arachidicola* Hori). Stromata present, slight to 100 μm in diameter, dark brown in colour. Conidiophores arranged in dense fascicles, pale olivaceous or yellowish brown in colour and darker at the base, mostly once geniculate, unbranched, 15-45 × 3-6 μm in size. Conidia sub-hyaline, slight olivaceous, obclavate, often curved, 3 to 12 septate, base rounded to truncate, tip subacute, 35-110 × .0-5.4 μm in size. The teleomorph is *Mycosphaerella arachidis* Deighton.

Late leaf spot. The anamorph is currently known as *Cercosporidium personatum* (Berk. & Curt.) Deighton. Stroma dense, pseudoparenchymatous, up to 130 μm in diameter; conidiophores numerous, pale to olivaceous brown, smooth, one to three geniculate, 10-100 × 3.0-6.5 μm in size, conidial scars conspicuous, prominent, 2 to 3 μm wide; conidia olivaceous, cylindrical, obclavate, usually straight or slightly curved, rounded at the apex, base shortly tapered with a conspicuous hilum, one to nine septa not constricted, mostly three or four septate, 20-70 × 4-9 μm in size. Perithecia scattered, mostly along lesion margins.

Disease cycle and management. Disease cycles for early and late leaf spot are shown in Figure 21.23. Since the teleomorphs of *C. arachidicola* and *C. personatum* are rarely observed, ascospores are probably not an important source of initial inoculum. Conidia produced on crop residue are probably the important source of initial inoculum.

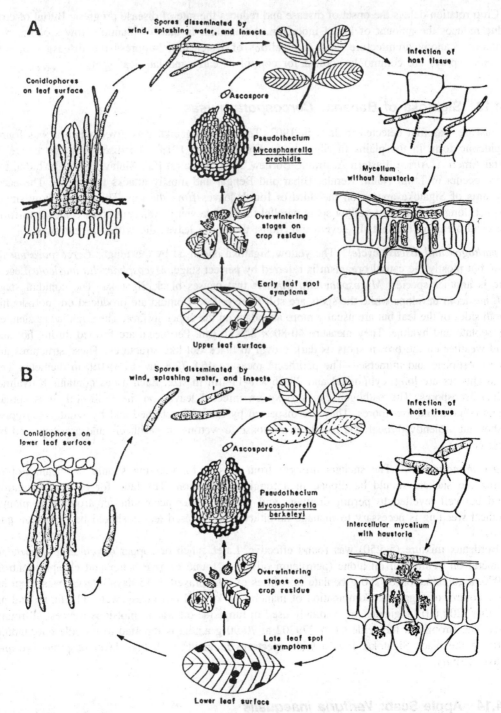

Figure 21.23 Disease cycle for early leaf spot caused by Cercospora arachidicola (A) and late leafspot caused by *Cerocosporidium personatum* (B). (*Source:* Smith, et al., 1992).

Crop rotation delays the onset of disease and reduces the rate of disease progress. Burial of crop residue reduces the amount of initial inoculum. Adjustment in date of planting, row spacing, row orientation, canopy architecture, and applications of water may suppress the disease progress. Fungicidal sprays are commonly applied for control of early and late leaf spots.

21.4.13 Sigatoka of Banana: *Cercospora musae*

This disease was first detected in Java in 1902. The name Sigatoka was given when it was found in epidemic form in the plains of Sigatoka in Fiji Island in 1913. The disease is destructive in Central America, Africa, Eastern Australia, Bornew, Java, Sumatra, Fiji, Malaysia, etc. In India, the disease occurs in Tamil Nadu, Kerala, Bihar and Bengal and mostly attacks the leaves. The early **symptoms** of Sigatoka appear on the third or fourth leaves from the top. The leaves show small, indistinct, longitudinal, light yellow spots parallel to the side veins. Adjacent spots coalesce to form large dead areas on the leaf. In severe infections, the entire leaves die within a few days.

The pathogen and disease cycle. The yellow Sigatoka is caused by the fungus *Cercospora musae* Zimm, but mostly the causal organism is referred by perfect stage, *Mycosphaerella musicola* Leach. There is another species, *Mycosphaerella fijiensis* that causes black Sigatoka. The conidial stage of *M. musicola* develops while the spots are still light yellow. Conidia are produced on sporodochia on both sides of the leaf but are usually more abundant on the upper surface. The conidia are slender, long, septate and hyaline. They measure $40\text{-}80 \times 2.5\text{-}3.6$ µm. Perithecia are formed during hot and humid weather on the brown spots as dark brown to black dot-like structures. These structures are globose, ostiolate and immersed. The perithecia measure 46.8-72.8 (av. 61.8) µm in diameter. The asci in clusters are long, cylindrical and $28\text{-}36 \times 8\text{-}11$ µm in size. Each ascus contains 8 hyaline, 2-celled ascospores. The pathogen can survive on infected leaves on the field soil. It is spread through conidia and ascospores. They are dispersed by raindrop splashed and by wind. Ascospores are shot out violently through the ostiole in response to wetting of perithecia and are dispersed by air currents.

Disease management. The suckers brought from outside for planting should be clean. Before planting the suckers should be dipped in a fungicidal solution. The land for banana plantation should be well levelled to permit drainage and prevent water accumulation around the plants. Periodical weeding is necessary to manage humidity. The diseased leaves should be picked up and destroyed.

Bordeaux mixture (5:5:50) was found effective. Later, zineb or copper oxychloride suspended in mineral oil or mineral oil alone (petroleum oil) were found to give better and cheaper control. In 1970, a combination of 250 g benlate in 6 litres of oil, sprayed at 15 days interval was reported to give control of Sigatoka. Combination of maneb (2.5 kg), oil (18 litres), water (12 litres) and an emulsifier (200 ml) fungicides are routinely used in fungicide-oil-water emulsions for best all-round results. The strobilurin fungicide CGA 279202 at 70-90 g a.i./ha is reported to provide outstanding control of the black Sigatoka. It is a wide spectrum fungicide with high level of protective and curative activity.

21.4.14 Apple Scab: *Venturia inaequalis*

Apple scab is an endemic disease of the apple growing areas of the world. Infection due to scab reduces fruit size, shelf-life and quality of the fruit while severe leaf infections result in reduced leaf areas, defoliation and poor yield. During epidemic years can go upto 70 per cent or even more. The geographical distribution of the disease is shown in Figure 21.24.

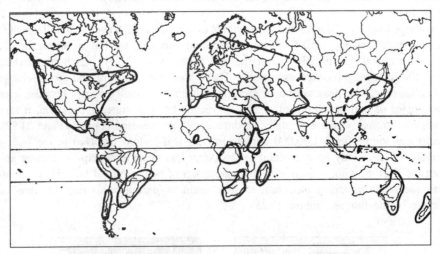

Figure 21.24 Geographical distribution of apple scab.

The symptoms are normally produced on foliage and fruits and are less common on twigs. The infected leaves show olive green round spots with a velvety, indistinct outline that later become brownish black (Plate 21.10). In aged infected leaves, the tissues adjacent to a lesion thicken and the leaf surface gets deformed. When there are many infections on young leaves, they become curled, dwarfed and are distorted. Heavily infected leaves show premature yellowing and defoliation (Plate 21.10). The twig lesions are small, 3-5 µm long and slightly raised which become blister and cause bursting of the bark. The infected fruits develop circular scab lesions; velvety and olive green initially but later become dark, scabby and sometimes cracked (Plate 21.10).

Plate 21.10 Symptoms of apple scab.

The pathogen. *Venturia inaequalis* (Cke,) Wint., completes its life cycle in two stages—the imperfect stage (*Spilocea pomi* Fr.) on living plant parts and perfect or perithecial (*Venturia inaequalis*) on dead fallen leaves. Out of the five races known globally, two races have been so far recorded in India.

The pathogen survives during the cold winter in the diseased leaves that fall on the orchards. As the temperature rises above 10°C in late January and February, the fungus enters the sexual stage and produces pseudothecia initials within the leaf tissue (Plate 21.11). Each pseudothecium may yield 800-1200 unequally bicelled ascospores. These ascospores mature and are discharged over a period of 5-9 weeks. The peak period of ascospore discharge usually occurs between pink and the full-bloom stages of bud development. Once the fungus has penetrated the cuticle, it ramifies into the subcuticular stroma, which eventually produce conidiophores and conidia (Plate 21.12). Conidia are the principal source (upto 1,00,000 conidia in each leaf lesion) involved in the build-up of the disease (Plate 21.12). Many such conidial cycles occur and these also help in creating an epidemic throughout the fruit-growing season with the production of new crops of conidia. Late infection on leaves provides over-wintering inoculum to start again as pseudothecial initials, thus completing the life cycle of the fungus (Figure 21.25).

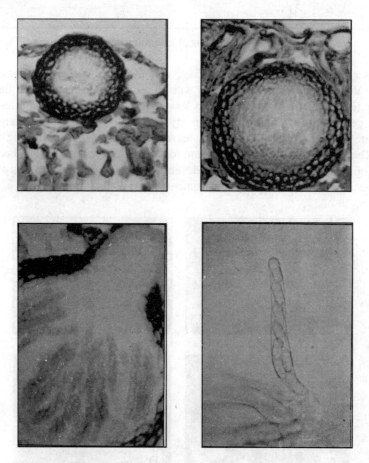

Plate 21.11 Development of pseudothecia, asci and ascospores.

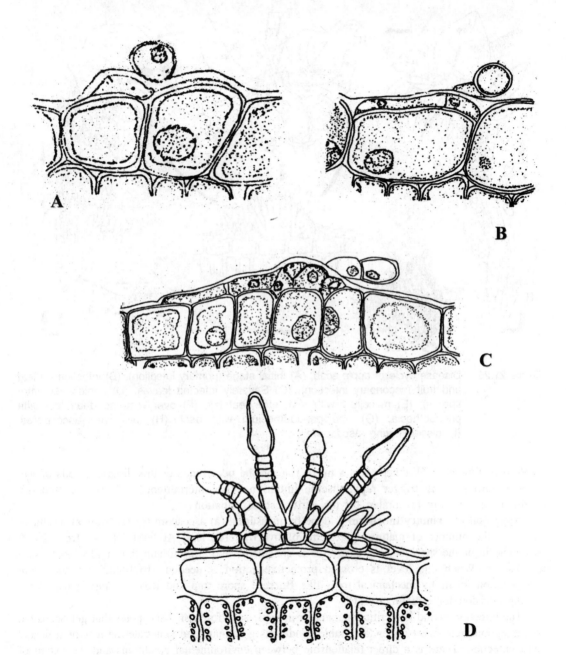

Plate 21.12 Initiation and development of infection by *V. inaequalis,* (A) conidial infection, (B) germination and penetration, (C) subcuticular mycelium, (D) production of conidiophore and conidia.

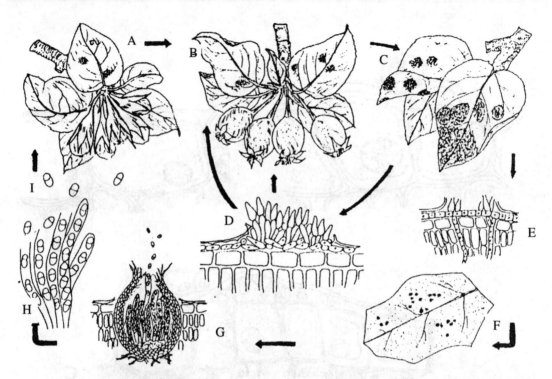

Figure 21.25   Disease cycle of apple scab, (A) initial stage (primary infection), (B) infection on leaf and fruit (secondary infection), (C) Severely infected leaves, (D) conidia (summer spores), (E) mycelium with leaf, after leaf fall, (F) over wintered dead leaf with pseudothecia, (G) ripe pseudothecium with asci, (H) asci with ascospores, (I) disseminating ascospores.

Apple scab forecast.   Weather plays a major role on the occurrence of this disease. Spells of wet weather during spring trigger rapid disease initiation. Also intermittent spells of wet and dry conditions are equally favourable for the early disease initiation.

Appraisal of primary inoculum is done by measuring (a) ascospore (sexual spores) discharge based on the number of mature spores/cm^2 of overwintered leaf. At least 20 asci from 20-25 pseudothecia or the spore bearing structures is considered as the minimum threshold level to start the disease. When this level is crossed protective action is needed. (b) Measuring ascospore concentration in air by mechanical traps like Burkard spore trap and Rotorod trap is useful for making decision for initiating sprays.

The infection period is a critical parameter in apple scab forecast. Ascospores that get deposited on susceptible host tissue under favourable conditions germinate and penetrate the leaf or fruit and cause infection. There is a direct relationship between environmental conditions and the extent of infection established. Extended wetting period at any temperature increases the number of infections as is evident from the Mills table (Table 21.3). Scab predictor analyses and makes a prediction on the incubation period and timing of a protective or eradicant fungicide spray is accordingly decided. For assisting in decision-making, various electronic predictors have been developed and sold in Europe and North America.

Table 21.3 Mills Table to arrive at Incubation Period based on Temperature and Leaf Wetness

Average daily temperature	Minimum wetting hours of leaves for infection			Infection period
0°C	Light	Moderate	Heavy	(Days)
17.2-23.4	9	12	18	9
16.7	9	12	19	10
16.1	9	13	20	10
15.6	9.5	13	20	11
15	10	13	21	12
14.4	10	14	21	12
13.9	10	14	22	13
13.3	11	15	22	14
12.8	11	16	24	14
12.2	11.5	16	24	15
11.7	12	17	25	15
11.1	12	18	26	16
10.6	13	18	27	16
10	14	19	29	17
9.4	14.5	20	30	17
8.9	15	20	30	Extended infection period

Scab warning service in India. Apple scab forewarning service currently carried out through this method is being followed. The infection periods of the pathogen are monitored by measuring leaf wetness period, ambient temperature and arriving through the Mills table (Table 21.3). Besides infection period, periodic information on the maturation and discharge of ascospores is also collected from orchards, forecasting the time and extent of primary infection. For the prediction of secondary infection and the build up of epidemic, monitoring of the infection period becomes most important. The information collected from field laboratories on the infection period is passed on to the orchardists. The message is flashed 2-3 times through 'All India Radio' on the urgent need to undertake immediate spray or to reschedule already recommended spray programme. Such forewarning has benefitted the growers in minimizing damages due to scab and also reduce fungicides usage.

Disease management. There are two approaches. (a) Interrupting the life cycle of the scab pathogen and (b) protection against primary and secondary infection.

Interrupting the life cycle. In order to interrupt the life cycle of the pathogen a spray of 5 per cent urea, shortly before general leaf fall is recommended for hastening the decomposition of the apple leaf that would fall down during autumn. Some of the fungicides (Baycor @ 0.2% or Saprol @ 0.2%) can also be sprayed in place of urea to reduce the level of infection. In addition, physically collecting and destroying the infected fallen leaves is also to be followed to reduce the disease development.

Protection of infection courts. The intensity of apple scab can be substantially reduced by timely application of fungicides that are either protective, curative or have eradicant action against the pathogen. Such spray strategies are in popular use (Table 21.4) in all apple-growing areas in India. These sprays are recommended at various susceptible phenological stages of apple trees.

Table 21.4 Apple Scab Control Spray Schedule for the Orchardists of Himachal Pradesh for the Year 1992

Schedule	Tree stage	Fungicide	Grams/100 litres
1	Silver tip to green tip	Chlorothalonil or	400.00
		Dodine or	100.00
		Mancozeb or	400.00
		Dithianon or	75.00
		Captan	300.00
2	Pink bud stage	Mancozeb + Sulfur	300+200
3	Petal fall stage	Carbendazim	50.00
4	Fruit set stage	Dodine or	75.00
		Bitertanol or	75.00
		Mancozeb or	300.00
		Captan	300.00
5	Fruit development stage	Carbendazim or	25.00
		Thiophanate methyl +	25.00+
		Mancozeb or	250.00
		Captan or	300.00
		Dithianon	50.00
6	Fruit development (after 14 days)	Mancozeb or	300.00
		Bitertanol or	75.00
		Captan	300.00
7	20-25 days before fruit harvest	Mancozeb or	300.00
		Captan	300.00
8	Pre-leaf fall	Urea	5000.00

Post symptom spray. Even after establishment of infection, certain measures can be taken. Fungicides like myclobutanil, fenarimil, carbendazim, dodine, etc. that have a high level of eradicant or antisporulant effect to inhibit the spore production and reduce new infections.

Breeding resistant varieties. Besides Prima, Priscilla and Sir Prize, six other scab resistant varieties namely Macfree, Coop-12, Red Free, Nova Easygro, Liberty and Freedom have also been introduced from USA and Canada in Himachal Pradesh. Among these, Coop-12 and Red Free have shown promise in mid-hills. These varieties are being utilized in hybridization programme for the development of scab resistant apple varieties of the Delicious group.

21.4.15 Ascochyta Blight of Gram: *Ascochyta rabiei*

Ascochyta blight of gram (Chickpea, Bengal gram, *Cicer arietinum* L.) is one of the important diseases of this crop. It occurs from northwest India through Pakistan to the countries bordering the Mediterranean seas and parts of Eastern Europe (Figure 21.26). Nene (1981) and Chaube (1987, 1992) had reviewed different aspects of the disease.

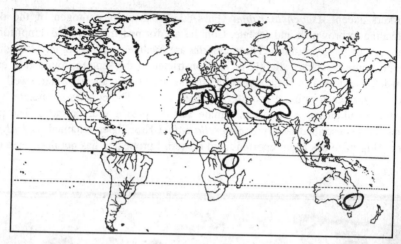

Figure 21.26 Geographical distribution of ascochyta blight of chickpea.

The early **symptoms** appear on leaves and pods (circular spots) and on petioles and stems (elongated spots). The depressed brown spots are surrounded by a brownish red margin. The spots may coalesce and the entire leaf turns brown, presenting a scorched appearance. On the green pods the pycnidia (black dot like bodies) arranged in concentric circles (Plate 21.13). Seeds within the pods may show lesions. When the spots on the stem completely girdle them, the parts above the lesion droop and wilt.

Plate 21.13 Symptoms of ascochyta blight of chickpea.

Most workers accept *Ascochyta rabiei* (Pass.) Labrousse, as pathogen of the disease. The mycelium is hyaline to brownish and septate. Conidia are formed from hyaline, ampliform phialides from the inner cells of the pycnidium. These conidia are hyaline, oval to oblong, straight or slightly curved, 1-septate, some 0-septate, slightly or not constricted at the septum, rounded at each end and measure 10-16 × 3.5 µm in size. If the pycnidia are moistened they absorb water, swell, and a slimy mass of conidia oozes out forming a spore horn (Plate 21.14). The conidia germinate by long germ tubes. Within the pycnidia the conidia can remain viable up to a year or more. The perfect stage of *A. rabiei* has been described as *Mycosphaerella rabiei* Kov., later renamed as *Didymella rabiei* (Kov.) von Arx. This stage has been reported from Eastern Europe and has not been seen in the Indian subcontinent

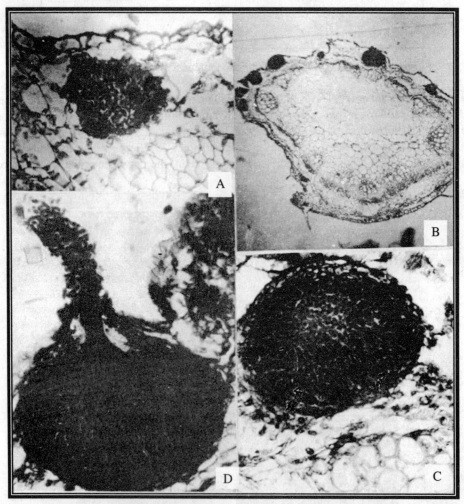

Plate 21.14 Development of pycnidium and release of conida of *A. rabiei,* (A) subepidermal aggregates of fungal mycelium, (b) developing pycnidium, (C) mature pycnidium, (D) mature pycnidium with pycnidiospores oozing out ot ostiole.J

Disease cycle and management. The fungus survives as pycinidia on diseased plant debris and also on seeds (Plate 21.15). However, affected seeds normally do not germinate. Pycnidial survival in debris depends on moisture, irrespective of temperature. It can survive for over two years at 10-35°C if relative humidity on soil surface is 0-3%. It loses viability rapidly if the humidity is 65 to 100% or if the debris is buried deep in the soil. On contaminated seed, 50% of the conidia (pycnidiospores) survive for 5 months at 25-30°C but only 5% at 35°C. Mycelium may also be present in the seed coat. If deep lesions are formed on the seed, pycnidia may be present in the seed coat (Figure 21.27).

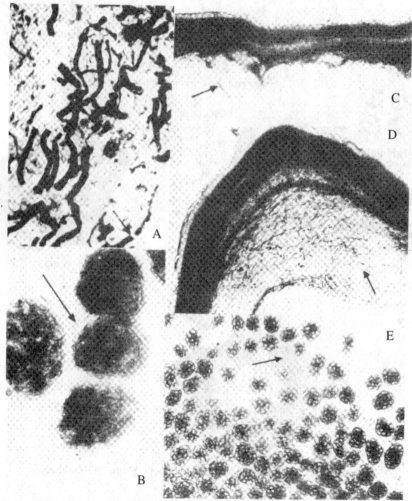

Plate 21.15 Location of *Ascochyta rabiei* in chickpea seeds, (A) mycelium in seed coat (whole mount) 675x, (B) mycelium in cotyledons (whole mount) 675x, (C) pycnidia in seed coat (V.S.) 150x, (D) mycelium in seed coat (V.S.) 150x, (E) mycelium in cotyledons (V.S.) 150x. (*Courtesy:* K. Vishunuvat)

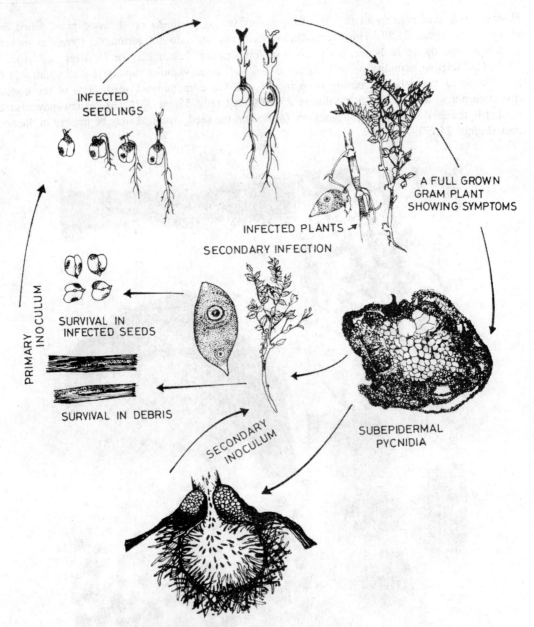

INFECTED
SEEDLINGS

A FULL GROWN
GRAM PLANT
SHOWING SYMPTOMS

INFECTED PLANTS

SECONDARY INFECTION

PRIMARY INOCULUM

SURVIVAL IN
INFECTED SEEDS

SURVIVAL IN DEBRIS

SECONDARY INOCULUM

SUBEPIDERMAL
PYCNIDIA

Figure 21.27 Disease cycle of ascochyta blight of chickpea.

The spread of the disease occurs through conidia disseminated by raindrop splashed in a windy weather, insects, contact between leaves and movement of animals through the field. The disease spread fast if wet weather with strong winds occurs in February and March when the temperature is around 22-26°C. Years of high rainfall during the crop season are conducive to epidemics of the disease.

1. Removal and destruction of dead plant debris, rotation and deep sowing, intercropping of gram with cereals to reduce spread and deep ploughing to bury the debris is recommended.
2. Seeds can be treated with copper sulfate, thiram, benomyl or calixin M. The last named fungicide is reported to completely eradicate the inoculum from the seed.

In mild attacks spraying with zineb, ferbam, maneb, captan and daconil is recommended. However, the disease spread is so fast that 4-6 spraying may be required and this will be costly.

21.4.16 Important Powdery Mildew Diseases

Powdery mildew of grapevines: Uncinula necator.   It occurs in mild to severe form in North and South America, Europe, parts of Africa and in Australia. The first diagnostic symptom is the appearance of white patches of powdery growth on both surfaces of leaves. Similar symptoms are also seen on young blossoms and young berries. Later infected berries turn dark, irregular in shape and develop cracks. Diseased vines appear wilted and dwarfed (Plate 21.16). *Uncinula necator* is the telomorphic stage of pathogen (anamorph: *Oidium tuckeri* Berk). Simple and erect conidiophores of *Uncinula necator* (Schw.) Bur. develop from the ectophytic hyphae. They bear a chain of 3-4 conidia, which are oval and measure 25-30 × 15-17 µm. Development of cleistothecial stage is uncertain. In India, perfect stage is not found. Fully mature ascocarps are black round bodies and measure 75-100 µm. The peridium is covered with 8-25 septate appendages, which are coiled at the distal end. Each cleistothecium contains 2-8 ovoid asci measuring 48-60 × 37-45 µm. In each ascus, there are 4-6 ascospores, which are oval and measure 21-31 µm (Plate 21.17).

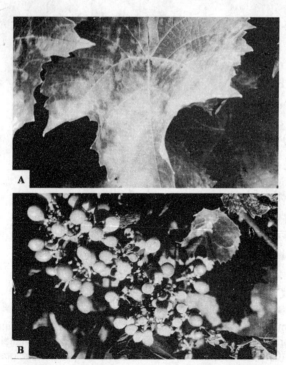

Plate 21.16 (A) Powdery mildew on grapevine foliage and (B) on grape berries.

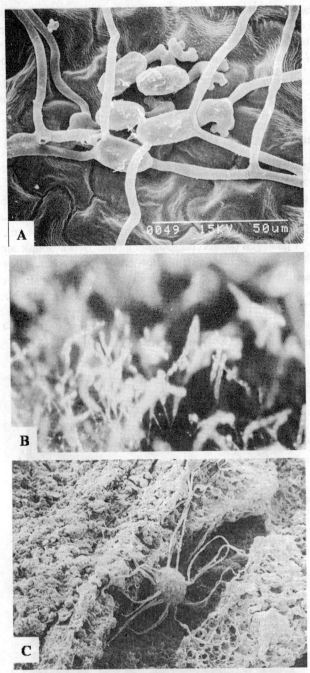

Plate 21.17 (A) Germinating ascospores of *Uncinula necator* showing young colony and appressoria, (B) epilluminescence micrograph of conidial chains of *Uncinula necator*, (C) cleistothecia of *Uncinula necator* on bark of grapevine.
(*Source:* R.C. Pearson and D.M. Gadoury, 1996)

Disease cycle and management. The pathogen perennates through mycelium in diseased buds, fallen berries and through cleistothecia, if formed. The fungus grows into the bud, where it remains in a dormant state on the inner bud scale until the following season. Shortly after bud break, the fungus is reactivated and shoots growing from infected buds become covered with white mycelium. Conidia are produced abundantly on these infected shoots (called flag shoot), and they are readily disseminated by the wind. Cleistothecia are washed by late summer and autumn rains to the bark of vine, where they overwinter.

Cultural practices like trimming of developing shoots to reduce shading and allow free ventilation are important. Pruning after shedding of leaves, thining out and cutting back of laterals, and removal and destruction of diseased parts are important to achieve reduction of inoculum. Dusting of vines thrice with sulfur (300 mesh) gives effective control. Foliar sprays of bayleton (triadimefon), karathane (dinocap), sulfex (0.25%), calixin (0.05%), topsin-M(0.1%), thiovit (0.25%) have been advocated.

Powdery mildew of apple: Podosphaera leucotricha. The disease is reported from almost all apple-growing areas (Figure 21.28). It is common in the apple orchards of North India. Nursery plants are damaged more than adult plants. The disease appears soon after the buds develop into new leaves and shoots. Early symptoms on such leaves consist of small patches of white/gray powdery masses on the surface of leaves and twigs. Later, the leaves turn brown from the tip downward. Severe attack results in partial defoliation of the tree. Fruit buds suffer more damage than the vegetative buds. Infected fruits remains small, deformed and tend to develop rough surface (Plate 21.18).

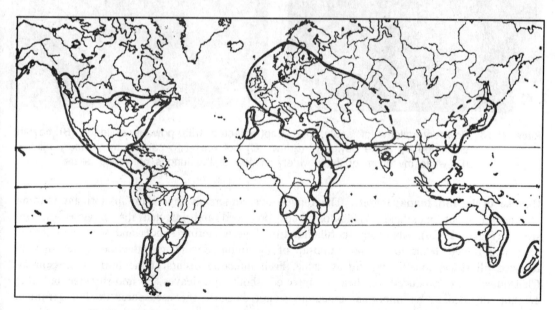

Figure 21.28 Geographical distribution of powdery mildew of apple.

The fungal pathogen *Podosphaera leucotricha* (Ell. & Ev.) Salm is the cause of disease. Aerial conidiophores bear a chain of conidia which are hyaline, oval and measure 25-30 × 10-12 μm. Development of ascocarp is rare particularly in India. The cleistothecia that develop are black globose and measure 75-96 μm. Two types of appendages are formed over the surface of the cleistothecia. Some are long and stiff while others are short and tortuous. Each cleistothecium contains a single ascus measuring 55-70 × 40-50 μm. Each ascus has eight ascospores.

Plate 21.18 Powdery mildew of apple, (A) shoot infected with powdery mildew, (B) flowers distoreted by apple powdery mildew, (C) net russeting caused by powsery mildew, (D) white mycelium of the powdery mildew of the fungus on young pears.

Disease cycle and management. The fungus overwinters as mycelium in dormant terminal and lateral shoot buds and in blossom buds produced and infected the previous growing season (Figure 21.29). Abundant sporulation from overwintering shoots and secondary lesions on young foliage leads to a rapid build-up of inoculum. Secondary infection cycles may be repeated till susceptible tissues are available. Fruit infection occurs at the time of blossoming. Cleistothecia are produced on heavily infected shoot and leaves in mid-summer but they are not regarded as an important inoculum source because the ascospores do not germinate readily.

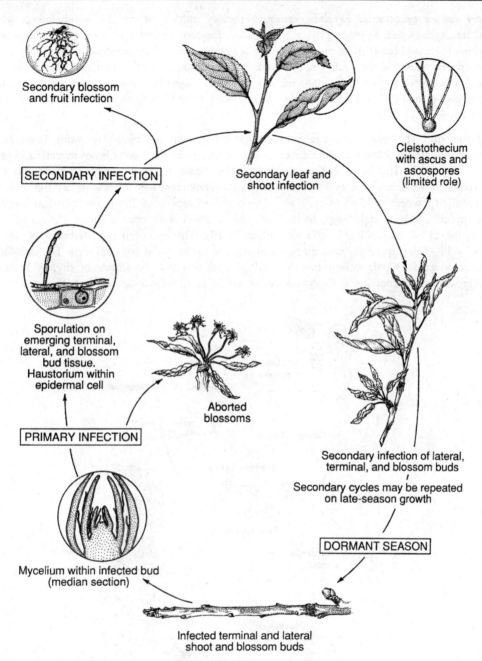

Figure 21.29 Disease cycle of powdery mildew of apple.

Four sprays of bavistin (0.05%) or morocide (0.1%) staring at bud swell stage and repeated at 15 days interval give good control. 0.05% triadimefon (Bayleton) gives best control as it persists on host surface by over 15 days. Sharma and Gupta (1994) observed maximum reduction in spore germination and germ tube growth by triforine, tridemorph, bitertanol and carbendazim.

Powdery mildew of cereals: Erysiphegramins. Powdery mildew of cereals, which infects wheat, barley, oats, rye, as well as many grasses (*Agropyron, Bromus, Dactylis, Elymus,* etc.), is distributed throughout the world but is more prevalent in the temperate zones. The **symptoms** are mostly visible on the upper surface of the leaf. Under favourable conditions, sheath, stem and glumes are also affected. The mycelial growth is white initially (conidial stage) but later on turns gray or reddish brown (cleistothecial stage). Infected plants are stunted. Infected leaves eventually become wrinkled, spirally twisted and deformed.

The pathogen. The fungus that cause the disease was known as *Erysiphe gramins,* however, the new name proposed is *Blumeria graminis* because of large ascocarps, two types of mycelia and grass-hosts (Speer, 1973). This heterothallic causal organism is now referred as *Blumeria graminis* f. sp. *tritici* (powdery mildew of barley), *B. graminis f.* sp. *avenae* (powdery mildew of oats), *B. graminis f.* sp. *secalis* (powdery mildew of rye), etc. The conidiophores arise from hemispherical swellings on the mycelial web, at right angle to the leaf surface. Each conidiophore forms a chain of 10-20 conidia, the eldest one being at the top (Plate 21.19). The ascocarp (cleistothecia) measuring 160-192 × 120-130 μm are globose, black and partly immersed in the mycelial weft. The cleiothecial surface is covered by pale yellow myceloid appendages that may be simple or slightly branched. Each cleistothecium contains 9-30 cylindrical or ovoid asci, measuring 40-60 × 25 μm.

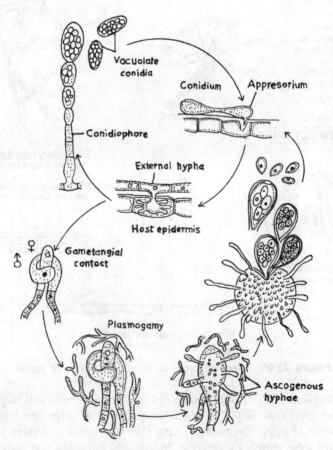

Plate 21.19 Life cycle of *Blumeria* sp.

Disease cycle and management. In temperate regions the fungus survives through cleistothecia formed in soil. At low temperature, the cleistothecia remain viable for about 13 years. According to Sharma, et al., (1992) the cleistothecia are the source of primary inoculum in temperate regions like Lahaul and Spiti in H.P. (India) whereas in other parts of North India, the conidia introduce the disease. The fungicides recommended for management of disease include ethirimol, dimethirimol, benlate (0.1%), karathane (0.1%), calixin, baytan, bayleton and vigil, HD 2204, HB 208, CPAN 1676, VL 401 and HD 2074 have been found to possess high degree of resistance.

Powdery mildew of peas: Erysiphe polygoni. This disease occurs throughout the world. In plains of India, the disease appears towards January end to February, when temperature starts rising, causing substantial loss almost every year. Munjal, et al., (1963) observed the same fungus on cabbage, sugarbeet, turnip, clover and lentil. Crop infection may reduce pod number by 21-31% and pod weight by 26 to 47% (Munjal, et. al., 1963). The early symptoms, scattered spots with white growth, appear on upper surface of leaves. The disease is severe on plants at flowering stage to pod formation. The powdery white spots completely cover the entire plant except roots. The plants and the whole field looks greyish white (Figure 21.30).

Figure 21.30 Powdery mildew of pea.

The pathogen, *Erysiphe polygoni* DC, is virtually an aggregate of several individual species. The species described under the name *E. polygoni*, on different hosts in India, comprise eight species namely, *E. polygoni*, *E. pisi*, *E. betae*, *E. heraclei*, *E. martie*, *E. renunculi* and *E. salvae*. Expect haustoria, the entire thallus develops on host surface (ectophytic growth). The mycelium is fine, hyaline, thick and persistent. Asexual sporophores and spores are produced in huge numbers. On short conidiophores, the conidial chains develop. The conidia are single celled, hyaline, elliptical to cylindrical. Sexual reproduction leading to formation of ascocarp and asci is not very common. The entire process of gametangial contact till formation of cleistothecia is supposed to take place in soil on fallen infected leaves. The cleistothecia measuring 90 mm bear myceloid appendages and 2-8 asci.

Disease cycle and management. The survival and carry over of inoculum from season to season is not yet fully known. Information pertaining to survival of the pathogen is summarized in the following flow chart:

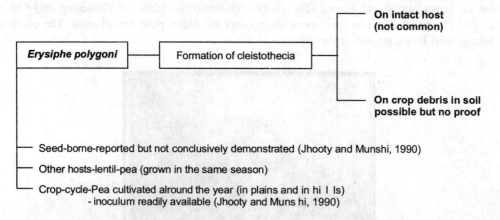

The analysis of the information available clearly reveals that asexual spores produced on the hill crops during summer cause infection on pea and lentil during winter when these crops are raised. Management of the disease has been studied extensively. Among the fungicides recommended are Sulfur dust (200 mesh) @ 25-30 kg/ha, elosal (0.5%), karathane WD (0.2%), morocide (0.1%), cosan (2 kg/ha), sulfex (0.25%), calxin (0.1%), bitertanol (Baycor), and triadimenol (Bayton). Several short duration varieties that mature before the onset of disease, escape infection though without genetic resistance.

Powdery mildew of cucurbits: Erysiphe cichoracearum. The disease is known to occur almost in all those areas where cucurbits are cultivated. Besides cucurbits, several other crops like potato and tobacco seedling, lettuce, sunflower, mango, castor, etc. are also attacked by the same pathogen. The initial symptoms include development of tiny, white, superficial spots on leaves and stems (Figure 21.31). The ectophytic growth turns powdery as the disease advances. Under favourable conditions, the entire host surface is covered with powdery growth of the fungus. Though not common under Indian conditions, black pin-point like bodies (cleistothecia) appear on infected parts, late in the season. Premature defoliation and undersized fruits are also observed, which may cause damage.

Figure 21.31   Powdery mildew of cucumber.

The pathogen. *Erysiphe cichoracearum* DC and *Sphaerotheca fuliginea* (Sc.) Poll. and *Sphaerotheca fuliginea* (Schlecht ex Fr.) Poll. are known to be associated with the powdery mildew of cucurbits in various parts of the world.

Erysiphe cichoracearum DC ex Merat–The mycelium is usually well developed. Ellipsoidal or barrel shaped conidia measuring 24 × 14-26 μm are formed in long chains. Cleistothecia formed are gregarious or scattered, globose and measure 90-135 μm in diameter. Appendages are numerous; basally inserted, myceloid, interwoven with mycelium and hyaline to dark brown. They are rarely branched, 10-25 asci develop in each cleistothecium. The asci are ovate to broadly ovate, rarely subglobose, more or less stalked, 60-90 × 25-50 μm in size. Ascospores two per ascus, rarely three, measure 20-30 × 12-18 μm.

Sphaerotheca fuliginea (Schlecht ex Fr.) Poll—Mycelium and conidia are similar to that of *E. cichoraciarum*. The cleistothecia that develop late in the season are comparatively smaller (66-98 μm). There is only one ascus per ascocarp. The asci are elliptical to subglobose and measure 50-80 × 60 μm. Each ascus has 8 ascospores, which are ellipsoid to nearly spherical and measure 17-22 × 12-20 μm. Three physiologic races of the pathogen have been reported (Kaur and Jhooty, 1985 and Khan and Sharma, 1993). Race 3 is most wide spread and infects most of the cucurbits.

Disease cycle and management.   The carryover of the pathogen from season to season is not fully known. It is postulated that the fungus survives through cleistothecia that are formed on stray cucurbit plants in isolated areas and serve as source of primary inoculum. In addition to this, the wild cucurbits and stray plants of cultivated cucurbits harbour the conidial stage of the fungus and release conidia for primary infection of the spring and summer sown cucurbits. Fungicides are the only available option for control of the disease. Spraying the crop with karathane (0.5-0.2%) is recommended.

Powdery mildew of mango: Oidium mangiferae: This is one of the devastating diseases of mango affecting almost all mango areas. First appearance of disease was recorded in Brazil in 1914. In India, the disease is widespread causing 20 to 90% losses in different parts and is a serious threat to mango production. The disease appears at the flowering time (January-March). The characteristic symptoms are the presence of white, superficial, powdery growth on all the aerial parts like inflorescence, leaves, stalk of inflorescence and young fruits. Mango flowers are attacked before fertilization, which results in dropping of infected, unfertilized flowers. Young fruits are covered entirely by mildew growth and it results in premature fruit drop at pea size stage (Plate 21.20). The disease is caused by *Oidium mangiferae* Berthet. The perfect stage belongs to *E. polygoni* (Palti, et al., 1974). Conidiophores emerging from the superficial mycelium are unbranched, 61-103 μm long and 18-22 μm wide. Conidia are borne singly, sometimes in pairs or in chains of 20-40.

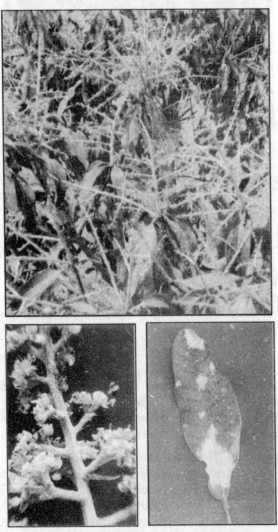

Plate 21.20 Symptoms of powdery mildew of mango.

Disease cycle and management. The pathogen perennates in intact malformed infected panicle mostly hidden under dense foliage where conidia are produced within the ensuring season. Abundant conidia are produced and blown over to the new flushes on young panicles. Spores germinate within 5-7 hrs. The germ tube produces haustoria inside the plant cells. Application of fungicides has been the only effective means to control the disease. Fungicides such as wettable sulfur, carbendazim, bitertanol, triadimefon, tridemorph and dinocap have given significant control.

21.4.17 Genera *Helminthosporium* and *Bipolaris* and Plant Diseases

In *Helminthosporium* conidiophores are determinate, ceasing growth with production of apical conidia, relatively short and simple or, sparingly branched. In *Bipolaris*, the conidiophores are simple or sparingly branched, indeterminate continuing growth sympodially. In *Bipolaris*, conidia are fusiform slightly curved germinating from the end cell only (Plate 21.21).

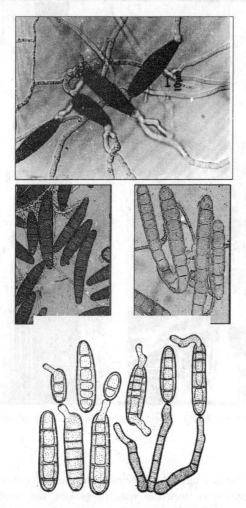

Plate 21.21 Anamorphs of *Cochlibolus* and *Pyrenophora*.

Helminthosporium and *Bipolaris* occur globally and cause leaf spots and blights on many important crop plants of the grass family. Among several diseases caused by these pathogens, three of them, brown spot or blight of rice, southern corn leaf blight and victoria blight of oats caused sudden and catastrophic epidemics that resulted in huge crop losses, human suffering, and new approaches to disease control.

Southern corn leaf blight is caused by *Cochliobolus heterostrophus*. The pathogen causes small (0.6 by 2.5 cm) numerous lesions that almost cover the entire leaf. Some races of the pathogen also attack stalks, leaf sheaths, ear husk, ears and cobs. Affected kernels are covered with a black, felty mould, and cobs may rot, or if the shank is infected early, the ear may be killed prematurely.

Brown spot of rice caused by *Cochliobolius miyabeanus* (anamorph: *Drechslera oryzae*). The symptoms of disease appear on coleoptile, the leaves, the leaf sheath and also the glumes. The spots are brown, small, all circular or oval. Badly affected leaves turn brown and dry out (Plate 21.22).

Plate 21.22 Symptoms of brown spot of rice.

Disease management

1. Management of diseases caused by *Pyrenophora* and *Cochliobolus* depends on the use of pathogen free seed, seed treatment with fungicides, hot weather ploughing, proper crop rotation and balanced fertilization.

2. Wherever, resistant/tolerant varieties are available, they should be grown that too under fungicide umbrella.

3. Several fungicides like chlorothalonil, iprodione, vinclozolin and maneb can be applied at the onset of the disease and then repeated at 10-15 days intervals.

21.4.18 Genus *Alternaria* and Plant Diseases

Fungus *Alternaria* belongs to fungi imperfectii group and is almost cosmopolitan in distribution. Some species like *Alternaria tenuis* or *Alternaria solani* have wide host-range but there are many, which are host specific and produce host specific toxins during pathogenesis. The disease first become visible as small, isolated, scattered pale brown spots on leaves and the leaflets. These spots become covered with greenish-blue growth of the fungus. Lower leaves are attacked first and the disease progresses upwards. In the necrotic tissue, concentric ridges develop to produce a target board effect the characteristic symptom (Plate 21.23). There is usually a narrow chlorotic zone around the spots.

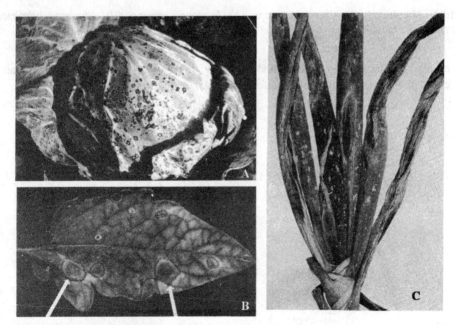

Plate 21.23 Symptoms caused by Alternaria spp. on (A) cabbage, (B) brinjal and (c) onion.

The pathogen. The mycelium consists of septate, branched, light brown hyphae which become darker with age. Conidiophores emerge through the stomata from the dead centres of the spots. They are short and dark coloured. Conidia are muriform, beaked and borne single or in chains. They develop from a bud formed by the apical cell of conidiophore. 3 to 10 or even more transverse septa and a few longitudinal septa are present in each conidium (Plate 21.24). *Alternaria* reproduces mainly asexually. The perfect stage known for *A. tenuis* is *Plespora* of ascomycota. *Lewia* is another teleomorph of *Alternaria* spp. causing leaf spores and blights.

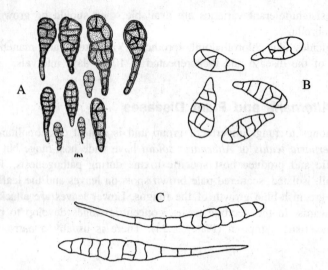

Plate 21.24 Morphology of Alternaria spore, (A) *Alternaria triticina*, (B) *Alternaria brissicicola*, (C) *Alternaria brassicae*.

Disease cycle. The fungus has several modes of survival, may be soil borne/seed borne/air borne. Disease cycle of Alternaria blight of crucifers is shown in Figure 21.32.

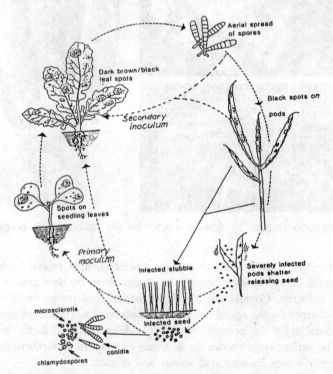

Figure 21.32 Disease cycle of *Alternaria* blight of crucifers.

The possible ways and venues involved in survival of inoculum are shown in the following flow chart.

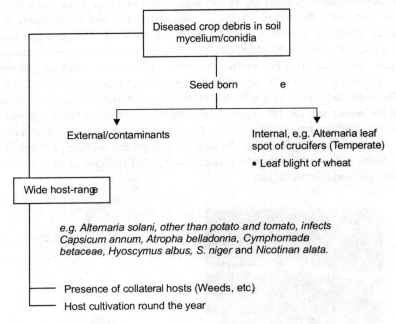

Important diseases and their causal agents

- Early blight of potato and tomato-*Alternaria solani*
- Alternaria leaf spot of crucifers
  - (A) *Alternaria brassicicola* (Schw) Wiltshire
  - (B) *Alternaria brassicae* (Berk.) Sacc.
  - (C) *Alternaria raphani* Groves & Skolko
- Leaf blight of wheat—*Alternaria triticina,* Prasad and Prabhu
- Purple blotch of onion—*Alternaria porri* (Ellis) Cif.
- Black rot of oranges—*Alternaria citri*
- Brown spot of tobacco—*Alternaria longipes*

Diseases management

1. Healthy and certified seeds should be used from fresh crop.
2. Field sanitation is essential. Diseased plants should be destroyed.
3. Appropriate and adequate nitrogen application.
4. Before sowing, the seeds should be treated with fungicides such as thiram, captan, rovral, etc. to protect the seed from soil borne inoculum.
5. Seeds may also be treated with formulations of bioagents like *Trichoderma harzianum, T. viride.*
6. Foliar sprays of a number of fungicides have been recommended. Dithane Z-78, dithane M-45, antrocol, captan, difolatan, blitox-50, etc., invariably 3-4 sprays are required at 10-15 days intervals.
7. Cultivate tolerant/resistant cultivars and varieties wherever and whenever available.

21.4.19 Genus *Sclerotinia* and Plant Diseases

Fungal genus *Sclerotinia*, especially *S. minor* and *S. sclerotiorum* cause destructive disease of numerous vegetable crops. Sclerotinia diseases occur worldwide and affect plants at all stages of growth, including seedlings, mature plants and harvested products. The pathogen has a very wide host range attacking more than 350 plant species belonging to more than 60 families. The damage caused may vary depending upon the weather conditions, host susceptibility and nature of infection. The symptoms caused by this fungus vary with the host plant or plant part attacked and with weather conditions. The Sclerotinia diseases are known under a great variety of names, such as cottony rot, stem rot, head rot, watery soft rot, crown rot, drop white mould, blossom blight and wilt (Plate 21.25). In some crops like sunflower the fungus causes head rot, stem rot and wilt. In others like chickpea, pea, tomato, etc., there may be fruit and blossom rot and general wilting of leaves. In cauliflower, it is curd rot. In oilseed crucifers, there is general wilting and collapse of the plant. Vegetables like tomato develop rot during transit also.

Plate 21.25 (A–B) Sclerotinia stem rot of chickpea, (C) sclerotinia white mould of bean, (D) sclerotinia cottony soft rot of carrot.

The most obvious and typical early symptoms of the disease is the appearance on the infected plant of a white fluffy mycelial growth (white mould) in which soon develop large, compact resting bodies or sclerotia later. On opening the dry portion of the stem, the pith can be seen full of sclerotia or they may also develop on the stem surface as white mycelial web sticking to the host surface. On pea pods, white mycelium develops on pod surface, mostly at the basal and distal ends causing necrosis. Later, the fungus enters the pods and rots the developing seeds.

The disease is caused by *Sclerotinia sclerotiorum*. The hyphae are closely septate, 9-18 µm broad, inter as well as intracellular. The sclerotia are pinkish white when young, becoming dark brown to black at maturity. They vary in size and shape, being flattened, elongated or roughly spherical, 2-12 mm in diameter.

Each sclerotium develops 2-5 columnar stripes on germination. Each stripe produces an apothecium at its tip. Apothecia are brownish or fawn coloured, funnel shaped and 6-10 µm wide. Several asci develop in each apothecial cup. The asci are cylindrical, 108-152 × 4.5-10 µm in size, unicellular, ovate and 7-16 × 3.6-10 µm in size. The ascospores are the chief means of spread of the disease. They are discharged violently through an apical pore in the ascus.

Disease cycle and management. The pathogen survives as sclerotia, present on soil surface or in crop debris or as admixture with the seed. In the next season, the crop becomes infected by ascospores produced after germination of the sclerotia (Figure 21.33). The pathogen spreads from field to field or from one area to another by wind-borne ascospores and soil adhering to seedlings, farm equipment, animals or man. The pathogen may also spread through manure, if the cattle are fed with contaminated feed. However, in cool and wet Tarai areas of U.P., sclerotia present on or in soil decompose rapidly, and only those present in stem of infected plant debris germinate in next season. In north India, outbreaks of the disease may occur by ascospores from germinating sclerotia during mid-winter. Apothecia formation occurs abundantly during winter, when suitable temperature, sunlight and moisture are most favourable for sclerotial germination.

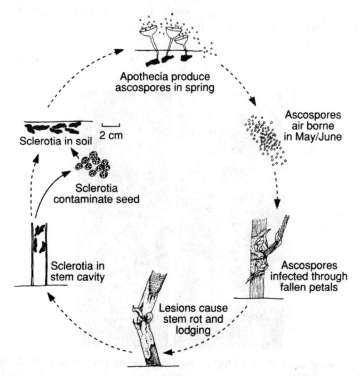

Figure 21.33 Disease cycle of *Sclerotiorum* (stem rot of oilseed rape).

Suitable cultural practices may help in reducing primary inoculum. These include removal of plant debris, ploughing of soil (deep burial of sclerotia), flooding of soil (reduces sclerotia), crop rotation (onion, spinach, maize, etc.) and soil solarization.

Sprays of fungicides, viz. benomyl, dichloran or thiophanate-methyl, iprodione and vinclozolin also have given good control. Biological control has also been achieved by using *Coniothyrium minitans*, *Gliocladium virens*, *G. roseum* and *Trichoderma viride*.

21.4.20 Genus *Botrytis* and Plant Diseases

Botrytis diseases are probably the most common and most widely distributed disease of vegetables, fruits, ornamentals and even some field crops. These diseases appear as blossom blight, fruit rots, damping off, stem cankers or rots, leaf spots and tuber and corn rot. Some of the major hosts affected by these diseases among vegetables and fruits. In field crops, chickpea gray mould has become an important disease in India. It was first reported from Pantnagar in 1969 (Joshi and Singh, 1969). Losses varying from 70 to 100% are still reported when weather is favourable for the disease (Mukherjee, *et al.*, 1997). The gray mould rot of apples is a serious problem in temperate climate.

Symptoms of gray mould rot vary with hosts and plant organs affected. In chickpea, the disease causes leaf blight and rotting including rot of the stem. A gray aerial growth covers the affected parts. Those that survive produce flowers, which are soon attacked by the mould, and there is blossom blight. In the lettuce damping off phase, seedlings collapse and topple over. Soon the dead seedlings are covered with the gray mould which is made up of conidiophores and conidia of the fungus. In bunch rot of grapes, infection can occur on young as well as relatively older leaves which show irregularly shaped necrotic spots. Infected berries become dark coloured and show typical gray mould symptoms, i.e., grayish, hairy mycelial growth all over the fruit surface. In severe attack, all the berries in a bunch are involved and totally lost. Infected berries are prone to attack of such secondary rot causing fungi as *Asperegillus*, *Penicillium* and *Trichothecium roseum*. These fungi give a bitter taste to the fruit. Losses are heavier if stalks of berries are infected (Plate 21.26).

Plate 21.26 Symptoms caused by **Botrytis**, (A) Gray mould of chickpea, (B–C) Botrytis leaf blight of onion, (D) infected bunch of grape.

The above diseases are caused by *Botrytis cinerea*. In onion, the disease is commonly known as blast and in addition to *B. cinerea*, many other species (*B. allii*, *B. byssoidea*, *B. squamosa*, *B. cepae*) are also involved. In culture, the mycelium is at first white but becomes dark with age. The hyphae are septate and 8-16 μm wide. The tall, erect, conidiophores arising from the mycelium are hyaline towards the tip but dark below. The tips give rise to sporogenous ampullae; each ampulla produces numerous conidia simultaneously (Figure 21.34). The whole structure looks like a bunch of grapes. The conidia are aseptate, ovate, and measure 11-15 × 8-11 μm (4-24 × 4-8 μm in grapes). The ascigerous stage of *Botrytis cinerea* is *Botryotinia fuckeliana* (de Bary) Whetzel. Generally the sclerotia of the fungus appear like a crust on the woody parts of the host but in some species fairly large, black sclerotia are produced. In addition to structures of survival, these sclerotia may produce spermatia that lead to the ascigerous stage.

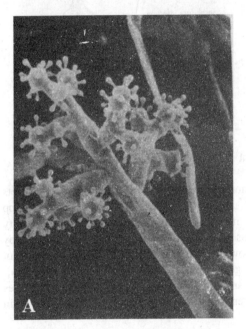

Figure 21.34 (A) Asexual structures of *Botrytis* spp., blastic origin of the conidium on the ampullae, (B) conidia of *Botrytis cinerea* showing the stergmata attachment to the ampullae.

Disease cycle and management. *Botrytis* can grow as a saprophyte on dead crop refuge. It survives as sclerotia and on weed hosts. Survival through seed is reported in chickpea but it is mostly in the form of contaminant, sclerotia-bearing debris is often carried with seed. Germination of sclerotia is myceliogenic-producing conidia, which are disseminated by wind. If the conidia fall on dead plant parts such as flowers and leaves, there also they grow and produce enormous numbers of conidia which are disseminated by wind to healthy leaves and blossom (Figure 21.35). Under field conditions, cool and foggy weather is ideal for development of gray mould.

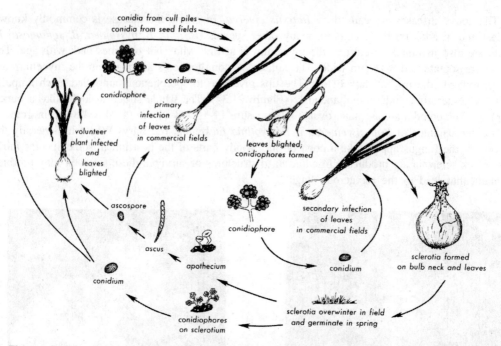

conidia from cull piles
conidia from seed fields
conidium
conidiophore
primary infection of leaves in commercial fields
volunteer plant infected and leaves blighted
leaves blighted; conidiophores formed
ascospore
conidiophore
secondary infection of leaves in commercial fields
ascus
apothecium
conidium
sclerotia formed on bulb neck and leaves
conidium
conidiophores on sclerotium
sclerotia overwinter in field and germinate in spring

Figure 21.35 Disease cycle of botrytis leaf blight of onion. (*Source:* J.W. Lorbeer, 1992).

In crops where damping off is a problem, solarization of the nursery bed soil under plastic sheets is an economical and highly effective measure. Field sanitation practices such as removal of crop debris including dead or rotting fruits reduces primary inoculum. In the field, reduction in humidity is one of the most important steps. Spacing in crops like chickpea and strawberry and canopy management in grapevines reduces humidity and allows quick evaporation of moisture on plant parts through aeration and sunlight. In chickpea gray mould, wide row spacing (60 cm), intercropping with dwarf or semi-dwarf wheat cultivars and uniform nipping of tender branches 45-60 days after planting not only reduce disease severity but also significantly increase the grain yield.

In grapevines a system of green pruning or leaf removal has been found very effective. Partial defoliation of basal portion of shoots near the clusters, performed shortly after bloom or done 2-3 times during season improves wind speed through the vines. This can cause as much as 69% disease reductions. *B.cinerea* quickly develops resistance to fungicides. Therefore, no effective and durable fungicide spray schedule has been found.

In gray mould of grapes, during the late 1950s and until 1968 captan, captafol, folpet, chlorothalonil and thiram were commonly used in vineyards but they gave only 20-50% control. After 1968, benzimidazole fungicides (benomyl, thiophanate methyl and carbendazim) were found to give consistently better control. By 1970, resistance to MBC in *B.cinerea* became common. Since 1976, the carboximide fungicides iprodione (rovral) and vinclozolin (ornalin, ronilan or vorlon) have exhibited good efficacy against botrytis disease. The post-harvest gray mould rot of grapes can be checked by periodical fumigation of bunches with sulfur dioxide. The use of neem (margosa) oil, horticultural oils, silicates, phosphates and carbonates is under trial for control of bunch rot.

In onion, spray of captan, ferbam or ziram at 7-10 days interval protects the foliage from initial development of blast. Excellent onion blast control has been obtained by mixing iprodione

(0.56 kg/ha) and chlorothalonil (0.87 kg/ha) with mancozeb (1.79 kg/ha). The mixture reduces the chances of resistance development in the fungus (Lorbeer and Vincelli, 1990).

In gray mould of chickpea, fungicidal control involves the dicarboximide vincolozolin (ronilan) and the benzimidazole (carbendazim). The fungus shows rapid development of resistance to benzimidazoles. Agarwal and Tripathi (1999) have reported the superiority of vinclozolin over other fungicides in suppression of gray mould. Effort on biological control using antagonistic strains of bacteria and fungi, the bacterial species *Bacillus mycoides, Pseudomonas syringae, Pseudonas, Pseudomonas fluorescence, etc.* have shown promise.

REFERENCES

Agrios, G.N., 1996, *Plant Pathology*, Academic San Diego, CA.

Alcorn, J.L., 1983, Generic concept in *Drechslera, Bipolaris* and *Exserohilum Mycotaxon*, 17:1.

Alcorn, J.L., 1988, The taxonomy of *Helminthosporium* species, *Annu. Rev. Phytopathol*, 26:37.

Alexopoulos, C.J., et al., 1996, *Introductory Mycology*, John Wiley and Sons, INC, New York.

Aust, H.J. and Hoynigen-Huene, J.V., 1986, Microclimate in relation to epidemics of powdery mildew, *Annu. Rev. Phytopathol*, 24:491.

Bailey, J.A. and Jeger, M.J., 1992, *Colletotrichum: Biology, Pathology and Control*, CAB International, Wallingford, U.K.

Bhatt, J.C. and Singh, R.A., 1992, Blast of rice, *In: Plant Diseases of International Importance*, Vol. I., U.S. Singh, et al. (Eds.), Prentice Hall, New Jersey.

Brawn, U., 1987, A monograph of the *Erysiphales* (Powdery Mildews), *Nova-Hedw*, 89:1.

Burgess, D.R. and Keane, P.J., 1997, Biological control of *Botrytis cinerea* on chickpea seed with *Trichoderma* spp. and *Gliocladium roseum* indigenous versus non-indigenous isolates, *Plant Pathology*, 46:910-918.

Burgess, D.R., Bretag, T. and Keane, P.J., 1997, Biocontrol of seed-borne *Botrytis cinerea* in chickpea with *Gliocladium roseum, Plant Pathology*, 46:298-305.

Chakrabarti, N.K. and Chaudhari, S., 1992, Brown spot of rice, *In: Plant Diseases of International Importance*, Vol. I, U.S. Singh, et al. (Eds.), Prentice Hall, New Jersey.

Chaube, H.S., et al., 1992, Greymould of chickpea, *In: Plant Diseases of International Importance*, Vol. I, Singh, U.S., et al. (Eds), Prentice Hall, New Jersey.

Chaube, H.S., et al., 1992, *Plant Disease of International Importance*. Vol. II, Diseases of vegetable and oil seed crops, Prentice Hall, Englewood Cliffs, New Jersey.

Chaube, H.S. and Mishra, T.K., 1992, Ascochyta blight of chickpea. *In: Plant Diseases of International Importance*, U.S. Singh, et al. (Eds.), Prentice Hall, New Jersey.

Coley-Smith, J.R., et al., 1980, *The Biology of Botrytis*, Academic Press, New York.

Gupta, G.K., Apple scab, *In: Plant Diseases of International Importance*, Vol. III, J. Kumar, et al. (Eds.), Prentice Hall, New Jersey.

Gupta, V.K. and Sharma, S.K., 2000, *Diseases of Fruit Crops,* Kalyani Publishers, New Delhi.

Haware, M.P., et al., 1991, Integrated biological chemical control of Botrytis gray mould of chickpea, *Indian Phytopath.,* 52:174

Hawksworth, D.L.B., et al., 1983, *Ainsworth and Bisby's Dictionary of the Fungi,* 7th ed., CMI, Kew, UK.

Jameel Akhtar, 2003, Studies on Phomopsis blight and fruit rot of brinjal, Ph. D. Thesis submitted to G.B. Pant Univ. of Agric. & Technol., Pantnagar 263145.

Jones, A.L. and Aldwinckle, H.S., 1990, *Campendium of Apple and Rear Diseases,* APS Press, St. Paul, Minnesota.

Kaur, S. and Singh, J., 1990, *Colletotrichum acutatum:* a new threat to chilli crop in Punjab, *Indian Phytopath,* 43:108.

Kolte, S.J., et al., 1984, *Diseases of Annual Edible Oilseed Crops,* Vol. I, *Peanut Diseases,* CRC Press Inc., Boca Raton, FL.

Kumar, J., et al., 1992, *Plant Diseases of International Importance,* Vol. III, Diseases of Fruit Crops, Prentice Hall, Englewood Cliffs, New Jersey.

Laha, S.K. and Grewal, J.S., 1983, Botrytis blight of chickpea and its perpetuation through seed, *Indian Phytopath,* 36:630

Lorbeer, J.W., 1992, Botrytis leaf blight of onion, *In: Plant Diseases of International Importance,* Vol. II, H.S. Chaube, et al. (Eds.), Prentice Hall, New Jersey.

Loveless, A.R., 1976, *Claviceps fusiformis* sp. Nov, The causal agent of an Agalactia of Sows, *Trans. Br. Mycol. Soc.,* 50:15.

Manion, P.D., 1991, *Tree Disease Concept,* 2nd ed., Prentice Hall, Englewood Cliffs, New Jersey.

Meredith, D.S., 1970, Banana leaf spot disease (Sigatoka) caused by *Mycosphaerella musicola. Commonw. Mycol. Inst. Phytopathol., Pap,* 11:1.

Mukhopadhyay, A.N., et al., 1992, *Plant Diseases of International Importance,* Vol. IV, Diseases of sugar, forest and plantation crops, Prentice-Hall, Englewood Cliffs, New Jersey.

Mukhopadhyay, A.N. and Pavgi, M.S., 1973, Cytology of chlamydospores development in *Protomyces macrosporus* unger, *Cytologia.* 38:467.

Nair, N.G. and Hill, G.K., 1992, Bunch rot of grapes, *In: Plant Diseases of International Importance,* Vol. III, J. Kumar, et al. Prentice Hall, New Jersey.

Ou, S.H., 1985, *Rice Disease,* UK Commonwealth Agricultural Bureaux.

Porter, D.M., Smith, D.H. and Rodriguez-Kabana, R. (Eds.), 1984, Compendium of peanut diseases, *American Phytopathological Society.*

Rotem, J., 1994, *The Genus Alternaria,* APS Press, St. Paul, MN.

Shurtleff, M.C., 1980, *A Compendium of Corn Disease,* 2nd ed., APS Press, St. Paul, MN.

Singh, K., et al., 1992, Red rot of sugarcane, *In: Plant Diseases of International Importance,* Vol. IV, A. N. Mukhopadhyay, et al., (Eds.), Prentice Hall, Englewood Cliffs, New Jersey.

Singh, M.K., 2002, Studies on *anthracnose* of chillies and its incitant Colletotrichum capsici, M.Sc. (Ag.) Thesis. Submitted to G.B. Pant Univ. of Agric. & Technol, Pantnagar 263145.

Singh, R.S., 1998, *Plant Diseases*, 7th edn., Oxford and IBH Publ., New Delhi.

Singh, R.S., 2000, *Diseases of Fruit Crop*, Science Publishers, Inc., Enfield (NH), USA.

Singh, U.S., et al., 1992, *Plant Diseases of International Importance*. Vol I, Diseases of cereals and pulses, Prentice Hall, Englewood Cliffs, New Jersey.

Smith, D.H., et al., 1992, Cercosporadium and cercospora leaf spots of peanut, *In: Plant Diseases of International Importance*, Vol. II, H.S. Chaube, et al. Prentice Hall, New Jersey.

Spencer, D.M., 1978, *The Powdery Mildew*, Academic Press, New York.

Stover, R.H., 1986, Disease management strategies and the survival of the banana industry *Annu. Rev. Phytopathol.*, 24:83.

Thakur, D.P., 1983, Epidemiology and control of ergot diseases of pearl millet, *Seed Sci. Technol*, 11:797.

Thakur, R.P. and King, S.B., 1992, Ergot of pearl millet. *In: Plant Diseases of International Importance*, Vol. I, Prentice Hall, Englewood Cliffs, New Jersey.

Thakur, R.P. and King, S.B., 1988, Ergot diseases of pearl millet, *Information Bull.*, No. 24, ICRISAT, Patancheru.

Thakur, R.P., Rao, V.P. and Williams, R.J., 1984, The morphology and disease cycle of ergot caused by *Claviceps fusiformis*, in pearl millet, *Phytopathology*, 74:201.

Tu, J.C., 1992, Bean anthracnose, *In: Plant Diseases of International Importance*, Vol. II, H.S. Chaube, et al. (Eds.), Prentice Hall, New Jersey.

Vishnuwat, K., 1992, Phomopsis blight and fruit rot of eggplant. *In: Plant Diseases of International Importance*, Vol. II, H.S. Chaube, et al. (Eds.), Prentice Hall, New Jersey.

Webster, R.K. and Gunnel, P.S., 1992, *Compendium of Rice Diseases*, APS Press, St. Paul, Minnesota.

Zheng, R.Y., 1985, Genera of Erysiphales, Mycotaxon, 22:209.

22 Vascular Wilts

22.1 INTRODUCTION

Sadasivan (1961) stated: *Despite many approaches that have been made to the problem of the 'cause and effect' of wilt pathogenesis, we have a long way to go before we understand many complex situations in the sequence of events that culminate in the syndrome.* This holds true even now despite the fact that many reviews have been written on the subject. Typically the wilt diseases are associated with plants that contain vessels in their xylem, that is, the angiosperms. While wilt, or loss of turgidity, is a common symptom of disease, it may result from one of many possible causes. The vascular wilts are set off as a group because of the association of symptoms with the presence of the pathogen in the vascular system of the host, usually in the xylem tissue. *Fusarium, Verticillium, Ceratocystis, Ophiostoma* are fungal genera that cause vascular wilts. Each of them causes wilt disease on several important crops, forest and ornamental plants. *Ceratocystis fagacearum* causes vascular wilt of oak trees. *Ophiostoma ulmi* causes Dutch elm disease. *Fusarium* causes vascular wilts of vegetables and flowers, herbaceous perennial ornamentals and plantation crops. Most of the wilt causing *Fusarium* belongs to the species. *F. oxysporum.* Different host plants are attacked by special forms or races of the fungus. *Verticillium* causes vascular wilts of vegetables, flowers, field crops, ornamentals, and fruit and forest trees. Two species, *V. albo-atrum* and *V. dahliae*, attack hundreds of kinds of plants.

22.2 CAUSES OF VASCULAR DYSFUNCTION

Probably no single factor is responsible for vascular dysfunction in the wilt disease (Figure 22.1). High resistance to the flow of the water through infected plants is probably the result of several factors. Some originate from the host as a result of response to the pathogen invasion and other due to the pathogen itself. The infected plant may contribute to the altered resistance to flow by virtue of the changes in vessel size that accompany infection and development of tyloses in conductive elements. These are: (a) collapse of vessels, (b) formation of tyloses, (c) the physical presence of the mycelium, production of bud cells, microconidia and macroconidia within the vessels, (d) altered viscosity of tracheal fluids and (e) plugging by compounds of high molecular weights, such as polysaccharides, polymerized melanoid pigments, gum, gels and pectins.

PATHOGEN FACTORS

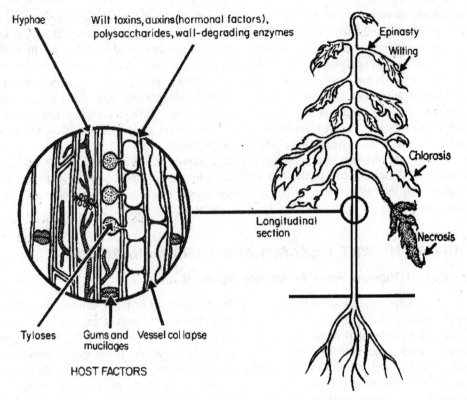

Figure 22.1 The vascular wilt syndrome. (*Source:* Dickinson and Lucos, 1982).

22.2.1 Plugging by High Molecular Weight—Polysaccharides

Polymerized melanoid pigments are compounds of high molecular weight. The walls of the conducting elements behave as ultra filters and remove materials of high molecular weight from the transpiration stream. In the process, the channels become plugged and this impedes the flow of water, and nutrients through vessels.

22.2.2 Blockage by Cell-wall Degrading Enzymes

The wilt pathogens, in common with many microorganisms, excrete extra cellular pectolytic and cellulolytic enzymes. The evidence of the role of these enzymes in pathogenesis is based upon their presence in diseased plants, the ability of pathogens to produce them in host tissues, microscopic and chemical evidences of degradation of middle lamellae and cell walls, and the presence in diseased vessels and pits of molecules representing cleavage products from cell walls and the ability of such products to produce vascular dysfunction.

22.2.3 The Toxin Theory

Toxins have been extensively investigated, especially in tomato wilt caused by *F. oxysporum* f. sp. *lycopersici,* in which Gottlieb (1943, 1944) showed that toxins might be involved. It is now known to play a pathogenic role in the wilt of tomato and cotton. Fusaric acid is called a **wilt toxin**, as it is now known to play a distinct role in the wilt of tomato and cotton plants. Even when the pathogen is restricted to the roots, symptoms like vein clearing and epinasty are seen in the leaves, reduction in respiration and growth, necrosis of cortical tissues overlying the vascular bundles (leading to the furrowing of the stem) and epinasty of petioles. This seems to be due to the toxic metabolites translocated to distant parts of the plant from the focus of infection. Pure toxin fusaric acid simulates some of the symptoms caused by the pathogen.

The toxin, lycomarasmine, is a polypeptide with a molecular weight of 277.3. The pathogenic effect of this toxin is partly due to the fact that its molecules, on their way through the infected plants, chelate iron ions in the host, which otherwise would not be able to migrate and transport themselves into the leaves in the form of lycomarasmine-iron complex.

22.3 IMPORTANT WILT DISEASES AND THEIR MANAGEMENT

22.3.1 Wilt of Pigeon Pea: *Fusarium udum* Butler

This is a very common disease. It is the worst disease of red gram in India, causing severe damage wherever the crop is grown, especially in Maharashtra, Madhya Pradesh, Uttar Pradesh, Bihar and Tamil Nadu. Geographical distribution of the disease is shown in Figure 22.2. The plant is susceptible to attack throughout its development. However, the symptoms are more pronounced and the damage greater after the rainy season. The main symptom of the disease is the wilting of seedlings and adult plants as if from water shortage even when plenty of it may be present in the soil. The wilting is characterized by gradual, sometimes sudden, yellowing, withering and drying of leaves followed by the drying of the entire plant or some of its branches (Plate 22.1). The main roots and base of the stem tissues are blackened either uniformly, or especially in the early stages, in streaks. If the stem is examined after it is broken and split, the black streaks may be traced up to a height of several feet on the stem. Partial wilting is also common because often only one side of the stem and root system is affected in which case the symptoms are found only on that side of the plant.

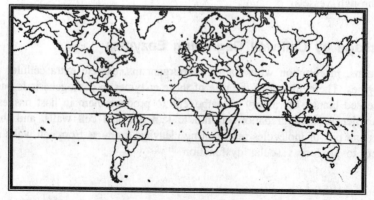

Figure 22.2 Geographical distribution of wilt of pigeon pea.

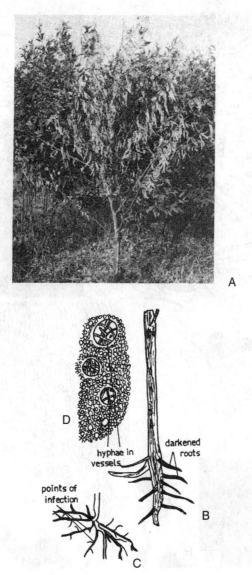

Plate 22.1 (A) Wilted pigeon pea plant in field, (B) stem in early stage of attack, (C) roots of wilted seedlings showing plants of infection, (D) hyphae in vessels.

The pathogen responsible for the wilt of pigeon pea is named *Fusarium udum* Butler. The fungus is mainly confined to the vascular tissues and is both inter and intracellular. The mycelium is hyaline and produces three types of spores. The microconidia are small, elliptical or curved, unicellular or with 1-2 septa and measure 5-15 × 2-4 μm. The macroconidia are long, curved, pointed at the tip, with 3-4 septa and measure 15-50 × 3-5 μm. The chlamydospores are formed in culture as well as in host tissues. They are spherical to oval, thick-walled, single or in chains of two to three, terminal or intercalary. All the types of spores germinate readily in water. Chlamydospores are believed to survive for a number of years (Plate 22.2).

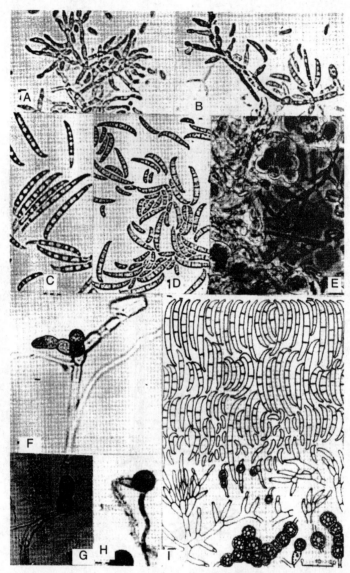

Plate 22.2 Asexual structures of *F. udum,* (A–D) conidiophores and conidia, (E) clumps and chains of chlamydospores, (F) chlamydospore formation, (G) intercalary chlamydospore, (H) one-celled terminal chlamydospore, (I) diagrammatic presentation of various structures of *F. udum.* (*Source: Upadhyay and Rai, 1992).*

The perfect stage *Gibberella indica* described by Rai and Upadhyay (1982) is usually found on exposed roots and collar region of the stem. The mature perithecia are superficial, subglobose to globose, sessile, smooth walled, dark violet and 350–550 μm in diameter. Asci are eight spored, subcylindrical, 60-80 × 6-10 μm. Ascospores are ellipsoidal to ovate, 10-17 × 5-7 μm, hyaline commonly two celled (Plate 22.3).

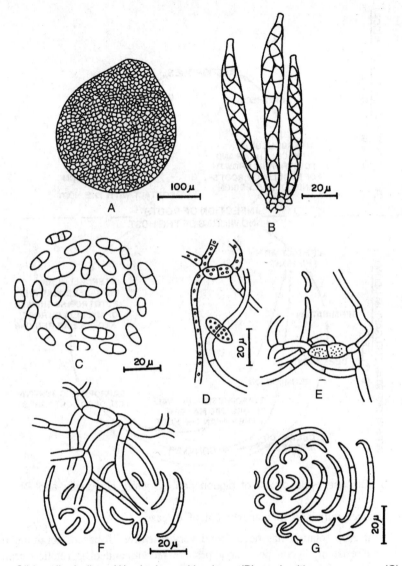

Plate 22.3 *Gibberalla indica,* (A) single perithecium, (B) asci with ascospores, (C) ascospores, (D) germinating ascospores, (E) microconidia produced on a germ hypha from ascospore, (F) germ hypha of ascospore producing micro and macroconidia, (G) micro and microconidia. (*Source:* Upadhyay and Rai, 1982).

Disease cycle and management. The pathogen is soil-borne and can survive in soil after the host crop has been removed. According to reports the pathogen can survive in soil for more than 10 years in the absence of its host. The pathogen has limited saprophytic survival that too due to continued presence of the dead host roots and other parts pre-colonized by the fungus. Apart from the saprophytic mycelium, the conidia of the fungus also remain viable for long periods while chlamydospores persist in dormant state for even longer duration. The above ground parts are never attacked. Secondary infection by conidia produced on aerial parts is rare. The disease cycle as conceived by Upadhyay and Rai (1992) is shown in Figure 22.3.

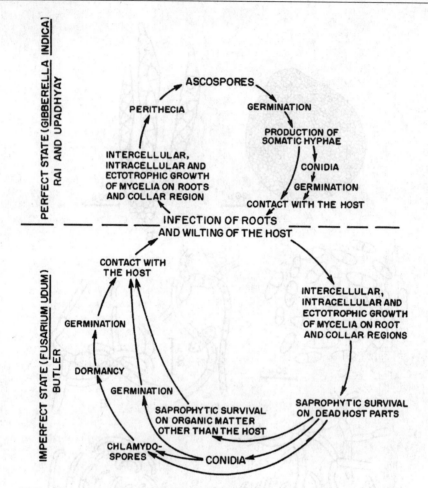

Figure 22.3 Disease cycle of wilt of pigeon pea. (*Source:* Upadhyay and Rai, 1983).

Following practices will help in management of disease.

1. A 4-5 year crop rotation has been found very effective. Tobacco, sorghum, pearl millet, cotton and resistant pigeon pea genotypes are recommended as rotation crops.
2. To reduce inoculum field sanitation (removal of affected plant parts with their roots and deep ploughing during summer is recommended).
3. Mixed cropping with sorghum provides the most effective and practical solution of this problem.
4. Infection of seedlings may be avoided by presoaking seeds in zinc or manganese solution.
5. Seed treatment with benlate + thiram (1:3) reduces wilt incidence
6. Introduction of green manure crop in the rotation and increasing soil organic matter content by other means seems desirable.
7. Varieties C-11, C-28, C-36, F-18, NP(WR)15, NP-41, T-17, and NP-38 has been considered resistant to wilt. In multi-locational trials (Conducted by ICRISAT), pigeon pea lines ICP4769, 0063, 9168, 10958, 11299 and cultivars C11 (ICP 7118) and BDNI (ICP 7182) were found resistant.

22.3.2 Chickpea Wilt: *Fusarium oxysporum* f. sp. *Ciceri* (Padwick) Snyd and Hans

The disease has been reported from several countries (Figure. 22.4). All types of chickpea irrespective of plant types and seed size succumb to the disease. Rough estimates indicate that losses may hover around 10-15% each year (Jalali and Chand, 1992). The disease symptoms can be observed in susceptible cultivar within 25 days after sowing in the field. Confusion may arise over seedlings that die due to the wilt disease with those that die due to root rots if not examined carefully. The affected seedlings show drooping of the leaves and paler colour than the healthy seedlings. They may collapse and lie flat on the ground. Such seedlings when removed from soil show shrinkage of the stem. The roots do not show any external rotting but look apparently healthy. Such roots, when split vertically from the collar region downward, show a brown discolouration of the vascular tissues.

Figure 22.4 Geographical distribution of chickpea wilt.

Adult plants show typical wilting, which may occur in the field up to podding stage. The initial symptom is drooping of petioles and rachis along with leaflets. Within 2 to 3 days drooping is seen on the entire plant. There is a slow fading of the green colour and the plant looks dull green. Gradually all leaves turn yellow and straw-coloured (Plate 22.4). Roots of the wilted plant show no external rotting, drying or discolouration. Root and stem of the wilted plant, when split vertically, clearly show internal discolouration of the pith and xylem tissues.

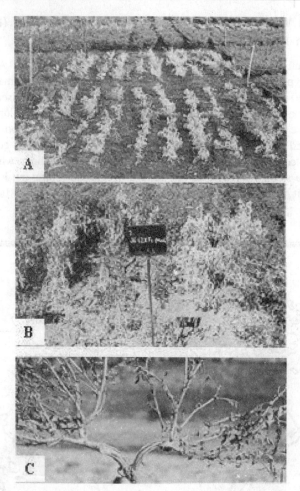

Plate 22.4 Symptoms of chickpea wilt. (A) fusarium wilt affected plants—a field view, (B) plants showing dropping of leaves and branches, (C) wilt affected internal structure of stem. (*Source: ICRISAT, 1997*)

Chickpea wilt is caused by *Fusarium oxysporum* f.sp. *ciceri* (Padwick) Snyd. and Hans. Microconidia are borne on simple short conidiophores, arising laterally on the hyphae. Micro and macroconidia are generally sparse on solid medium. They are formed abundantly on potato-sucrose broth. Microconidia are oval to cylindrical, straight to curved and 2.5-3.5 × 5-11 µm. Macroconidia are lesser in number than microconidia, borne on branched conidiophores, thin-walled, 3 to 5 septate, fusoid and pointed at both ends, and measure 3.5-4.5 × 25-65 µm. Chlamydospores are formed in old cultures (20 d), smooth or rough walled, terminal and intercalary; and may form singly or in pairs or in chain.

Disease cycle and management. The fungus may be seed-borne and may survive in plant debris in soil. The primary infection is through chlamydospores or mycelium. The conidia are shortlived; however the chlamydospores can remain viable upto next crop season. Disease cycle with various steps is shown in Figure 22.5.

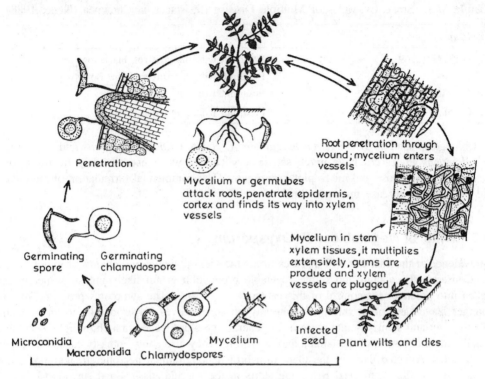

Penetration

Mycelium or germtubes
attack roots, penetrate epidermis,
cortex and finds its way into xylem
vessels

Root penetration through
wound; mycelium enters
vessels

Mycelium in stem
xylem tissues, it multiplies
extensively, gums are
produed and xylem
vessels are plugged

Germinating
spore

Germinating
chlamydospore

Microconidia

Macroconidia   Chlamydospores

Mycelium

Infected
seed

Plant wilts and dies

Infected plant parts remain in soil . Pathogen lives
saprophytically and forms various types of spores and mycelium .
In infected seeds , the pathogen survives in the form of
chlamydospore .

Figure 22.5 Disease cycle of chickpea wilt. (*Source:* Jalali and Chand, 1992)

Seed-borne infection is observed in seeds from plants which wilt after pod formation. Rouging wilted plants at harvest may help reduce chances of seed transmission. Haware, *et al.,* (1978) demonstrated that Benlate T (a mixture of 30% benomyl and 30% thiram) could completely eradicate seed-borne inoculum. It is important to treat the seeds to stop spread of the pathogen through seed and to facilitate the international movement of the germplasm and breeding material needed for chickpea improvement work. Some other recommendation for disease management includes: delayed sowing, plants spaced at 7.5 cm, planting of seeds at proper depth (10-12 cm), planting of seed with "pora" method using lower seed rate, one irrigation before flowering, and mixed cropping of chickpea with wheat and barseem. On the basis of multi-locational testing, several stable and durable sources of resistance have been identified. Some of these express resistance against other diseases also (Table 22.1).

Table 22.1 Some Examples of Multiple Disease Resistance in Chickpea (Nene, 1988)

Cultivars	Resistance to
ICP 12237-12269	Fusarium wilt, dry root rot, black root rot
ICC 1069	Fusarium wilt, Ascochyta blight, Botrytis gray mould
ICC 10466	Fusarium wilt, dry root rot, stunt
ICC 858, 959, 4918, 8933, 9001	Fusarium wilt, Sclerotinia stem rot

Several bioagents such as *Trichoderma harzianum, T. viride, Gliocladium virens* and several strains of *Pseudomonas fluoresces* have given satisfactory control when used as seed treatment or soil application in glass-house and micro-plot experiments. The commercial formulation of the bioagents should be used for disease management.

22.3.3 Wilts of Vegetables: *F. Oxysporum*

The prevalence of the vascular wilt diseases limits the yield potential and quality of major vegetable crops. Consequently, a high and stable vegetable production is not likely unless proper measures are taken into practices for control of this category of diseases. The symptoms progress from older to younger leaves and often starting unilaterally on some leaves corresponding to an infection of part of the root and stem vascular system. In general, the older leaves first show light vein clearing (of small veins), chlorosis of the lamina and/or wilting. They also show epinasty caused by drooping of the petioles. Affected parts of the plant turn brown; longitudinal necrotic streaks appear on the stems and spread the stem apex. Browning starts in the vascular tissues and spreads to the cortex in the later phase of infection. Plants of all ages are infected. But symptoms may not appear on plants that grow in cool soil until the soils warm up rather close to the time of crop maturity. Some other symptoms on some hosts are occasional formation of adventitious roots and more intense yellowing on one side of a midrib than on other. Plants affected at the seedling stage usually wilt and die soon after appearance of first symptoms.

The pathogen. All vascular wilts have certain characteristics in common. But the strain of the causal fungus that attacks a particular plant species is different from the one that attacks the other. These differences are not apparent in the appearance of the fungus, so that the various strains are classified as one species. A strain that can infect a group of plants is often designated as "special form" of the fungus (*forma specialis* in Latin). The pathogens (special forms) attacking important host plants are indicated in Table 22.2.

Table 22.2 Wilt Pathogens and their Distribution in Vegetable Crops

F. oxysporum	Main host	Geographical occurrence
f. sp. *batatas*	Sweet potato(*Ipomoea batatas*)	USA, Africa, China, India, Australia
f. sp. *betae*	Beet (*Beta vulgaris*)	Widely spread
f. sp. *coriandriei*	Dhania (*Coridandrum sativum*)	India
f. sp. *cucumerrinum*	Cucumber (*Cucumis sativus*)	USA, South Africa, Iraq, Japan, Thailand, England, France, Norway, Canada, Australia

(Contd.)

Table 22.2 Wilt Pathogens and their Distribution in Vegetable Crops (*Contd.*)

F. oxysporum	*Main host*	*Geographical occurrence*
f. sp. *conglutinans*	Cabbage and other crucifers	Africa, China, Japan, Australia, Newzealand, France, USA, Central America, West Indies, Brazil
f. sp. *cumini*	Cumin (*Cuminum cyminum*)	India
f. sp. *fabae*	Broad bean (*Vicia faba*)	USA
f. sp. *lagenariae*	Calabash gourd (*Legenaria vulgaris*)	USA
f. sp. *luffae*	Vegetabie sponge *Luffa* species	Africa, USA
f. sp. *lycopersici*	Tomato (*Lycopersicon esculenttus*)	Africa, Asia, North and South America, Europe,
f. sp. *melonis*	Muskmelon/cantaloupe (*Cucumis melo*)	Canada, USA, Europe, Iraq, Japan, India, Philippines, Australia
f. sp. *melongenae*	Egg plant *(Solanum melongena)*	Japan, India
f. sp. *niveum*	Watermelon (*Citrullus lanatus*)	Argentina, South Africa, Chile, South Europe, India
f. sp. *phaseoli*	Kidney bean (*Phaseolus vulgaris*)	Widely distributed
f. sp. *pisi*	Pea (*Pisum sativum*)	Widely distributed
f. sp. *raphani*	Raddish (*Raphanus sativus*)	Japan, USA
f. sp. *spinaciae*	Spinach (*Spinacia oleracea*)	India
f. sp. *tracheiphilym*	Cowpea (*Vigna sinensis, V. unguiculata*)	USA, South Africa, Colombia, Russia, India, Australia
f. sp. *vasinfectum*	Okra	India, USA

Disease cycle and management. The pathogen is a soil inhabitant. It survives long periods in soil as chlamydospores. It can colonize host and non-host tissues and can compete successfully with other soil fungi. The pathogen can occur at high population levels in surface soil near diseased plants presumably from macroconidia produced on stem lesions. The macroconidial cells are transformed into resistant chlamydospores. Generally, seed as a source of primary inoculum has been overlooked or underestimated because of the predominance of soil as a source of inoculum. However, the fungus laying deep in the seed coat in the form of chlamydospores show high tolerance to the long-term storage of the seed; but the surface borne conidia and mycelium die out when seed is stored for 4 months at 35°C and above. Some of the seeds carry the pathogen in their internal tissues. Seeds collected from tomato fruit borne by infected plants show infection at a rate of 2.0-16.0 per cent. Chances that seed is a source of inoculum are high and appear to be more in matured (ripened) fruits than in unripe fruits borne on diseased plants.

When healthy plants grow in infested soil, the germ tubes of spores (the mycelium) penetrate the host through root tip meristematic zone and the epidermis of the roots formed in the root elongation and maturation zone. It can also enter the root through wounds or ruptures caused by new lateral roots. Penetration can also be assisted by nematode attack especially *Meloidogyne* species. The mycelium then advances through the root cortex intercellularly and when it reaches the xylem vessels, it enters them through the pits. The mycelium then remains exclusively in the vessels and travels through them mostly upward towards the stem and crown of the plant. While in vessels, the mycelium penetrate the upper wall of the vessels, and more microconidia are produced in the next vessel. The mycelium also advances laterally into the adjacent vessels penetrating them through the pits. Thus, the wilt symptoms appear in each leaf in acropetal succession.

1. Use of resistant varieties.   The use of resistant varieties offers the most promising method for control. The successful examples are available. Resistance is reported to be governed by dominant genes: 1-3 genes. Such reports are available in the case of *Fusarium* wilt of cowpea, melons, cabbage and tomato.

2. Breeding.   Breeding in cowpea using iron genotype shows development of resistance to all the known three races of *F. oxysporum* f. sp. *tracheiphilum*. The breeding programme is, however, complicated by development of newer races and presence of plant parasitic nematodes (*Meloidogyne* spp.).

In some cases grafting with a high level of broadly based resistance can give good results. Grafting has provided not only a practical method for diseases resistance but also several other benefits such as ease in transplanting seedlings and tolerance to low temperature. Some examples are given in Table 22.3.

Table 22.3   Examples of Grafting on a Rootstock

Crop/Plant	Fusarium-wilt resistant root-stock
Watermelon	*Lagenaria siceraria, Benincasa hispida*, shintosa (*Cucurbita maxima* × *C. moschata*), Shirokikuza (*C. moschata*)
Cucumber	kurodane (*C. ficifolia*), Shintosa
Musk melon	BF Okitus 101, LS89, Walter, KNVF, Fukuju 2
Egg plant	*Solanum integrifolium, S. gilo, S. mammosum, S. torvum*, Shiko No 1

3. Selection of seed and seed treatment.   Seed should be saved only from plant free from *Fusarium*. Hot water treatment can be used. All *Fusaria* are killed when seeds are kept for drying at 40°C for 24 hrs in order to reduce the moisture content of the seed. Alternatively seeds may be treated with a mixture of carbendazim + thiram or thioplanate methyl + thiram @0.2 to 0.3%.

4. Biological control.   (a) *Soil organic amendment*–Various forms can be useful. Sun-Huang mixture known as S-H mixture is able to convert conducive soils to suppressive soils reducing the watermelon wilt by 93.8% in sandy soil and by 73% in loamy soil in Taiwan/Japan. Similar methodology can be useful under Indian condition. The composition of S-H mixture is: 4.4% bagasse, 8.4% rice husk, 4.25% oyster shell powder, 10% KNO_3, 13.6% calcium super phosphate, 8.25% urea and 60% mineral ash. The S-H mixture is used @1%.

(b) *Soil suppressiveness*–Some soils are naturally suppressive to *Fusarium* wilt pathogens and this suppressive effect can even be transferred to conducive soil and established there. This opens prospects for biological control. Fluorescent pseudomonas induces suppressiveness in soil, as they produce iron-acquiring compounds called **siderophores**. Siderophores have a higher iron-binding constant than the hydroxymate siderophores produced by *Fusarium oxysporum*, species i.e. the fungal pathogens. Therefore, in alkaline soils (pH 8), with low availability of iron, rhizosphere-competent fluorescent pseudomonas may compete with and deprive *Fusarium* wilt pathogen of this essential element.

5. Soil solarization. The soil is mulched with thin transparent polyethylene sheets or other plastic material (vinyl chloride). The basic process involved is heating of the soil to 50°C in the upper 30 cm (e.g. watermelon wilt, pea wilt).

6. The integrated control. Various components individually effective against the pathogen (disease development) can be brought into an unified treatment combination for much more economical and efficient disease management strategy. (Chattopadhyay and Sen, 1996).

22.3.4 Guava Wilt: *F. oxysporum* f. sp. *psidii*

This disease is very destructive and is known to occur in whole of northern India. The disease was first observed in U.P. in 1935 and is now present in approximately 51,200 sq. km. area of the state. In central and eastern part of the state, the disease is estimated to cause an annual tree mortality of 5-10%. It appears to be a wilt complex of fungal invasion, insect attack and nutritional disorder. Guava wilt is reported from other countries also.

The **symptoms** of the fungal wilt caused by *Fusarium* appear during the rainy season. The affected plants are lusterless with brown leaves. The symptoms of disease are browning and wilting of leaves, stem discolouration coupled with death of the branches on one side. Sometimes the whole plant may show wilting. The whole plant may even finally die (Plate 22.5). Das Gupta and Rai (1947) and Prasad, *et al.,* (1952) attributed the guava wilt disease in UP to infection of *F. oxysporum* f. sp. *psidii*. In West Bengal, Chattopadhyay and Bhattacharya (1968) attributed the wilt to *Fusarium solani* under high moisture conditions and to *Macrophomina phaseolina* in dry soils.

Plate 22.5 Symptoms of guava wilt.

Disease cycle and management. The fungus survives in roots of dead trees and through chlamydospores. The infection is through root hairs or through wounds or natural openings. The disease is more common in alkaline soils with moderate soil moisture. Recovery of affected trees has been claimed by some scientists who have used an integrated approach involving.

Following practices will help in management of disease:

1. Pruning to remove branches 30-40 cm from discoloured conducting vessels in March.

2. Drenching of soil around the pruned trees with 10-15 litres of 0.2% carbendazim solution per tree in March, June and September.

3. Spray of 0.05% metasystox and 0.3% zinc sulfate twice a year (March and September).

4. Use of nitrate nitrogen for fertilization.

5. Application of lime or gypsum to soil (1 kg/tree) or margosa seed cake (10 kg/tree) after exposing the roots to a depth of 15 cm.

6. Select only healthy seedling for planting in orchards.

7. Do not use the same site for new planting.

8. Resistant varieties of guava include Banarasi, Dholak Sind, Nasik, White Guava No. 6299, Supreme, Cone 32-12 and Lucknow-49.

22.3.5 Panama Disease of Banana: *Fusarium oxysporum* f. sp. *cubense*

The disease is widespread throughout Africa, Asia, Australia and Oceania, West Indies and North, Central and South Africa. **Symptoms** (Plate 22.6) are most clear on plants that are at least five months old. Sudden wilting of the plant or individual leaves is a characteristic symptom of the disease. Leaf symptoms appear after the fungus has spread through the corm. In young plants, the first signs are on the unfurling leaf, which turns yellow and dies. In older plants, the leaves collapse at the base of the petioles and branches hang down and wither. Often, all the leaves except the youngest ones collapse. Any new leaves, which are produced, are blotchy and yellow with the wrinkling of the lamina. The pseudostem later splits and the vascular symptoms extend up the pseudostem.

In Gros Michel, a very susceptible variety, the lower leaves become yellow and the petioles collapse around the pseudostem from the base to the top. If the base of the plant is cut open vertically, numerous brown and black lines can be seen running in all directions through the corm and upwards into the leaf bases and petioles.

Reaction to the two clonal groups of cultivars differ to this disease.

1. 'Inodoratum' or yellowing strain, which is characterized, by a strong yellowing of erect leaves is not found in Costa Rica, Panama, Columbia and Ecuador.

2. 'Odoratum' is found in the Caribbean Islands, Honduras and Guatemala. Plants do not yellow but suffer from the collapse of the petiole. The cut smells badly of rotten fish.

Plate 22.6 Symptoms of fusarium wilt of banana, (A) internal vascular discolouration of the pseudostem, (B) marginal chlorosis of the lamina of a leaf that has also buckled at the petiole base, (C) damage ultimately caused in a mature plantation (note surviving, non-symptomatic suckers), (D–F) inconspicuous, subepidermal vascular discolouration of outer leaf sheaths of a pseudostem that the first symptoms evident above ground. Note dull discolouration of thin vascular strands in (D) in the area cut out of the pseudostem in (E) and (F). (*Source:* Ploetz, 1992)

The **pathogen** responsible for wilt of banana is *Fusarium oxysporum* f. sp. *cubense*. (E.F.S.) Snyder and Hansen. The hyphae of the pathogen are present both inter and intracellularly in the host tissue. They are largely confined to the vascular bundles, often filling the cavity of the vessels. When once inside the vascular bundles, the pathogen spreads in a systemic manner and extends into the infected rhizomes and the suckers. The fungus produces numerous micro- and macroconidia and chlamydospores, which are characteristic of the genus. The sporodochium arises from a globose mass of pseudo-parenchymatous tissue and bears the conidiophores. Conidiophores measure 70×4 µm. The macroconidia are sickle-shaped, hyaline; thin walled, 2-5 septate and measure $22\text{-}36 \times 4\text{-}5$ µm. The chlamydospores are oval to spherical often paired and measure $7\text{-}13 \times 7\text{-}8$ µm.

Disease cycle and management. The pathogen is soil borne and invades the plant mainly through the roots or wounds in the rhizomes. The fungus colonizes the vascular bundles and produces masses of mycelium, which bear both macro- and microconidia and the chlamydospores. The chlamydospores can survive in the soil for a long period. The pathogen can also survive in the diseased rhizomes and other plant parts saprophytically for a long period. The disease can easily spread in infected banana trash and soil carried in surface flooded water. Suckers used for planting from diseased areas to other areas spread the disease easily. The entry of the pathogen in the host is helped by the incidental wounds and insect injuries on the rhizomes. The disease is favoured by high soil moisture, light soils, bad drainage and the strong development of new roots, for example, after a nematode attack. (Figure 22.6).

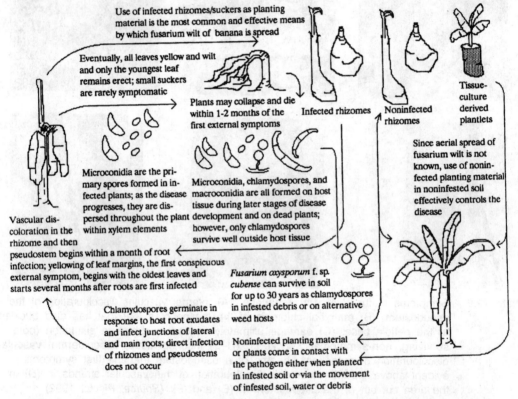

Figure 22.6 Disease cycle of panama disease of banana. (*Source:* Ploetz, 1992).

Following practices will help in management of disease.

1. Flood fallowing has been found to be the most effective method of reclaiming infested soil. In flooded soils the fungus is believed to be eliminated due to the effect of toxic substances (such as acetic acid) produced in the soil and also due to the low oxygen availability in the soils. The carbon dioxide in submerged soils causes continued germination of the conidia but prevents the chlamydospores from developing.

2. The amendment of the soil with carbohydrate sources and plant tissues reduces the population of the fungus by stimulating chlamydospores germination and the lysis of the germ tubes and conidia, and by inhibiting further chlamydospores formation.

3. Soil fumigation has also been suggested but it is not economically feasible. A solution of 5% phenol or 5% formaldehyde is useful.
4. Infected plants should be eradicated by weed killer.
5. The planting material should be dipped in allyl alcohol.
6. Resistant varieties should be cultivated. Gros Michel is very resistant but Cavendesh strains are also resistant.

22.3.6 The Verticillium Wilt

Verticillium wilt occurs worldwide but is economically important in temperate regions only. More than 200 plants species are attacked by species of the fungus. In some hosts, *Verticillium* wilt develops primarily in seedlings, which die after infection. More common are late infections which cause upper leaves to droop and other leaves to develop irregular chlorotic patches that become necrotic. Infected plants are usually stunted and their vascular tissues show discolouration. Two species of *Verticillium*, *V. albo-atrum* and *V. dahliae* cause wilts in most plants. Both produce conidia that are shortlived. *V. dahliae* produces microsclerotia whereas *V. albo-atrum* produces dark, thick-walled mycelium but not microsclerotia.

Disease cycle and management. *V. dehaliae* overwinters in the soil as microsclerotia, which can survive up to 15 years. Both species, however, can overwinter as mycelium within perennial hosts, in propagative organs or in plants debris. Contaminated seed, vegetative cuttings and tubers, wind, surface water and movement of soil spread the pathogen. Following practices will help in management of wilt diseases:

1. Planting disease-free plants in inoculum free soil.
2. Using resistant varieties, and avoiding the planting of susceptible crops.
3. Soil solarization has proved effective in regions with high summer temperatures and low rainfall.
4. To protect high value crops, soil fumigation may be profitable.

REFERENCES

Agrois, G.N., 1997, *Plant Pathology,* 4th ed., Academic Press, New York, London, p. 635.

Beckman, C.H., 1987, *The Nature of Wilt Disease of Plants,* APS, St. Paul, Minnesota.

Booth, C., 1971, *The Genus Fusarium,* Common Wealth, Mycol. Inst. Kew, UK.

Chattopadhyay, C. and Sen, B., 1996, Integrated management of Fusarium wilt of musk melon caused by *Fusarium oxysporum* f. sp. *Melonis, Indian J. Mycol Plant Pathol.,* 26(2):162-170.

Dimond, A.E., 1970, Biophysics and biochemistry of vascular wilt syndrome, *Annu. Rev. Phytopatho*logy 8:301-320.

Gottlieb, D., 1944, The mechanism of wilting caused by *Fusarium bulbigenum* var. *lycopersici, Phytopathology,* 44:41.

Gottlieb, D., 1943, The presence of a toxin in tomato wilt, *Phytopathology,* 43:535.

Haware, M.D., et al., 1978, Eradication of *Fusarim oxysporum* f. sp. *ciceri* transmitted in chickpea seed, *Phytopathology,* 68:1364.

Jalali, B.L. and Chand, H., 1992., Chickpea wilt, *In: Plant Diseases of International Importance*, Vol. I, U.S. Singh, et al. (Eds.), Prentice Hall, New Jersey.

Nene, Y.L., 1988, Multiple disease resistance in grain legumes, *Annu. Rev. Phytopathol,* 26:203.

Oloetz, R.C., 1990, *Fusarium Wilt of Banana,* APS Press, St. Paul, Minnesota.

Pegg, G.F., 1974, Verticillium Diseases, *Rev. Plant Pathol,* 53:157.

Rai, B. and Upadhyay, R.S., 1982, *Gibberella indica*: the perfect state of *Fusarium udum*, *Mycologia,* 74:343.

Sadasivan, T.S., 1961, Physiology of wilt diseases. *Annu. Rev. Plant Physiol,* 12:449.

Singh, R.S., 2000, *Diseases of Fruit Crops,* Science Publishers, Inc. Enfield (NH) USA, Plymouth, UK.

Upadhyay, R.S. and Rai, B., 1992, Wilt of pigeon pea, *In: Plant Diseases of International Importance,* Vol I., U.S. Singh, et al. (Eds.), Prentice Hall, New Jersey.

23 Phylum: Basidiomycota and Plant Diseases

23.1 INTRODUCTION

Basidiomycota the second biggest group of fungi, which includes about 1100 genera, and 16000 species. The group consists of forms like rusts, smuts, jelly fungi, mushrooms, toadstools, puffballs, stinkhorns, bracket fungi, and birds nest fungi. These are highly evolved fungi and important characteristics include (a) the presence of basidium and basidiospores, (b) the extensive dikaryophase, (c) the clamp connections and (d) the dolipore septum.

23.2 GENERAL CHARACTERISTICS

The mycelium is composed of well-developed, septate and branched hyphae, which are either white, yellow-orange, deep brown, or charcoal black. In some forms rhizomorphs develop. The mycelium of most heterothallic basidiomycetes passes through three distinct stages of development the primary, the secondary, and the tertiary before the fungus completes its life-cycle. As most basidiomycetes are heterothallic, the formation of secondary mycelium or heterokaryon involves an interaction between two compatible homokaryotic mycelia. This is achieved either through spermatization or more commonly through the fusion of two uninucleate cells of the compatible homokaryotic mycelia. Thus, in a heterokaryotic, often binucleate cells are established from this cell. In majority of basidiomycetes the secondary mycelium is characterized by the presence of hyphal connections known as **clamp connections** (Plate 23.1) by which the nuclei arising from conjugate division of a dikaryotic cell are separated into the daughter cell. The tertiary mycelium is represented by organized, specialized tissues that comprise the basidiocarp of the more complex species. Such sporophores originate when the secondary mycelium forms complex tissues. Studies on the structure of septa have revealed that in basidiomycetes, the septa are generally laid in the middle surrounded by a double membrane on each side forming a barrel shaped structure with a minor pore in the centre open at both ends. This type of septum is known as **dolipore septum**, through which cytoplasmic continuity is maintained between adjacent cells but migration of nuclei is prevented.

23.3 REPRODUCTION

23.3.1 The Basidiocarp

Most basidiomycetes produce their basidia in fruiting bodies of various types called **basidiocarp** (*Gr. Basidion* = small base, basidium + *karpos* = fruit). Such fruiting bodies are not formed in rust

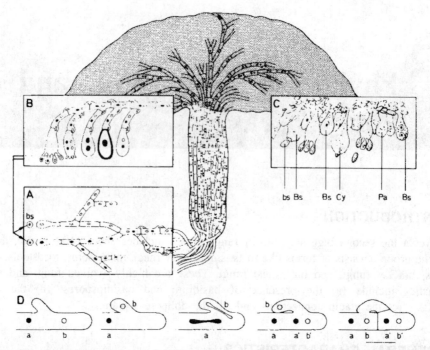

Plate 23.1 Developmental cycle of basidiomycetes, (A) development of septate hyphae from basidiospores (bs) and plasmogamy with subsequent clasp formation, (B) formation of basidia with sequential stages of basidiospore formation, (C) longitudinal section through a hymenium, with basidiospores (bs), basidia (Bs), cyst (Cy) and paraphyces (Pa), (D) development of clamp connection.

and smuts. Basidia are produced in hymanium (layer comparable to ascus wall). Along with basidia, are interspersed sterile hyphal structures called **paraphyses**. Some sterile hyphae (paraphyses) assume larger and swollen shapes and then are called **cystidium** (Plate 23.1).

23.3.2 Development of Basidium and Basidiospores

From the terminal of binucleate hypha, a simple club shaped structure further develops to become basidium. After its separation by septa formation, it enlarges and becomes broader (Plate 23.1). Two nuclei present in swollen structure (basidium) undergo karyogamy and the zygote formed undergoes meiosis giving rise to four haploids. During the nuclear division, four small outgrowth structures called **sterigmata** are formed. Thereafter, vacuoles develop at the base of basidium as contents along with nuclei are pushed to periphery where autogrowths have developed. One nucleus then moves into each of the four basidiospores. The basidiospores eventually are discharged. It should be emphasized here that not all basidia bear four spores. Some may produce only two while others produce more than four. The basidium (*pl.* basidia, *Gr. Basidion* = a small base); it is a structure bearing on its surface a definite number of basidiospores (*Gr. Basidion* = small base + spora), i.e., a meiospore borne on the outer side of a basidium, following karyogamy and meiosis.

Asexual reproduction takes place by means of budding, by fragmentation of the mycelium and by production of conidia, arthrospores or oidia. Sexual reproduction in basidiomycetes culminates in the production of basidia bearing basidiospores. As already described, karyogamy and meiosis take place within basidium. Compatible nuclei (functional gametes) are, however, typically brought together by fusion of compatible primary mycelium. In some basidiomycetes, oidia produced fuse with somatic hyphae to give rise to heterokaryotic mycelium. Sex organs—spermatia and receptive hyphae are formed only in rusts.

23.4 THE CLASSIFICATION

Alexopoulos et al. (1996) have discussed the evolution of basidiomycetes. They have proposed a hypothesis given below, based on information generated by researchers in areas like electron microscopy, rDNA, etc. (Figure 23.1).

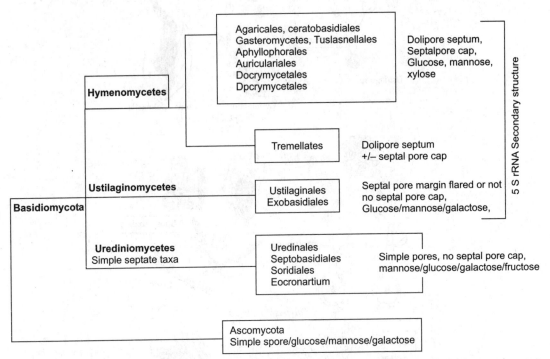

Figure 23.1   Hypothesis of basidiomycetes evolution based on morphological characters and rDNA sequence analysis (Alexopolous, et al., 1996).

23.5 ORDER: USTILAGINALES; THE SMUTS AND BUNTS

The order Ustilaginales includes plant parasitic fungi referred as smut and bunt fungi. The order is characterized by the production of sessile basidiospores, which are released passively. Teliospores are formed from intercalary as well as terminal cells of the dikaryotic secondary mycelium. These arise like chlamydospores by rounding up of the cells and formation of a thick dark wall. About 1200 species of smut fungi belonging to more than 50 genera, attacking about 4000 species of angiosperm belonging to over 75 plant families, is the statistics showing wide distribution and potential parasitism.

23.5.1   Important Pathogens

The life cycles of smut fungi is simpler. Only teliospores are formed which on germination give rise to basidiospores. The mode of germination of teliospores forms the basis of segregation of these fungi into two families—Ustilaginceae and Tilletiaceae. In the former, teliospores form upon germination, a tubular outgrowth that bears spores termed as **sporidia**. Promycelia and sporidia are analogous to basidia and basidiospores, respectively. The diploid nucleus moves from the spores into the promycelium and undergoes meiosis. Three septa form in the promycelium separating the 4 haploid nuclei. Finally basidiospores are formed (Plate 23.2).

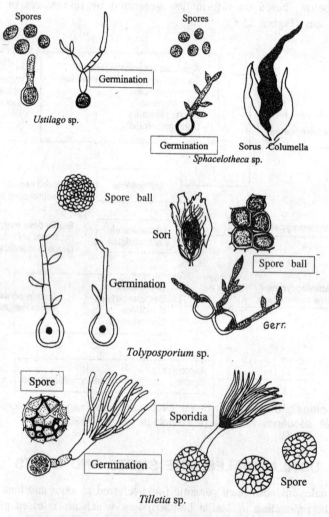

Plate 23.2   Spores of smut and bunt fungi.

In Tilletiaceae, the epibasidium is hollow, bearing variable number of basidiospores only terminally (Plate 23.2). The basidiospores also called **sporidia** multiply by budding *in situ* or after separation from the epibasidium. On germination, basidiospores give rise to monokaryotic primary hyphae, which except in *U. maydis*, exist only for a very short duration. It has been observed that even though the primary hyphae may initiate infection, dikaryotic hyphae are essential for parasitic colonization of host tissues. The dikaryotic hyphae which grow intercellularly in the host tissues may be localized or systemic and feed on the host through haustoria. The infected plants usually do not show much morphological changes until the teliospore formation.

The members of Ustilginceae produce septate promycelium bearing terminal and lateral basidiospores. In Tilletiaceae, the pro-mycelium is aseptate and bears only terminal basidiospores. The identification of genera and the species is based on: (a) Teliospores characteristics, (b) The type and site of sorus development and (c) Host range. The important parasitic genera of the family Ustilaginaceae are:

Ustilago. The teliosorus without a peridium; the black dusty teliospores covered by a membrane of host origin, spores small and less than 20 μm in diameter.

Sphacelotheca. The genus produces sori in the florescence, predominantly in the ovaries. The sori are covered with a definite pseudomembrane composed of largely or entirely sterile fungus cells. The membrane later breaks away exposing the dusty spore mass and central columella composed of host tissues. Spores are free, single, developed in somewhat centripetal manner.

Tolyposporium. Spores in the balls held together by interconnected thickenings of the exospore walls; germination as in *Ustilago*.

In the family **Tilletiaceae,** the teliospores germinate to produce non-septate promycelium, basidiospores in a terminal cluster. Important genera are *Tilletia, Neovossia, Entyloma,* and *Urocystis.* Genus *Tilletia* produces large spores measuring 16-54 μ in diameter, exospore reticulate, smooth and verrucose. *Neovossia* sori are more or less dusty at maturity. Spores have large hyaline appendages and confined to *Gramineae. Entyloma* is another genus. In this fungus sori are formed in most plant parts except roots. These sori tend to remain embedded in the host tissue after maturity forming distinct spots on the infected plant parts. The fourth genus is *Urocystis.* In this fungus, spore balls are formed in the saccate cavities in galls. The balls consist of one to several fertile spores surrounded by bladder-like sterile cells.

23.5.2 Important Plant Diseases

Loose smut of wheat. Loose smut occurs throughout the world (Figure 23.2), including all the wheat growing states of India. However, its incidence is more in cool and moist northern states. In India, 2-4 per cent losses occur annually but in isolated field the incidence may go as high as 50 per cent.

Symptoms. Normally the infected ear heads emerge earlier than the healthy ones. In the infected plants, the ears are transformed into a black powdery mass consisting of smut spores, which are initially covered by a delicate papery grayish membrane. The thin membrane soon ruptures and the spores are released. Subsequently, all these spores are dislodged by the wind leaving behind the naked rachis (Figure 23.3).

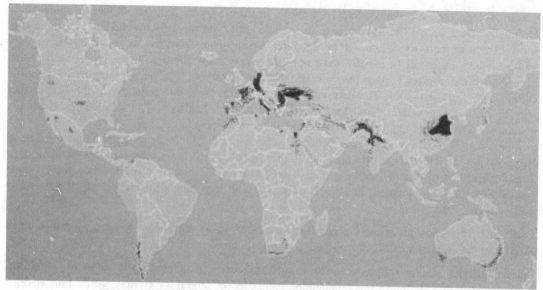

Figure 23.2 Worldwide distribution of loose smut of wheat.

Figure 23.3 Symptoms of loose smut of wheat.

The pathogen. *Ustilago segatum* Var. *tritici* (Syn. *Ustilago tritici*). Teliospores are olivaceous brown, spherical to oval and measure 5-9 μm in diameter. The teliospores germinate to form a germ tube which develops into promycelium (basidium) with four uninucleate cells. No formation of sporidia occurs. The infection hypha is produced from the promycelial cell after dikaryotization. The teliospores are known to remain viable for 5-6 months.

Disease cycle. The fungus perpetuates in the form of dormant mycelium inside the embryo of the infected seeds. At the time of seed germination, the mycelium becomes active and grows along with the seedlings in the meristematic tissues without producing any visible symptoms. When it reaches the ears, the mycelium invades all the young spikelets, where it grows intercellularly and destroys most of the tissues of ear except rachis. Further details are shown in Figure 23.4.

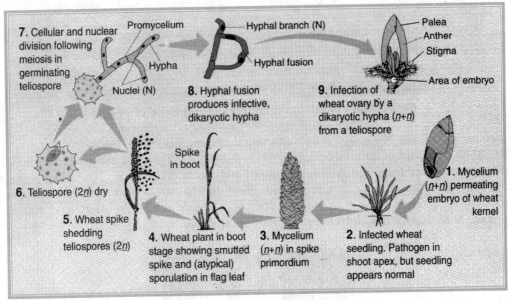

Figure 23.4   Disease cycle of loose smut of wheat. (*Source:* Wilcoxon and Saari, 1996, CIMMYT)

Disease management

1. Vitavax is widely used for the management of this disease and is very popular in seed industry. Seed treatment with Vitavax (carboxin)@2.5 g/kg seed or raxil (tebuconazole) @ 1.5 g/kg seed is highly effective.
2. Joshi, et al. (1983) reported that dwarf varieties like PBW-65, PBW-181, HW-517, Raj-2296, VL-614, HW-888 and HD-4502 are fairly resistant.

Flag smut of wheat.   This has been reported from almost all the wheat growing regions in the world (Figure 23.5). In India, the disease leads to considerable reduction in crop yield due to complete loss of productivity of infected plants.

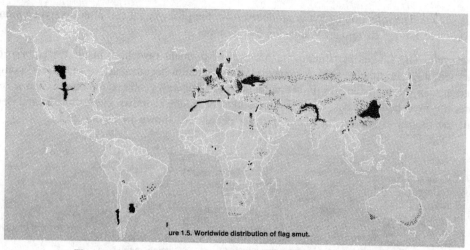

ure 1.5. Worldwide distribution of flag smut.

Figure 23.5 Worldwide distribution of flag smut of wheat.

Symptoms. Flag smut is a serious disease affecting the leaves, leaf sheath, culms and stem of wheat plants. There is twisting of the affected leaves, which droop down like a flag and finally wither away. The fungus produces linear sori on leaf blades and leaf sheath (Plate 23.3). The sori of pathogen are formed on the leaves in the mesophyll tissue under the epidermis. The epidermis later ruptures exposing black powdery mass of the spores. The culms remain sterile and plants do not produce any grain. Sometimes a few shriveled grains may be produced.

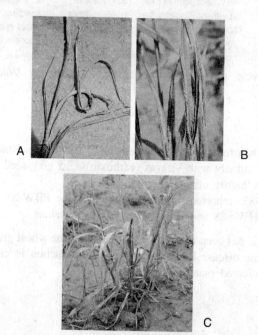

A

B

C

Plate 23.3   Symptoms of flag smut of wheat, (A) twisted foliage and dark linear sori, (B) white striations, upright growth and dark linear sori, (C) stunted plant, tillering, necrotic lower leaves, yellow striations on upper leaves and dark linear sori.

The pathogen. *Urocystis agropyrii* causes this disease. The spores of the fungus are borne in tiny balls (Figure 23.6). Each ball may have 1-6 spores but normally three are present. These are surrounded by a layer of flattened sterile cells. The spore balls are globose, ellipsoidal to oblong, golden brown and 35-40 × 18-34 μm in size (average 32 × 24 μm) (Figure 23.6).

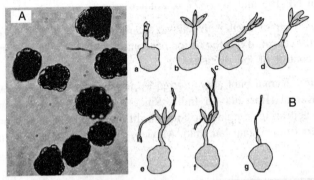

Figure 23.6 (A) spore balls of *U. agropyri* showing dark pigmented telliospore areas and sterile peripheral cells, (B) germinating teliospores of *U. agropyri* showing (a) promycelium and nuclei, (b) sporidia with nuclei on promycelium, (c) lateral sporidium and secondary sporidia, (D) fusion of sporidia with nuclei, (e) infection hyphae from sporidia, (f) fusion of infection hyphae, (g) infection hypha from promycelium. (*Source:* Wilcoxon Coxson and Saari, 1996, CIMMYT)

Disease cycle. The disease is both seed and soil borne. Wheat seeds contaminated by the smut spores at the time of harvest and soil infested by smut spores released from crop residue during tillage are the major sources of inoculum. Air borne smut spores can also reach distant fields. The smut spores can survive in the soil upto four years but the viability decreases logarithmically during that time, thus reducing the inoculum potential and disease severity. After a pre-wetting period, the smut spores germinate and infect the cuticle of coleoptiles before the emergence of seedling (Figure 23.7).

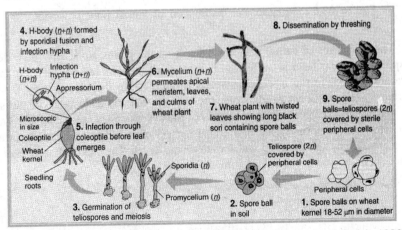

Figure 23.7 Disease cycle of flag smut of wheat (*Source:* Wilcoxon and Saari, 1996, CIMMYT)

Disease management

1. *Cultural*–Burning of stubbles, shallow sowing (less than 1.5 cm) and one to two-year rotation with crops other than wheat and deep ploughing reduces infection and disease severity.

2. *Resistance*–Resistant cultivars are also effective in controlling the disease. Resistance to flag smut has been observed in NP-165 and WG-377 wheat varieties.

3. *Chemical*–The treatment of seed with Vitavax (carboxin) @ 2.0 g/kg seed or fenpropimorph, triadimefon, benomyl, butrizol, oxycarboxin or penconazole @ 1.5 g/kg seed reduces the inoculum and results in good control of the disease.

Karnal bunt of wheat. Karnal bunt also referred as new bunt or partial bunt was first reported by Mitra (1931) from Karnal (Haryana) in India. Since then the disease appeared sporadically for sometime but started appearing in epidemic form in different parts of India from 1976. The disease has also been reported from Afganistan, Iraq, Mexico, Nepal, USA and Pakistan (Figure 23.8).

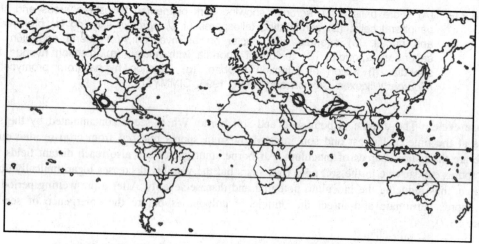

Figure 23.8 Geographical distribution of karnal bunt of wheat.

Symptoms. The symptoms of karnal bunt are evident on the grains alone after their development. Only a few spikes in an ear head are affected. In a stool all the ears are not infected and in ear all the grains are not bunted. In the infected spikelets (Figure 23.9), the glumes may flare to expose the bunted grains. The infection spreads along the grooves but the endosperm of the smooth side of grain may not be bunted. Since the embryo is not always damaged, such partially bunted grains can germinate. However, in severely infected grains most of the seed tissues are converted into bunt spores, leaving intact only the pericarp and the aleuronic layer. The infected seed emit foul odour due to production of a volatile chemical trimethylamine.

Figure 23.9 Symptoms of karnal bunt of wheat, karnals showing different levels of infection, wheat spike infected by *T. indica.* (*Source:* Willcoxson and Sarri, 1996, CIMMYT)

The pathogen. *Tilletia indica* (Syn. *Neovossia indica*) causes this disease. Teliospores of the fungus are produced as dark brown to black mass and are held together by the pericarp emitting a typical smell. The teliospores are produced singly at the end of fertile hyphae and are dark brown in colour, ellipsoidal to spherical and measure 24-47 average (35) μm in diameter (Figure 23.10). The teliospores have a characteristic apiculus, arising from the episporium. The episore is reticulate with curved spines, which are covered by a thin hyaline perisporium or sheath. This sheath remains persistent after the maturity of the spores (Figure 23.10). Sporidia are long, sickle shaped and do not fuse together in pairs. They germinate by a germ tube, which acts as an infection hyphae. The unicellular primary sporidia contain one haploid nucleus each, which on germination develop into monokaryotic mycelium or secondary sporidia. The compatible sporidia/mycelium fuse and produce dikaryotic mycelium or sporidia which can initiate infection.

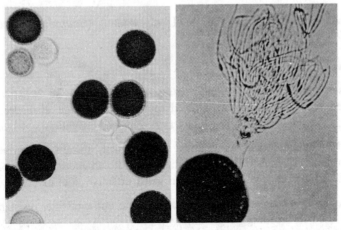

Figure 23.10 Teliospores and sterile cells of *T. indica,* germinated teliospore of *T. indica.* (*Source:* Wilcoxon and Saari, 1996, CIMMYTT)

Disease cycle and epidemiology. The teliospores reach the soil during harvest and threshing of the crop together with infected or contaminated seeds. On germination in soil, the spore produces a promycelium bearing 60-125 primary sporidia at its tip. The primary sporidia germinate while still attached to the promycelium on the soil surface producing allantoid (banana shaped) and filiform secondary sporidia. The allantoid sporidia are released forcibly and become air-borne. Further details of disease cycle is shown in Figure 23.11.

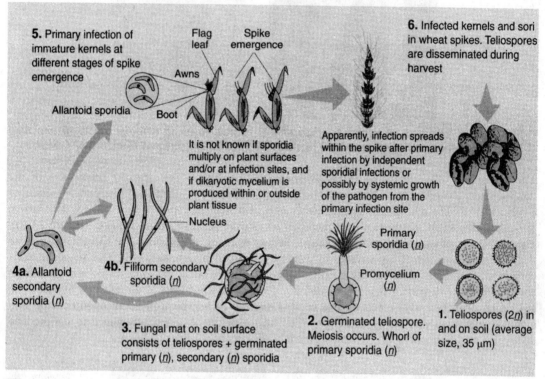

Figure 23.11   Disease cycle of karnal bunt of wheat. (*Source:* Wilcoxon and Saari, 1996, CIMMYT)

Disease management

1. *Cultural.* Disease-free seed should be used for sowing and more so in a seed multiplication programme. Infected seed should not be allowed to move over large distances. At the time of anthesis, avoid the excessive use of nitrogenous fertilizers and irrigation.

2. *Chemical.* Seed treatment with compounds like butrizol, thiram or carbendazim reduces germination of teliospores adhered to the seed. Foliar spray of carbendazim, mancozeb, hexacnazole or propiconazole @ 0.1 per cent at anthesis stage gives effective control.

3. *Resistance.* Since the resistant varieties to karnal bunt are not available, resistant donors HD 29 and HD 30 can be used in breeding programme.

Common/Hill bunt or stinking smut of wheat. The disease has been of much historical significance in the development of plant pathology as a science. The disease is known to be widely distributed in all wheat-growing areas of the world (Figure 23.12). In India, the disease is restricted to cooler regions such as western U.P., parts of Punjab, H.P. and Kashmir.

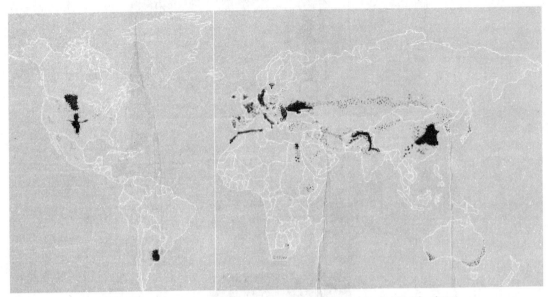

Figure 23.12 Geographical distribution of common bunt of wheat.

Symptoms. The infected plants may become stunted and markedly shorter than the normal unaffected plants (Plate 23.4). The normal green colour of the plant may also change to bluish green to grayish green. Diseased plants produce smaller heads. Plants affected by bunt ripen a little earlier and the ears assume a dark green colour and are more open (loose) than the normal ones. A few days prior to emergence of head from the boot, striking difference can be seen between smutted and normal florets. The carpel of the affected heads is larger with fairly longer ovary than the normal one and of green colour instead of white. The glumes spread apart (more evident in *Vulgare* types) forming a greater angle with the main axis of the head. The smutted ears are darker green than normal ones. The smutted grains yield a soft black paste-like mass. In mature grains the black paste-like interior changes to an oily powder, that characteristic feature of the spore mass. The grain is full of bunt balls.

As a rule, all the ears in a smutted plant are attacked, and all the grains in an ear are turned into bunt balls, though exceptions occur. The bunt balls in the ears are not irregular, but occur in more or less regular manner, one above the other (Plate 23.4). If a mature ball is squeezed it burst open, exposing a greasy, dusty powder composed of teliospores and smelling strongly of rotten fish. The presence of the smut in the field can be detected by the foul smell of a volatile compound, trimethylamine in the spore mass. It is this smell of rotten fish that gives the name stinking smut to the disease.

Plate 23.4 Symptoms of common/hill bunt of wheat, (A) dwarfing of wheat seedling infected with
T. controversa (left) compared to a healty seedling, (B) early symptoms of infection
by *T. controversa* on wheat seedling leaves, (C) flaring of awns on a spike due to
infection by *T. controversa* (right) compared to a healthy spike and (D) sori of
T. controversa.

The pathogen.   The common bunt of wheat is caused by two smut fungi, *Tilletia caries* (=*T. tritici*)
and *T. foetida* (=*T. laevis*). These two species may sometimes occur in the same grain. A dwarf bunt
caused by *Tilletia controversa* occurs on winter wheat in temperate countries only. Morphological
features (Plate 23.5) and disease cycle of the two smut fungi causing the common bunt is more or
less similar. The main difference between the two is in the spore wall. The wall of teliospores of
Tilletia caries has reticulations whereas in *T. foetida*, they are irregular in shape and 17-22 μm in
diameter.

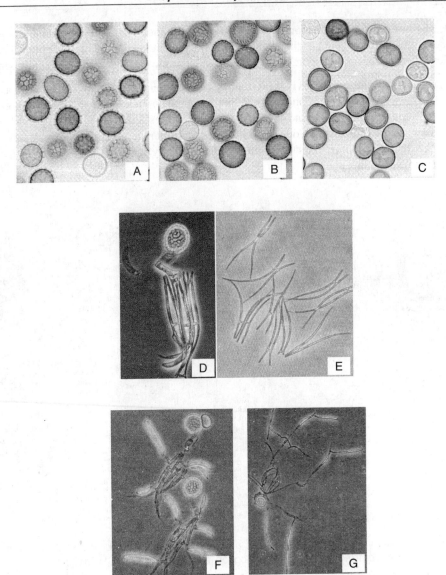

Plate 23.5 The features of spores and their germination in *Tilletia caries* and *T. controversa*, (A) teliospores and sterile cells of *T. controversa*, (B) teliospores and sterile cells of *T. tritici*, (C) teliospores and sterile cells of *T. laevis*, (D) germinated teliospore of *T. tritici* showing promycelium, primary sporidia and H-bodies that formed by fusion of sporidia, (E) H-bodies of *T. tritici*, (F) alletoid secondary sporidia of *T. tritici*, (G) filiform secondary sporidia of *T. tritici*.

The teliospores on germination produce a short hyaline, stout promycelium bearing a cluster of 8-16 filiform, hyaline, primary sporidia. The primary sporidia fuse in pairs to form characteristic H-shaped structures (Plate 23.5). These dikaryotic structures germinate by a hypha which then produces dikaryotic secondary sporidia. These secondary sporidia are sickle-shaped and hyaline and germinate to form dikaryotic infection hypha. This hypha invades the tissues of young seedling. The fungus then spreads inside the seedling and later throughout the plant. The mycelium then enters the ovaries where it forms teliospores. The disease is systemic and generally externally seedborne.

Disease cycle. The pathogen survives as teliospores on contaminated seeds as well as in soil (Figure 23.13). The latter form of inoculum is not common in India, and the disease is externally seed borne. The teliospores germinate with the young seedlings and form basidia, primary sporidia and secondary sporidia. The dikaryotic mycelium formed after germination of secondary sporidia penetrates the young seedlings directly. It grows intercellularly and invades developing leaves and the growing points of the plant.

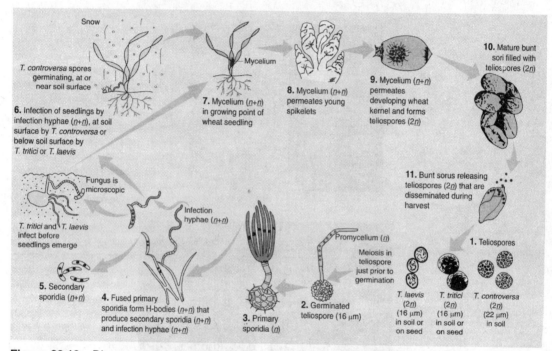

Figure 23.13 Disease cycle of common bunt of wheat caused by *T. tritici* and dwarf bunt caused by *T. controversa*. (Source: Wilcoxon and Saari, 1996, CIMMYT).

Disease management

1. The most effective method is to use disease resistant varieties. In India, several wheat varieties resistant to this bunt has been developed. Some of these are S 227, PV 18, HD 2012, HD 4513, HD 4519, Kalyan Sona, UP 2002, HB 383, WL 410, WL 885, WL 1581, IWP 72, IWP 87, IWP 127 and IWP 129.
2. Crop rotation, modification in soil temperature and moisture through alteration in date and depth of sowing and destruction of crop debris help in reducing the soil-borne inoculum.
3. Seed treatment with benlate (0.3%) and vitavax (0.2%) have given complete control of the disease. Recently a triazole, bitertanol has been found very effective for seed treatment to eradicate seed borne inoculum.

Smut of pearl millet. Smut, caused by *Tolyposporium penicillariae* Bref., is a widespread disease of pearl millet [*Pennisetum glaucum* (L.) R. Br]. The disease has been reported from Pakistan, India and the United States, and from many countries in Africa.

Symptoms. In the infected florets, ovaries are converted into structures called **sori** (singular sorus). The sori are larger grains and appear as enlarged than grains, oval to conical bodies projecting somewhat beyond the glumes in place of grains. Initially the sori are bright green (Figure 23.14) but later they turn brown to black (Figure 23.14). The sori are usually 3-4 mm long and 2-3 mm broad at the top; they are covered by a thin membrane, which often breaks at maturity to release brown to black spore balls.

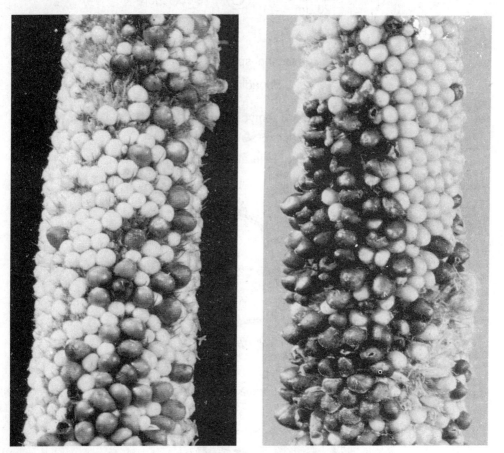

Figure 23.14 Symptoms of smut of pearl millet, (A) shiny green smut sori on an infected panicle of pearl milet, (B) matured dark brown smut sori on an infected panicle of pearl millet.

The pathogen. The accepted name of the causal fungus is *Tolyposporum penicillariae* Bref. The teleutospores occur in compact, ball like masses called **spore balls**, measuring 42-325 × 50-175 µm in diameter (Figure 23.15).

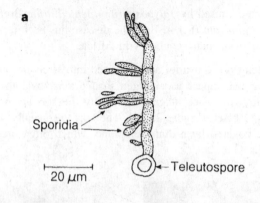

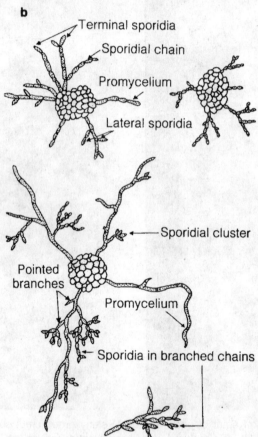

Figure 23.15 Fate of germinating teliospores of *T. penicillarie* (A) a germinating teliospore producing four-celled promycelium and sporidia, and (B) variation in germination patterns of teliospores while they are held in spore balls (Note: production of sporidia in chains on branched mycelia).

Disease cycle. The primary inoculum source is spore balls in the soil from the previous infected crop and surface contaminated seed used for sowing. Teleutospores germinate following rain showers and produce numerous air-borne sporidia that infect the pearl millet crop at flowering. Two sporidia of compatible mating types are required to form a dikaryotic infection hypha (Figure 23.16). *T. penicillariae* is not internally seed borne but external contamination of seed with spore balls from ruptured sori in the field and on the threshing floor is common. Teleutospores remain viable in soil at depths up to 22.5 cm for about one year.

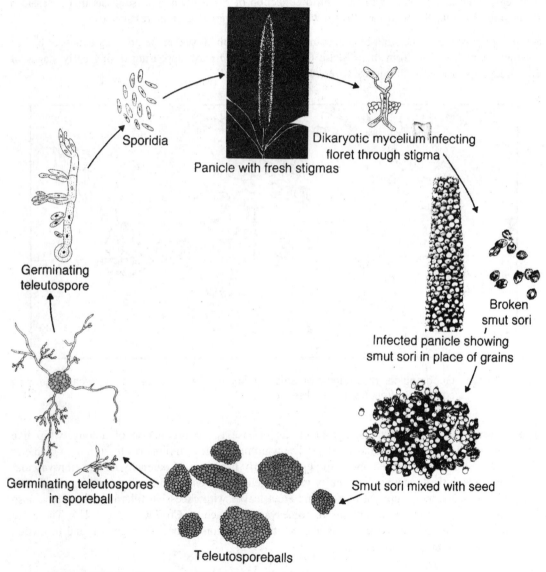

Sporidia

Panicle with fresh stigmas

Dikaryotic mycelium infecting floret through stigma

Germinating teleutospore

Broken smut sori

Infected panicle showing smut sori in place of grains

Germinating teleutospores in sporeball

Smut sori mixed with seed

Teleutosporeballs

Figure 23.16 Disease cycle of smut of pearl millet caused by *T. penicillariae*.

Disease management

Chemical control. Various non-systemic fungicides, including, zineb, and mancozeb, the systemic fungicides plantvax, vitavax and benlate, and antibiotics heptanes and aureofungin have been tried either as seed, foliage or panicle spray treatments with limited success, even under low disease pressure. Effective control by foliar and panicle sprays with plantvax and Vitavax is reported. Four sprays with captafol, zineb and heptanes have also been reported effective.

Host resistance. Growing disease-resistant cultivars is the most economical and feasible method of disease control. The work with the world collection of *Pennisetum* spp., suggests that accessions from Mali, Nigeria, Senegal and Zimbabwe have some degree of smut resistance.

Smut of sugarcane. The smut of sugarcane is reported from all sugarcane growing countries except Australia, which is free from this disease (Figure 23.17). Disease appearing during early stages of 40-60 days of crop growth causes severe losses.

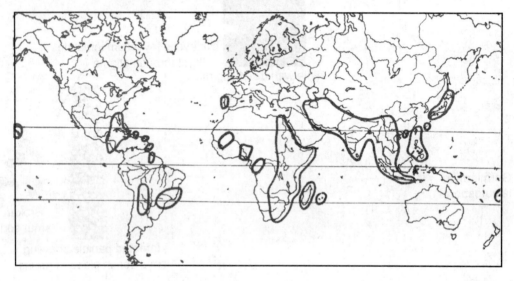

Figure 23.17 Geographical distribution of smut of sugarcane Australia, a sugarcane growing country, is free from this disease.

Symptoms. The characteristic symptom of the disease is the production of a long, whip like structure from the apex of the attacked stalk. The whip may be few millimetres to 20 mm in diameter (Figure 23.18). It is unbranched and made up of a fairly hard core of parenchyma and fibrovascular element in which the fungal hyphae ramify with the teliospores enclosed in a thin silvery membrane. The diseased plant shows upright narrow and erect leaves with excessive tillering. There have also been reported some unusual symptoms in some varieties such as Co 740 and Co 419. These are formation of multiple buds, adventitious leaves, stalk distortion, galls and outgrowth and formation of whips beneath leaf sheaths.

Figure 23.18 Symptoms of sugarcane smut.

The pathogen. The disease is caused by *Ustilago scitaminea,* described for the first time as *Ustilage sacchari* in 1870 by Rabenhorst. From India, the disease was first recorded by Sydow and Butler in 1906. The pathogen is a true culmicolous (stem infecting) smut. The teliospores are spherical, light brown and 10.5–17.04 µm in diameter. Soon after their release they are easily disseminated by wind and germinate without rest period to produce four-celled promycelium. Four sporidia (basidiospore) are produced, one from each cell of the promycelium. Sometimes teliospores germinate to give rise a narrow septate hypha which elongates and branches. Dikaryotic phase is established through fusions between sporidia, between cells of promycelium or between cells of hyphae developing from the germinating teliospores. The dikaryotic infection hypha invades the host tissue. When the whip is fully emerged, the membrane ruptures releasing teliospores in the air.

Disease cycle. The seed pieces are the source of primary inoculum. The soil borne inoculum has very little role in epidemiology. The disease spreads centrifugally in the field. The air-borne inoculum increases sharply between June and August with emergence of whips after primary infection. A second large peak appears after October at the second flush due to secondary infection

(Figure 23.19). In India, since there is no dead season for sugarcane crop, the host is available to the pathogen round the year.

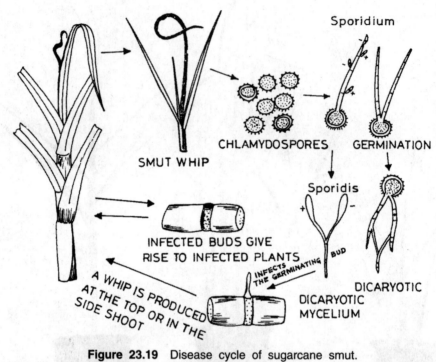

Figure 23.19 Disease cycle of sugarcane smut.

The pathogen spreads in several ways. These are: (a) planting of sets of smutted canes containing mycelium of the fungus, which spreads disease to new areas, (b) planting of sets with buds carrying the teliospores, thus spreading the disease to new areas, (c) infection of buds on nearby standing canes by teliospores released from whips in the field during the growing season (secondary infection), (d) ratooning the smutted canes.

Disease management

1. The seed sets should be selected from healthy field or from a crop with an infection levels below 5%. This reduces secondary infection. The crop with high levels of disease should not be ratooned.
2. Sets before planting be subjected to physical or chemical treatment. Physical methods include hot water as well as moist hot air treatment. For hot water treatment, the sets are dipped in water at 55°C to 60°C for 10 minutes. Exposure of sets to moist hot air at 54°C for eight hours is also very effective.
3. Some systemic fungicides like vitavex, benlate, bavistin, triadimephon (bayleton) have proved very effective eradicants. These systemic fungicide give still very effective control when used in combination with physical treatment (hot water, hot air). Bayleton added to hot water treatment tank is reported to have controlled the smut completely. Hot water plus 0.1% bavistin or bayleton at 50°C completely eliminated the smut from sets. Bayleton

treatment also eradicated smut development in systemically infected seed pieces. Bayleton (0.1%) incorporated in to water at 51°C for 2 hours completely eliminated seed borne infection.

4. Source of resistance to smut have been reported in *Saccharum spontaneum, S. barberi, S. sinense* and *S. robustum*. These have been used to develop several smut-resistant cultivars of sugarcane. Some of the resistant varieties are: Co 49, Co 527, Co 658, Co 974, Co 1148, Co 6806, Co 7108, Co 7319, BO 11, BO 22, BO 24, Co Lk 7807, 8001, 8004, 8102, 8402, CoH 29, Cos 8214, S 3-7, S 4-7, S 4-12, S 15-7, S 15-9, S 20-2 and S 22-9.

23.6 ORDER: UREDINALES; THE RUST FUNGI

The order Uredinales includes plant parasitic fungi commonly referred as rust fungi. Rusts are considered elite among plant pathogens where presence on the host is known not by "symptoms" but by the "signs" of their own "sori" (Plate 23.6). It is estimated that there are approximately 5000 species belonging to about 140-150 genera of rust fungi. They parasitize green plants ranging from the ferns and conifers to most of the highly evolved families of both dicotyledons and monocotyledons.

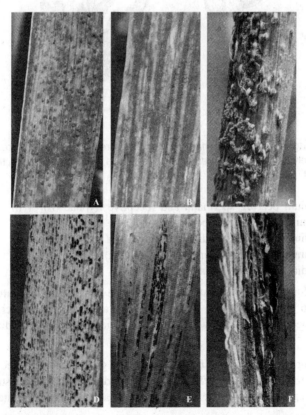

Plate 23.6 Symptoms of wheat rusts (A-C) uredinium bearing urediniospores (D-F) telium bearing teliospores.

23.6.1 Important Pathogens

The spore stages. Most rust fungi exhibit complicated life cycles. Rust produces more than one type of spores. The basic or full life cycle consists of five spore stages (Plate 23.7) but some genera produce few or only one type of spores, the teliospores. The spore stages are designated by roman numerals in addition to their specific names. The spore stages are:

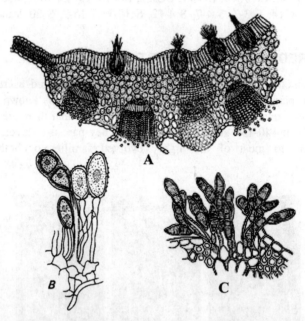

Plate 23.7 Spore stages of *P. graminis* (A) pycniospores and aeciospores on barberry leaf, respectively, (B) and (C) urediniospores and a teliospore arising from the same sorus on wheat plant.

Stage 0	Pycnium bearing spermatia and receptive hyphae (n) or (n')
Stage I	Aecium bearing aeciospores $(n + n')$
Stage II	Uredinium bearing urediniospores $(n + n')$
Stage III	Telium bearing teliospores $(n + n' \rightarrow 2n)$
Stage IV	Basidia bearing basidiospores $(n) + (n')$

The rusts, which form all the spore stages on the same host are called **autoecious**, while those that form them on two hosts, alternating with each other, are called **heteroecious**. In heteroecious rusts, the pycnial and aecial stages are always formed on one host and the uredinial and telial stages on the other.

Life cycle. Depending upon the spore stages present, the genera and the lifecycles are designated as: *macrocyclic*, *demicyclic* and *microcyclic*. Rust fungi producing all the five stages or lacking only the pycnial stage are called **macrocyclic**. Genera which lack the uredinial stage (Pycnia may be present or absent) are called **demicyclic**. These too, like the macrocyclic rusts, may be autoecious or heteroecious. The microcyclic rusts possess only the telial stage. A general life cycle of a rust fungus is illustrated in Figure 23.20.

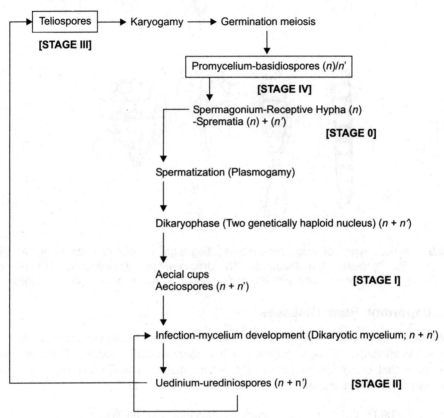

Figure 23.20 Nuclear pattern of spores produced and their nuclear status in a rust fungus.

The classification. There is little agreement regarding division of Uredinales into families. Over the years, various workers have proposed from two to fourteen families. The limited information that is available supports the division of Uredinales into the families Pucciniaceae and Melampsoraceae. These families are characterized on the basis of teliospore characteristics (Plate 23.8).

Family: Pucciniaceae. The stalked teliospores constitute the characteristic feature of this family. The genera are based on teliospores morphology, aecial characteristics and life-cycle pattern. The teliospores are one celled in *Uromyces*, and *Hemileia*, bicelled (sometimes a few three celled) in *Puccinia* and *Gymnosporangium*, and many celled in *Phragmidium* and *Ravenelia*.

Family: Melampsoraceae. It includes genus (e.g. *Melampsora*) forming sessile, single celled teliospores in palisade layers. The telia are erumpent or crustose lying covered by the host epidermis.

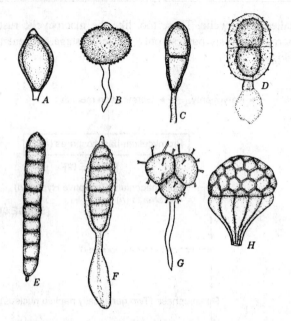

Plate 23.8   Various types of teliospores representing eight genera of rusts fungi, (A) Uromyces, (B) Pileolaria, (C) Puccinia, (D) Uropyxis, (E) Xenodochus, (F) Phragmidium, (G) Nyssopsora, and (H) Ravenelia. (*Source:* Alexopolouse, et at., 1996)

23.6.2 Important Rust Diseases

The cereal rusts.   The genus *Puccinia* infects a number of crops belonging to the family *Gramineae* and others. Occasionally, the same pathogen infects more than one species. There are three types of wheat rusts that occur almost universally. Symptomatology and other characteristics of the pathogen and the diseases are summarized in Tables 23.1 and 23.2.

Table 23.1   Disease Caused by *Puccinia* spp. on Winter Cereals

S. No.	Crop	Disease	Causal agent
1.	Wheat(*Triticum* spp.)	Black (stem) rust, Brown (leaf) rust, Yellow (stripe) rust	*Puccinia graminis Pers.* f. sp. *tritici* Eriks. and Henn., *P. recondita* Rob. Ex. Desm. f. sp. *tritici* Eriks. (syn. *P. triticina, P. rubigo*vera var. *tritici*), *P. striiformis* West. f. sp. *tritici*
2.	Barley(*Hoardeum vulgare*)	Black rust, Leaf rust, Yellow rust	*P. graminis* Pers. f. sp. *tritici* Eriks. and Henn., *P. hordei* Otth. (syn. *P. anomala* Rostr.), *P. striiformis* West, f. sp. *hordei*
3.	Oat (*Avena sativa*)	Black rust, Crown rust	*P. graminis* f. sp. *avenae* Eriks. and Henn., *P. coronata* **cda**. f. sp. *avenae* Fraser and Lingham.
4.	Rye (*Secale cereale*)	Stem rust, Brown rust	*P. graminis* Pres. f. sp. *secalis, P. recondita* Rob. Ex Desm. f. sp. *secalis (P. dispersa)*

Table 23.2   Comparative Features of Three Rusts of Wheat

Differentiating characters	Black rust (Puccinia graminis f. sp. tritici)	Brown rust (Puccinia recondita f. sp. tritici)	Yellow rust (Puccinia striiformis f. sp. tritici)
Suitable temperature range	25°C	20°C	10–15°C
Severity	More severe on stalks than on leaf sheaths, leaves, ear heads	Infects leaves, exclusively, rarely on leaf sheath and stalks	Infects leaves and when severe, leaf sheaths, stalks and ears also.
Urediopustule	Large elongated, dark brown, bursting early, throwing epidermal fringes in the process	Small, oval, light brown, do not run together, burst early with mild displacement of epidermis, found chiefly on upper surface of leaves.	Arranged in rows of lemon yellow coloured sori, epidermal rupture not visible
Urediniospore	Brown, oval, thickwalled, tiny spines, 25–30 × 17–20 µm, having 4 germ pores at equatorial plane.	Brown, spherical, minutely echinulated, 16–28 µm, 7–10 germ pores dispersed all over	Spherical to ovate, spore wall colourless, contains yellow oil globule, minute echinulation, 23–35 × 20–25 µm, 6–10 germ pores dispersed all over
Teliopspustule	Black, found on all aerial parts, mainly stem	Pustules do not burst epidermis, found chiefly on leaf surface	Sori are flattened and dull black, chiefly on lower surface and do not burst open easily
Teliospores(Two celled)	40–46 × 15–20 µm	35–63 × 12–20 µm	35–63 × 12–20 µm
Alternate hosts	Species of *Berberis, Mahonia, Mahoberberis*	*Isopurum fumarioides, Thalictrum* spp., *Clematis* spp., *Anchusa* spp.	Not known
Collateral hosts	*Bromus cooratus, B. carinatus, B. japonicus, B. moillis, B. patulus, Hordeum distichon, H. murinum, H. stenostachys, Lolium perenie, Hilaria jamesii Aegilops squarrosa, A. ventricosa, A. trinecilis*	*Aegilops* spp.	*Bromus catharticus, B. japonicus, Hordeum murinum, Muehlenbergia hugelii*

Stem rust. *P. graminis tritici* produces teliospores late in the crop season. These require a dormancy period before germinating into a four celled promycelium bearing single celled globose basidiospores, on short sterigmata. Prior to germination, fusion of nucleus (karyogamy) takes place in the teliospores (Figure 23.21). This diploid nucleus undergoes meiosis, forming four daughter haploid nuclei that migrate one each into the basidiospores. The basidiospores are of two different strains, namely +ive and -ive, each being self-incompatible.

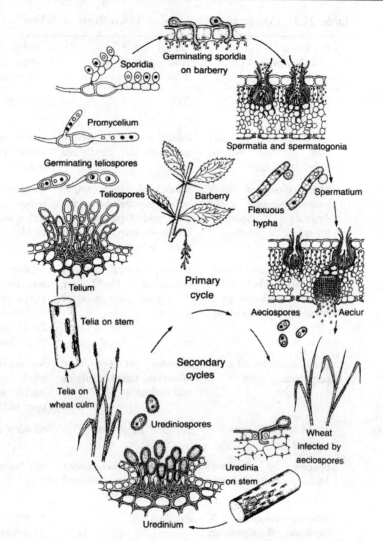

Figure 23.21 Life cycle of stem rust fungus *Puccinia graminis tritici*.

The basidiospores are windborne, and if deposited on young barberry leaves, germinate and infect the leaf at 12–21°C. Spermagonia are produced near the upper epidermis after few days of infection. Spermatia are produced on stalks. The mycelium producing spermatia also produce receptive hyphae carrying the same factor. While feeding on the fragrant nectar, insects transfer the spermatia soaked in nectar on to the receptive hyphae of another factor. The hyphae protrude out through the ostiole, facilitating easier fertilization. The spermatial contents pass into the receptive hyphae through a pore by dissolving the wall at the place of contact. The dikaryotic mycelium formed thereafter proliferates and forms aecial cups rupturing the lower epidermis. These cups contain chain of aeciospores in palisade layers borne on short stalk. The aeciospores are ejected from the lower side of leaves in high humidity and thus differ in the mode of spore liberation when compared to the urediniospores (Figure 23.21). Aeciospores are incapable of infecting *Berberis*. Mature aeciospores get blown off infect wheat to produce crops of urediniospores. About 83 species of *Berberis* are known to be infected by the stem rust pathogen.

Mehta (1929, 1940) showed that under Indian conditions, alternate hosts are not functional. The survival and perpetuation of the pathogen, therefore, occur through repeated urediniospores. In fact, alternate hosts are of no consequence in the recurrence of stem rust in India. So far four aecial stages have been recorded on *Berberis* but are connected with the hosts other than wheat.

Brown rust. Jackson and Mains (1921) demonstrated *Thalictrum* spp. as the alternate host for *P. recondita tritici*. Later *Isopyrum fumarioides* in Siberia, *Clematis* spp. in Italy, and *Anchusa* spp. in Portugal were also found to serve as alternate hosts. The life cycle of *P. recondite tritici* is like that of *P. graminis tritici*. An aecial stage found on *Thalictrum javanicum* in India is that of *Puccinia persistens* and therefore, does not infect wheat. A few species of *Aegilops* also become infected by *P. recondite tritici* (Nagrajan, et al., 1992).

Yellow rust. Although heteroecious, there is still no alternate host for the yellow rust pathogen. In India, the primary inoculum for the Indo-Gangatic plain comes each year from the Himalayan hills. In the temperate countries, volunteer plants or the "green bridge" and collateral hosts help in the annual perpetuation of the pathogen. In the absence of a fungional alternate host, perpetuation of the pathogen is accomplished by repeated urediocycles. When temperature is low, infections remain latent for an unusually long time and burst open suddenly when favourable conditions return (Nagrajan, et al., 1992).

International spread. Cereal rusts particularly the wheat rusts are notorious international travellers. The pathogen propagules spread hundreds and thousands of kilometres each year. In many cases, the source and target area of the organism are distinct and the spread of the pathogen is facilitated by the coincidence of certain favourable weather patterns, direction of winds, inoculum load, plant age and type of host variety at the target area (Nagrajan, et al., 1992). Long distance dispersal of rust pathogens have been discussed in Chapter 7 pertaining to disease development in populations.

(a) *Australia and New Zealand.* Wheat growing areas within Australia are separated by long distances. Post harvest rains in the eastern part of the country facilitate the survival of pathogens on volunteer plants and *Agropyrn scabrum* Beauv. (rough wheat grass). Western Australia, the other wheat area, is separated from the east by 1,300 km of desert, yet an occasional exchange of inoculum between these regions occurs. Stem rust strains move north and south and east and west over the Australian continent in which aerial transport of spores plays a major part. Studies spanning a period of 40 years revealed the long-distance spread of *P. graminis tritici* urediniospores. Strain 21-ANZ, 2 spread between New South Wales and South Victoria, over a distance of 1,450 km. Earlier observations suggest that west to east movements are rare however, the epidemic of 1973-74 was a result of these movements (Nagrajan, et al., 1992). The information on population of *P. graminis tritici* in New Zealand clearly reflect a resemblance of race flora to Eastern Australia. This information can be further validated by the occurrence of a new strain in Northern New Zealand undoubtedly detected earlier in Queensland. Such virulence spreads across the 2,000 km distance of ocean from Australia to New Zealand (Nagrajan, et al., 1992).

(b) *United States.* In the United States, 80% of the wheat area is winter wheat, and the rest consists of spring types. Stakman and his co-worker (1923) demonstrated the northerly movement of the stem rust pathogen from its overwintering sources in Southern Texas and Northern Mexico. From this over-wintering area, the wind-borne inoculum sweeps through the United States, crossing Rockies and infecting the fields in the Dakotas, Minnesota and across the Canadian border (from Mexico to the Prairie, covering a distance of 4,000 km). Favourable winds carry innumerable spores back into the Southern United States and Mexico during autumn, therefore, the movement of the stem rust is **bi-directional Puccinia Pathway.** The race 15 B of *P. graminis tritici* is known to swept across the United States in a single year.

(c) *South Asia. Berberis/Thalictrum* spp., the alternate hosts for black and brown rusts, are non-functional in Asian context. In the Indo-Gangetic plains during the warm postharvest summer months, the rust pathogens are eliminated due to the high temperature. There is no local inoculum left in the Indo-Gangetic plain to cause fresh infections during succeeding wheat season. In the Himalayas during the May-November period summer crops of wheat and "green bridges" are available. The Nilgiri and Palney hills of Southern India where wheat is available round the year, above 2,200 m altitude, serves as the source area for the inoculum for the southern and central Indian crop. It is believed that the rust inoculum from Himalayas plays a very minor role in the recurrence of epidemics for northern India. Inoculum that is available in the Southern India hills is carried further north by tropical cyclones and are deposited along with rains over one month–old central Indian wheat crops. Such deposition, which occurs during November as a consequence of tropical cyclones are capable of epidemic initiation. Spread of stem rust from central India to other parts of northern India is favoured by the repeated passage of "western disturbances" linking both areas. The associated winter rainfall permits nation wide appearance and buildup of stem rust. A set of three weather situations that favour a northerly movement of the stem rust urediniospores have been identified as that Indian stem rust rules (Nagrajan and Singh, 1975).

Wheat growing areas are relatively cooler over northwest India and Pakistan; hence, yellow rust of wheat (*P. striiformis tritici*) is more important. During both 1976 and 1980 serious epidemics of yellow rust on wheat in Pakistan caused food deficits. *P. striiformis tritici* is not a regular long distance traveller, and from over summering areas in Hindukush, Sulaiman ranges and in the Himalayas, the pathogen spreads up to a few hundred kilometres. Epidemic size and the terminal disease severity are greatly dependent on the number and frequency of western disturbance.

Management of wheat rust

(a) *Cultural.* Excessive use of nitrogenous fertilizers should be avoided as these enhance foliar growth and make plants more prone to rust infection, whereas on the other hand, phosphatic fertilizers hasten maturity and hence reduce the chances of infection. Diversity in cultivars grown on a farm and mixed cultivation of different varieties and/or crops will reduce the multiplication of inoculum resulting in slow development of rust.

Destruction of collateral hosts/alternate hosts and volunteer wheat plants/green bridges might reduce the initial inoculum and delay the epiphytotic. *Barberry* eradication was visualized as a means of breaking the stem rust cycle. Such an eradication done in the United States drastically delayed disease onset, reduced initial inoculum level, decreased the number of physiologic races, and reduced the frequency of stem rust epidemics. Coupled with better varieties and plant protection operations, the *barberry* eradication substantially reduced the frequency of stem rust in the United States.

(b) *Host resistances.* Various disease management approaches are in practice using host resistance such as multiline, varietal mixture, gene cycle, pyramiding resistance genes, and using slow rusting or adult plant resistance. Releasing and cultivating a number of varieties with differing resistance genes create a diverse mosaic pattern. Such patterns minimize the chances of widespread epidemic. Wheat rust epidemics can be checkmated by quick varietal changes along the path of the pathogen dispersal "Gene zone". A rapid change in cultivars averted or delayed the possible epiphytotic of 1976 in India, while in adjoining Pakistan, where cultivars were not changed, a severe leaf rust epidemic occurred (Nagrajan and Joshi, 1985).

(c) *Biological control. Sphaerellopsis filum* (perfect state *Eudarluca filum*), an ubiquitous hyperparasite, is associated with *P. coronata, P. graminis, P. recondita, P. striiformis, P. sorghi*, and species of *Cronartium*. In Kenya, *S. filum* was found in about 99% of the rust sori. *Gonatobotrys simplex* and *Verticillium lecanii* are also known to infect *P. graminis* f. sp. *avenae*, and *P. recondita* f. sp. *tritici* by preventing production of urediniospores, and so only teliospores are produced. The biological control needs special attention as not much work has been done for exploitation of bioagents.

(d) *Chemical control.* From early days of chemical control using sulfur to the present era of systemic fungicides, much advancements have been made, which have resulted in reducing the amount of fungicide and reducing the number of sprays needed to keep disease below the economic threshold. In India, even in the highly productivity north western regions, the chemical control is not very popular. However, several fungicides have been found effective. These include dithiocarbantes (zineb, maneb, mancozeb), plantvax, etc. Some recently introduces include triazole fungicides like triademefon, trianimol and fenapanil. Bayleton and propiconazole (tilt) have also been found effective.

Rust of groundnut. Rust of groundnut (*Arachis hypogaea* L.) caused by *Puccinia arachidis* Spegazzini was largely confined to South and Central America, with occasional outbreaks occurring in the southern USA. The worldwide spread of rust (Figure 23.22) has resulted in its establishment in many countries of Asia and Africa (McDonald and Subrahmanyam, 1992).

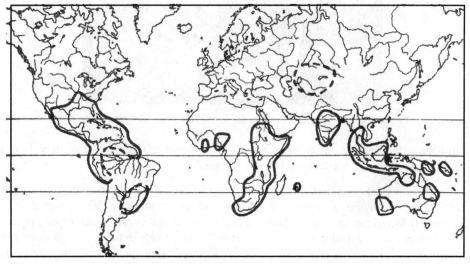

Figure 23.22 Geographical distributio of rust of groundnut.

Symptoms. Rust can be easily recognized when the orange-coloured pustules (uredinia) appear on the lower (abaxial) surfaces of leaflets and rupture to release the reddish-brown urediniospores (Figure 23.23). The pustules, which develop on all aerial plant parts except flowers, are usually circular and range from 0.5 to 1.4 mm in diameter. Pustules may also develop on shells of developing pods.

Figure 23.23 Rust pustules on lower surface of groundnut leaf.

The pathogen. *Puccinia arachidis* is causal organism. Stages 0 (spermagonia), stage I (aecia) and stage IV (metabasidia and basidiospores) are not known.

Stage II. The uredinial stage is the most commonly observed stage. The uredinia are scattered or irregularly grouped, elliptical, round or oblong, subepidermal in origin, covered by a thin membranous net-like peridium and is blister-like when immature, becoming erumpent, powdery and dark. Urediniospores are broadly ellipsoid or obovoid, thick, finely echinulate with mostly two and occasionally three or four, nearly equatorial, germ pores. Teliospores may be intermixed with urediniospores (Figure 23.24).

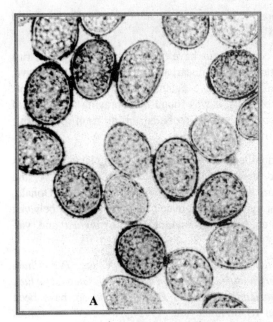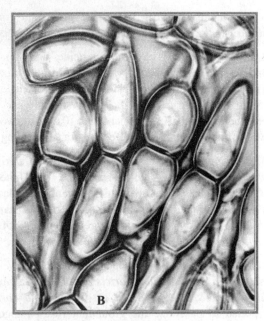

Figure 23.24 Urediniospores (A) and teliospores (B) of groundnut rust.

Stage III. Telia are chiefly hypophyllous, 0.2 to 0.3 mm in diameter, scattered, prominent, chestnut-brown or cinnamon-brown. The ruptured epidermis is prominent; teliospores are oblong, obovate or ellipsoid, with rounded to acute and thickened apex, predominantly two-celled (Figure 23.24), sometimes with one, three or four cells, wall smooth, light or golden-yellow or chestnut-brown, 0.7-0.8 (-1.0) μm thick at sides, 2.5-4.0 (–5.0) μm thick at top, apical thickening almost hyaline, pedicel thin walled, usually collapsing laterally, hyaline.

Disease cycle and epidemiology. The role of pycnia and alternate host is not established in the life cycle. It would appear that urediniospores are the main, if not the only, means of dissemination and spread of groundnut rust. There is no record of the occurrence of any collateral hosts of groundnut rust outside the genus *Arachis* (McDonald and Subrahmanyam, 1992). Urediniospores are shortlived in infected crop debris in the tropics, and the fungus is unlikely to survive from season to season during post harvest conditions. The practice of continuous cultivation of groundnut without any significant break in parts of India, Vietnam, and China could be an important factor in the perpetuation of groundnut rust in those countries (McDonald and Subrahmanyam, 1992). Subrahmanyam and McDonald (1982) suggested that groundnut crops in southern India may act as a reservoir of rust inoculum from which spores are carried by monsoon winds to infect the groundnut crops in Northern India. Long-distance dissemination of the pathogen may be by air borne urediniospores, by movement of infected crop debris or by movement of pods or seed surface contaminated with viable urediniospores.

Disease management

1. *Cultural measures.* Eradication of groundskeepers and volunteer groundnut plants is important in reducing the primary sources of inoculum. Field management should include a time gap of at

least a month, between successive groundnut crops. Existing plant quarantine procedures should suffice to prevent spread of the pathogen on pods or seeds.

2. *Chemical control.* Several fungicides and their combinations have been tested for control of rust and leaf sport together. Sprays of bordeaux mixture and dithiocarbamates were found effective. Tridemorph is effective against rust. Chlorothalonil is effective against both rust and leaf spots (Smith and Litterll, 1980). Based on several years of trials, it was found that spraying a mixture of carbendazim (0.05%) and mancozeb (0.2%) at two to three week intervals starting from four to five weeks after planting was effective for controlling rust and leaf spots.

3. *Breeding for resistance.* At ICRISAT, the world collection of over 12,000 germplasm accessions were screened in the field for resistance. The United States Development of Agriculture (USDA) and ICRISAT released fourteen rust-resistant germplasm lines jointly (Subrahmanyam and McDonald, 1983). It is interesting that most of the rust-resistant genotypes originated in Peru, which is believed to be one of the secondary "gene centres" of cultivated groundnut (var. *hypogaea* and var. *fastigiata*).

4. *Biological control.* Mycoparasites such as *Verticillium lecanii* (Zimmerm.) Viegas, *Penicillium islandicum* Sp. *Eudarluca caricis* (Fr.) *O.* Ericks, *Acremonium persicinum* (Nicot.) W. Gams, *Darluca filum* (Biv. & Bern ex Fr.) Cost *Tuberculina costaricana* Syd., and *Hyalodendron* sp. have been reported to parasitize the groundnut rust pathogen (Subrahmanyam, 1992). However, no serious attempts have been made to use any of these organism on biological control of groundnut rust at the field level.

Sunflower rust. The sunflower rust was first described by Schweinitz as *Aecidium helianthi-mollis* in 1882. Later, the pathogen was renamed *Puccinia helianthi-mollis* (Schw.) Arthur and Bisby. The pathogen has been commonly referred to as *Puccinia helianthi* Schw. Sunflower rust occurs worldwide, reported from 33 countries (Figure 23.25). Rust is a serious disease of cultivated sunflower and causes yield losses ranging from 11 to 50% and reduces seed quality and yield.

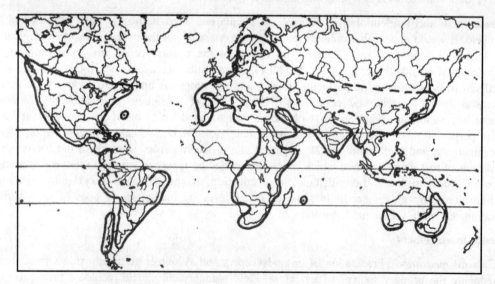

Figure 23.25 Geographical distribution of sunflower rust.

Symptoms. The sunflower rust symptoms appear just as small chlorotic leaf sports, which become cinnamon, cinnamon-brown or orange when they are actively producing urediniospores. Uredial pustules appear on both leaf surfaces, but more commonly on the lower surface, and may be surrounded by yellow halo. Pustules may coalesce to occupy most of the leaf surface. The uredial stage is the most conspicuous and damaging stage of sunflower rust and during severe infections pustules may occur on petioles, stalks, bracts and floral parts. The telial stage produces black-coloured pustules later in the growing season or when plants are under physiological stress.

The pathogen. Sunflower rust caused by *P. helianthi*, is a typical macrocyclic, autoecious rust. Telial, pycnial, aecial and uredial stages are produced on sunflower. The telia are usually hypophylous, scattered or gregarious, confluent, oval, 2 to 3 µm in diameter, compact and chocolate brown. The teliospores are two-celled, slightly constricted at the septum, oblong-elliptical or pear-shaped, obtuse or rounded above and below, and vary considerable in size from $18\text{-}30 \times 30\text{-}58$ µm (average 23.9×39.1 µm). The pycnia (spermatia) are flask-shaped, amphigenous, occur in small clusters, and frequently occur on the cotyledon or on first and second true leaves. The pycniospores are small, oval, hyaline and appear shiny and viscous in mass.

The aecia are frequently hypophylous, in cluster, occurring opposite or nearly opposite a cluster of pycnia. The aecia are orange-red with white laciniate margins. Aeciospores are orange-red to pale orange, typically ellipsoidal, and finely echinulate with four median germ pores. They vary in size from $21\text{-}28 \times 18\text{-}20$ µm. The wall of aeciospores is colourless and 1 to 1.5 µm thick. The uredia are chestnut, cinnamon, cinnamon brown or orange. They are round and occur scattered on leaves petioles and stems. The urediniospores are yellowish-brown, vary from subglobose to obovate, are flattened laterally, and measure $17\text{-}26 \times 23\text{-}34$ µm (average 20.8×23.7 µm).

Disease cycle. In United States, *P. helianthi* overwinters as mycelia in the tissues of perennial sunflower, as urediniospores on infected tissues in regions where winters are mild or as teliospores on the crop residues in northern regions. Teliospores adhering to sunflower seed during harvest are long lived and may germinate after the seed is planted. Each cell of the teliospores may germinate in the spring by producing a promycelium which produces four haploid sporidia (basidiospores) of two mating groups, +ive and –ive, via meiosis (Stage IV). Further details of the disease cycle are explained in Figure 23.26.

Epidemiology. In early spring, numerous aeciospores and urediniospores are produced on wild and volunteer sunflower. These spores are readily transferred to the cultivated sunflower by wind, where they initiate disease. With the onset of unfavourable conditions for development of uredial stage, telia (overwintering stage) quickly develop, and the perpetuation of the pathogen is guaranteed until the return of suitable growing conditions. However, the majority of teliospores germinates over a long period, and abundant inoculum is always available (Yang and Dowler, 1992).

Disease management

1. Use of host resistance is the best method to control sunflower rust. Several sources of rust resistance are known, and the resistance genes Pu_1 and Pu_2 have already been incorporated into many commercial sunflower cultivars (Yang and Dowler, 1992).

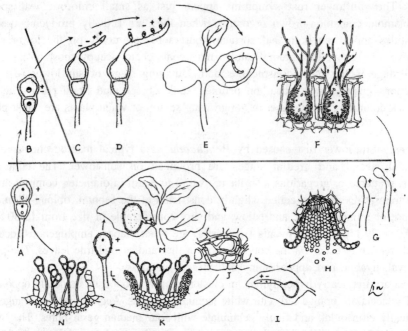

Figure 23.26   Disease cycle of sunflower rust, (A) dikaryotic phase of teliospore, (B) diploid phase of teliospore, (C) germination of teliospores by producing promycelium, (D) haploid basidiospores, (E) a basidiospore infects cotyledons of sunflower, (F) pycnia of two mating groups + and – side by side, (G) pycniospores united with receptive hyphae of the opposite mating group, (H) aeciospores in a aecium, (I) germination of aeciospore showing binuclears, (J) binucleate mycelium in the infected tissue, (K) uredium with urediniospores, (L) single celled urediniospore in a stalk, (M) germination of urediniospore, (N) telium and teliospores. (*Source:* Yang and Dowler, 1992)

2. The wild *Helianthus* spp. can provide a breeding sanctuary for development of new mutant/virulence. Therefore, early elimination of volunteer and wild sunflower near production fields will help in long term management.

3. Crop rotation and fungicide applications should also be a component of sunflower rust management.

Coffee rust.   Leaf rust of coffee is classic among example of annihilating plant diseases. The disease wiped out coffee plantations in Sri Lanka in nineteenth century. In the Western Hemisphere, coffee rust was first reported in Brazil in 1970 and since then spreading there also. In India, the disease was first recorded in 1870 and occurs in Karnataka, Kerala and even M.P. where coffee is grown in a small tract.

Symptoms.   The infection is restricted to leaves only, although sometimes symptoms can be seen on tender shoots and berries. The pustules appear as small spots, 1-2 mm in diameter. In early stages, the spots are yellowish becoming orange coloured with increase in size. On upper surface, the colour is often brownish (Figure 23.27). The infected leaves are defoliated which affects the yield (Figure 23.27).

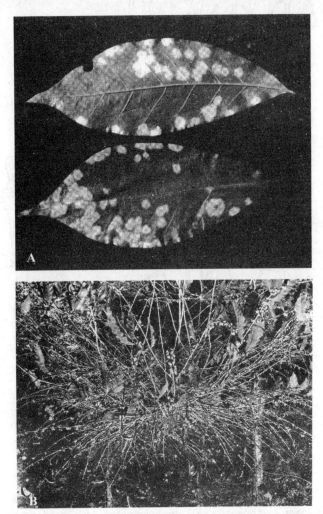

Figure 23.27 (A) Arabica coffee leaves infected by *H. vestatrix,* (B) a coffee bush defoliated due to leaf rust.

The pathogen. Two species of *Hemileia* infect coffee: *H. vastatrix* Berk. and Br, which is commonly reported, and *H. coffeicola* Maube and Roger, which occurs only in west and central Africa and as a minor disease of Arabinca coffee, occasionally becoming serious under very wet conditions. *Helmileia* means "half moon". The urediniospores are *cuniform* with the convex surface (Figure 23.28) ornamented with spines or warts. *H. vastatrix* occasionally produces teliospores which germinate and produce basidium and basidiospores (Figure 23.28). They do not infect coffee or any other host. No alternate host has been found.

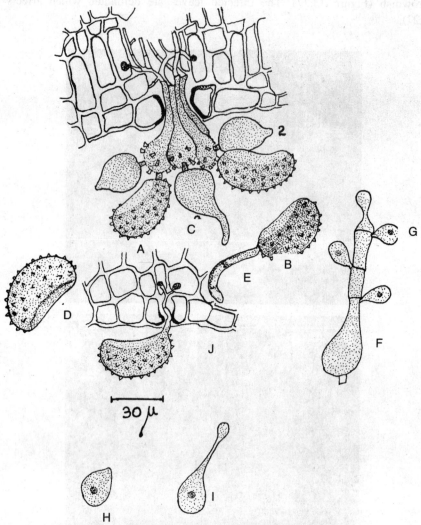

Figure 23.28 The spores of *Hemileia vastarix* Berk, & Br., the coffee leaf rust fungus, urediniosorus showing (A) urediniospores, (B) teliospores, (C) germinating teliospores, (D) urediniospore, (E) germinating urediniospore, (F and G) germinating teliospore with basidiospores, (H) basidium, (I) germinating basidiospore and (J) urediniospore infecting coffee leaf through stomata. Notice haustoria in the cells.

Disease cycle. For a tropical evergreen perennial shrub like coffee, it would appear that there is no epidemiological necessity of alternate host, despite its role in sexual recombination. The carry over of inoculum between rainy seasons is critical: in areas of unimodal annual seasons, the longer dry season would reduce fungal survival. Mayne (1971) attributes the lesser severity in Northern India compared with Southern India to reduced inoculum survival during the long dry season

(Figure 23.29). At the beginning of rainy season new leaves are produced, which are most susceptible when, they are maturing. The rate of infection is high during the mid to late rainy season but with onset of dry weather, as the growth of plants slows down; the infection also ceases.

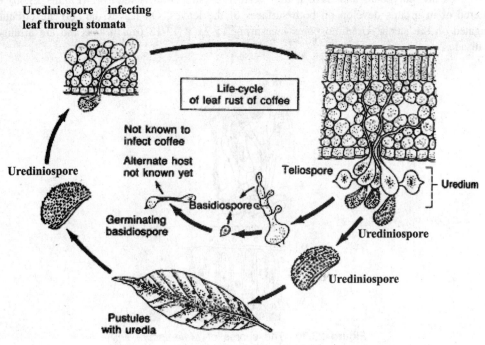

Figure 23.29 Disease cycle of coffee rust.

Disease management

1. Sanitation in coffee plantation is essential. Fallen leaves should be destroyed.
2. In South India, bordeaux mixture (2:2:40) has been in use. Two sprays are given, one during April-June and the other during September-November. Oxycarboxin (vitavax 75 WP) used at 0.03% a.i. gives significant control up to 50 days. The triazole fungicide; triadimenol (bayton) applied to coffee seedlings disrupts the hyphae in the host tissues.

Rust of linseed and flax. The disease is common on linseed in North India and also occurs in other linseed growing areas of the world including USA, Europe, South America, Canada, Africa and Australia. According to Saharan (1988) the loss in yield depending upon the severity of the disease varies form 16 to 100 per cent. Flax- *M. lini* system was used by H. H. Flor (1942-56) to study genetics of host-pathogen system, which ultimately gave the concept of gene for gene hypothesis. Flor choose the system, probably, as the pathogen autoecious. Several generations can be studied on same plant, successive inoculations can be made on new emerging leaves on the same plant.

Symptoms. Characteristic bright orange coloured, minute pustules (uredosori) are produced on the leaves and stems. As the disease advances, the pustules turn black with the production of the telial stage. Both the spermagonial and aecial stages develop on the same host, mostly on the leaves. In cases of severe infection the plants look sick and stunted, even from a distance.

The pathogen. *Melampsora lini* (Pers.) Lev. is an autoecious rust fungus, all spore stages occurring on linseed. Pycnial morphology and mating types have been described by Lawrence (1988). The subepidermal pycnia are flask shaped and pale yellow. The pycniospores are ovate to globose. The aecia are orange yellow, scattered on the under surface of the leaves and also on the stems. The aeciospores are polygonal and have a thin verrucose outer wall. Uredosori (Figure 23.30) either scattered or in groups develop on both surfaces of the leaves. On leaves the sori are circular but elongated on the stems. Urediniospores measuring 15-25 × 13-18 μm in size and are arranged in a palisade.

Figure 23.30 The spores of *Malampsora lini.*

Disease cycle. In India, where the linseed is grown in winter and the diseased plant are exposed to summer heat, the telial stage do not play any role in perennation of this pathogen. Urediniospores are also inactivated during summer. It is presumed that the pathogen survives on linseed and other suitable hosts in its uredial or telial stage at high altitudes (1200-1800 m). From these sources, the urediniospores are blown to the plains by wind to initiate the disease (Singh, 1998).

Management of the disease

1. Sanitary practices such as destruction of diseased crop debris and weed hosts have been advocated.
2. Cultivation of resistant varieties is the most appropriate method to combat the disease. In India resistance has been located in many lines and varieties have been developed for different regions. Cultivars LC-216, LC-255, and LC-256 are resistant to all races prevalent in the hills (Saharan, 1991).

23.7 DISEASES CAUSED BY *RHIZOCTONIA* AND *SCLEROTIUM*

The sterile fungi *Rhizoctonia* and *Sclerotium* are soil inhabitants and cause serious diseases on many hosts by affecting the roots, stems, tubers, corms and other plants parts that develop in or on the ground.

23.7.1 *Rhizoctonia* and Plant Diseases

Rhizoctonia solani Kuhn causes economically important diseases throughout the world and on almost all vegetables, ornamentals, several field crops, turf grasses, shrubs and trees. The most common symptoms on most plants are damping-off, root-rot, stem rot, stem-canker, scurf, foliage blights, spots, etc.

Stems canker and black scurf of potato. Potato plants attacked by the fungus are characterized by a general lack of vigour. Few top symptoms appear if the underground parts of a stem are only partly girdled. Often small, green or reddish aerial tubers are formed (Plate 23.9). Long brown lesions can occur on infected stems, before they reach the surface of the soil or the roots may be severely killed. The most common symptom is the presence of numerous, hard, small, dark-brown to black resting bodies called **Sclerotia** on the surface of mature tubers. Other tuber symptoms include russeting, cracking, knobbiness and dwarfing.

Plate 23.9 Rhizoctonia stem canker and black scurf of potato.

Sheath blight of rice. Lesions are formed on the leaf sheath and culms (Plate 23.10). The spots on the leaf sheath are first ellipsoid or ovoid, about 10 mm long, and greenish grays. They enlarge and may reach 2-3 cm in length and become irregular in outline. The centre of the spots becomes white with brown or purplish margins depending on the host genotypes. Outer leaves may fall off, plants look yellow and may ultimately wilt. Under favourable conditions, the infection may spread up to the culms, killing the entire leaves.

Plate 23.10 Sheath blight of rice.

Banded leaf and sheath blight of maize. It is the banded appearance and presence of these sclerotial bodies, which gives the name "Banded Sclerotial disease". The disease occurs in almost all maize growing states of India, particularly severe in Tarai region. Losses in grain yield due to this disease have been estimated in the range of 23–97% depending upon disease severity. **Symptoms** are present on all parts of the plant. Disease starts from the lowest sheath, which is in contact with the soil and travel up to ear. The disease symptoms are characterized by the presence of alternate bleached area or bands on leaf sheath and leaves. Olive green and brown large continuous patches on stalks can be seen immediately below the diseased leaf sheath, presence of sclerotia on diseased parts which are initially brown in colour turn blackish later on is also a characterized symptom (Plate 23.11). The fungus produces brown sclerotia.

Plate 23.11 Banded leaf and sheath blight of maize.

The pathogen. *Rhizoctonia* sp. consists of a large, diverse and complex group of fungi. Mycelial cells of the most important *Rhizoctonia*, *R. solani* are multinucleate, whereas mycelial cell of several other *Rhizoctonia* species are binucleate. The mycelium which is colourless when young but turns light browns with age, consists of long cells and produces branches that grow at approximately right angles to the main hypha, are slightly constricted at the junction, and have a cross wall near the junction. Under certain conditions the fungus produces sclerotia like tufts of short, broad cells that function as chlamydospores or eventually the tufts develops into rather small, loosely formed brown to black sclerotia.

Rhizoctonia species infrequently produce a basidiomycetous perfect stage. The perfect stage of multinucleate *R. solani* is *Thanatephorus cucumeris*, whereas that of binucleate *Rhizoctonia* is *Ceratobasidium*. A few multinucleate *Rhizoctonia* spp. (*R. zeae* and *R. oryzae*) have *Waitea* as their perfect basidiomycetous stage. It is now evident that *R. solani* and other species are "collective" species consisting of several more or less unrelated strains. The *Rhizoctonia* strains are distinguished from one another because *anastomosis* (fusion of touching hyphae) occurs only between isolates of the same *anastomosis* group. The existence of anastomosis groups in *R. solani* represents genetic isolation of the populations in each group.

Although the various anastomosis groups are not entirely host specific, they show certain fairly well defined tendencies:

- Isolates of AG1 cause seed and hypocotyls rot and aerial (sheath) and web blights of many plant species.
- Isolates of AG2 cause canker of root crops, wire stems on crucifers and brown patch on turf grasses.
- Isolates of AG3 affect mostly potato causing stem cankers and stolen lesions and producing black sclerotia on tubers.
- Isolates of AG4 infect a wide variety of plant species, causing seed and hypocotyls rot on almost all angiosperm and stem lesions near the soil line on most legumes, cotton and sugarbeet.

Six more anastomosis groups are known with *R. solani* and many more in other *Rhizoctonia*.

Disease cycle.   The pathogen over seasons normally as mycelium or sclerotia in the soil and in or infected perennial plant or propagative material such as potato tubers. In some hosts the fungus may even be carried in the seed. The fungus is present in most soils and, once established in a field remains there indefinitely.

Disease management.   Because of wide-host range and prolonged survival in soil and plant parts, control of *Rhizoctonia* diseases has always been a challenge. However, some of the practices that have been recommended include:

1. Proper drainage conditions should be developed.
2. Seeds and planting materials must be free from the pathogen.
3. Wide spacing among the plants (row to row and plant to plant) is recommended.
4. Crop rotation (3-4 year) with suitable crop may be valuable.
5. *Rhizoctonia* is one of the causal agents for pre- and post-emergence damping-off. Mulching of the plot for 4 to 8 weeks with certain plants materials or plastic (preferably photodegradable) gives significant control.
6. Several biocontrol agents such as *Trichoderma harzianum, T. viride, Gliocladium virens, Bacillus subtilis and Pseudomonas fluorescence* have been evaluated. Research results invariably convey that *Rhizoctonia* can be managed satisfactorily by using these bioagents. They should be used as seed treatment, soil treatment or as foliar application.
7. Fungicide application with some contact (iprodione, chlorothalonil) and systemic fungicides (carboxin, triadimefon, thiophanate-methyl) seem to provide effective control.
8. Research reports indicates that *Rhizoctonia* often suffers by the so called *Rhizoctonia* decline, which is caused by two or three infectious dsRNAs. These RNAs, through anastomoses, spread from infected hypovirulent *Rhizoctonia* individuals to healthy virulent ones and reduce both their ability to cause disease and their ability to survive.

23.7.2 *Sclerotium* and Plant Diseases

The species of genus *Sclerotium* cause damping-off, stem canker, crown rot, root rot, bulb/tuber rot and fruit rot diseases in many plants particularly those grown in warm climates.

Symptoms.   In general, the pathogen attacks young, immature and succulent plant parts. In most crops the infection begins on the succulent stems as a dark brown lesion just below the soil line. Thereafter, first the lower leaves and then the upper leaves turn yellow or wilt or die back from the tips downwards. In plants like tomato with harder stems, the infected stems stand upright but subsequently wilt. The fungus moves downward into the roots and destroys the root system (Plate 23.12). On all infected host tissues, and even on the near by soil fungus produces numerous small round sclerotia of uniform size that are white when immature, becoming dark brown to black on maturity.

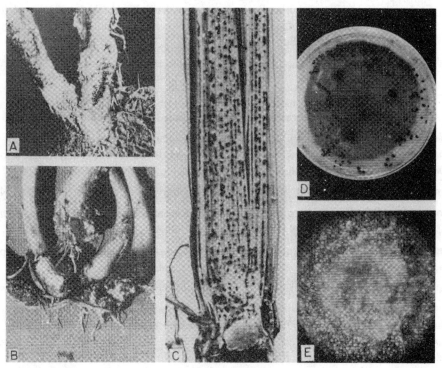

Plate 23.12 Symptoms produced by *Sclerotium* (A) stem blight of tomato caused by *S. rolfsii,* (B) onion white rot caused by *S. Cepivorum* (C), stem rot of rice caused by *S. oryzae* (D), mycelium and scelerotia of *S. rolfsii* in culture and (E) cross-section of sclerotium showing the compact mass of mycelial cell.

The pathogen. Sclerotium sp. produces abundant white, fluffy, branched mycelium that forms sclerotia. *S. rolfsii* occasionally produces basidiospores at the margins of the lesions under humid conditions (Agrios, 1997). Its perfect stage is *Aethalium rolfsii. S. bataticola,* which causes diseases in several hosts, occasionally produces conidia in pycnidia and is now known as imperfect fungus *Macrophomina phaseoline. S. cepivorum,* which causes the white rot disease of onion and garlic, in addition to sclerotia also produces occasional conidia on sporodochia; these conidia, however, seem to be sterile (Agrios, 1997). The fungus survives mainly as sclerotia. It is spread by moving water, infested soil, contaminated tools, infected transplant seedlings, infected vegetables and fruits, and in some hosts, as sclerotia mixed with the seed.

Disease management

1. The management of diseases caused by species of *Sclerotium* has always been a difficult preposition. Some of the cultural practices such as crop rotation, deep/hot weather

ploughing, application of nitrogen through ammonium sources, and use of calcium compounds have been recommended but only partial control has been achieved.

2. In the last one decade research reports have indicated the soil solarization if practiced properly gives satisfactory control. It should be practiced in nurseries to manage damping-off diseases as *S. rolfsii*, and *M. phaseolina* are among the causes of damping-off of seedlings.

3. Several biocontrol agents like *Trichoderma* spp. have invariably been claimed to provide satisfactory management of sclerotial diseases. Wherever, commercial formulations of such bioagents are available, they should be tried.

REFERENCES

Agrios, G.N., 1997, *Plant Pathology*, Academic Press, San Diego, London, New York.

Aleander, K.C. and Padmanabhan, 1992, Smut of sugarcane. *In*: *Plant Diseases of International Importance,* Vol. II, A.N. Mukhopadhyay, et al., (Eds.), Prentice Hall, Englewood Cliffs, New Jersey.

Alexopoulos, C.J., et al., 1996, *Introductory Plant Pathology*, John Wiley & Sons, INC, New York.

Anderson, N.A., 1982, The genetics and pathology of *Rhizoctonia solani*, *Annu. Rev. Phytopathol.,* 20:324.

Bahadur, P., et al., 1994, Management of wheat rusts: A revised strategy for gene deployment, *Indian Phytopath.*, 47:41.

Burpee, L. and Martin, B., 1992, Biology of *Rhizoctonia* species associated with turf grasses, *Plant Dis.*, 76:112.

Costanho, B. and Butler, E.E., 1978, *Rhizoctonia decline*: A degenerative disease of *Rhizoctonia solani* II. Studies on hypovirulence and potential use in biological control III. The association of double stranded RNA with *Rhizoctonia* decline, *Phytopathology*, 68: 1505,

Dasgupta, M.K., 1992, Rice sheath blight: The challenge continues, *In*: *Plant Diseases of International Importance*, U.S. Singh, et. al. (Eds.), Vol. I, Prentice Hall, New Jersey.

Flor, H.H., 1971, Current status of the gene for gene concept, *Annu. Rev. Phytopathol.*, 9:275.

Goel, R.K., 1992, Flag smut of wheat, *Indian. J. Mycol. Plant Pathol.*, 22:113.

Jackson, H.S. and Mains, E.B., 1921, Aecial stage of the orange leaf rust of wheat, *Puccinia triticina Eriks J. Agric. Res.*, 22:151.

Joshi, L.M., et al., 1983, Status of rust and smut disease of wheat in India, *Plant Dis. Reptr.*, 54:391.

Joshi, L.M., et al., 1983, Karnal bunt: a minor disease that is now a threat to wheat, *Bot. Rev.*, 49:309.

Lucas, P., et al., 1993, Decline of *Rhizoctonia* root rot on wheat in soil infested with *Rhizoctonia solani* AG8, *Phytopathology*, 93:260.

Malik, V.S. and Mathre, D.E. (Eds.), 1997, Bunts and smut of wheat: An international symposium, North American Plant Protection Organization, Ottawa, Canada.

Mayne, W.W., 1971, The control of coffee diseases in South India, *World crops*, 23:206.

McDonald, D. and Subrahmanyam, P., 1992, Rust of groundnut, *In: Plant Diseases of International Importance*, Vol. II, H.S. Chaube, et al. (Eds.), Prentice Hall, New Jersey.

Mehta, K.C., 1929, Annual recurrence of rusts on wheat in India, *Proc. 16th Ind. Sci. Congr.,* 199.

Mehta, K.C., 1940, Further studies on cereal rusts in India, *Sci. Mongr No. 14, Imperial Council Agric. Res.,* India, 1.

Mitra, M., 1931, A new bunt on wheat in India, *Ann. Appl. Biol.,* 18:178.

Nagrajan, S. and Joshi, L.M., 1985, Epidemiology in Indian Subcontinent, *In: The Cereal Rusts,* Vol. II, A.P. Roelfs and W.R. Bushnell (Eds.), Academic Press, New York.

Nagrajan, S. and Singh, H., 1975, The Indian stem rust rules: A concept on the spread of stem rust. *Plant Dis. Rep.,* 59:133.

Nagrajan, S., et al., 1992, Wheat rusts, *In: Plant Diseases of International Importance*, Vol. I, U.S. Singh (Ed.), Prentice Hall, New Jersey.

Ogoshi, A., 1987, Ecology and pathogenicity of *Rhizoctonia solani* Kuhn, *Annu. Rev. Phytopathol.,* 25:125.

Parmeter, J.R., Jr. (Ed.), 1970, *Rhizoctonia Solani, Biology and Pathology*, Univ. of California Press, Berkeley and Los Angeles.

Punja, Z.K., 1985, The biology, ecology, and control of *Sclerotium rolfsii, Annu. Rev. Phytopathol,* 23:97.

Saharan, G.S. 1991, Linseed and flax rust, *Indian J. Mycol. Pl. Pathol.,* 21:119.

Singh, A., 1994, Epidemiology and Management of karnal bunt disease of wheat, *Res. Bull. No. 127,* p. 167, Directorate of Exp. Sta., G.B. Pant University, Pantnagar, India.

Singh, R.S., 1998, *Plant Disease*, Oxford and IBH Publ. Comp Pvt. Ltd., New Delhi.

Smith, D.H. and Littrell, R.H., 1980, Management of peanut foliar diseases with fungicides, *Plant Disease,* 64:356.

Sneb, B., et al., 1991, Identification of *Rhizoctonia* species, APS Press, St. Paul, MN.

Stakman, E.C., et al., 1923, Spores in upper air, *J. Agric. Res.,* 24:599.

Subrahmanyam, P. and McDonald, D., 1983, Rust disease of groundnut, *Information Bull No. 13,* ICRISAT, Pathancheru, India.

Subrahmanyam, P. and McDonald, D., 1982, Groundnut rust: its survival and carryover in India, *Proc. Ind. Acad. Sci. (Plant Sci.),* 91:93.

Thakur, R.P. and King, S.B., 1988, Smut disease of pearl millet, ICRISAT, *Information Bulletin No. 25,* ICRISAT, Patancheru, AP, India.

Warham, E.J., 1992, Karnal bunt of wheat, *In: Plant Disease of International Importance*. Vol. I. U.S. Singh, et al. (Eds.), Prentice Hall, New Jersey.

Wiese, M.V., 1987, Compendium of wheat diseases, *Am Phytopathol. Soc.,* St. Paul, Minnesota, USA.

Wilcoxson, R.D., and Soari, E.E. (Eds.), 1996, Bunt and smut diseases of wheat: Concepts and methods of disease management CIMMYT, Mexico.

Yang, Shaw-Ming and Dowler, W.M., 1992, Sunflower rust, *In: Plant Disease of International Importance*, Vol. II, H.S. Chaube, et al. (Eds.), Prentice Hall, New Jersey.

24 Bacteria and Plant Diseases

24.1 INTRODUCTION

Most of the bacteria are strictly saprophytic and help decompose large quantities of organic wastes, only 200 of 1600 bacterial species are known to infect various kinds of plants. Many bacterial species are beneficial to humans because of their role in building up the nutritional level of the soil. Bacteria are simple in structure: they may be rod-shaped, spherical, ellipsoidal, spiral, comma shaped or filamentous. The bacterial cells may be enveloped by a thin or thick slime layer made of viscous gummy materials. The slime layer may also be found as a larger mass around the cell called **capsule** (Figure 24.1). Most of the plant pathogenic bacteria are motile, and the flagella may be present either single or in groups or distributed over the entire cell surface (Figure 24.2). The bacterial colonies may vary in shape, size, colour, elevation, form of edges, etc. The size of colony may vary from 1 mm to several centimetres in diameter, and they may be circular, oval or irregular, with smooth, wavy or angular edges. The colonies may have flat, raised, dome-shaped or wrinkled elevation and are of different colours: white, yellow, red or gray.

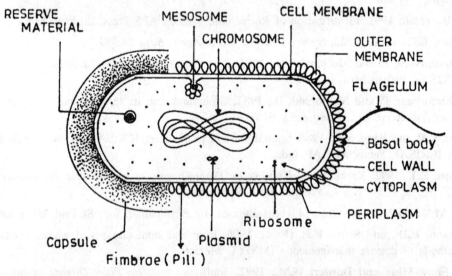

Figure 24.1 Schematic structure of gram negative bacteria.

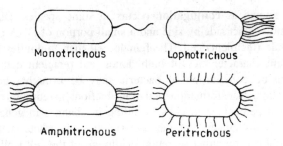

Figure 24.2 Flagellation in bacteria.

24.2 REPRODUCTION IN BACTERIA

Rod-shaped plant pathogenic bacteria reproduce asexually by the process referred to as fission or binary fission. During this process, the cytoplasmic membrane grows towards the centre of the cell, forming a transverse membranous partition dividing the cytoplasm into approximately two equal parts. Between the two layers of cytoplasmic layers, two layers of cell wall material, continuous with the outer wall, are laid down. As the formation of these cell walls is completed, they separate, splitting the two cells apart. The nuclear material is also duplicated (Figure 24.3). The bacteria can divide at an astonishingly rapid rate, dividing once in every 20 min under favourable conditions.

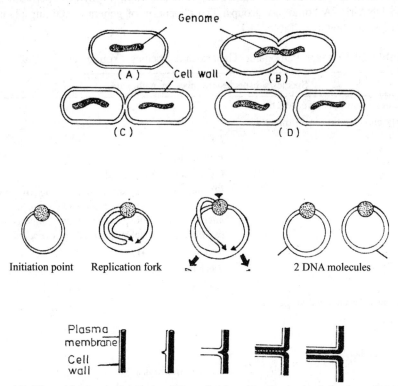

Figure 24.3 (A) Binary fission in bacteria, (B) replication (duplication) of the bacterial chromosome, (C) septum and cell wall formation during cell division, (D) Two independent daughter bacterial cells.

The sexual process known as **conjugation** occurs in some species. During this process, two compatible cells come into contact side by side and a small portion of DNA of the male cell (donor) is transferred to the female (recipient) cell. The female cell then multiplies by fission, resulting in daughter cells that contain characteristics of both donor and recipient cells.

Variation in the genetic constitution of bacteria may be brought about by three different phenomena, viz. conjugation, transformation and transduction, in addition to mutation. Mutation may occur in a very small percentage of cells, resulting in changes in genetic material leading to permanent changes in certain characters of the bacteria. In some bacteria, the genetic material is liberated from one bacterial cell by either secretion or rupture of the cell wall. A portion of this free genetic material (DNA) gets entry into a genetically compatible bacterium of the same or closely related species, making the recipient cell become genetically different. Transduction requires a bacteriophase as a vector for the transfer of genetic material of the infected bacterium, where it becomes integrated with the DNA of the recipient bacterium. Thus, different characters may be transferred from one bacterial cell to another. The ability of bacteria to multiply very rapidly and reach high populations within a short period makes them an important factor to be considered in any ecosystem in general and as plant pathogens in particular.

24.3 THE CLASSIFICATION AND IDENTIFICATION

The class Proteobacteria is divided into subclasses (Stackebrandt, 1980) or superfamilies (De Ley, 1978) based on DNA-rRNA homology groups. The allocation of genera containing plant pathogens to these subclasses is shown in Table 24.1.

Table 24.1 Plant Pathogenic Genera and Species (Young, et al., 1992)

	Species/subspecies (number of pathovars)
Division: Firmicutes (Gram-positive genera)	
Family: no family classification in Firmicutes	
Arthrobacter	*Ilicis*
Bacillus	*megaterium* (1)
Clavibacter	(1) *iranicus, rathayi, tritici*
	(2) *michiganensis* subsp. *michiganensis*, *michiganensis* subsp. *insidiosus*, *michiganensis* subsp. *nebraskensis*, *michiganensis* subsp. *sepedonicus*, *michiganensis* subsp. *assellarius*, *xyli* subsp. *xyli* subsp. *cynodonlis*
Curtobacterium	*flaccumfaciens* (4)
Nocardia	vaccinii
Rhodococcus	fascians
Division: Gracilicutes (Gram-negative genera)	
Class: Protebacteria	
Alpha subclass	
Family: Acetobacteriaceae	
Acetobacter	*aceti, pasteurianus*
Family: Rhizobiaceae	

(Contd.)

Table 24.1 Plant Pathogenic Genera and Species (Young et al., 1992) (*Contd.*)

Species/subspecies (number of pathovars)	
Agrobacterium Family: Not classified	*rhizogenes* (2), *rubi*, *tumefaciens* (2), *vitis*[b]
Rhizomonas Beta subclass Family: Comamonadaceae	*suberifaciens*[c]
Acidovorax (*Pseudomonas*)	*avenae* subsp. *avenae*[d] (syn. *rubrilineans*[d]), *avenae* subsp. *cattleyae*[d], *avenae* subsp. *citrulli*[d], *konjaci*[d] (syn. *avenae* subsp. *konjaci*[d])
Xylophilus Family: Not named	*ampelinus*
Pseudomonas	*andropogonis, caryophylli, cepacia, gladioli* (3), *glumae, plantarii, solanacearum, syzygii, rubrisubalbicans*
Gamma subclass Family: Enterobacteriaceae	
Enterobacter	*cancerogenus, dissolvens, nimipressuralis*
Erwinia	(1) *amylovora*, "*nulandii*", *mallotivora, nigrifluens, psidii, quercina, rubifaciens, salicis, stewartii, tracheiphil* (2) *aananas, herbicola* (2), *uredovora* (3) *cacticida, carotovora* subsp. *carotovora, carotovora* subsp. *atroseptica, carotovora* subsp. *betavasculorum, carotovora* subsp. *wasabiae, chrysanthemi* (7), *cypripedii, rhapontici*
Family: Pseudomonadaceae (needs emendation)	
Pseudomonas	(1) *agarici, asplenii*, "*blatchfordae*", *fuscovaginae*, "*gingeri*", *marginalis* (3), *tolaasii* (2) *amygdali* (3) *caricapapayae*[g], *ficuserectae*[h], *meliae*[h], *syringae* (45), *viridiflava* (4) *cichorii* (5) *corrugate*
Family: Not named	
Xanthomonas	*albilineans, axonopodis, campestris* (143), *fragariae*, "*graminis*"[l], *oryzae* (2)[j], "*populi*"
Family: Not classified	
Xylella Division: Tenericutes Class: Mollicutes Family: Spiroplasmataceae	*factidiosa*
Spiroplasma Genera of uncertain affinity	*citri, kunkelii, phoeniceum*
Rhizobacter	*dauci*
Streptomyces	spp.[k]

(*Contd.*)

Table 24.1 Plant Pathogenic Genera and Species (Young et al., 1992) (*Contd.*)

Species/subspecies (number of pathovars)	
Species that are misclassified	
Pseudomonas	*betle* (?*Xanthomonas*[l])
Pseudomonas	*ciccicola* (Generically misclassified; ?*Agrobacterium*[m]; ?*Xanthomonas*[n])
Pseudomonas	*flectens* (Generically misclassified)
Pseudomonas	*hibiscicola* (?*Xanthomonas*[l])

24.3.1 Identification of Bacteria

The major characteristics of common plant pathogenic bacterial genera are summarized in and Plate 24.1 and Table 24.2.

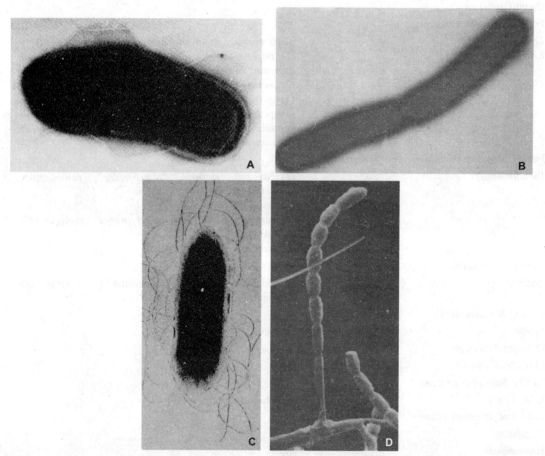

Plate 24.1 Some important plant pathogenic bacteria, (A) *Agrobacterium,* (B) *Xylella,* (C) *Erwinia,* (D) *Streptomyces..*

Table 24.2 Salient Features of Plant Pathogenic Genera of Bacteria

Genus or trivial name	Gram stain	Flagellation	Morphology and size	Colony and pigmentation	G-C mol%	Habitat and disease symptom	Reactions
Agrobacterium	Negative	Peritrichous	Rods, 0.8×1.5–3 μm	Smooth, non-pigmented	60–63	Rhizosphere and soil inhabitants, causes hypertrophy	On carbohydrate media abundant polysaccharide slime produced
Clavibacter (Corynebacterium)	Positive	None or Polar	Straight/curved, pleomorphic, (0.5–0.9×1.5–4.0 μm)	Stained pigments or granules and club shaped swelling	53–55	Soil-borne, produce canker, wilt, rots and fasciations	
Erwinia	Negative	Peritrichous	Straight to curved rods, 0.5–1.0×1.0–3.0 μm	None or yellow blue pink pigmentation	50–57	Facultative anaerobes, necrosis, wilt diseases and soft rots	'Carotova' group has strong pectolytic activity. The 'amylovora' group lack it
Pseudomonas	Negative	One/many polar flagella	Straight to curved rods, 0.5–1.0×1.5–4.9 μm	None or green blue	57.7–67	Inhabitants of soil, cause leaf spots, galls, wilts, blight, canker, etc.	Soluble pigments produced P. syringae produce yellow green diffusible fluorescent pigments
Streptomyces	Positive	None	Slender, branched hyphae, 0.5–1 μm in diameter, spores formed	Colonies are small (1–10 mm) smooth surface, with a weft of aerial mycelium wide variety of pigments formed	69–73	Soil inhabitants, cause scab disease	Produced one or more antibiotics active against bacteria, fungi, etc.
Xanthomonas	Negative	Polar	Straight nods, 0.4–1.0×1.2–3.0 μm	Growth on agar media usually yellow	63–69	Cause leaf spot, blight, canker, etc.	Produce acid from lactose
Xylella	Negative	Non-motile aflagellate	Straight rods, 0.3 × 1–4.0 μm	Colonies small, with smooth or finely undulated margins, non-pigmented	—	Strictly aerobic, nutritionally fastidious, habitat is xylem of plant tissue	—

24.4 SURVIVAL AND DISPERSAL

Ecology deals with interactions between organisms and relations between organisms and environments, comprising abiotic and biotic components. The survival of plant pathogenic bacteria, in addition to their soil phase and subsequently their spread in nature is summarized in the following flow chart.

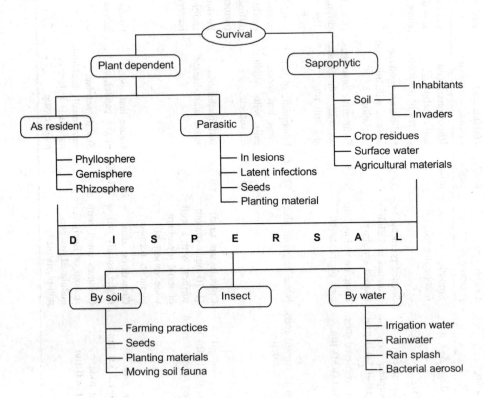

Factors affecting survival in soil. One of the most important factors affecting survival of plant pathogenic bacteria in soil is that of nutrient availability. Host plant debris serves, as a food base for many of the soil invading bacteria and longevity of these bacteria is contingent on persistence of host debris. Subsequent to degradation of host tissue, survival depends on innate characteristics of the microorganisms themselves and a larger number of variable properties of the edaphic environment. Moreover, the microbial flora and fauna of the soil have a profound effect on survival. Environmental factors in addition to having a direct effect on survival of plant pathogenic bacteria also have an indirect effect by affecting antagonistic and competing microorganisms. The complex interactions among environmental, biotic, and abiotic variables that influence survival of plant pathogenic bacteria in soil is illustrated in Figure 24.4.

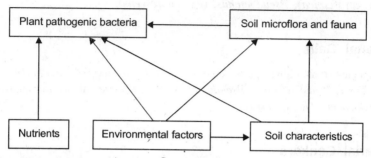

Figure 24.4 Interaction of major factors affecting survival of pathogenic bacteria.

24.5 SYMPTOMS CAUSED BY BACTERIA

Plant pathogenic bacteria cause a variety of symptoms on their hosts (Table 24.3).

Table 24.3 Important Plant Pathogenic Bacteria and Kinds of Symptoms Induced by Them

Bacterial genus	*Kinds of symptoms*
Agrobacterium	Galls (crown, twig, cane)
Clavibacter	Spots, ring rot, canker, wilt, fasciations
Erwinia	Blight, wilts, soft rots
Pseudomonas	Leaf spots, blight, galls, wilts, canker
Xanthomonas	Leaf spots, blights, cankers, rots
Streptomyces	Scab, soft rot

24.6 MAJOR GROUPS OF BACTERIAL DISEASES

24.6.1 Bacterial Spot and Blights

Several pathovers of the bacteria *Pseudomonas syringae* and *Xanthomonas campestris* cause spots and blights on a variety of crop plants.

24.6.2 Bacterial Vascular Wilts

Vascular wilts are caused by five bacterial genera. Mostly herbaceous plants such as vegetables, field crops, ornamentals and tropical plants are affected. The pathogens causing important vascular wilts include: *Clavibacter (Corynebacterium)*, *Curtobacterium (Corynebacterium) flaccumfaciens*, *Erwinia (E. tracheiphila, E. stewartii, E. amylovora)*, *Pseudomonas*, (*Ps. solanacearum*/*Ralstonia solanacearum*) and *Xanthomonas*, (*X. campestris* pv. *campestris*).

24.6.3 Bacterial Soft Rots

Bacteria are invariably associated with rotting host tissues in the field or in storage. The bacterial pathogens causing important soft rot diseases include *Erwinia*, (*E. carotovora* pv. *carotovora*, and *E. carotovora* pv. *atroseptica*), *Pseudomonas*, (*Ps. fluorescens*).

24.6.4 Bacterial Galls

The bacterial species that cause galls include: *Agrobacterium* (*A.tumifaciens* or biover 1, *A. rhizogenes* or biover 2 and *A. rubi*), *Pseudomonas* (*Ps. syringae* subsp. *savastanoi*), *Rhizobacter* (*R. daucus*), *Rhodococcus* (*R. fascians*).

24.6.5 Bacterial Cankers

There are several canker diseases of plants which are widespread and economically important. The bacteria and the important canker diseases they cause include: bacterial canker of stone and pome fruit trees (*Pseudomonas syringae* pv. *syringae*, and *Ps. syringae* pv. *morsprunorum*) and bacterial canker of citrus (*Xanthomonas axonopodis*, formely *X. campestris* pv. *citri*).

24.6.6 Bacterial Scab

Bacterial scabs are caused by species of *Streptomyces*. The most important ones are the *common scab of potato* (*Streptomyces scabies*) and *pox of sweet potato* (*S. ipomoea*).

24.7 IMPORTANT BACTERIAL PLANT DISEASES

24.7.1 Bacterial Leaf Spots and Blights of Cereals

Several pathovers of *Pseudomonas* and *Xanthomonas* species infect cultivated cereals, and some of them are economically important. The common bacterial disease of cultivated cereals are bacterial stripe of sorghum and corn (*Ps. andropogonis*), leaf blight of all cereals (*Ps. avenae*), red stripe and top rot of sugarcane (*Ps. rubrilineans*), basal glume rot of cereals (*Ps. syringae* pv. *atrofaciens*), halo blight of oats and other cereals (*Ps. syringae* pv. *corohafaciens*), bacterial blight, stripe or streak of several cereals (*Xanthomonas campestris* pv. *translucens*), bacterial leaf blight of rice (*X. oryzae* pv. *oryzae*) and leaf scald of sugarcane (*X. albilineans*).

Common bacterial leaf blight of rice. It is among most important diseases, particularly in Southeast Asia. Bacterial blight is widely distributed and devastating diseases of rice. It has been reported from several countries (Figure 24.5). Yield losses range from 20 to 30% in severely infected fields and may go up to 50%. Losses ranging from 6% to 60% have been reported in India (Devadath, 1992).

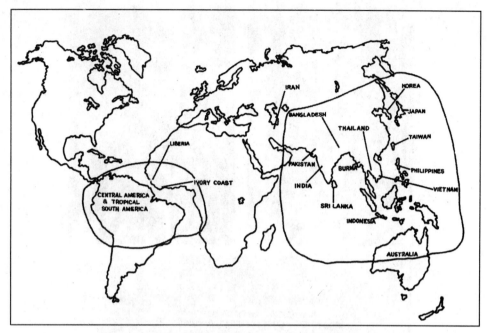

Figure 24.5 Distribution of bacterial blight of rice.

Symptoms. It vary considerably with the stage of infection and the prevailing weather conditions. Leaf blight phase is most commonly seen. A little below the tip of the leaves, water soaked lesions, appear at the margin. The lesions enlarge both in length and width with a wavy margin and turn straw yellow within a few days covering the entire leaf (Plate 24.2). Milky or opaque bacterial exudate is observed in the morning hours when relative humidity is high and then dry up forming pale yellow, small, spherical beads (Plate 24.2). Kresek or pale yellow symptoms are also noticed in tropics. In the Kresek symptoms (Plate 24.2), tips of the leaves are trimmed off before transplanting. One or two weeks after transplanting, infection starts from the cut ends of the leaves as green water soaked spots, becomes grayish green and folds up and rolls along midrib. The rolling and withering of the entire leaf, including leaf sheath follows. A pale yellow leaf is another type of symptom sometimes observed. The youngest leaf is pale yellow or has a yellow or greenish yellow broad stripe while the older leaves are green. When leaf bits from freshly infected leaf are mounted in a drop of water and examined under microscope, bacterial streaming from the veins is always observed. Yellowish sticky bacterial ooze is observed when the lower end of Kresek plant is cut and squeezed between the fingers.

The pathogen. It is gram-negative, non-spore forming, short rods with rounded ends measuring $1-2 \times 0.8-1$ μm with monotrichous polar flagellum. The bacterial cells are capsulated and are joined to form an aggregated mass. Colonies are circular, convex with entire margins; whitish yellow or straw yellow later and opaque.

Plate 24.2 Symptoms of bacterial leaf blight, (A) development of bacterial blight on rice leaves, (B) rice crop severely affected by bacterial blight, (C) bacterial exudate on the diseased leaf, (D) Potted plants showing kresek symptoms.

Disease cycle. There are several modes of perpetuation of the bacterium from season to season. In India many grass hosts have been identified. These include *Cyperus rotundus*, *C. defformis*, *Leptocorsia acuta* and *Leersia hexandra*. According to Trimurthy and Devadath (1981), leaves of *Paspalum scrobiculatum*, *Leersia hexandra*, *Panicum repens* and *Cyperus rotundus* harbour the bacterium without showing blight symptoms. In double cropped areas, volunteer rice seedlings also perpetuate the pathogen. The perennation of the pathogen in infected rice straw left in the field is also reported. There is evidence that seeds from infected crops are one of the major sources of primary inoculum. The secondary spread is brought about through wounds and stomata by bacterial cells disseminated by wind borne rain drop splashes, by irrigation water or rain water coming from infected fields and by contact between diseased and healthy leaves. The leaf hopper (*Nephotettix viriscence*) and the grass hopper (*Hieroglyphus banian*) can transmit the bacterium mechanically on their body.

Disease management

1. Several bactericides are being used to control the disease but none is very effective. However, soaking seeds for 8 hours in Agrimycin (0.025%) and Wettable ceresan (0.05%) followed by hot water treatment for 10 minutes at 52-54°C eradicates the bacterium in the seed. A mere soaking of seeds for 8 hours in ceresan (0.1%) and streptocycline (3 g in 11 litres of water) is also recommended.

2. Spraying with copper fungicides alternately with streptocycline (250 ppm) is reported effective in controlling the disease.

3. Varieties like TKM6, TR42 and chinsurah Boro II are tolerant to both Kresek and leaf blight phases of the disease.

Common bacterial blight of beans. Common blight occurs in temperate, subtropical and tropical regions (Figure 24.6) and can cause significant losses in these regions. The disease is particularly serious in the tropics. Most characteristic and diagnostic **symptoms** are on trifoliate leaves (Figure 24.7) but symptoms also occur on primary leaves. Initially, small water-soaked lesions develop on the undersurface of leaves. As these lesions expand, the lesion centre becomes necrotic and lesions become surrounded by a conspicuous yellow halo (Figure 24.7). As the disease progresses, these lesions may coalesce. The symptoms on pods starts as small, water-soaked spots that expand to form dark, reddish, water-soaked blotches. In severe infection, pod lesions become sunken and under very humid conditions may exude a yellow slime that can dry and appear as a yellow crust. Seeds become infected from inoculum originating from pod lesions or internally via systemic inoculum. In case of heavy infection, pods and seeds may shrivel and die.

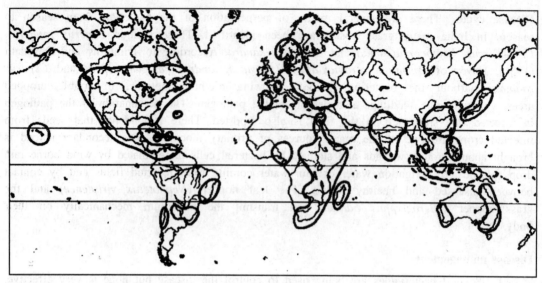

Figure 24.6 Distribution of common bacterial blight of bean.

A

B

Figure 24.7 Symptoms of common bacterial blight of bean, (A) leaf symptoms, (B) pod symptoms.

The pathogen. Common blight bacteria are typical member of the species *X. campestris*. *X. campestris* strains that induce disease on different host plants are indistinguishable by morphological, biochemical or physiological characteristic.

Disease cycle. Contaminated bean seed plays crucial role in the life cycle (Figure 24.8) and provides a dual function for blight bacteria: dissemination and survival. Blight bacteria can survive for as long as 30 years in infected seed. The most likely other source of inoculum is infested plant debris.

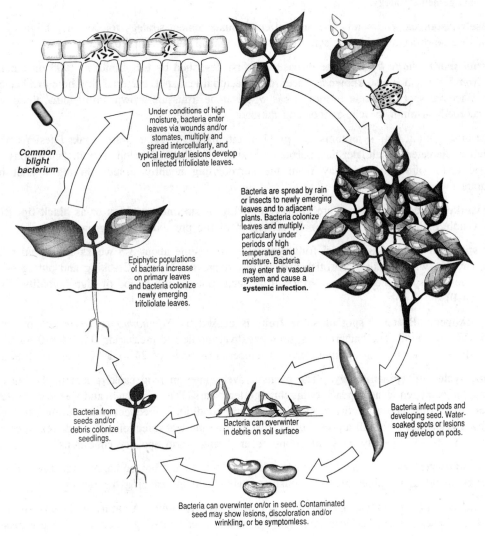

Figure 24.8 Disease cycle of common blight of bean. (*Source:* Gilbertson and Maxwell, 1992).

Management. Common blight continues to be very difficult to control. This is due to the seed-borne nature of the bacteria and to the lack of high levels of disease resistance in *P. vulgaris*.

Chemical control. Various chemicals have been applied to seed and/or foliage in attempts to control common blight. Because of the expense of these chemicals, particularly for subsistence farmers in the tropics, chemical control is not a feasible method of control. As part of an integrated approach to disease management, however, chemicals are tool that can be used in special conditions.

Cultural practices. An effective management strategy must use pathogen free seed. Sanitation can be used as a management tool for the disease. Deep plowing of debris and crop rotation can be used as a management strategy.

Disease resistance. Ultimately, the most effective management strategy for common blights is the use of disease-resistant cultivars, particularly for the small farmers in tropical regions.

Bacterial spot of stone fruits. The disease was first described by E.F. Smith in 1903 on Japanese plum from USA and is also known as bacteriosis, bacterial leaf spot, bacterial shot hole and bacterial crack. Bacterial spot is present in most areas where stone fruits are grown. From India, the disease was recorded on plum, peach, apricot and almond.

Symptoms. Initial leaf symptoms are grayish, circular to angular, water-soaked lesions about 1-5 mm in diameter, which later turn purple or brown. Often halos develop around such lesions. The necrotic lesion areas break away from the surrounding healthy tissues, giving a shot hole appearance.

Twig canker. Lesions on twigs are known as **spring** or **summer cankers** or as **black tip**. Black tip is visible in late winter on terminal bud region of the previous year's growth.

Fruit spot and gummosis. Initial fruit symptoms are visible about 3-5 weeks after petal fall as small, circular, water-soaked, brownish and slightly depressed lesions. Cracking and pitting occurs around the fruit spots and gum may exude from such spots during period of high humidity (Jindal et al., 1990).

The pathogen. Bacterial spot of stone fruits is caused by *Xanthomonas arboricola* pv. *pruni* (Smith) Vauterin et al. The bacterium is gram-negative, motile rod measuring $0.2-0.4 \times 0.8-1.0$ μm. It is a strict aerobe with an optimum growth temperature range of 24 to 29°C (Agrios, 1997).

Disease cycle and epidemiology. The bacteria over-winter in twig cankers and in the buds. In autumn, the pathogen invades peach twigs through leaf scars. The occurrence and spread of bacterial spot of stone fruits depend entirely on environmental conditions. Frequent rains during late bloom to a few weeks after petal fall are very conducive to fruit and leaf infections. Wind driven rains may increase the disease severity. Few infections occur during warm and dry conditions.

Disease management. *Cultural practices.* Use of bud wood from orchards with diseased trees should be avoided. Keeping trees vigorously growing help in reducing the disease.

Chemical control. Chemical sprays have not been very effective. Autumn application of fixed copper fungicides prevent leaf scar infection and reduce over-wintering inoculum. Because most of the stone fruits are sensitive to copper fungicides, their use is limited to dormant and early season sprays.

Resistant varieties. Where bacterial spot occurs, planting highly susceptible varieties should be avoided. Resistance occurs in large number of varieties of peach, nectarine and Japanese plum.

Other bacterial diseases of pome and stone fruits

Diseases	Pathogen
Leaf spot of apple	*Pseudomonas cichorii* (Swingle) Stapp.
Bacterial canker of almond	*Pseudomonas amygdale* Psallidas & Panagoupoulos
Leaf necrosis and rot of almond and peach	*Pseudomonas syringae* pv. *marginalis* (Brown) Stevens
Leaf spot of apricot and peach	*Pseudomonas viridiflava* (Burkholder) Dowson
Almond leaf scorch	*Xylella fastidiosa* Wells, et al.
Phony peach	*Xylella fastidiosa* Wells, et al.
Plum leaf scald	*Xylella fastidiosa* Wells, et al.

Fire blight of apple and pear. Fire blight of apple and pear was the first bacterial plant disease to be reported. In 1878, T.J. Burrill in Illinois demonstrated that fire blight of pear and apple is caused by bacterium. The disease has been reported from 31 countries and is of major concern wherever pome fruits are grown (Figure 24.9). In countries like India, where the occurrence of this disease has not been confirmed, strict quarantine measures have been enacted to prevent its entry. Fire blight has been instrumental in establishing many new concepts in plant pathology. *Erwinia amylovora* was the first bacterial plant pathogen to cause a disease and it was also the first disease where insects were shown to be vectors.

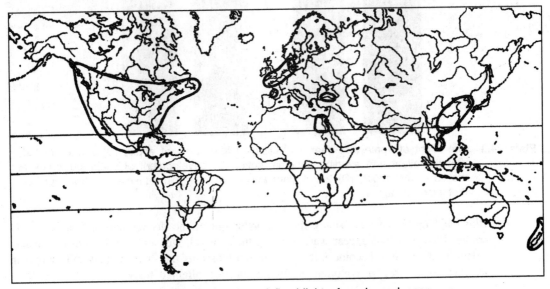

Figure 24.9 Distribution of fire blight of apple and pear.

Symptoms. The name fire blight is descriptive of the most characteristic symptoms of this disease—a blacking of twigs, flowers and foliage as though they had been scorched by fire (Plate 24.3). The fire blight syndrom may show any or all of the following symptoms.

Plate 24.3 Fire blight of apple and pear, (A) killing of fruit spurs of apple, (B) apple infected with fire blight and exuding bacterial ooze, (C) development of shepherd' crook at the tip of the shoot, (D) active (left) and dormant (right) cankers, (E) fire blight on root stock of apple.

(i) *Blossom blight.* This is usually the first symptom of the disease and is found in early spring. Blossoms first appear water-soaked, then shrivel, wilt and turn brownish to black. Young fruitlets often become infected. Infected blossoms and fruitlets may fall or remain attached to the tree, a symptom useful in detecting blighted trees.

(ii) *Twig and leaf blight.* After the blossoms, in a few days, infection can move 15-30 cm or more into the twig. Infected shoots, bark and leaves usually appear light to dark brown in apples and dark brown to black in pears. Blighted twigs and waterspouts often form a cane like or shepherd's crook at their tips, a characteristic symptom of the disease. During humid conditions drops of bacterial ooze frequently appear on the blighted shoots.

(iii) *Fruit blight.* Fruit blight symptoms are common in immature fruits. The infected parts appear brown to black and appear oily or water-soaked. A sticky, milky to amber coloured fluid collects at the core and sometimes oozes from the lenticels.

(iv) *Limb and trunk blight.* The disease symptoms may advance downward from the blossoms, shoots or fruit through the larger twigs and branches causing stem cankers. The cankers may be slightly sunken, varying in size and surrounded by irregular cracks in the bark. Active fire blight cankers have a dark, water-soaked appearance.

(v) *Collar and root blight.* These two types of fire blight symptoms can be most destructive and frequently cause the immediate death of tree. Fire blight cankers at the collar region are usually referred as collar blight. It may spread from the collar into the roots or sometimes from the roots into the collar.

The pathogen. *Erwinia amylovora* Burr. (Winslow et al.) is a rod shaped bacterium (1.1-3.0 µm × 0.5-1.2 µm) with rounded ends, gram-negative and motile by many peritrichous flagella. In addition to these small wild type cells, *E. amylovora* also produces filamentous cells, which are equally virulent. Colonies of virulent isolates are small, rough and white with typical glistening shine (Deckers, 1990). Bacteriophages specific to *E. amylovora* seem to be relatively common on diseased parts of apple and pear trees.

Disease cycle. The bacteria over-winter at the margin of cankers and possibly in buds and apparently healthy woody tissues. In the spring, the bacteria become active, multiply and spread into healthy tissues. During wet weather, bacterial ooze exudes through lenticels and cracks. From these sites wind, rain and insects to blossoms or young tender tissues of shoots carry bacteria where infection may start (Figure 24.10).

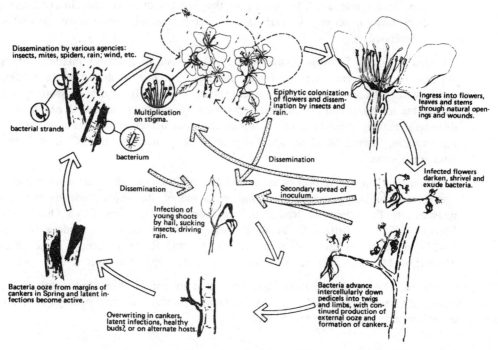

Figure 24.10 Disease cycle of fire blight of apple and pear. (*Source:* Thomason, 1992)

Disease management. Experience reveals that the best way to manage the disease is through the integrated programme of chemical use combined with sanitation, pruning, eradication, tree nutrition and insect control (Van der Zwet and Keil, 1979).

(i) *Quarantine measures.* The most effective quarantine is to strictly prohibit importation of all fruit, seed, bud wood and other plant parts of all rosaceous plants from any country or region having fire blight. Clonal or seedling stocks and bud wood should be taken from plants free of the disease.

(ii) *Cultural practices*

- **Pruning:** During the winter all blighted twigs, branches and cankers should be cut out about 10 cm below the last point of visible infection and burned. Since in spring and summer bacteria are very active so pruning should be done about 30 cm below the point of visible infection. Ten per cent sodium hypo-chlorite should be used to disinfest the tools as well as the large cuts made by the removal of cankered branches.
- **Tree nutrition:** To reduce excessive succulence, trees should be grown in light soil and should receive balanced fertilization. Higher potassium and manganese application also leads to fire blight resistance. Sprinkler irrigation, which wets the foliage and blossom, increases the disease spread. Overhead irrigation should not be used where fire blight is a problem.
- **Insect vector control:** Aphids, flies, ants, plant bugs and leaf hoppers have been implicated in the spread of fire blight. These insects should be kept under control with insecticide applications. The activity of the insect vectors is also closely intertwined with pollination activity so early season vector control during boom period is not recommended.

(iii) *Chemical control.* Dormant sprays with copper sulfate or bordeaux mixture offer some but not much protection for fire blight. Bordeaux mixture is also effective as blossom spray. Among the antibiotics, streptomycin sulfate is generally used as blossom sprays and later in the season. In number of orchards, streptomycin resistant *E. amylovora* strains have developed making these antibiotics ineffective. In such orchards oxytetracycline, fosetyl-Al, kasumin, flumequine (Firestop) and oxanilic acid analogue (S-0208) have been used with some success.

(iv) *Resistance varieties.* No pear or apple varieties are immune to fire blight when conditions are favourable and pathogen is abundant. Some of the apple varieties which have resistance to fire blight are Red Delicious, Northwest Greening, Cox's Orange Pippin, Stayman, Winesap, Britemac, Carroll, Primegold, Pricilla, Quinte, Splendour and Viking. Highly resistant varieties of pear include Orient, Richard Peters, Waite, Maxine, Moonglow, Mac and Spartlet (Van der Zwet, et al., 1993; Thomson, 1992).

Biological control. Some investigators have attempted to control fire blight with biological means. Strains of *Erwinia herbicola* and *Pseudomonas fluorescens*, non-pathogenic epiphytic bacteria are effective in controlling fire blight.

24.7.2 Bacterial Wilts

Bacterial wilt of potato. Bacterial wilt/brown rot is the most destructive and is wide spread in tropics, subtropics and warm temperature regions. In different countries it is known by several names such as bacterial wilt, brown rot, Granville wilt, ring disease, slime disease. It may damage the crop in two ways, i.e., premature wilting of standing crop and rotting of tubers both in field and stores.

Symptoms. The first symptom is slight wilting of the leaves at the end of branches during the hottest part of the day. Leaves of affected plants become pale green and then the leaflets take on a bronze colour (Figure 24.11). Affected plants recover during cool night temperatures, but the wilting is progressive and becomes more pronounced each day until finally the plants die. The vascular bundles in the stems turn brown when they become clogged with bacteria. When vascular bundles of the affected parts are cut, the bacteria, as white slimy ooze from the cut surface. The first symptom of the disease in the tubers is a brown circle, more or less slightly underneath the skin (Figure 24.21). This circle can be readily seen around the eyes and at the stem end of affected tubers.

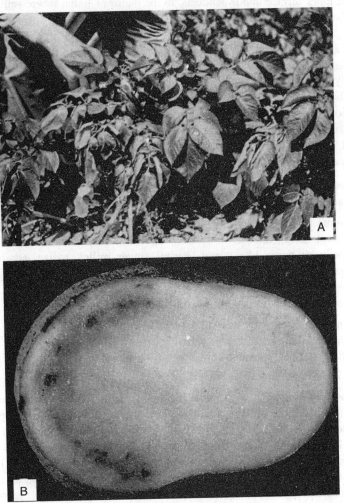

Figure 24.11 Bacterial wilt of potato, (A) wilted plants, (B) infected tuber.

The pathogen. With the introduction of molecular techniques, generic nominal of the wilt pathogen changed from *Pseudomonas* to *Burkholderia* to *Ralstonia*. *Ralstonia solanacearum* which causes this disease is a gram-negative rod, measuring approximately 0.5- 0.7 × 1.5–2.5 μm. Virulent isolates are mainly non-flagellated, non-motile and are surrounded by extra cellular slime.

Disease cycle. The pathogen survives between crop seasons in soil, seed tubers and on alternate cultivated or wild host plants. Population of bacterium can survive on roots of non-host plants as wheat, sorghum and maize. Soil is considered as a potential source of primary inoculum. In cultivated soil, survival of the bacterium has been reported for a period of more than two years. In the north Indian hills, the potato crop is cultivated during March-September. Since, the weather during off season (Sept. March) remains cool and humid, the pathogen may survive in plant debris under such conditions. In the Nilgiri Hills, the bacterium may survive on potato crops grown throughout the year. Potato tubers carry the bacterium in three ways: in vascular tissues (active infection), on the tuber surface and in lenticels. In the plains of India, where soil survival is doubtful, infected and/or surface contaminated potato seed tubers appear to be the only source of primary inoculum.

The major economic hosts include tomato, brinjal, chillies, ginger, groundnut, sesame and banana. According to Kelman (1953), representatives of more than 35 plant families are affected by the disease. Haywards (1991) also reported six economically important plant families that are infected by the bacterium. There are considerable differences in the host range of individual strains. In general the potato race (Race 3) is restricted to potato and a few other alternative hosts. On the contrary the Solanaceous race (Race 1) has a wide host range and is commonly found in tropical and sub-tropical climates. Under such situation, therefore, alternative hosts play an important role in survival of the bacterium.

Disease management. This disease has been considered to be a difficult one to control. However, the following can be effectively used:

1. Agronomic practices and stable bleaching power can reduce disease by 70-100% (Shekhawat, et al., 2000).
2. Rotation with crops like wheat, barley, finger millet, maize, sorghum, onion, garlic, cabbage, cauliflower knol khol, carrot, lupine and horse gram can reduce wilt incidence substantially.

The disease management efforts should be based on the following:

1. Escaping the disease by adjusting planting time
2. Utilizing resistant/tolerant cultivars
3. Reduction in field spread by disinfecting implements
4. Development of biological control

Moko disease (wilt) of banana. Moko wilt also known as **bacterial wilt of banana** caused havoc in the Moko planting during 1890 in Trinidad. The disease occurs chiefly in parts of central and south America and th West Indies. In India, the disease was first reported by Chattopadhya and Mukhopadhyay (1968) from West Bengal. Later on, Gnanamanickam et al. (1979) reported the occurrence of bacterial wilt on cv. Robusta of banana in Tamil Nadu (Figure 24.12). In Honuras and the Pacific Coast banana zones of Costa Rica and Panama, the Moko disease is one of the major diseases of commercial plantation which add to the cost of production approximately $400,000 annually in terms of control measures (Stover, 1972). The disease appeared in epidemic form during 1960s in the Amazon basin. In India, the crop losses due to this disease were upto 70 per cent during 1977-78.

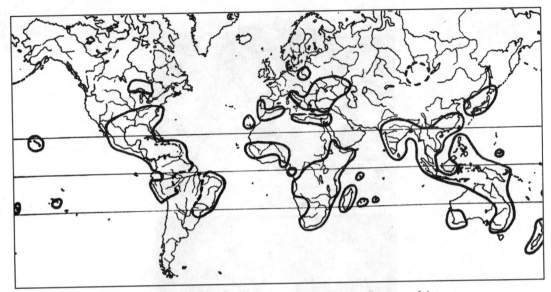

Figure 24.12 Geographical distribution of Moko disease of banana.

Symptoms. The symptoms of Moko disease are sometimes confused with Panama wilt as both the diseases cause wilting of plants. On young plants, the newly emerged leaves turn pale green or yellow and collapse near the point of attachment of the lamina and the petiole. The whole leaf may collapse within a week after infection (Gnanamanickam and Anuratha, 1992). The disease also affects the suckers and the affected suckers are blackened, get twisted and remain stunted. These are the characteristic symptoms of the disease (Figure 24.13). The sucker leaves, if present turn yellow and become necrotic. The internal symptoms are the presence of vascular discolouration in pseudostem, which may be concentrated more near the centre than periphery. The fruits are also affected and fruit bunches are transformed into yellow fingers. The individual fruits are brown coloured with discolouration and dry rot symptoms. The fruit symptoms readily distinguish Moko wilt from Panama wilt.

The pathogen. Moko disease is caused by bacterium *Ralstonia solanacearum* (Smith) Smith. Race 2 of the bacterium has been found responsible for infection in *Musa* and *Heliconia*. The race further comprises several strains, which differ in virulence and transmissibility. These strains affect musaceous host such as plantain, banana and *Heloconia* spp.

Disease cycle and epidemiology. The pathogen is transmitted from plant to plant by pruning machetes. The bacteria are also carried by insects from open wounds formed on pseudostems of older diseased plants to the disease free suckers. The bacterial ooze from infected male flower bracts and carried to new sites by visiting insects. Some strains of the bacterial causing Moko disease can persist in soil for 12-18 months (Stover, 1972). The disease spreads through infected suckers, soil and irrigation water from sick soil (Figure 24.14).

Figure 24.13 (A) Moko disease of banana plants in a plantation, (B) cross-section of pseudostem showing internal vascular discoluration and bacterial ooze.

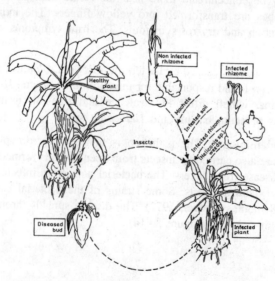

Figure 24.14 Disease cycle of Moko disease of banana. (*Source:* Gnanamanickam and Anuratha, 1992)

Disease management

(i) *Cultural practices.* Kelman (1953) suggested the use of disease free suckers against this disease. The diseased plants should be detected and destroyed alongwith the adjacent healthy plants (Stover, 1972). After eradication of diseased plants, the area must remain fallow for a year to eliminate the bacteria. The pruning machetes and other farm tools used in infested area should be disinfected with formaldehyde. The male flower buds should be removed after emergence of female hands to avoid infection by insects.

(ii) *Chemical control.* Moko disease can not be controlled effectively by chemical means. Although chemical soil disinfectants and fumigants have been used by various workers, yet none has prevented infection in diseased areas when replanted with bananas.

(iii) *Resistant varieties.* All the commercial cultivars of banana in Latin America were found susceptible to the bacterial strain (Stover, 1972). In Honduras, Pelipita was found resistant and was recommended as a substitute for the susceptible variety Bluggoe (Stover and Richardson, 1968). In India, commercial cultivars like, Monthan and Poovan were found resistant while Dwarf Cavendish, Robusta, Nendran and Peyan were susceptible to the disease

(iv) *Biological control.* Kelman (1953) reported various fungi, actinomycetes, and bacteria exhibiting antibiotic effect against the pathogen. Anuratha and Gnanamanickam (1990) found that application of bacterization procedures with efficient strains of *Pseudomonas fluorescens* resulted in increased survival of plants with enhanced plant height and biomass. This treatment also protected the pathogen-inoculated plants from stuntedness.

Bacterial wilt of cucurbits. Bacterial wilt was observed near Washington, DC in 1873. It is widespread in North America and also occurs in Europe and Asia. Losses vary from occasional plants up to 75% of a crop. Many wild cucurbit species are susceptible and could be involved in the disease cycle.

Symptoms. Wilt symptoms appear first on leaves but soon they affect lateral roots and finally entire plants. Wilted leaves shrivel and dry up; affected stems first become soft and pale but later they too, shrivel and become hard.

The pathogen. *Erwinia tracheiphila* is a bacterium that differs from other *Erwinia* spp. because it is a vascular pathogen. The cells are slender rods about 1 to 2.5 × 0.6 µm; as cells age, they may become round.

Diseases cycle. The bacterial wilt organism apparently overwinters in cucumber beetles. Bacteria are most prevalent in the mid intestine and appear to multiple in the beetle. The bacteria be spread to other susceptible cucurbits when beetles feed. The bacteria are not seed-borne or soil-borne. Secondary cycles begin when beetles feed on newly infected plants. Inoculation is accomplished by the striped cucumber beetle, *Acalymma vittata*, and 12-spotted cucumber beetle, *Diabrotica undecimpunctata howardi.*

Disease management. Control methods are aimed at preventing primary cycles from starting-by controlling beetles before they feed on plants, and by use of resistant varieties. Secondary cycles are also slowed by rouging diseased plants to reduce secondary inoculum, controlling beetles to reduce spread, and spraying with bactericides to kill bacteria when they are carried to plants by beetles. Beetle control depends on fast-acting insecticides. Sprays with methoxychlor, carbaryl, and endosulfan have been used; most recently, soil treatment at planting with a systemic, carbofuran, has provided excellent beetle control.

Trap cropping to attract beetles, followed by insecticide control on the trap crop, has been used to reduce beetle populations before a main crop emerges or is transplanted in an adjacent area. Resistance to bacterial wilt in cucumber is known and should be used depending upon local availability.

24.7.3 Bacterial Cankers

Citrus canker. Canker was recognized as a new disease in citrus in 1913 in Florida as it was earlier confused with citrus scab (*Elsinoe fawcetti*). In USA, a campaign to eradicate citrus canker in southern states of America began in 1915 and the disease was declared to be eradicated from these areas by 1947. This achievement has been regarded as a rare instances of successful eradication of plant disease that had once been established in certain ecosystem. In India, citrus canker was first reported from Punjab in 1940 (Luthra and Sattar, 1940).

Symptoms. The symptoms of the disease are observed on all the aerial parts including leaves, twigs and fruits as necrotic brown spots having a coarse raised surface. On young leaves, the lesions appear as small white specks at the very early stage. Later on, these lesions develop into brown necrotic spots (1-2 μm in dia). The lesions further enlarge and become white or grayish, which give a rough, corky and crater like appearance (Plate 24.4). The lesions are surrounded by a yellowish halo. The cankers are irregular, rough and more prominent on twigs and branches. The lesions on fruits are almost similar to those present on leaves, however, the yellow halo is absent and the crater like depression in the centre is more pronounced.

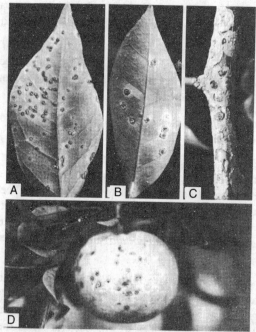

Plate 24.4 Symptoms of canker on *Citrus natsudaidai*, (A) erupted spongy lesions developed on leaf under dry conditions, (B) enlarged lesions with collapsed centre and greasy margin developed under humid conditions, (C) enlarged twig lesions developed on seedlings, (D) fruits lesions. (*Source:* Masao Goto, 1992)

The pathogen. The disease caused by *Xanthomonas campestris* pv. *citri* (Hasse) Dye., is now referred as *X. axonopodis*. Three distinct corms (A, B and C) of the bacterium have been reported to exist on the basis of geographical distribution and host range of the pathogen (Stall and Seymour, 1983). The canker A bacterium known as **Asiatic canker** or true canker is widely distributed and has a broad host range (Goto, 1992). The bacterium is gram negative and straight rod measuring 1.5-2.0 × 0.5-0.75 µm with a polar flagellum.

Disease cycle and epidemiology. Since citrus is a perennial plant, there is no problem for the survival of the bacterium, which easily over-winters on cankered lesions on the leaves, twigs and fruits (Figure 24.15). The bacterial cells start multiplying inside the tissue during the onset of spring and ooze out in large numbers. The cells are splashed onto young tissues through rain water. The bacteria enter the plant tissue through stomata on leaves or small wounds created due to thorn bruising and insects. Free moisture and strong winds favour the spread of the bacteria. The disease seems to be much more severe in areas experiencing high rainfall with high mean temperature. Nirvan (1961) reported the dissemination of bacteria through leaf minor (*Phyllocnistis citrella*). The long distance dissemination is through the transfer of diseased planting material.

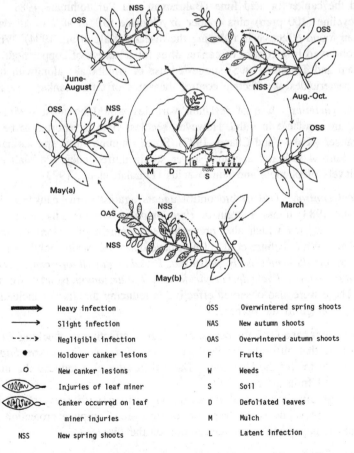

━━➤ Heavy infection	OSS Overwintered spring shoots
───➤ Slight infection	NAS New autumn shoots
----➤ Negligible infection	OAS Overwintered autumn shoots
● Holdover canker lesions	F Fruits
○ New canker lesions	W Weeds
Injuries of leaf miner	S Soil
Canker occurred on leaf	D Defoliated leaves
miner injuries	M Mulch
NSS New spring shoots	L Latent infection

Figure 24.15 Disease cycle of citrus canker. (*Source:* Masao Goto, 1992).

Disease management

(i) *Quarantine measures.* In canker free citrus producing areas, strict quarantine measures are practiced to exclude the pathogen. All efforts must be made to eradicate the canker bacterium from infested areas.

(ii) *Cultural control.* Raising canker free nursery plants is the first essential step in citrus canker management. The infected plant parts should be pruned out and destroyed. This is useful to reduce the inoculum density. Disease free nursery stock should be used.

(iii) *Chemical control.* Prevention of primary infection on new shoots is one of the most important practice in the reduction of the disease and must be emphasized once the infection is established. Application of bordeaux mixture (4:4:50) or copper compounds (Cu content 50%) with $CaCO_3$ in late March has been recommended by Goto (1992) against the disease. In addition two pruning, alongwith four sprays of copper oxychloride (0.5%) or bordeaux mixture (1%) have been reported to be effective against the disease by Kishun and Chand (1987) under Indian conditions. Streptomycin sulfate is specifically recommended against this disease and six sprays at 1000 ppm along with two prunings reduced the canker in acid lime (Balaraman and Purshothman, 1981). Foliar sprays of Streptocycline (100 ppm) plus copper oxychloride (0.1%) at 7 or 15 days interval have also been found effective in reducing the disease (Kale et al., 1994). While Zhang et al., (1996) observed best control of canker after foliar sprays of copper hydroxide (800 ppm). Gottawald and Timmer (1995) suggested use of windbreaks alongwith the application of copper bactericides as effective control measures of citrus canker.

(iv) *Resistant varieties.* Use of resistant varieties would be most desirable but no such varieties are available in India. However, seedless lime is reported to be resistant against citrus canker (Kishun and Chand, 1987). Some immune citrus species have been reported to have narrow stomatal aperture, lower stomatal frequency (Pullaiah et al., 1994) and higher levels of phenols and amino acids (Pullaiah et al., 1993).

(v) *Biological control.* Use of biocontrol agents against citrus canker is in a preliminary stage. Ota (1983) found a strain of *Pseudomonas syringae* antagonistic to *Xanthomonas campestris* pv. *citri* which also prevented enlargement of lesions on infected leaves in citrus plants. While Pabitra et al., (1996) have observed *in vitro* inhibition of *X. campestris* pv *citri* by *Bacillus subtilis*, *B. polymyxa*, *Pseudomonas fluorescens*, *Serratia macescens*, *Aspergillus terreus*, *Trichoderma viride* and *T. harzianum* isolates from phylloplane of lemon. These were also observed effective in reducing the disease incidence when applied over crop foliage in the orchard.

Application of neem cake (160 lbs per acre) is highly effective in checking the disease. Akhtar et al., (1997) observed that diffusates of *Phyllanthus emblica*, *Acacia nilotica*, *Sapindus mukorossi* and *Terminalia chebula* inhibit the bacterium. These diffusates also reduced the number of lesions on detached leaves and fruits of grapefruits.

To summarize all this, pruning of infected twigs along with sprays of Bordeaux mixture alternating with streptomcycline is the best control measure. Complete protection is thus required throughout the season depending upon appearance of the disease.

24.7.4 Bacterial Rots

Soft rot of potato. Bacterial soft rot is an important disease of potato occurring at all stages, viz. planting, emergence, growth, harvesting, curing, grading, handling, transportation, storage and even at consumer's level. Soft rot is found both in hills and plains and is a major cause of spoilage of large percentage of tubers stored at ambient temperature of above 15°C.

Symptoms. Initially a small area of tuber tissue around lenticels or stolen attachment point becomes water soaked and soft. Under low humidity, the initial soft rot symptoms may be restricted to sunken type of lesions, while under high humidity, the lesions enlarge and typical soft rot symptoms develop. Secondary organisms usually invade tubers in advanced stages of decay and because of such invasion, the decaying tissues become slimy and foul smelling and a brown liquid oozes out. The skin of the tuber remains intact and sometimes the rotted tubers are swollen due to gas formation.

The pathogen. Potato tubers carry a wide range of pectolytic bacteria in a latent or quiescent form in both tropical and temperate climate. Several of these bacteria viz., *Erwinia carotovora* var. *carotovora*, *E. c.* var. *atroseptica*. *Bacillus polymyxa, B. subtilis, B. mesentericus. B. megatherium, Pseudomonas marginalis, P. viridiflava, Clostridium* spp., *Micrococcus* spp. and *Flavobacterium* spp. have been found associated with tuber decay. Shekhawat and Perombelon (1985) concluded that tuber decay in temperate climate is caused by Erwinias and to some extent by pectolytic *Clostridium* spp. but *Bacillus polymyxa* and *Pseudomonas marginalis* predominate in hot climates. Shekhawat et al., (1982) reported following features to distinguish tuber rot by different bacteria:

E. carotovora	Complete rot of slices no discolouration of tissues, bacterial growth transparent, shining and slimy
P. marginalis	Complete rot of slices profuse creamish and shining bacterial growth on slices
B. subtilis	Partial rot profuse white, rough wrinkled andmatted bacterial growth on rotted tissue
B. polymyxa	Complete rot of slices exposed surface turns black
B. sphaericus	Partial rot, no discolouration, shining transparent bacterial growth on slices

Disease cycle. The main source of contamination is the decaying mother tubers in soil, which contaminate the progeny tubers. The pathogen enters through lenticels, wounds or injuries in freshly harvested tuber. In black leg infected plants, the pathogen may reach the progeny tubers through stolen. During storage the disease spreads by contact of brownish liquid oozing out of the diseased tuber. The maximum infection is in vascular tissues followed by in tuber lenticels and on tuber surface. Cutting knife can transmit soft rot bacteria from infected to healthy tuber. A species of mite has also been found to transfer bacteria from rotted to healthy uninjured tubers. The mite colonizes on tuber eyes from where the rot initiates.

Disease management

1. *Host resistance.* Kufri Dewa had good resistance to soft rot and could be stored for 7–8 months at room temperature in plains. Late blight infected tubers are more susceptible and therefore most of the late blight resistant varieties develop very little soft rot.

2. *Chemical treatment of seed-potato.* Several chemicals found effective include: streptocycline, agrimycin-100, stable bleaching powder 0.05 and 0.10%, boric acid 3 and 4%, thiabendazole

flowable 1.0%, copper sulfate 2.0% 30 min dip. Only bleaching powder or boric acid should be used for treating tubers. Application of bleaching powder (Klorocin) 17 kg/ha in soil before planting or with first or last irrigation reduces bacterial soft rot in storage by 80%. The best tuber treatment for control of soft rot is tuber dip in 3% boric acid for 30 min. This treatment has also been found effective for other tuber diseases like common scab, black scurf and dry rot and has been recommended for control of tuber diseases.

3. *Cultural operations.* Careful selection of uninjured and healthy tubers for storage helps in satisfactory management of soft-rot. Application of high doses of nitrogen (200-300 kg/ha) to the crop increases the soft rot incidence in produce during storage in country store. Source of nitrogen applied also affect soft rot incidence during storage. Ammonium chloride is reported to induce highest incidence (32.0%), followed by ammonium sulfate (23.5%), calcium ammonium nitrate (20.5%) and least by liquid nitrogen fertilizer (16.0%). The differences in soft rot incidence among different sources of nitrogen might be related with the accompanying ions. Fertilizers containing chloride ions increase water content and decrease dry matter in potato tubers, which might be responsible for increased rotting.

Time of harvesting. In country stores (from April to September) late harvested (i.e. in March) tubers have highest incidence of soft rot followed by February and January harvested tubers. In cold storage the incidence is negligible but when such tubers are planted in field, the emergence is 5-10% lower in late harvested crop.

Storage. In different methods of storing potatoes, soft rot is the biggest problem. Pit storage of potato during the hot weather was satisfactory especially in dry areas.

24.8 FASTIDIOUS VASCULAR BACTERIA

The fastidious vascular bacteria (earlier known as Rickettasia like organisms, or RLOs) that cause plant disease can not be grown on simple culture media in absence of host cells, and some of them are yet to be identified, named and classified. Fastidious phloem limited bacteria were observed first in 1972, in the phloem of clover and periwinkle plant affected with the clover club leaf disease and, later, in citrus plants affected with the greening disease and in alfalfa affected with alfalfa dwarf. Since then similar organisms could be detected in the xylem of plants affected with one of more than 20 other diseases.

24.8.1 General Characteristics

The fastidious vascular bacteria are generally rod shaped cells 0.2 to 0.5 µm in diameter by 1 to 4 µm in length. The cell contents are bound by a cell membrane and a cell wall, although in the phloem-inhabiting bacteria the cell wall appears more as a second membrane than as a cell wall. They lack flagella and the cells are usually undulating or rippled (Figure 24.16). Nearly all-fastidious bacteria are gram negative. Several such xylem-limited bacteria have been placed in recently created genus *Xylella*. Only the xylem inhabiting bacteria causing sugarcane ratoon stunting disease and Bermuda grass stunting disease are Gram-positive, and they are classified as members of the genus *Clavibacter* (formerly *Corynebacterium*). None of the phloem inhabiting bacteria has been grown in culture so far, but all the xylem inhabiting bacteria can be grown in culture on complex nutrient media.

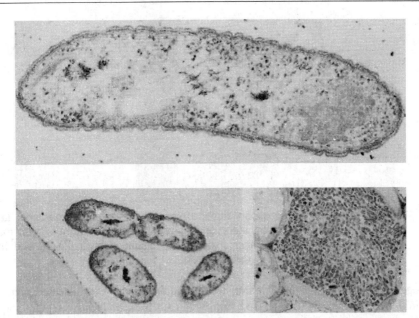

Figure 24.16 Morphological, multiplication, and distribution of plant pathogenic xylem-inhibiting bacteria, the causal agent of Pierce's disease of grape (A) A typical cell showing rippled cell wall, (B) Fastidious bacteria in xylem vessel, one of them undergoing binary fission, (C) Fastidious bacteria in a tracheary element of a leaf vein. (Source: G. N. Agrios, 1997)

All gram-negative xylem inhabiting fastidious bacteria are transmitted by xylem feeding insects such as sharpshooter, leafhoppers and spittlebugs. So far, no insect vector is known for the gram-positive xylem inhabiting fastidious bacteria. Although fastidious vascular bacteria are sensitive to several antibiotics such as tetracycline and penicillin, chemotherapy of infected plants in the field has proved impractical (Agrios, 1997). These bacteria are sensitive to high temperature. Among the most important plant disease caused by fastidious xylem limited, Gram-negative bacteria are Pierce's disease of grape, citrus variegation chlorosis, phony peach disease, almond leaf scorch and plum leaf scald. They are all caused by forms of the bacterium *Xylella fastidiosa*, which also causes leaf scorch diseases on elm, sycamore, oak and mulberry. Ratoon stunting disease of sugarcane is caused by xylem limited, gram-positive bacterium *Clavibacter xyli* sub. sp. *xyli*. Phloem limited bacteria are so far known to cause citrus greening and some minor diseases of clover and periwinkle.

24.8.2 Important Plant Diseases

Ratoon stunting of sugarcane. Ratoon stunting disease (RSD) has been found in the majority of the sugarcane growing areas of the world. The RSD pathogen is frequently present in seed cane and, therefore, has very probably been spread from country to country during the exchange of sugarcane germplasm. RSD has caused reductions in sugarcane yield. Losses may reach levels of 30% or more in some years.

Symptoms. As the name implies, the external symptoms involve less than optimum growth. Microscopic examination of the region of mature nodal symptoms shows that the larger xylem vessels coloured gummy substance (Figure 24.17).

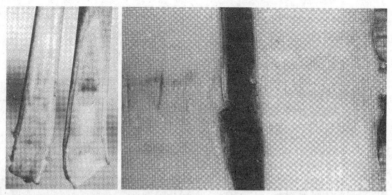

Figure 24.17 Internal symptoms of ratoon stunting disease in stalks of sugarcane. *Left:* Juvenile symptoms with diseased stem on left and healthy on right, *Right:* mature nodal symptoms of ratoon stunting disease with diseased stalk on left and healthy stalk on right. (Gillaspie and Davis, 1992)

The pathogen. In 1973, a small bacterium was found associated with diseased plant. In culture, the bacterium which measures 0.25 to 0.35 mm by 1 to 4 mm, divides by septum formation. The bacterium is coryneform, having straight or slightly curved cells with occasional swellings at the tip or in the middle (Figure 24.18). Taxonomic studies have designated the RSD bacterium as *Clavibacter xyli* sub sp. *xyli*.

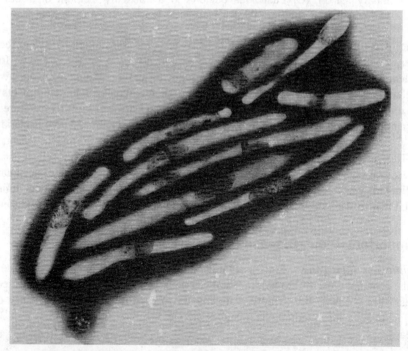

Figure 24.18 Negative stained cells of *Clavibacter xyli* subsp. *xyli* showing septa, swellings and mesosomes. (Gillaspie and Davis, 1992)

Disease cycle. The pathogen occupies a very narrow ecological niche. It apparently cannot survive outside the host for any substantial period of time. It is transmitted through wounds from plant to plant. The pathogen over seasons in infected sugarcane plants and propagative material such as seed cane.

Disease management. Control of this disease depends on the use of disease free cane, heat treatment of suspected infected cane, sanitation of cutting equipment and use of resistant cultivars.

Citrus greening disease. Citrus greening occurs widely in India and appears to be even more dangerous than tristeza virus. A synergism between the causal agents of two diseases has been indicated and the two being jointed responsible for citrus die back.

Symptoms. Characteristic yellow type of symptoms are produced and leaf chlorosis is the main symptom, that resembles the zinc deficiency symptom. Scattered green islands are visible in the yellow area of leaf lamina. Leaf size is reduced and the leaves become thicker and more or less erect. Due to shortening of internodes, the branches give a bushy appearance. Numerous extra buds develop on these branches which later leads to die back. The attacked trees look stunted, flowering earlier and produce smaller fruits.

The pathogen. In 1972, the disease was reported to be caused by a phloem inhabiting fastidious bacterium in which cell wall appears more as a second membrane than as a cell wall. The bacterium is gram negative, non-motile, rigid rod, measuring $1\text{-}2 \times 0.2\text{--}0.5$ µm. The cells occur in mature sieve elements, irregularly distributed among vascular bundles.

Disease management. Diseased plants should be removed from the orchard and healthy grafts from disease free trees should be used. Insect vectors should be eradicated by using diazinon (0.02%) or parathion (0.02%). Spraying affected trees with a mixture of bavistin and leadermycin (500 ppm each) six times at 10 days intervals brings recovery.

REFERENCES

Agrios, G.N., 1997, *Plant Pathology*, 4th edn., Academic Press, New York.

Anuratha, C.S. and Gnanamanickam, S.S., 1990, Biological control of bacterial wilt caused by *Pseudomonas solanacearum* in India with antagonistic bacteria, *Plant and Soil*, 124:109.

Balaraman, K. and Purshothman, R., 1981, Control of citrus canker on acid lime, *South India Hortic.*, 29(4):175-177.

Beattie,W. A. and Lindow, S.W., 1995, The secret life of foliar bacterial pathogens on leaves, *Annu. Rev. Phytopathol.*, 33, 145.

Bradhury, J.E., 1986, *Guide to Plant Pathogenic Bacteria*, CAB Int. Mycol. Inst., Kew, Surrey, England.

Buddenhagen, I.W. and Kelman, A., 1964, Biological and physiological aspects of bacterial wilt caused by *Pseudomonas solanacearum, Annu. Rev. Phytopathol.*, 2:203.

Chattopadhya, S.B. and Mukhopadhyay, N., 1968, Moko disease of banana: a new record, *FAO Plant Prot. Bull.*, 16:52.

Coerper, F.M., 1919, Bacterial blight of soyabean, *Phytopathology*, 10, 119.

Crosse, J.E., 1966, Epidemiological relation of the pseudomonad pathogens of deciduous fruit trees, *Annu. Rev. Phytopathol.,* 4, 291.

Daft, G.C. and Leben, C., 1973, Bacterial blight of soyabeans: field-overwintered *Pseudomonas glycinea* as possible primary inoculum, *Plant Dis. Reptr.,* 57:156.

Daft, G.C. and Leben, C., 1972, Bacterial blight of soyabean: epidemiology of blight outbreaks, *Phytopathology,* 63, 57.

Danos, E., Berger, R.D. and Stall, R.E., 1984, Temporal and special spread of citrus canker within Groves, *Phytopathology,* 74, 904.

Davis, M.J., et al., 1978, Pierce's disease of grapevine: isolation of the bacterium, *Science,* 199:175.

Davis, M.J., et al., 1984, *Clavibacter:* a new genus containing some phytopathogenic coryneform bacteria including *Clavibacter xyli* subsp. *Cynodontis* subsp. nov. pathogens that cause ratoon stunting disease of sugarcane and Bermuda grass stunting disease. *Int. J. Syst. Bacteriol.* 34:107.

Davis, M.J., et al., 1980, Ratoon stunting disease of sugarcane: isolation of the causal bacterium, *Science,* 240:1365.

Davis, M.J., et al., 1980, Ratoon stunting disease of sugarcane: Isolation of the causal bacterium, *Science,* 240, 1365.

DeCleene, M. and DeLey, J., 1981, The host range of infectious hairy root. *Bot. Rev.,* 47:147.

DeCleene, M. and DeLey, J., 1976, The host range of crown gall, *Bot. Rev.,* 42:389.

DeCleene, M. and DeLey, J., 1981, The host range of infectious hairy root. *Bot. Rev,* 47:147.

Drummond, M., 1983, Crown gall disease – A case study, *In:* J.A. Callow (Ed.), *Biochemical Plant Pathology,* John Wiley & Sons, Chichester, p. 65.

Fahy, D.C. and Persley, G.F. (Eds.), 1983, *Plant Bacterial Diseases: A diagnostic Guide,* Academic Press, New York.

Fett, W.F., 1979, Survival of *Pseudomonas glycinea* and *Xanthomonas phaseoli* var. *sojensis* in leaf debris and soyabean seed in *Brazil, Plant Dis. Reptr.,* 63, 79.

Gillaspie, A.G., Jr. and Davis, M.J., 1992, Ratton stunting of sugarcane, *In: Plant Diseases of International Importance:* disease of sugar, forest and plantation crops, A.N. Mukhopadhyay, J. Kumar, H.S. Chaube, and U.S. Singh, (Eds.), Vol. 4, Prentice-Hall, Englewood Cliffs, New Jersey.

Gnanamanickam, S.S. and Anuratha, C.S., 1992, Moko diseases of banana, *In:* J. Kumar, H.S. Chaube, U.S. Singh and A.N. Mukhopadhyay (Eds.). *Plant Diseases of International Importance,* Diseases of fruit crop, Vol. III, Prentice Hall, Englewood Cliffs, New Jersey, p. 283.

Gnanamanickam, S.S., Lokeshwari, T.S. and Nandini, K.R. 1979, Bacterial wilt of banana in southern India, *Plant Dis. Rep.,* 63:525.

Goodman, R.N., 1983, Fire blight—A case study, *In:* J.M. Ogawa, E.I. Zehr, G.W. Bird, D.F. Ritchie, K. Urin and J.K. Uyemoto (Eds.), *Compendium of Stone Fruit Diseases,* American Phytopathological Society Press, Minnesota, p. 48.

Goto, M., 1992, *Fundamentals of Bacterial Plant Pathology,* Academic Press, San Diego.

Goto, M., 1992, Citrus canker, *In*: J. Kumar, H.S. Chaube, U.S. Singh and A.N. Mukhopadhyay (Eds.), *Plant Disease of International Importance*, Diseases of fruit crop, Vol. III, Prentice Hall, Englewood Cliffs, New Jersey, pp. 170-208.

Gottwald, T.R., Timmer, L.W., and McGuire, R.G., 1989, Analysis of disease progress of citrus canker in nurseries in Argentina, *Phytopathology*, 79, 1276.

Graham, J.H., 1953, Overwintering of three bacterial pathogens of soyabeans, *Phytopathology*, 42:189.

Grogan, R.G., et al., 1971, Angular leaf spot of cucumber in California, *Plant Dis. Rep.*, 55:3.

Habte, M. and M. Alexander, 1975, Protozoa as agents responsible for the decline of *Xanthomonas campestris* in soil, *Appl. Microbiol.*, 29:159.

Hayward, A.C., 1991, Biology and epidemiology of bacterial wilt caused by *Pseudomonas solanacearum*, *Annu. Rev. Phytopathol.*, 29, 65.

Hirano, S.S. and Upper, C.D. 1983, Ecology and epidemiology of foliar bacterial plant pathogens, *Annu. Rev. Phytopathol.*, 21:243.

Hopkins, D.L., 1989, *Xylella fastidiosa:* xylem limited bacterial pathogens of plants, *Annu. Rev. Phytopathol.*, 27, 271.

Hopkins, D.L. and Mollenhauer, H.H., 1973, Rickettsia-like bacterium associated with Pierce's disease of grapes, *Science*, 179, 298.

Johnson, J. and Coerper, F.M., 1917, A bacterial blight of soyabean, *Phytopathology*, 7:65.

Jones, D.A. and Kerr, A., 1989, *Agrobacterium radiobacter* strain 1026, a genetically engineered derivative of strain K84, for biological control of crown gall, *Plant Dis.*, 73:15.

Karwasara, S.S. and Parashar, R.D., 1988, Bacteria associated with soft rot of potato tubers affecting disease development, *Indian Phytopath.*, 41:270.

Kaul, J.L. and Sharma, R.C., 1994, Pear diseases and their management, *Int. J. Trop. Plant Diseases*, 12:139.

Keil, H.L. and Van der Zwet, T., 1975, Fire blight susceptibility of dwarfing apple root stocks, *Fruit Var. J.*, 29:30.

Kerr, A., 1980, Biological control of crown gall through production of agrocin 84, *Plant Dis.*, 64:25.

Kishun, R. and Chand, R., 1986, Studies on bacterial diseases of fruit crops, *Annu. Rep. IIHR*, Bangalore, p. 60.

Kishun, R. and Chand, R., 1994, Epiphytic survival of *Xanthomonas campestris* pv. *mangiferae indicae* on weeds and its role in MBCD, *Plant Dis. Res.* 9:35.

Kreig, N.R. and Holt, J.G., 1984, *Bergey's Manual of Systematic Bacteriology*, Vol. I, Williams and Wilkins, Baltimore, M.D.

Leu, L.S. and Su, C.C., 1993, Isolation, cultivation and pathogenicity of *Xylella fastidiosa*, the causal bacterium of pear leaf scorch disease in Taiwan, *Plant Dis.*, 77, 642.

McKeen, C.D., 1973, Occurrence, epidemiology and control of bacterial canker of tomato in southwestern Ontario, *Can. Pl. Dis. Survey*, 53:127.

Mew, T.W., 1987, Current status and future prospects of research on Pohronezny, K., et al., 1992, Sudden shift in the prevalent race of *Xanthomonas campestris* pv. *vesicatoria* in pepper fields in Southern Florida, *Plant Dis,* 76, 118.

Mishra, A.K. and Prakash, O., 1992, Bacterial canker of mango: incidence and control, *Indian Phytopathol.,* 45:172.

Mount, M.S. and Lacey, G.H. (Eds.), 1982, *Phytopathogenic Prokaryotes,* Vols. I and II, Academic Press, New York.

Nagaich, B.B., et al., 1980, Studies on bacterial soft rot, *Ann. Sci. Rept.* CPRI, Shimla, 1978.

Nagaich, B.B., et al., 1980, Studies on bacterial soft rot, *Ann. Sci. Rept.,* CPRI, Shimla, 1979.

Nelson, P.E. and Dickey, R.S., 1990, Histopathology of plants infected with vascular bacterial pathogens, *Annu. Rev. Phytopathol.,* 8, 259.

Nirvan, R.S., 1961, Citrus canker and its control, *Hortic. Advance,* 5:171.

Onasando, J.M., 1988, Management of black rot of cabbage caused by *Xanthomonas campestris* pv. *campestris* in Kenya, *Acta Hort.,* 218:311.

Park, E.W. and Lim, S.M., 1985, Overwintering of *Pseudomonas syringae* pv. *glycinea* in the field, *Phytopatholgy,* 75:520.

Perombelon, M.C.M. and Kelman, A., 1980, Ecology of the soft rot Erwinias, *Annu. Rev. Phytopathol.,* 18, 361.

Prakash, O. and Srivastava, K.C. 1987, *Mango Diseases and Their Management,* A World Review, Today and Tomorrow's Printer, New Delhi.

Purcell, A.H., 1982, Insect vector relationships with prokaryotic plant pathogens, *Annu. Rev. Phytopathol.,* 20, 397.

Raju, B.C. and Wells, J.M., 1986, Disease caused by fastidious xylem-limited bacteria and strategies for management, *Plant Dis.,* 70, 182.

Ream, W., 1989, *Agrobacterium tumefaciens* and inter-kingdom genetic exchange. *Annu. Rev. Phytopathol.,* 27:583.

Ream, W., 1989, *Agrobacterium tumefaciens* and interkingdom genetic exchange, *Annu. Rev. Phytopathol.,* 27, 583.

Shekhawat, et al., 1984, Studies on bacterial soft-rot of potato, *Ann. Sci. Rept.,* CPRI Shimla, 1982.

Shekhawat, G.S., Gadevar, A.V. and Chakravarti, 2000, Potato bacterial wilt in India, *Tech. Bull (No. 38),* CPRI, Shimla.

Shekhawat, G.S., Nagaich, B.B. and Kishore, V., 1976, Bacterial top rot—a new disease of the potatoes, *Potato Res.,* 19:241.

Shekhawat, G.S., Piplani, S. and Ansari, M.M., 1984, Endophytic bacterial flora of potato plant in relation to soft rot disease, *Indian Phytopath.,* 37:501.

Sherf, A.F. and Macnab, A.A., 1986, *Vegetable Disease and Their Control,* John Wiley and Sons, New York.

Singh, U.S., Mukhopadhyay, A.N., Kumar, J. and Chaube, H.S., (Eds.), 1992, *Plant Diseases of International Importance,* Vols. I-IV, Prentice Hall, Englewood Cliffs, New Jersey. (Extensive chapters on blackrot of crucifers and fire blight of apple and pear)

Smith, M.A., 1944, Blister spot, a bacterial disease of apple, *J. Afric. Res*, 68:269.

Stall, R.E. and Seymour, C.P. 1983, Canker, a threat to citrus in the Gulf-coast states, *Plant Dis.*, 67:581.

Stall, R.E. and Civerolo, E.L. 1991, Research relating to the recent outbreak of citrus canker in Florida. *Annu. Rev. Phytopathol.*, 29, 399.

Starr, M.P., 1984, Landmarks in the development of phytobacteriology, *Annu. Rev. Phytopathol.*, 22, 169.

Starr, M.P., 1983, *Phytopathogenic Bacteria,* selections from *The Prokaryotes* Springer-Verlag, Berlin and New York.

Thomason, S.V., 1992, Fire blight of apple and pear, *In*: J. Kumar, H.S. Chaube, U.S. Singh and A.N. Mukhopadhyay (Eds.). *Plant Diseases of International Importance*, Diseases of fruit crops, Vol. III, Prentice Hall, Englewood Cliffs, New Jersey, p. 32.

Thyr, B.D., et al., 1973, Tomato bacterial canker: control by seed treatment, *Plant Dis. Rep,* 57:974.

Van der Zwet, T., 1993, Worldwide spread and present distribution of fire blight—an update, *Acta Hortic*, 338:29.

Vander, Zwet, T., and Keil, H.L., 1979, Fire blight—A bacterial disease of rosaceous plant, *U.S.D.A. Handb.* 510, p. 200.

Vaughan, E.K., 1944, Bacterial wilt of tomato caused by *Pseudomonas solanacearum, Phytopathology*, 34:443.

Vidaver, A.K., 1976, Prospects for control of Phytopathogenic bacteria by bacteriophages and bacteriocins, *Annu. Rev. Phytopathol.*, 14, 451.

Watterson, J.C., et al., 1971, Response of cucurbits to *Erwinia Tracheiphila Plant Dis. Rep.*, 55:816.

Wells, J.M., et al., 1987, *Xylella fastidiosa*, Gen. Nov., gram-negative, xylem limited, fastidious plant-bacteria related to *Xanthomonas* spp, *Int. J. Syst. Bacterial*, 37:136.

Williams, P.H., 1980, Black rot: A continuing threat to world crucifers, *Plant Dis.*, 64, 736.

Wills, A.B. and Walker, J.C., 1952, Epidemiology and control of angular leaf spot cucumber, *Phytopathology*, 42:105

Wormald, H., 1931, Bacterial disease of stone fruit trees in Britain III, The symptoms of bacterial canker in plum trees, *J. Pomol*, 9:239.

Young, J.M., Takikawa, Y., Gardan, L. and Stead, D.E., 1992, Changing concept in the taxonomy of plant pathogenic bacteria, *Annu. Rev. Phytopathol,* 30, 67.

Zhang, K., He, S. and Huang, Z., 1996, Effect of several fungicides for control of citrus canker (*Xanthomonas citri* Hasse Dowson), *South China Fruits*, 25:20.

25 Viruses and Plant Diseases

25.1 INTRODUCTION

Viruses are unique class of pathogens. They are simple in structure, cannot be seen with microscope, yet cause dangerous diseases in animals (Polio, Rabies, AIDS, Influenza) and plants (mosaics, yellows, stunting/dwarfing, leaf roll/leaf curl, curly top/bunchy top, etc.). Viruses attack wide variety of biological systems including single cell bacteria and highest evolved biological systems, i.e., animals and human being. Approximate number of viruses known is 2000 and about 977 are known to parasitize plants (Agrios, 1997). One pathogenic virus can attack several plant genera, also several viruses attacked same plant species. Viruses behave like parasite inside living cells by utilizing the cell systems and cell resources for their own multiplication, thus exhausts the animal/plant cells. Outside living cells the viruses behave like chemical molecules (TMV can survive in dried tobacco leaves for decades). In fact viruses have characteristics common to both living and non-living systems.

25.2 CHARACTERISTICS OF PLANT VIRUSES

Plant viruses are so simple that they have hardly any morphological features of significance. Basically they are composed of nucleic acid core (genetic material) enveloped by a protein coat. Complete virus particle is known as **virion.** Virus particles are mostly rod shaped or polyhedral with some modifications. In viruses only one type of nucleic acid (RNA/DNA) is present and mostly they have one kind of protein. Viruses do not have cell or any organization like that.

Particle composition and structure. Virus particles can be either rod shaped (rigid rods or flexuous threads) or spherical in shape (isometric or polyhedral). Some have cylindrical shape also. The elongated viruses may vary from 15×300 nm (rigid rods) to 10×2000 nm (flexible threads). The bacillus like, cylindrical rod shaped particles measure $52\text{-}75 \times 300\text{-}380$ nm. The spherical viruses have diameter from 17 nm to 60 nm. Some viruses consist of more than one unit, i.e. two or more distinct nucleic acid strands enveloped in same protein coat, even though, they may vary in size. Alfalfa mosaic virus has four components of different sizes. Similarly, spherical (isometric) viruses may have two or more components. In any multi-component viruses (rod/spherical) all nucleic acid strands must be present in plant cell for biological activities. The protein coat, covering genetic material, makes the outer surface of virus particles. This is made up of definite number of protein subunits. Some spherical virus particles are provided with an outer membrane (lipoprotein envelope). Virus particles are made up of one type of nucleic acid (5-40%, RNA/DNA) and protein (60-95%). The elongated viruses have lower level of nucleic acid as compared to spherical viruses.

Nucleic acid. Viruses contain either RNA/DNA as genetic material. Most of plant viruses contain RNA (ssRNA/dsRNA), about 80 plant viruses contain DNA (50 ssDNA and 30 dsDNA). The RNA/DNA are long macromolecule made up of nucleotide subunits. The nucleotide unit consists of a ring (the base) attached to ribose (a five carbon sugar) in RNA and DNA has deoxyribose sugars, which are attached to phosphoric acid (Figure 25.1). The RNA or DNA strands are formed as the sugar of one nucleotide reacts with phosphate of another nucleotide (Figure 25.1) two pyrimidine bases, **adenine** and **guanine**, interact with two purine bases **uracil** and **cytosine** in RNA strand. In DNA, the oxygen of one sugar hydroxyl is missing and the base uracil is replaced by the base **thiamine** (methyl uracil).

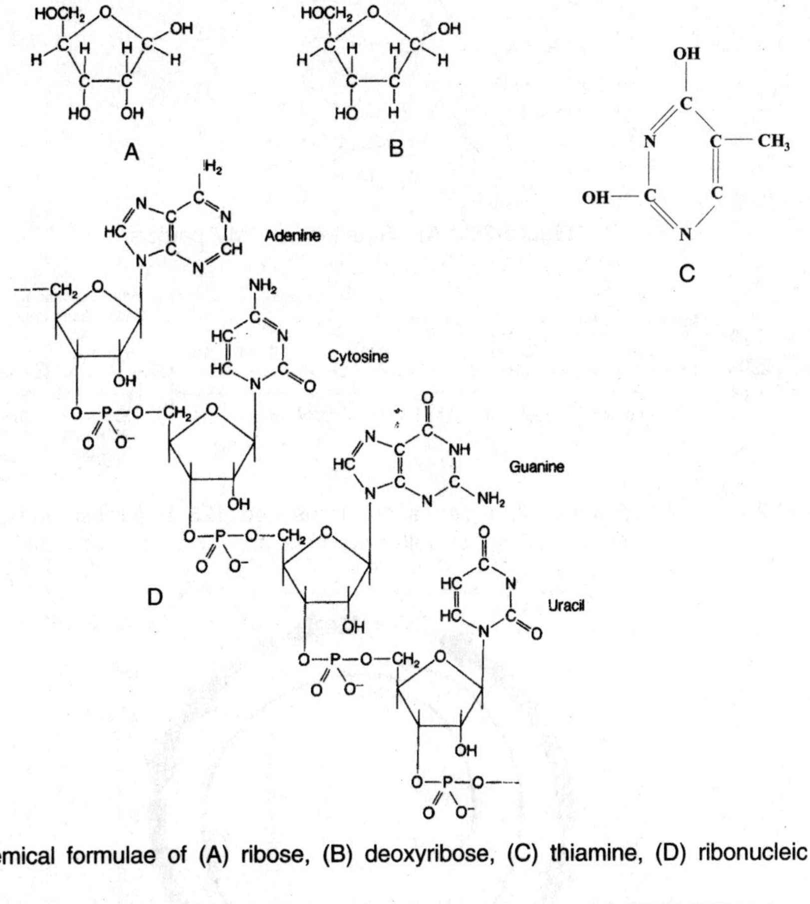

Figure 25.1 Chemical formulae of (A) ribose, (B) deoxyribose, (C) thiamine, (D) ribonucleic acid.

Viral proteins. Protein makes coat or shell, covering the genetic material (RNA/DNA) in a virus particle. The proteins are made up of amino acids. The genetic material governs the amount and sequence of amino acids in protein, which differ for different viruses. The TMV protein subunits (158 amino acids in a fixed sequence; mass 17,600 Daltons) are arranged in a helix containing 16 1/3 subunits per turn (49 subunits per three turns). The central hole of virus particle has a diameter of 4 nm while the diameter of virus particle is 18 nm. Each TMV particle has approximately 130 helix turns of protein subunits. The nucleic acid (RNA) is tightly packed between the helices of protein subunits [Figure 25.2(A)]. Figure 25.2(B) presents the details of TMV genome where three major genes encode for three proteins, viz. replicase (126 K), movement protein (30 K) and coat protein (17 K). In polyhedral plant viruses, the protein subunits are tightly packed in arrangements that produce 20 facets of a shell. Within the shell the nucleic acid is arranged. Figure 25(C) shows the genetic map of cauliflower mosaic virus, where DNA is genetic material.

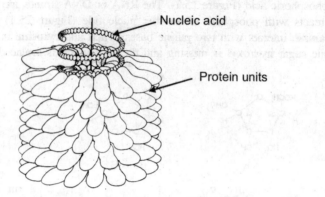

Figure 25.2(A) Structure of TMV particle.

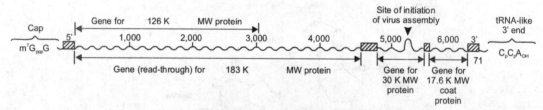

Figure 25.2(B) TMV genome—four genes are translated 126 K largest proteins as replicase, 30 K protein for cell to cell movement and 17 K is coat protein.

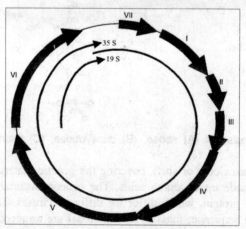

Thick arrows ━━━▶ represent open reading frames (ORF$_s$),
Thin arrows ───▶ are for two major transcripts.
The thin lines ─── are intergenic regions.

(**Source**: Stephane Blanc, et al., 2001, Caulimoviruses. *In: Virus- Insect-Plant Interactions*, Harris et al., (Eds.)
Figure 25.2(C) Genetic map of caulimoviruses (Cauliflower mosaic virus).

The genome of caulimoviruses contains seven major ORF$_s$:

ORF I; codes for protein (P$_1$) involved in cell to cell movement and systemic spread.

ORF II; encodes for CaMV helper protein (P$_2$) which is also known as aphid transmission factor (ATF).

ORF III; product protein (P$_3$) is involved in aphid transmission.

ORF IV; codes for a precursor protein (P$_4$), which gives a set of structural polypeptides that make the viral capsids.

ORF V; codes for the reverse transcriptase, and is also involved in P$_4$ maturation.

ORF VI; codes for multifunctional protein (P$_6$). It is translated from 19$_s$ RNA. P$_6$ trans-activates the expression of other genes from polycistronic 35s RNA.

ORF VII; The product of ORF VII has not been found in plants, thus no role for this gene is assigned.

Satellite viruses and satellite RNAs. Satellite viruses are associated with typical plant viruses and depend on them for multiplication and infection of host plant. They may adversely affect the typical virus, with which they are associated. The satellite viruses may be considered as 'parasite' on plant viruses. The satellite RNAs are small, linear strands of RNA present in virus particles. They may decrease the effect of virus or may be result of host response to virus infection (satellite RNA may be related to host RNA).

25.3 VIRUSES AND PARASITISM

The ancient Romans used the word virus for a poison, later during 19th century it was used to mean 'poisonous elements by which infection is communicated.' Beijerink (1890) for the first time used the word 'virus' to describe '*contagium vivum fluidum*' (infectious living fluid), which was demonstrated to be the cause of mosaic disease of tobacco. Some of the definitions used to describe 'virus' are as follows:

Luria (1953): Submicroscopic entities capable of being introduced into specific living cells and reproducing inside such cells only.

(1978): Entities whose genomes are elements of nucleic acid that replicate inside living cells using cellular synthetic machinery and leading the synthesis of virion (complete virus particles).

Bawden (1964): Obligate parasite pathogens with dimensions of less than 200 nm.

Mathews (1981): Set of one or more template molecules normally encased in a protective coat or coats of protein or lipoproteins which is able to organize its own replication only within suitable host cells.

Boss (1983): Infectious agent, submicroscopic, small enough to pass through a bacterial filter, lacking metabolism of their own and depending on living host cell for multiplication.

Kassanis (1984): Parasitic nucleic acids, normally contained within proteinaceous envelope, which use their own template molecule to replicate within living cell alone or with the help of another virus.

Singh (1989): Found 'almost similar theme' in all the definitions proposed. He listed the following essential characteristics of viruses:

1. Viruses contained one or more pieces of a single type of nucleic acid.
2. This nucleic acid carries the genome of the virus, which differs from one virus to another.
3. The genome in the nucleic acid strand directs the synthesis of specific proteins for the coat, which must be present in all viruses throughout their active phase except at the time of replication.
4. Viruses rely on living host cells for most of the enzymes necessary for their replication.

Our understanding about viruses and the infection process will be better if we understand the parasitic relationship with host plants. Conventionally, parasite is defined as, *organism which grows at the expanses of other living organism (host)*. It derives its nutrients from the host. Since viruses neither draw nutrients nor they grow, they are not considered as parasites. In fact, viruses are not considered as cellular organism or living organism. But viruses behave like organisms when inside living host cells through the expression of their genome, multiplication of nucleic acid, synthesis of viral proteins and assembly of virions. Thus, the viruses can be accepted as parasites at genetic level (Singh, 1999).

25.4   THE VIRUS CYCLE

Viruses behave like organisms while inside living host cells. In this parasitic mode they replicate (production of replica), multiply (grow in number), mutate and even recombine to give rise to new forms (strains: create variability). As regards the reproduction, viruses differ from other cellular organism; prokaryotic (binary fusion) and eukaryotic (sexual and/or asexual), as they lose their identity due to disassembly of virion inside host cell. The protein coat is removed and lost in plant cell. Then viral genome is replicated by host cell machinery. Recent studies on behaviour of virus particles inside host cell has been conducted on isolated protoplasts (plant cells without cell wall), callus tissues and the cells of vector. Following steps are described to give readers incite into virus cycle (Figure 25.3): Hamilton (1974) described replication of plant viruses.

25.4.1   Inoculation and Entry

Life activities of virus particles are confined only inside living host cells and viruses depend on some agency to get entry into host cell. The mechanically transmitted viruses require some minor injury to plant cell, which facilitate their entry into cell system. During experimental inoculations some abrasive agents (carborandum powder) are added to inoculum. This creates minor entry points for the viruses. In nature large number of viruses depend for their spread (horizontal movement) and entry (inoculation) on minor natural injuries or insect vectors, which 'transmit' them (place directly inside/cell) while feeding on plants. Viruses placed on intact plant surface fail to cause infection, as they are unable to enter the host cell. When virus comes in contact with protoplast they may get in through pinocytes, the small perforations in all membrane.

25.4.2   Uncoating of Viral Genome

In early stages of infection process the protein coat of virus particle is removed, thus nucleic acid (genome) becomes free (in TMV, within 10 minutes of inoculation). This is a prerequisite step for

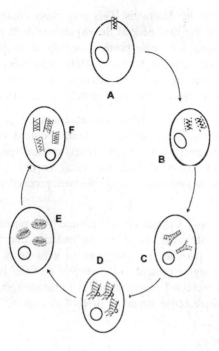

Figure 25.3   General scheme for virus cycle in host cell, (for +ve sense RNA virus; TMV), (A) entry of virus through wound, (B) uncoating of viral genome (RNA), synthesis of viral nucleic acid strands, (D) synthesis of viral proteins, (E) assembly of virions, (F) virions in infected host cell.

activity (replication/expression) of genome. It is believed that removal of protein coat is both physical as well as enzymatic process; however the exact place of uncoating is not fully known. The rod shaped viruses attach to some sites on cell membrane. The ability and process of uncoating will largely depend on structure of virus particles (coat-proteins).

25.4.3 Synthetic Phase

Once the virus genome (RNA/DNA) is free, from the protein envelop, the synthetic phase (parasitic phase) starts under which the genetic material replicates (many replicas produced) and synthesis of viral protein takes place.

Replication of viral genome

(i) Positive sense ssRNA virus.   Replication in ssRNA, mono-partite viruses (TMV) is a simple process. The single chain of nucleotides (RNA) is known as **+ive sense strand** and functions directly as messenger RNA and genetic information can be directly translated using host system (ribosomes, t-RNA and amino acids). First synthetic activity is the production of protein enzyme (replicase/ polymerase) required for replication of viral RNA. With the help of specific enzyme the +ive sense parent RNA replicates to produce a negative sense RNA strand, which acts as template for synthesis of progeny of positive sense viral RNA strands. This way many copies of viral RNA are produced for multiplication of virus inside the host cell, at the expanse of host metabolites. The viral nucleic acid can be mono-cistronic (coding for single protein) or poly-cistronic (coding for many proteins). In multi-component positive strand ssRNA viruses (alfalfa mosaic, brome mosaic and cucumo viruses) different parts of genome code for coat proteins and enzymes. Replication of each RNA segment is performed through a separate negative template, transcribed from parent strand.

(ii) Negative sense ssRNA virus. Some RNA viruses contain negative sense strand and cannot directly act as mRNA, for synthesis of enzyme proteins required for replication. These viruses (lettuce necrotic, yellow mosaic and potato yellow dwarf) require specific transcriptase/polymerase (from host cell), which is incorporated into the virus particle. Now positive strand RNA, complementary to parent RNA, is synthesized and infection proceeds in same way as described in case of +ive sense ssRNA virus.

(iii) Double stranded RNA virus. Certain viruses contain both positive and negative RNA strand, thus in virions, RNA is double stranded (wound tumor and rice dwarf). There are 10-12 segments of RNA, all contained in same particle, each segment of genome is separately transmitted into a single mRNA using replicase enzyme present in the core of particle. Each mRNA is monocystronic and encodes for single type of protein. In early stages of replication, the strands of dsRNA separate. During transcription only negative sense strand of dsRNA is copied. The positive sense strand has following roles to play:

(a) Translated into proteins
(b) Act as template for negative strand RNA

(iv) DNA viruses. Cauliflower mosaic virus was demonstrated to have DNA as genetic material instead of RNA. Once DNA is free from coat protein it can replicate, using replicase from host cell. The caulimoviruses have dsDNA; only one strand is transcribed into mRNA, using host enzymes. The mRNA is translated (polycistronically) into many types of viral proteins. The Gemini viruses contain ssDNA.

Protein synthesis. The viral RNA acts as mRNA and gets translated at ribosome for production of proteins, which are specific to each virus species. The host amino acids are arranged in a specific sequence, aided by tRNA and factors required for initiation and termination of protein synthesis. The protein coat of virus particles is thus synthesized at the expense of host plant cells.

25.4.4 Assembly of Virions

At the end of synthetic phase (production of viral nucleic acid and protein) the assembly of virus particles (virions) takes place. The assembly may be in nucleus (complete virus particles-virions: come out) or in cytoplasm or in *'viroplasm'* (electron-dense mass). Once nucleic acid and viral proteins are synthesized, the assembly seems to be a spontaneous process, but there must be some information needed for their assembly. This may be due to aggregation of protein subunits around nucleic acid (elongated or helical viruses). Formation of isometric virus is more complex and mechanism not properly understood. Nucleic acid may fix initial proteins at specific points and later more proteins may aggregate to give virions a particular shape. The nucleic acid is packed inside protein coat, *the virion assembly is irreversible.* The virus cannot enter another reproductive/ infective cycle inside same cell.

25.4.5 Site of Replication

Cell nucleus, nucleolus and cytoplasm are the sites for viral replication. The caulimoviruses and Gemini viruses, potex viruses and tobamoviruses replicate inside nucleus and viruses move out into cytoplasm. The bromoviruses, potyviruses, nepoviruses and comoviruses replicate in cytoplasm.

25.5 TRANSMISSION OF PLANT VIRUSES

Viruses are active (parasitic) only inside living host cells. Viruses cannot move on their own, movement of virions may be within plant tissues or outside plants aided by various agencies (Essau, 1967). The short and long distance dispersal (transmission) employs various agencies depending upon nature of crop and relationship with vector. Efficiency of virus vectoring agency is the most important aspect of viral epidemiology. In addition to vectors, the other important means of virus spread is via propagating material (seed/vegetative parts) and by contact (mechanical transmission).

25.5.1 Movement of Viruses within Plant

The viruses have to move out of infected host cells for causing new infections. Cell to cell movement of viruses within plants is through plasmodesmata (the connection between adjacent cells). Approximate movement of viruses is 1.0 r.im per day. For faster movement of viruses within plants, they enter and move through phloem. After being loaded in phloem, the viruses become systemic and move towards the sink tissues (growing apical tissues, fruits or storage roots/stems). From phloem the virus can move into adjacent parenchymatous cells, thus enter the new tissues for further spread. Viruses causing mosaic type symptoms may be confined in certain cells/tissues. The localization of virus may produce different patterns. Actively growing apical tissues and true seeds generally do not favour the multiplication of viruses (except viruses in legume seeds). Localization of viruses in infected/invaded cells or tissues results in formation of local lesions. Sometimes the lesions created by viral infection may continue to enlarge. There are indications that the viruses continue to spread beyond the borders of the lesions. Hull (1989) reviewed information on movement of viruses in plants.

25.5.2 Mechanical Transmission

Mechanical or sap transmission of plant viruses is one of the important means of field spread of viruses. Physical contact/rubbing of infected parts facilitate the transfer of virus in sap and similar mechanical contact or rubbing with healthy tissue provide opportunity of inoculation, through minor injuries. Sap or mechanical transmission is one of the easy ways to establish presence of virus in some suspect plant specimens. Comparatively high concentration of virus particles (1000 or more) is required for each infection. Certain host plants, which are extra sensitive or local lesion hosts are used as indicator plants. These are used to verify presence of a particular virus, based on known reaction.

25.5.3 Transmission Through Propagative Material

Most plant viruses associated with diseased plants are systemic, thus present in all plant parts/cells.

The viruses may spread with seed or vegetative plant parts. If plant cuttings or buds, grafts are used as means of propagation, there are fair chances of spread of plant viruses. Important commercial crops (sugarcane, potato and ornamentals) face the problem of quality/disease free seed/planting material.

Transmission with seeds. Plant viruses may be carried on the seed coat, as surface contaminants (TMV on tomato seeds) or inside the seed (endosperm/embryo). Viruses considered under true seed transmission are carried in embryo. For this the early infection of plant and invasion of embryonic tissue by virus, prior to pollination and formation of female gametes is required. After fertilization, the embryonic sac (containing embryo and endosperm) is separated from direct vascular connection of mother plants. Majority of unstable viruses are lost. These reasons explain why majority of plant viruses are not transmitted through seeds. Table 25.1 gives list of plant viruses transmitted through seeds or pollen.

Table 25.1 Example of Plant Viruses Transmitted Through Seed and Pollens

Virus	Host species	True seed transmission (%)	Pollen transmission
Abutilon mosaic	*Abution* spp.	14–24	4
Alfalfa mosaic	*Medicago* sativa	10–50	–
Barley stripe	*Hordeum* vulgare	15–100	+
Bean common mosaic	*Phaseolus* vulgaris	1–93	+
Bean yellow mosaic	*Pisum sativum*	10–30	+
Black gram mottle	*Vigna mungo*	8	–
Cowpea mosaic (common bean)	*Vigna unguiculata*	25–40	–
Cowpea mosaic (Banding)	*V. unguiculata*	2.7–19	–
Cowpea mosaic (Chavali)	*V. unguiculata*	17–23	–
Cucumber mosaic	*Stellaria media*	21–40	–
Elm mosaic	*Ulmus americana*	1–3	+
Lettuce mosaic	*Lactuca sativa*	3–10	+
Lychnis ring spot	*Lychnis divaricata*	58	+
Mungbean and Urdbean mosaic	*Vigna radiate*	20	–
Pea early browning	*P. sativum*	37	–
Pea enation mosaic	*P. sativum*	1.5	–
Pea seed-borne mosaic	*P. sativum*	0–100	–
Peanut (groundnut) Indian clump	*Arachis hypogaea*	12	–
Peanut mottle	*A. hypogaea*	9	–
Peanut stunt	*A. hypogaea*	0.1	–
Prune dwarf	*Prunus cerasus*	3–30	+
Raspberry ring spot	*Fragaria* spp.	50	+
Southern bean mosaic	*V. unguiculata*	3–7	+
Soyabean mild mosaic	*Glycine max*	22–70	–
Soyabean mosaic	*G. max*	30	+
Soyabean stunt	*G. max*	39	+
Tobacco ring spot	*G. max*	78–82	+
Tomato black ring	*Rubus* spp.	5–19	+
Urdbean leaf crinkle	*Vigna mungo*	18	–
Vicia cryptic	*Vicia faba*	Varying	+
White clover mosaic	*Trifolium repens*	6	–

25.5.4 Transmission Through Insects

As discussed earlier the viruses cannot move on their own, the vectors help in their dispersal or transmission to ensure the continuity of infection chain. In fact, *epidemiology of virus disease depends on behaviour of vector.* Thus, the study of the virus-vector relationship is important biologically, ecologically and economically. Insects and mites play the role of vectoring viruses efficiently or viruses have used the plant-insect/mites relationship for a 'ride' from source (diseased plants) to targets (healthy tissue/plants). Figure 25.4 gives some information on various groups of insects/mites involved in transmission of various viruses.

In 1895-1901, Japanese workers first studied transmission of rice dwarf virus by leaf lopper (*Inazuma dorsalis* and *Nephotetix cicticeps*). Later beet curly top virus (leaf lopper, *Circulifer tenellus*-1915), cucumber mosaic viruses (aphid, *Aphis gossypi*–1951) and potato leaf roll viruses (aphid, *Myzus persicae*–1920) were reported. Harris (1981) described arthropods and nematode vectors of plant viruses.

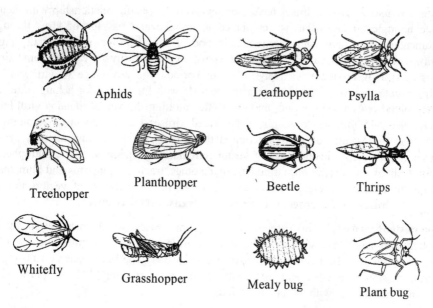

Figure 25.4 Groups of insects/mites involved in transmission of viruses.

Virus-vector relationship: Involvement of vectors (living organism) in host-pathogen interaction complicates the process of viral disease development. Whether it is by chance or by design, viruses have developed a specific relationship with their vectors, which plays important role and influence the host range, the disease development and to some extent the evolutionary process in long-term. For specific description of virus-vector relations following terms are commonly used:

Acquisition feeding period–The time period for which virus free vector must feed on a virus infected plant to acquire virus.

Acquisition access period–Period for which vector is allowed to feed on source of virus.

Latent period–Duration after which a vector becomes able to transmit virus (viruliferous).

Inoculation access period–The time period for which vector must feed before it is able to inoculate viruses into plants (inoculation feeding period).

Transmission threshold period–Minimum period required by vector for acquisition and subsequent transfer to a virus free plant.

Depending upon the duration for which the vectors could transmit viruses and the intimacy of their relationship, three categories have been identified:

(a) Non-persistent viruses. The acquisition and inoculation periods are very small (few seconds to a minute). Vectors acquire viruses during probing or feeding on surface infected cells (epidermal). Without any latent period, vector can transmit virus and the period of retention (persistence) is also very brief. It is basically a mechanical association and virus is lost during molting. Aphids are commonly involved in non-persistent transmission and fasting before feeding increases their transmission efficiency.

(b) Persistent viruses. These viruses have more evolved or specific relationship with their vectors. An intimate biological relationship is anticipated in up-take and passage of virus through insect system (alimentary canal, gut wall, circulation in body fluid-haemolymph and finally coming out with saliva). These are also called **circulative virus**. Persistent viruses require some time to go through insect system, so there is always a latent period. The advantage to virus, in persistent relationship, is that once acquired, they remain (persist) with the vector for a long time (life time) and are transmitted over a long period, and even after molting the vector remains viruliferous. The vectors may take 5-15 minutes to acquire deep-seated viruses (from phloem or adjoining tissues). Depending upon the amount of viruses acquired the vector is able to transmit persistent viruses. Some viruses even multiply inside body of vector (circulative-propagative). The multiplication may take place in cells of muscles, brain, fat bodies, mycetomes, trachea, epidermis and alimentary canal. Rice dwarf virus and wheat streak viruses are passed to next generation of vectors through eggs. The passage of viruses to the progeny is known as **transovarial transfer**.

(c) Semi-persistent viruses. This category has the plant viruses, which share certain features with non-persistent and persistent viruses. They take a little longer to acquire viruses (3-4 min), suggesting that virus may be neither circulative nor persistent. The pre-acquisition fasting does not improve transmission efficiency and infectivity is lost after molting. Phloem borne viruses are picked up and transmitted without latent period.

Specificity of virus-vector relationship. The virus-vector relationship is more than chance carryover. Since it has developed over long period of time, the relationship has become specific or specialized. The following facts about viruses give some indications about specificity in virus-vector relationship:

- Potato virus X and potato virus Y together cause rugose mosaic disease. Out of these PVX is sap or mechanically transmitted and vector aphids (Myzus persicae) transmit only PVY and not PVX.
- PVS along with PVA cause crinkle of potato. PVS is sap transmitted while M. persicae transmit only PVA.
- Aphids, M. ornatus, pick and transmit only cauliflower mosaic virus and not cabbage ring spot virus from a mixed inoculum but M. persicae can not differentiate, thus transmits both.

The mechanism underlying the observed phenomena of specificity is not known. The location of viruses (epidermal cells or phloem) and the feeding behaviour of insect vector may influence specificity. The role of specific protein shell and involvement of transmission factor have also been speculated. Presence of one virus (helper virus) may facilitate the transmissibility of another virus, e.g. presence of vein distorting virus helps in aphid transmission of tobacco mottle virus, which is only sap transmitted.

25.5.5 Transmission by Mites

The eriophyed mites and spider mites (8 legged) suck the cell contents. The mites acquire viruses and wind may help in spread of disease to distances. *Aceria tulipae* transmits wheat streak mosaic and *A. cajani* transmits pigeon pea sterility mosaic viruses* (*viral nature not yet confirmed). Nymphs of mite acquire wheat streak mosaic virus and transmit in persistent manner, also survives molting.

25.5.6 Transmission by Nematodes

Nematodes are silent but important soil borne vectors of some viruses. Role of nematodes as vector has been discussed in Chapter 4 on disease development.

25.5.7 Transmission by Fungi

Soil borne fungi, belonging to Olpideaceae and Plasmodiophorace (Chytirids) are known to carry plant virus and during infection the zoospores facilitate the entry of virus inside plant cells. The fungal transmission is more prevalent under cool wet conditions (temperate climate). *Olipidium brassicae* (Tobacco lettuce big vein and tomato stunt virus necrosis virus- TMV) and *O. radicale* (cucumber necrosis virus) are examples of fungus born viruses.

Polymyxa graminis	: wheat mosaic
Polymyxa betae	: beet necrotic yellow vein
Spongospora subterranea	: potato curly top virus

25.5.8 Transmission by Dodder

Dodder (*Cuscuta* spp.) is total plant parasite absorbing plant nutrients through modified roots (haustoria). They have wide host range also. Several plant viruses are passively transported from diseased plants to other plants by thread like tubular structure of dodder. Certain viruses multiply in dodder. Virus transmission through dodder is a useful tool in experimental virology. The passage of virus from infected to test plants and the symptom development can be studied using dodder as transporting channel.

25.6 NOMENCLATURE AND CLASSIFICATION OF PLANT VIRUSES

Viruses are so simple, in structure and/or function that they do not provide much morphological, physiological or biochemical features of taxonomic importance. Thus, basic features, based on composition of virions, are used to group plant viruses. The features used include: type of nucleic acid (RNA/DNA), number of strands (single/double), negative sense/positive sense, shape and symmetry (rod, thread, circular, isometric or bullet shaped), number of components in virions (mono or multi-partite). Agrios (1997) proposed a classification of viruses associated with plant diseases (Figure 25.5).

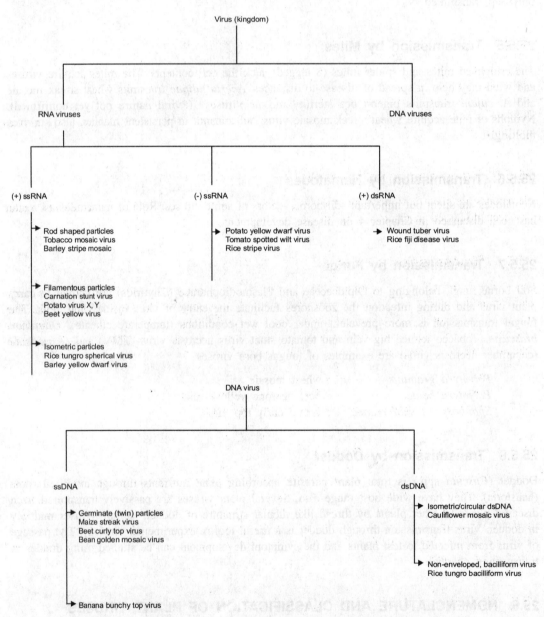

Figure 25.5 Scheme for grouping of plant viruses. (*Source:* Agrios, 1997).

Nomenclature of viruses has been tried by scientists in different ways. As a result, same virus, e.g. potato virus Y is also named as potato acropetal necrosis virus, potato severe mosaic virus, tobacco vein banding virus, Solanum virus-2, *Marmor upsilon*. Potato leaf roll virus (PLRV) is also called potato virus-1, Solanum virus-1, *Carium solani* Holmes. This created a state of confusion. It was realized that a virus should be described on certain lines, e.g. particle morphology, number of particles in multi-particle virus, comparative serology, methods of purification, diagnostic and assay hosts, transmission, thermal inactivation and dilution end points. Gibbs and Harrison (1968) proposed use of *system of cryptograms* for description of viruses. These cryptograms were based on four pairs of symbols, viz. TMV cryptogram is **R/1:2/5:E/E:** S/O, with following description;

First pair: **R/1** for RNA or DNA respectively/strandedness (1 or 2),

Second pair: **2/5** is for molecular weight of nucleic acid in millions/percentage of nucleic acid in particle.

Third pair: **E/E** defines the outline of particle/outline of nucleo-capsid. (E = elongated, S = spherical)

Fourth pair: **S/O** is the kind of host (S = seed plants)/kind of vector in nature.
Vector symbols: O = spreads without vector, Ac=mite,
A1 = whitefly, Ap = aphids, Au = hoppers, Fu = fungus,
Ne = nematode, Th = thrips).

The symbol * is written for unknown property of virus/un-confirmed information.

Cryptograms for groups of viruses and the type virus are given below:

Virus group	Cryptogram	Type virus
Tombus viruses	R/1: 1.5/18: S/S: S/*	Tomato bushy stunt
Tobacco necrosis virus	R/1:1.5/19:S/S: S/Fu	Tobacco necrosis
Caulimovirus	D/2: 4.5/16:S/S: Sap	Cauliflower mosaic
Comoviruses	R/1: 1.4/24+2.1/34: S/S: S/c1	Cowpea mosaic
Tobraviruses	R/1: 2.3/5: E/E: S/Ne	Tobacco rattle
Tobamoviruses	R/1: 2/5: E/E: S/O	Tobacco mosaic
Potexviruses	R/1: 2,2/6: E/E: S/O	Potato virus *X*
Potyviruses	R/1: 3.0-3.5/5-6: E/E: S/O, AP	Potato virus *Y*
Luteobviruses	R/1: 2/*: S/S: S/AP	Barley yellow dwarf
Geminiviruses	R/1: */*: S/S: S/A1	Maize streak

The International Committee on Nomenclature of Viruses was formed in 1966, with separate subcommittees for vertebrates, invertebrates, bacteria and plants. In 1975, this committee was called **International Committee on Taxonomy of Viruses** (ICTV). In its Sixth Report (May, 2000), ICTV established nine families and 33 genera. A database of 864 plant viruses has been developed. Summary of the characteristics of some plant virus genera are given in Table 25.2.

Table 25.2 Characteristic of Plant Virus Genera

Genome	Family	Genus	Type species
DNA	Caulimoviridae	Caulimovirus	Cauliflower mosaic virus
		'RTBV-like'	Rice tungro bacilliform virus
	Geminiviridae	Curtovirus	Beet curly top virus
		Begomovirus	Bean golden mosaic virus
dsRNA	Reoviridae	Phytoreovirus	Wound tumour virus
		Varicosavirus	Lettuce big-vein virus
(-)ssRNA	Rhabdoviridae	Nucleohabdovirus	Potato yellow dwarf virus
	Bunyaviridae	Tospovirus	Tomato spotted wilt virus
(+)ssRNA	Bromoviridae	Cucumovirus	Cucumber mosaic virus
		Alfamovirus	Alfalfa mosaic virus
	Closteroviridae	Closterovirus	Beet yellows virus
	Comoviridae	Comovirus	Cowpea mosaic virus
	Luteoviridae	Polerovirus	Potato leaf roll virus
	Potyviridae	Potyvirus	Potato virus Y
		Bymovirus	Barley yellow mosaic virus
	Sequiviridae	Waikavirus	Rice tungro spherical virus
	Tombusviridae	Tombusvirus	Tomato bushy stunt virus
	Unassigned	Tobamovirus	Tobacco mosaic virus
		Hordeivirus	Barley stripe mosaic virus
		Potexvirus	Potato virus X
		Foveavirus	Apple stem pitting virus
		Vitivirus	Grapevine virus A

25.7 PATHOGENICITY TEST IN VIRUSES/VIROIDS

Since viruses/viroids are active only inside living cell and cannot be isolated, grown and multiplied on any cell-free media, it is not possible to establish Koch's postulates (to establish the pathogenicity) as is the case of conventional plant pathogens. Boss (1983) redefined and modified postulates to be accepted as proof of pathogenicity.

- The virus must be concomitant with virus disease.
- It must be isolated from diseased plant and multiplied in a propagative host, purified physico-chemically and identified for intrinsic properties.
- When inoculated onto a healthy host plant, it must reproduce the disease.
- The same virus must be demonstrated to occur in and must be re-isolated from experimental host.

25.8 VIRUSES AT THE THRESHOLD OF LIFE

Once TMV was established to be the cause of mosaic disease of tobacco, plant viruses were considered to be living, like other fungal and bacterial pathogens. Stanley in 1935 purified and crystallized the virus particles from infected sap of tobacco leaves, thus, the TMV was considered as 'molecule or macromolecule'. Molecules cannot be living. Thus, the living status of viruses was questioned. But purified and crystallized TMV particles retained two important characters of living organism, i.e., mutation and reproduction. Thus, there was confusion, whether the viruses should be considered as living or non-living. The living organisms are expected to exhibit the features of life which include

- Metabolism (assimilation and release of energy)
- Growth
- Reproduction
- Mutation
- Response to environment (stimulus)

The viruses do not share these characteristics of life in true sense. Moreover, living organisms must be independent for structures and function and have definite structures, while viruses do not have these characteristics. Thus, viruses cannot be taken as organism. However, the ability to reproduce (multiply), mutation, infectious nature do suggest that viruses can be considered as organism. Thus, at present state of information about plant viruses and our understanding about the infection process, the virus can be safely placed *at the threshold of life*. Some workers have coined the group meso-biotic (for virus/virus like organisms) to be placed between abiotic and biotic pathogens.

25.9 VIROIDS AND VIRUSOIDS

In 1967, Diener and coworkers reported that the potato spindle tuber disease was caused by an agent much smaller than known viruses (250-400 base long). It was naked, single-stranded, circular molecule of infectious RNA, which they named **viroid.** So far about 20 plants diseases are known to be caused by viroids (Table 25.3). No animal or human disease is reported to be caused by viroids.

Table 25.3 Diseases Caused by Viroids

Diseases	Abbreviated names	Etiology established	Distribution
Avocado sun blotch	ASBV	1971	Australia, Israel, Peru, South Africa, USA, Venezuela
Burdock stunt	BSV	1983	China
Carnation stunt	CarSV	1983	Italy, USA
Citrus exocortis	CEV	1972	Argentina, Australia, Brazil, Corsica, Israel, Japan, Spain, South Africa, Taiwan, USA
Chrysanthemum chlorotic mottle	CCMV	1975	USA
Chrysanthemum stunt	CSV	1973	Australia, Canada, China, India, Japan, The Netherlands, United Kingdom, USA
Columnea viroids	ColV	1978	USA
Coconut cadang cadang	CCCV	1975	Philippines
Cucumber pale fruit	CPFV	1974	The Netherlands
Grapevine	GV	1985	Japan
Hop stunt	HSV	1977	Japan
Potato spindle tuber	PSTV	1971	Argentina, Brazil, Canada, China, Chile, Peru, USA, USSR, Venezuela
Tomato apical stunt	TASV	1981	Ivory coast
Tomato planta macho	TPMV	1982	Mexico

180

Viroids differ from viruses for following two points:

- They lack protein coat, thus viroids are naked nucleic acid (RNA).
- Size of viroids RNA (250-370 bases) is too small as compared to viruses.

The viroids have single stranded circular RNA with extensive base pairing, which gives a hairpin structure (Figure 25.6). Each viroid consists of five structural regions, which include left and right hand terminal domains (A & E), one central conserved core (C), the crucial pathogenicity regions (B) and variable region (D). The mode of viroids replication is not fully understood. The RNA in viroids is unable to act as mRNA in *in vitro* protein synthesizing system. It is believed that viroids RNA replicate by direct copying. All components required for replication, (including RNA polymerase), are provided by the host cell. Diener, et al. (1993) discussed how do viroids make plants sick.

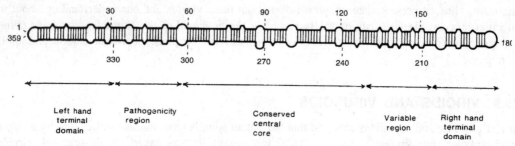

Figure 25.6 Structure of PSTV indicating composition of left terminal domain, right terminal domain and pathogenicity region.

Viroids can be separated into six groups based on their nucleotide sequence. The groups are represented by potato spindle tuber viroids (PSTV), coconut cadang cadang viroid (CCCV), hop stunt viroid (HSV), apple scar skin viroid (ASSV), avocado sun blotch viroid (ASBV) and hop latent viroid (HLV). The nucleotide homology within group ranges from 65% to 100% while intergroup similarity is 39-60%.

This is also not clear, how viroids cause disease? The symptoms produced resemble with those produced by viruses. Although the viroids use host cell resources for multiplication, but the amount of viroids present in infected cells do not support the view that viroid multiplication will starve host cells of RNA nucleotides. It is suspected that the activation of the protein kinase represents the triggering event in viroids pathogenesis and disease development in plants. Generally viroids spread by mechanical means, although, they are also known to be transmitted through pollen and seeds, in addition to vegetatively propagated plant parts. No specific insect vectors are known to transmit viroids. The management of viroids mainly depends on production of disease/viroids free propagating material and suitable cultural practices to prevent spread. Host resistance to viroids is another good proposition.

Virusoids. Virusoids, like viroids, are naked ssRNA, which are associated with plant diseases. They are virus satellite RNAs. Although they are low molecular weight, naked, covalently closed, circular RNA molecules (324-388 nucleotides) yet they differ from viroids. Virusoids exists in solution as rod shaped structures. Table (25.4) gives more information on some of the virusoids.

Table 25.4 List of Virusoids

Virusoids	Abbreviation	Number of nucleotides
Lucerne transient streak virus RNA 2	vLSTV	324
Solanum nodiflorum mottle virus RNA 2	Vsnmv	378
Subterranean clover mottle virus RNA 2	V (388)SCMoV	388
Subterranean clover mottle virus RNA 2	V (332)SCMoV	332
Velvet tobacco mottle virus RNA 2	vVTMoV	366, 367

25.10 VIRAL DISEASES OF POTATO AND MANAGEMENT

25.10.1 Potato Viral Diseases

Potato is an important crop occupying fourth position, after rice, wheat and corn. The crop suffers serious damage, some time unnoticed, due to several viral diseases, which assume significance as potato is vegetatively propagated. The potato crop is attacked by some 36 viruses and viruses like organisms (Khurana, 1999). Viruses are largely responsible for crop losses along with degeneration of seed stocks (annual losses: 30-40% infection causing 25-30% yield losses in India). Viruses are responsible for causing crop losses upto 50% in tuber yield in Indian plains (Pushkarnath, 1967). An average 5-10% viral infection hardly affects crop yields but early and severe infection does cause appreciable yield losses (10-60%).

Potato mosaics

(i) Latent mosaic. The disease and the pathogen, potato virus X (PVX), are worldwide in distribution. It alone can cause 15-20% yield loss but combined infection with other potato viruses (PVA and PVY) cause severe losses (Khurana and Garg, 1992). Symptoms produced by PVX causes faint mottle or interveinal mosaic in early stage of plant growth (Figure 25.7).

Pathogen. PVX (Potex virus) or potato mild mosaic virus is filamentous particle (515 × 13 nm). PVX is highly contagious, spread in field by contact or by cutting of seed tubers. Symptoms are masked in vigorously growing plants above 21°C.

Host range. Potato, tomato, tobacco, eggplant, pepper, *S. nigrum*, *Petunia* spp., *D. stramonium*, *G. globosa*, *Chenopodium amaranticolor.*

(ii) Severe mosaic/Rugose mosaic. This disease is worldwide in distribution, caused by different strains (PVY-O, worldwide, PVY-C Australia and India, PV2-N Africa, Europe, South America) of potato virus Y (PVY). Yield losses may vary from 30-80%. More serious damage when potato plants are co-infected with PVA or PVX. PVY infected plants are more susceptible to late and early blights (Singh and Khurana, 1993). The characteristic symptoms include severe mosaic, necrosis along veins (vein banding virus) and may also induce rugosity, drying and dropping of leaves (Figure 25.7). Plants from infected mother tubers are stunted with brittle and crinkled leaves (primary symptoms).

Pathogen. Potato virus Y (Poty virus) *Solanum virus* 1, severe mosaic viruses or potato vein banding virus is flexuous filamentous (740 × 11 nm) and helically structured. PVY is transmitted by aphids (*Myzus persicae* and *Aphis gossypii*) in non-persistent manner. Some isolates (N) are known to be transmitted through contact.

Host range. PVY mainly attacks members of family Solanaceae, other hosts include *Nicotiana glutinosa*, *N. tabacum* and *Datura stramonium*.

Figure 25.7 Symptoms on potato caused by different virsus, Potato leaf roll on leaves (A) and in tuber (B), mosaics (C, D, E and F) and rugose mosaic (G).

Potato leaf roll. Potato leaf roll is worldwide in distribution and reported to cause upto 90% yield losses (Khurana, 1999), depending upon the percentage of the seed stock infection. The *primary symptoms* (on plants from infected mother tubers) are seen as chlorosis of top leaves, late in season the top leaves show rolling and erect habit (Figure 25.7). The *secondary symptoms* include stunting of shoots, upwards rolling of older leaflets, which may turn chlorotic (Figure 25.7), leathery and brittle. Severe infection, in some cultivars, shows net necrosis in tuber flesh (phloem tissues). Aerial tubers are also formed due to blockage of phloem by viral infection.

Pathogen. The potato leaf roll virus (PLRV), potato virus-1, Solanum virus –1 or potato phloem necrosis virus is the causal agent. PLRV (Lutero virus) has isometric particles (24 nm in diameter), which are confined to phloem tissue. Under natural conditions PLRV is confined to *Solanum* spp. (narrow host range). *Gomphrena globose, Capsella bursa-patoris* and *Mantia perfoliata* are other hosts. Several aphid species (*M. persicae, Aphis gossyspi, Macrosiphum euphorbie* and *Aulacorthum solani*) transmit virus.

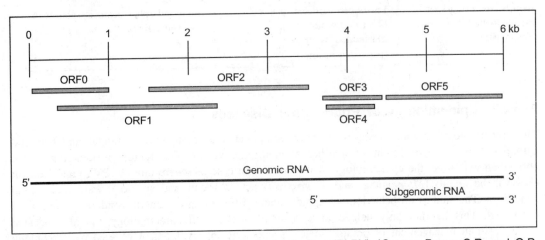

Figure 25.8 Genomic organization of potato leaf roll virus (PLRV) (*Source:* Brown C.R. and O.P. Smith, 2001. Genetically engineered potatoes. In: Virus-Insect- Plant Interactions, eds., Harris et al., Academic Press.)

Genomic organization of potato leaf roll virus (PLRV) reveals that single-stranded positive sense RNA is organized into six open reading frames (ORFs). The product of ORF1 and ORF2, a fusion protein, functions as RNA replicase. The translation product of ORF4 functions as movement protein. ORF3 encodes the coat protein (CP) of PLRV whereas read-through protein is encoded by ORF5. No function has been attributed to ORF0, although roles in host recognition and symptom expression have been suggested.

Other viral diseases of potato. In addition to PVX, PVY and PLRV some other viruses also cause variable damage to potato crop. Table 25.5 gives information on these potato viruses.

Table 25.5 Potato Diseases, the Pathogens and Other Features of Potato Diseases Caused by Minor Viruses

Disease	Pathogen	Features
Latent/faint mosaic (PVS: Carla virus)	Flexuous particles (66 × 12 nm), Highly contagious, contact/mechanically transmitted, (non-persistent), *Myzus persicae*	Frequently found worldwide, co-infection with PVX:10-20% yield loss
Leaf rolling mosaic (PVM-Carla virus)	Slightly curved filamentous particles (650 × 12 nm), mechanically and aphid transmitted (non-persistent).	World wide but important in eastern Europe and Russia.
Super mould mosaic virus (PVA: Poty virus)	Flexuous filament (730 × 11 nm), aphids (*M. persicae*) in non-persistent manner.	Worldwide, co-infection with PVX or PVY upto 30-40% yield losses
Stem necrosis/ring spot, tomato spotted wilt virus: (Tospo virus)	Enveloped particles spherical (70-110 nm diameter), transmitted by thrips (persistent manner)	Stem and foliar necrosis spots with concentric rings

25.10.2 Epidemiology of Potato Viral Diseases

The epidemiology of viral diseases is more complicated as compared to fungal and bacterial pathogen, due to involvement of another element: the vector. The factors influencing vector population will affect the epidemiology of the disease. In case of severe mosaic (PVY) and leaf roll (PLRV), the aphids (*M. persicae* and *A. gossypii*) act as vector and spread disease under field conditions. The studies on behaviour of aphids, under different agro-climatic conditions, have been conducted. This has not only helped in understanding the viral epidemiology, but also became useful input in management of potato viruses, particularly in development of seed plot technique for production of virus free seed stocks in NW/NE plains of India.

The PVX, PVS and PSTV are transmitted through infected tubers, from season to season while under field conditions the virus spreads through contaminated hands and tools (mechanical/sap transmission). The highly contagious virus spread rapidly in 3-4 years (more than 50%), grown from successive seed. PSTV is highly contagious, spreads through seed tubers, through sap transmission and also readily get transmitted through pollen and true potato seed. The weed hosts harbouring the viruses and/or aphids also seem to have some epidemiological significance in over-wintering aphids and consequent virus spread (Singh and Boiteau, 1988; Garg, et al., 1990).

Studies of Verma and Vashisth (1985) revealed prevalence of aphid populations in Northern plains of India (Figure 25.9). It was concluded, from these studies, that with certain precautions seed potato crop can be grown in northern plains of India by keeping aphids below critical level (20 aphids per 100 compound laves). They reported that quality seed stocks can be produced by adopting practices like rouging, insecticide application and de-haulming. Based on this information primary and secondary seed production centres have been identified in India.

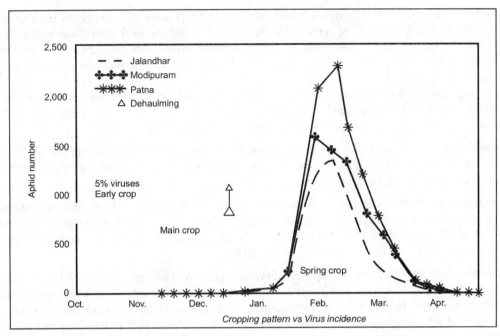

Figure 25.9 Prevalence of aphid populations in Northern plains of India. (*Source*: *Technical Bulletin No.* 26 (1999), CPRI Shimla)

25.10.3 Management of Potato Viral Diseases

Potato, an important cash crop, suffers moderate to heavy losses due to viral infections under field conditions. Since there is no viricide available the damage due to viruses can be minimized by managing the host genotype and the cultural practices. Production and use of virus and viroids-free propagating materials is an important component of integrated strategy. Some general practices involve quarantine, sanitation, eradication, avoiding/managing vector, seed certification and resistance breeding (including biotechnology). In a country like India where seed replacement rate is 15-20%, it becomes more imperative to manage the incidence of viral diseases. Some of the practices involved in integrated management of potato viruses are as follows:

Quarantine. Most of potato viruses are tuber borne (PSTV is also carried with true potato seed). The National Quarantine Programme, at CPRI, Shimla is operating and many potential viruses, viz. andean potato latent, tobacco ring spot, potato virus T, PST viroid, etc. were intercepted in imported consignments (Singh and Khurana, 1993). A large number of viruses, which do not occur in country, are to be kept out by following strict quarantine measures to protect potato crop against 'potential pathogens'.

Sanitation. Several potato viruses (PVX, PVS and PSTV) are contagious, i.e., they spread by contact. This calls for adopting various sanitation practices such as clean seed, rouging, disinfestations methods, isolation of seed and ware crop for minimizing field spread. The use of 30% trisodium phosphate or common bleach (Sodium hypochloride) solution can be used for surface inactivation of viruses.

Virus free seed production. Diseased mother tubers not only produce diseased plants but also serve as a source of inoculum for field spread. The importance of healthy seed stocks was realized very early and the efforts made by a group of Indian scientist resulted in development of **seed plot technique** (Pushkarnath, 1967). CPRI, Shimla, has developed a scheme for field multiplication of seed potato as foundation and certified seed under inspection by the certifying agencies. Virus free plants, regenerated from meristem tips, are genetically stable and yield true-to-type plants. A modified scheme 'multi-meristem culture', developed at CIP, Lima, has increased rate of multiplication by inducing production of multiple shoots (Rocca et al., 1978).

Thermotherapy. PVY and PVA are easily eliminated at 36-39°C. PSTV is eliminated by chilling (5-6°C for 8-12 weeks). PVX and PVS by 29°C treatment for 20-24 weeks. However, PVS and PSTV are difficult to eradicate by heat treatment.

Chemotherapy. Certain chemicals and antiviral agents are known to reduce viral concentration (pre-treatment to meristem tissue or added in culture medium). Growth promoting agents (cytokinin) and GA were reported effective against PVY. Incorporation of riboside in medium helps in eradication of PVY and PLRV (Khurana, et al., 1996).

Avoidance and management of vector. Several aphid species are responsible for spread/transmission of potato viruses (PVY, PVR, PVM) from diseased to healthy potato tissue (non-persistent manner). Thus, avoiding or management of aphid population will have direct bearing on status of viral infection in potato crop. Verma and Vashishth (1985) found at Jalandhar that planting in first 10 days of October and de-haulming in first 10 days of January gives good yield of quality seed tubers.

Forecasting of viruses. The factors related with host, viruses, insect vector and environment decide the outcome of interaction. Based on aphid migration, prevailing temperature and host age the prediction of PVY has been attempted. Exposing the bait plants and determining percentage of viruliferous aphids have been used to forecast PVY in potato crop. Such models will have significant role in epidemiology and management of potato viruses. Weeds in potato field do not seem to play any significant role in epidemiology of potato viruses.

Aphids are not pests of potato; yet they are important due to their involvement in spread of viruses. Systemic insecticides are applied in soil at planting/earthing time. Foliar spray of contact insecticide in December/January helps to prolong the vector-free crop period, i.e., delays the onset of *critical date*. The use of resistance var. and suitable cultural practices are also recommended. Trivedi, et al. (1998), developed a model for forecasting aphid population (*M. persicae*) so that de-haulming date could be properly determined. Following is the relationship:

$$Y = a + b \cos \left(\Sigma c_i \times i \right) + e$$
$$i = 1$$

where

Y = Aphid population of current week

x_i = Minimum temperature of previous week

a, b, and c are constants to be estimated and e is the error term.

The R^2 value for the model was 0.74, which suggests that model is appropriate (74% observed variability explained).

Host resistance and transgenic potato. Although host resistance appears to be most logical way to manage viral problem but not many resistant varieties are available in India (Khurana, 1992). Some of old days popular cultivars Craig's Defiance, Up-to-date, Great Scot and Katahdin had resistance against viruses. Sources of resistance to potato viruses have been identified in *S. tuberosum S. andigena, S. berthaulti* and *S. acaule.*

At CPRI, Shimla, the resistance against aphid vectors has been intercorporated in potato cultivars, viz. K. Jyoti, K. Shakti and K. Badshah while new cultivars K. Ashoka, K. Jawahar, K. Pukhraj have tolerance to PVX and PVY. Beekman (1987) reported that single dominant gene controls resistance to PVX and PVY while PLRV is believed to be under polygenic control. This explains why breeding for PVX and PVA is easy as compared to PLRV. Jayasinghe et al., (1989) reported that PLRV resistance is ineffective in clones that were susceptible to PVX and PVY. Thus, it is important to incorporate PLRV resistance in potato material that has immunity/resistance to both PVX and PVY. Recently resistance to viruses PVX, PVY and PLRV has been engineered in commercial cultivar by using biotechnology (Khurana, et al., 1997). Following transgenic strategies have been proposed to develop resistance in potato (Brown and Smith, 2001).

(i) Coat protein mediated resistance. Beachy et al., (1990) reviewed the information on coat protein mediated resistance, which interfered with the virions disassembly, multiplication, expression and spread of virus. CP-mediated resistance is not specific (Mandhar and Khurana, 1998) and has been incorporated in transgenic potato plants, which show high degree of resistance to aphid inoculations. Major problem with this strategy is that resistance is not functional when plants are inoculated with naked viral RNA or high concentration of intact virus. Commercial release of CP-engineered potato is withheld, probably due to such reasons.

(ii) Movement protein mediated resistance. The investigations on intra or intercellular movement of viruses have revealed that certain movement proteins (MP) help in cell to cell movement of viruses, and transgenic plants expressing a defective MP could block the movement of viruses. This MP-mediated resistance is of a broad spectrum. Transgenic potato plants expressing a MP of PLRV showed resistance to PVX and PVY also.

(iii) Antisense technology. Antisense RNA is a strand of RNA, which is complementary to the messenger RNA that is translated to viral protein. The antisense RNA hybridize with the corresponding mRNA to form double stranded RNAs that are susceptible to degradation by cellular RNA (Nicholson, 1996). Antisense constructs targeted against the viral coat protein as well as replicase have been successfully used against PVX, PVS and PLRV (Kawchuk, et al., 1991).

(iv) Non-pathogen derived resistance. Genes from systems other than potato have been used to induce resistance against potato viruses. The gene encoding ribosome-inactivating protein (RIP), from pokeweed, has been transferred in transgenic potato. Transfer of a mammalian gene (coding for oligonucleotide synthetase), which confers resistance to PVX in potato plants under field conditions has been reported.

25.10.4 Potato Seed Production and Certification

In potato cultivation, seed is an important input for getting optimum production. In India, 1.4 million ha area is under potato cultivation. Out of which 22% is under seed production programme. Total seed production is 4.6×10^6 tons. Quality seed production in potato is both technical and specialized operation.

Basic requirements for seed production

- Fields free from serious soil borne pathogen and pests.

- Low aphid period (minimum 75 days) from October to March
- Healthy seed available to start the programme

Seed plot technique (SPT). Importance of quality seed was realized at very early stages of potato research. The efforts of CPRI scientists, led by Pushkarnath (1967), developed SPT for production of quality seed in India. The data from surveys conducted revealed (1967) that in north-west Indo-Gangetic plains, a suitable period (75-80 days) has low aphid population. The SPT has the following salient features:

- Adoption of 2-3 years crop rotation (no Solanaceous crops)
- Isolation distance of minimum 25 m from ware crop
- Healthy seed from reliable source (right physiological state)
- Planted between 15th-25th October (Punjab, Haryana, Rajasthan Western, U.P.) and by 5th Nov. (Eastern U.P., Bihar, Bengal, Orrisa)
- Systemic granular insecticide applied at planting and earthing up time
- Pre-sprouted (multiple sprouts) healthy whole tubers planted
- Full earthing up and use of herbicides
- Normal recommended plant protection measures for foliar pathogens
- Spray Rogor or Metasystox (1.2 l/ha) at 10 days interval from 1st week of December in plains to control aphids
- Stop irrigation 10 days before haulm killing/cutting
- Haulm killing or cutting on critical date. No re-growth allowed
- Harvesting done 15-20 days after haulm cutting
- Curing of harvested tubers, by keeping in heaps in cool shady place, for 15-20 days
- Seed crop should be inspected 3 times at 50, 65 and 80 days for rouging (off-types and diseased plants should be removed along with tubers)

Seed certification standards. Seed certification is a way of monitoring the quality of seed crop so that seed stocks remain free from degenerative viral diseases, tuber born fungal and bacterial diseases and off-types (varietal mixture). Objective is to produce healthy tubers true to type, with high vigour and productivity. Seed certification standard/permissible limits of purity/diseases in seed crop is given below in the following chart:

Permissible Limits of Diseases and Damages in Potato Seed Programme (Per cent Incidence of Foliar and Tubers Diseases)

Grade of seed	Off type	Mild mosaic	Severe mosaic (PVY& PLRV)	Total virus	Brown Rot	PSTV
Foundation 1	0.05	1.0	0.5	1.0	—	—
Foundation 2	0.05	2.0	0.75	2.0	3 plants/ha	—
Certified	0.10	3.0	1.0	3.0	–do–	—
Grade of seed	**Common scab**	**Black scurf**	**Cut/bruised (Injuries)**	**Late blight**	**Dry rot**	**Total diseases**
Fs 1	5.0	5.0	1.0	1.0	1.0	5.0
Fs 2	5.0	5.0	1.0	1.0	1.0	5.0
Certified	5.0	5.0	5.0	5.0	1.0	5.0

25.11 VIRAL DISEASES OF TOMATO AND THEIR MANAGEMENT

Tomato (*Lycopersicon esculentum* Mill.) is an important vegetable crop cultivated throughout the world. In India about 50,00,000 metric tones of tomato is produced annually. The crop is affected by several major pathogens including viruses (36 viruses affect tomato crop).

25.11.1 Tomato Viral Diseases

Tomato mosaic. It is most common viral disease of tomato caused by tomato mosaic virus (TMV) belonging to genus Tobamo virus. It is reported to reduce yields upto 23% (Rast, 1975). The characteristic symptoms are mottled areas of light and dark green colour on leaves (Figure 25.10). Some strains may cause yellow mottling also. Leaves may be reduced in size and may be curled. Severe infection may cause necrosis of leaf and stem. The fruits before ripening also show symptoms on the surface as well as internal browning and collapse of cells.

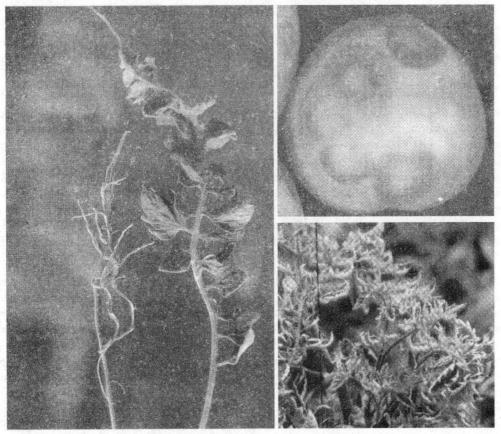

Figure 25.10 Shoestring of tomato leaves caused by tomato mosaic virus (left) and tomato fruits showing ring-spotting and yellow hallow caused by tomato spotted wilt virus (right top) and tomato leaf curl virus symptoms (bottom right).

The pathogen. Tomato mosaic was earlier supposed to be caused by TMV, CMV, PVX or PVY. Now, Tomato mosaic virus (ToMV) is established a separate virus, though closely related with CMV (both are Tobamo virus). ToMV is a RNA containing straight rod particle (about 300×18 nm). The virus remains active in extracted host plant juice upto 50 years. The virus can survive in soil (dry or wet) and plant debris for more than two years. Seed borne ToMV is considered to be main source of primary inoculum, in addition to root debris left in soil. It is contagious and can spread in field easily by sap or contact/mechanical transmission. Operations during transplanting and training are chief means of spread.

Tomato yellow leaf curl. Tomato yellow leaf curl is a common disease in tropical and sub-tropical countries. It is most serious disease of tomato in India, especially in summer and rainy season crops. It has been reported to cause 75-96% yield losses (Kalloo, et al., 1986).

Symptoms. These include mosaic, interveinal yellowing, vein clearing, crinkling and puckering of leaves. Inward rolling of leaf margins may also be observed. Early infection cause stunting of plants, the older leaves become leathery and brittle, the dropping of flowers is commonly observed. The disease is caused by tomato yellow leaf curl virus (TYLCV). The virions measures 20×30 nm, are monopartite and have ssDNA (a Gemini virus). It is transmitted by white flies (*B. tabaci*) in circulative but non-propagative manner. The experimental hosts include (15 species in 5 families) *Lycopersicon esculentum, L. pennellic, L. hirsutum, L. peruvianum, L. pimpinellifolium, Nicotiana glutinosa, N. tabacum* and *Datura stramonium.* Tobacco is symptomless carrier of virus. TYLCV is not reported to be seed borne in tomato

Tomato spotted wilt. The disease caused by tomato spotted wilt virus (TSWV) is characterized by bronze coloured marking on upper side of young leaves. Leaves may also show slight downwards curling. Stiffening of leaflets, formation of small circular necrotic spots on leaves with upward marginal rolling are other symptoms. The necrosis on stem, near tips, may cause wilting of infected plants. The fruits on infected plant show pale red or yellow or sometimes white areas on normal red skin (Figure 25.10). The *pathogen*, TSWV (tospo virus), is a RNA virus with membrane envelope surrounding protein coat. It has very wide host range (300 plant species belonging to mono and dicots). Weeds and perennial ornamentals are reservoirs of virus. The virus is transmitted by thrips (*Thirips tabaci*) in persistent manner. It is also transmitted by tomato seeds. MacKenzie and Ellis (1992) developed resistance in transgenic tomato plants expressing viral nucleoprotein gene.

Management of tomato viral diseases. Tomato viruses have wide host range and weeds/volunteer plants serve as reservoirs, these should be eradicated to reduce load of initial inoculum. Several practices have been recommended for management of vectors (aphids, thrips, etc.). Barrier crops (corn, non-susceptible, tall crops) break the flight of insects. Reflective mulches on earth repel insect vector from the fields (yellow sticky polythene) and reduces TSWV upto 64% (Sharma, 1999). Use of insecticides thimet, phorate, malathion, pyrethrum, demelon, parathion and disulfolon has been recommended (Azam, et al., 1997). Host resistance is the most important component of management strategy. Sources of resistance to TYLCV have been identified in wild tomato. Most of cultivated varieties are susceptible. Gene Tm^{-1} and Tm^{-2} have been used for developing genetic resistance in hybrids. Transgenic plants resistant to ToMV have been released (Asakawa, et al., 1993). Kim, et al., 1994 developed genetically engineered tomato plant resistant to TSWV (expressing the antisense RNA and coat protein gene). Kunik, et al. (1994) developed transgenic tomato plants expressing the tomato yellow leaf curl virus capsids protein and were resistant to virus.

25.12   VIRAL DISEASES OF CHILLIES AND MANAGEMENT

Chillies (*Capsicum annuum* L.) is an important crop, grown worldwide, for vegetable (bell type) as well as spices (pungent type). More than 20 viruses in different locations affect the crop. The leaf curl (Tobacco leaf curl virus) and mosaics, caused by poty and cucumo virus, are major yield reducing factors.

25.12.1   Mosaic Diseases

Chilly mosaics are caused by potyviruses, cucumovirus and tobamo virus. Seven distinct viruses, viz. TMV, CMV, PVY, pepper vein banding virus, pepper mottle virus and pepper severe mosaic virus are involved. These viruses are easily sap transmissible. In addition, aphids (*M. persicae, A. gossypii, A. craccivora*) transmit viruses in non-persistent manner. The variability in mosaic symptoms is due to crop factor (cultivar and age), virus (es)/strains involved, and the environmental factors. Characteristic symptoms associated with viruses are described as follows:

Potato virus Y.   Vein-banding, necrosis of veins, petioles and stem.

Pepper venial mottle virus.   Mosaic mottling, distortion of leaves (filiform), bushy appearance.

Pepper mottle virus.   Systemic mottling and leaf deformities. Systemic necrosis of leaves causing death.

Pepper severe mosaic virus.   Mosaic mottle, vain clearing and dark green vein banding, cupping and necrosis of leaf lamina, brown lesions on branches and ring line pattern on fruits.

Chilly mosaic virus.   Mosaic mottling, reduced size and distortion of leaves (filiform) and plants become stunted.

Management.   The spread and severity of chilly mosaic depends on population and behaviour of vector (aphids). Management of aphid population by employing barrier crops (sunflower, sesame, corn, sorghum, pearl millet, snap bean) helps in reducing disease severity.

25.12.2   Chilly Leaf Curl

It is a serious disease of chillies and infection at early stages of plant growth may cause heavy damage. Disease is caused by tobacco leaf curl virus (Bigemini virus) consists of geminate isometric particles (18-20 nm in diameter), the virus has wide host range and is transmitted by white flies (*B. tabaci*). The leaves are reduced in size with curling of lamina, with pale yellow colour. The internodes are short and the plant gives stunted (witches broom) appearance. In severe infection, fruits may be rudimentary and distorted. The virus may survive on tobacco; tomato or papaya round the year and gets further spread is by white flies.

Management.   Since Gemini viruses are transmitted by white flies in persistent manner, timely spray (at regular interval) of insecticide is required to check the vector population. Spraying should be stopped 15-20 days before fruit harvest. Yellow traps may also reduce vector populations. Single gene (recessive) resistance is reported; several chilly cultivars show good level of resistance.

25.13 VIRAL DISEASES OF PEAS AND MANAGEMENT

25.13.1 Pea Enation Mosaic

The enation mosaic of pea is known to occur in USA, Germany, Holland, UK and India. The early infection may cause distortion and death while the surviving diseased plants show stunting and chloretic flecks. The name 'enation' comes from the tissue proliferations on infected pods and along leaf veins. The seeds from infected pods are reduced in size and of low quality. The pathogen, pea enation mosaic virus (PEMV) contains ssRNA. The virion consists of two types of 28 nm isometric particles. The PEMV is transmitted by aphids (pea aphid: *Acrythosiphon pisium*) in persistent manner. The host range of virus is restricted to legumes only, which include cicer, lathyrus, lens, lupins, medicago, phaseolus, trifolium and pisum. The aphid vectors play major role in annual spread while annual and perennial legume plants serve as virus reservoirs. The flights of aphids, during spring and early summer spread virus to surrounding fields. The management of PEMV can be achieved through use of tolerant cultivars and control of aphids by application of insecticides. Care should be taken to eradicate off-season reservoirs of PEMV.

25.13.2 Pea Seed Borne Mosaic

It is an important disease where virus is transmitted through seed at high frequency. This makes exchange of germplasm (seeds) a risky venture from quarantine point of view. The pea seed borne mosaic virus (PsbMV) is reported from the erstwhile Czechoslovakia, Yugoslavia, Canada, Poland, Switzerland, New Zealand, UK, India, Morocco and France (Maury and Khetrapal, 1992). The PsbMV infected pea seeds can be recognized by reduced size and necrotic symptoms on seed coat. The disease is reported to cause 10-35% reduction in yield. The initial symptoms include chlorosis and stunting of infected plants. The leaflets are narrow and show downward rolling (Figure 25.11). The apical malformation (no setting and tendril curling) is observed in late stages of disease development. The mosaic symptom may or may not be pronounced, though vein clearing is observed. Symptomless pea plants also carry PsbMV. The PsbMV (poty virus) is a flexuous particle (780 nm) containing ssRNA. It is transmitted through seeds (as the name indicates), aphid vectors (pea and potato aphids) and has a wide host range belonging to legume plants. Comparatively higher temperature (28-32°C) favour disease progress. The chances of seed transmission are increased if infection takes place before flowering.

Figure 25.11 Leaf roll symptoms induced by PsbMV on pea (Left, diseased and Right, healthy).

Management. Strict seed certification and quarantine measures should be adopted. The resistant variety may help in management of PsbMV.

25.14 VIRAL DISEASES OF BEAN AND MANAGEMENT

25.14.1 Bean Common Mosaic

Legumes are important group of dicotyledonous plants belonging to family Leguminosae, subfamily Papilionoidae has several plants of economic importance used for human food (vegetable and grain legumes). *Phaseolus vulgaris* (French or snap bean) is grown world over. Allen (1983) described important pathogen and their management of French bean. Bean common mosaic virus (BCMV) causes stunting, mottling and leaf malformation. Irregular shades of yellow or green are observed on infected leaves (Figure 25.12). Factors related with host (age), pathogen (strains) and environment might influence symptoms. BCMV may also produce leaf crinkling, chlorosis and dwarfing. The infected pods have few seeds of smaller size, which may be malformed or aborted. Virus has very wide host range (44 genera in 9 families). BCMV is flexuous filament (730-750 × 12-15 nm). The BCMV is transmitted by several species of aphids in non-persistent manner. The incidence of seed transmission is high (0-93%), which makes this virus an important one.

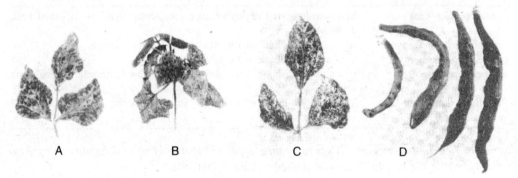

A   B   C   D

Figure 25.12   Symptoms caused by bean common mosaic virus, (A) BCMV, (B) BYMV, (C) UMV, (D) bean pods infected by BCMV.

Management

- Chemical (insecticides) control of aphid vectors
- Changes in cropping to avoid peak aphid activity periods
- Use of virus free healthy seeds
- Use of resistant cultivars

25.14.2 Bean Yellow Mosaic

The fields infected with bean yellow mosaic virus (BYMV) can be identified from distance. Foliar mosaic contrasting dark and yellowish green areas mixed with yellow sports are characteristic symptoms of disease (Figure 25.12). Variability in symptoms (mild and diffused mottle to coarse mosaic and rugosity) is associated with type of viral strains. In certain varieties necrotic spots, venial and apical necrosis, wilting and premature death may be recorded. Infected plants are stunted and give bushy appearance. BYMV (Poty virus) is elongated flexuous filament (750-780 × 11-15 nm). It is readily transmitted by sap and several aphid species in non-persistent manner but not through seeds. French bean and other collateral hosts have primary inoculum, which can assume epidemic proportion due to field spread by aphids.

Management

- Chemical control of aphids
- Elimination of collateral hosts

25.15 VIRAL DISEASES OF CUCUMBER AND MANAGEMENT

Cucumbers, comprising variety of fruits and vegetables, are affected by wide varieties of viruses/strains from different locations. The damage caused by these viruses varies from 10-15 to even 90%. Table 25.6 gives the summarized information on important viruses of cucumber.

Table 25.6 Symptoms of Some Viral Diseases of Cucumber

Virus/pathogen	Symptoms
(a) Cucumber mosaic virus	Severe wilting and drying of cucumber, (virus survives in wilted host, weeds, seeds).
(b) Cucumber green mottle virus	At low temp: green mosaic Above 25°C: white mosaic
(c) Cucumber ring spot virus	Yellow green mosaic with reduced growth.
(d) Water melon mosaic virus	Internodes shorting, severe mottling and dry brittle necrotic lesions along veins.
(e) Muskmelon mosaic virus	Yellow leaves green vein banding, increased curling, Necrotic spots and venial necrosis.

Management of cucumber viruses. Host resistance is not stable due to wide variability in viruses. Emphasis should be on healthy seed and suitable cultural methods.

25.16 SOME OTHER IMPORTANT PLANT DISEASES CAUSED BY VIRUSES

25.16.1 Yellow vein mosaic of Okra

Okra, (*Abelmoschus esculentus* L. Moench.) is common vegetable (Bhindi) extensively grown in different parts of world. Viral diseases are a serious threat to okra cultivation. Yellow vain mosaic, enation leaf curl, okra mosaic and okra leaf curl are some common viral diseases of okra. Yellow vein mosaic is most serious and 50-95% yield loss are reported in India. Disease is characterized by yellow network of veins and veinlets (Figure 25.13). The inter-venial area may become chlorotic, thus whole leaf becomes yellow. Fruits are yellowish green dwarfed and malformed with very low market value. The yellow vein mosaic virus (YVMV: Bigemini virus) measures 18 × 30 nm. YVMV is transmitted by white fly (*B. tabaci*). It is neither sap nor seed transmissible.

Figure 25.13 Yellow vein mosaic of okra.

Management. Efforts are being made to develop host resistance to YVMV but management of vector population is the only way out at present.

25.16.2 Bunchy Top of Banana

It is an important disease of banana, reported from all banana-growing areas, except Central and South America. Disease causes significant loss, as diseased plants produce no fruits. The leaves on disease plants show dark green streaks on petioles and veins while the margins show chlorosis. The top leaves are upright, narrow and closely packed, to give bunchy appearance. In case of early infection, the inflorescence and fruits do not emerge out of banana pseudostems. Banana bunchy top virus (BBTV) is present in petiole, midrib and veins. The phloem cells of BBTV infected plants produce a specific fluorescence. The virus also affects ornamental *Canna* sp. BBTV is ssDNA virus. Banana being vegetatively propagative (rhizome and suckers), provides the opportunity for long distance travel to virus. The field spread of BBTV is aided by banana aphids (*Pentalonia nigronervosa*) in persistent manner. Volunteer bananas/left over pseudostems support the large populations of viruliferous aphids. The management of BBTV has to be based on preventive measures. The production of virus free propagating material, control of aphid population and other cultural practices to keep banana plantation free of infected plants will help in disease management.

25.16.3 African Cassava Mosaic

Cassava is common source of carbohydrates in African and Asian countries. The cassava mosaic disease occurs in sub-Sahara Africa, India and certain island of southern Asia. It is known to cause yield losses up to 50%, annually losses upto 2 billion US Dollars are reported (Agrios, 1997). Infected cassava plants show mild to severe mosaic symptoms. The plants are stunted with narrow leaves and produce small tubers. African cassava mosaic virus is Gemini virus having two circular ssDNA. ACMV is transmitted by *Bemisia* spp. The replication of gemini virus genome in plant cells seems to take place through formation of double-stranded DNA intermediate via a rolling cycle mechanism. The use of virus free propagating material (stem cuttings) can help in management of ACMV. Planting new cassava crop at distance and with time interval from previous harvested crop may help to reduce severity of disease. Management of white fly population is another crucial aspect of disease management.

25.16.4 Citrus Tristeza

The disease (chronic tree decline) occurs in all citrus growing areas and on all kinds of citrus plants. The citrus tristeza virus affects both quality and quantity of citrus fruits. It also induces quick or chronic decline and ultimate death of infected trees. The rootstocks of sour orange, more susceptible to CTV, should be avoided for propagation. The disease is responsible for death of millions of citrus plants in South Africa, Argentina, Brazil, Colombia and Spain. Citrus aphid, *Toxoptera citricida*, is considered most efficient vector of CTV. The declining trees shed yellow leaves and later wilt (Figure 25.14). The severe strains of CTV may also cause stem pitting (longitudinal pits on wood below bark), the twigs become brittle and break easily. CTV is +ive sense ssRNA virus particle, thread like (2000 nm × 12 nm). CTV is transmitted by budding or grafting and by several aphids, semi-persistent manner. Management of CTV is difficult and warrants strict quarantine measures, where disease is absent. Only certified bud wood should be used for propagation. Sour orange rootstocks should be avoided (in Florida about 20 million citrus trees are raised on sour orange stocks). Citrus trees can be protected by employing cross protection; inoculation with mild CTV strains protects plants for long time against severe CTV strains. Bar-Joseph et al., (1989) reviewed information on management of citrus tristeza virus.

Figure. 25.14 Chronic decline of sweet orange tree.

25.16.5 Tungro Disease of Rice

It is a serious disease in South and South East Asia (Pakistan to Philippines). This degenerative disease of rice was reported from Japan (Rivera and Ou, 1965) and Southern and Southeast Asian countries, China and Italy. Characteristic symptoms of disease include stunting of rice plants, discolouration of leaves (yellowing) and reduced tillering (Figure 25.15). Certain varieties may show vein clearing or have small, rusty or necrotic spots. Rice tungro is caused by two distinct viruses.

Rice tungro bacilliform virus (RTBV) and *rice tungro spherical virus* (RTSV) are involved in disease development. RTSV has an isometric capsid, 30 nm in diameter (ssRNA) and RTBV has a bacilliform capsid (130 × 30 nm) having dsRNA. RTSV and RTBV have no serological relationship. Both RTBV and RTSV can multiply independently and both viruses are transmitted by green leafhopper (*Nephotettix virescems*). RTSV is transmitted independently while RTBV require RTSV or RTSV related helper factor for transmission by green leafhoppers. Limited transmission by *N. nigropictus* has also been reported. Both the adults and nymphs can transmit virus but adults are more efficient. The transmission by green leafhopper is non-persistent type.

Figure 25.15 Rice tungro disease.

The epidemics of rice tungro depend on varietal response, the virus strains and availability of viruliferous vectors. Several rice varieties carry virus with very mild or no symptoms, e.g., IR-20, IR-30, IR-36, IR-442-58, Vijoya, Cauvery, Ratna, Bala, Krishna, etc. (Mukhopadhyay, 1999). The viruses survive in diseased rice plants, which serve as reservoir. Two or three rice crops in a year may help the continuity of inoculum availability. As in West Bengal and Orrisa, spread of rice tungro is directly dependent on availability of viruliferous leafhoppers, i.e., for tungro epidemics to occur, presence of both rice tungro viruses and vector population is essential. The vector can spread virus from source plant upto a distance of 250 m.

Management. The strategy for rice tungro management has to be an integrated one, which should involve the following:

(a) **Eradication of source of virus.** Destruction of natural source(s) of primary inoculum (rice stubbles and other host plants) will help to contain the disease progress.

(b) **Cultural practices.** Suitable adjustment in crop calendar (intercrop period between rice crops), age of seedlings at transplanting time (to avoid vector population pressure) can be exploited for management of rice tungro. Safe distance (10 m) between seedbed and standing crop along with two insecticide applications in seedbed are recommended.

(c) **Host-resistance.** Several sources of resistance to tungro virus have been identified and utilized to breed tungro resistant variety of rice which are in cultivation. It has been reported that low level of disease in some cultivars is due to resistance to vectors (Rapusas and Heinrich, 1982).

(d) **Vector management.** Use of insecticides to keep vector population under check is important for field management of disease. There should be a monitoring system for recording population of green hoppers. The seedling should be kept free from vectors 45-50 days after transplanting, if need be, the insecticide should be applied. Satapathy and Anjaneyulu (1986) found cypermethrin and carbofuran very effective. Carbofuran as root zone application was superior to broadcast application in keeping green leafhopper and rice tungro disease under check.

Green leafhopper does fly and have definite nocturnal flight activity. They stick to host plant during daytime and disperse during night, i.e., 5 hr after sunset to 2 hr before sunrise (Mukhopadhyaya, 1997). This behaviour is related to the lunar periodicity. This behaviour should be critically examined for further exploitation of this information for management of tungro virus.

25.17 DISEASE CAUSED BY VIROIDS

25.17.1 Potato Spindle Tuber Disease

Potato spindle tuber disease was the first plant disease reported to be caused by viroids (Diner, 1971). The disease occurs in North America, Canada, Russia and South Africa and causes serious economic losses by affecting yield and quality of seed potato. Infected potato plants are dwarf and show erect habit, leaves are reduced in size and dark green. They are spindle shaped (Figure 25.16). The eyes are more prominent. Disease causes about 25% yield losses. Potato tuber spindle viroid (PSTV) consists of 359 nucleotides RNA. It is heat stable, as sap remains infectious after 10 minutes heating at 75-80°C. Thus heat treatment (dry/wet) will not eliminate PSTV from plant tissues. PSTV is

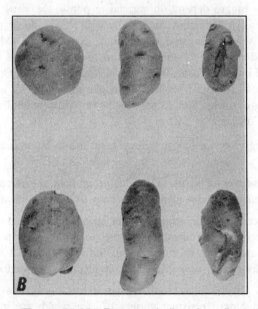

Figure 25.16 Potato spindle tuber disease.

mechanically transmitted, i.e. it spreads through workers' hands, clothes, machines, knives and other tools. Potato tubers, pollen and botanical seed (true potato seed-TPS) are also known to transmit PSTV. This makes potato spindle tuber disease and PSTV a significant case of quarantine significance. The grasshoppers, flea beetles and bugs, not considered to be vectors of PSTV, transmit PSTV by contaminated mouthparts. PSTV can be effectively managed by integrated practices like production of disease free seed, strict quarantine and seed certification, and suitable cultural practices to minimize field spread by mechanical means.

25.17.2 Coconut Cadang Cadang Disease

This premature decline of coconut palm was first reported from Philippines in 1937. Initial incidence was 25%, which gradually increased. Coconut and other related plants in Philippines are damaged, in millions, due to coconut cadang cadang (dying) viroids (CCCV). The disease is of great economic importance as it is annually killing about 1 million palm trees, a commodity of subsistence value for local population. Development of disease is very slow (10-15 years). The symptoms observed very late (after flowering). The leaves show yellow spots, coconuts become round, inflorescence is killed and plants do not produce fruits. In about 5-7 years, the growing bud dies, the crown falls and coconut trunk stands like a pole (Figure 25.17). Palm trees die 5 years before maturity, and new plantation takes 5-8 years to fruit. Thus, 13 years production is lost.

Figure 25.17   Early (E), medium (M) and late (L) stages of cadang cadang disease. Cocunut plantation seriously affected (Right side).

Management of CCCV has not been successful so far as the disease spreads slowly from the focus of infected plants (500 metres per year). The manifestation of symptoms is very slow. The leaves from infected palms are thinner with yellow spots on expanding leaves. Rasa (1968) reported phloem necrosis in apical meristem of diseased plants. There is reduction in front and crown size accompanied by slow growth. Inflorescences are not produced on infected trees.

Randles, et al. (1975) first detected two RNAs from infected palm trees, where infectivity was established in 1985 (Mohamed, et al.). Two associated RNAs with disease were isolated, which were monomeric and dimeric forms of CCCV, respectively. Both are naked, single stranded RNA, circular and infectious. The smaller (246/247 nucleotide molecules) is detected in young infected fronds and as disease progresses the larger (287/296/300/nucleotide molecules) are isolated more. In later stage of infection, after more than a year, only larger molecules are detected. Hanold and Randles (1991) described coconut cadang cadang and its viroid agent. The method of viroid replication is not known, however, with progress of disease and increase severity of disease a gradual increase in CCCV is observed. The frequency of seed transmission is low (17%). Exact means of CCCV spread is not known, probably, CCCV spreads by mechanical transmission or through pollen. The disease incidence/severity is related with age of plants. Incidence was negligible in plantation of age below 10 years; but after this a linear regression of incidence on age was observed cadang cadang. It can be considered as an endemic disease in Philippines but reaching epidemic proportion in certain established pockets (Albay province; 1951-1957).

Management.   No management recommendation at present, possible avenues for future may include:

Replanting.   Replacement of infected plants in new sites may help to sustain coconut production.

Eradication.   Removal of infected trees markedly reduce the rate of disease in initial years, which later picks up.

Resistance.   Development of field resistance may be very effective, efforts are on but no reasonable sources have been identified. Efforts are being made to produce viroid free seedlings, testing them by using electrophoresis and nucleic acid probes and planting in new distant locations.

25.17.3 Chrysanthemum Stunt

Dimock in 1947 described Chrysanthemum stunt as an infectious disease based on graft transmission. Stunt agent was found unusually heat stable and infectivity was not lost even after boiling of infectious extracts. But infectivity was lost by treating agent by RNase. Etiology of disease was established by Diener and Lawson (1973) who demonstrated that 'causal agent' was a low molecular weight RNA or a 'viroid'. The main **symptoms** include chloretic blotching on leaves, stunting, premature blooming, inferior flower quality and lack of root formation in cuttings. CSV is reported to be transmitted through sap. The CSV RNA has 356 nucleotide residues. CSV shares 60-70% nucleotide homology with PSTV.

Management.   The viroids generally get carried with planting material and are highly contagious. Thus, use of viroid free planting material, disinfecting all tools and hands (with 25% sodium hypochlorite) and use of proper cultivation practices are some useful means to contain spreads of diseases caused by viroids. Seed certification and quarantine regulation have helped in eradicating potato spindle tuber and chrysanthemum stunt viroids. Cross protection and thermotherapy are not effective in case of viroids, as in plant viruses.

REFERENCES

Agrios, G.N., 1997, *Plant Pathology*, 4th ed., Academic Press, New York.

Allen, D.J., 1983, *The Pathology of Tropical Food Legumes, Disease Resistance in Crop Improvement,* John Wiley and Sons, Chichester, p. 413.

Asakawa, Y., et al., 1993, Evaluation of the impact of the release of transgenic tomato plants with TMV resistance on the environment, *Jpn. Agric. Res. Quart,* 27:126-136.

Azam, K.M., Razvil, S.A., Zouba A. and AL-Raeesi, A.A., 1997, Management of whitefly (Bemisia tabaci Gennadius) and tomato leaf curl virus in tomato crop, *Arab. Near East Plant Prot. Newsl.* 25:27.

Bar-Joseph, M., Marcus, R. and Lee, R.F., 1989, The continuous challenge of citrus tristeza virus control, *Annu. Rev. Phytopathol,* 27:291-316.

Beachy, R.N., Loesche-fries, S. and Turker, N.E., 1990, Coat protein mediated resistance against virus infections, *Annu. Rev. Phytopathol,* 28:451–474.

Beekman, A.G.B., 1987, Breeding for resistance, *In: Viruses of Potatoes and Seed Potato Production* De Dokx JA and Van Der Want JPH, (Eds.), PUDOC, Wageningen, pp. 162-174.

Boss, L., 1983, Ecology and control of virus disease of plants: a critical synopsis, *Adv. Appl. Biol.,* 7:105-173.

Boss, L., 1978, Symptoms of Virus Diseases in Plants, Oxford and IBH Publishing Co., New Delhi, p. 225

Brown, C.R. and Smith, O.P., 2001, Genetically engineered potatoes, *In: Virus Insect Interactions,* Haris et al., (Eds.), Academic Press.

Chenulu, V.V., 1984, Plant virology in India—post, present and future, *Indian Phytopath.,* 37:1-20.

Clark, M.E., 1981, Immunosorbent assays in Plant Pathology, 27:291–316.

Diener T.O., Owens, R.A. and Hammond, R.W., 1993, Viroids: The smallest and simplest agents of infection disease, How do they make plant sick, *Intervirology,* 35:186-195.

Diener, T.O., 1972, Viroids, *Adv. Virus Res.,* 17:295-313.

Essau, K., 1967, Anatomy of plant virus infection, *Ann. Rev. Phytopathol.,* 5:45-70.

Garg, I.D., Khurana, S.M., Paul and Singh, M.N., 1990, Common weed reservoirs of potato viruses X, S and Y in Shimla hills, *Plant Dis. Res.* (Spl.), 5:84-86.

Gibbs, A.J. and Harrison, B.D., 1968, Realistic approaches to virus classification and nomenclature, *Nature,* 218:927-929.

Gibbs, A.J. and Harrison, 1976, Plant virology—The principles, Edward Arnold, p. 292

Gierer, A. and Schramm, G., 1956, Infectivity of ribonucleic acid from tobacco mosaic virus, *Nature,* 177:702-703.

Hamilton, R.L., 1974, Replication of plant viruses, *Ann. Rev. Phytopathol.,* 12:223-245.

Hanold, D. and Randles, J.W., 1991, Coconut cadang cadang disease and its viroid agent, *Plant Disease,* 75:330–335.

Harris, K.F., 1981, Arthropod and nematode vectors of plant viruses, *Ann. Rev. Phytopathol.,* 19: 391-426.

Hull, S.A., 1989, *Methods in Plant Virology,* Blackwell, Oxford.

Jayasinghe, U., Chuqullanqui, C. and Salazar, L.F., 1989, Modified expression on virus resistance in mixed virus infection, *Am. Potato J.,* 66:137-144.

Kalloo, G., Banerjee, M.K. and Dudi, B.S., 1986, Leaf curl virus resistance in tomato (*Lycopersicon* spp.), *Proc. Natl.Symp.New Horizons Resistance Breeding Vegetable Crops,* Jabalpur, India.

Kawchuk, L.M., Martin R.R. and McPherson, J., 1991, Sense and antisense RNA mediated resistance to potato leaf roll virus in russet Burnank potato plants, *Mol. Plant Microbe Interactions,* 4:247–253.

Khurana, S.M., Paul, 1997, Genetic manipulation of potato varieties for virus resistance, pp.173-180. *In: Glimpses in Plant Science,* K.R. Aneja, M.V. Charaya, A. Aggarwal, and D.K. Hans, (Eds.), Prof. R.S. Mahrotra, Comm. Vol.

Khurana, S.M., Paul and Garg, I.D., 1992, Potato mosaics, *In: Plant Diseases of International Importance,* Vol. II, H.S. Chaube, U.S. Singh, A.N. Mukhopadhyay, J. Kumar (Eds.), Prentice Hall Inc. New Jersey.

Khurana, S.M., Paul, 1999, Virus and virus-like disease of potato and their control, *In: Disease of Horticultural Crop* (Vegetables, Ornamental and Mushroom), L.R. Verma and R.C. Sharma, (Eds.), Indus Publication Company, New Delhi, pp. 82–120.

Khurana, S.M., Paul, Chandra, R. and Dhingra, M.K., 1996, Potato viruses and their eradication for production of virus free seed stocks, pp. 195-218, *In: Disease Scenario in Crop Plants,* Vol. I, Fruits and Vegetables, Agnihotri, V.P., Om Prakash, Ram Kishan and Mishra, A.K. (Eds.), IBPSS, New Delhi.

Khurana, S.M., Paul, 1992, Potato viruses and viral diseases, *Tech. Bull. No. 35,* CPRI, Shimla, p. 23.

Khurana, S.M., Paul, 1997, Genetic manipulation of potato varieties for virus resistance, *In: Glimpses in Plant Science,* K.R. Aneja, M.V. Charaya, A. Agarwal, and D.K. Hans (Eds.), Prof. R.S. Mehrotra, Comm. Vol. 1, pp. 173-180.

Kim, J.W., Sun, S.S.M. and German, T.L., 1994, Disease resistance in tobacco and tomato plants transformed with tomato spotted with virus necleocapsid gen, *Plant Dis.,* 78:615-621.

Kunik, T., et al., 1994, Transgenic tomato plants expressing the tomato yellow leaf curl virus capsid protein are resistant to virus, *Bio/Technology,* 12, 500-504.

Mandhar, C.L. and Khurana, S.M., Paul, 1998, Role of biotechnology in controlling plant diseases, *In: Pathological Problems of Economic Crops: Plants and Their Management,* Khurana, S.M., Paul (Eds.), pp. 637–648, Scientific Publishers, Jodhpur.

Maury, Y. and Khetrapal, R.K., 1992, Pea seed-borne mosaic virus, *In: Plant Diseases of International Importance,* Vol. II , H.S. Chaube and U.S. Singh (Eds.), Prentice Hall, New Jersey, 377.

Mitra, M., 1929, Report of the imperial mycologist scientific reports of the agricultural research institute, Pusa, pp. 58-71,

Pushkarnath, 1967, Seed potato production in the sub-tropical plains of India, *Am. Potato J.,* 44:429-441.

Randles, J.W., Boccardo, G. and Imperial, J.S., 1975, Detection of the cadang-cadang RNA in African oil palm and buri palm, *Phytopathol.,* 65, 163,

Rapusas, H.R. and Heinrich, E.A., 1982, Plant age and levels of resistance to green leafhopper, *Nephotettix virescens* (Distant), and tungro virus in rice varieties, *Crop Prot.,* 1:91.

Rasa, E.A., 1968, Anatomic effects of cadang-cadang disease on coconuts, *Plant Dis. Rep.*, 52, 734.

Rivera, C.T., and Ou, S.H., 1965, Leafhopper transmission of tungro disease of rice, *Plant Dis. Rept.*, 49:127.

Rocca, W.M. No. Espinoza, Roca, M.R. and Bryan, J.E. 1978, A tissue culture method for rapid propagation of Potatoes, *Ann. Potato J,* 55:691-701.

Satapathy, M.K. and Anjaneyulu, A., 1986, Prevention of rice tungro virus disease and control of the vector with granular insecticides, *Ann. Appl. Biol.*, 108:503.

Sharma, P.K., 1999, *Identification and Management of Viruses infecting Tomato in Himachal Pradesh*, Ph.D. Thesis, UHF, Solan, India, p.129.

Singh, R.A. and Khurana, S.M., Paul, 1993, Viral and allied disease of potato, pp. 491-528, *In: Advances in Horticulture. Potato*, Vol. 7, K.L. Chandha and J.S. Grewal (Eds.), Malhotra Publ. House, New Delhi.

Singh, R.S., 1989, *Plant Pathogens: The viruses*, p. 176, Sarita Prakashan, New Delhi.

Trivedi, T.P., et al., 1998, Development of forewarning system for aphids, *Myzus persicae* on potato, *In: Proc. Entomology in 21st Century*, RCA, Udaipur, p. 256.

Verma, A.K. and Vashisth, K.S., 1985, Manipulation of planting and haulms cutting dates for better health standards in seed potato crop, *Indian J. Virol.*, 1:54-60.

26 Mollicutes and Plant Diseases

26.1 INTRODUCTION

Mollicutes is a class of pathogens, which contain prokaryotic cells that lack walls. In 1967, Doi and co-workers found wall-less microorganism in phloem cells of mulberry plants showing yellows type symptoms. Later, they were also reported to be occurring in other diseased plants such as potato witches broom, aster yellows and paulownia witches broom and also inside bodies of insect vectors. More than 200 plant diseases are caused by mollicutes. These diseases were earlier described to be caused by viruses. Maramorosch and Raychaudhuri (1981) described diseases caused by mycoplasmas in plants. The observed wall less mollicutes were initially called Mycoplasma like organisms (MLOs) due to their resemblance to mycoplasmas. Bove (1984) described walliess prokaryotes in plants. Later mollicutes associated with diseased plants were grouped into phytoplasmas and Spiroplasmas.

26.2 PHYTOPLASMAS AND PLANT DISEASES

Round to elongated mollicutes (Plate 26.1) have been found in diseased plants, e.g. aster yellows, apple proliferation, apricot chlorotic leaf roll, coconut lethal yellowing, elm yellows, peach yellows, pear decline, big bud diseases of solanaceous plants, grape yellows, X-disease of peach, etc. Phytoplasmas can not be grown on artificial nutrient medium and so far Koch's postulates have not been established in "true sense", i.e., by inoculating phytoplasmas from diseased plant, no disease could be reproduced in healthy plants.

The phytoplasmas lack cell walls and are bound by unit cell membrane, which surrounds the cytoplasm containing ribosomes and nuclear material (unorganized nucleus of prokaryotic cells). They may be spheroidal or ovoid, tubular or filamentous. They can be separated from intact phloem sieve tubes of diseased plants by using cell wall degrading enzymes (cellulase). They can also be detected in sieve tubes by dark-field light microscopy. The ultra structure of phytoplasmas reveals the following:

1. A triple layered membrane (7.5–10 nm in width).
2. Cytoplasm containing ribosomes and fibrillar strands of nuclear material.
3. There are no other organelles in cytoplasm.

The major symptoms produced by phytoplasmas include yellowing or reddening of leaves, smaller leaves, shortening of internodes and stunting of the plants, excessive proliferation of shoots and production of witches brooms, sterility of flowers, rapid dieback, decline and death of plants. The accumulations of cellulose in sieve tubes and necrosis have been reported during pathogenesis.

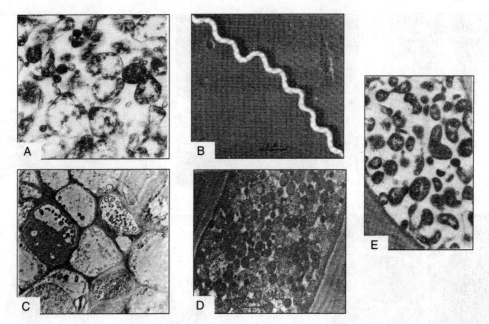

Plate 26.1 (A) Typical large mycoplasma like bodies bound by a unit membrane and containing standards resembling DNA. The smaller particles contain ribosomes, (B) replicative form of *Spiroplasma citri* isolated from stubborn-infected citrus. Platinum shadowing from a log-phase culture fixed with glutaraldehyde, (C) distribution of the peach yellow phytoplasma within vascular tissues of diseased cherry showing symptoms, (D) longitudinal section of a sieve cell profusely filled with MLOs, (E) several polymorphic phytoplasmas and some apparently undergoing binary fission or budding.

Significant changes in hormonal status are supposed to be responsible for stunting/proliferation/ witches broom/big bud type symptoms (Plate 26.2).

The transmission of phytoplasmas involves insect vectors (leaf hoppers, psyllids and plant hoppers), and phytoplasmas can be detected in the body tissues of insect vectors. The vectors require long incubation period (10-45 days), which may be influenced by prevailing temperature. The vectors, once acquire, can transmit phytoplasmas throughout their life. The pathogen survives the moults, but do not pass through eggs. Thus, the nymphs must feed on infected plants to transmit the pathogen. Good amount of information has been developed on serological and nucleic acid techniques and being used for detection, identification, classification and management of diseases caused by phytoplasmas (Prince, et al., 1993). Specific antibodies, DNA probes, RFLP profiles have been extremely useful (Sinha and Chiykowski, 1984).

The management of diseases caused by phytoplasmas should involve direct as well as indirect measures. The mollicutes are sensitive to antibiotics (tetracycline group). The application of these antibiotics may delay the appearance or suppress the symptoms but the symptom soon reappears when the treatment is stopped. Soil and foliar treatment of infected plants in growth chambers (30-37°C) or dipping dormant parts in hot water (30-50°C) are effective methods for curing plant/ plant parts. Since phytoplasmas are transmitted through insect vectors, the management of vector

Plate 26.2 Symptoms of phytoms of phytoplasmal plant diseases, (A) on carrots. Note thte bushy tops and the stunted, hairy, tapered roots of the infected carrots, (B) on onion. diseased flower cluster showing varying degrees of distortion and sterility, (C) sweet orange trees showing extreme dwarfing, (D) corn stunt disease. plant showing chlorotic streaks, stunted growth, proliferation and sterile tassel, (E) corn stunt spiroplasmas as seen in phloem tissue, (F) Lethal yellowing affected coconut palm in late stage of decline.

population may help in containing diseases as well as losses. Suitable cultural practices, e.g., weeding, altering, sowing and harvesting time may reduce the yield losses.

26.2.1 Aster Yellows

The phytoplasmas induce general yellowing and dwarfing in plants such as carrots, onion, tomato and lettuce. The hormonal alternations during pathogenesis also induce symptoms like abnormal production of shoots, malformation of organs and sterility of flowers, thereby, reducing the quality and quantity of yield. Losses may be 10-20 to 80-90 per cent. This disease is more damaging in carrots where it also causes unpleasant flavour. The phytoplasmas are present in phloem tissue, sieve tubes, from where they are picked up by leafhoppers, which play important role in disease development. Budding or grafting can also transmit the pathogen. Phytoplasmas survive in perennial ornamentals. There is more reliance on host resistance supported by management of vectors and weed plants.

26.2.2 Lethal Yellowing of Coconut

The coconut palm trees infected by phytoplasmas decline and die showing yellowing symptoms. Diseased trees have premature fruit drop also. The inflorescence is also affected (flowers die). The yellowing is observed on lower leaves. The death of vegetative bud leads to toppling of entire top crown and trunks remains standing like poles. The phytoplasmas are present in phloem tissue from where plant hopper (*Myndus crudus*) is believed to transmit the pathogen. Injecting antibiotics (tetracycline) and use of resistant plant type can help in reducing the damage by disease.

26.2.3 Peach X-Disease

The initial symptoms are seen on leaves (reddish/purple spots), which later form short holes, by dropping the dead tissue. The leaves show yellowing, reddening and roll upward. Later, leaf fall takes place, which is followed by fruit drop from infected branches. The pathogen, a phytoplasma, present in phloem tissue is transmitted by several species of leaf hopper of genera *Colladonus* and *Scaphytopius*. Budding or grafting also contributes in transmission of pathogen. General control measures like use of healthy buds and resistant rootstock, management of vector and weed populations may help in management of disease. The tetracycline injections may temporarily suppress the symptoms.

26.2.4 Pear Decline

Disease is common in North America and Europe. The phytoplasmas may cause slow and progressive decline or a quick, sudden wilting and death of pear trees. Between 1959-1962 the disease was catastrophic, killed more than 1 million pear trees in California. The slow decline is characterized by progressive weakness of trees. The leaves are few, pale green or turn reddish in late summer before dropping prematurely. Blossoms are few with very less number of small fruits. Feeder roots also die, leading to death of plants. In slow decline it takes few years before death of plant while in quick decline or sudden wilting (within few weeks) there is degeneration of phloem tissue. The phytoplasma, in phloem tissues, are transmitted by budding or grafting and by pear psylla (*Psylla pyricola*), which is responsible for natural spread of disease.

26.3 SPIROPLASMAS AND PLANT DISEASES

Mollicutes associated with plant diseases having spiral or helical structure (Plate 26.1) were called **spiroplasmas**, e.g., citrus stubborn and corn stunt. Spiroplasmas have been grown on artificial nutrient media and inoculations on healthy plants have resulted in diseases development. The agents causing citrus stubborn and corn stunt are placed in genus *Spiroplasma*, within the class mollicutes (Tully and Whitcomb, 1983).

The mollicutes that have spiral or helical morphology were termed as **spiroplasmas.** The agents causing citrus stubborn and corn stunt are described under genus *Spiroplasma*, class Mollicutes. *Spiroplasma citri*, causal agent of citrus stubborn, has also been reported in other plants like crucifers, lettuce and peach. The spiroplasma cells (100-240 nm in diameter) may be spiral or helical and branched, non-helical filamentous during active growth phase. They lack true walls, surrounded by unit membrane and multiply by fission. Helical filamentous spiroplasmas are motile.

Spiroplasmas, unlike phytoplasmas, can be grown on artificial nutrient media. They produce 0.2 mm diameter colonies, which have fried egg appearance. Spiroplasmas are resistant to penicillin but sensitive to tetracycline. They are transmitted by insect vectors.

L-form bacteria. The normal bacteria often produce mutants or variants that lack cell wall. The cell wall synthesis may be inhibited, *in vitro* or *in vivo,* due to presence of some cell wall inhibiting drugs (penicillin). This L-form bacterium resembles the mycoplasmas or phytoplasmas and may revert back to normal walled cells anytime. The plant pathogenic bacteria which produce L-form include *Erwinia caratovora* pv. *Atroseptica.*

26.3.1 Citrus Stubborn Disease

This disease of citrus/sweet oranges and grape fruit is a serious threat in hot and dry areas, e.g. Mediterranean countries, South Western United States (California), Brazil and Australia. Due to the slow progress of disease the infected plants live for long time but there is drastic reduction in yields. The infected trees show bunchy, upright growth of twigs and branches, with short internodes and excessive number of shoots. The die-back in affected twigs is also observed. Plants are stunted; the leaves are small, mottled and chlorotic and fall during winters. Only few fruits are produced, which are small with thin rind and show prominent greening. The fruits drop prematurely. The seeds, inside affected trees, are poorly developed or aborted.

The pathogen, *Spiroplasma citri,* is confined in phloem sieve tubes. They are spherical to ovoid or elongated. The pathogen grows best at 30-32°C (range is 20-37°C) and is highly sensitive to tetracycline and insensitive to penicillin. *S. citri* is transmitted by budding and grafting. The natural spread is by several leafhoppers (*Circulifer tenellus, Scaphytopius nitrides* and *Meoaliturus haemoceps).* The management of the disease should involve use of pathogen free budwood and root stocks. Tetracycline, though experimentally proved effective but not used at commercial scale for disease management.

26.3.2 Corn Stunt

The disease of corn is confined in USA. The infected plants show yellowing streaks on young leaves, which later turn more yellow to reddish purple. Plants are stunted due to short internodes. The small ears bear few or no seeds. The tassels are usually sterile. Roots of infected plants are proliferated. The pathogen is similar to agent causing citrus stubborn. Chen and Liao (1975) described different aspects of corn stunt including pathogenicity. The spread of disease under field conditions is facilitated by leafhoppers (*Dalbulus elimatus* and *D. maydis*) with incubation period of 2-3 weeks. Host resistance (hybrid corn) is the only practical measure for disease management.

REFERENCES

Bove, J.M., 1984, Wallless prokaryotes of plants. *Annu. Rev. Phytopathol.*, 22:361-396.

Chen, T.A. and Liao, C.H., 1975, Corn stunt spiroplasma: isolation, cultivation and proof of pathogenicity. *Science*, 88:1015-1017.

Da Graca, J.V., 1991, Citrus greening diseases. *Annu. Rev. Phytopathol.,* 29:109-136.

Doi, Y., et al., 1967, Mycoplasm or PLT group like microorganisms found in the phloem elements of plants infected with mulberry dwarf, potato witches-broom, aster yellows, or paulownia witches' broom, *Ann. Phytopathol., Soc. Jpn.,* 33:259-266.

Maramorosch, K. and Raychaudhuri, S.P., 1981, *Mycoplasma Diseases of Trees and Shrubs,* Academic Press, New York.

Nienhaus, F. and Sikora, R.A., 1979, Mycoplasmas, spiroplasmas and rickettasia like organisms as plant pathogens, *Annu. Rev. Phytopathol.,* 17:37-58.

Prince, J.P., et al., 1993, Molecular detection of diverse mycoplasma like organisms (MLOs) associated with grapevine yellows and their classification with aster yellows, X-diseases and elm yellows MLOs, *Phytopathology,* 83:1130-1137.

Sinha, R.C. and Chiykowski, L.N., 1984, Purification and serological detection of mycoplasma like organism from plants affected by peach eastern X-disease, *Can. J. Plant Pathol.,* 6:200-205.

Tully, J.G. and Whitcomb, R.F., 1983, The genus *Spiroplasma., In: Phytopathogenic Bacteria,* M.P. Starr (Ed.), p. 2271, Springer-Verlag, Berlin and New York.

27 Nematodes and Plant Diseases

27.1 GENERAL CHARACTERISTICS

27.1.1 Morphology

With some exceptions, adult plant parasitic nematodes are elongated worms ranging in length from about 0.30 mm to over 5.0 mm. The anterior end tapers to a rounded or truncated lip regions, the body is more or less cylindrical, and posterior end tapers to a terminus, which may be pointed or hemispherical (Figure 27.1). Proportions of the elongated body vary greatly, some species being

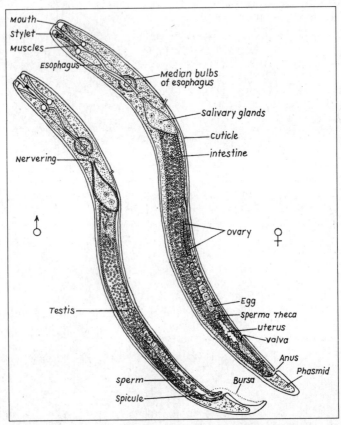

Figure 27.1 Morphology and main characteristics of male and female plant parasitic nematodes.

more than 50 times longer than wide, others being only about 10 times longer than wide. Females have greatly expanded bodies, sometimes nearly spherical but always with a distinct neck (Plate 27.1). The adult males are always slender worms. Plant parasitic nematodes have no appendages. The mouth of a nematode is at anterior end, and the terminus is at the posterior end. The excretory pore, vulva and anus are on the ventral side and the opposite side are called **dorsal** (Figure 27.1). The right and left sides are called **lateral**. The cuticle is attached to several other layers of tissue which are separated laterally, dorsally and ventrally by chords. These contain nerves, excretory organ and separate four bands of muscles, which move the body.

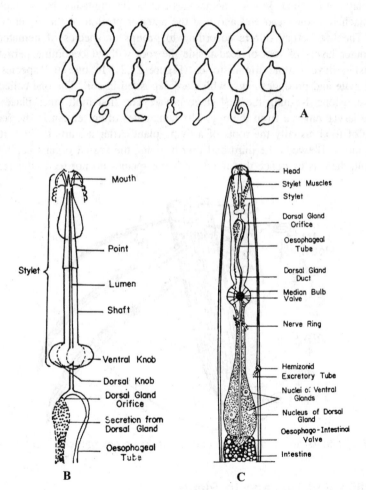

Plate 27.1 (A) Shapes of female nematodes, (B) stylet and associated structures, (C) anterior end.

27.1.2 Reproductive System

Reproductive system of plant parasitic nematodes is of three general types, varying with species, in hermaphroditic species, the female produces both eggs and sperms. In parthenagentic species, the eggs develop without fertilization. The sex ratio varies according to reproduction types. It ranges from about equal number of males and females in species, which are bisexual to very few or no males, which are hermaphroditic, or parthenagentic. Some bisexual species may also reproduce parthenogenetically.

27.1.3 Life Cycle

The life history of plant parasitic nematodes is usually very simple, with five distinct stages, the first four of which end in a molt. Nematodes molt by forming a new cuticle, after which the old cuticle may or may not be shed. Molting nematodes can be distinguished by the fact that the cuticle is not closely attached at the head end and that the anterior portion of the stylet is attached to the molted cuticle. The life-history differs according to groups or species of nematodes. Nematodes which feed on outer layers of root or feed inside the root without becoming permanently attached (migratory parasite) have simple life histories (Figure 27.2). In bisexual species, the female is fertilized by the male and produces eggs, which are deposited in soil. The one-celled egg undergoes a series of cell divisions, forming the first stage larvae. The first molt takes place in the egg, and the second stage larvae emerge from the egg. The nematodes often remain in the second stage until it finds a source of food, usually the roots of a living plant. After it starts to feed, it passes through three additional molts. Between the third and fourth molts, the sexual organs begin to develop; and at the fourth molt, there is evidence that males of some species do not feed after reaching the adult stage.

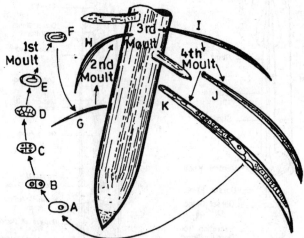

Figure 27.2 Life cycle of migratory endoparasitic or ectoparasitic nematode species.

27.1.4 Feeding and Damage to Plants

The mechanical injury directly inflicted upon plants by the nematodes during feeding is slight. Most of the damage seems to be caused by secretion injected into plants while the nematodes are feeding. This secretion called *Saliva* is produced in three glands from which it flows forward into the oesophagus and then injected through the stylet. Some nematodes are such rapid feeders that in a matter of few minutes they pierce a cell, inject saliva, withdraw the cell contents, and move on. Others feed more leisurely and may remain at the same juncture for hours or a whole day.

Members of family *Heteroderidae*, show the greatest morphological adaptation to parasitism. At the feeding site, a group of cells develop into characteristic synchytia around the head of the parasite. The cytoplasm becomes dense and the size of nuclei and nucleoli enlarges considerably. The cell walls are usually altered. Species of *Meloidogyne* induce hyperplasia in the pericycle, which results in the formation of galls. *Heterodera* species do not induce excessive/extensive hyperplasia. *Nacobbus* sp. forms galls on sugarbeet roots due to hypertrophy of cortex and epidermal cells.

Synchytial mass is formed by the alteration of cells immediately adjacent to the nematode's head and extends longitudinally along the root (Plate 27.2). In *Heterodera* infection synchytium is formed as a result of the enlargement of nuclei, incomplete dissolution of cell walls, disintegration of nucleoli, thickening of cell walls and by the cytoplasm becoming dense and granular (Plate 27.2). Giant cells of *Meloidogyne* are formed as a result of the enlargement of nuclei and the cells become polyploid and undergo synchronous mitosis. The cytoplasm of these cells becomes granular and new cells are incorporated by cell wall dissolution. The walls of the synchytium become thickened and the cells of pericycle divide repeatedly (Plate 27.2).

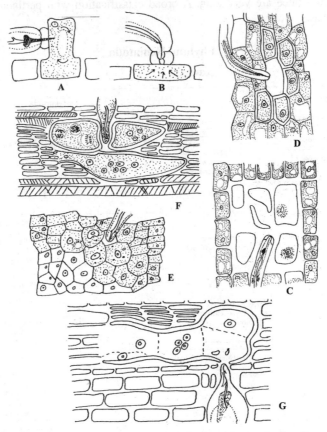

Plate 27.2 (A) No visible destructive effect, (B) immediate removal of cell content, (C) cell lysis, (D) nurse cells of Tylenchulus, (E) Synchytium of Nacobbus, (F) Synchytium of Heterodera, (G) Giant cells of Meloidogyne.

27.2 THE CLASSIFICATION

Plant parasitic nematodes are distinguished from non-parasitic forms by the presence of a stylet. For convenience, nematode parasites of plants are sometimes classified as endoparasites or ectoparasites, and as sedentary or migratory. Taxonomically, plant parasitic nematodes are classified in two large groups. About 1000 of the approximately 1100 described species belong to the order Tylenchida. The reminder belongs to Dorylaimida. The differences between the two is based essentially on the structure of stylet and of the oesophagus, though there are many other differences, for example, Tylenchida always have annulus, where as Dorylaimida do not. Most Tylenchida have stylets with knobs. An oesophageal tube is attached to the stylet, and they have a median bulb with valve. While there is great variation in size and shape of the stylet, the oesophageal tube, and the median bulb, they are nearly always present and easy to see. They are absent or very difficult to see in males of some genera, such as *Radopholus*, *Pratylenchus*, *Hemicycliophora* and *Criconemoides*. The plant parasitic nematodes of the Dorylaimida group have an entirely different type of oesophagus. It consists of a narrow anterior portion and a thicker posterior portion, and is without valve. The four plant parasitic genera of this group are *Xiphinema*, *Longidorus*, *Paralongidorus*, and *Trichodorus*. The stylets of the first three are very long. A broad classification with pertinent examples is given in the following chast:

Phylum–Nematoda

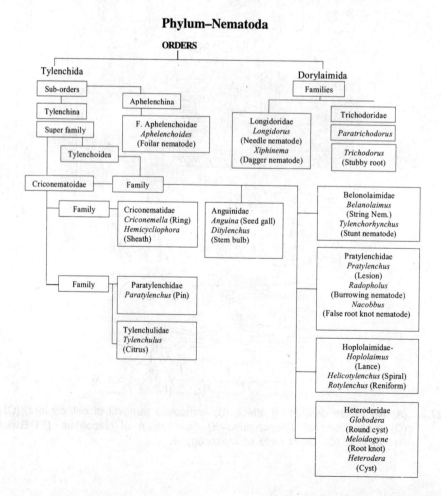

27.3 IMPORTANT PARASITIC NEMATODES AND PLANT DISEASES

27.3.1 Cyst Nematodes: *Globodera* and *Heterodera*

Cyst nematodes cause variety of diseases. The round cyst nematode, known as **golden nematode**, that is particularly severe on potato, tomato and brinjal is *Globodera rostochiensis*. *Heterodera* is another cyst nematode. Important hosts of this nematode are cereals (*H. avenae*), soyabeans (*H. glycines*), sugarbeet (*H. schachtii*), tobacco (*H. tabacum*), clover (*H. trifolii*), etc.

Beet cyst nematode. *Heterodera Schachtii* is widely distributed throughout the temperate zones of the world and has been found in almost all areas where sugarbeet is grown intensively. The nematode also affects spinach and crucifers. The nematode causes yield losses of 25 to 50% or more, especially in warmer climates or late planted crops.

Symptoms. Damage to sugarbeet crops usually first becomes apparent to the growers are a patch or patches of plants that wilt readily in warm weather (Figure 27.3). Severely affected plants are stunted and giving them a bearded appearance (Figure 27.3). Infestation can usually be confirmed in the field by the presence of white or brown females or cysts which are attached to the roots and just visible to the naked eyes. Other symptoms include an elongation of the petioles and reduction of leaf size.

Figure 27.3 *Heterodera schachtii* on sugarbeet (A) patch of wilting, stunted plants in a heavily infested field, (B) affected plant showing excessive lateral root formation, (C) white and brown cysts on lateral roots.

The pathogen.   *H. Schachtii* is the type species of the genus *Heterodera*. The cysts (Plate 27.3) are the most easily recognized stage in the life cycle of *H. schachtii* and together with its enclosed eggs and juveniles is the most useful for diagnostic purpose. It is brown and lemon shaped with a prominent neck anteriorly and a vulval cone posteriorly. Other morphological details are illustrated in Plate 27.3.

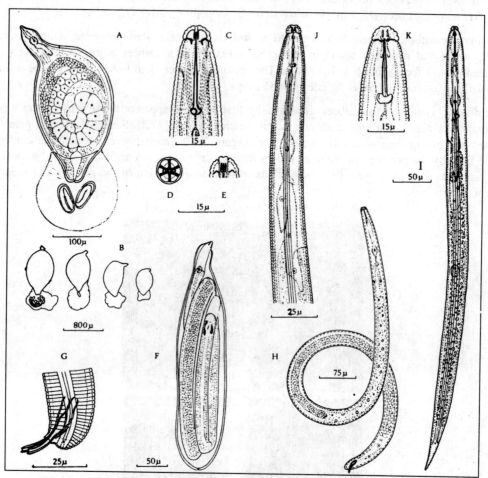

Plate 27.3 Morpholoyg of *Heterodera schachtii,* (A) adult female with egg sac, (B) cysts with egg sacs, (C) head of male showing anterior and posterior cephalids, (D) end on view of male head, (E) dorsoventral view of male head showing amphid opening, (F) fourth stage of male molting, (G) male tail, (H) male, (I) male esopageal region, (J) head of second stage juvenile, (K) second stage infective juvenile. (*Source:* M.T., Fraklin, *Heterodera schachtii*, Description of Plant Parasitic Nematodes, set 1, no. 1, Commonwealth Institute of Helminthology, 1972).

The resistant stage in the life history of *H. schachtii* is the brown cyst, in which upto 600-second stage juveniles, each enclosed in an egg cell, can remain dormant in the soil (Figure 27.4). The juveniles hatch from the egg by cutting a slit in the shell and escape into the soil. Hatching can occur over a wide range of temperatures but the optimum is 20-25°C and least at and below 10°C. In waterlogged soils hatch is decreased. The root exudates of all host crops of *H. schachtii* appear to contain hatching factors. Hatching is also stimulated by root exudates from some non-host plants. Other stages in the life cycle of the nematode are shown in Figure 27.4.

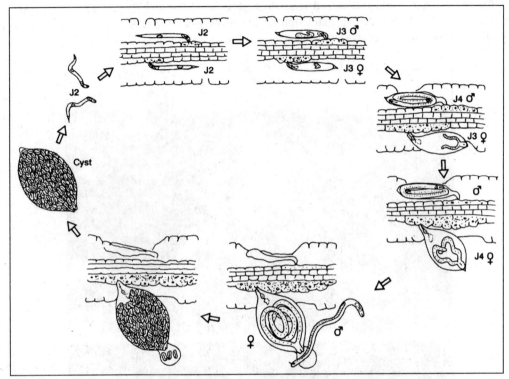

Figure 27.4 Schematic representation of life cycle of *Heterodera schachtii*. (Redrawn after a diagram by F. Grundler).

Management. Control of sugarbeet nematode is based on several practices:

- Early sowing so that plants can grow as much as possible at temperatures at which the nematodes are relatively inactive
- Crop rotation with alfalfa, cereals, or potatoes which are non-host of *H. schachtii*
- Fumigation with nematicides

Soyabean cyst nematode. Among the nematode parasites of plants, cyst nematode is one of the most devastating. Soyabean production in many areas of the world is reduced by cyst nematode. Cyst nematode's adaptability, capacity to survive for long periods without a host and reproductive ability in the presence of host make it a serious threat to crop production and very difficult to control. *Heterodera glycines* was discovered in United States in 1954, it is now present in 27 countries.

Symptoms. Soyabean cyst nematode feeding disrupts the function of the soyabean root and reduces its ability to translocate water and nutrients to the top of the plant. Severely damaged plants are stunted, discoloured (leaves may be yellow green) and look unthrifty (Figure 27.5). Leaves of infected plants wilt more readily than those of healthy plants in the mid-day summer sun and may defoliate prematurely. Infected roots are stunted, necrotic and usually have fewer rhizobium nodules than healthy roots. Reduced nodulation enhances foliar yellowing because the plants are staved for nitrogen. The most characteristic symptom of this disease is the presence of cysts attached to the root. Cysts are small, white-yellow and protrude slightly from the root (Figure 27.5). Old cysts are brown and usually detach during extraction of the roots from the soil. Yields may be reduced depending on the amount of nematode damage, and some plants may die.

Figure 27.5 (A) (Left) Susceptible soyabean cultivar showing typical symptoms of *Heterodera glycines* damage. (Right) Resistant cultivar, (B) white cysts of *Heterodera glycines* and brown *Rhizobium* nodules attached to soyabean roots. (After Wrather and Rao-Arelli, 1992)

The pathogen. *Heterodera glycine* is a member of the order *Tylenchida* and family *Heteroderidae*. All of the more than 45 species in this genus are characterized by cyst-forming females; *cyst* refers to the hard walled body of the female that encapsulates her eggs. The egg is ca. 100×47 μm, the second-stage juveniles 450×18 μm, the mature male 1300×30 μm, and the cyst 47-790 × 210-580 μm. Variations in size may be due to the host, environment, and the qualitative or quantitative structures of the nematode population.

Management. A quarantine enacted in 1957 to prevent the spread of this pest did not work. Soyabean cyst nematode can move through the soil only a few centimetres a year on its own efforts but gets easily spread over long distances in soil. Anything that moves soil is capable of moving cysts, and that includes wind, water, machinery and animals. The quarantine was lifted in 1972. Damage due to *Heterodera glycines* can be managed by planting resistant cultivars, practicing crop rotation, and temporarily protecting the young plants from *H. glycines* by nematicides. The grower must take many factors into account when deciding which single measure or combination to use, but the final decision is based on economics.

Crop rotation. Alternate planting of susceptible and non-host crops are an effective measure for controlling *H. glycines*. Planting a non-host crop for one to two years results in a decrease in soybean cyst nematode populations and an increase in yields of subsequent soyabean crops.

Nematicides. Farmers may need to use nematicides for control of *H. glycines* if resistant cultivars are not available. The use of fumigant nematicides—halogenated aliphatic hydrocarbons (e.g., ethylene dibromide)—has been suspended by the EPA. Non-fumigant nematicides such as oxime carbamates (e.g.,aldicarb) and carbamates (e.g., carbofuran) can be used for control of soyabean cyst nematode. The non-fumigants move with water through the soil and kill larvae on contact or disrupt their behaviour (movement, root penetration, etc.).

Biological control. Natural enemies of soyabean cyst nematode offer considerable promise in managing nematode populations. Hartwig (1981) observed a decline in soyabean cyst nematode populations after five years of continuous cropping with a susceptible cultivar and speculated that decline was due to a parasite. Fungi such as *Fusarium oxysporum*, *F. solani* and *Exophiala pisciphila* have been found to infect eggs and cysts in Alabama.

27.3.2 Root Knot of Vegetables

Root-knot nematodes, due to their worldwide distribution, exceedingly wide host range and interactions with other plant pathogens, are one of the major groups of plants parasitic nematodes affecting the world's food production. Root-knot disease is common on an array of economically important crops. The attacked crops suffer both quantitatively and qualitatively. Vegetables are the most preferred group of host crops of root-knot nematodes in different agroclimatic zones of the world.

Out of nearly 72 species of *Meloidogyne* described, the four major species are worldwide in distribution. *M. incognita* with its four races (Races 1, 2, 3 and 4), *M. javanica*, *M. arenaria* with its two races (Races 1, 2) and *M. hapla* attack vegetables commonly in various parts of the world. *M. incognita* and *M. javanica* are more prevalent species on vegetable crops than *M. arenaria* and *M. hapla*. *M. incognita* is most common.

Many vegetable crops belonging to the families Solanaceae, Cucurbitaceae, Fabaceae, Liliaceae, Chenopodiaceae, Asteraceae, Apiaceae, Brassicaceae, and Malvaceae suffer great damage due to root-knot nematodes in subtropics and Mediterranean climates. *M. incognita* cause yield losses of about 50% to canning tomato in southern Italy and to table tomato in Malta. Yield losses of 30 to 60% in eggplant resulted from attack of *M. incognita* in southern Italy. Cucumber, squash and vegetables marrow are severely damaged by *M. incognita* wherever grown. Occasionally, crops of cucumber are completely destroyed. Okra, sweet potato and carrots are also attacked severely. *M. javanica* is another species which affects various vegetables such as tomato, eggplant, beans, squash, okra, carrot, etc. on subtropical and Mediterranean climates. *M. arenaria* is also a problem on vegetables under such climate conditions.

Symptoms. The root-knot disease develops with the formation of giant cells and ancillary hypertrophy and hyperplasia of adjacent cells resulting in root galling. Root galls or knot are the most recognizable and characteristic symptoms of the disease (Plate 27.4).

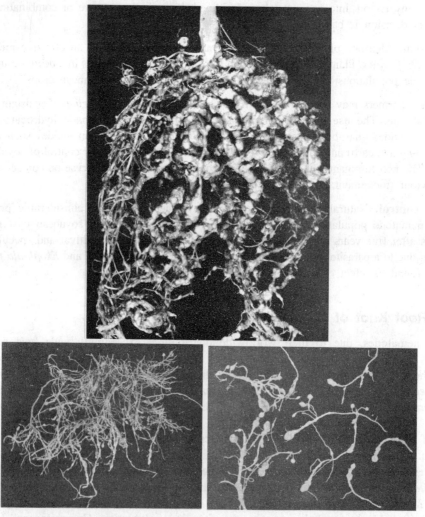

Plate 27.4 Symptoms and root knot caused by *Meloidogyne*.

Heavily infected roots become shorter with fewer branched roots and root hairs. In some vegetables, like cabbage and cauliflower, root become bushy in appearance. As the whole root system is affected and become deformed, its efficiency decreases, causing reduction in top growth, stunting, chlorosis, yellowing, loss of vigour, premature leaf drop and wilting, especially in hot and dry weather. Growth of plants is uneven and yield is very much reduced. Chlorotic patches of plants in field are obvious field symptoms. In case of heavy infestation, yellowing and other deficiency symptoms are evenly distributed throughout the field. In some vegetables, galls may be produced on trailing stems. Galls develop also on underground plant parts like tubers, rhizomes, etc.

The pathogen. The root-knot disease in vegetables is caused by species of *Meloidogyne,* although a number of species are reported to attack vegetables, four major species of *Meloidogyne, M. incognita, M. javanica, M. arenaria* and *M. hapla,* are more commonly involved in the disease than others.

Identification of the root-knot nematode species. Morphological characters that are valuable for identification of four major species include perineal patterns, female stylet, male heads and stylets and heads and stylets of second stage juveniles. Of these, morphology of perineal patterns is the most important. Morphological characters of these structures in four major species are as follows:

M. incognita. Perineal patterns have a high, squarish arch, often with a distinct whorl in the tail terminal area. Striate are smooth to wavy, sometimes zigzagged. Distinct lateral lines are absent; the lateral field may be marked by breaks and forks in striate (Plate 27.5). Stylets of females are curved dorsally. The anterior half of the cone is cylindrical, and the posterior half is conical; knobs are set off from the shaft, anteriorly indented, and transversely elongate.

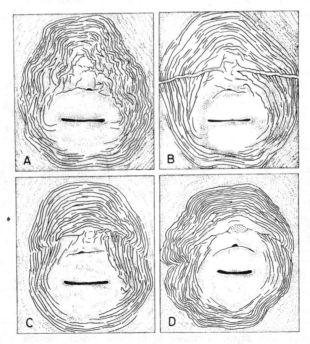

Plate 27.5 Perineal patterns of the four major species of root-knot nematodes, (A) *M. incognita,* (B) *M. javanica,* (C) *M. arenaria,* (D) *M. hapla.*

Heads of males have a large, round a labial disc raised above the median lips. The labial disc is concave to flat. The head cap is high and as wide as the head region in lateral view. The head region is marked by two or three incomplete annulations. The head region is not distinctly set-off from the rest of the body. The stylet has a blunt, blade like tip, which is wider than the medial portion of the cone; the shaft is usually cylindrical and often narrowed near the knobs. Knobs are large, rounded to transversely ovoid, sometimes anteriorly indented, and set-off from the shaft (Plate 27.6).

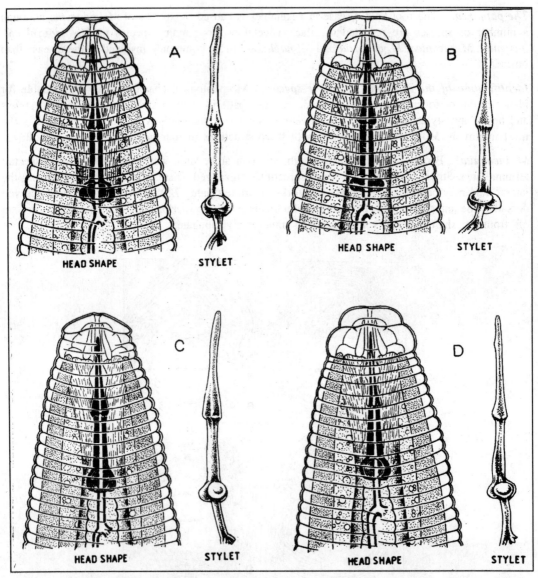

Plate 27.6 Head shape and stylet of males of the four major species of root knot nematodes, (A) *M. incognita*, (B) *M. javanica*, (C) *M. arenaria*, (D) *M. hapla*.

In second juveniles, labial disc and median lips are fused to form one smooth continuous, elongated structure. The head region is smooth or marked by one to three incomplete to complete annulations. The stylet has prominent knobs, posteriorly rounded and distinctly set off from the shaft; the cone and shaft gradually increase in width posteriorly.

M. javanica. The perineal pattern has distinct lateral lines dividing the dorsal and ventral striate. Lateral lines run the entire width of the pattern and gradually disappear near the tail terminus. The dorsal arch is low and rounded to high and squarish, and often with a whorl in the tail terminal area. Striate are smooth to slightly wavy (Plate 27.5)

Female stylets are similar to *M. incognita* except the one, which is slightly curved dorsally, and the shaft, which is more cylindrical. Knobs are transversely elongated but not deeply indented anteriorly. Male heads have a high, rounded head cap distinctly set off from the head region. The labial disc and medial lips are fused to form one smooth, continuous structure, almost as wide as the head regions in lateral view. The head region is smooth or marked by two or three incomplete head annulations. The stylet has very broad, elongated stylet knobs. The anterior two thirds of the cone gradually increase in width; the posterior one third widens rapidly. The shaft is cylindrical; the knobs are low and wide, sometimes indented, and always set off from the shaft (Plate 27.6).

The head shape of second stage juveniles is very similar to *M. incognita* and is not diagnostic. The head cap is anteriorly flattened but posteriorly rounded; labial disc and medial lips are fused to form one smooth, continuous elongated structure. The head region is usually smooth but may have one to three incomplete annulations. The stylet has transversely elongated knobs; other characteristics are similar to *M. incognita*.

M. arenaria. Perineal patterns have a low dorsal arch, slightly indented near the lateral fields to form rounded shoulder. Dorsal and ventral striate often meet at an angle. Distinct lateral lines absent, but short, irregular and forked striate mark the lateral fields. Striate are smooth to slightly wavy; some bend towards the vulva. Sometimes patterns extend laterally to form one or two wings (Plate 27.5). The stylet of females is very characteristic. The whole stylet is broad and robust, and the wide, rounded, backward-sloping knobs gradually merge with the shaft.

Male heads have a low head cap sloping at the posterior. Labial disc and medial lips fuse to form one smooth, continuous structure, nearly as wide as the head region in the lateral view. The head region is marked with one to three incomplete annulations and is generally smooth. The stylet of males is relatively straight, broad and robust; the posterior two thirds of the cone gradually increase in width, and the posterior one third widens rapidly. The posterior portion of the cone is much broader than the anterior portion of the shaft. The shaft is cylindrical. The knobs are large, posteriorly rounded and gradually merged with the shaft (Plate 27.6). The head shape of second stage juveniles is similar to *M. incognita* and *M. javanica*, anteriorly flattened and posteriorly rounded. Labial disc and medial lips fuse to form one smooth, continuous elongate structure. The head region is generally smooth and may be marked by one to three incomplete annulations.

M. hapla. Perineal patterns are rounded hexagonal to flattened ovoidal and have very fine striate and sub-cuticular punctuations in the smooth tail terminus area. The dorsal arch is low and rounded but may be high and squarish. Lateral lines are absent but lateral fields are marked by irregularities in striate. Dorsal and ventral striate often meet at an angle. Striate are smooth to slightly wavy; some patterns are winged on one or both lateral sides (Plate 27.5). Stylets of females are narrow and delicate. The cone is slightly curved dorsally; the shaft is a little broader posteriorly. The knobs are small, round and set off from the shaft.

Male heads have a high and narrow head cap and are set-off from the head regions. Labial disc and medial lips fuse to form one smooth, continuous structure much narrower than the head regions. The head region is without annulations, distinctly set off from the body annulations. Stylets of the male are narrow and delicate. The cone gradually increases in width, and the base of the cone is only slightly wider than the anterior portion of the shaft (Plate 27.6). Second stage juveniles have a narrow head cap and a round head region, much different from the other three species. Labial disc and medial lips fuse to form one smooth, continuous, narrow head cap. The head region is anteriorly rounded and free of annulations. The stylet has a narrow cone and shaft, and minute, rounded knobs set off from the shaft.

Life cycle. The life cycle of *Meloidogyne* species starts with an egg, usually in the one-celled stage, deposited by a female which is completely or partially embedded in a root of a host plant. The eggs are deposited into a gelatinous matrix, which holds them together in egg masses or egg sacs. More than 1000 eggs have been found in one egg mass, and it may be larger than the female body. Egg development begins within a few hours after deposition, resulting in multiplication of cells, until a fully formed larva with visible stylet lines is coiled in the egg membrane. This is the first larval stage (Plate 27.7). It can move in the egg but is not very active. The first molt takes place in the egg, and it is not difficult to see the separated first stage cuticle protruding beyond the head of the second stage larva (Plate 27.8). Shortly after, the larva hatches, emerging through a hole made in the end of the flexible eggshell by repeated thrusting with the stylet.

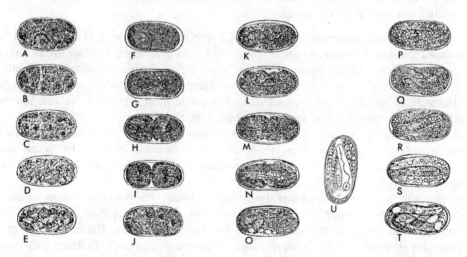

Plate 27.7 Development of eggs of a *Meloidogyne* speices, (A-S) stages in development from one cell to second stage larva, (T) second stage larva, (U) second stage larva showing molted cuticle (A-T) from Saigusa, 1957; (U) from Christie and Cobb, 1941.

Second-stage infective larvae usually penetrate roots just above the root cap. They move mostly between undifferentiated root cells, and finally come to rest with heads in the developing stele near the regions of cell elongation and bodies in the cortex (Figure 27.5). Cells walls are pierced with stylets, and secretions from the esophageal glands are injected. These secretions cause enlargement of cells in the vascular cylinder and increased rates of cell division in the pericycle (Figure 27.6). This leads to the formation of giant cells (also called syncytia), formed by enlargement of cells (hypertrophy), possible dissolution of cell walls, enlargement of nuclei and changes in the composition of the cell contents. At the same time, there is intense cell multiplication (hyperplasia) around the larval head. These changes are usually, but not invariably, accompanied by enlargement of the root to form distinct galls (Figure 27.6). On small roots, galls containing only one female are round to fusiform and may be one to three millimetres in diameter.

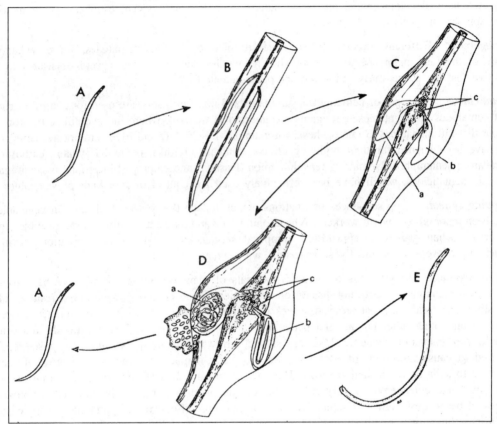

Figure 27.6 Life cycle of a *Meloidogyne* species (Schematic), (A) Pre-parasitic second-stage larva, (B) two larvae which have entered a root, become statinoary, and started to feed, (C) start of gall formation, development of larvae (a, b) and giant cells (c), (D) gall with mature female and egg mass (a), male after metamorphosis (b), and giant cells (c) (E) male free in soil (De Guiran and Netscher, 1970).

While the giant cells and galls are forming, width of larvae increases. And there is considerable enlargement of the esophageal glands. The cells of the genital primordium divide and genital primordium enlarges, becoming distinctly the two pronged in the female or forming on elongated body in the male. Six rectal glands begin to enlarge in the nearly, hemispherical posterior part of female body. As the second stage larvae continue feeding, body size increases, bodies become flask-shaped, and the gonads lengthen.

With the second and third molts completed by the female, the stylet and median esophageal bulb disappear. Shortly after the fourth molt, the stylet and median bulb are regenerated, the uterus and vagina are formed, and a perineal pattern becomes visible. Further development of the two female gonads is difficult to see as they elongate and become folded in the nearly globular or slightly elongated body with a neck which may be short and stout or nearly as long as the body. Just before the second molt, the male gonad is near the posterior end of the body and the rectum is visible. After the second and third molts, no stylet is visible, the median esophageal bulb has degenerated, and only the gonad has enlarged. Then there is a rather rapid metamorphosis as the elongated body develops inside the larval cuticle, complete with stylet, esophagus with median bulb, spicules and sperm in the testis.

Management. Different measures are suggested to manage root-knot nematodes. The polyphagous nature of the four major species of root knot nematodes does not allow several measures to be effective that are successfully employed for other nematodes.

Nematicides. Two types of nematicides, fumigants and non-fumigants, are used for control of root-knot nematodes on vegetables. Fumigants are injected in the soil, where they volatilize to produce vapour that kill nematodes. Some of these, for example, DBCP, DD and EDB, are not available now and have been banned for their polluting effects. Aldicarb (Temik), oxamyl (Vydate), carbofuran (Furadan), phenamiphos (Nemacur), fensulphothion (Dasanit) and ethprop (Mocap) are non-fumigant systemic nematicides, which have been effectively used for control of root knot of vegetables.

Cropping system. Crop sequences or rotations, which reduce the root-knot disease on vegetables, have been reported by several workers. Wheat, onion, rice and maize are known to increase the yield of tomato when grown in appropriate temporal sequences. Most common rotations involve sequencing of vegetables, mostly solanaceous, with cereals.

Soil amendment. Applications of organic materials of plant or animal origin have been found effective in reducing the root-knot disease on vegetables. Green manures, mature crop residues like rice straw, rye straw and oat straw, oilcakes of margosa, peanut, linseed, castor and cottonseed, cellulose and other amendments like paper, rotten wood, shavings and sawdust; oils and other organic amendments like bone meal, sewage sludge, farmyard manure, horse dung, compost, etc. are reported to cause inhibition of root knot besides other nematodes. Addition of most of these materials to soils serves a dual purpose. They act as manure as well as reduce root-knot disease intensity. Once considered as very promising management measure, it is now not favourably suggested because of high cost input. Oilcakes, found most effective, are particularly very costly, and a huge quantity is required for field applications. Their prohibitive prices have overshadowed their use as profitable measures for management of root-knot nematodes.

Biocontrol. Several fungi, bacteria and sporozoan are known to reduce nematode populations. In the past, all experiments with nematode trapping fungi failed to yield desired results. However, in recent years, the discovery of *Paecilomyces lilacinus*, a soil fungus, as an efficient parasite of eggs of *Meloidogyne* started a new phase in efforts of biocontrol of root-knot nematodes. The fungus was found successful in several green house experiments. Field application of *P. lilacinus* controlled root knot on potato. *P. lilacinus* is a saprophytic fungus but becomes parasitic when nematodes or their eggs are available. The bacterium, *Pasteuria penetrans*, is an obligate parasite of *Meloidogyne*. Spores are attached to the outer cuticle of the juveniles and germinate about eight days after the infected juveniles penetrate the root system. The germ tube penetrates the cuticle. The bacterium proliferates and fills the body of the developing females. Upon decomposition of dead females, spores are liberated in soil. This organism is also considered as an effective biocontrol agent of root-knot nematodes.

Host resistance. Host resistance is an effective and economic means of reducing losses from root-knot nematodes. This measure has become further significant in recent times because of polluting effects related to manufacturing and use of nematicides. Resistance against root-knot nematodes has been detected or introduced in vegetable cultivars.

Integrated management. In integrated management, a variety of measures are used to manage one or more diseases. This approach increases the efficient production of crops and reduces the overall unfavourable effects of the various measures. Cultural practices like crop rotation, fallowing, application of nematicides, use of biocontrol agents and cultivation of resistant cultivars can be integrated to control root-knot nematodes on vegetables.

27.3.3 Citrus Root Nematode (*Tylenchulus semipenetrans*)

The citrus root nematode was first noticed in 1912 on orange trees in California (USA). The nematode is present throughout the world wherever citrus is grown. In India, where the nematode was first reported in 1961, up to 80% orchards were found infested in certain areas. The pathogen causes slow decline of citrus trees with die-back of twigs and debilitation of the trees.

Symptoms. In early stages of root infection, no above-ground signs are visible. Affected trees show reduced terminal growth, chlorosis, shedding of terminal leaves, dieback of branches and reduction in number and size, of fruits. Infected roots show brownish discolouration. Ultimately the roots decay.

Morphology and life cycle. *Tylenchulus semipenetrans* is a sedentary semi-endoparasite of roots. The juveniles and males are worm like, but the female body is swollen irregularly behind the neck (Figure 27.7). The nematodes measure about 0.4 mm long by 18 to 80 µm in diameter, with the larger diameters being found only in the maturing, and mature females. The females lay eggs in a gelatinous substance. The life cycle of the nematode is completed within 6 to 14 weeks at 24°C. The male juveniles and the adults do not feed and apparently do not play a role either in disease development or the reproduction. The second stage female juvenile is the only infective stage and usually attacks young feeder roots. They undergo three additional molts and produce females. The young females then penetrate deeper into the cortex and may reach the pericycle. The head of the nematode develops a tiny cavity around it and feeds on enlarged parenchyma cells. Later on, the cells around the feeding site become disorganized and ultimately break down.

Disease management
1. Citrus nurseries should never be established on or near old citrus orchard.
2. Nursery soil should be fumigated or solarized before planting for rootstock is done.
3. Suspected rootstock should be denematized by hot water at 45°C for 25 min.
4. The seedling roots can also be treated by root dip in nematicides such as zinophos.
5. DBCP (Nemagon) @15-45 lit/ha has been very effective.
6. Dimethoate at 16 ml a.i. per tree and phorate (Thimet) at 15 g a.i./tree followed by light irrigation are also reported to reduce nematode population significantly. Fensulfothion (Terracur P or Dasanit) at 24.7 kg a.i./ha, and dichlorofenthion at 27.8 kg a.i./ha give effective control.

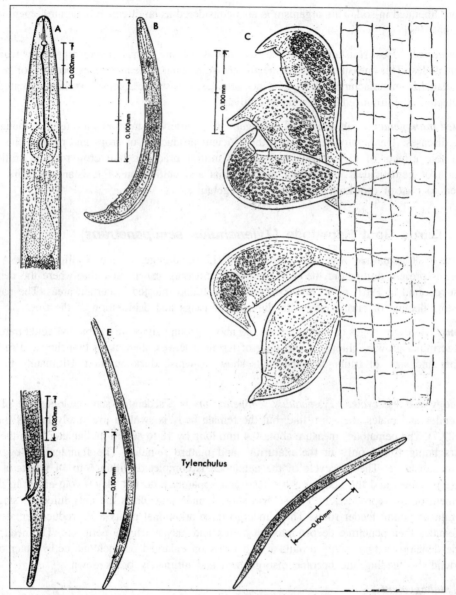

Figure 27.7 *Tylenchulus (Citrus-root nematodes and related speices),* (A) young female, anterior part, (B) young female, full length, (C) mature females with anterior portions embedded in citrus root, (D) male, posterior part, (E) male, full length, (F) larva, full length.

7. Organic amendment of orchard soil has also been recommended for nematode management. Steer manure, chicken manure, cotton waste, sugarbeet pulp, lucern hay and caster cake are reported to reduce the population of citrus nematode.

8. Trifoliate orange *Poncirus trifoliate* and Troyer citrange (*P. trifoliate* × *C. sinensis*) are resistant and their use as rootstock is one way of managing this nematode.

27.3.4 The Burrowing Nematode: *Radopholus*

Radopholus (the burrowing nematode) occurs widely in tropical and subtropical countries. *R. similes* causes banana root rot, blackhead toppling disease or decline of banana. It also causes decline of avocado and of tea, and the yellow disease of black pepper. It is also parasitic on coconut, coffee, ornamentals, forest trees, sugarcane, maize, vegetables, grasses and weeds. Another closely related species *R. citrophilus*, causes the spreading decline of citrus in Florida (USA). This species also infects several other cultivated crops and ornamentals.

Root and rhizome rot of banana

Symptoms.   Wounding of banana roots by *R. similes* usually induces reddish brown cortical lesions which are diagnostic features of the disease. These lesions are clearly seen after the affected root is split longitudinally. Varying degree of growth retardation, leaf yellowing and eventually the established plant fall-off manifests root and rhizome necrosis.

Life cycle.   *R. similis* has a migratory endoparasitic habit. Although the stages remain vermiform throughout, sexual dimorphism is apparent with adult males being somewhat degenerated. Eggs are normally laid in infested tissues. The life cycle from one egg to the next extends over 20-25 days with eggs taking 8-10 days to hatch and the larva, 10-13 days to mature. The incidence of Panama wilt of banana is almost doubled in the presence of the nematode. The nematode spreads from one locality to another through corms. *R. similes* may be disseminated when water draining from infested areas gets recycled into irrigation system. Soil that adheres to implements may also spread the nematode. The nematode does not seem to have any special adaptation for survival in the absence of a susceptible host. Free living stages and the eggs do not survive for more than 12 weeks. After a plantation is removed, the nematodes in the corms may probably survive for as long as these remain succulent.

Management.   The population density of nematode in soil may be reduced either by fallowing, crop rotation or intercropping. The banana biotype of *R. similes* has a narrow host range and limited survival period in soil in the absence of host. Therefore, distraction of pseudostem either mechanically or through herbicides is practical approaches to rehabilitate the infested plantations. After this practice, planting of cover crops like *Panicum maximum* var. *trichoglume* and *Phaseolus atrapurpureus*, which do not support the nematode, help in containing their population. Planting sugarcane following the destruction of bananas eliminate *R. similes* after 10 weeks.

Rotations of banana with *panola* grass, sugarcane, sorghum, tobacco, cassava, and grape fruit increase yield and control *R. similes*. Fallowing for a period of 3 months, and flood fallowing for 5 months after banana effectively suppress the nematode populations. Banana intercropped with *Crotalaria* reduce *R. similes*. Application of neem cake at 400 g/plant once at planting and second after 4 months reduce *R. similes* and increase yield.

To avoid introducing inoculum into new plantations, banana sets should be disinfested by dipping them in hot water bath at 55°C for 25 min. Certified nematode free sets can be obtained by this method. Application of D-D, EDB or DBCP@300 lit/ha at planting time gives good disease management for one year but the treatment is to be repeated the following year. These fumigants are now generally not recommended. Charles et al., (1985) reported that application of Carbofuran @1 g a.i./ plant at planting and again after 3 months gives satisfactory control.

According to Umesh, et al. (1988) VAM fungus *Glomus fasciculatum* suppresses multiplication of *R. similes*. Tetraploids selected from crosses between wild banana (diploid male parent) and Gros Michel (triploid female parent) show considerable resistance to *R. similes*.

Spreading decline of citrus.   The disease appears in citrus orchards as groups of stunted or unthrifty trees with sparse foliage, small fruits and retarded terminal growth. Leaves have a tendency to wilt during hot and dry periods and new branches do not come out. Examination of the root system reveals that below 50 cm of soil young feeder roots are considerably reduced.

Management.   Pull and treat method followed for control involves pulling out and destroying the infected trees and fumigating the soil. D-D@ 672 kg/ha has been used for fumigation. The land is either left fallow, keeping weeds out by herbicides or such antagonistic crops as asparagus or marigold are cultivated for two years before replanting of citrus. To prevent introduction of the disease in disease free areas through planting stock, bare rooted citrus plants should be treated with hot water at 50°C for 10 min before planting.

27.3.5   Stem or Bulb Nematodes (*Ditylenchus dipsaci*)

This problem occurs in many countries but usually it is important economically only in areas where onions are grown intensively. The disease was first described in the Netherlands in 1883 and in the United States in 1931. Since then it has been reported in several areas of the world. The pathogen *Ditylenchus dipsaci* can attack over 400 plant species belonging to more than 40 families. However, only certain physiologic races of the nematode cause disease of onion.

Symptoms.   Plants can be invaded at any growth stage, although most penetration occurs in young tissue. When young seedlings are invaded, they become dwarfed, twisted and abnormally white and they develop swollen areas where the epidermis sometimes splits. When sets are planted into infested soil, the first symptoms are stunted plants and yellowish speckles on new leaves. In older onion bulbs, tissue softens near the top of the bulb or at the base of the leaves. This does not become evident until the onion is handled; then the softness becomes apparent, and the outside dry scales fall off. If the first fleshy scale of such an onion is torn open, it will appear as white, loose weft of tissue or as a lacelike resembling thick frost. The tops of such plants usually are stunted; an abnormal number of cracked or double bulbs occur. Many species of fungi and bacteria follow nematode invasion and in wet weather, injured bulbs rot and often produce a foul odour. Plants outside the onion family exhibit the same stunting of tops, twisting or crinkling and yellowing of foliage, and swelling and cracking of swollen petioles. The crown of the main roots usually are discoloured, furrowed and cracked.

Life cycle.   *Ditylenchus* over-winters in a number of ways. Live nematodes may be present on some stored seeds and can be disseminated with seed. Nematodes are also spread in diseased hyacinth and narcissus bulbs. Individual nematodes remain alive in onion bulbs left in the field. Such discarded onions often produce volunteer plants for several years in succession and supply food for *Ditylenchus*. Weeds also harbour the nematode. Soon after the nematode larvae hatch, they penetrate susceptible plants and burrow in the soft parenchyma tissue. Here they feed and multiply rapidly. The plant cell enlarges abnormally until they reproduce most rapidly in onion seedlings. Seedlings mortality is most prevalent, and 'bloat' symptoms are most severe. Moisture probably is the most important single environmental factor affecting the nematode; free moisture is vital for its activity.

Management. A long rotation of crops using spinach, carrots, beets, crucifers, lettuce or grains has proved effective. Complete removal and destruction of old infested crop bulbs is necessary. Only healthy onion seed and sets should be used. Infestation of seed and sets can be eliminated by soaking them in 115°F water for 60 minutes. Garlic cloves can be disinfested by presoaking at 100°F for 30 minutes in a 1% formalin + 0.1% detergent solution for 150 minutes followed by a 20 minute soak in the same solution at 120°F. Onion seed can be fumigated with methyl bromide to eradicate the nematode. Fumigation with dichloropropene-dichloropropane (D-D) mixture has given excellent field control.

27.3.6 Lesion Nematodes (*Pratylenchus penetrans*)

Although there are at least 66 species of *Pratylenchus* that occur in all temperate and subtropical areas of the world, *P. penetrans* is the best-known and most serious one on vegetables, including potatoes. The species has been recorded on over 350 hosts including most vegetables except beet, curled mustard, rutabaga, yam, okra, sweet potato, lettuce, radish and sweet corn. It is essentially a parasite of the root cortex.

Symptoms. Affected roots first show tiny, water soaked yellowish spots that soon turn brown or black. These lesions appear mainly on the young feeder roots. They finally coalesce and girdle the entire root, causing it to die. Infected roots are often invaded by root pathogen such as *Aphanomyces* and *Fusarium* on peas and *Verticillium* on eggplant, pepper, tomato, potato and strawberry. The severity of damage is variable and hard to estimate but affected plants grow poorly, produce poor yield and often die before they can mature.

The pathogen and life cycle. *Pratylenchus penetrans* is an obligate parasite and has a simple life cycle with sexual reproduction. After fertilization, the female lays 1 to 6 eggs per day singly in the roots or soil and continues to do so until she dies. The first molt occurs in the egg, and the second stage juvenile that hatches from the egg molts three more times between intervals of feeding. A complete life cycle requires from 30 to 90 days depending on soil temperature, and it is shortest around 86°F. All larval stages and adults can invade roots. *Pratylenchus* is most common in light or sandy loam soils, and it reproduces best between pH 5.2 and 6.4 at temperature between 70 and 80°F, on hosts growing under unfavourable light, and on hosts low in nitrogen, potassium or calcium.

P. *thornei* was first reported in California in 1953 and is associated with sugarbeet, nectarine, grape, bean, strawberry, walnut, grass and oak. It has also been reported on tomato, bean, wheat and tea. *P. zeae* is mainly a pest of tobacco, sugarcane, sorghum and rice. Other minor host includes soyabean, tomato, millet, rye, oat, sweet potato, peaches, peanut, barley, strawberry, wheat and cowpea.

Management. The best control of root lesion nematodes comes from overall or row treatment with nematicides. These include DD, chloropicrin, metham-sodium, aldicarb, prophos, phorate, di-trapex, dazomet, fensulfothion, methomyl, carbofuran or phenamiphos. Rotations with resistant crops such as oats may reduce nematode populations greatly. Also in hot, dry climates, fair control results from summer fallow.

27.3.7 Ear Cockle Nematode: *Anguina*

Seed-gall nematodes, the first recorded plant parasitic nematodes were discovered in 1743, in UK. The wheat seed gall nematode, responsible for the ear cockle or *Sehun* disease of wheat is now known to be present in all major wheat-growing regions of the world. But it is more common in Eastern Europe and in parts of Asia and Africa. From India, the disease was first reported in 1919 from Punjab and is now known to be occasionally widespread in Haryana, Delhi, H.P., Punjab, Rajasthan, Maharashtra, M.P., U.P. and Bihar. The nematode is very often present in association with the bacterial yellow ear rot or tundu diseases of wheat.

Symptoms. Symptoms appear on all above-ground parts stem, leaf and floral organs. Infected seedlings as well as adult plants are more or less severely stunted and their leaves show characteristic rolling or twisting. A rolled leaf often traps the next emerging leaf or the inflorescence within it and causes it to become looped or bent and badly distorted. Stems are often enlarged near the base, frequently bent, and generally stunted. Diseased heads are shorter and thicker than normal ones, with their glumes spread farther apart by the nematode filled grain galls. A diseased head may have one, a few or all of its kernels transformed into nematode galls. Diseased heads remain green longer than normal ones and galls are shed of the heads more readily than kernels. Thus, grains in the diseased ear are replaced by galls (cockles) of the nematode.

The pathogen and disease cycle. The disease is caused by the nematode, *Anguina tritici*. In a diseased head, grains are replaced by nematode galls (cockles). Each gall is shiny green at first, turning brown or black as the hard, dark, rounded and shorter than normal wheat kernels and often resembles cockle seeds, smutted grains or ergot sclerotia. The galls are filled with nematode larvae, which can be seen by soaking the galls in water and then macerating them. Each gall may contain 10,000 to 30,000 or more larvae.

The pathogen is a large nematode, in which adult females are about 3.2 mm long and 120 µm in diameter. They lay eggs and produce all the juvenile stages and adults in seed galls. The larvae (second stage juveniles) have extreme longevity (of upto 28 years under dry conditions) in wheat galls. Thus, nematode survives as second stage larvae in infected seed galls. These galls fall to the ground. Galls fallen to ground or sown with seed soften during warm, moist weather and release infective second stage juveniles. When a film of water is present on the surface of the plants the juveniles swim upward and feed ecto-parasitically on the tightly compacted leaves near the growing point, causing the leaves and the stem malformed. As the inflorescence begins to form, the juveniles enter the floral primordia and produce third and fourth stage juveniles within 3-5 days of invasion. These become adult males and females. Each infected floral primordium becomes a seed gall and may contain 80 or more adults of both sexes. Each female lay up to 2000 eggs within freshly formed galls over several weeks so that each gall contains 10,000 to 30,000 eggs. The adults die soon after the eggs are laid. The eggs hatch and first stage larvae emerge. However, these larvae molts soon produce second stage juveniles by the time of crop harvest. These second-stage larvae are resistant to desiccation and can survive in galls for 28-30 years. The seed gall nematode produces only one generation per year. Some etiological relationship of this nematode with a bacterium, *Clavibacter tritici* causing tundu disease of wheat has also been observed. The presence of this nematode has been shown to be essential for the development of tundu in wheat. The bacterium is said to be unable to produce tundu independently.

Management. Clean, nematode-free seeds must be used. The seeds should be free of nematode galls. Contaminated seeds can be cleaned with sophisticated equipment or by sieving and floating in fresh water. The seeds are placed in 20% common salt solution and stirred vigorously. The galls being lighter float on the water surface and can be removed and destroyed. Hot water treatment is also recommended. The seeds are first soaked in water for 4-6 hours at room temperature and then treated at 54°C for 10 minutes. Diseased ear heads should be picked up and destroyed.

Crop rotation with barley and oat for 2-3 years is also effective. During rotations, seasonal wetting of gall ensures release of larvae, which die in absence of host (wheat). Cultural practices, like early sowing of wheat and use of resistant varieties have also proved useful. Early sown crops usually escape infection. Chemical treatment of soil with nematicides has also been recommended when there is heavy soil infestation. Nemaphos (Zinophos), aldicarb or thionazin can be applied to soil. Nemaphos applied @10 kg a.i./ha has given good control of ear cockle and tundu of wheat.

REFERENCES

Baldwin, J.G., 1992, Evolution of cyst and non-cyst forming Heteroderinae, *Annu. Rev. Phytopathol.*, 30:271.

Brodie, B.B. and Mai, W.E., 1989, Control of the golden nematode in the United States, *Annu. Rev. Phytopathol.*, 27:443.

Brown, R.H. and Kerry, B.R., (Eds.), 1987, *Principles and Practices of Nematode Control in Crops*, Academic Press, Sydney.

Chaube, H.S. and Singh, U.S., 1991, *Plant Disease Management: Principles and Practices,* CRC Press, Boca Raton, Boston, USA. p. 319.

Chaube, H.S., Singh, U.S., Mukhopadhyaya, A.N. and Kumar, J., 1992, *Plant Diseases of International Importance*, Vol. II, Diseases of vegetables and oilseed crops, Prentice Hall, Englewood Cliffs, New Jersey, USA, p. 376.

Dropkin, V.H., 1980, *Introduction to Plant Nematology,* Wiley, New York.

Duncan, L.W., 1991, Current options for nematode management, *Annu. Rev. Phytopathol.*, 29:145.

Goswami, B.K. and Chenulu, V.V., 1974, Interaction of root-knot nematode, *Meloidogyne incognita* and tobacco mosaic virus in tomato, *Indian J. Nematol.*, 4:69.

Hussey, R.S., 1989, Disease-inducing secretions of plant parasitic nematodes, *Annu. Rev. Phytopathol.*, 27:127.

Khan, F.A. and Khan, A.M., 1973, Studies on the reniform nematode, *Rotylenchulus reniformis*, I, Host range population changes, *Indian J. Nematol.*, 3:24.

Khan, R.M., Saxena, S.K., Khan, M.W. and Khan, A.M., 1980, Interaction of *Meloidogyne incognita* and *Phomopsis vexans*, *Indian J. Nematol.*, 10:242-4.

Kumar, J., Chaube, H.S., Singh, U.S. and Mukhopadhyay, A.N., 1992, *Plant Diseases of International Importance*, Vol. III, Disease of fruit crops, Prentice Hall, New Jersey, USA, p. 456.

Macdonald, D., 1979, Some interactions of plant parasitic nematodes and higher plants in *Ecology of Root Pathogens*, Kreepa, S.V. and Dommergues, Y.R., (Eds.), Elsevier, 281.

Mamiya, Y., 1983, Pathology of the pine wilt disease caused by *Bursaphelenchus xylophilus*, *Annu. Rev. Phytopathol.*, 21:201.

Mankau, R., 1980, Biological control of nematode pests by natural enemies. *Annu. Rev. Phytopathol.*, 18:415.

McKay, A.C. and Opfel, K.M., 1993, Toxigenic Clavibacter/Anguina associations infecting grass seedheads, *Annu. Rev. Phytopathol.*, 31:151.

Mishra, C. and Das, S.N., 1977, Interaction of some plant parasitic nematodes on the root-knot development in brinjal, *Indian J. Nematol.*, 7:46.

Mukhopadhyay, A.N., Kumar, J., Chaube, H.S. and Singh, U.S., *Plant Diseases of International Importance*, Vol. IV, Diseases of sugar, forest, and plantation crops, Prentice Hall, New Jersey, USA, p. 376.

Nath, R., Khan, M.N., Wanshi, R.S.K. and Dwivedi, R.P., 1984, Influence of root-knot nematode, *Meloidyne javanica* on pre and post emergence damping off of tomato, *Indian J. Nematol.*, 14:135.

Nickle, W.R., (Ed.), 1991, *Manual of Agricultural Nematology*, Dekker, New York.

Sasser, J.N., et al., 1983, The international *Melodogyne* project—Its goals and accomplishments, *Annu. Rev. Phytopathol.*, 21:271.

Sayre, R.M. and Walter, D.E. 1991, Factors affecting the efficacy of natural enemies of nematodes, *Annu. Rev. Phytopathol.*, 33:37.

Seddiqi, M.R., 1974, *Tylenchulus semipenetrans*, Commonwealth Institute of Helminthology Descriptions of Plant Parasitic Nematodes, Set 3, No. 34. ST. Albans, England.

Sikora, R.A., 1992, Management of the antagonistic potential in agricultural ecosystems for the biological control of plant parasitic nematodes, *Annu. Rev. Phytopathol.*, 30:245.

Singh, D.B., Parvatha Reddy, P., and Sharma, S.R., 1981, Effect of the root-knot nematode, *Melodogyne incognita* on Fusarium wilt of French beans, *Indian J. Nematol.*, 11:84.

Singh, R.S. and Sitaramaiah, K., 1971, Control of plant parasitic nematodes with organic amendments of soil, *G.B. Pant Univ. Expt. St. Res. Bull.*, 6:289.

Singh, U.S., Mukhopadhyay, A.N., Kumar, J. and Chaube, H.S. 1992, *Plant Diseases of International Importance*, Vol. I, Diseases of cereals and pulses, Prentice Hall, Englewood Cliffs, New Jersey, USA.

Striling, G.R., 1991, *Biological Control of Plant Parasitic Nematodes*, CAB Int., Wajlingford, England.

Sturhan, D. and Brzeski, M.W., 1991, Stem and bulb nematodes, *Ditylenchus* spp, *In: Manual of Agricultural Nematology,* W.R.Nickle, (Ed.), p. 423, Dekker, New York.

Van Gundy, S.D., 1985, The life history of the citrus nematode *Tylenchulus semipenetrans*, *Nematologica*, 3:283.

28 Phanerogamic Plant Parasites

28.1 INTRODUCTION

More than 2500 species of flowering plants are known to be parasitic on economic plants and cause considerable damage. Important plant families that have such parasites are: *Cuscutaceae* (genus *Cuscuta*, the dodders), *Orobanchaceae* (genus *Orobanche*, the broomrape), *Scrophulariaceae* (genus *Striga*, the witchweed), and *Viscaceae* (genus *Arceuthobium*, the dwarf mistletoes; *Phoradendron*, the American true mistletoes; *Viscum*, the European true mistletoes) (Plate 28.1).

28.2 CUSCUTA (DODDER, AMARBEL)

There are about 100 species of *Cuscuta* attacking trees, clover, alfalfa, onion, sugarbeet, potatoes and several ornamental plants. *C. gronovei* is the most common dodder in India. Dodder is a slender, twining leafless plant. The stem is tough, curling, threadlike, and leafless, bearing only minute scales in place of leaves. The stem is usually yellowish or orange coloured, sometimes tinged with red or purple; sometimes it is almost white, bearing clusters of tiny flowers. The flowers are white, yellowish or pinkish in colour. Gray to brown seeds are produced in abundance and mature within a few weeks after bloom.

Dodder seeds over winter in infested fields or mixed with the crop seeds germinate and produce shoot without roots. This leafless shoot rotates as if in search of a host. Once in contact with susceptible host, it encircles the host plant, sends haustoria into it, and begins to climb the stem. The haustoria penetrate the host tissue (stem or leaf) and reach into the vascular tissues, from which they absorb nutrients and water.

Cuscuta is best managed by preventing its introduction in the field, by use of dodder-free seed. In case dodder is already established in the field/garden, the scattered patches may be contained early in the season with contact herbicides. When infestations are already widespread in the field, *Cuscuta* can be controlled by frequent tillage, flaming, and use of herbicides that kill the dodder plant on its germination but before it becomes attached to the host.

28.3 *DENDROPHTHOAE* (GIANT OR LEAFY MISTLETOES)

Dendrophthoae is a common phanerogamic parasite of fruits and roadside trees and wastelands. In ancient Sanskrit literature it is mentioned *Vrikshabhaksh*, eater of trees. This describes the damage done by the parasite. In India mango trees are the worst sufferers. In northern India 60-90% of the old, tall 'desi' (indigenous) type of mango trees and a large number of other trees are heavy or

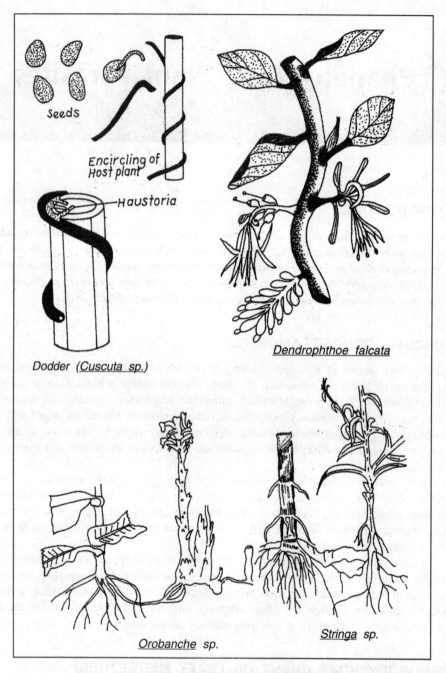

Seeds

Encircling of
Host plant

Haustoria

Dodder (*Cuscuta sp.*)

Dendrophthoe falcata

Orobanche sp.

Stringa sp.

Plate 28.1 Phanerogamic plant parasites.

moderately infected. Where there is no timely eradication of the parasite the entire tree becomes uneconomical. The parasite spreads from tree to tree and a major portion of orchard may be affected.

Dendrophthoae spp. (Loranthaceae-Viscoideae) is a warm climate shrub found in India and Malaysia. Its allied genus, *Phoradenedron* (*Serotinum*) is found in North America and *Viscum album* in California, Europe and many other countries. These are semi-parasites of tree trunks and thick branches. The leathery and evergreen leaves possess chlorophyll and synthesize carbohydrate constituent to meet their requirement. Since the parasite attacks the aerial parts of the host trees, situated far above the soil level, they are devoid of a true root system and they are dependent on the host for water and mineral nutrients. Other manufactured food from the host also passes into the parasite. They obtain these by developing suckers (haustoria) which grow into the host tissue and become intimately associated with the vascular elements of the host.

Dendrophthoae falcate, the common species in India, is a strongly branched and glabrous shrub. The stem is thick, erect or flattened at the nodes and appears to arise in clusters at the point of attack. These clusters form a dense and bushy growth, which can be easily spotted on the trees. The point, at which the haustorium penetrates, often swells to form a tumor. These tumors vary in size according to the age of the parasite. Sometimes, the parasite, instead of confining its attack to one point, produces a creeping branch, which grows closely along the host stem and forms haustoria at intervals. The flowers are borne in clusters. They are long and tubular, usually greenish white or red in colour according to species. The fruit is fleshy and contain a solitary seed. It is sweet and eaten by birds, cattle and other animals.

The parasite spreads by dispersal of its seed mostly by birds and to some extent by other animals. The birds are attracted by brilliant colour of the fruit. The pulp is sticky and thus the seeds are easily carried by birds. When seeds are deposited on other trees, at the junction of branches with the trunk, they germinate and give rise to haustoria, establishing the parasite. Droppings of birds containing seeds also help in dissemination of the parasite.

The commonly known method of control of the parasite is to top off the affected branches. It is important that the branches should be cut sufficiently low so that all vestiges of the haustorial system of the parasite are eradicated. In the early stages of the growth of the parasite, it can be easily detached from the host without damaging the latter. If the tumor is on one side of the branch then the wood just below the tumor may be sawed off. Injection of copper sulfate and 2, 4-D into affected branches has been found effective in many hosts. A spray of diesel oil emulsion in soap water is also effective in eradicating the parasite from mango trees.

28.4 STRIGA (THE WITCH WEED)

Several species of *Striga* parasitize important economic plants like corn, sugarcane, cereals and tobacco. Three species like *S. densiflora, S. asiatica* and *S. euphrasiodes* are well known semi parasites in India. Affected plants remain stunted, turn yellow and wilt. Infected roots bear a large number of witchweed haustoria, which are attached to the root and feed on it. *Striga* is a small plant. It produces a bright green, slightly hairy stem and leaves and grows 15-30 cm high. The leaves are rather long and narrow in opposite pairs. The flowers are small, red or yellowish or white, always having yellow centres. Flowers appear just above the leaf attachment to the stem, each fruit contains more than a thousand tiny brown seeds. Witchweed over winters as seeds, most of which require a rest period of 15-18 months before germination. Seeds close to the host roots germinate and move towards the roots under the influence of root exudates. Once haustorium is formed, it eventually penetrates the host roots and reaches the vessels of the host roots and absorbs water and nutrients.

To mange this parasite, its introduction should be avoided at all costs. Trap crops, consisting of host plants should be used to stimulate germination of *Striga* seeds, and the witchweed plants can be destroyed by ploughing under or by the use of herbicides. Trap crops consisting of non-host legumes may also be used to stimulate germination. Since *Striga* can not infect these non-hosts, it will be starved to death. Use of resistant cultivars, seed treatment with herbicides of differential toxicity and use of bioagents (fungal pathogens) of *Striga* are other possible means to manage this parasite.

28.5 *OROBANCHE* (THE BROOMRAPES)

Orobanche spp. are total root parasites affecting several species of herbaceous dicotyledonous crop plants. In India, *O. aegyptiaca* parasitizes many crops. Affected plants usually occur in small patches and may be stunted to various degrees. The pathogen is a whitish to yellowish annual plant 15-50 cm tall. It has a fleshy stem and scale like leaves and produces numerous pretty, white, yellow-white or slightly purple snapdragons like flower. The broomrapes produce seed pods about 5 mm long, each containing several hundreds minute seeds.

Broomrapes over winter as seeds, which may survive in soil for more than 10 years. Seeds germinate only when roots of certain plants grow near them. On germination a radical is produced which grows towards the root of host plant and becomes attached, and produces a shallow cup-like appressorium that surrounds the root. From the appressorium, a mass of undifferentiated cells penetrates the host and reaches the xylem to absorb water and nutrients. Some undifferentiated cells also become attached to phloem cells. Subsequently, the parasite begins to develop on stem and other parts.

Management of broomrapes depends on preventing the introduction of its seeds in disease free areas, planting non-susceptible crops in infested areas, and frequent weeding and removal of *Orobanche* plants before they produce new seeds. If feasible, fumigating soil with methyl bromide may give good control. It has been reported that flax serves as a trap crop. Its root exudates stimulate broomrape seed germination. Later, the broomrape infects flax but do not flower on it. Some plant varieties are resistant to broomrapes.

REFERENCES

Kuijt, J., 1967, *The Biology of Parasitic Flowering Plants*, Univ. California Press, Berkeley.

Kuijt, J., 1977, Haustoria of phanerogamic parasite, *Annu. Rev. Phytopathol,* 17:91.

Berner, D.K., et al., 1994, Relative roles of wind, crop seeds and cattle in dispersal of *Striga* spp. *Plant Dis.,* 78:402.

Berner, D.K., Kling, J.G., and Singh, B.B., 1995, *Striga* research and control: A perspective from Africa, *Plant Dis.,* 79:652.

Eplee, R.E., 1981, *Striga's* status as a plant parasite in United States, *Plant Dis.,* 65:951.

Hawksworth, F.G., and Wiends, D., 1970, Biology and taxonomy of the dwarf mistletoes, *Annu. Rev. Phytopathol.,* 8:187.

Musselman, L.J., 1980, The biology of *Striga, Orobanche* and other root parasitic weeds, *Annu. Rev. Phytopathol.,* 18:463.

Musselman, L.J. (Ed.), 1987, *Parasitic Weeds in Agriculture*, Vol. I, CRC Press, Boca Raton, Florida.

Thoday, M.G., 1991, On the histological relations between *Cuscuta* and its host, *Ann. Bot.,* 25:655.

29 Post-Harvest Diseases

29.1 INTRODUCTION

Plant pathogens are well known for causing various types of losses to crop plants, fruit and forest trees under field conditions. The association of the pests and pathogens with plant products continues even after harvest, and during post-harvest period the biotic and abiotic agents cause significant losses, which mostly go unrecorded or even unnoticed. Post-harvest diseases develop on plant products during harvesting/threshing/grading, packing, transportation, storage and marketing or before utilization by the consumers. The infections leading to these losses may be initiated in field (pre-harvest) or take place during post harvest phase. Good amount of information is available on post harvest damage to grains (cereals, legumes), which are stored generally in bins or warehouses.

29.2 IMPORTANCE OF POST-HARVEST LOSSES

Average losses of 10-20% are reported depending upon the storage conditions in Africa, Asia and Latin America. Moisture state in grains as well as the place of storage play vital role. At 12-14% moisture, no or least damage is done to grains but 25% or more moisture results in serious damage to grains due to attack of fungal pathogens, causing both quantitative (decay/rotting) and qualitative (mycotoxin production) losses. A conservative estimate suggests that in the tropics around 25% of all perishable food crops harvested are lost between harvest and consumption. Perishable /semi-perishable plant products, which are tender or succulent having greater water content (>50% moisture) are more susceptible to post- harvest diseases. The fleshy fruits, vegetables, cut flowers, bulbs/corms/tubers, etc., are prone to infections during or after harvesting, leading to huge losses in quantity and/or quality of products due to physical, physiological and pathological damage.

29.3 CAUSES OF POST-HARVEST DISEASES

All durable and dried agricultural commodities if not properly dried after harvest are subject to attack by fungal moulds. Fungal attack is more common in the humid tropics where fungal growth is stimulated by high ambient temperatures and relative humidity. Moulds most commonly encountered include species of *Aspergillus*, *Penicillium*, *Mucor* and *Rhizopus*.

29.3.1 Physical Damage

Loss due to mechanical damage occurs in both durable and perishable produces but because of their higher moisture content and loose mechanical strength, perishable products are generally more susceptible. Mechanical injury occurs at all stages from pre-harvest operations, through harvesting, grading, packing, transport to exposure in the market and domestic activities. Losses caused by such injury predispose produce to enhanced secondary physiological and pathological loss. For example, as much as 33% of the potato crops can be so seriously damaged through harvesting and grading as to be fit only for stock feed, while a further 12% loss can occur during transit to market. In bananas, which are commercially harvested unripe, all mechanical injuries, not apparent on the green fruit may lead to downgrading or total loss of the ripe fruit. Exposure to low or high temperature radiation also disrupts tissues and can lead to physiological changes that reduce quality and storage life.

29.3.2 Physiological Losses

Physiological losses are diverse in nature. Because the produce is alive, endogenous respiratory losses of dry matter and loss of water through transpiration always occur in perishable produce but the magnitude of these varies with the crop and is greatly influenced by the storage. Storage life is short when produce is stored in the tropics at high ambient temperature without refrigeration. The storage life of different commodities varies inversely as the rate of evolution of heat. Generally respiration is maximum during the first 24 hours after harvest in vegetables. Fruits generally have a gradually increasing rate of respiration as they ripen. Moisture loss represents a reduction in saleable weight and losses of 3-6% are generally enough to cause a marked decline in quality.

29.3.3 Pathological Attack

Attack by microorganism (fungi, bacteria and to a lesser extent viruses) is probably the most serious cause of post-harvest loss in perishable produce, although physical and physiological damage frequently predisposes material to pathogenic attack. The pattern of attack is usually initial infection by one, or a few, specific pathogens followed by massive infection by broader spectrum secondary invaders such as species of *Fusarium*, *Botrytis*, *Rhizopus*, *Botryodiplodia* and *Erwinia*. These are generally weakly pathogenic or are saprophytic on the dead or moribund tissue remaining from the primary infection. Many microorganisms responsible for post-harvest pathology originate in the field and either infect the produce before or during harvest or are present as surface contaminants. Contamination with pathogens may also occur during post-harvest operations. However, some pre-harvest infections produce latent infections, which only become active following ripening or damage as in the case of anthracnose, whether infection occurs at or after harvesting, it is mostly at the sites of mechanical injury inflicted during harvesting and handling operations. Bacterial pathogen are often the most important causal agents in the spoilage of vegetables particularly the soft-rot bacteria, e.g., *Erwinia*. Virus diseases, while not normally of post-harvest significance, may detract from the market value of produce, for example, internal cork in sweet potatoes, internal brown spot of yams, apple ring spot and stony pit virus of pears. A list of some of the major market diseases and their causal agents is given in Table 29.1.

Table 29.1 Post-harvest Diseases of Some Perishable Crops

Commodity	Disease/Disorder	Causal organism or condition
Apple	Blue mould	*Penicillium expansum*
	Brown rot	*Monilinia fructigena*
	Bitter rot	*Glomerella cingulata*
	Bitter pit	Calcium imbalance in field
Banana	Anthracnose	*Colletotrichum musae*
	Crown rot	*Botryodiplodia theobromae*
		Colletotrichum musae
		Fusarium palidoroseum
		Verticellium theobromae
	Pitting disease	*Magnaporthe grisea*
Cassava	Primary deterioration	Cassava brown streak virus
	Secondary deterioration	Secondary invaders or weak pathogens
Citrus	Alternaria black rot	*Alternaria citri*
	Blue mould	*Penicillium italicum*
	Green mould	*Penicillium digitatum*
	Brown rot	*Phytophthora citrophthora*
	Scab	*Elsinoe fawcetti, E. australis*
	Stem-end root	*Diaporthe citri*
	Internal gumming	Boron deficiency
Crucifers	Alternaria leaf spot	*Alternaria* spp.
	Bacterial soft rot	*Erwinia carotovora* sub sp. *carotovora*
	Soft rot	*Rhizopus* spp.
	Watery soft rot	*Sclerotinia sclerotiorum*
	White rust	*Albugo candida*
Cucurbits	Anthracnose	*Colletotricum orbiculare*
	Bacterial soft rot	*Erwinia* spp.
	Black rot	*Didymella bryoniae*
	Charcoal rot	*Macrophomina phaseolina*
	Fusarium rot	*Fusarium* spp.
	Leak	*Pythium* spp.
	Sclerotium rot	*Corticium rolfsii*
	Soft rot	*Rhizopus* spp.
	Root rot	*Thanatephorus cucumeris*
	Stem-end rot	*Botryodiplodia theobromae*
Grapes	Alternaria rot	*Alternaria* spp.
	Downy mildew	*Plasmopara viticola*
	Grey mould	*Botryotinia fuckeliana*
	Rhizopus rot	*Rhizopus stolonifer*
Mango	Anthracnose	*Glomerella cingulata*
	Black rot	*Aspergillus niger*
	Stem-end rot	*Botryodiplodia theobromae*
Onions	Bacterial soft rot	*Erwinia carotovora* sub sp. *carotovora*
	Black rot	*Aspergillus niger*
	Grey mould/neck rot	*Botrytis allii*
	Smudge	*Colletotrichum circinans*
	White rot	*Sclerotium cepivorum*

(Contd.)

Table 29.1 Post-harvest Diseases of Some Perishable Crops (*Contd.*)

Commodity	Disease/Disorder	Causal organism or condition
Papaya	Anthracnose	*Glomerella cingulata*
	Black rot	*Phoma caricae-papayae*
	Ripe/ fruit stem-end rot	*Botryodiplodia theobromae*
Pear	Bitter rot	*Glomerella cignulata*
	Blue mould	*Penicillium* spp.
	Late storage rot	*Nectria galligena*
	Bitter pit	*Calcium imbalance*
Pineapple	Black rot	*Ceratocystis paradoxa*
	Brown rot	*Gibberella fujikuroi*
	Fruitlet core rot	*Penicillium funciculosum*
Potato	Bacterial wilt/brown rot	*Ralstonia solanacearum*
	Bacterial ring rot	*Clavibacter michiganensis* subsp. *sepedonicus*
	Blight	*Phytophthora infestans*
	Dry rot	*Fusarium* spp.
	Gangrene	*Phoma* spp.
	Pink rot	*Phytophthora erythroseptica*
	Soft rot	*Erwinia* spp.
	Tuber rot	*Corticium rolfsii*
	Wart	*Synchytrium endobioticum*
	Watery wound rot	*Pythium* spp.
Stone fruit	Brown rot	*Sclerotinia* spp.
	Rhizopus rot	*Rhizopus stolonifer, R. nigricans*
Strawberry	Gery mould	*Botryotnina fuckeliana*
	Rhizopus rot	*Rhizopus* spp.

29.4 MYCOTOXINS AND MYCOTOXIOCES

During 1960, in England, nearly 10,000 young turkey fowls were killed due to an 'X' disease which was due to feeding them with groundnut meal infected by *Aspergillus flavus*. Alfatoxins is the collective name proposed for a number of toxic products, which have been first discovered from and named after *A. flavus*. Now more commonly, the generic name *mycotoxins* has been proposed for the group. Mycotoxins are considered responsible for mycotoxicoses. Mycotoxins have been associated with diseases often leading to mortality in swine, cattle, poultry, horses and sheep as well as causing some human diseases such as respiratory allergy, ergotism, dermatitis, liver cirrhosis and so forth. Some fungi causing post-harvest diseases of perishables, viz. *Absidia cerymbifera, Rhizopus oryzae, Mucor* spp., *Aspergillus* spp., *Penicillium* spp., *Curuvularia geniculata, Fusarium* spp. are known to attack both man and animal.

29.5 MANAGEMENT OF POST-HARVEST PROBLEMS

Post-harvest diseases may be managed or avoided by various physical, chemical or biological means. Currently biocontrol is not commercially exploited and more emphasis is given over host plant resistance to post harvest diseases in the management of the diseases.

29.5.1 Avoidance

Immediately processing the produce into some easily preserved inert form can avoid the need for good storage and the risk of losses due to post-harvest problems. The continuous demand for a particular plant produce requires adoption of a strategy of production, storage and transportation.

29.5.2 Physical Methods

The correct stage of produce and method of harvesting are important factors, which determine extents of post-harvest losses. The physical and physiological conditions and health of produce when it is placed in store are major factors governing losses during storage.

Proper handling. The reduction in losses can be achieved by careful handling and improved packaging techniques in order to avoid mechanical injury. Produce should be transported and stored in containers with good ventilation, adequate cushioning materials, stacking strength, and durability to withstand crushing pressure and high humidity conditions. In the majority of starchy root crops the adverse effects of injury may be reduced by a simple process of curing through exposure to a warm, well aerated but humid environment. This promotes cell suberization and the formation of cork layer over wounds, which not only reduce moisture loss but also acts as a physical barrier against wounds pathogens. For example, the average storage loss of 33% in sweet potatoes in USA was reduced by curing to 17%. Careful attention must always be paid to general sanitation and cleanliness of implements, handling machinery, containers and stores.

Temperature. Longevity of harvested produce (shelf-life) as well as extent of losses are influenced by prevailing temperature. The cool chains and refrigerated storage are probably most important means of reducing post harvest losses in perishable produce. Moisture loss from fresh produce is largely determined by the difference between the vapour pressure of the product and that of the surrounding air (vapour pressure deficit – VPD). The drier the air the more rapid is the water loss and as VPDs are lower at lower temperatures, moisture loss is less at lower temperatures. Onions, for example, when kept in open air stores in Israel, lost 42% of their original weight within four weeks, but only 2.7% when kept in sheds protected from high ambient temperature, and 1.4% in cold stores at 0°C. The optimum relative humidity for the storage of most perishable produce is 85-95%. Durable or dried perishable produce should be stored in a dry and cool environment to prevent mould growth.

Radiation treatment. Radiation is used for food preservation, e.g., grain disinfestations, the inhibition of sprouting in potatoes and onions, and delayed ripening in mangoes and bananas. Under certain conditions, radiation can kill insects, reduce populations or eliminate microorganisms and retard physiological processes such as ripening and sprouting.

Chemical treatments. Use of chemical pesticide should be avoided for management of post-harvest diseases as the toxic residues may cause health hazards. For optimum use of chemical agents for avoiding losses a thorough knowledge of the etiology and epidemiology of the diseases involved is required. For diseases where infection occurs in the field prior to harvest, chemical control measures should normally be used for preventing field infection before harvest (pre-harvest infections). **Fumigants** are used in closed treating containers used for produce to be transported or stored. Fumigants have the advantage of greater power of penetration. The best-known fumigant is sulfur dioxide (SO_2) used primarily to control *Botrytis* and other rots of grapes. This gas may be applied directly from cylinders, by burning sulfur or by release from sodium acid sulfate. Overtreatment results in loss of flavour and bleached skin spots; SO_2 is phytotoxic to most fruit and vegetables, and the gas is highly corrosive. Other fumigants include ozone and nitrogen trichloride (NCl_3; poisonous in high concentrations). It has been successfully used to control stem-end rot, and blue and green moulds of citrus and common post-harvest diseases of cantaloupe melons, tomatoes and onions.

Chemically treated wraps have been used predominantly in the citrus and apple industries for localizing diseases and preventing the development or spread of diseases. Treatments are more effective when the chemical also acts as a vapour phase (fumigant), e.g., biphenyl impregnated wrappers. Other chemicals used to impregnate wraps are pine oil, sodium-o-phenyl, phenyl phenol esters, copper sulfate, and some active halogen compounds. Some success has also been obtained in treating container liners or shredded paper packaging material, instead of individual wrappers. Waxes are used to improve the appearance and to reduce moisture loss. Waxes are used commercially on citrus, cucumbers, and to a lesser extent on other crops such as sweet peppers, tomatoes, melons and apples.

29.5.3 Biological Control

The manipulation of antagonistic fungi and bacteria is likely to find a prominent place in management of post-harvest diseases. Biocontrol agents are safe for consumers and the environment. Direct application of antagonists to harvest produce as dips or sprays is a relatively straightforward technique but methods that establish populations of antagonists on fruit surfaces prior to harvest are also being worked out.

29.6 SOME IMPORTANT POST-HARVEST DISEASES OF FRUITS

29.6.1 Fruit Rot of Papaya

The post-harvest diseases of papaya are due to various fungal pathogens. However, those caused by *Macrophomina*, *Rhizopus* and *Phomopsis* spp. are important and most commonly reported. Symptoms of three important diseases (Plate 29.1) are described. *Macrophomina* rot appears as small water-soaked spots on fruit surface. Gradually, such spots become deeper and sunken causing rotting of inner tissues. Subsequently, small sclerotia develop on these spots. The inner tissues of such fruits develop brownish-black colour having dark mycelial growth. *Rhizopus* rot or watery fruit rot develops on the injured fruits, which develop irregular watersoaked lesions. These lesions in due course are covered with whitish fungal growth which later on turns dark brown. The fruits become watery and emit foul smell. Infection spreads quickly to the adjoining fruits. In *Phomopsis fruit rot*, initially water-soaked spots appear which may become sunken and dark brown to black. Sometimes, white raised tissues on the sides surround such spots. The whole area becomes soft and pulpy giving the typical appearance of soft rot.

Causal organisms. Large number of fungi have been found associated with papaya fruits. Important amongst these are: *Rhizopus stolonifer*, *Macrophomina phaseoli*, *Phomopsis caricaepapayae*, *Colletotrichum gloeosporioides*, *Botryodiplodia theobromae*, *Phytophthora palmivora*, *Cladosporium cladosporioides*, *Alternaria alternata*, *Ascochyta caricae*, *Aspergillus flavus*, *A. fumigatus*, *A. nidulans*, *A. niger*, *A. terreus*, *Cochliobolus spicifer*, *Curvularia lunata*,

Cladosporium cucumerinum, Corynespora cassiicola, Penicillium implicatum, etc. Out of these *Macrophomina phaseoli, Rhizopus stolonifer* and *Phomopsis caricae-papayae* are important ones.

Management

(i) Preventive measures. As papaya fruits are highly perishable, therefore, proper handling of fruits during harvesting, grading, packing and transportation helps in avoiding bruising or injuries to the fruit. Removal and destruction of the rotting fruits from packing sheds also help to reduce sources of inoculum for new infections.

(ii) Chemical control. Kapoor and Chohan (1974) reported that pre-harvest sprays of ziram, captan and ferbam control the rot effectively in storage also. Similarly, benomyl, captan and mancozeb have also been found effective in preventing symptoms development due to *Phomopsis* infection (Dhingra and Khare, 1971). Field sprays of mancozeb reduces Rhizopus soft rot incidence by reducing field initiated fruit disease whose lesions serve as the source of infection (Nishijima et al., 1990).

(iii) Hot water/air treatment. Dipping of fruits in hot water at 49°C for 20 min has been found effective to control rot due to various pathogens (Pathak et al., 1972). With the use of recently, developed quarantine treatment by a forced hot air (48.5°C for 3-4 hours) combined with thiabendazole (TBZ) (4 g ai/l) application or hot water immersion (49°C for 20 min), the incidence of most post-harvest diseases can be reduced (Nishijima et al., 1992). The hot water treatment combined with the vapour treatment provides adequate control of stem end rot due to *Botryodiplodia thebromae, C. gloeosporioides* and *Fusarium* sp. The double hot water dip (42°C for the 30 min.) followed by 49°C for 20 min, treatment used in Hawaii also control post-harvest diseases. Forced air-dry heat or vapour heat treatments are currently used in United States. Both treatments take 6 hours of gradually increasing temperature and are completed when the internal temperature of fruits reaches 47.2°C.

29.6.2 Stem-end Rot of Pineapple

The disease is also known as **core rot, base rot** or **black rot**. In India, Mehta first reported the disease in 1940. It is serious in transit and storage and losses upto 15 per cent have been reported. Symptoms appear as small circular, water-soaked spots near the stem end, which gradually enlarge and coalesce forming black patches. The underneath surface also becomes black, soft and exude juice upon little pressing. In advanced stage such rotten fruits emit foul characteristic smell of ethyl acetate. *Ceratocystis parasoxa* (Doidge) C. Morean is responsible for causing this disease.

Management. Post-harvest dipping of fruits for 5 minutes in TBZ (1000 ppm) or benomyl (200 ppm) has been observed to reduce storage decay (Sridhar, 1975). Dusting of fruits with benzoic acid (0.1%) coated in kaolin also reduces this disease in transit (Mallikarjunaradhya, et al., 1979). In addition to these chemical measures, certain preventive measures should also be followed to avoid losses. Diseased plant should be removed and destroyed. The harvested fruits should be dried in sun for 2 hours and the packing boxes should be sprayed with 3 per cent formaline.

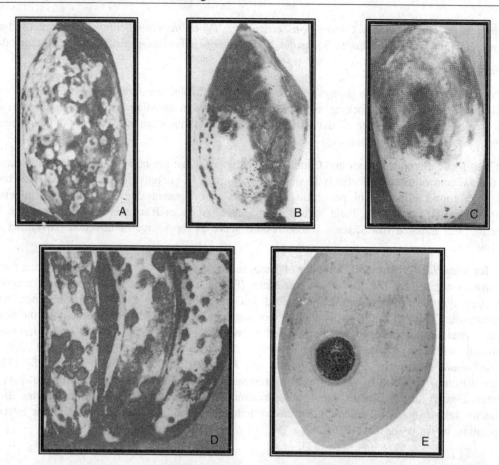

Plate 29.1 Symptoms of post-harvest diseases of fruit, (A) rot of papaya caused by *Cladosporium herbarum*, (B) post-harvest sympotms showing black spots on mango fruits, (C) symptoms of stem-end rot of mango due to *Diplodia natalens*, (D) storage rot of banana caused by *Verticilium theobromae*, (E) fruit rot of papaya.

29.6.3 Post-Harvest Diseases of Mango

Anthracnose (Colletotrichum gloesporioides – Glomerella cingulata). It is also known as **blossom blight**, **leaf spot** or **fruit rot** and is the most common and widespread fungal disease of mango. The disease appears on all the aerial plant parts including leaves, stems, inflorescence and fruits. Anthracnose of ripening fruits is characterized by the development of black spots of varying forms which may be slightly sunken or may show cracks. Finally, the entire fruit is covered by spots and shows fruit rot symptoms.

Management. Instantaneous dip of fruits in 1000 ppm benomyl or 2000 ppm thiobendazole before storage is reported to give a good control of fruit rot.

Black mould rot of mango. It is a disease of wide occurrence. The disease has been reported from Philippines, Venezuela and India (Srivastava, et al., 1965; Srivastava, 1968). The pathogen has been reported to cause losses from 20-35 per cent. The disease is severe during storage and marketing processes. The affected fruits show yellowing of the base along with development of irregular, hazy, grayish spots. These spots coalesce and produce dark brown or black lesions. The skin of the fruits becomes soft and sunken. These spots are later covered with sooty mass of black spores. The stalk end infection results in premature fruit drop (Plate 29.1). *Aspergillus niger* is responsible for black mould rot.

Management. Incidence of black mould rot may be reduced by pre-harvest fungicidal sprays as well as post-harvest fruit dip in hot water and/or fungicides. Pathak and Shekhawat (1976) found that hot water treatment (55°C for 5 minutes) delayed the rot for 6 days. Similarly, careful handling is necessary at all stages after harvesting to prevent mechanical damage to the fruit. Storage at temperatures between 10°C and 15°C prevents development of black mould rot. Post harvest dip treatment with fungicide like benomyl@1500 ppm (Bhargava and Singh, 1975) or triforine (100 ppm), delan @ 1250 ppm (Pandey et al., 1980) could reduce the disease.

Soft rot. Disease appears in the form of light brown circular patches on fruit surface. The intensity of the colour varies according to the variety infected and time after infections. The lesion grows in regular manner and form large circular patches. The skin of the fruit becomes soft. In severe cases, watery ooze comes out. In later stages, fluffy growth of the fungus occurs over the fruit. *Rhizopus arrhizus* is responsible for causing soft rot of mango.

Management. The dipping of mango fruits in 2-aminothiazole with 2-aminopyridine (each in 5% concentration) has been reported to protect fruits for about 20 days. Pathak et al (1972) further found that dipping of fruits in a combination of oils like mustard oil, castor oil and paraffin each at 75% concentration with 1% soap solution is effective in preventing fruit infection.

Stem-end rot. Besides India, the disease is known to occur in Burma, Sri Lanka, USA, Philippines and Mauritius. Four to six per cent fruits are normally spoiled every year in the Indian markets. In the initial stages of infection, epicarp of the fruit around the base of the pedicel darkens. Within few hours, the affected area enlarges to form a black circular patch which, under humid conditions, extends rapidly and within two or three days the whole fruit turns black (Plate 29.1). The pulp in the diseased fruit softens and turns brownish. The infected fruits lose ascorbic acid rapidly and have low content of non-reducing sugars in the pulp.

Management. Pre-harvest spray of carbendazim (0.1%) can be effective. Harvesting of fruits should be done on a clear dry day and immediately after harvest, the fruits should be covered and brought to the ripening houses. Care should be taken to prevent shaping off of the pedicle and injuries should be avoided during handling. Pedicle or stem-end scar can be coated with Chaubattia paste. Fruits can also be given post-harvest dip with borax at 43°C for 3 minutes.

29.6.4 Fruit Rot of Banana

Fruit rot of banana is also known as **finger rot**. The fungi *Botryodiplodia theobromae, Rhizopus oryzae, Aspergillus niger, A. flavus* and *Fusarium equiseti* have been associated with premature ripening and storage rots. The initial symptom includes discoloured fruit rind followed by appearance of water-soaked spots. Infection starts from distal end and gradually the rotting progresses to the stalk end. Finally, the fruits turn dark brown in colour. The fruit pulp is converted to black watery mass, emitting sweetish odour. In advanced stages white or light gray cottony mycelial growth appear on the rotten tissues followed by development of pycnidia. Wounds provide the avenues for the entry of the pathogen. High temperature ranging from 25-30°C favour disease development.

Management. It includes preventive measure. Fruits should be harvested at proper stage of maturity and ripening during transit should be avoided. Care must be taken to prevent bruising of fruits. Thiabendazole @ 300-500 ppm reduces the incidence of the disease and controls latent and apparent infections.

29.6.5 Fruit Rot of Citrus

The fruit rot of citrus is also known as **gray mould** or **blue mould rot of citrus**. It occurs during the transit, storage and in the markets. Mature fruits fall on the ground. The disease incidence may vary from 0-100 per cent depending upon the storage condition. In Maharashtra losses of 43 and 47 per cent of mandarins in trucks and train transport, respectively, have been reported (Naqvi and Dass, 1994). Disease symptoms can be seen on any part of the fruit. The infected fruits become brownish and watery, which may crack easily, even with little pressure. Such fruits are later covered with green (*P. digitatum* Sacc.) or blue mouldy growth (*Pencillium italicum* Whemer) depending upon the causal fungus involved. Gradually, the entire fruit rots may be reduced to decomposed mass, producing numerous conidia that act as source of secondary inoculum. Wounds provide the avenues for the entry of the fungus. Stem end is the common entry point for both the organisms. Long storage periods also enhance susceptibility.

Management. Management: The management of citrus fruit rot requires combinations of chemical, biological and host resistance. Washing or dipping of fruits in bleaching powder (2%) for five minutes or flit 406 (0.2%) for 10 minutes and subsequent storage at 2-4°C helps in reducing the incidence of disease. TBZ incorporated in Waxol –12 or prestorage dip in TBZ (500 ppm) for 2-3 minutes provides good control. Imazalil WP and EC formulations have been found quite effective for long-term storage. Treatment of lemons with fenpropimorph and flutriafol at a packing house reduce post-harvest decay upto 94% by arresting lesions and sporulation at inoculation sites. Fumigation of packinghouses with formaldehyde and driol for 4 hours has been reported to reduce number of viable spores on culture and plastic surface (Chitzanidis, et al., 1987). Chemical impregnated wraps such as diphenyl wraps (320 mg/300ml acetone, 40 mg/wrap) provide complete control of blue mould in Kinnow fruits (Mishra, 1989). Treatment of oranges with sodium O-phenyl phenate (SOPP) for three minutes, heated to 45°C resulted in 87.94% reduction in the incidence of decay (Barkai and Apelbaum, 1991).

Curing of sealed citrus fruits at 32-36°C enhances resistance, lignification and anti-fungal metabolite production. Exposure of lemon fruits to ultraviolet radiations also enhances the level of scoparone and illuminated fruits have reduced susceptibility of *P. digitatum*. Giberelic acid dip @ 500 ppm for 2 minutes inhibits decay development of stored fruits.

Biological control has been found effective. Several antagonists, e.g., yeasts (*Debaryomyces hansenii* and *Aureobasidium pullulans*) and bacteria (*Pseudomonas cepacia* and *P. syringae*) have been used. The bacterium grows rapidly in wounds and causes no visible injury to the fruit. Another bioagent *Bacillus pumilus* provides significant control of *P. digitatum* infection in Valencia orange which is as effective as imazalil (500 ug/ml) and is significantly better than benomyl treatment (500 ug/ml) (Huang, et al., 1992).

29.6.6 Fruit Rot of Guava

Fruit rot of guava is caused by many pathogens, which are capable of infecting fruits during transit and storage. In Bangladesh, the disease is quite serious where almost 90-100 per cent fruits have been found infected with fungi, namely *Pestalotiopsis psidii, Colletotrichum gloeosporioides* and *Botryodiplodia theobromae* (Hossain and Meah, 1992). Fruit rots also result in reduced ascorbic acid, sugars, proteins and total phenols (Majumdar and Pathak, 1989). Symptoms produced on guava fruit depend upon the pathogen involved; however, ultimate end result is rotting of fruit. In case of *Colletotrichum*, small, circular dark brown lesions are produced on the fruits. The mesocarp beneath these spots turns hard and corky after developing cracks. In *Botryodiplodia* fruit rot, the affected fruits show brownish discolouration first at stem end, proceeding to rest of the fruit in the wavy fashion, followed by appearance of small pycnidia on the entire fruit surface.

Number of post-harvest fungi such as *Phoma psidii, Macrophomina allahabadensis, Phytophthora nicotianae* var. *parasitica, Pestalotiopsis psidii, Colletotrichum gloeosporioides, Rhizopus stolonifer, Botryodiplodia theobromae* and *Aspergillus niger*, have been reported to cause fruit rot of guava. Fruit rot of guava due to *Pestalotiopsis psidii* can be managed with the sprays of benomyl. Hot water treatment of infected fruits at 50°C for 5 min has been found to reduce disease severity by Majumdar and Pathak (1991). Gamma radiations (100 kr) inhibit germination and elongation of germ tube of conidia of *Colletotrichum gloeosporioides* and help in preventing post-harvest decay of guava fruits (Gupta and Chatrath, 1973).

29.6.7 Post-Harvest Diseases of Pome and Stone Fruits

Like other fruits, pome and stone fruits also suffer post-harvest losses. Plate 29.2 presents the symptoms of post-harvest problems. Important diseases during storage and transit are summarized as follows:

Bitter rot. The disease is severe in warm and humid areas. Slightly sunken areas/brown spots extend in concentric shape. Minute dark acervuli develop. *Glomerella cingulata (Collectotrichum gleosporioides)* is the causal organism. Perennial cankers on limbs and mummified fruits are source of inoculum. Disease management includes pruning of dead wood and removal of mummified fruits, pre-harvest fungicide spray and post-harvest treatment.

Grey mould rot. Basically a problem of storage and transportation may start as calyx end rot, further grows as soft brown rot affecting the fruits. Under humid conditions, gray-brown spores are produced on rotten host surface. The pathogen *Botryotinia fuckeliana (Botrytis cinerea)* survives in soil or debris as sclerotia. The conidia infect dying blossom or fruits. Disease can be managed by sanitation, fungicide spray and post-harvest treatment with fungicides or *Trichoderma viridae*.

Rhizopus rot. Brown coloured, circular water soaked areas appear on fruit skin. Soft and watery rot of tissue with fermented/acidic odour is commonly found. *Rhizopus stolonifer* (stone) and *R. arrhizus* (apples) are responsible for heavy post-harvest losses. *Rhizopus*, a wound parasite, is favoured by high humidity and high temperature. Pre-harvest fungicide spray and proper cold storage (4-5°C) reduce the incidence.

Blue mould rot. Most important post-harvest problem of apples *Penicillium expansum* attacks only injured or over mature fruits. Prevention of physical injuries, post-harvest cleaning and disinfestations help in reducing incidence.

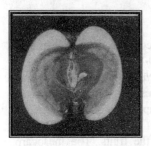

(A) rot of an apple caused by the bulls eye rot fungus *Pezicula malicorticis*

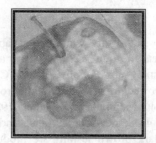

(B) bull's-eye rot of Golden Delicious apples, producing lesions with light coloured centres

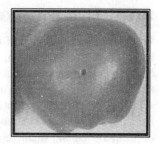

(C) Alternaria rot in wounds on Delicious apples

(D) blue mould on a Golden Delicious apple

(E) blossom-end rot (gray mould) of a Granny Smith apple

Plate 29.2 Symptoms of post-harvest diseases of apple.

REFERENCES

Barkai, G.R. and Apelbaum, A., 1991, Synergistic effect of heat and sodium o-phenyl phenate treatments to inactivate *Penicillium* spores and suppress decay in citrus fruits, *Trop. Sci.*, 31:229.

Booth, R.H., 1974, Post-harvest deterioration of tropical root crops: losses and their control, Trol, *Sci.*, 16:49.

Burton, W.G., 1974, Some biophysical principles underlying the controlled atmosphere storage of plant material, *Annals of Applied Biology*, 78:149-168.

Chitzanidis, A., Riethmacher, G. and Kranz, J., 1987, *Pencillium* contamination and effectiveness of chemical disinfection in citrus packing houses in Greece, *Annales-de-1 Institute-Phytopathologique–Benaki*, 15:109.

Dennis, C., 1983, *Post-harvest Pathology of Fruits and Vegetables,* Academic Press, London, p. 257.

Dhingra, O.D. and Khare, M.N., 1971, A new fruit rot of papaya, *Curr. Sci.*, 40:612.

Eckert, J.W. and Ogawa, J.M., 1985, The chemical control of post-harvest diseases: subtropical and tropical fruits, *Annu. Rev. Phytopathol.*, 23:421.

Eckert, J.W. and Ogawa, J.M., 1988, Chemical control of post-harvest diseases: delicious fruits, berries, vegetables and root/tuber crops, *Annu. Rev. of Phytopathol.*, 26:433.

Ellis, M.A. and Barrat, J.G., 1983, Colonization of Delicious apple fruits by *Alternaria* spp. and effect of fungicides sprays on mouldy core, *Plant Dis.*, 67:150.

Gupta, J.P. and Chatrath, M.S., 1973, Gamma radiation for the control of post-harvest fruit rot of guava, *Indian Phytopathol.*, 26:506.

Harvey, J.M., 1978, Reduction of losses in fresh market fruits and vegetables, *Annu. Rev. Phytopathol.*, 16:321.

Hossain, M.S. and Meah, M.B., 1992, Prevalence and control of guava fruit anthracnose, *Trop. Pest Management*, 38:181.

Huang, Y., Wild, B.L., and Morris, S.C., 1992, Post-harvest biological control of *Pencillium digitatum* decay on citrus fruit by *Bacillus pumilus*, *Ann. Appl. Biol.*, 120:367.

Kapoor, S.P. and Chohan, J.S., 1974, Evaluation of fungicides for the control of fruit rot of papaya caused by *Macrophomina phaseoli*, *Indian Phytopathol.*, 27:251.

Lonsdale, J.H., Saaiman, W.C. and Smith, D.C., 1994, *An Effective Pre-harvest Spray Programme for the Control of Post-harvest Mango Diseases,* Yearbook—South African Mango Grower's Association, 14:52.

Majumdar, V.L. and Pathak, V.N., 1989, Changes in nutritional value of guava fruits infected by major post-harvest pathogens, *Plant Foods Hum. Nutrit.*, 39:311.

Majumdar, V.L. and Pathak, V.N., 1991, Effect of hot water treatment on post-harvest diseases of guava fruits, *Acta Botanica India.*, 19:79.

Mallikarjunaradhya, A.V., et al., 1979, Control of fungal stem-end rot during Transport of Pineapples, *J. Food Sci. Tech.*, 16:232.

Mishra, B.P., 1989, A note on control of blue mould of Kinnow fruits caused by *Penicillium italicum* through diphenyl wrappers, *Haryana. J. Hortic. Sci.*, 18:65.

Naqvi, S. and Dass, H.C., 1994. Assessment of post-harvest losses in Nagpur mandarin a pathological perspective, *Plant Dis., Res.*, 9:215.

Nishijima, W.T., 1995, Effect of hot air and hot water treatment of papaya fruits on fruit quality and incidence of diseases, *Acta Hortic.*, 370:121.

Pathak, V.N. and Shekhawat, P.S., 1976, Efficacy of some fungicides and hot water in control of Anthracnose and Aspergillus rot of mango fruits, *Indian Phytopathol.*, 37:682.

Pathak, V.N. Sharma, H.C. and Bhatnagar, L.G., 1972, Efficacy of fungicides and hot water for control of Fusarium and Rhizopus rot of papaya, *Int. Sym. Sub. Trop. Hortic,* Bangalore, p. 118.

Rao, N.N.R., 1984, Effect of post-harvest fungicidal treatment of citrus fruits against the control of green mould rot, *J. Food Sci. Tech.*, 21:25.

Schirra, M., Mulas, M. and Baghino, L., 1995, Influence of post-harvest hot dip fungicide treatments on Redblush grapefruit quality during long term storage, *Food Sci. Tech. Int. Ciencia-Y-Technologi-de-Alimentos*, 1:35.

Smilanick, J.L. and Denis, A.R., 1992, Control of green mould of lemons with *Pseudomonas* species, *Plant Dis.*, 76:481.

Thakur, D.P. and Chenulu, V.V., 1970, Chemical control of soft rot of apple and mango fruits caused by *Rhizopus arrhizus, Indian Phytopathol.*, 23:58.

Villiers, E.E.D.E. and Korsten, L., 1994, *Biological Treatments for the Control of Mango Post-harvest Diseases*, Yearbook—South African Mango Grower's Association, 14:48.

Wilson, C.L. and Chalutz, X., 1989, Post-harvest biological control of Penicillium rots of citrus with antagonistic yeasts and bacteria, *Scientia Hortic.*, 40:105.

Yaguchi, Y. and Nakamura, S., 1993, Effect of hot water and vapour heat treatments on the control of stem end rot of papaya, *Japanese J. Trop. Agric.*, 37:167.

30 Plant Diseases of Unsettled Etiology

30.1 INTRODUCTION

There are some plant diseases whose causal agent (s) are yet to be conclusively and precisely identified and established. Several possible causes of such concerned plant diseases have been described. In this chapter three such diseases of economic and national importance are briefly described.

30.2 MANGO MALFORMATION

Mango, *Mangifera indica*, is one of the most precious fruit grown in subtropical and tropical zones. In different agro climatic zones, number of stresses, both pathological and physiological, have been recognized in mango, which adversely affect its productivity. Mango malformation, an age old disease, is one of the most threatening disease of recent times primarily because of its destructive and widespread nature. Although the disease was recognized as early as 1891 by Maries in India, some attention was devoted to it only in mid 1950s when it started assuming serious proportions in other parts of the country. Presently, the disease is known to occur in most of the mango growing areas of the world (e.g., Pakistan, the Middle East, South Africa, Brazil, Central America, Israel, Mexico and USA). The Indian mango industry is badly hit by this malady, as more than 50% of trees are affected, causing heavy losses in yield, particularly in northern parts of India.

30.2.1 Symptoms

Mango malformation appears at two stages: (a) vegetative malformation (Plate 30.1) and (b) floral malformation (Plate 30.2).

Vegetative malformation. Vegetative malformation is more pronounced on young seedlings but may also appear on mature trees. Young seedlings show symptoms when about five months old. In the initial stages of symptoms development, vegetative buds in the axils of leaves or at the apex of seedlings swell and produce small shootlets bearing small, scaly leaves. In such seedlings, apical dominance is lost and as a result numerous vegetative buds sprout, producing hypertrophied growth, which constitutes vegetative malformation. More than one vegetative bud at one point gets activated, and as a result, small shootlets arise bearing very small rudimentary leaves at short internodes. These leaves get crowded so that shootlets and their branches are not distinguishable, and the whole mass of rudimentary leaves gives a bunch like appearance. Such symptoms, when present at the apex of the seedlings, are referred to as bunchy-top (BT) stage. In some cases, thick

645

Plate 30.1 Vegetative malformation, (A) a young mango seedling showing bunchy top symptoms, (B) a vegetatively malformed seedling showing sprouting of vegetative buds at various sites of internodes, (C) bunchy top symptoms on the branch of a tree, (D) transformation of malformed panicles to vegetatively malformed apices.

shootlets arise from the swollen axillary buds, which ultimately have secondary branches that elongate further and bear small rudimentary leaves at the internodes. Collectively, the whole structure looks like a witch's broom. In other cases, the vegetative buds get activated throughout the length of internodes and produce small, scaly leaves, (Plate 30.2).

Floral malformation. The disease makes its appearance with the emergence of inflorescences on the shoots. Normally, the healthy panicles emerge from terminal buds and bear hermaphrodite and male flowers, which vary from 6 to 8 mm in diameter. Contrarily, the flowers in the diseased panicles are greatly enlarged, which constitutes a malformed inflorescence. At maturity, such panicles appear hypertrophoid, though diameter of the main and secondary axis does not always increase as compared with a healthy inflorescence. Such panicles are heavier and generally much greener as compared to healthy ones.

Great variation in symptoms is observed in a malformed panicle, depending on the cultivar, degree of hypertrophy and severity of symptoms. Healthy branches may also be present in a malformed panicle. Such partially infected panicles bear fruits, which may even attain maturity. (Plate 30.2).

Plate 30.2   Floral malformaiton, (A) a malformed panicle showing the formation of numerous small heads due to clustering of hypertrophied flowers, (B) a partially infected panicle showing healthy (H) and malformed (D) flowers.

30.2.2   Etiology

Symptoms and the effects of mango malformation have been studied exhaustively but the actual cause of the disease has been very controversial. On the basis of symptoms and physiological changes in the tissues, the disease was considered a physiological disorder (Khan and Khan, 1963; Majumdar, et al., 1970). It was suspected a viral disease, but no organism had been isolated from the diseased organs and symptoms resembled leafhopper transmitted virus diseases (Singh, et al., 1961). The malformation was also considered due to toxemia resulting from the feeding of eriophyed mites (Narasimhan, 1954; Nariani and Seth, 1962; Summanwar and Raychaudhuri, 1968). None of these reports could provide conclusive proof of pathogenicity. Indications about hormonal imbalance had prompted the use of indole acetic acid as a control measure and some relief was claimed. Manipulation of macro and micronutrients has not been able to reduce disease incidence or recovery of plants. Electron microscope studies could not reveal presence of virus particles or phytoplasmal bodies. Use of acaricides, could provide only temporary relief.

In the last two decades, the published findings suggest indirect effects of one or more fungi. Several workers (Bhatnagar and Beniwal, 1977; Chakrabarti and Ghosal, 1985; Summanwar, et al., 1968; Verma, et al., 1974) reported constant association of *Fusarium moniliforme* and *Fusarium oxysporum* with diseased plant organs. However, Koch's postulates or the test of pathogenicity has not yet been demonstrated.

Kumar and Beniwal (1992) after their exhaustive investigations put forth the hypothesis in support of the role of *Fusarium*, particularly *F. moniliforme* var. *subglutinans*, which is taken up by the wounded mango roots from the soil and are apoplastically transported to the growing points (shoot tips, auxiliary buds, etc.) where they multiply and gradually release 'malformation inducing principles' (MIP) for an extended period of time. This principle induces hormonal imbalance and conditions the host cells to produce malformed growth. Once the growth phase of the fungus is over due to nutrient depletion, it produces secondary metabolites which are translocated in the plant and result in toxicity symptoms such as reduced growth and necrosis of malformed tissue, seedling necrosis and loss of flowering.

Several workers (Kumar and Ram, 1999; Pandey and Ram, 1995; Raina and Ram, 1991; Ram and Bisht, 1984; Singh and Dhillon, 1987) proposed the presence of 'malformin like substances' in malformed mango tissues as well as in culture filtrates of *Fusarium*. Majumdar and Singh (1972) studied seasonal variation in disease incidence and suggested a correlation between disease incidence and ambient temperature at flowering. The disease incidence was less when temperature was artificially raised around the trees during the flowering period and flower buds appearing early showed more disease than those appearing late. The incidence of disease is most common where mean temperature during winter is 16°C. Incidence of disease is low in South India where winter temperate remains relatively high. From the available information one may be tempted to conclude that *Fusarium* sp., particularly *F. moniliforme* var. *subglutinans* is the most likely cause of mango malformation (Kumar and Beniwal, 1992) as:

1. It is most often isolated from malformed tissues where its population is much higher than the healthy tissues.
2. Its conidia are taken up by the damaged roots and are translocated to different plant parts except leaves.
3. Physiology of the fungus and/or its metabolic products may explain several physiological alterations observed in the infected tissues some of which individually or collectively may constitute malformation inducing principle (MIP). Culture filtrates of the fungus, when inoculated on seedlings or flower buds, produce similar toxicity symptoms as induced by the extracts of malformed tissues. Therefore, it may also serve as a source of toxicity principle (TP). These toxicities may be the part of malformation syndrome.
4. These is no strong evidence to refute the involvement of fungus, more specifically *F. moniliforme* Var. *subglutinans*, as the causal agent of mango malformation.

Unfortunately, none of the aforementioned characteristics are associated exclusively with *F. moniliforme* var. *subglutinans* except for its invariably higher population in infected as compared to healthy tissues. However, this could be a consequence of malformed growth. Conidia of the fungus are already present in the vascular system of plant as they are taken up from the soil through the damaged roots. In one of the opinion surveys involving 20 mango pathologists from all over India unanimous conclusion was that, 'mango malformation should still be considered a disease of unknown etiology'.

30.2.3 Disease Cycle

In early stages not many experiments were successful in producing infection either of vegetative or floral malformation following inoculations. Therefore, sufficient information on the causal organisms, its biology and infection court, mode of entry, mechanism of dissemination, etc. have not been generated. Nevertheless, the recorded developments towards establishing the cause have put forth growing evidences on the involvement of fungus-induced principles in the etiology of the malady. Until then, a cycle is proposed (Kumar and Beniwal, 1992) that gives at least the chain of events in the rapid development of disease in newer areas (Figure 30.1).

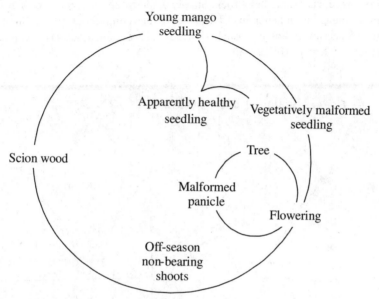

Figure 30.1 Chain of events in development of mango malformation disease (After Kumar and Beniwal, 1992).

30.2.4 Management

Although, the etiology of disease is not known, it did not prevent the attempts for its management. Several fungicides, nutritional amendments, growth regulators (IAA) and many cultural practices such as root pruning, all have failed to give a lasting control of the mango malformation disease. An integrated schedule consisting of pruning of affected parts, sprays of mangiferinzinc or copper chelates and acaricides (three applications: pre-bud burst, after emergence, and pre-blossom stages) is reported to give significant reduction in malformation and increase in the number of healthy inflorescences and fruit set. These can be probably only additive steps to more workable solutions. On the basis of information available it can be visualized that the first step in the malformation management strategy should be to raise seedlings from a nursery where soil is free from fungi suspected to be involved in the disease. Fumigation of nursery soil with fungicides such as vapam may be useful in preparing soil for raising seedling. In addition to seedlings being free from vegetative malformation, it should also be ensured that scions selected from trees which are completely free from vegetative and floral malformation. Injury to roots during planting in the orchard should be minimized.

30.3 COCONUT ROOT (WILT) DISEASE

The root (wilt) disease of coconut is an important threat to coconut plantations in central Kerala. The disease was independently reported from kaviyoor-kallooppara and karunagappally, approximately 50 km away from each other (Figure 30.2). The disease subsequently started spreading to adjoining areas from these foci. Survey undertaken in recent years reveals that the disease occurs in a contagious manner in 4.1 million ha affecting about 59.2 million fruit bearing and 32.4 million non-bearing palms (Jayasankar, 1992). The disease tract has a contiguous core in the southern districts of Kerala (Figure 30.3).

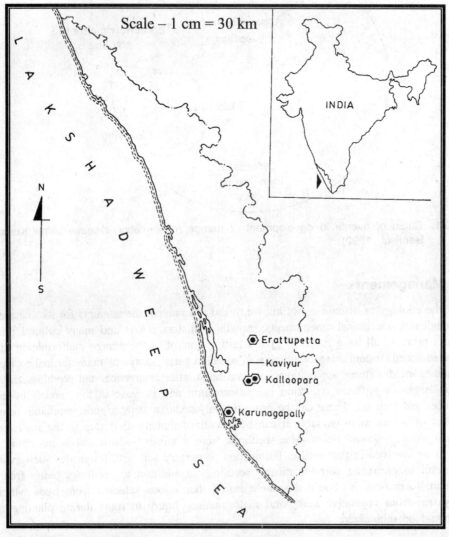

Figure 30.2 Origin and distribution of coconut root (wilt) disease. (*Source:* Jayasankar, 1992).

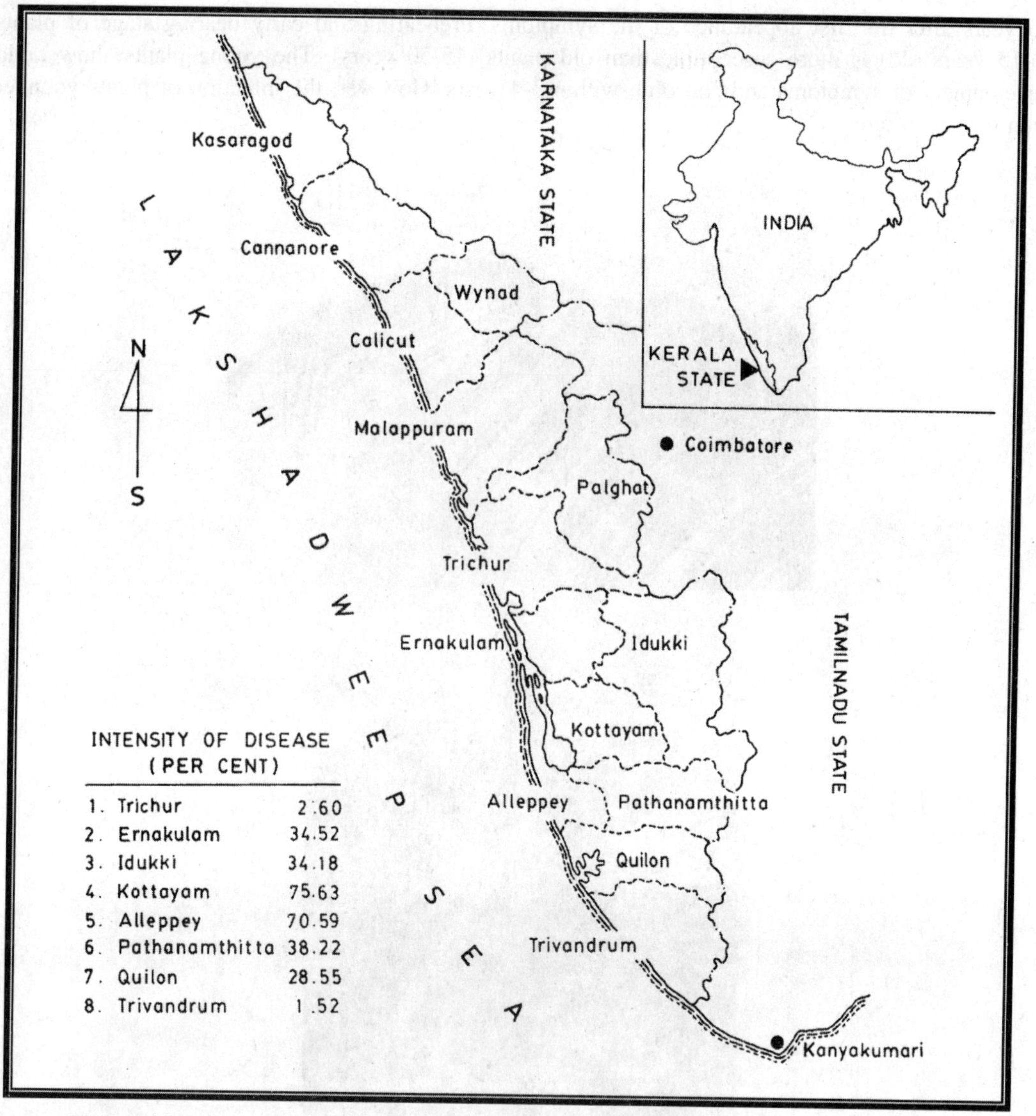
Kasaragod
Cannanore
Wynad
Calicut
Malappuram
Palghat
Trichur
Ernakulam
Idukki
Kottayam
Alleppey
Pathanamthitta
Quilon
Trivandrum
Kanyakumari
Coimbatore
KARNATAKA STATE
TAMILNADU STATE
INDIA
KERALA STATE
LAKSHADWEEP SEA
N
S
INTENSITY OF DISEASE (PER CENT)
1. Trichur 2.60
2. Ernakulam 34.52
3. Idukki 34.18
4. Kottayam 75.63
5. Alleppey 70.59
6. Pathanamthitta 38.22
7. Quilon 28.55
8. Trivandrum 1.52

Figure 30.3 Intensity of coconut root (wilt) disease. (*Source:* Jayasankar, 1992)

30.3.1 Symptoms

The characteristic symptom of the disease is slow wilting of the foliage. The earliest symptoms are flaccidity and ribbing of leaflets accompanied by an abnormal bending of petiole (Figure 30.4). Later, yellowing of the outer whorl of leaves and marginal necrosis of leaflets occurs. Rotting of roots is an important feature of the disease. In root rot, a major portion of the root system is destroyed. Many of the main and lateral roots start drying from the tip backward. The cortex turns brown and gradually dries. A very high percentage of root decay is common in old trees and loss of 50% root system is not uncommon even in healthy plants. The affected plants may survive for

15 years after the first appearance of the symptoms. Prebearing and early bearing stage of plants (6-15 years old) is more susceptible than old plants (15-50 years). The young plants show rapid development of symptoms and succumb within 3-4 years. However, the infection of plants younger than 4 year is rare.

A

B

Figure 30.4   (A) Flaccidity: earliest consistent foliar symptoms of the disease, (B) a plant in the advanced stage of coconut root (wilt) disease. (*Source:* Jayasankar, 1992)

30.3.2 Etiology

Etiology of disease is not very clear (Lal, et al., 1970). Earlier the melody was attributed to nutrients deficiency, waterlogging and other soil conditions. Virological investigations gained accent since 1952 with successful transmission of disease mechanically and by banana lacewing bug *Stephanitis typica*. Sap transmissible agent has been demonstrated by production of transmissible symptoms on cowpea (Shanta and Menon, 1960). Holmen, et al., (1965) suggested that the agent might be a virus like spirochete or a protozoan.

Summanwar, et al. (1969, 1971) attributed disease to the presence of tobacco mosaic virus (TMV). Maramorosch and Kondo (1977) reported the presence of two types of submicroscopic particles identified as Phyloferritin and icosahedral virus. Further investigations on all aspects of viral etiology recorded inconsistent results and, therefore, viral etiology was ruled out. A *fungiod concept* was proposed in 1906. Possible association of *Botryodiplodia*, *R. solani* and *R. bataticola* were reported. Later, some other fungi like *Fusarium equiseti*, *Cylindrocarpan effusum* and *C. lucidum* were investigated. None of these fungi could fulfil Koch's postulates. Thus, any primary role of fungi in inciting the disease has been ruled out. The bacterium (*Enterobacter cloacae*) too was investigated. The bacterium was inoculated alone and in combination with other associated biotic agents in one year old seedlings. Symptoms were not produced and the involvement of the bacterium too was ruled out (Jayasankar, 1992).

Investigations of the involvement of nematodes have yielded 35 genera of nematodes from the root zone of coconut. They include *Xiphinema*, *Longidorus* and *Radopholus similis*. Subsequently, the investigations centred on *R. similis*. In a pathogenicity trial initiated in 1982, the production of typical disease symptoms even after six years was absent. As such *R. similis* is not involved as an incitant in the etiology of root (wilt) disease. Against the background of the investigation carried out from different angles on the etiology of the disease, Solomon, et al. (1983) observed association of mycoplasma like organisms (MLOs) in diseased tissues while such bodies were conspicuous by absence in sample from healthy palms. The constant association of MLOs has subsequently been established in a large number of diseased palm tissues (Figure 30.5). The intensified search for insect

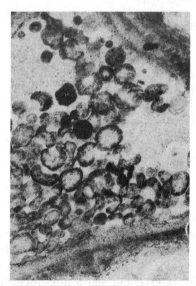

Figure 30.5 MLOs in sieve tubes of diseased plant tissues. (*Source:* Jayasankar, 1992)

vectors in this context, besides the lace bug, *S. typica*, a leafhopper, *Sophonia greeni* (Distant) and a plant hopper, *Proutista moesta* (westwood), were recorded. Electron microscopic observations of the lace bugs that had a sufficient acquisition plus incubation period on diseased coconut palms (18-23 days) revealed the presence of structures resembling MLOs in the salivary glands and brain tissues (Figure 30.6), which were not observed in the bugs collected from disease free areas.

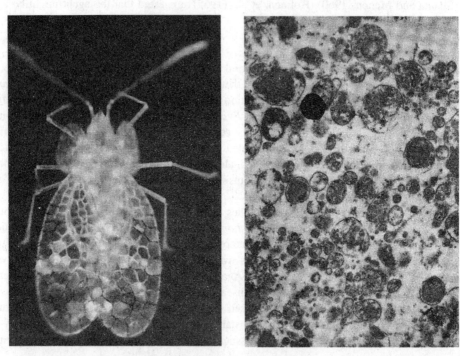

Figure 30.6 (A) *Stephanitis typica*, the lace wing bug, (B) structures resembling MLOs in salivary glands of *Stephanitis typica*. (*Source: Jayasankar, 1992*).

The lace bug *S. typica* is not a conventional phloem feeder but the insect feeds through the stomata and its stylets reach the phloem of palm leaves. Regarding the hoppers, electron microscopic studies located the presence of MLOs in the salivary gland of *P. moesta* with an acquisition plus incubation period above 40 days. Renewed attempts were made in this direction employing refined techniques under controlled conditions; MLOs were observed in all the four experimental seedlings, and in two seedlings flaccidity of leaflets was observed by the 17th month, unlike in the control seedlings.

The role of MLOs in the etiology of coconut root (wilt) disease gains additional support from the response of the disease to OTC. It was observed, even prior to the implication of MLOs with the disease as dealt with earlier, that the application of OTC prevented the deterioration of the diseased condition of experimental palms, while the untreated control palms showed deterioration. The field trial started in 1984 with OTC, neomycin, penicillin, and distilled water control indicated after a span of 3 years that the fresh set of leaves had remission of symptoms in 53% of the palms treated with high concentration of OTC (3g and 6 g a.i.). On the other hand, palms treated with distilled water and penicillin deteriorated significantly compared with the control palms (Jayasankar, 1992).

To sum up, the constant association of MLOs in diseased palm tissues combined with their total absence in healthy palms, the establishment of the role of vector (*S. typica*) through transmission trials, and the positive response of diseased palms to OTC, suggest a mycoplasmal etiology of coconut root (wilt) disease.

30.3.3 Management

Definite strategies have crystallized on the basis of scientific investigation by Muralidharan et al., (1986) to manage coconut root (wilt) disease. In the heavily diseased tract all diseased juvenile palms, irrespective of the intensity of the disease, and all adult palms in the advanced stage of the disease need eradication. By a process of systematic replanting and under planting, the number of palms in a unit area is restricted to the optimum level of 175 palms/ha. Proper fertilization (0.5 kg N, 0.3 kg P_2O_5, 1.0 kg K_2O and 0.5 kg MgO in two split doses) with farmyard manure and compost at the rate of 50 kg/palm/year and the raising of green manure crops like *Pueraria* are important components of management strategy. Intercropping with the least competing crops (yams, ginger, colocasia) in rotation or mixed farming with fodder crops and milch cows in diseased coconut gardens with the recycling of organic matter will be beneficial. The control of leaf rot disease and pests, the prevention of waterlogging and the lack of aeration in the soil, and the regulation of excessive shading are the other required factors in the package.

The earliest attempt to prevent the recurrence of the disease in mildly affected areas by the removal of the foci of infection was in 1971 (Bavappa et al., 1986), when uprooting and burning of three diseased palms prevented recurrence. A total of 730 palms in 341 gardens in 10 villages were eradicated and the boles and roots burned *in situ* during 1979 to 1982. The recurrence of disease has been limited to 21 palms spread over 15 gardens in 3 villages. This essentially forms the basis of the strategy recommended for the sparsely affected isolated pockets away from the contiguous core.

The suppression of insect vector(s) can perhaps result in economic control of the disease. The possible application of the ELISA and western blot techniques for rapid diagnosis need attention in the light of a positive serodiagnostic test. The exclusive selection and propagation of MLO specific clones by the application of the monoclonal antibody technique are worth elucidation. There is a need to develop a suitable strategy for ill drained low lands and coastal soils, and the existing management devices can be improved by reducing the cost to greatest possible extent. Host plant resistance will be the best solution to the malady. High yielding mature palms are often located in heavily diseased coconut gardens that are tolerant to wilt disease. Improved progenies for evaluation, selection and hybridization can be generated. DNA hybridization techniques to locate MLOs in plants and insects can be ideal for screening varieties.

30.4 STERILITY MOSAIC OF PIGEON PEA

Sterility mosaic is one of the most serious diseases of pigeon pea in India, first reported by Mitra (1929) from Pusa (Bihar). In spite of extensive research work, during last 50 years, etiology of disease is not understood. Capoor (1952) established the infectious nature of disease through graft transmission. The disease is confined in Asian countries, and is reported from India, Bangladesh,

Burma, Sri Lanka, Thailand and Nepal. The disease can cause upto 90% yield loss, mainly due to partial/complete sterility. A loss of 205,000 tons of grains is reported from India alone (Ghanekar, et al., 1992). The infected pigeon pea plants have bushy appearance due to excessive secondary branching from leaf axils. The leaves are reduced in size and became pale green. Due to sterility of infected plants and mosaic type of appearance on the leaves, the disease is called sterility mosaic. Three types of symptoms are noticed during screening of pigeon pea germplasm:

- Severe mosaic pattern with complete sterility
- Ring spots on leaves without sterility
- Mild mosaic on leaves with partial sterility

30.4.1 Transmission of Agent

Although, the causal agent of sterility mosaic of pigeon pea is not yet established, Capoor (1952) established graft transmission. Later the role of mite vector was reported (Seth, 1962). The disease is neither sap nor seed transmitted. Eriophyed mite (*Aceria cajani*) has major role in field spread of disease. The mites transmit the agent in persistent manner but not transmitted through eggs.

30.4.2 Disease Cycle and Management

There are gaps in our knowledge about the nature of pathogen, its transmission and survival in nature. The disease is seen more in rainy season, probably through mites (*A. cajani*), since mites transmit the agent in persistent manner; its survival during summer can help in perpetuation of causal agent of sterility mosaic. The mite population is seen during summers in wild pigeon pea plants. In addition, the discarded diseased pigeon pea plants may be the other potential source of inoculum. The long duration of pigeon pea crop, in north India, may help in survival of pathogen Figure 30.7. The experiments at ICRISAT established that disease could spread up to 2 km towards wind direction from inoculum source and about 200 m against wind direction. In absence of information about causal agent, use of resistant varieties and management of vector population are important components for management of the disease. The intensive and systematic efforts at ICRISAT resulted in identification of resistance/tolerant lines, which were used for breeding programme at ICRISAT as well as traditional programme in India. The ICP 786, ICP 10976 and ICP 10977, found resistant in multi-location trials, were used as donor parents. Many of the resistant sources identified, do not favour mite multiplication (Reddy and Nene, 1980). Seed dressing with higher doses of carbofuran 3 G (25%) has been reported to protect the plants from sterility mosaic upto 45 days after planting. Soil application of carbofuran (40 kg/ha) and temic 10 G (15 kg/ha) at planting time gives protection to pigeon pea against sterility mosaic for 75 days after sowing (Ghanekar, et al., 1992). Spraying of pigeon pea with acaricides from early stages protects the crop from sterility mosaic, through management of vectors.

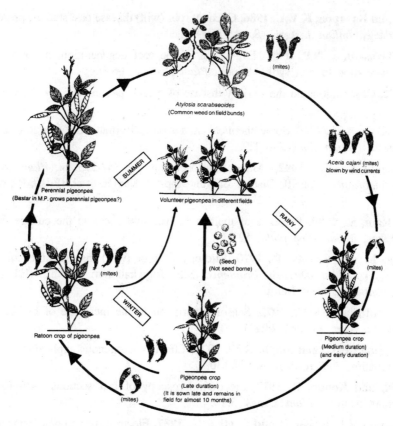

Figure 30.7 Disease cycle of sterility mosaic of pigeon pea. (*Source:* Ghanker, et al., 1992)

REFERENCES

Bhatnagar, S.S. and Beniwal, S.P.S., 1977, Involvement of *Fusarium oxysporum* in causation of mango malformation, *Plant Dis. Rep,* 61:894.

Chakrabarti, K.K. and Ghosal, S., 1985, Effect of *Fusarium moniliforme* var. *subglutinans* infection on mangiferin production in the twigs of *Mangifera indica, J. Phytopath.*, 113:47.

Ghanekar, A.M., Sheila, V.K., Beniwal, S.P.S., Reddy, M.V. and Nene, Y.L., 1992, Sterility mosaic of pigeon pea, *In: Plant Diseases of International Importance*, U.S. Singh, A.N. Mukhopadhyay, J. Kumar, and H.S. Chaube (Eds.), Vol. I, Prentice Hall Inc., New Jersey.

Holmes, F.O., 1965, Reports to the Government of India on investigation on the etiology of coconut root (wilt) disease, Report No. 1958, Project No. India/TC/RL, 13.

Jayasankar, N.P., 1981, Research on coconut root (wilt) disease current status, *paper presented at the Internet. Conf. on Tropical Crop Protection*, Lyon, France.

Jayasankar, N.P., and Radha, K., 1982, Coconut root (wilt) disease—a practical approach to contain the disease and live with it, The *Bull. No. 8*, Central Plantation Crops Research Institute, Kararagod, India.

Jayasankar, N.P. and Bavappa, K.V.A., 1986, Coconut root (wilt) disease past studies, present status and future strategy, *Indian J. Agric. Sci.,* 50:309.

Joseph, T. and Jayasankar, N.P., 1981, Evaluation of the root degeneration in coconut (*Cocos nucifera* L.) in relation to root (wilt) disease, *Plant Disease,* 66:666.

Kapoor, S.P., 1952, Observations on the sterility disease of pigeon pea in Bombay, *Indian J. Agric. Sci.,* 22:271.

Khan, M.D. and Khan, A.H., 1963, Some chemical studies on malformation of mango inflorescence in West Pakistan, *Punjab Hort. J.* 3:229.

Kumar, J. and Beniwal, S.P.S., 1992, Mango malformation, pp. 357-393, *In: Plant Diseases of International Importance,* Vol. III, Disease of fruit crops, J. Kumar, et al. (Eds.), Prentice Hall, New Jersey.

Kumar, N. and Ram, S., 1999, Presence of malformin like substances in the culture filtrates of *Fusarium* species, *Indian Phytopath.,* 52:134.

Lal, S.B., Radha, K. and Shanta, P., 1970, Etiology of root (wilt) disease of coconut palms, pp. 662-669. *In: Plant Disease Problems,* S.P. Raychaudhuri, et al. (Eds.), *Indian Phytopathological Soc.,* New Delhi.

Majumdar, P.K. and Sinha, G.C., 1972, Seasonal variation in the incidence of malformation in *Mangifera indica, Acta. Hortic.,* 24:221.

Majumdar, P.K., Sinha G.C. and Singh, R.N., 1970, Effect of exogenous application of NAA on mango malformation, *Indian. J. Hort.,* 27:130.

Maramorosch, K. and Kondo, F., 1977, Electronmicroscopy of leaf sections from Kerala wilt diseased coconut palm, *J. Plant. Crops,* 5:20.

Mathen, K., Solomon, J.J., Rajan, P. and Geetha, L., 1987, Electron microscopic evidence on the role of Stephantis is typica (Distant) as vector of coconut root (wilt) disease, *Curr. Sci.,* 56:1339.

Menon, K.P.V. and Shanta, P., 1962, Soil transmission of the coconut root (wilt) virus, *Curr. Sci.,* 31:153.

Mitra, M., 1929, Report of the imperial mycologist, *Scientific reports of the Agricultural Research Institute,* Pusa, pp. 58-71,

Muralidharan, A., Narir, M.G. and Jayasankar, N.P., 1986, Response of coconut root (wilt) disease to management practices, *Indian Cocon. J.,* 3.

Narasimhan, K.J., 1954, Malformation of panicles in mango induced by a species of *Eriophyes, Curr. Sci.,* 23:297.

Nariani, T.K. and Seth, M.L., 1962, Role of eriophyid mites in causing malformation disease in mango, *Indian Phytopath.,* 14:231.

Nene, Y.L. and Reddy, M.V., 1976, A new technique to screen pigeon pea for resistance to sterility mosaic, *Trop. Grain Legume Bull,* 5:23.

Pandey, G. and Ram, S., 1995, Presence of malformin like activity in culture filtrate of *Fusarium moniliforme* var. *intermedium, Indian J. Hort.,* 51:1.

Peethambaran, C.K., 1989, Disease of arecanut and coconut palms, pp. 227-239, *In: Perspectives in Plant Pathology,* V.P. Agnihotri, et al. (Eds.), Today and Tomorrow Printers and Publishers, New Delhi.

Raina, K. and Ram, S., 1991, Occurrence of malformin-like substances in malformed mango seedlings, *Acta Hotic.*, 291:272.

Ram, S. and Bisht, L.D., 1984, Occurrence of malformin like substances in malformed panicles and control of floral malformation in mango, *Scientia Hortic.*, 23:331.

Ramadasan, A., 1970, On the nature of wilt in the root (wilt) disease of coconut palm, pp. 670-675, *In: Plant Disease Problems*, S.P. Raychaudhuri, et al. (Eds.), Indian Phytopathological Society, New Delhi.

Reddy, M.V. and Nene, Y.L., 1980, Influence of sterility mosaic resistance pigeon pea on multiplication of the mite vector, *Indian Phytopathol.*, 33:61.

Sahasranaman, K.N., Radha, K., and Pandalai, K.M., 1964, Effect of manuring and intercultivation in the field of coconut in relation to leaf rot and root (wilt) disease, *Indian Cocon. J.*, 18:3.

Seth, M.L., 1962, Transmission of pigeon pea sterility by an eriophyid mite, *Indian Phytopathol*, 15:225.

Shanta, P., Menon, K.P.V. and Pillai, K.P., 1960, Etiology of root (wilt) disease, Investigations on its virological nature, *Indian Cocon. J.*, 13:56.

Shanta, P., and Menon, K.P.V., 1960, Cowpea (*Vigna sinensis* Endl.) as indicator plant for the coconut wilt virus, *Virology*, 12:309.

Shanta, P., et al., 1975, Possible association of tobacco mosaic virus with the root (wilt) disease of coconut, *J. Plant. Crops,* 3:77.

Shanta, P., and Radha, K., 1975, Recent studies on root (wilt) disease, *FAO Tech. Wkg. Pty. Cocon. Prod. Prot. and Processing*, Kingston, Jamaica, 1.

Singh, L.B., Singh, S.M. and Nirvan, R.S., 1961, Studies on mango malformation: review, symptoms, extent, intensity and cause, *Hort. Adv.*, 5:197.

Singh, Z. and Dhillon, B.S., 1987, Occurrence of malformin-like substances in seedlings of mango (*Mangifera indica* L.), *J. Phytopath.*, 120:245.

Solomon, J.J. and Sasikala, M., 1980, A serological appraisal of the connection of the tobacco mosaic virus isolate with the root (wilt) disease of coconut, *Phytopath. Z.*, 99:26.

Solomon, J.J., Govindankutty, M.P. and Nienhaus, F., 1983, Association of mycoplasma-like organisms with the coconut root (wilt) disease in India, *Z. Pfl. Krenkh.Pfi. Shutz.*, 90:295.

Summanwar, A.S., et al., 1917, Further studies on coconut root (wilt) disease, *2nd Internal. Symp. on Pl. Path.*, New Delhi, India.

Summanwar, A.S., et al., 1969, Virus associated with coconut root (wilt) disease, *Curr. Sci.*, 38:208.

Summanwar, A.S., Raychaudhuri, S.P. and Pathak, S.C., 1966, Association of the fungus *Fusarium moniliforme* Sheld. With the malformation in mango, *Indian Phytopath.*, 19:227.

Verma, A., et al., 1974. Mango malformation: A fungal disease, *Phytopath. Z.*, 79:254.

31 Non-Infectious Disorders

31.1 INTRODUCTION

Non-infectious disorders differ from infectious diseases as no living agent (pathogens) are involved and situations do not lead to fast spread (epidemic). However, physiological disorders may predispose plants to infection by other parasites or even to saprophytes. Non-infectious disorders in which no primary parasite/pathogen is involved, and are brought about by abnormal conditions of temperature, light or atmospheric factors, nutritional and water imbalances, chemical toxicities and physical injuries, due to wind and lightning (Plate 31.1). The symptoms produced often confuse with certain symptoms induced by pathogen. Thus, very critical and careful observations are required to correctly identify the disorders and their corrections. Another limitation in diagnosis is total absence of any causal agent or structure related to cause, which could help in positive confirmation of diagnosis made. The chemical analysis of soil and leaf samples may help up to some extent in diagnosis of non-infectious disorders. The physical characteristics of soil and prevailing environmental conditions may also be helpful.

31.2 COMMON NON-INFECTIOUS DISORDERS

31.2.1 Temperature Induced Disorders

Every living system carries out normal biological activities within a range of temperature, known as cardinal points (minimum to optimum and maximum temperature for various growth/reproduction related activities). Since plants grow in open fields, they can tolerate wider fluctuations in temperature, but beyond the tolerable limits extreme low or high temperature may induce disorders in plant structures and functions. Sometimes these may be due to indirect effects of other factors coming into play. At low temperature, potato tubers are sweetened, due to conversion of starch into sugar while at very high temperature, in storage as well as soil, potato tubers develop "black heart" due to insufficient availability of oxygen for cellular respiration. Some plants/crops are more sensitive to low temperature and frost. Thus, freezing injuries are commonly observed in temperate zones or tropical plant grown at high altitude. Some crops such as banana, citrus, cucurbits, eggplants, pepper, sweet potato and tomato, suffer injuries when exposed to low temperature. The disorders induced by high temperature are complex, as they create imbalance in plant water relationship, which may further be complicated due to involvement of certain pathogens/pests. High temperature and bright sunshine may cause sunscald of fruits and leaves or cankers of stem at soil level. Seeds may fail to germinate if soil temperature is too high (may be due to lack of soil moisture).

Plate 31.1 (A) Effect of ozone injury on potato leaves, (B) freezing necrosis injury (Net type), (C) potato tuber showing hollow heart, (D) freezing necrosis injury (Vascular ring type), (E) lightining injury to potato plants.

31.2.2 Moisture Induced Disorders

The symptoms induced due to soil-water-plant imbalance may be the result of lack of moisture and excess of water (supersaturated soil) for prolonged periods. In later situations the disorder may be due to lack of oxygen supply to roots and/or the salt injuries to underground plant parts. Frequent but regulated irrigations and well drained soils are good for normal plant growth. Water stress, due to high temperature, may also aggravate the pathogen induced wilting of plants. In addition, these may provide entry opportunities to weak pathogens or saprophytes. Charcoal root rot (*Macrophomina phaseolina*) of several crops in semi arid tropics, is often associated with low soil moisture.

31.2.3 Air Pollution: Effects and Injuries

Crop plants and their produce may suffer disorders due to extraneous gases or the volatile byproducts of industry or gaseous emissions of automobiles. There is now abundant evidence that the major effect of most air pollutants on plants is invisible rather than visible and due to long-term chronic exposures rather than isolated and often accidental acute exposures. This physiological invisible injury often causes significant losses of yield and reductions in biomass formation and has been traced to a variety of changes. Principal among these are changes in stomatal behaviour, which can disturb both photosynthesis and transpiration, direct losses in photosynthetic capacity, failure to provide sufficient antioxidant protection, imbalances and accumulations of certain metabolites or nutrients (e.g., S and N) and disturbances to the translocation of photosynthate (Wellburn, 1994).

Influencing factors. A large number of studies of chronic low level fumigations of plants with different air pollutants have shown that poor root growth is a common outcome (Darrell, 1989). As a consequence, root: shoot ratios are lower and such exposed plants; although usually not showing visible injury, are highly susceptible to subsequent drought. Different parts of the foliage are affected by acute exposures to particular air pollutants. Younger tissues are affected by HCl, SO_2 and oxides of nitrogen and immature tissues are sensitive to HF whereas ethane causes epinasty to expanding leaves. Ozone generally affects intermediate and older leaves. Dose responses to air pollutants are sigmoid in shape. Generally, very low dosages do not produce visible symptoms and losses are very little. However, all relationship differs between species and often within species. Plants are usually more sensitive at higher temperatures but conifers, cabbages, etc., exposed to NH_3 in winter are the exception. Seasonal changes in sensitivity are also possible. Excesses and deficiencies of soil nutrition can also affect the sensitivity of vegetation to air pollution injury but this depends on type of air pollutant. By stripping away the protective boundary layer of still air around leaves, wind has a pronounced effect on air pollutant uptake and hence sensitivity. There is a pronounced genetic element within species, which determines sensitivity towards air pollutants. This has resulted in the availability of both sensitive and tolerant cultivars of the same species.

Types of visible injury. There is a wide range of visible injury caused by acute concentrations of different air pollutants on various species and there is no substitute for a colour photograph in each case to describe the symptoms. Such a compendium does not exist and useful photographs are scattered around the literature. The best examples, in terms of quality, are provided by Treshow (1980) and Wellburn (1994), but the most comprehensive are those of Taylor et al., (1989). They have the advantage of being published alongside examples of possible confusions with other causative factors. Taylor et al., (1989) also provide comprehensive tables of species response to each type of air pollutant, the symptoms found, the concentrations known to cause injury to different species and the relative sensitivities of various species to sulfur dioxide, hydrogen fluoride, oxides of nitrogen, chlorine, hydrochloric acid, ammonia, ethane, dust and particulates, acid mist, hydrogen sulfide, carbon mono oxide, vapours of mercury, ozone, bromine and peroxy-acetyl nitrate (PAN). However, the relative sensitivities and symptoms of easily recognized species to acute concentrations of different gases is an important first step towards identification and elimination of possible air pollutants causing problems in the fields (Table 31.1). Special mention, however, must be made of the visible injury caused by chronic exposures of certain plants to O_3, which have enabled surveys of this gas to be made over large areas. Current-year needles of certain sensitive long needle pines show chlorotic mottling or banding, which form as the needles elongate during exposure of high O_3. Broad-leaved plants also show visible injury after long-term chronic exposures to O_3. The best-known example is that of black cherry (*Prunus serotina*) in the Great Smoky Mountains of the eastern USA.

Mention has already been made of bioindicator surveys using sensitive and of certain species have been made for suitable species for surveys in Europe (Table 31.2).

Table 31.1 Relative Sensitivity and Responses of Some Common to Acute Concentrations of Common Air Pollutants (Adapted from Taylor, et al., 1989)

Species	SO_2	F, HF	NO_2	Cl_2	HCl	NH_3	C_2H_4	O_3	PAN
Apple	I	I	Sn	Sn	-	Sd	T	-	-
Ash	T	Snt	-	-	-	Sd	-	Ss	-
Aspen	I	Sn	-	-	Sc	Sb	-	Sn	-
Barley	Sn	Snt	Sn	Sn	Sc	Sc	T	Sc	T
Bean	Snc	I	Sn	I	Sn	Sd	Sa	Sn	Sg
Birch (Silver)	I	T	Sn	-	I	Sn	-	T	-
Blackberry	I	T	-	Snc	-	-	-	-	-
Carrot	I	I	Sn	-	Sc	I	I	I	I
Cherry	I	I	-	-	Sc	Sn	-	Sb	-
Chickweed	Sn	I	T	-	-	Sd	-	-	Sg
Clover	Sn	Sc	Sn	-	-	I	T	Sc	Sg
Cocksfoot	I	Sc	I	-	-	I	-	Sb	-
Dandelion	Sn	T	I	I	I	I	T	-	-
Fathen	I	I	T	Sc	I	Sd	Sa	T	I
Fir (Douglas)	I	Snc	Sa	Sn	Stb	I	T	T	-
Iris	I	St	-	T	I	-	-	-	-
Larch	Sc	I	Sna	-	St	T	-	I	-
Lettuce	Sf	I	Sa	Sn	-	Sd	-	T	Sg
Lilac	T	Sd	-	Sn	-	Sn	-	Sl	-
Lucerne	Sb	I	Sn	Sn	Sn	I	Sa	Sn	I
Oak	T	Sn	T	-	Sc	T	-	T	-
Oat	I	I	Sn	Sn	-	-	T	Sc	Sy
Onion	T	Sgt	T	Sn	-	I	T	Sf	T
Pea	Sn	I	Sn	-	-	Sd	Se	I	-
Pear	I	T	Sn	-	I	Sd	T	-	-
Petunia	I	T	I	I	-	I	Si	Sb	Sg
Potato	T	I	T	-	Sc	Sn	Sa	Sb	-
Privet	T	T	I	I	-	Sd	Sa	I	-
Radish	Sn	-	Sn	Sn	Sn	Sd	T	Scn	T
Raspberry	I	T	-	-	Sc	Sd	-	-	-
Rose	I	I	Sn	Ss	Sn	T	Scn	-	-
Ryegrass	Sn	T	I	-	-	I	T	-	-
Smooth-stalked meadow grass	Sn	I	I	Sn	-	T	T	-	-
Spruce	I	Snt	I	Sn	I	Sd	T	T	-
Sunflower	Sn	I	Sn	Sn	-	Sd	T	T	-
Sweet pea	Sn	T	Sn	-	-	Sd	Se	-	-
Wheat	I	I	I	-	-	-	-	Sc	I
Willow	I	T	-	-	Sa	Sb	-	-	-

S Sensitive, **I** Intermediate, **T** Tolerant, —, No information, **a** Abscission, **b** Bronzing, **c** Chlorosis, **d** Discolouration, **e** Epinasty, **f** Shot holing, **g** Glazing, **i** Inhibition of flowering, **l** Leaf curling, **n** Necrosis, **s** Stippling, **t** Tip burning, **y** Yellow or white banding

Table 31.2   List of Plant Species Suitable for Use as Air Pollution Bio Indicators in Europe (After Steubing and Jager, 1982)

Pollutant	Species and variety
SO$_2$	Lucerne *(Medicago sativa* L. cv. Du Puits), Clover *(Trifolium incamatum* L.), Pea *(Pisum sativum* L.), Backwheat *(Fagopyrum esculenutum* Moench.)
NO$_2$	Wild celery *(Apium graveolens* L.), *Petunia* sp., Ornamental tobacco *(Nicotiana glutinosa* L.)
O$_3$	Tobacco *(Nicotiana tabacum* L. cv. Bel W3)
PAN	Small nettle *(Urtica urens* L.), Annual meadow grass *(Poa annua* L.)
HF, fluorides	*Gladiolus gandavensis* L. cv. Snow Princess), Tulip *(Tulipa gesneriana* L. cv. Blue Parrot)
General accumulators	Italian rye grass *(Lolium multiflorum* Lam. Ssp. *Italicum*), Cabbage *(Brassica oleracea* L. cv. Acephala)
Bark accumulators	Rose *(Rose rugosa)* Thunb *(Thuja orientalis* L.)

31.2.4   Toxicity of Minerals

Soils often contain excessive amounts of certain elements, which at higher concentration may be injurious to plants. For instance, excessive nitrogen induces deficiency of calcium in the plant while the toxicity of Cu, Mn, or Zn is both, direct on the plant and induces a deficiency of iron in the plant. Excessive amounts of sodium salts, especially sodium chloride, sodium sulfate and sodium carbonate, increase soil pH and affect plant growth directly or indirectly. The injuries vary in different plants and may range from chlorosis to stunting, leaf burning, wilting to outright death of seedlings and young plants. Some plants, e.g., wheat and apples, are very sensitive to alkali injury while sugarbeet, alfalfa and several grasses are quite tolerant. On the other hand, when soil is too acidic, the growth of some kinds of plants is impaired and various symptoms may appear. The pH influences plant growth indirectly by affecting nutrients availability and microbial ecology. For example, blue berries grow well in acidic soil (pH 4 to 5.2) primarily because of the effect of pH on soil microflora and on the form of nitrogen. Blue berries use nitrogen as NH$_4^+$ ions more efficiently than NO$_3^-$ ions. At low pH, nitrifying bacteria (*Nitrosomonas* and *Nitrobacter*), which convert NH$_4^+$ to NO$_3^-$ are less active, thus nitrogen remains as NH$_4^+$. Hydrogen ions also affect the ionic form and solubility of several elements and thus influence the availability of the elements. At low pH, Zn, Mn and Fe exist in relatively soluble forms but at higher pH they exist in less soluble forms. Consequently, at lower pH, excessive amounts of these elements may become available to plants. In contrast, at higher pH they may be so insoluble that they are unavailable. Toxicity symptom consists of root discolouration, distortion, chlorosis and browning of older leaves.

31.2.5   Herbicide Injury

Pesticides, especially herbicides cause injury to plants when they are used incorrectly, i.e., on sensitive plants, at wrong time, under improper environmental condition or at wrong dosage. Pesticide injury is often associated with cultural practices during spraying, planting or cultivation. However, some pesticides may be transported by air or water. For example, 2,4-D (2,4 dichlorophenoxy acetic acid), a common broad leaf herbicide, is volatile and may drift to some distance. Sensitive plants such as grapes, sunflower, etc., have been injured when growing far away from the site of application. Among the common symptoms observed are smaller leaves, narrowed interveinal areas, rolled leaves, distorted petioles, yellowing of veins, leaf distortions, hypertrophied inflorescence, etc. Some symptoms of herbicide injuries on various plants have been described by Streets (1972) and Lockerman et al., (1975) and should be referred to and consulted if herbicide injury is expected to be involved. Use of pre-plant or pre-emergence herbicides through applications to the soil before or at planting time often affect seed germination and growth of seedlings. Some herbicides persist in soil for pretty long and sensitive plants grown in such fields may grow poorly and produce varying symptoms.

31.2.6 Nutritional Deficiencies

Crop plants and fruit trees suffer nutritional disorders due to inadequate supply or excess of certain minerals. Antagonistic or synergistic interactions among mineral elements have also been reported in soil or in plant system. The term macro and micronutrients are used to denote collectively groups of chemical elements, which are indispensable for optimal growth and which plants absorb primarily through roots. Nitrogen, phosphorus and potassium, required in larger quantities, are known as **macronutrients** while iron, copper, magnesium, manganese, sulfur, zinc, boron and calcium, required in smaller amounts, are termed as **micronutrients**. The micronutrient deficiency symptoms are described in Table 31.3.

Nitrogen deficiency (N). Nitrogen is an integral part of plant tissues (0.2-4.1% N on dry matter basis), which is required for proper photosynthesis by green tissues. Nitrogen is absorbed by roots, as ammonium or nitrate form, and translocated through xylem to all photosynthesizing parts in the form of amino acids (ammonical form) and nitrate salts. Nitrogen deficiency results in pale green leaves and reduced shoot growth. Plants grow poorly and are of light green colour. The lower leaves turn yellow or light brown and stems are short and slender. Nitrogen insufficiency is expressed by the reductions in the shoot: root ratio. In stone fruits under low nitrogen conditions, anthocyanin production is encouraged and fruits are more coloured than those with high nitrogen status.

Phosphorus deficiency (P). Phosphorus, another macronutrient, is important for normal plant growth and reproduction. Deficiency causes a reduction in plant growth through slower leaf production. Older leaves exhibit marginal chlorosis along with purplish brown flecks, which gradually increase. Chlorosis spread inwards from the midrib, sometimes leaving areas of healthy green tissues. Necrosis of tissue leads to withering of leaves and breaking petioles at the pseudostem. The distance between leaves on the pseudostem is shortened giving a 'rosette' appearance. Younger leaves do not exhibit symptoms.

Potassium deficiency (K). Potassium is vital for affecting normal growth and development of plants, in addition it also influences the ghost reaction (resistance) to various pests/pathogens. K stimulates early shooting and time required for fruit maturity. The potassium deficiency leads to small sized leaves accompanied by premature yellowing (starting from tips and distal margins), which may be followed by necrosis and desiccation. Purplish brown patches may appear at the base of petiole and in severe cases water soaked areas may be seen. Fruits are deformed and poorly filled.

Table 31.3 The Symptoms Induced by Micronutrient Deficiencies in Plants

Nutrients	Symptoms
Boron	The bases of young leaves of terminal buds become light green and finally breakdown. Stems and leaves become distorted. Plants are stunted. Fruits, fleshy roots or stem etc., may crack on the surface and/or rot in the centre, e.g., heart rot of sugarbeets.
Calcium	Young leaves become distorted, with their tips hooked back and the margins curled, leaves may be irregular in shape and ragged with brown scorching or spotting, terminal buds may die and plants have poor root system, e.g. blossom end rot of many fruits.
Copper	Tips of young leaves of cereals wither and their margins become chlorotic, leaves may fail to enroll and appear wilted, heading reduced and the heads are dwarfed and distorted. Citrus, pome and stone fruits show dieback of twigs in summer, burning of leaf margins, chlorosis, resetting, etc.
Iron	Young leaves become severely chlorotic but main veins remain green, sometimes brown spots develop, part or entire leaf may dry and leaves may be shed.
Magnesium	First the older, then the younger leaves become mottled or chlorotic, then reddish, sometimes necrotic spots appear. The tips and margins of leaves may turn upwards and the leaves may appear cupped, leaves may drop off.
Manganese	Leaves become chlorotic but their smallest veins remain green and produce a checked effect, necrotic spots may appear scattered on the leaf, severely affected leaves turn brown and wither.
Sulfur	Young leaves are pale green or light yellow without any spots. The symptoms resemble those of nitrogen deficiency.
Zinc	Leaves show interveinal chlorosis. Later they become necrotic and show purple or reddish pigmentation. Leaves are few and small, internodes are short and shoots from rosettes and fruit production is low. Leaves are shed progressively from base to tip.

REFERENCES

Altman, J. and Campbell, C.L., 1977, Effect of herbicides on plant diseases. *Annu. Rev. of Phytopathol.*, 15:361.

Basra, A.S. and Basra, R.K., 1997, *Mechanisms of Environmental Stress Resistance in Plants,* Harwood Academic Publishers, Amsterdam, Netherlands, p. 407.

Bennett, W.F., 1993, *Nutrient Deficiency and Toxicities in Crop Plants,* APS Press, Minnesota, USA, p. 202.

Bhargaba, B.S. and Raghupathi, H.B., 2000, Nutrient deficiency and toxicity disorder in tropical and sub-tropical fruits, *In: Diseases of Fruit Crops*, V.K. Gupta, and S.K. Sharma (Eds.), Kalyani Publisher, New Delhi, p. 279.

Dohroo, N.P., Bharat, N.K. and Sushma Nayar, 2000, Nutrient deficiency and toxicity disorder in temperate fruits, *In: Diseases of fruit crops,* V.K. Gupta, and S.K. Sharma (Eds.), Kalyani Publisher, New Delhi, p. 279.

Griffiths, E., 1981, Iatrogenic plant diseases, *Annu. Rev. of Phytopathol.*, 19:69.

Lockerman, R.H., et al., 1975, *Diagnosis and Prevention of Herbicide Injury*, CES, *Bull., E. 809,* East Lansing.

Shurtleff, M.C. and Averre, C.W., 1997, The plant disease clinic and field diagnosis of abiotic diseases, *American Phytopathological Society*, St. Paul, USA, p. 245.

Steubing, L. and Jager, H.J., 1982, *Monitoring of Air Pollutants by Plants, Methods and Problems.* Dr. W. Junk, The Hague.

Streets, R.B. Sr., 1972, *The Diagnosis of Plant Diseases,* CES, AES, Univ. of Arizon, Tucson.

Tattar, T.A., 1980, Non-infectious diseases of trees, *Journal of Agriculture,* 6:1, 1.

Taylor, H.J., Ashmore, M.R. and Bell, J.N.B., 1989, *Air Pollution Injury to Vegetation,* HM Health and Safety Executive, IEHO, London, UK.

Tickell, Sir C., et al., 1993, The impact of global change on disease, *Parasitology,* 106:SUPPL, S1-S107.

Treshow, M., 1980, *Air Pollution and Plant Life,* John Wiley and Sons, UK.

Weinstein, L.H. and Laurence, J.A. (1981), Impact of air pollutants on plant productivity, Annu. Rev. Plant Pathology, 19:257.

Wellburn, A.R., 1994, *Air Pollution and Climate Change: The Biological Impact,* Longmans, Harlow, UK.

Glossary

Abiotic: Non-living agents viz., nutritional deficiencies/toxicities or environmental factors (Temperature, light, water, air) causing disorders in plants.

Acervulus: A subepidermal, saucer-shaped, asexual fruiting-body producing conidia on short conidiophores.

Acquired resistance: Plant resistance to infection/disease activated after inoculation of plant with certain microorganisms or treatment with certain chemical compounds.

Actinomycetes: Formerly, a group of bacteria forming branched filaments.

Adaxial: The side next to the long axis; toward the axis or central line.

Aeciospore: A spore borne in an aecium (rust fungi).

Aecium, pl. aecia: A cup-shaped fruiting body containing aeciospores.

Aerobic: A microorganisms that lives or a process that occurs in the presence of molecular oxygen.

Agar: A gelatine like material obtained from seaweed and used to solidify culture media on which microorganisms are grown.

Allele: One of two or more alternate forms of a gene occupying the same locus on a chromosome.

Alternate host: One of the two kinds of host plants required by a parasitic fungus (e.g., *P. graminis tritici*) to complete its life cycle.

Anaerobic: A microorganism that lives or a process that occurs in the absence of molecular oxygen.

Anamorph: The imperfect or asexual stage of a fungus.

Anastomosis: The union of a hypha with another resulting in intercommunication of their genetic material.

Antheridium: The male sexual organ/gametangium found in some fungi.

Anthracnose: A disease characterized by black and sunken lesion on leaf, stem or fruit, caused by fungi that produce their asexual spores in acervulus.

Antibiotic: A chemical compound produced by some microorganisms, which inhibits or kills other microorganisms.

Antibody: A protein produced in a warm-blooded animal in reaction to an injected foreign antigen and capable of reacting specifically with that antigen.

Antigen: A substance, usually a protein, that induces the formation of an antibody in a warm-blooded animal.

Antiserum: The blood serum of a warm-blooded animal that contains antibodies.

Apothecium: An open cup- or saucer-shaped ascocarp of some ascomycetes.

Appressorium: The swollen tip of a hypha or germ tube that helps during attachment and penetration of the host surface by the fungus.

Ascocarp: The fruiting body of ascomycetes bearing or containing asci.

Ascogonium: The female gametangium or sexual organ of ascomycetes.

Ascomycetes: A group of fungi producing their sexual spores (ascospore) within asci.

Ascospore: A sexually produced spore borne in an ascus.

Ascus: A saclike structure, which contains the ascospores.

Asexual reproduction: Type of reproduction not involving the union of gametes or meiosis.

Autoecious: A rust fungus completing its life cycle on one host plant.

Avirulent: Lacking virulence, on a particular host genotype.

Bactericide: A chemical compound that kills bacteria.

Bacteriocins: Bactericidal substances produced by certain strains of bacteria and active against other strains of same or closely related species.

Bacteriophage: A virus that infects bacteria and usually kills them.

Bacteriostatic: A chemical or physical agent that prevents multiplication of bacteria without killing them.

Basidiomycetes: A group of fungi producing their sexual spores, basidiospores, on basidia.

Basidiospore: The sexually produced spores borne on a basidium.

Basidium, pl. basidia: A structure on which basidiospores are borne.

Bioassay: Quantitative estimation of biologically active substance by testing its effect on living organism under standardized conditions.

Biotechnology: The use of genetically modified organisms and/or modern techniques and processes with biological systems.

Biotroph: An organism that lives and multiplies only on another living organism in nature (obligate parasite).

Biotype: A subgroup within a biological species or race usually of a single or a few new characters.

Blight: A disease characterized by rapid and extensive discolouration, necrosis, wilting, and death of plant tissues.

Blotch: A disease characterized by large and irregular shaped, spots or blots on leaves, shoots and stems.

Bunt: A disease caused by the fungus *Tilletia/Neovossia* in which the contents of the grains are replaced by odorous smut spores.

Canker: A definite, relatively localized, necrotic lesion, on a tree.

Capsid: The protein coat of viruses forming the closed shell or tube that contains the nucleic acid (RNA/DNA).

Capsule: A relatively thick layer of mucopolysaccharides that surrounds some bacterial cells.

Chemotherapy: Cure of diseased plant with chemicals (chemotherapeutants) that are absorbed and translocated in plant system.

Chlamydospores: A thick-walled asexual resting spore formed by the modification of a fungus cell.

Chlorosis: An abnormal yellowing of foliage, often a symptom associated with reduced chlorophyll content.

Chronic symptoms: Symptoms that develop over a long period of time.

Circulative viruses: Viruses that are acquired by their vectors, passed through their tissues and inoculated into plants via the mouthparts of vectors.

Cleistothecium: An entirely closed fruiting body (ascocarp).

Conidiophore: A specialized hypha on which one or more conidia are produced.

Conidium: An asexual spore produced at the tip of a conidiophore.

Conjugation: A process of sexual reproduction involving the fusion of two gametes. Also, in bacteria, the transfer of genetic material from a donor cell to a recipient cell through direct cell-to-cell contact.

Cross protection: The phenomenon in which plant infected with one virus are protected from infection by other more severe strains of the same virus.

Culture: The process of growing fungi or other microorganisms upon artificial media.

Cyst: An encysted fungal zoospore; in nematodes, the body of dead adult females of the genus *Heterodera* or *Globodera* which may contain eggs.

Damping-off: Death of seedlings near the soil line, resulting in falling over on the ground.

Dieback: Progressive death of shoots and branches, generally starting at the tip.

Dikaryotic: Mycelium or spores containing two sexually different compatible nuclei per cell.

Diploid: A cell having the double number of chromosomes ($2n$) in the nucleus.

Disease cycle: The chain of events involved in recurrence of disease, including the stages of development of the pathogen, survival and dispersal.

Disinfectant: An agent that kills or inactivates pathogens in the environment or on the surface of a plant or plant organ.

Disinfestant: A physical or chemical agent that frees a plant, organ, or tissue from infestation.

Dormancy: Reversible interruption of phenotypic development.

Downy mildew: A plant disease characterized by appearance of downy growth, sporangiophores and sporangia of the fungus on the surface of leaves, stems and fruit, caused by fungi in family Peronosporaceae.

Echinulate: Covered with small or finely pointed spines.

Ectoparasite: A parasite feeding on the host surface.

Egg: A female gamete.

Elicitor: Molecule produced by the pathogen which induces a response in the host.

ELISA: A serological test in which one antibody carries with it an enzyme that releases a coloured compound; enzyme linked immuno-sorbant assay.

Endocyclic: The rusts fungus having a life cycle with spermogonial and aecial spore stages only, in which the aeciospores function as teliospores.

Endoparasite: A parasite which enters a host and feeds from within.

Enzyme: A protein produced by living cells that can catalyze a specific biological reaction.

Epidemic/Epiphytotic: A widespread and destructive outbreak of a disease of plants most of individuals in a population are affected by disease.

Epidemiology: The study of factors affecting the outbreak and spread of infectious diseases in plant population.

Epiphytically: Existing on the surface of a plant or plant organ without causing infection.

Eradicant: A chemical substance that destroys a pathogen at its source.

Eradication: Eliminating the pathogen after it is established or eliminating the plants that carry the pathogen.

Etiolation: The elongation and yellowing of a green plant through lack of sunlight. Stem internodes may be elongated.

Etiology: In pathology, the study of a disease dealing with the causal agent, the pathogen, and its relations with the host.

Facultative parasite: A saprophyte having the ability to live as parasite also.

Fertilization: The sexual union of two haploid (*n*) nuclei resulting in doubling of chromosome numbers (2*n*).

Fission: Transverse splitting in two of bacterial cells, asexual reproduction.

Flagellum: A thread like structure projecting from a bacterium or zoospore and functioning as an organ of locomotion.

Forma specialis (f. sp.) pl. *formae speciales*: A taxonomic sub-division of species or variety, differing only in host range.

Fructification: Production of spores by fungi in closed fruit like structures (Fruiting body).

Fumigation: Application of a fumigant (volatile chemical) for disinfestations of an area.

Fungicide: Any agent (chemical compound) toxic to fungi, which can kill fungi.

Fungistatic: A compound that temporarily prevents fungus growth/germination without killing the fungus.

Gall: A swelling or overgrowth produced on a plant as a result of infection by certain pathogens.

Gametangium: A cell containing gametes or nuclei that act as gametes.

Gamete: A male or female reproductive cell or the nuclei within a gametangium.

Gene cloning: The isolation and multiplication of an individual gene sequence by its insertion into a system (bacterium) where it can multiply.

Gene: A linear portion of the chromosome which determines one or more hereditary characters. The smallest functional unit of inheritance.

Genetic engineering: The alternation of the genetic composition of a cell by various procedures (transformation, protoplast fusion, etc.) in tissue culture.

Genotype: The genetic constitution of an organism.

Genus, pl. genera: A division in the classification of living organisms (plants and animals); a genus consists of related species.

Germ theory: The theory states that the infectious and contagious diseases are caused by germs (microorganisms).

Girdle: To destroy living tissue (bark, cambium) in a ring around a stem or branch; usually resulting in the death of the distal parts of the tree or branch.

Growth regulator: A natural substance that regulates the enlargement, division, or activation of plant cells.

Gummosis: Production of gum by or in a plant tissue.

Habitat: The natural place of growth of a living organism.

Haploid: Having the single (*n*) number of chromosomes in a cell/nucleus.

Haustorium, pl. haustoria: The hypha of a parasitic fungus which acts as a penetrating and absorbing organ within a host.

Hermaphrodite: An individual bearing both functional male and female reproductive organs.

Heteroecious: The rust fungus completing its life cycle on two unrelated plants (alternate hosts).

Heterokaryosis: The condition in which a cell/mycelium contains two genetically different nuclei per cell.

Heterothallic fungi: Fungi producing compatible male and female gametes on physiological distinct mycelia/thalli.

Homothallic fungus: A fungus producing compatible male and female gametes on the same mycelium/thallus.

Horizontal resistance: Non-differential resistance that is uniform effective against all races of a pathogen and reduces the rate of disease development.

Host: A living organism harbouring a parasite.

Host range: Various kinds of host plants that may be attacked by a parasite/pathogen.

Hyaline: Clear and colourless; appearing white; transparent or translucent.

Hybridization: The crossing of two individuals differing in one or more heritable characteristics.

Hybridoma: A hybrid animal cell produced by the fusion of a spleen cell and a cancer cell, which is able to multiply and produce monoclonal antibodies.

Hydathodes: Structures with one or more opening that discharge water from the interior of the leaf to its surface at the leaf edge.

Hyperparasite: An organism parasitic on another parasite.

Hyperplasia: A plant overgrowth due to increased cell division.

Hypersensitivity: Excessive sensitivity of plant tissues to certain pathogens. Affected cells are killed quickly, blocking the advance of obligate parasites (defence mechanism).

Hypertrophy: Abnormal growth of cells, causing enlargement of some part of a plant.

Hypha, pl. hyphae: A filament of a fungus; an aggregation of hyphae is called mycelium.

Hypovirulence: Reduced virulence of a pathogen strain as a result of the presence of transmissible double stranded RNA.

Immunity: The state of being immune, i.e., exempt from infection.

Imperfect fungus: A fungus that is not known to produce sexual spores.

Imperfect state (or stage): A phase of the life cycle of a fungus in which only asexual spores are produced.

In vitro: In culture. Outside the host.

In vivo: In the host, i.e., colonization of host tissue.

Inclusion bodies: Crystalline or amorphous structures in virus-infected plant cells that are produced by and consist largely of viruses and are visible under the compound microscope.

Incubation period: The period of time between inoculation of a host by a pathogen and the first appearance of symptoms on the host.

Indexing: A procedure to determine whether a given plant is infected by a virus. It involves the transfer of a bud, scion, sap, etc. from one plant to one or more kinds of (indicator) plants that are sensitive to the virus.

Indicator: A plant that reacts to certain viruses or environmental factors with production of specific symptoms and is used for detection and identification of these factors (bioindicator).

Infectious diseases: A disease that is caused by a pathogen, which can spread from a diseased to a healthy plant.

Infested: Containing number of insects, mites, nematodes, etc. as applied to an area or field. Also applied to a plant surface, soil, container, or tool contaminated with bacteria, fungi, etc.

Injury: Damage of a plant by an animal, or a physical or chemical agent.

Inoculate: To bring a pathogen into contact with a host plant or plant organ.

Inoculum: The infectious pathogen or its parts, e.g. spores, mycelium, or virus particles that are capable of infecting plants.

Standard IPM: The attempt to minimize pathogen, insects, and weeds from causing economic crop losses by using need based management methods that are cost effective, ecofriendly and harmonious to ecosystem.

Invasion: The spread of a pathogen within the host tissue.

Isolate: A single spore or culture and the subcultures derived from it. Also used to indicate collections of a pathogen made at different times/places.

Isolation: The separation of a pathogen from its host and its culture on a nutrient medium.

Juvenile: The life stage of a nematode between the embryo and the adult: an immature nematode.

Latent infection: The state in which a host is infected with a pathogen but does not show any symptoms.

Latent virus: A virus that does not induce symptom development in its host.

Leaf spot: A self-limiting lesion on a leaf.

Lectins: A group of plant proteins that binds to specific carbohydrates.

Lesion: A circumscribed, well delimited diseased area.

Life cycle: The stages in life span of an organism (plants/animals) till reappearance of the same stage.

Local lesion: A localized spot produced on a leaf upon mechanical inoculation with a virus.

Macrocyclic, long-cycled (of rusts): Life cycle of rust fungus involving the aecial, telial, basidial, and usually the spermogonial and uredinial spore states.

Masked symptoms: Virus-infected plant symptoms that are suppressed under certain environmental conditions but appear when the host is exposed to certain conditions of light and temperature.

Mechanical inoculation: Inoculation of a plant with a virus through transfer of sap from a virus infected plant to a healthy plant.

Microcyclic, short cycled (of rusts): Life cycle involving only the telial and basidial (and sometimes the spermogonial) spore states.

Microscopic: Very small; can be seen only with the aid of a microscope.

Middle lamella: The cementing layer between adjacent cell walls: it generally consists of pectinaceous materials, except in woody tissues, where pectin is replaced by lignin.

Mildew: A fungus disease of plants in which the mycelium and spores of the fungus are seen as a whitish growth on the host surface (Powdery/Downy mildew).

Molt: The shedding or casting off of the cuticle.

Monoclonal antibodies: Identical antibodies produced by a single clone of lymphocytes and reacting only with one of the antigenic determinants of a pathogen or protein.

Monocyclic: Having one cycle per season. Disease without secondary infection during crop season.

Mosaic: A variegated pattern of greenish and yellowish shades on leaves: usually caused by affected chlorophyll content.

Mottle: An irregular pattern of indistinct light and dark areas.

Mould: Any profuse or woolly fungus growth on damp or decaying matter or on surfaces of plant tissue.

Mummy: A dried, shrivelled fruit.

Mutant: An individual possessing a new, heritable characteristic as a result of a mutation.

Mutation: Appearance of a new characteristic in an individual as the result of a sudden heritable change in a gene or chromosome.

Mycelium: A mass of interwoven threads (hyphae) that make-up the vegetative body of a fungus.

Mycoplasma like organisms: Microorganisms found in the phloem and phloem parenchyma of diseased plants and assumed to be the cause of the disease; they resemble mycoplasmas in all respects except that they cannot yet be grown on artificial nutrient media. Now called phytoplasmas or spiroplasmas.

Mycorrhizae: A symbiotic association of a fungus with the roots of a plant.

Mycotoxicoses: Diseases of animals and humans caused by consumption of feed and foods invaded by fungi that produce mycotoxins.

Mycotoxins: Toxic substances produced by several fungi in infected seeds, feed or food, and capable of causing illness of varying severity or death of animals and humans that consume such substances.

Necrosis: Death of cells, especially when tissues become dark in colour.

Nomenclature: A system of names or naming, as applied to the subjects in any science, botany and/or zoology.

Non-infectious disease: A disease/disorder that is caused by an abiotic agent. It does not spread from diseased to healthy plants.

Nucleoprotein: Referring to viruses: consisting of nucleic acid and protein.

Obligate parasite: A parasite that in nature can grow and multiply only on or in living organisms.

Oogonium: The female gametangium of oomycetes containing one or more female gametes.

Oomycete: A fungus like chromistan that produces oospores. A water mould.

Oospore: A sexual spore produced by the union of two morphologically different gametangia (oogonium and antheridium).

Operon: A cluster of functionally related genes regulated and transcribed as a unit.

Osmosis: The diffusion of a solvent through a differentially permeable membrane from its higher concentration to its lower concentration.

Ovary: The female reproductive structure that produces or contains the egg.

Parasexualism: A mechanism by which recombination of hereditary characters occurs within fungal heterokaryonts.

Parasite: An organism that lives on or in a living plant or animal (host) and obtains all or part of its nutrients from the host.

Pathogen: An organism/virus capable of causing disease (pathogenesis).

Pathogenicity: The capability of a pathogen to cause disease.

Pathovar: In bacteria, a subspecies or group of strains that can infect only plants within a certain genus or species.

Pectin: A methylated polymer of galacturonic acid found in the middle lamella and the primary cell wall of plants.

Pectinase: An enzyme that breaks down pectin.

Penetration: The initial invasion of a host by a pathogen, i.e., entry of pathogen in host tissue.

Perfect stage: The period of life of a fungus during which sexual spores are produced.

Perithecium: The globular or flask-shaped ascocarp of the Pyrenomycetes, having an opening or pore (ostiole).

Phage: A virus that attacks bacteria; also called bacteriophage.

Phenotype: The external visible appearance of an organism.

Phloem: Food-conducting tissues, consisting of sieve tubes, companion cells, phloem parenchyma and fibres. Part of vascular system in plants.

Phylogeny: The history of the descent and evolution of plants and animals.

Phytoalexin: A substance which inhibits the development of the fungus on hypersensitive tissue, formed when host plant cells come in contact with the parasite/other incitants.

Phytopathogenic: Term applicable to a microorganism that can incite disease in plants.

Phytoplasma: Mollicutes that infect plants and cannot yet be grown in culture.

Plant pathogenesis-related proteins (PR proteins): Groups of proteins with different chemical properties, produced in a cell within minutes or hours following inoculation, but all being more or less toxic to pathogens.

Plantibodies: Antibodies produced in transgenic plants expressing the antibody-producing gene(s) of mouse that had been previously injected with a pathogen (usually a virus) that infects the plant.

Plasmalemma: The cytoplasmic membrane found on the outer side of the protoplast adjacent to the cell wall.

Plasmid: A self-replicating, extra-chromosomal, hereditary circulary DNA found in certain bacteria and fungi, generally not required for survival of the organism.

Plasmodesms (Plural = plasmodesmata): A fine protoplasmic thread like tubes connecting two protoplasts and passing through the cell wall which separates two protoplasts.

Plasmodium: A naked, slimy mass of protoplasm containing numerous nuclei.

Plasmolysis: The shrinking and separation of the cytoplasm from cell wall due to exosmosis of water from the protoplast.

Polyclonal antibodies: The antibodies present in the serum of the blood of an animal that had been injected with a pathogen or protein that generally has many antigenic determinants.

Polycyclic: Completes many disease cycles in one year/season.

Polyetic: Requires many years to complete one life or disease cycle.

Polygenic: A character controlled by many genes.

Polyhedron: A particle or crystal with many planes faces.

Polymerase chain reaction: A technique that allows an almost infinite amplification (multiplication) of a segment of DNA for which a primer (short piece of that DNA) is available.

Polymerase: An enzyme that joins single small molecules into chains of such molecules (e.g., DNA, RNA).

Polysome (or polyribosome): A cluster of ribosomes associated with a messenger RNA.

Precipitin: The reaction in which an antibody causes visible precipitation of antigens.

Primary infection: The first infection of a plant by the overwintering or oversummering pathogen, i.e., primary inoculum.

Primary inoculum: The overwintering or oversummering pathogen, or inoculum that causes primary infection.

Probe: A radioactive nucleic acid used to detect the presence of a complementary strand by hybridization.

Prokaryote: A microorganism whose genetic material is not organized into a membrane-bound nucleus, for example bacteria and mollicutes.

Promycelium: The short hypha produced by the teliospore; which acts as basidium.

Propagative virus: A virus that multiplies in its insect vector.

Propagule: The part of an organism that may be disseminated and reproduce the organism.

Protectant: A chemical applied to a plant in advance of the pathogen to prevent infection.

Protoplast: A plant cell from which the cell wall has been removed. The organized living unit of a single cell; the cytoplasmic membrane and the cytoplasm, nucleus and other organelles inside it.

Pseudothesium: The ascocarp of the Loculoascomycetes (ascostreomatic ascomycetes) in which the asci are formed directly in cavity within a stroma (matrix) of mycelium. Pseudothecium is also called an ascostroma.

Pustule: Small blisterlike elevation of epidermis created as spores form underneath push outward (rust diseases).

Pycnidium: An asexual, spherical or flask-shaped fruiting body lined inside with conidiophores producing conidia.

Pycniospore: A spore produced in pycnium (Spermatium).

Pycnium: In basidiomycetes, it contains the spermatia and receptive hyphae (spermagonium).

Quarantine: Regulation of import and export of plants/plant products to prevent spread of pathogens and pests.

Race: A subgroup within a species of fungus, bacterium, nematode or virus that differs in virulence from other races in the same species.

Recognition factors: Specific receptor molecules or structures on the host or pathogen that help in recognition.

Resistance: Inherent ability of a host plant to suppress, retard or prevent entry or subsequent activity of a pathogen or other injurious factors.

Resting spore: A sexual or other thick-walled spore of a fungus that is resistant to extremes in temperature and moisture.

Rhizoid: A short, thin hypha growing in a rootlike fashion toward the substrate.

Rhizosphere: The soil zone under the influence of living root.

Rickettsiae: Microorganisms similar to bacteria in most respects but generally capable of multiplying only inside living host cells: parasitic or symbiotic.

Ringspot: A circular area of chlorosis with a green centre; a symptom of many viral diseases.

Rosette: Short, bunchy habit of plant growth.

Rot: The softening, discolouration, and often disintegration of a plant tissue as a result of fungal or bacterial infection.

Russet: Brownish roughened areas on skin of fruits as a result of cork formation.

Rust: The disease symptom caused by fungi of the order Uredinales.

Sanitation: A term used for any methods that reduce initial inoculum before infection.

Saprophyte: An organism that feeds on dead organic matter, as opposed to a parasite that feeds on living tissue.

Scab: A roughened, crustlike diseased area on the surface of a plant organ.

Sclerotium: A compact mass of hyphae with or without host tissue, usually with a darkened rind, and capable of surviving under unfavourable environmental conditions.

Scorch: "Burning" of leaf margins as a result of infection or unfavourable environmental conditions.

Secondary infection: Any infection caused by inoculum produced as a result of a primary or a subsequent infection; an infection caused by secondary inoculum.

Secondary inoculum: Inoculum produced by infections that take place during the same growing season.

Serology: A method using the specificity of the antigen-antibody reaction for the detection and identification of antigenic substances and the organisms that carry them.

Serum: The clear, watery portion of the blood remaining after coagulation.

Sexual: Participating in or produced as a result of a union of compatible nuclei (gametes), which is followed by meiosis.

Shot-hole: A symptom in which small diseased portion of leaves fall of and leave small holes in their place (part of plant defence mechanism).

Signal molecules: Host molecules that react to infection by a pathogen and transmit the signal. It activates proteins and genes in other parts of the cell and plant so they will induce the defence reaction.

Slime moulds: Pseudofungi of the class Myxomycetes; also, superficial disease caused by these pseudofungi on low-lying plants.

Smut: A disease caused by the smut fungi (Ustilaginales); characterized by mass of dark, powdery and sometimes odorous spores.

Soft rot: A rot of a fleshy fruit, vegetable or ornamental in which the tissue become disintegrated by the enzymes of the pathogen.

Soil inhabitants: Microorganism able to survive in the soil indefinitely as saprophytes.

Soil solarization: A technique based on hydrothermal process in which soil is mulched with transparent polythene sheet to capture and sustain solar radiation resulting in increased soil temperature.

Soil transients: Parasitic microorganism that can live in the soil for short period.

Sooty mould: A sooty coating on foliage and fruit formed by the dark hyphae/spores of fungi that live on the honeydew secreted by insects such as aphids, mealybugs, scales and whiteflies.

Sorus: A compact mass of spores or fruiting structure found especially in the rusts and smuts.

Species (sp.): Group of genetically and morphologically similar individuals (part of population) a division of a genus.

Spermatium, pl. spermatia (pycniospore): A sex cell borne in a spermogonium; spermatia do not cause infection.

Spermogonium, pl. spermogonia (pycnium): A fruit body containing spermatia, produced in the life cycle of a rust fungus.

Spiroplasmas: Pleomorphic, wall-less microorganisms that are present in the phloem of diseased plants. They are often helical in culture and are thought to be a kind of mycoplasma.

Sporangiophore: A specialized hypha bearing one or more sporangia.

Sporangiospore: Non-motile, asexual spore borne in a sporangium.

Sporangium: A container or case of asexual spores. In some cases, it functions as a single spore.

Spore: A propagative unit of a fungus or bacterium that functions as a seed but differs by not containing a preformed embryo.

Sporodochium: A fruiting structure consisting of a cluster of conidiophores woven together on a mass of hyphae.

Sporophore: A hyphae or fruiting structure bearing spores.

Stem-pitting: A symptom of some viral diseases characterized by depressions on the stem of the plant.

Sterigma: A slender protruberance on a basidium that supports the basidiospore.

Sterile fungi: A group of fungi that are not known to produce any kind of spores.

Sterilization: The elimination of pathogens and other living organisms from soil, containers, surface, etc., by means of heat, chemicals or radiations.

Strain: The decendants of a single isolation in pure culture; an isolate. Also a group of similar isolates; In plant viruses, a group of virus isolates having most of their antigens in common.

Stroma: A mass of vegetative hyphae, with or without tissue of the host, in or on which fruit bodies and/or spores are produced.

Stylet: The hollow needle-like proboscis of an insect or the hollow feeding spear of a nematode; both are used for feeding and can function in inoculation.

Suppressive soils: Soils in which a disease/pathogen is suppressed because of unfavourable conditions or presence in soil of microorganisms antagonistic to the pathogen.

Suscept: Any plant that can be attacked by a given pathogen; a host plant.

Susceptibility: The inability of a plant to resist the effect of a pathogen or other damaging factor.

Susceptible: Lacking the inherent ability to resist disease/pathogen or a damaging factor.

Symbiosis: A mutually beneficial association of two or more different kinds of organisms.

Symptom: The visible expression and internal alterations of a host-pathogen interaction (pathogenesis).

Symptomatology: The science of symptoms; which describes the symptoms of diseases.

Symptomless carrier: A plant which, although infected with a pathogen (usually a virus), produces no visible symptoms.

Syncytium: A multinucleate mass of protoplasm surrounded by a common cell wall, at nematode feeding sites.

Synergism: The concurrent parasitism of a host by two pathogens in which the symptoms or other effects produced are of greater magnitude than the sum of the effects of each pathogen infecting alone.

Telemorph: The sexual or so-called perfect growth stage or phase in fungi.

Telial: Pertaining to telium or the spore state in which telia are formed.

Telium: The fruiting structure in which rust teliospores are produced.

Tolerance: The ability of a plant to sustain the effects of a disease/pathogen without dying or suffering serious injury or crop loss.

Toxin: A compound produced by a microorganism and being toxic to a plant or animal.

Transduction: The transfer of genetic material from one bacterium to another by means of a bacteriophage.

Transformation: The change of a cell through uptake and expression of additional genetic material.

Transgenic (or transformed) plants: Plants in which genes from other plants or other organism have been introduced through genetic engineering techniques and are expressed.

Transmission: The transfer or spread of a virus or other pathogen from diseased plant to another.

Tumor: An uncontrolled overgrowth of tissue or tissues.

Tylosis: An outgrowth of the protoplast of a parenchyma cell into adjacent xylem vessel or tracheid (part of defence mechanism).

Urediniospore (urediospore, uredospore): Spore borne in a uredinium and capable of infecting the same host on which produced.

Uredinium, pl. uredinia (uredium): A fruit body containing urediniospores, produced in the life cycle of a rust.

Variety (var.): A division of a species, based on minor morphological characters; an intraspecific rank in taxonomic classification.

Vertical resistance: Complete resistance of host plant some races (avirulent) of a pathogen but not to others (virulent). Also called differential or discriminatory.

Vesicle: A bubblelike structure produced by a zoosporangium and in which the zoospores are released or are differentiated.

Virion: A complete virus particle.

Viroids: Low molecular weight ribonucleic acids (RNA) capable of infecting certain plant cells, replicating, and causing disease.

Virulence: The relative capacity of a pathogen to cause disease on known host variety/cultivar.

Virulent: Capable of causing infection/disease.

Viruliferous: Said of a vector containing a virus and capable of transmitting.

Viruses: Sub-microscopic, filterable obligate parasites. They are high molecular weight nucleoproteins capable of multiplying and acting like living organism when in plant or animal cells.

Virusoid: The extra-small circular RNA component of some isometric RNA viruses.

Wilt: Loss of rigidity and drooping of plant parts generally caused by insufficient water in the plant.

Witches' broom: An abnormally bushy, local growth of shoot, characterized by short internodes and proliferation of twigs (brooming).

Yellows: A plant disease characterized by yellowing and stunting of the host plant.

Zoosporangium: A fungal structure (sporangium) that contains zoospores.

Zoospore: A spore bearing flagella and capable of moving in water.

Zygospore: The sexual or resting spore of zygomycetes produced by the fusion of two morphologically similar gametangia.

Zygote: A diploid cell resulting from the union of two gametes.

E-References

Annual Review of Phytopathology
http://phyto.annualreviews.org

Phytopathology
mundtc@science.oregonstate.edu

Molecular Plant Pathology
http://www.bspp.org.uk/mypol

Plant Pathology
http://www.blackwellscience.com

Plant Diseases
http://www.apsnet.org

IJMPP
http://www.geocities/rainforest/canopy/6125

Indian Phytopathology
http://www.ipsdis.com

European Journal of Mycology
www.wkap.nl/

Index